CW01655730

Water Marks

Art in East Anglia

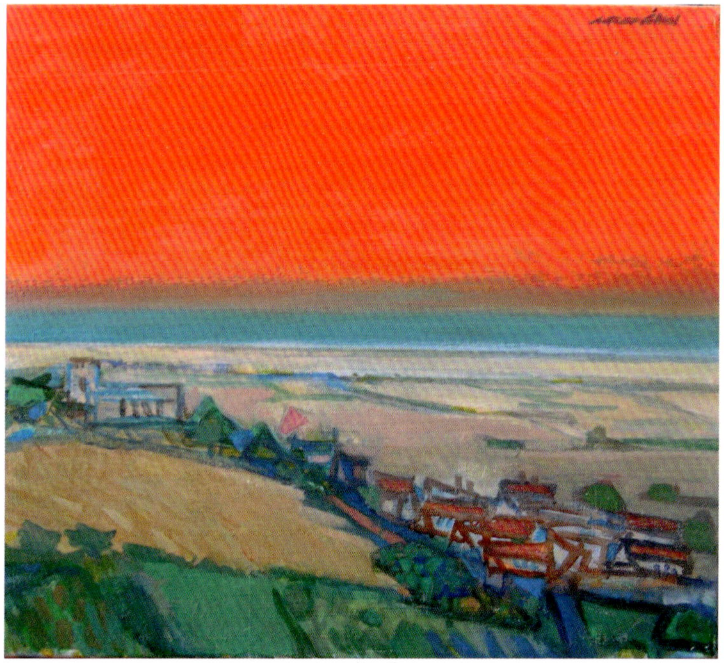

IAN COLLINS

BLACK DOG
BOOKS

This book is for

Ronald Blythe

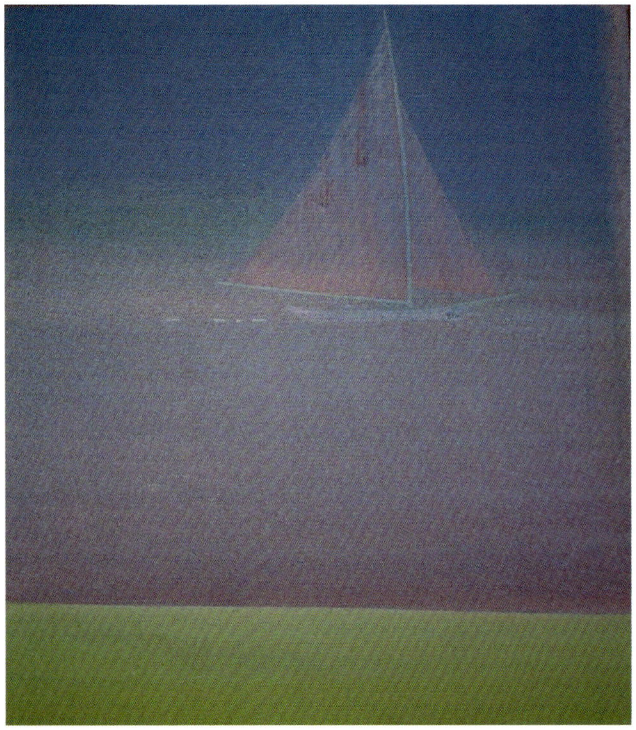

Yacht in Sea Mist (Walberswick), Derrick Greaves, 1977, acrylic on canvas (above)

Salthouse, Alfred Cohen, 1986, oil on canvas (previous page)

Blyth River (Walberswick), Katherine Hamilton, 2002, oil on canvas (opposite)

Published in 2010 by Black Dog Books,
104 Trinity Street, Norwich, NR2 2BJ

Text copyright © 2010 Ian Collins

ISBN 978-0-9549286-8-1

All rights reserved. No part of this publication may be reproduced, stored in a retrieval system or transmitted in any form or by any means, electronic, mechanical, photocopying, recording or otherwise, without the prior permission of the publisher.
Whilst every effort has been made to ensure that the information given in this book is correct at the time of going to press, no responsibility can be accepted by the publisher for any errors or inaccuracies that may appear.

Printed by Butler Tanner & Dennis Ltd, Frome, Somerset

Typeset in Times New Roman and Trade Gothic Light

CONTENTS

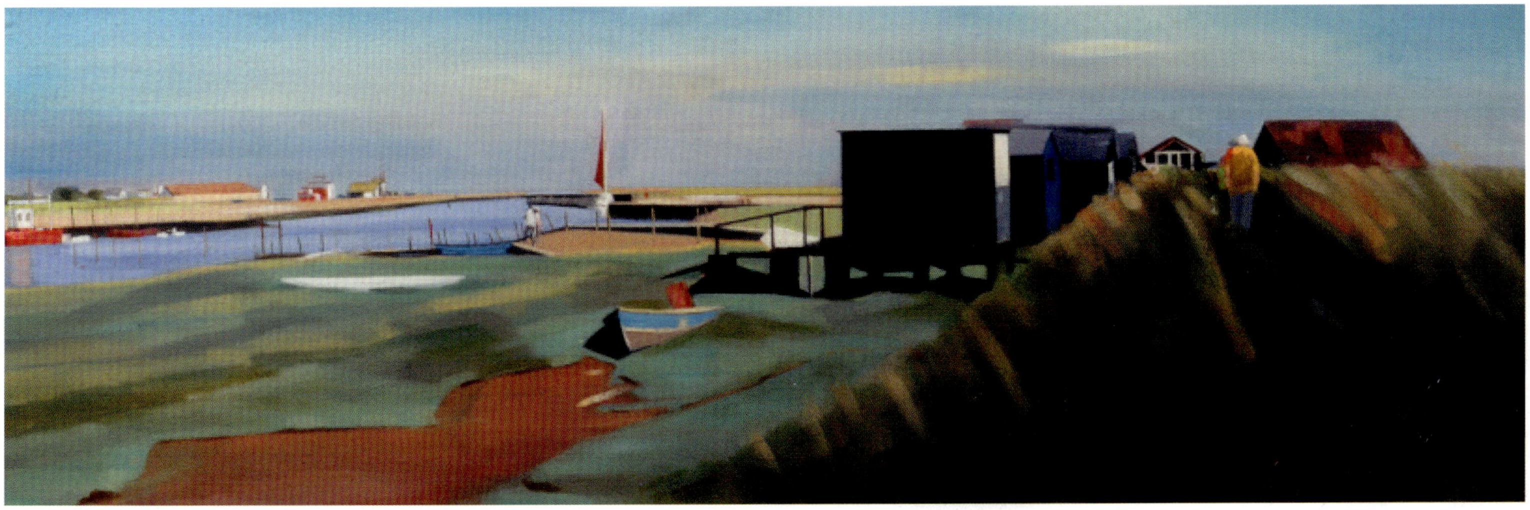

Norfolk River, Afternoon, John Crome, 1812-19, oil on canvas, Norwich Castle Museum

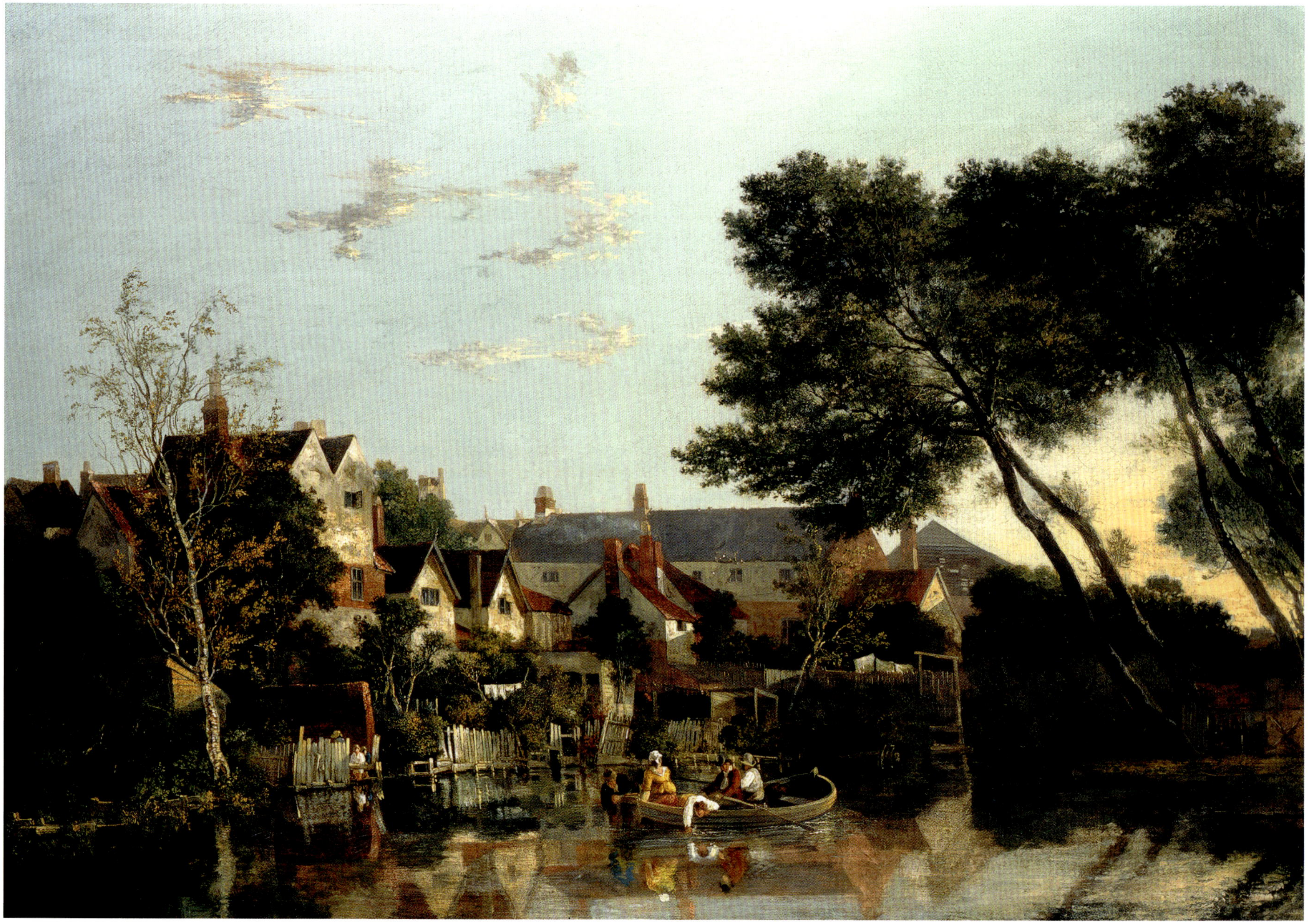

Introduction

Art in East Anglia is as old as human settlement here. The fields remain rife with ancient relics. As a child I filled pockets with pieces of decorated Roman pottery, and dreamed of Celtic torcs and the treasures of Angle ships berthed in burial mounds.

During the so-called Dark Ages the highest spirit of humanity remained illuminated in the manuscripts and stained glass of local monasteries. And in the Stour Valley church of Wiston a mural of St Francis preaching to the birds was painted by a master from the monastic art school at Colchester within a few decades of the saint's death. However remote, our region was never beyond the reach of creative currents abroad.

For the last 250 years East Anglia has acted as a powerful lure for visual artists. Such success has come despite a lack of those dramatic features traditionally linked in art to the picturesque or sublime. Though far from the uniformly flat terrain caricatured by Noel Coward, the nearest we get to a mountain range is a gentle undulation.

But admiration of the cool and quiet landscapes of northern Europe marked a major advance for art in the 17th century. East Anglia came to appeal a century later chiefly because of its affinity with the Netherlands. Dutch art hung in the homes of certain local collectors – where, doubtless, some of it was seen by a Sudbury-raised lad named Thomas Gainsborough. Looking to the local landscape he found his first and last love.

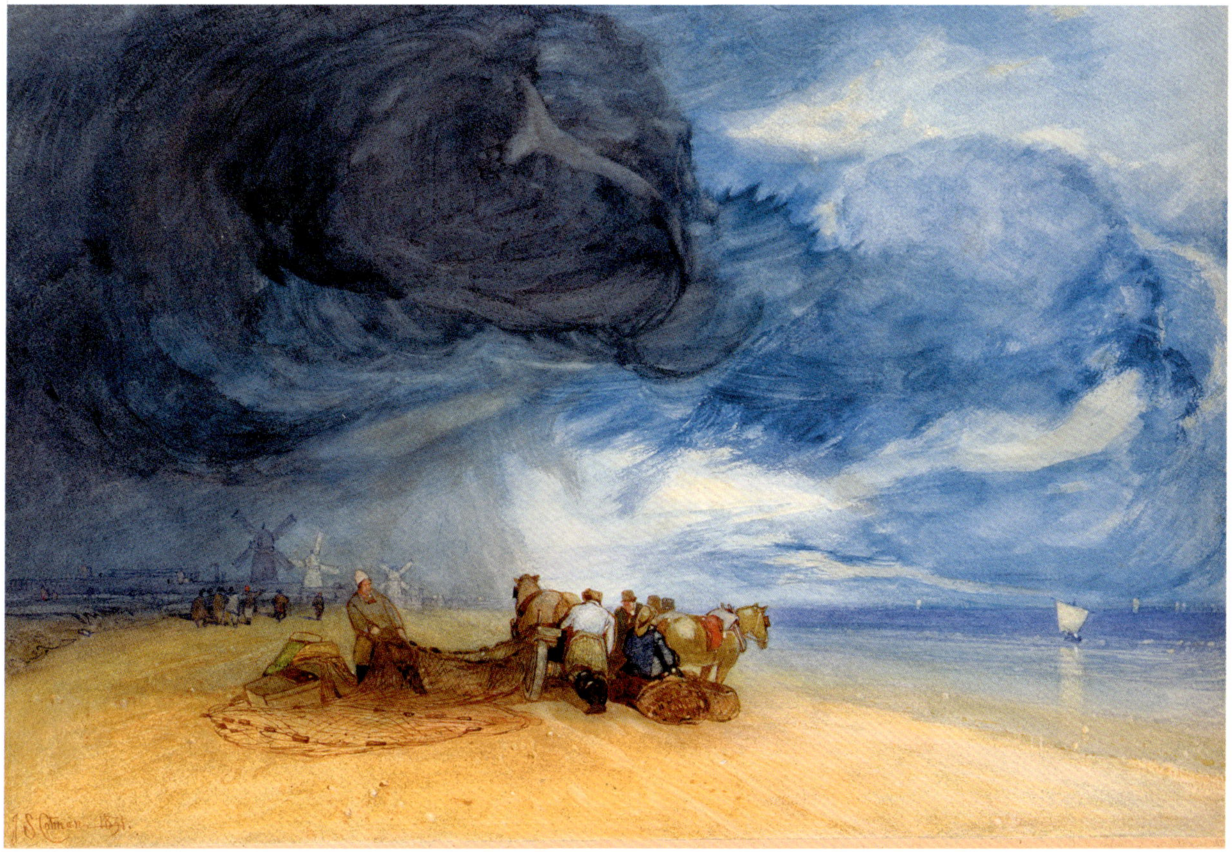

Storm on Yarmouth Beach,
John Sell Cotman,
1831, watercolour,
Norwich Castle Museum

Gainsborough's belief in the power and glory of the unclassical East Anglian countryside inspired one of the most radical artists Britain has ever produced: John Constable. Summing up his childhood haunts of East Bergholt, Dedham and the Stour Valley – an area little changed to this day save for more trees and the teeming jungle of the A12 – he wrote, 'These scenes made me a painter, and I am grateful.'

While Constable celebrated the agrarian and riparian landscape where Suffolk and Essex meet, John Crome and John Sell Cotman were leading the Norwich School of Artists into a discovery of magical Norfolk wilderness – Broadland, Breckland, Mousehold Heath – and of architectural ruins. Again, the Netherlands had set the scene. And a long-overlooked and

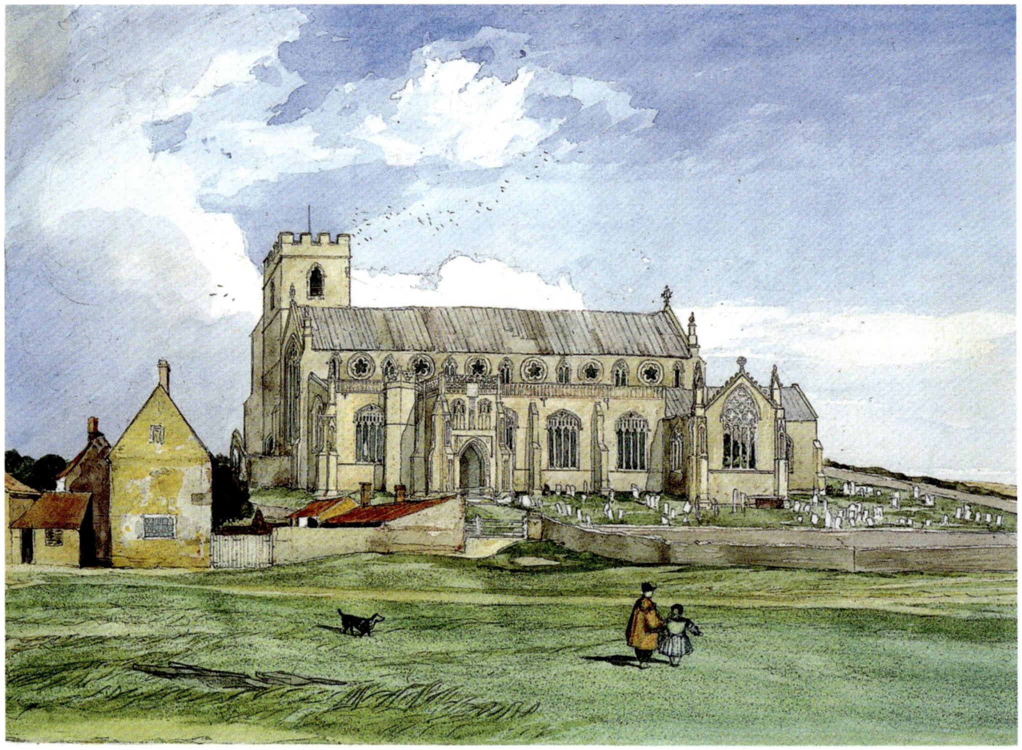

Cley Church, James Bulwer, 1849, watercolour, Norwich Castle Museum

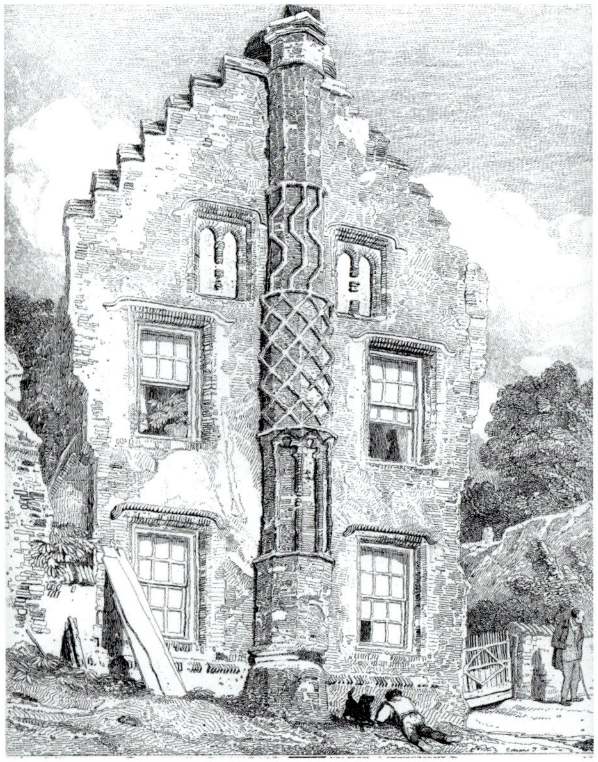

Old Rectory, Methwold, J S Cotman, 1812, etching

watery world was best evoked, it seemed, by a long-underrated but quicksilver medium: watercolour.

Retaining a sense of awe in the face of nature, Constable caught the myriad effects of light and atmosphere which are the true joy of soggy, sunken and sky-dominated East Anglia. He was ridiculed or ignored by local and national audiences for his pains (then again, Turner, who had also wandered the East Anglian coastline, spent his final years of embittered rejection living under an assumed name). But those revolutionary pictures lit a fire in France. A torch carried by Corot was taken up by several pioneering painters who decamped to the village of Barbizon, where

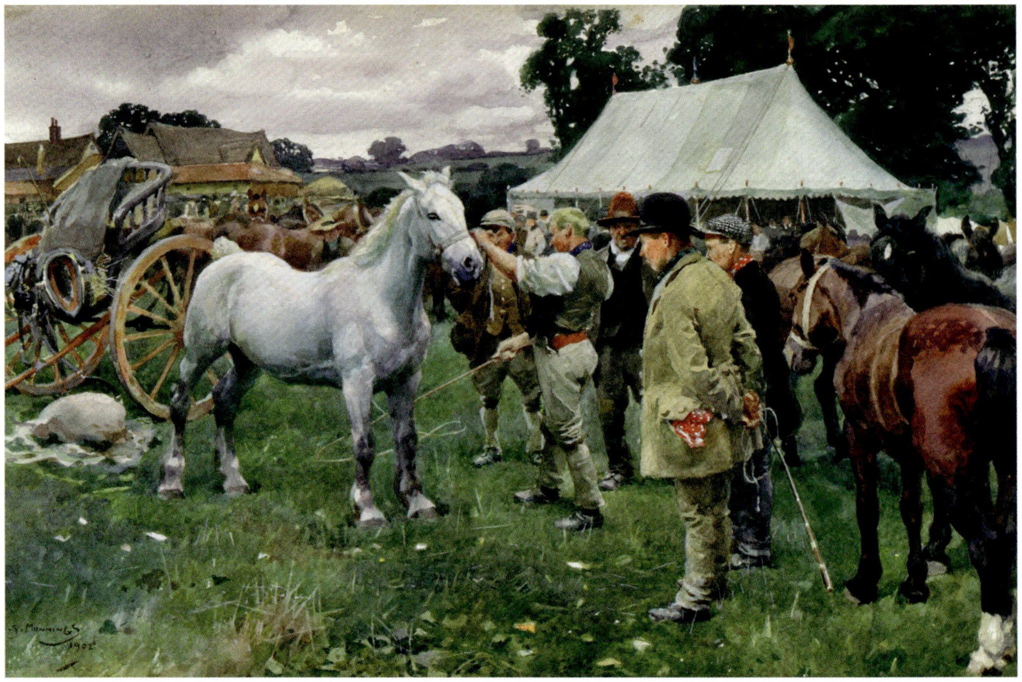

Horse Sale, Alfred Munnings, 1902, watercolour, Norwich Castle Museum

their experiences led in turn to the emergence of Impressionism.

An experiment begun in East Anglia was to return in 1884 when Philip Wilson Steer, fresh from France, spent the first of several summers in Walberswick and Southwold. Here he made notes and sketches for some of the most beautiful pictures known to British art, an air of eerie enchantment enhanced by the fact that the paintings were completed in wintry Chelsea. Girls with golden hair, pink sashes and – as someone said – long legs like Sheraton tables played beside the sea in a kaleidoscope of light and colour. The broken brushstrokes and vivid, unmixed colours of Impressionism captured the sun-drenched scene perfectly. How Steer came to develop this daring technique on the Suffolk coast – and why he abandoned it within a decade, as he moved elsewhere – remains unclear. His best pictures were hard to sell and easily mocked: his confidence was knocked. A recent novel and film suggested a passing love affair. Certainly there was an unparalleled passion in his East Anglian pictures of the period.

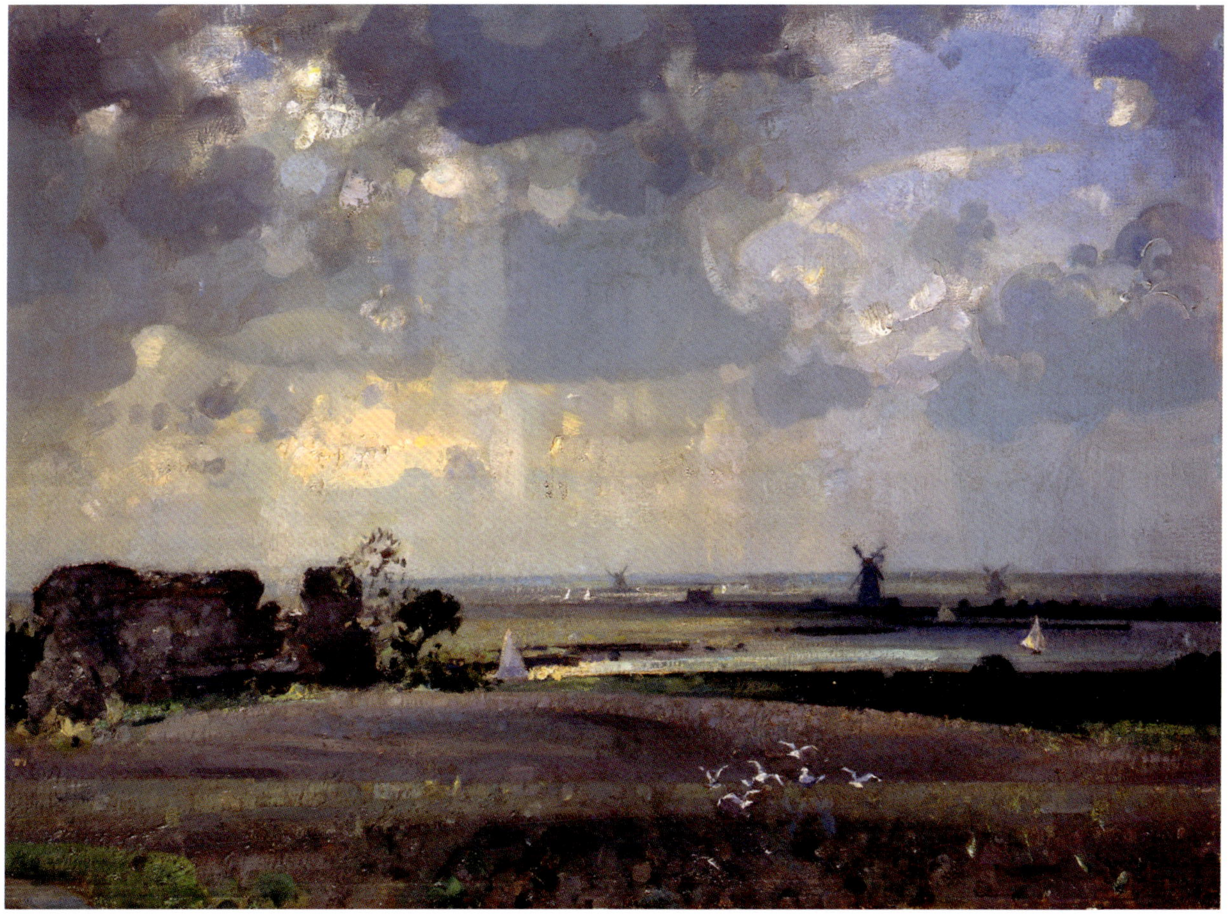

The Marshes from Burgh Castle,
John Alfred Arnesby Brown,
1939, oil on canvas,
Norwich Castle Museum

Walberswick and Southwold have attracted wave after wave of artists who have responded to the sparkling eastern light and wild sea and marshscapes without ever constituting a formal school. Along with the climate, the warmth of the local welcome has varied enormously. When a rejected Charles Rennie Mackintosh fled to Walberswick from Glasgow in the summer of 1914, and unwisely stayed on when World War One started, he took long evening walks in the sand dunes and collaborated with his wife Margaret on ravishing watercolour drawings of local flowers. But the 'foreign' artist was rumoured to be a spy who flouted black-out rules to signal to ships at sea – and correspondence with the Viennese Secession (alien revolutionaries!) appeared to provide proof of treachery. Mackintosh was arrested and allowed to continue a southward flight only

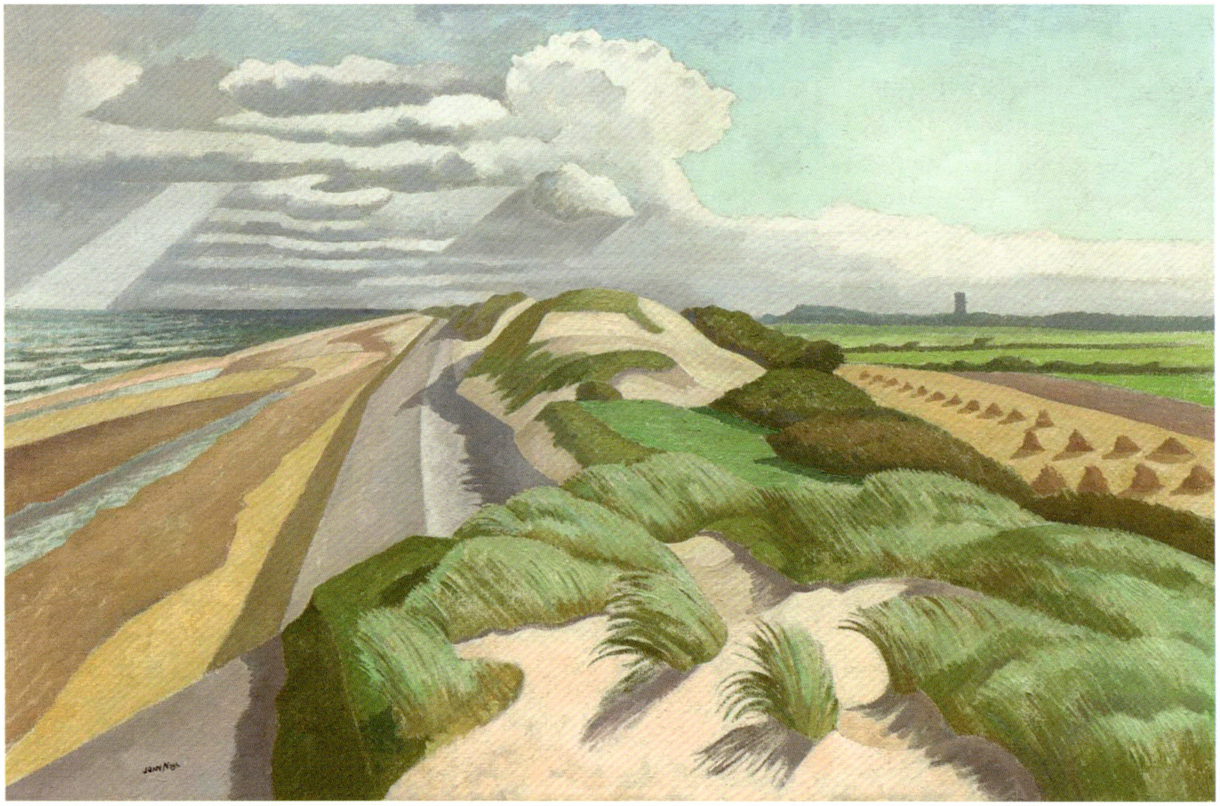

Norfolk Coast
(Waxham to Winterton),
John Nash, oil on canvas

after high-placed friends in London had intervened on his behalf.

World War One also brought an outpost of Bloomsbury to Wissett, near Halesworth, when the pacifist painters Duncan Grant and Vanessa Bell, and writer David Garnett, left the jingoism of London to struggle with a wayward smallholding. Such a haven proved illusory, despite warm praise from a visiting Virginia Woolf, who began drafting her novel *Night and Day* there. The men were threatened with jail terms by the Blything Tribunal before an appeal panel in Ipswich (mindful of a defence from Maynard Keynes) granted exemption from military service but banned self-employment. The artists moved to farm labour, and creation of the celebrated Charleston household, in Sussex.

War-time land work had taken a young Hilda Carline to Suffolk. When she married Stanley Spencer, in 1925, the service was held at Wangford, near Southwold, where she had been happy. They both painted pictures of local landscapes during their honeymoon, and it may not be fanciful to observe that a shadowy and tangled scene produced by the bride prefigured later mental turmoil. But Stan was in ecstasy – with an imprinted memory of guests leaving the church after the Wangford wedding in clusters and attitudes like the figures in his great *Resurrection* painting now in the Tate.

By the summer of 1937 Stanley Spencer was

Ives Farmhouse, Great Bardfield,
Edward Bawden, c.1956, linocut,
Cecil Higgins Art Gallery, Bedford

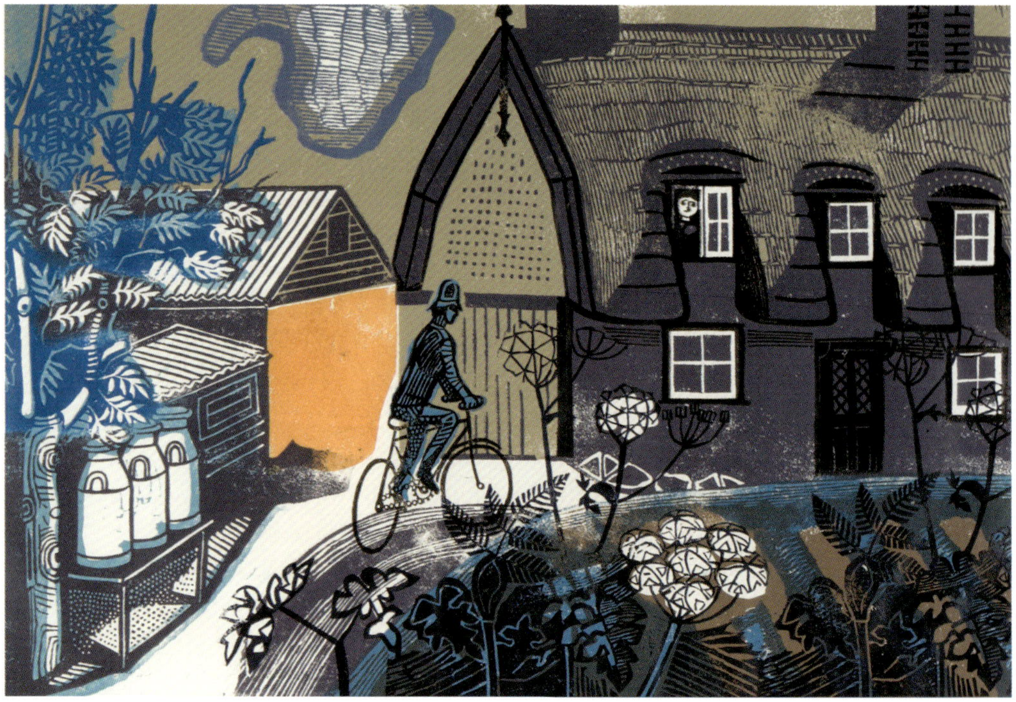

reluctantly divorced from Hilda, and already estranged from new wife Patricia Preece. He returned to the scene of his greatest romance and painted a brilliant picture of Southwold beach. The 'dirty-washing colour' sea was 'splashed by homely aunties' legs and the air was full of suburban seaside abandonment,' he

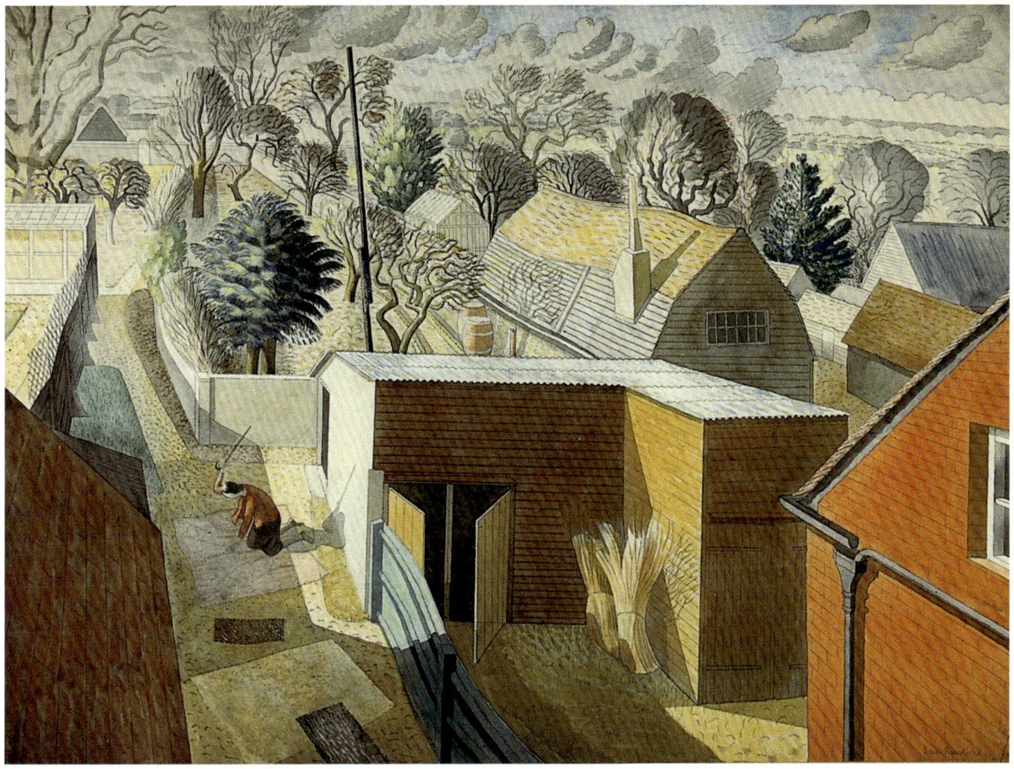

Prospect from an Attic,
Eric Ravilious, c. 1932,
watercolour,
Scarborough Art Gallery

wrote, having regained his vantage point each morning by measuring the distance between dog messes. Beneath a breezy surface it was a view from a wistful outsider.

In 1950 a passer-by spotted Spencer nudes in a London gallery window and pressed a prosecution for obscenity (causing the pictures to be destroyed). This was Sir Alfred Munnings, president of the Royal Academy. The previous year he had fulminated against Picasso. But the Waveney miller's son had not always been such an arch reactionary. Training as a poster designer in Norwich at 14, and losing an eye to a Norfolk briar at 20, he captured early horse-centred scenes with a bright impressionism. Despite an ongoing cloud over his reputation, he has some claim to being England's Degas.

Peaceful, private, isolated – yet with a network of rural rail links until the 1960s era of Dr Beeching – rural East Anglia has been hugely popular for holidays and hideaways. The sense of being a world away, on one of the edgiest edges of England, could be achieved within striking distance of London. Many have come here for health reasons. Between the wars Mark Gertler had three spells in the tuberculosis sanatorium at Mundesley on the windswept North Norfolk coast. With good reason travel posters of the time proclaimed the slogan: 'Come To East Anglia. It's So Bracing!'

Finance has been a factor. Local patrons of the arts have long been active. Certain artists have lived in grand style, migrating between London and the countryside according to season and whim. Until recently, others were able to live cheaply in simple cottages and on the fruits of land and sea. Some rural painters, like the prolific Harry Becker (1865-1928), were at times too poor even to buy canvas – being as impoverished as the farm labourers they depicted. Bills may be bigger now, in an age of high utility costs, steep rents and stratospheric property prices, but while the regional cost of living has risen sharply, the quality of life has remained higher still. The inward flow of artists continues. And if the luminaries are more often migrant than native, we have still nurtured the likes of Michael Andrews (linked to the School of London) and Pop Art's Colin Self.

Remoteness has appealed to reclusive spirits, but East Anglia has also offered more communal activities. The closest we came to a formal 20th-century arts colony was a motley assembly of artists and craftspeople around Edward Bawden and Eric Ravilious – themselves masters of lino-cuts and watercolours respectively – between the wars at Great Bardfield (with work now showcased in the wonderful Fry Art Gallery at Saffron Walden). Art schools and societies, arts festivals and now open studio schemes, have all added to the attraction. Often in Aldeburgh as a set-designer, John Piper criss-crossed the region as part of a self-appointed task to chart Britain's natural and architectural heritage. His fluent pen and brush encompassed noble halls and humble cottages, but lingered longest in and around churches – the beacon towers of the Fens looming loveliest among dozens of recorded East Anglian landscapes and landmarks.

In what Sickert so erroneously dubbed 'the sucked orange' of the Stour Valley, landscape painters have continued to find fresh inspiration in familiar scenes. Distinguished help has often been at hand – with the painter-plantsman John Nash once numbered among tutors at the Flatford Mill Field Studies Centre. And for decades from the 1930s Cedric Morris and Lett Haines ran the famous (in some circles, infamous) East Anglian School of Painting and Drawing along French and Bohemian lines. First at Dedham, and latterly at Hadleigh, the school drew students from Lucian Freud to Glyn Morgan and Maggi Hambling who were encouraged to portray each other, the iris-rife garden and the fields beyond. When depicting the smouldering wreck of the first school (ruin possibly wrought by a Freudian fag-end) the

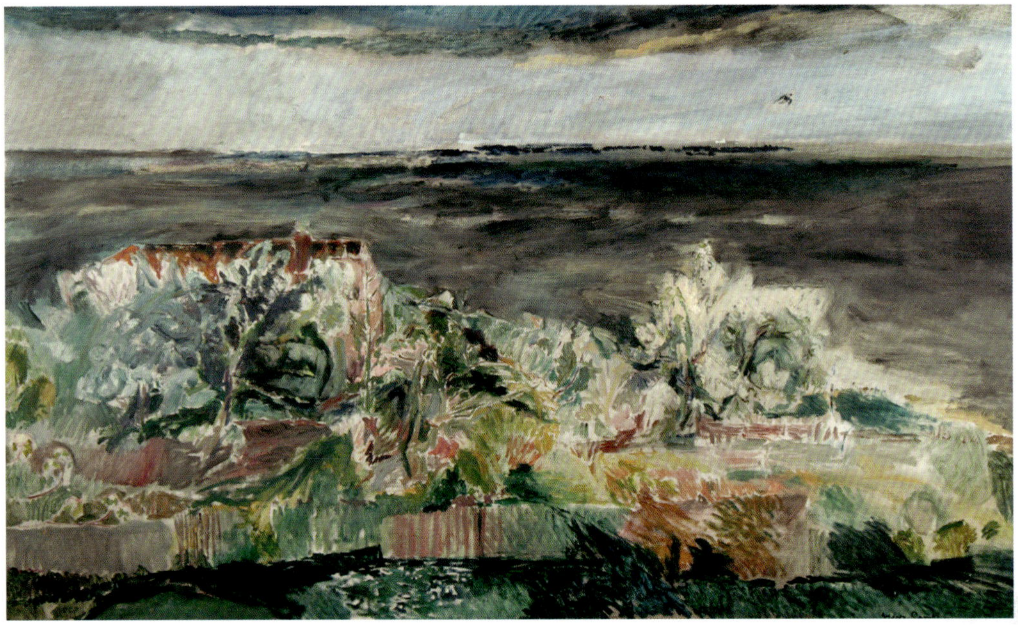

Black North Sea, Jeffery Camp, 1959, oil on board, King's Lynn Museum

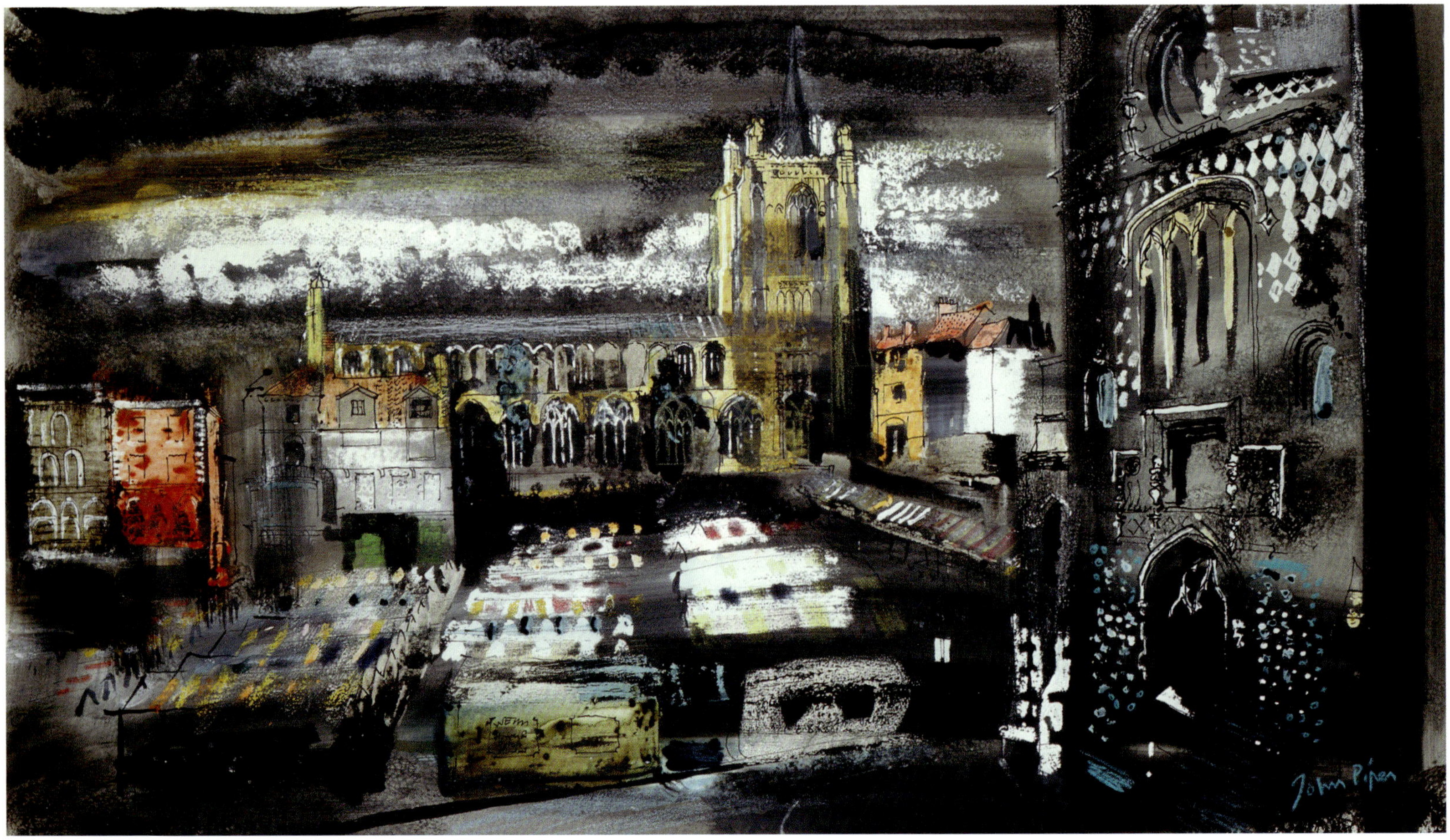

Norwich Market Place, John Piper, 1950, watercolour and chalk, Norwich Castle Museum

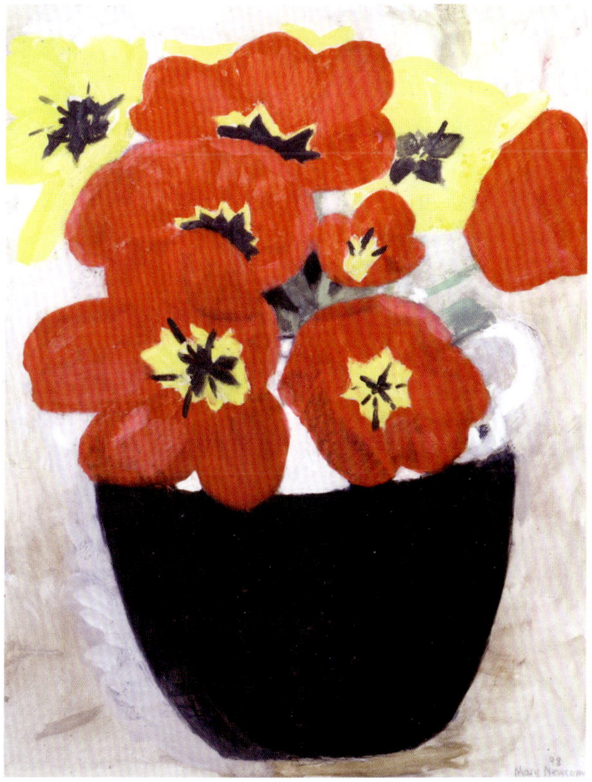

Red and Yellow Tulips, Mary Newcomb, 1998, oil on board

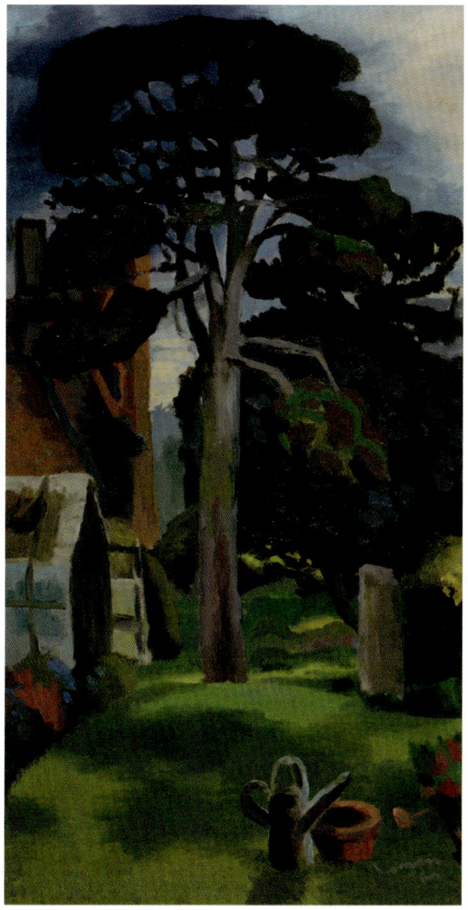

Benton End (Cedric Morris's garden), Glyn Morgan, c. 1957, oil on board

company was assailed by a passing Munnings, who lived nearby in what is now a museum to his memory, crying 'Down with modern art!' The same sentiment gripped a section of Aldeburgh opinion more than 60 years later when Maggi Hambling, lately relocated to a village near Snape, and long memorialising notable people from Beccles-raised scientist Dorothy Hodgkin to the dying Cedric Morris, designed a Scallop tribute to Benjamin Britten for the brow of the beach towards Thorpeness. The steely monument remains a controversial tourist attraction.

Another Flatford Mill Field Studies Centre tutor was the bird painter Eric Ennion, who in 1946 taught the science-minded Mary Slatford the art of intensely observing nature. As a farmer's wife in the Waveney Valley, the future Mary Newcomb evolved a painterly vision of deceptive naivety – a personal pictorial poetry firmly rooted in rural reality. A kindred evolution is now working through her daughter, Tessa. Similar (and yet absolutely singular) journeys from representational Suffolk towards a universal abstraction can be clearly traced in the work of Mary Potter, Pears and Britten's great friend, who spent her last three decades dissolving matter into light in Aldeburgh. It is less obvious in, but also fundamental to, the early art of Prunella Clough, who spent much of her childhood in Southwold and who then painted the local fishermen and turned the twisted shapes of war-time coastal defences into spiky abstraction. On the other side of Suffolk, at Little Thurlow, a young Elisabeth Frink would consign to memory a landscape dotted not with horses but airbases. She vividly remembered crippled bombers limping home, or occasionally crashing in the fields. The angular forms of some of her bird sculptures from the 1950s would be likened to the jagged fuselage of wrecked planes.

Then there are the complete oddities – such as Arthur Boyd, who crossed the world to Constable Country for the inspiration to paint his native Australia. Fiery images of the Outback filled his nest-like thatched studio at Ramsholt, on a bank of the River Deben. Part of a distinguished artistic dynasty, Boyd was brother-in-law to Sidney Nolan, who came to Aldeburgh in Britten's wake. He might also be a kindred spirit to John Bellany and Anthony

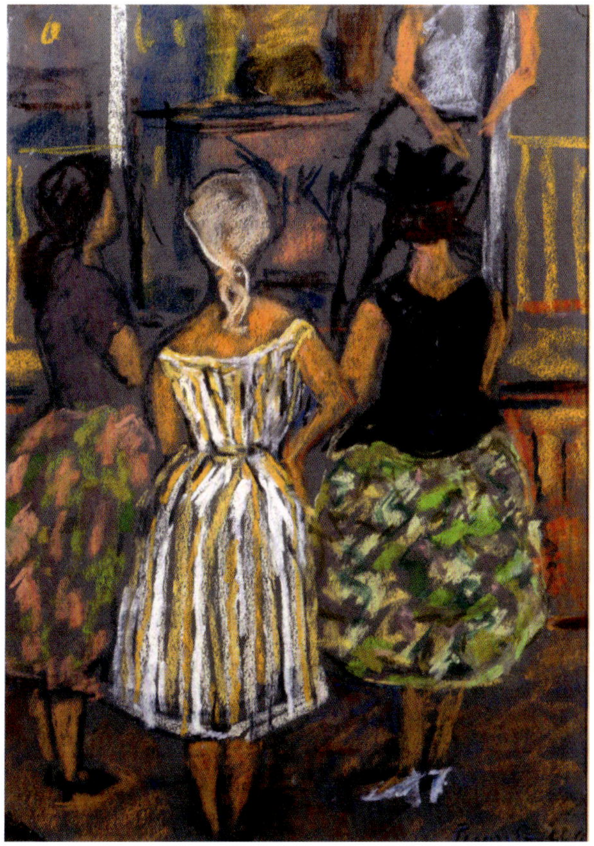

Three Girls at Aldeburgh Fair, Peggy Somerville, 1958, pastel

Green, memoirists and mythologists of faraway places who found the space for dreams in unlikely corners of rural Essex and Cambridgeshire respectively.

Overall, we can fairly claim that East Anglia has attracted more and better artists down the generations than any other English region, save for Cornwall. But as well as savouring such a fertile record, we may also ponder what might have been.

When the last war threatened, Adrian Stokes and his wife Margaret Mellis searched for a safe house in the country where they were to be joined by a couple of friends and fellow artists. The Norfolk and Suffolk coasts were scoured in vain before a refuge was found in Cornwall. Ben Nicholson and Barbara Hepworth arrived as planned, and the rest is art history. Today we could have been visiting a Tate Aldeburgh rather than a Tate St Ives.

Ironically, Margaret Mellis was to live in Suffolk from 1950 with her second husband, the collagist Francis Davison. From a harbourside shack at Walberswick and then a Syleham smallholding, they gravitated to Southwold, where Margaret continued in her widowhood to create abstract constructions from driftwood. Friends came in her wake – Roger Hilton very nearly moving to East Anglia (before preferring rugged Cornwall to a region where 'the trees look like parsley'). Guy Taplin, relocating permanently from London to Wivenhoe, a move Francis Bacon managed only briefly, came to share thoughts on the found wood from which he carved talismanic birds. And here a teenage fan of Davison and Mellis, who also tried his hand at driftwood constructions, saw things 'that blew me away'. His name was Damien Hirst.

The lure continues. Alison Wilding has worked at Snape. Louise Wilson has lately haunted the nuclear testing ground turned nature reserve of Orford Ness. And now Hirst's close friend Sarah Lucas lives in Britten's old house near Eye, having been drawn here by his music.

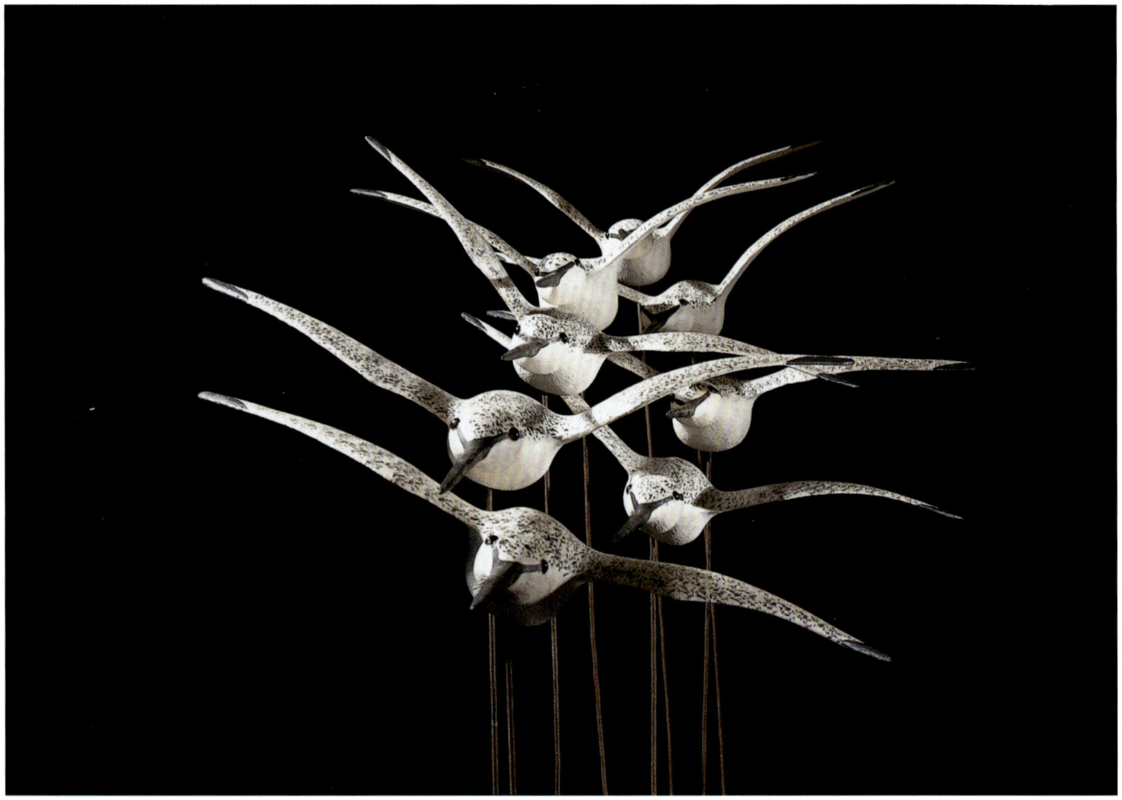

Sanderlings, Guy Taplin, painted wood

NORTH NORFOLK COAST

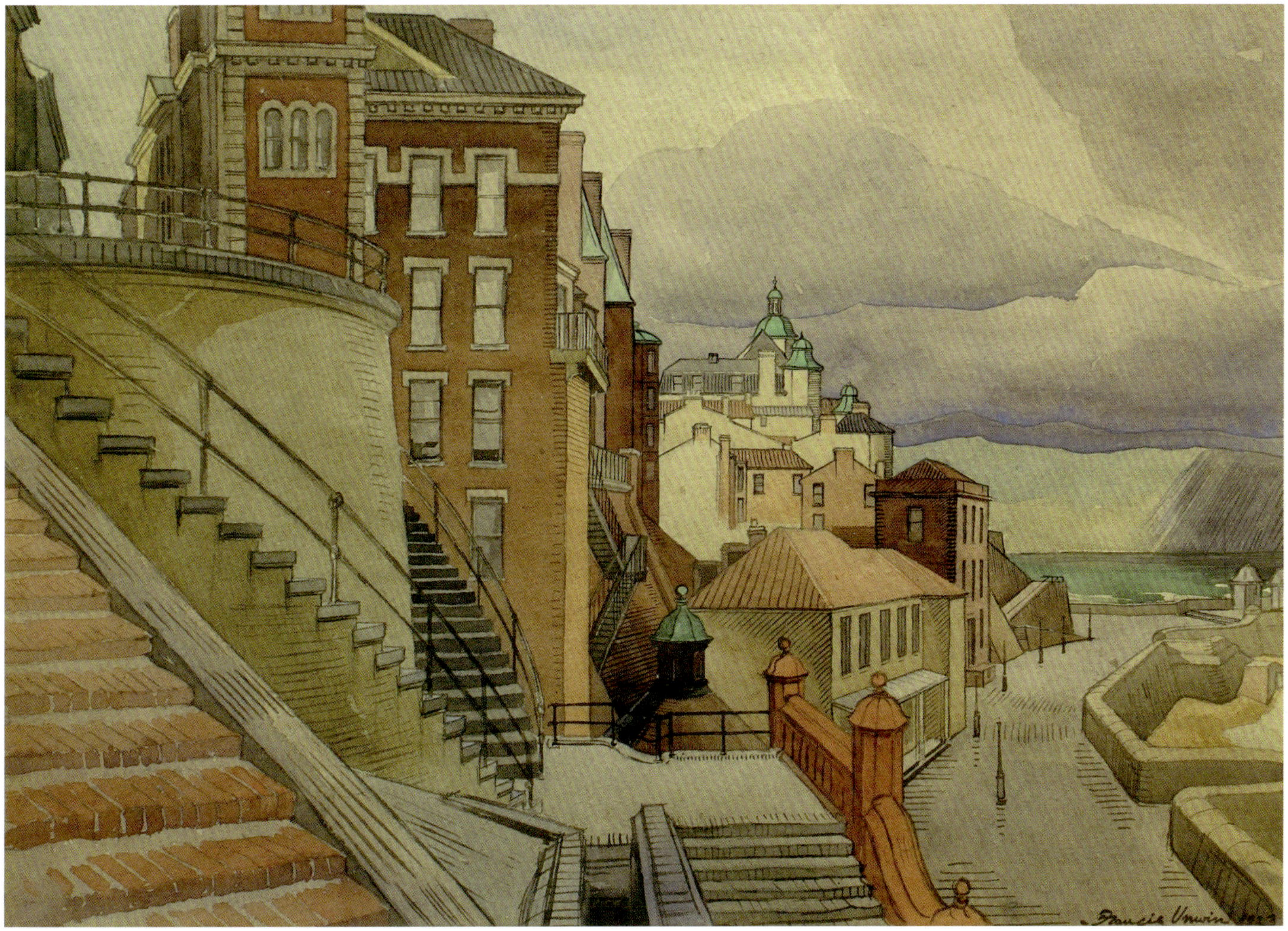

Cromer, Francis Unwin, 1923, watercolour

Latterly a librarian in Bury St Edmunds, Brenda Rawnsley was a young war widow when perfecting plans hatched with her aviator husband to make art accessible to everyone. Knowing little of art or commerce, she drew on expert advice but the drive was hers alone.

The first result, in 1945-6, was a 23-print series produced in large numbers and sold at low cost for classrooms. The School Prints project included East Anglian scenes by John Nash and Michael Rothenstein and – best of all – *Fairground*, by **Barbara Jones**.

Losing heavily on a sequel series of international images involving Moore, Picasso, Braque and Matisse, the arts campaigner pressed on with schemes to lend pictures to hospitals, offices and factories.

Fairground,
School Print Lithograph (First Series No. 2), 1945-6

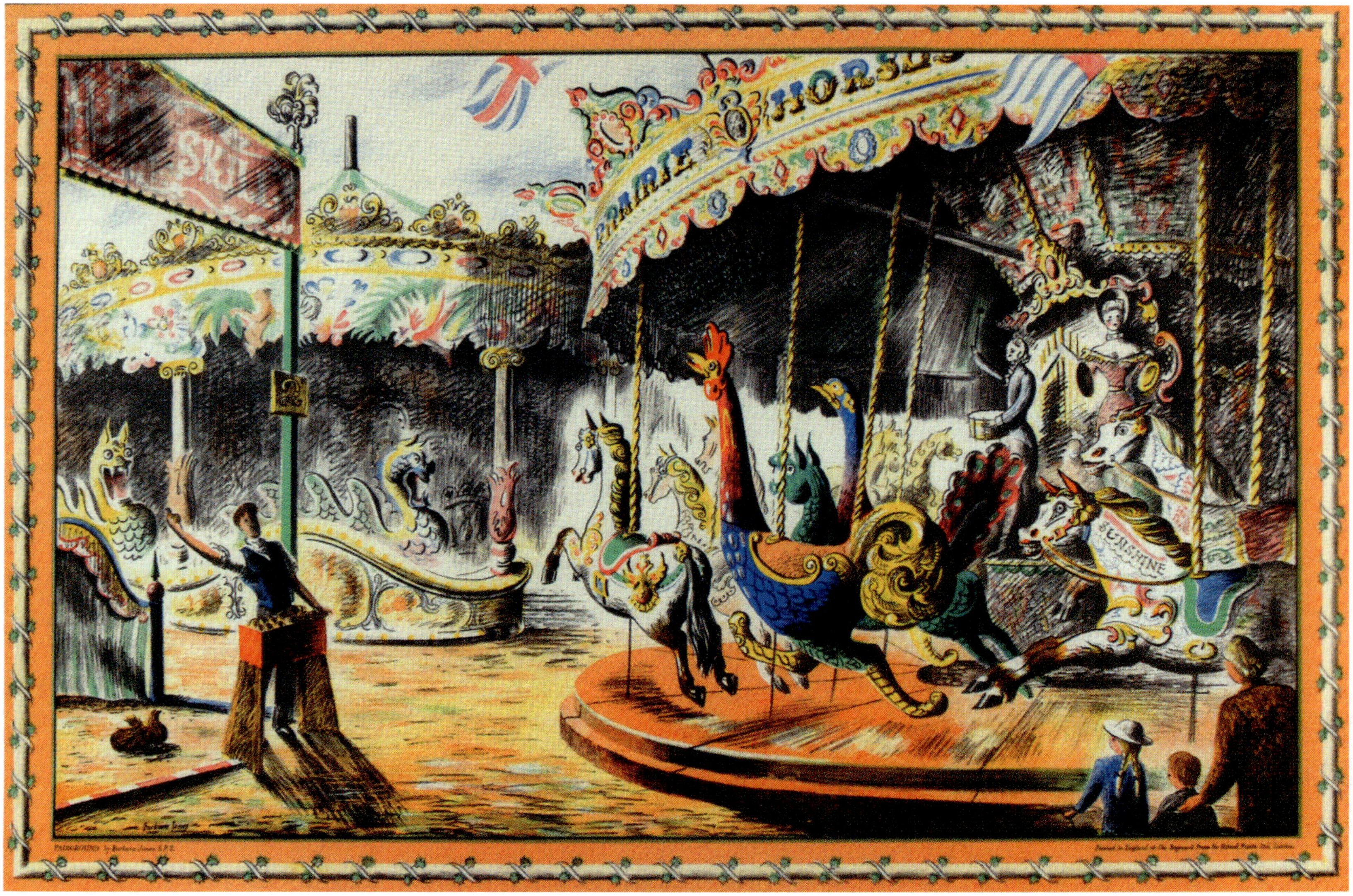

Fairground Fantasies

Savages of Lynn and Barbara Jones

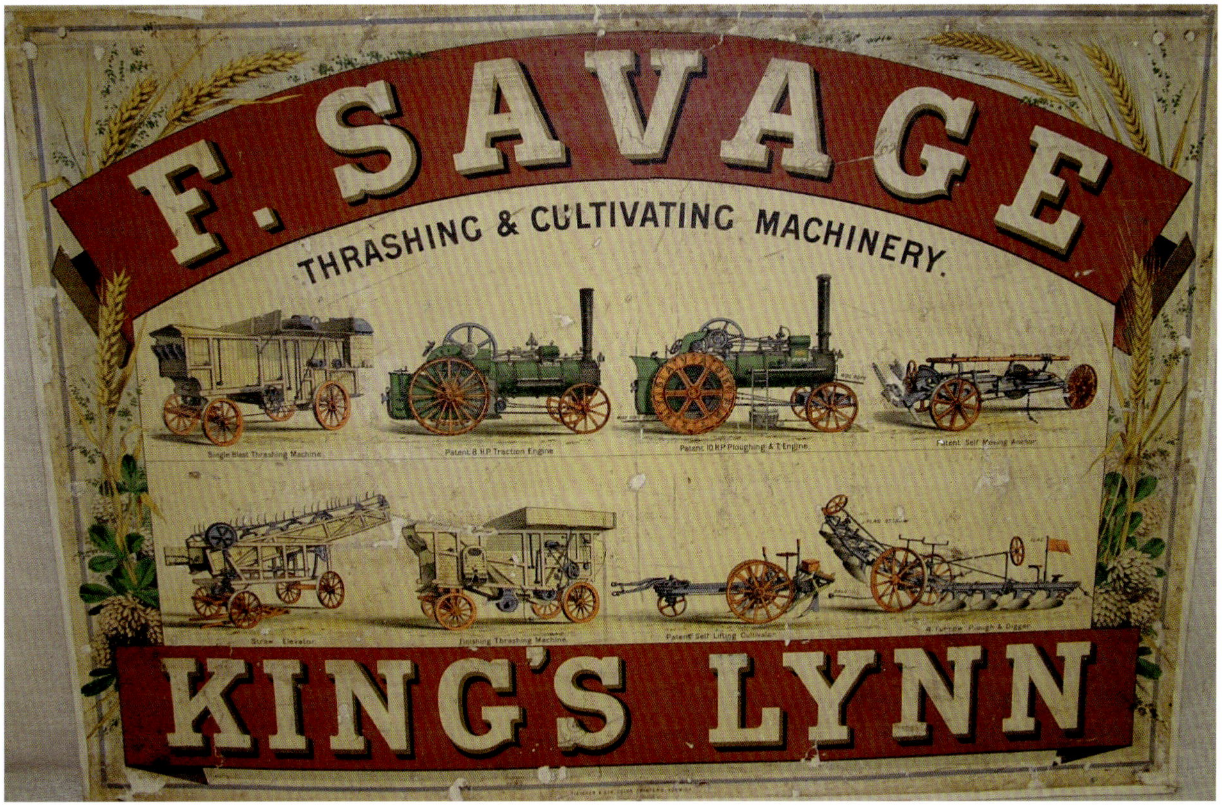

Savage advertising poster, c.1880

Roll up, roll up for the most flamboyant Victorian marriage of engineering, craftsmanship and art – courtesy of Frederick Savage of King's Lynn, whose fairground merry-go-rounds, switchback rides and showman's engines wowed the world from America to Australia.

Born in 1828, the son of hand-loom weavers in the mid-Norfolk village of Hevingham, he knew dire poverty when his father was deported to Tasmania for poaching. From ten he made fencing hurdles and scared rooks, but then was taken on by a Dereham ironsmith and machine-maker.

At 20 he continued his apprenticeship in King's Lynn, setting up his own business in 1850 to make and repair farm implements. Steam power was draining the Fens and aiding a wider flood of demand for ploughing, threshing and carting machinery which Savage was swift to meet via traction, or self-moving, engines. Expanding steadily, he built the St Nicholas Ironworks from 1872 where up to 400 employees with the high skills of precision engineering – draughtsmen, pattern makers, foundry workers – realised amazing dreams of the steam age.

Steam railways spread distribution networks which altered rural fairs forever. These ancient markets and employment exchanges now cranked up former side-lines in entertainment – and Frederick Savage was in on that game too. Less an inventor than a brilliant engineer and entrepreneur, he probably saw, at Aylsham Fair in the 1860s, a steam organ engine and

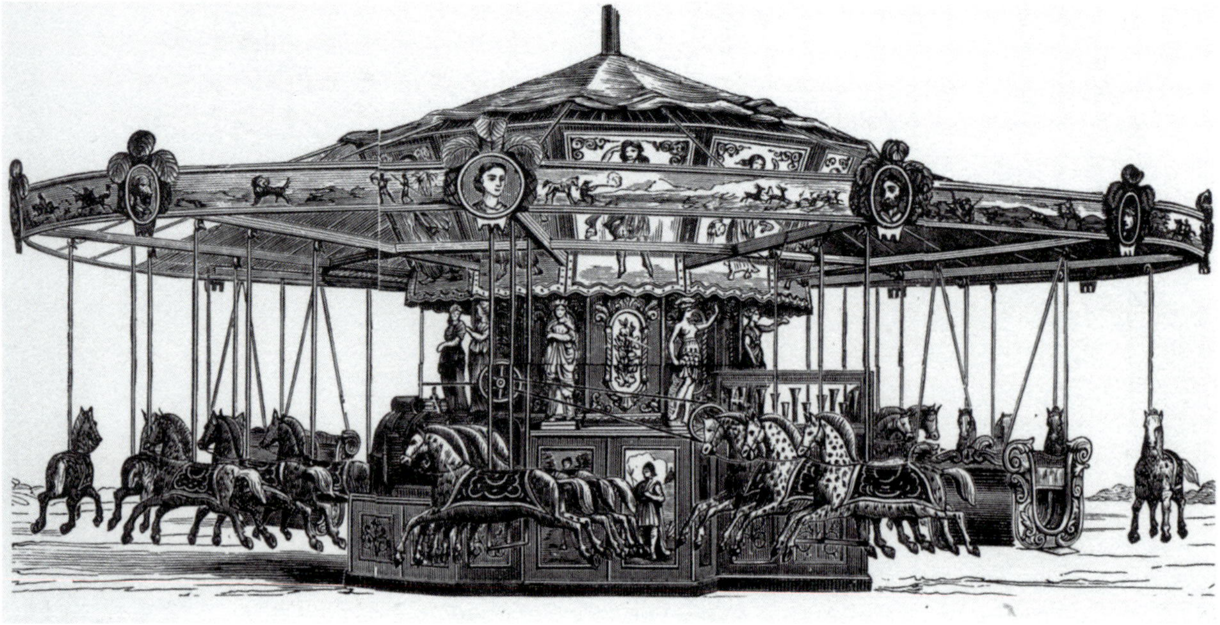

A Savage carousel, c. 1880-90

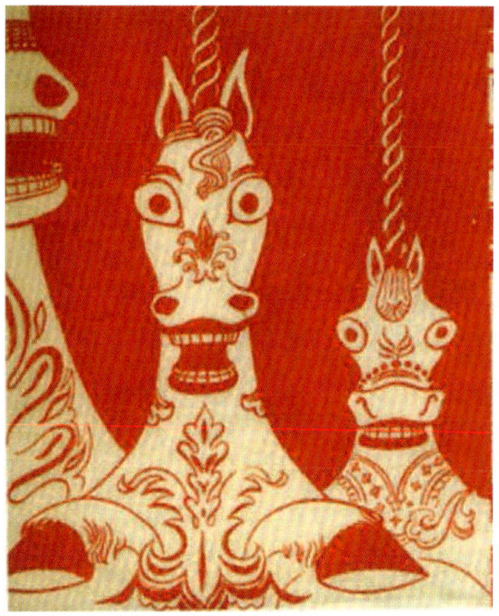

The Unsophisticated Arts, Barbara Jones, 1951, rear dust jacket

roundabout devised by Sidney George Soame of Marsham. Soon he had annexed and extended that basic design to become king of the carousels.

Velocipedes and Dobby Horses were marketed nationally after successful launches at the Lynn Mart, and then came the most marvellous of all merry-go-rounds: Gallopers. From a steam engine in the middle driven by a revolving centre, steel shafts like wheel-spokes supported a platform and up to 56 four-abreast horses cranked to move up and down as well as round, while Savage's patent 'platform slide' made them swing out concentrically as the machine gathered speed.

A galloping horse took ten long days to build, carve and paint. Each body consisted of nearly 30 pieces of best Siberian yellow pine, with beech or elm favoured for the legs. Necks bore individual names and heads were topped off with cast iron ears as grips for the riders. All parts save for glass eyes and horsehair tails were made at St Nicholas Ironworks.

With enchantment resting on novelty, Savages came to offer not just racing horses but prancing peacocks, turkeys, ostriches and cockerels – the birds cross-breeding to produce startling hybrids – as well as jumping cats and flying pigs. Pine rounding boards fixed to the ends of the spinning frame and shutters screening the engines were faced with canvas before being painted by Savage's Norfolk craftsmen or Italian artists brought up from the London works at Islington. These might depict bucolic landscapes or beastly struggles in lush green Rousseau-like jungles, each gory or

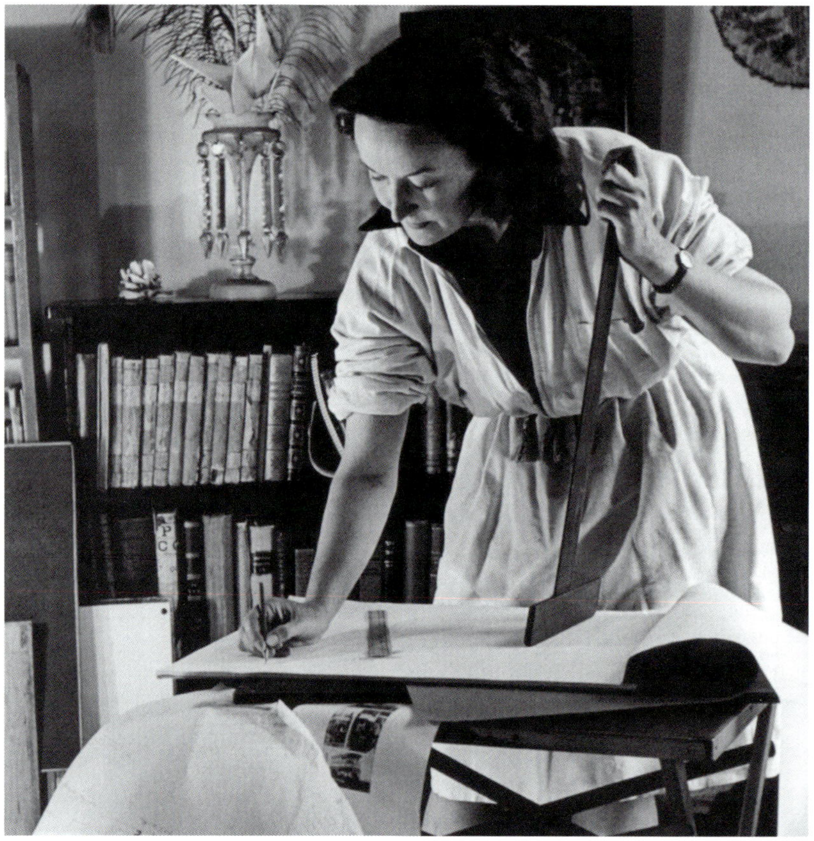

Barbara Jones in her studio

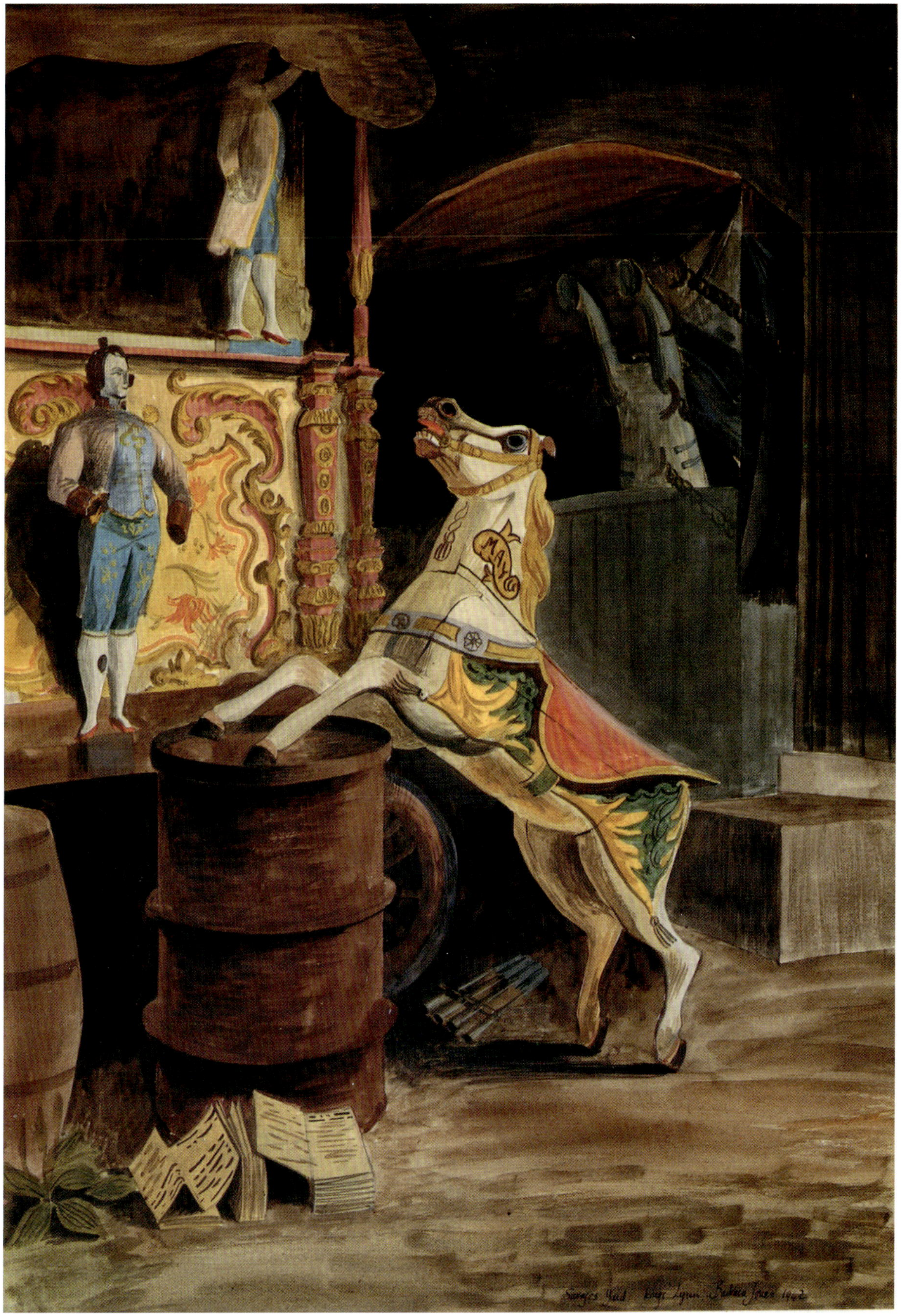

Savage's Yard, King's Lynn, Barbara Jones, 1942, watercolour, Victoria & Albert Museum glorious scene rendered with the same innocent gusto.

And then engraved mirrors, barley-sugar brasswork, plush upholstery, elaborate scrollwork bearing slogans such as Good Riding for all Classes and Patronised by Royalty, gaudy gilding, melodious organs bearing automaton musicians and, in time, Savage Sparklers – steam-powered electric light engines – all combined to lift poor folk into baroque fantasies for one or two pennies a fling.

From 1888 the fairground range included switchback rides, where groups of cars ran on an undulating track, with a third compensating rail added for front wheels only and then run out of sequence. Dipping and turning carriages became fabulous creations from ornate gondolas to bat-winged dragons and new-fangled motor cars. The company sales list also ran to Steam Yachts, Sea on Land (patented jointly with showman William Sanger), Tunnel Railway, Razzle Dazzle, Roley Poley, Wheely Whirly, Cakewalk and Aeroflyte. Savages designed special traction engines to pull these transports of delight from site to site, sending bright processions along the roads of pre-World War Two Britain at up to 15 miles per hour.

But Frederick Savage had died in 1897 – his craftsmen carving his coffin – and his sons were declared insolvent by 1910. Saved by a local consortium, the company limped on until closure in 1973. The St Nicholas Ironworks were then demolished and replaced by new factory units.

Lynn Museum has a few exquisite carvings and 30,000 engineering patterns, while antique roundabouts still spin in Norfolk steam centres at Bressingham and Thursford. The latter includes a three-abreast Gallopers ride of 1896, with an original Orton and Spooner painted hunting scene on the

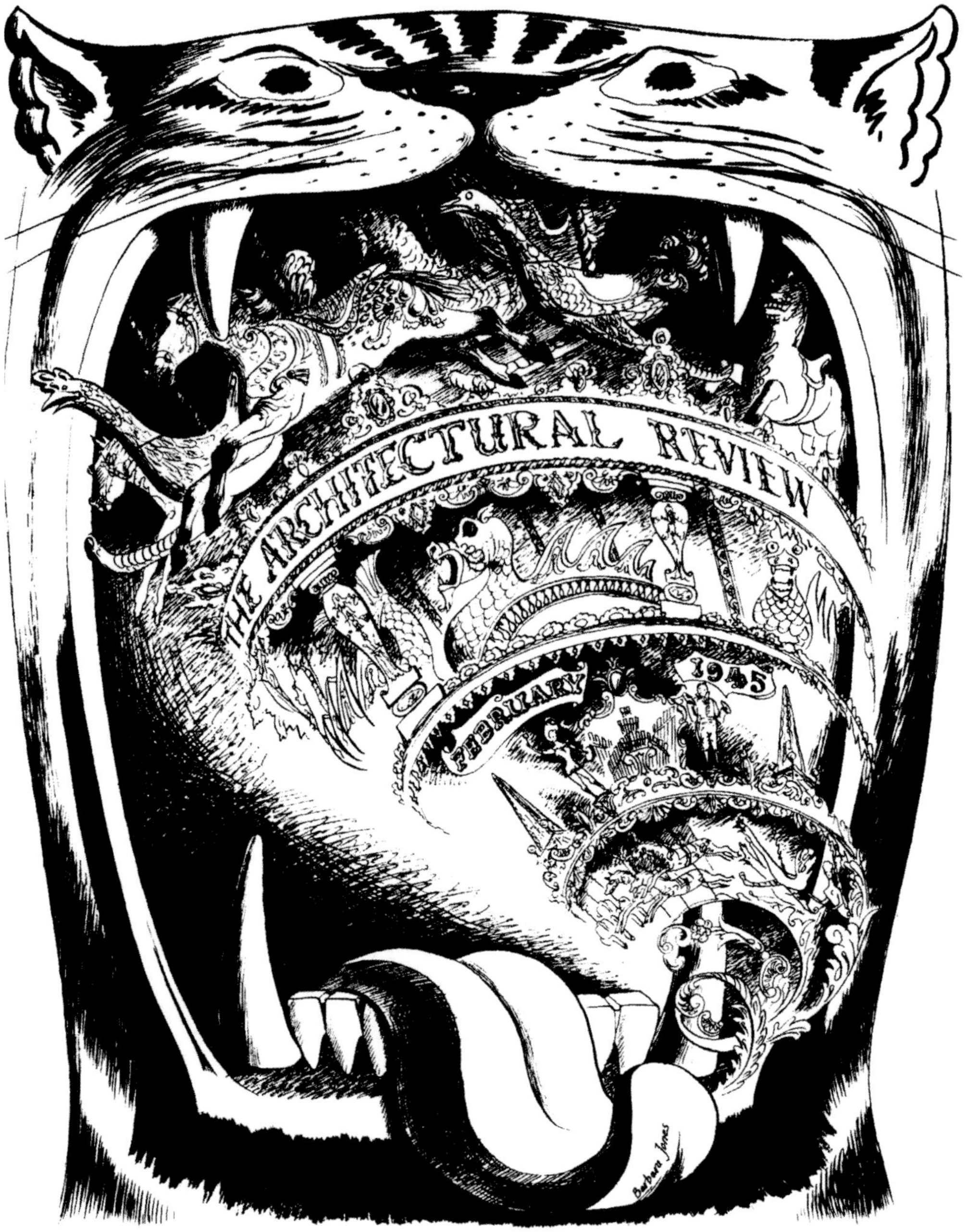

Architectural Review, cover, February 1945, Barbara Jones

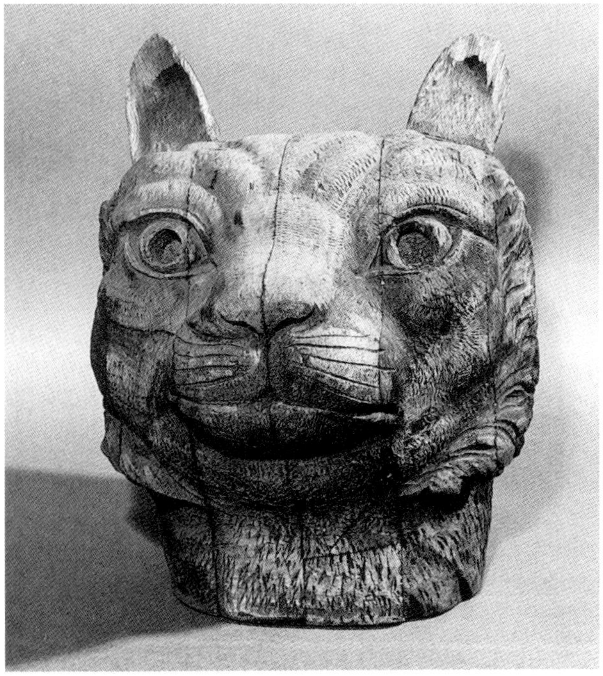

A wooden cat's head from Savage's workshop, prototype for Le Fevre's Jumping Cats roundabout

rounding board, which operated on Hampstead Heath from new until 1983 – and where an annual fair was staged for wounded soldiers during World War One. It may have inspired Mark Gertler's great anti-war painting *Merry-go-Round* of 1916, with riders locked in frozen screams. Now in the Tate, the picture was rolled away in the artist's Hampstead studio during his inter-war bouts in Mundesley Tuberculosis Sanatorium, to be rescued only after his suicide in 1939.

In 1940 the Ministry of Labour and the Pilgrim Trust launched a scheme to chart the special features of Britain at risk from Hitler's bombs, resulting in a Domesday record of more than 1,500 watercolour images. The project

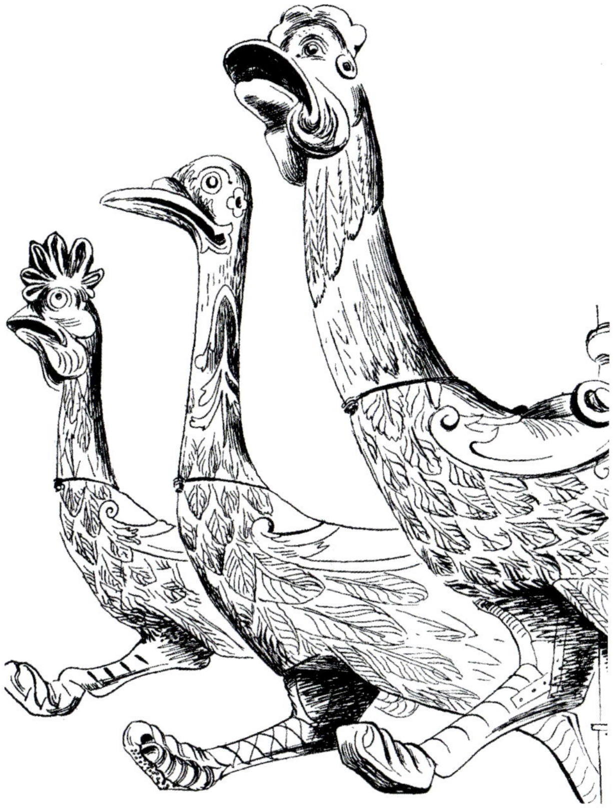

Roundabout cockerels, Barbara Jones, line drawing (right)

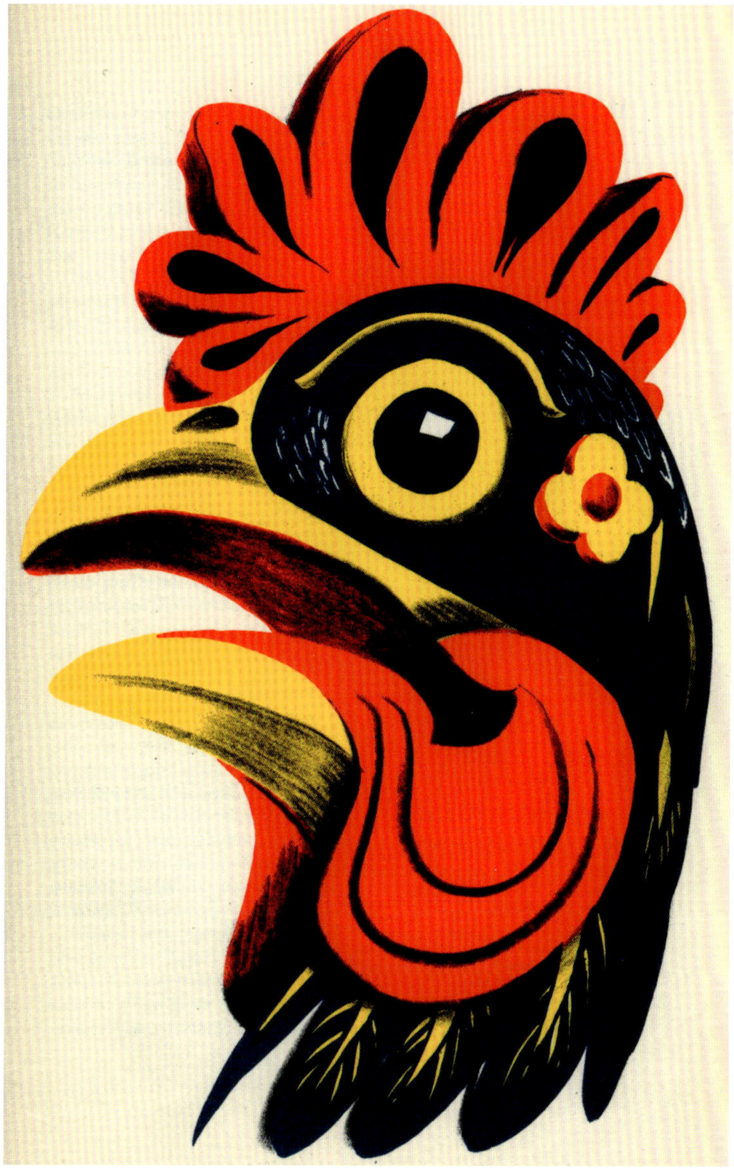

Roundabout cockerel, Barbara Jones, 1953, lithograph, from *English Fairs and Markets*

involved John Piper and Kenneth Rowntree, who would be very active in East Anglia, and a now almost-forgotten phenomenon named **Barbara Jones**.

A hugely prolific jobbing artist, Barbara Jones (1912-1978) is rightly described by biographer Ruth Artmonsky as 'a snapper up of unconsidered trifles' – with the rider: 'She chose to spread her talents widely – painter, muralist, illustrator, exhibition designer, curator, historian, collector, writer, broadcaster, evangelist – and, as with the adage, too widely may have been too thinly. People who knew her as a watercolourist of quaint and eccentric architecture may have been completely unaware of her prodigious output as a designer of book jackets.' All her fields of interest converged in King's Lynn.

In 1942 she produced a sadly surreal watercolour of Savage's Yard in which illusions are stripped bare. A study in decaying junk centres on a crudely modelled horse, whose features are formed chiefly in thin paint. This was an inner-circle horse and gorgeous styling was reserved for the steeds of the outer-ring, which lured fair-goers to part with their pennies. The card like a broken concertina in the foreground is a length of mechanical organ music with slits for notes, and the mutilated automata on the organ itself would have struck drums, bells or cymbals before the instrument ran out of steam.

But in a 1945 article for the *Architectural Review* called Roundabouts: The Demountable Baroque, she hailed such survivals as prime examples of popular art – paying a special tribute to Savage's in a cover drawing showing a

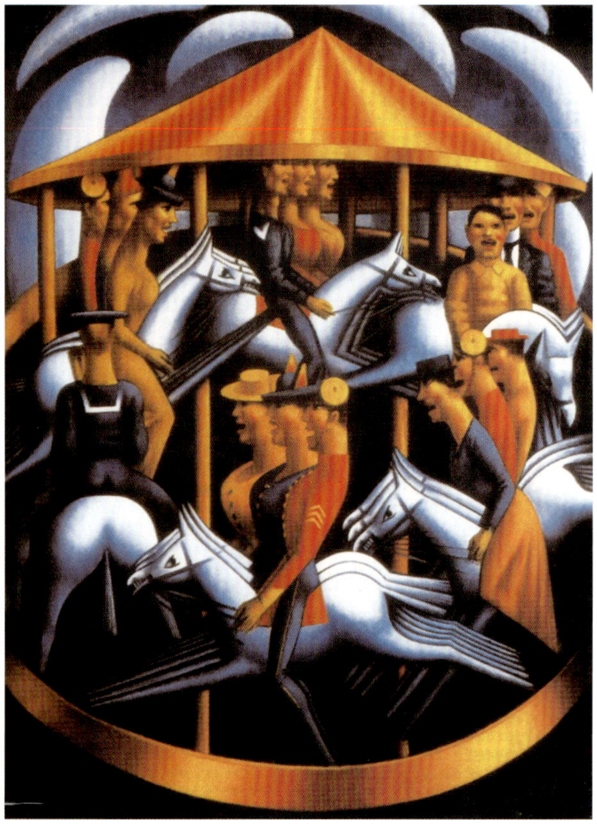

Merry-go-Round,
Mark Gertler, 1916,
oil on canvas,
Tate Britain (left)

whole fair of Norfolk-made carousels revolving within the mouth of a jumping cat. And she proved the point the following year in picture number two in the first School Prints series: *Fairground.* This triumphant image celebrates two hallmark Savage's rides.

Barbara Jones had a Savage horse's head named Norah on a wall in her Hampstead home – part of an eclectic collection of folk art, bric-a-brac and curios which she raided for her 1951 Whitechapel Gallery exhibition Black Eyes and Lemonade, and which thrilled visitors including the future Pop Artist Peter Blake. That was part of the Festival of Britain celebrations for which

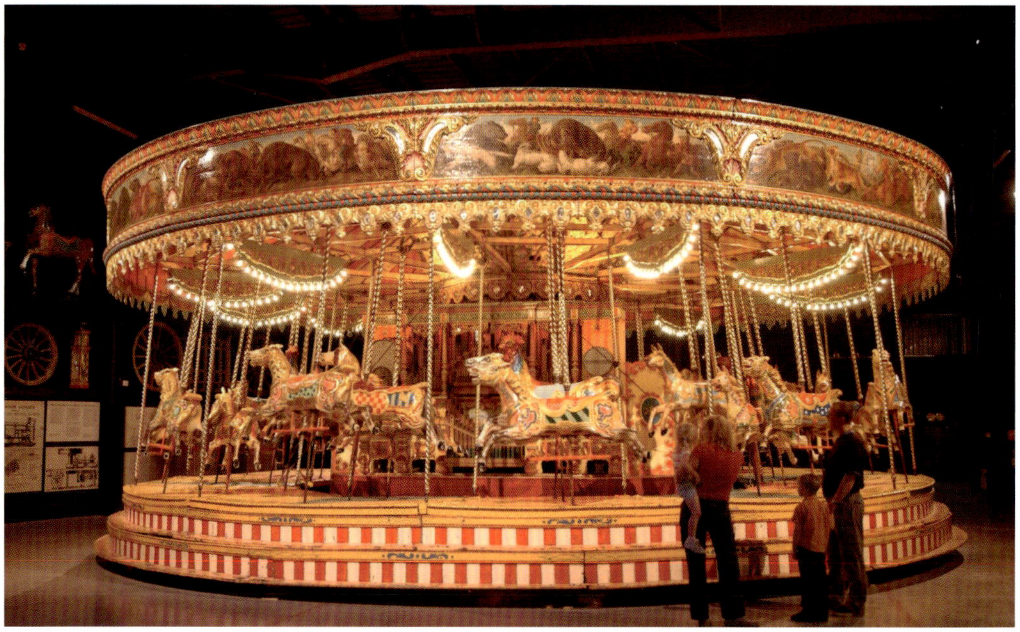

Gallopers ride, 1896,
The Thursford Collection

she also designed a gigantic Coastline of Britain diorama for the South Bank and the title page for East Anglia in the *About Britain* guides. Sadly her plan for a water roundabout of baroque shells manned by cat-gondoliers was rejected. But from that same stellar year the back cover of her influential book *The Unsophisticated Arts* boasts a trio of Savage horses.

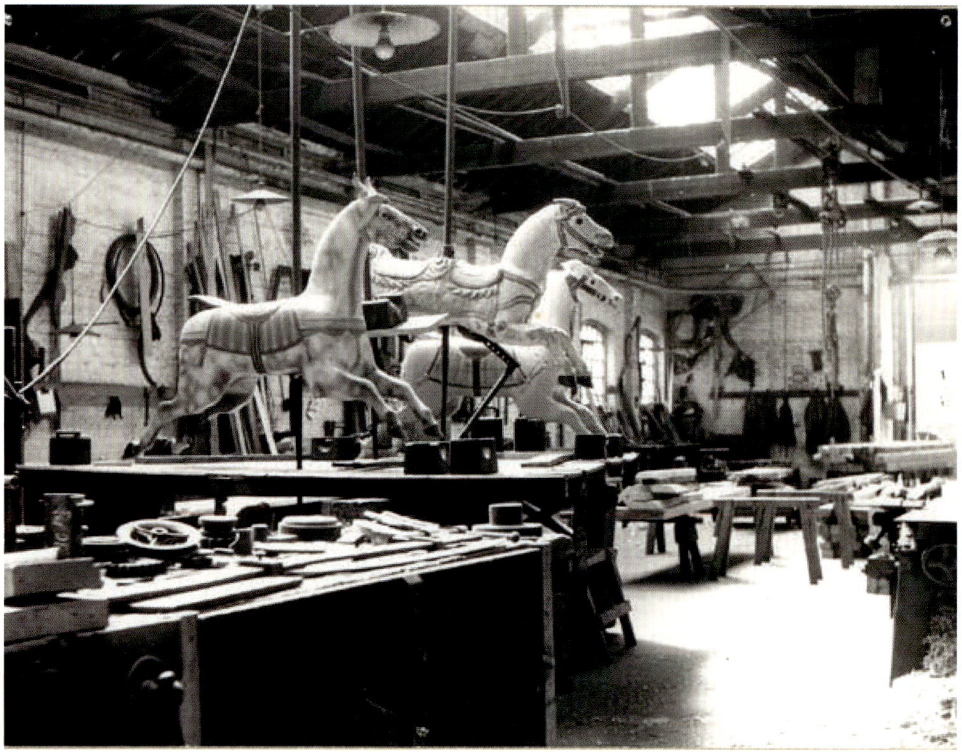

Savage's St Nicholas Ironwork's carving shop, with fairground gallopers, c 1910

Beastly Brilliance

Fabergé at Sandringham

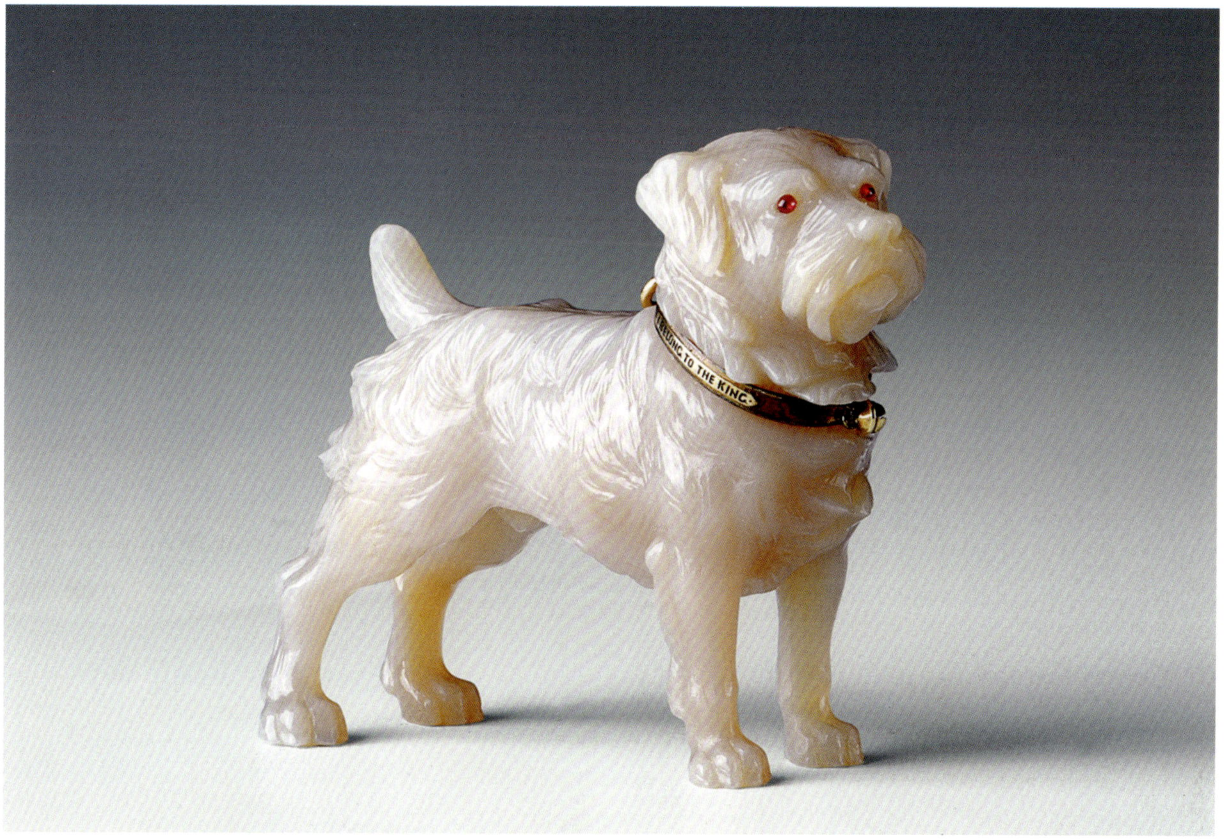

Caesar, c. 1907,
King Edward VII's favourite dog,
Royal Collection

In the spring of 1863 the first Royal train arrived at Wolferton station, on the branch line from King's Lynn, bringing the Prince of Wales and his bride, Alexandra, home from honeymoon to their new country estate at Sandringham. In the dying days of 1925 the body of the late queen dowager left the same rural halt for burial at Windsor.

Over those seven decades processions of eminent rail travellers were driven on through rhododendron avenues and birch and pine woods to a red-bricked neo-Elizabethan pile like a large railway hotel astray from that little station.

Royals (including Germany's last Kaiser and the last ruling Tsar of Russia and his family), nobles and notables here for house parties and shooting parties found themselves amid a menagerie of horses, dogs, birds, farm breeds and exotic beasts. Alexandra, neglected by her husband, came to depend on the loyalty of animals.

In 1907 the then King Edward VII commissioned **Carl Fabergé** to produce portrait sculptures of favourite dogs and horses at Sandringham as a present to the queen – an idea apparently suggested by his cleverest mistress, Alice Keppel. After a visit from the manager of the Russian court jeweller's London branch, the project was extended to cover the Norfolk estate's beastly gamut and resulted in at least 100 figures in the Royal

Collection plus others now all over the world.

The best animal sculptors on the books, including the Swiss Frank Lutiger and the Swede Boris Froedman-Cluzel, were despatched from St Petersburg, probably joined by England's Alfred Pocock. For several months they were honoured guests on the Norfolk estate, but toiling daily until, on 8 December 1907, the sculptors staged a show of wax models in the dairy which, after Royal approval, and suggestions for a few amendments, were then taken to Russia for production in hardstones, gems, gold and silver. At that viewing Edward was accompanied by his most beloved pet, Caesar, who would be wrought in ruby-eyed chalcedony and with a golden collar inscribed I BELONG TO THE KING. In May 1910 the Norfolk terrier walked behind his master's coffin from Westminster to Paddington, with his marble likeness eventually sitting at the feet of the king on the tomb in St George's Chapel, Windsor.

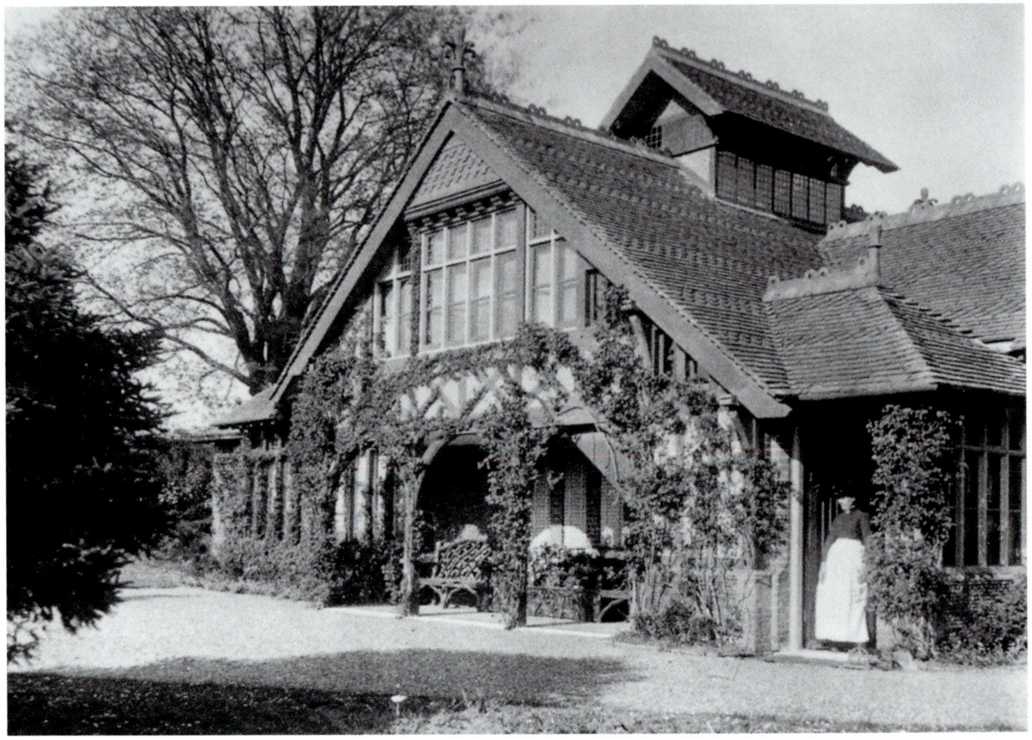

The dairy at Sandringham, c. 1900

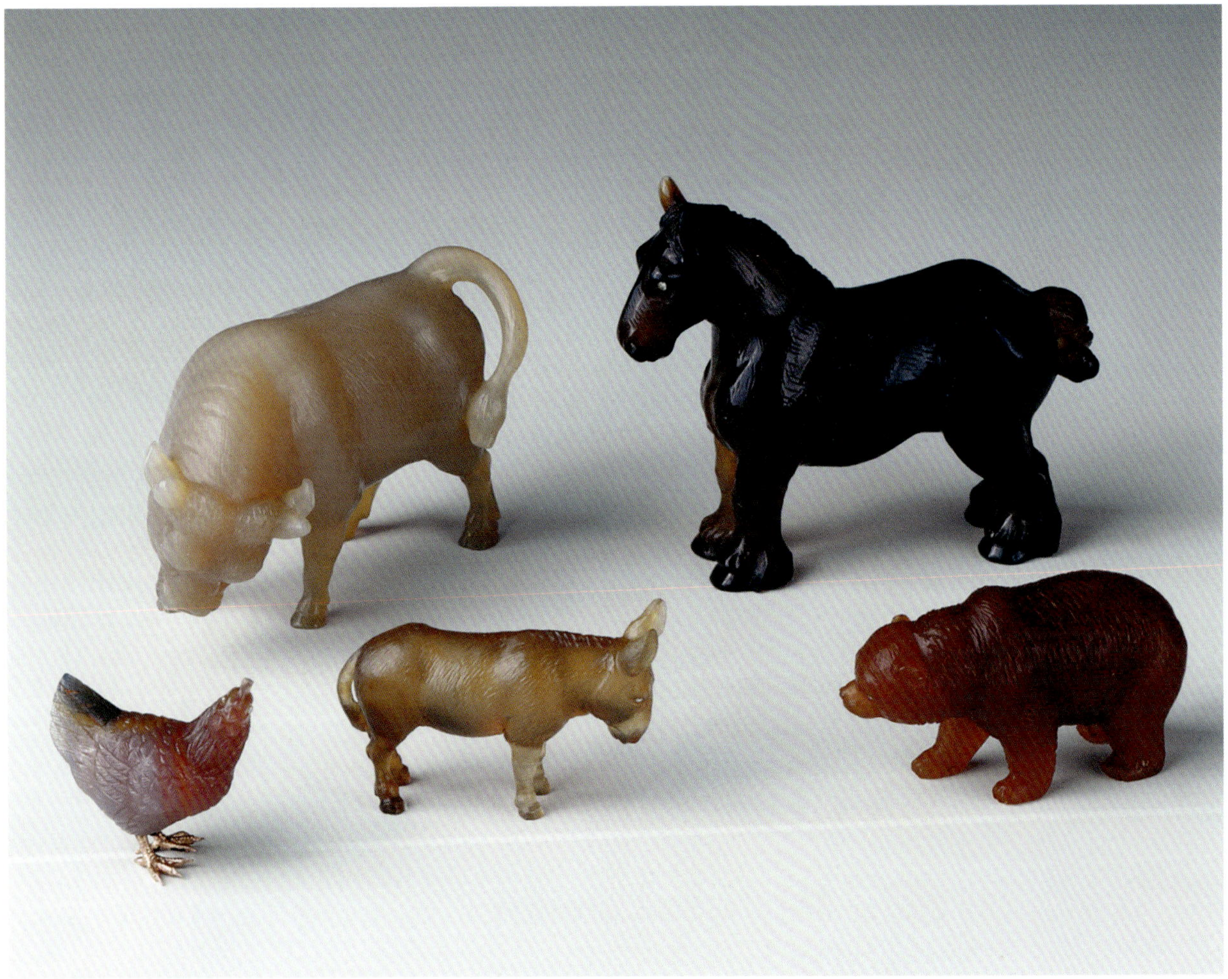

Sandringham farm animals commissioned by King Edward VII, c. 1907, Royal Collection

Meanwhile, the Fabergé carvers had had the run of Sandringham's 26 kennels housing great danes, borzois, bulldogs, basset hounds, Clumber and Japanese spaniels, pugs, chows, labradors, terriers, dachshunds, Pomeranians, Pekineses, St Bernards, Samoyeds, Siberian sledge dogs and motley mongrels. They had toured the estate with the royal commissioners for the pick from barns, fields, cages, pens, dovecots and pigeon lofts for the precious and precise tally of delicate models that were often like Japanese netsuke. Birds from reared pheasants to wild owls and a corncrake on a wheatsheaf – the latter still a common sight and a deafening sound in Edwardian Norfolk – were also featured.

Back in St Petersburg Carl Fabergé himself selected the hardstone blocks for each creature – obsidian for Norfolk black turkeys and Dexter bulls, chalcedony for cattle and donkey, agate for Shire horse, brown bear and hens, banded agate for racing pigeons, adventurine quartz for pink pigs and yellow ducklings.

After carving and polishing, figures might gain emerald, ruby, aquamarine or rose diamond eyes while birds were set on golden feet. The wax model of Persimmon, Edward VII's most successful racehorse, latterly the star of the Sandringham stud farm, went to the Moscow silver workshops, with a further six copies cast in bronze for royal gifts.

Many miniaturist marvels were presented to the queen, while Alexandra and her children George and Victoria bought more examples from the London store until it closed down with the onset of World War One. The Fabergé workshops could not survive the Bolshevik Revolution, though Carl Fabergé himself escaped to Switzerland.

These exquisite bibelots were the ultimate symbols of luxury at its most royal. Much of the hardstone had been mined at Ekaterinburg where, in July 1918, Russia's no-longer-ruling family, whose patronage had underpinned the enterprise, were brutally murdered in a basement.

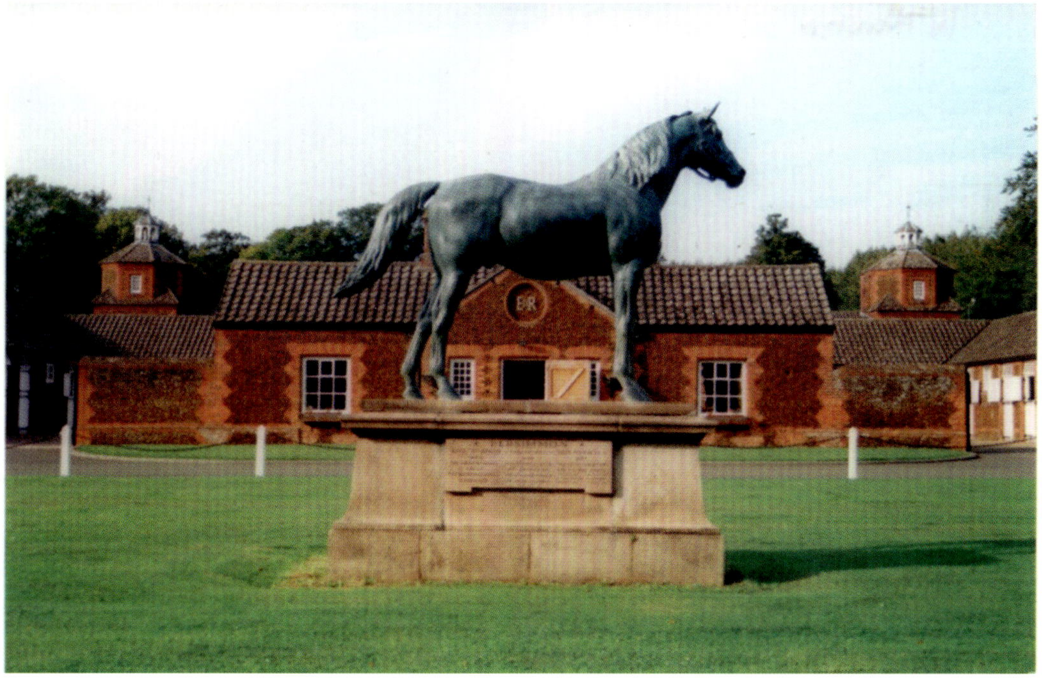

Persimmon,
Adrian Jones, bronze

Wildfowl (below) and *Whooper Swans* (opposite),
2009, linocuts, for *Wildfowl*, New Naturalist Library 110

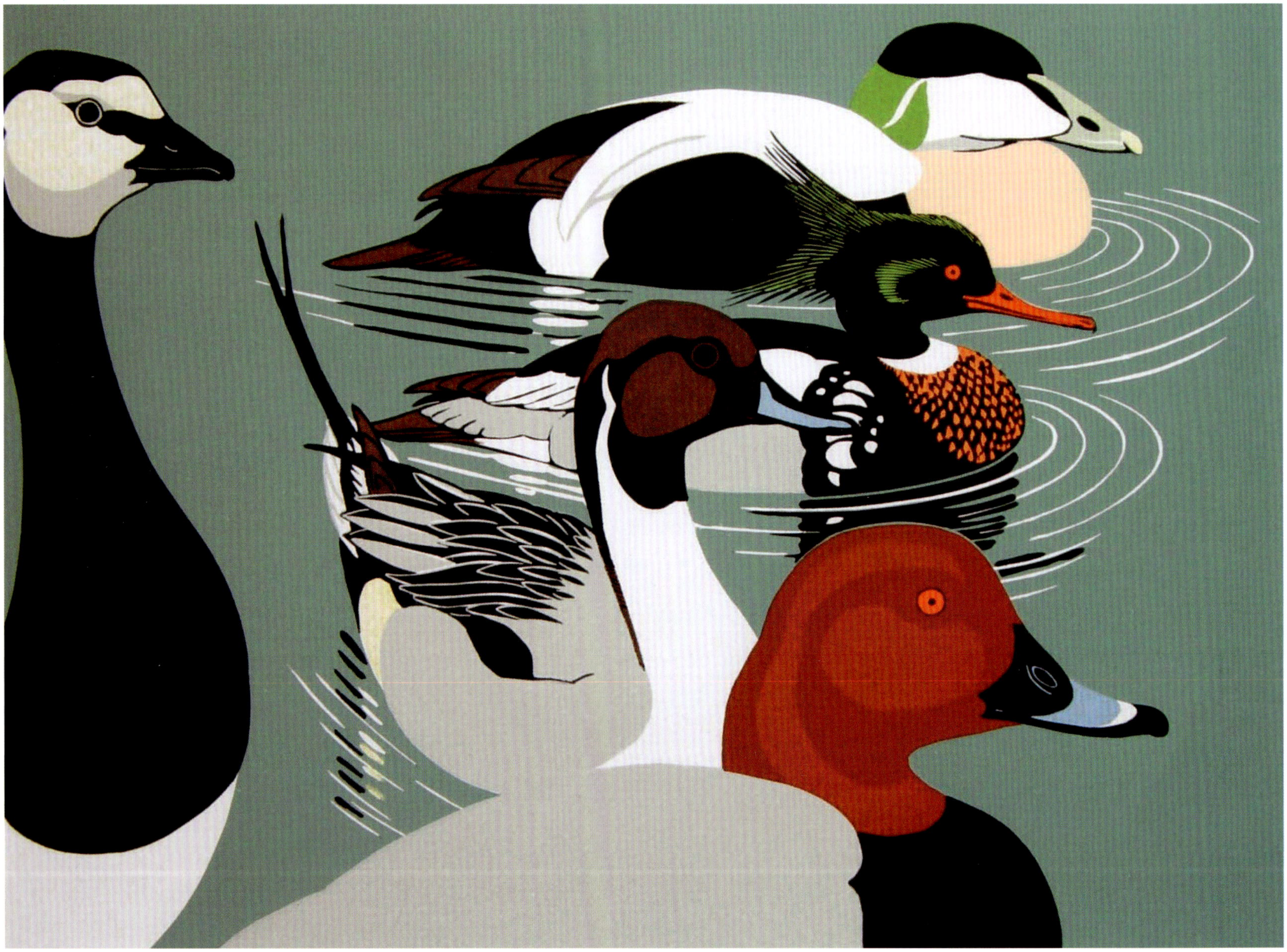

Wildlife Covers

Robert Gillmor and the New Naturalist Library

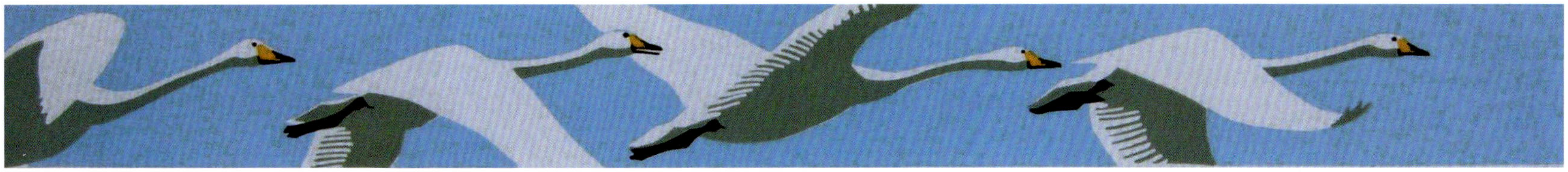

RSPB

RSPB avocet logo, Robert Gillmor

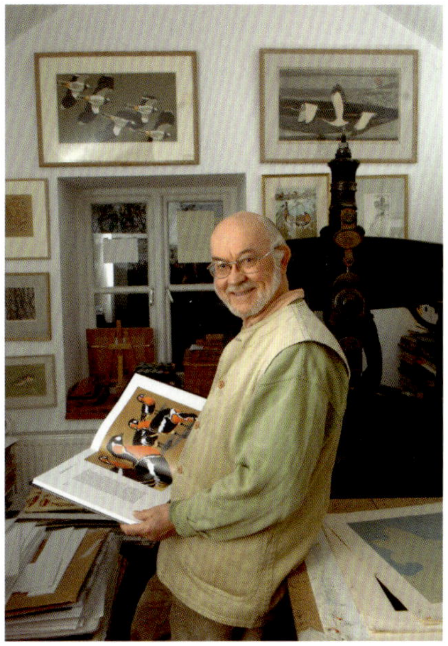

Robert Gillmor in his studio

Picture what has been likened to a paper rainbow – celebrating nature in these islands – beginning its brilliant arc in the ruins of wartime London. Publisher William Collins set up a New Naturalist Board to plot a sequence of books 'to interest the general reader in the wildlife of Britain by recapturing the enquiring spirit of the old naturalists'.

This meant the reverential spirit of peasant poet John Clare and Selborne parson Gilbert White, rather than the shot and chloroform of later trophy hunters. Hatched in the depths of the Blitz, like National Parks and nature conservation planning, the project was to be about life rather than death.

The publisher insisted that the series should have jackets illustrated by artist-designers Clifford and Rosemary Ellis, and booked the Ellises for six colourful jackets at 12 guineas a time. The first dramatic and eccentric image – for E B Ford's *Butterflies,* 1944 (right) – focused on the spectacular swallowtail of Broadland, but especially on its green-and-black-banded and orange-horned-and-spotted caterpillar. Mr Collins felt the subject too rare, before bowing to a bold design.

That initial batch of six jackets eventually extended to 92, and ended only with Clifford's death in 1985 when the baton passed to **Robert Gillmor** who, by 2009, had added another 44.

Born in Berkshire, Robert Gillmor studied and taught in Reading until fledging as a full-time illustrator in 1965. Since his first tome, on blackbirds, he has become one of Britain's best and most prolific depicters of birds.

Influenced by his artist grandfather Allen Seaby, and by Fens doctor turned ornithological illustrator Eric Ennion, he first spied a New Naturalist book at the age of ten. John Steers' *The Sea Coast*, published in 1953, helped him with A-level geography.

For the first 17 of his Collins jackets, the artist kept to the Ellis formula, using four colours – one of which was always black. More hues came in the mixing, with white from bare paper. So each design consisted of four black drawings, to be turned into four lithographic

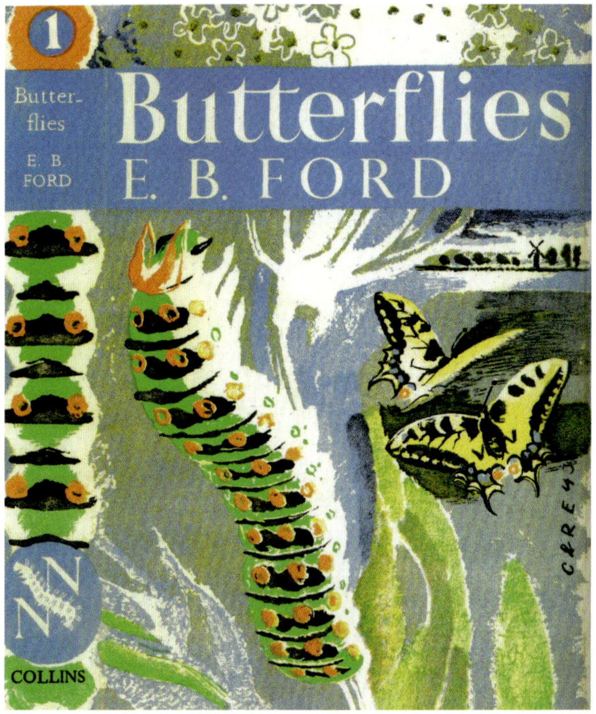

Butterflies, Clifford and Rosemary Ellis, 1944, New Naturalist Library 1

plates from which the colours were printed. He says: 'Usually there would be a careful pencil drawing, in pure line, over which I taped a transparent plastic sheet.

'The area for a particular colour would be filled in with black Indian ink. When that was dry another sheet of plastic would be taped on top and the next colour drawn or painted on. And so on, twice more. By working carefully on the overlays the four blocks should, and usually did, register accurately.'

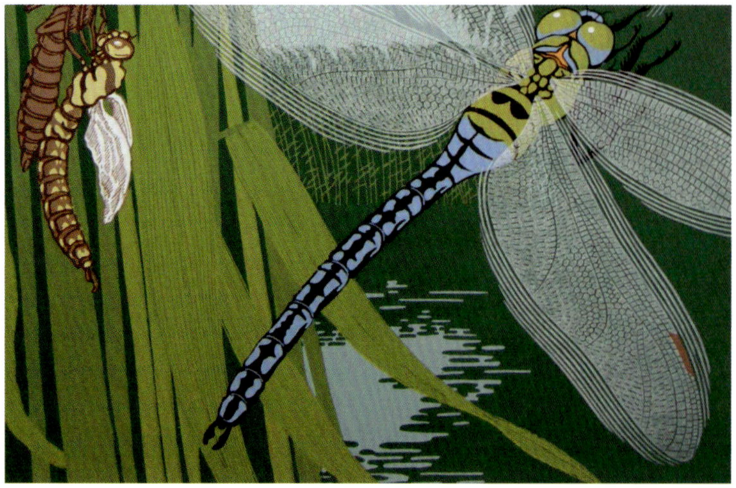

Dragonflies, 2008,
New Naturalist Library 106

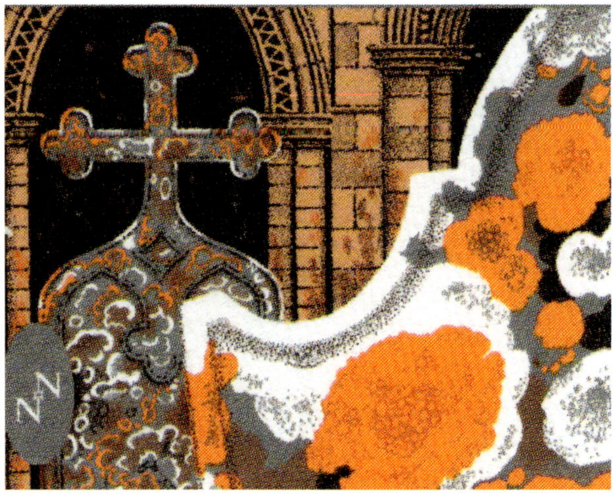

Lichens, 2000,
New Naturalist Library 86 (left)

Since moving to Norfolk in 1998 with his wife Susan Norman, herself an accomplished pastel and oil painter, Robert Gillmor has returned to the medium of linocut, favoured by school art classes of old and mastered over 20th-century decades by East Anglia's Edward Bawden. Each composition in this demanding but delightful medium is doubly difficult. It has to be formed in reverse since what will be printed is a mirror image.

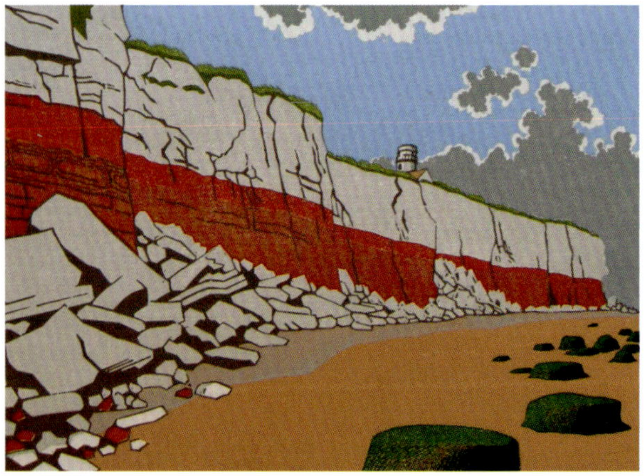

Southern England, 2008,
New Naturalist Library 108 (left)

Since *Seashore* (Peter J Hayward, 2004) all Gillmor jackets have been full-colour linocut designs. So now he cuts into a lino block for each colour – using up to 15 blocks in all. The blocks for each image are printed in sequence, using water-based inks, with additional colours achieved by over-printing. The entire process is carried out by hand using an 1860 Albion Press. Stand-alone prints are produced in editions of 65 or fewer.

Inspiration is all around. *Lichens* (Oliver Gilbert, 2000) shows Binham tombstones blotched orange, white and grey against the façade of the ruined priory with a tiny black-and-white moth, beautifully camouflaged against the lichen.

British Bats (John Altringham, 2003) salutes the pipistrelles which live in the Cley studio roof and, together with natterers, cause despair among the village's church cleaners, though his batty cover design actually portrays Wiveton church.

He says: 'When illustrating the *Handbook of British Mammals*, my studio was full of boxes and cages containing a variety of small mammals modelling for my drawings. This mini menagerie included a pipistrelle which fed enthusiastically on mealworms as I held him in my hand.'

The bracket fungus creeping up the spine of *Fungi* (Brian Spooner and Peter Roberts, 2005) sprouted from a dying apple tree in the Gillmor garden. And for *Bumblebees* (Ted Benton, 2006) he had only to step from his studio to study a typical Norfolk flint wall running the full length of the garden but virtually hidden by a great growth of honeysuckle.

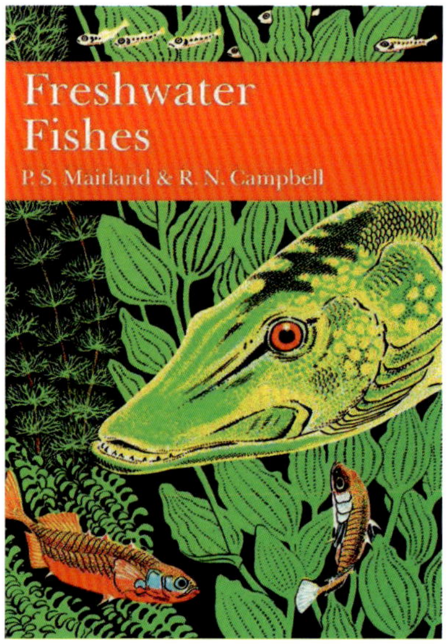

Freshwater Fishes, 1992,
New Naturalist Library 75

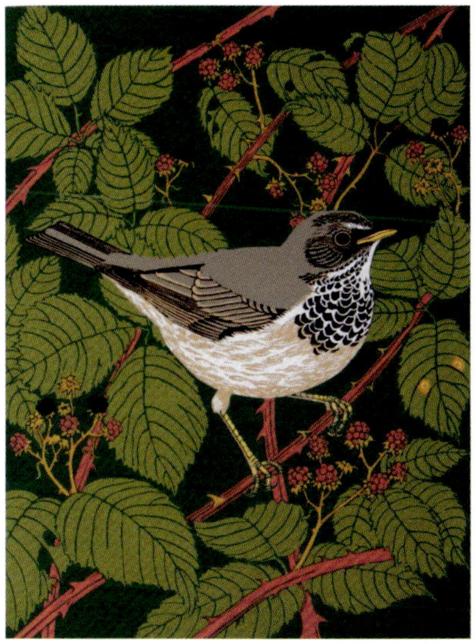

Black-throated Thrush,
Birds New to Norfolk, 2009

Whooper Swans, 2001 (right)

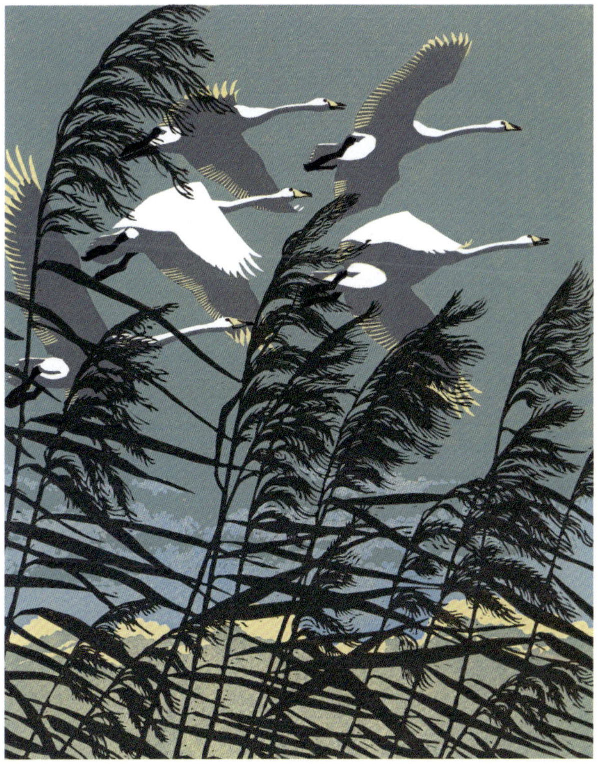

'During the late spring, summer and autumn, this is a well-attended restaurant for a multitude of insects,' he says. 'Bees, butterflies, flies and moths, including the exotic hummingbird hawk moth, throng to feed at the glorious white, trumpet-like flowers. Some minutes looking and then collecting a few sprigs to draw, and the basic idea was settled. The elegant flutes of the honeysuckle made a pleasing contrast to the heavy, clumsy bumbling bee (*Bombus hortorum*), with its furiously buzzing little wings somehow keeping it aloft.'

In 2007 he heard from an old friend – Peter Friend, to be precise – last encountered on an expedition to Spitsbergen, in 1957. Now this leading light at Cambridge University's Department of Earth Sciences had been commissioned to write the New Naturalist volume *Southern England* and his manuscript persuaded the artist to visit Hunstanton.

He was drawn to a town 'famous for the three differently coloured layers of bedrock in its cliffs: a layer of Late Cretaceous white chalk overlies an Early Cretaceous layer of brown sandstone (Carstone), with a thin layer of red chalk between them. The detached and fallen blocks of white chalk at the base of the cliff show that the cliffs are collapsing and moving inland all the time. The regular rows of weed-covered Carstone blocks in the lower part of the beach show how the storm waves have created a wave-cut platform with a regular system of joints (cracks).'

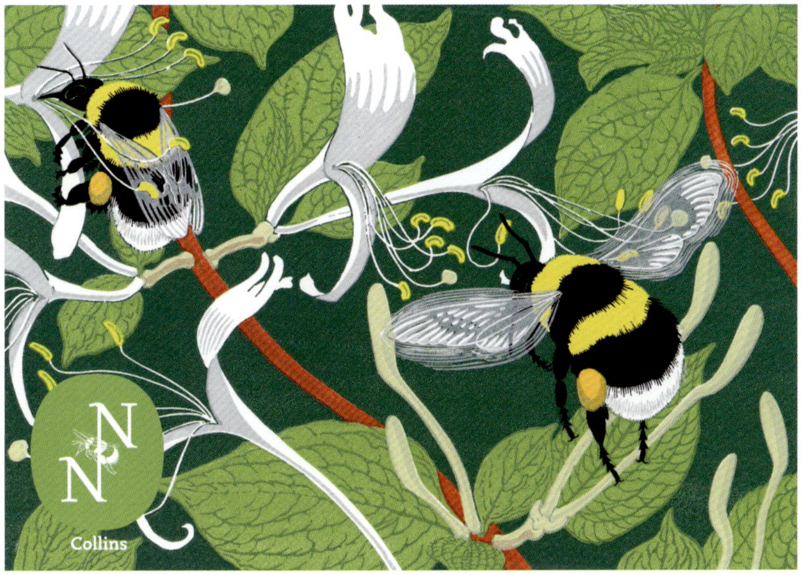

Bumblebees, 2006,
New Naturalist Library 98

Robert made drawings, took photographs and 'watched the fulmars flying up and down the cliffs, occasionally landing to cackle noisily with mate or neighbour'. Away from all human beings, save for a distant dog-walker, he found the perfect cover image.

This founder member of the Society of Wildlife Artists is, after all, most at home with birds. Winner of the RSPB medal for his outstanding contribution to bird conservation, he also designed the society's avocet logo.

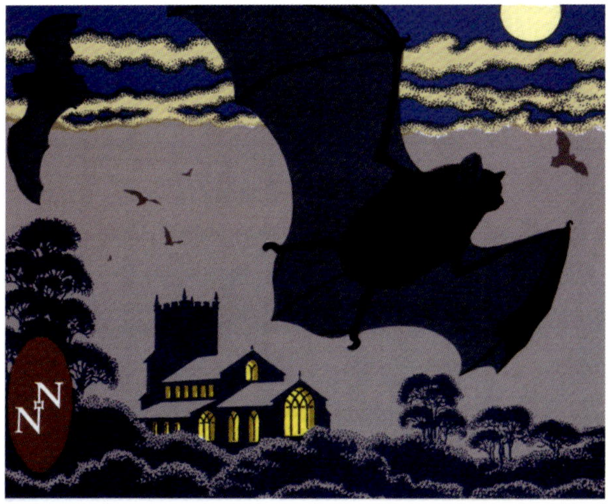

British Bats, 2003,
New Naturalist Library 93 (right)

Blakeney, Floodtide, 2005, watercolour

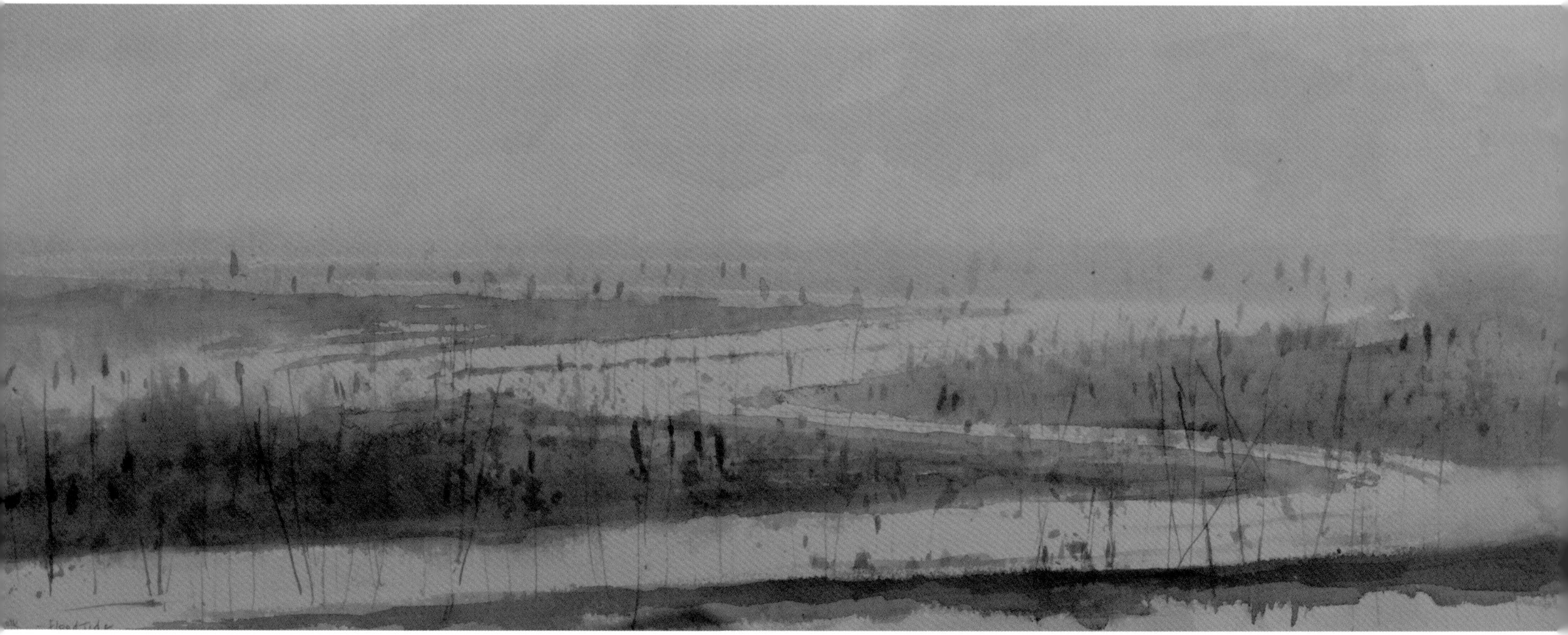

Energy on the Edge

Norman Ackroyd

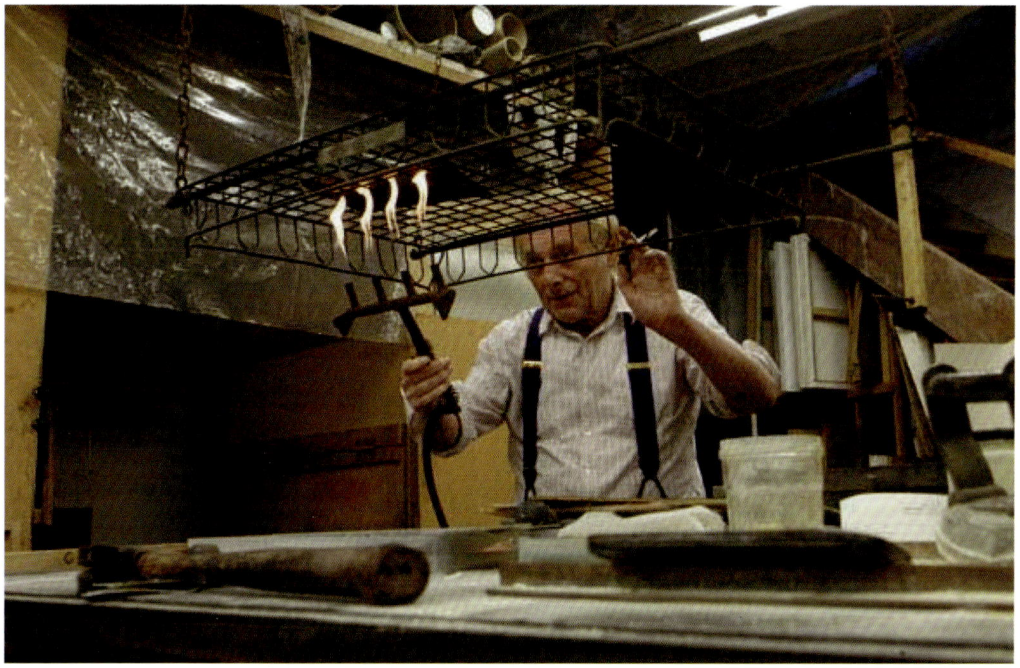

Norman Ackroyd
in his London studio

Some reckon Royal Academician **Norman Ackroyd** now the leading print-maker in the land. All his work, from etchings to watercolours and paintings, is rooted in travels across and around the landscape.

As a boy growing up in a working-class district of Leeds, in the drab decade after the last world war, his aim to be an artist was deemed 'outrageous'. But, inspired by bike rides into the Yorkshire Dales, he was determined to set down a passionate response to weather and wilderness. 'Even then I felt it was transient – we have a short life, you're catching at a moment,' he says.

He found his medium – etching – early but veered as an art student towards then-fashionable Pop Art before being lambasted by tutor Cecil Collins to work on what really touched his heart and soul. So, edging towards remoter parts of these islands, he came to focus on what seemed most sublime in the world around him. Taken under the wing of print-maker Julian Trevelyan, he then perfected a technique to match the lyrical immediacy of his vision.

The third and greatest role model for Norman Ackroyd, as for so many others, has been J M W Turner. Criss-crossing Britain two centuries ago, the master stuffed his pockets with sketchbooks, pencils and watercolours to record all that he saw and held in awe. What Turner did in watercolour, Ackroyd is doing – has done – in etching. The result is a ravishing record.

More than a thousand prints, plus hundreds of associated paintings, have now emerged from his journeys to seek out the most dramatically beautiful scenery across the UK and Ireland – from Cornwall to Cumberland and from Caithness to Connemara. Like the early 19th-century master, he has been drawn to rugged and jagged views, where rivers roar and mountains rise up and tumble into the sea.

He has ventured even further than Turner, to St Kilda and Rockall, sometimes setting down his impressions from the precarious vantage point of a bobbing boat. He is fascinated by geology and mythology and ancient ruins. He loves to work with poets – combining with Burnham Market's Kevin Crossley-Holland for the 2006 volume celebrating North Norfolk: *Moored Man*.

Most of all, his work is about evoking what it feels like to be immersed in a particular scene, and experiencing sun, rain, gale and sleet – whatever weather the brilliantly fickle British climate cares to throw at him and us. Therefore his printed plates are largely or entirely produced in the open air, directly in front of the subjects.

His essential travelling kit includes bottles of water and saturated sugar solution, pens, brushes, small copper plates and a mirror.

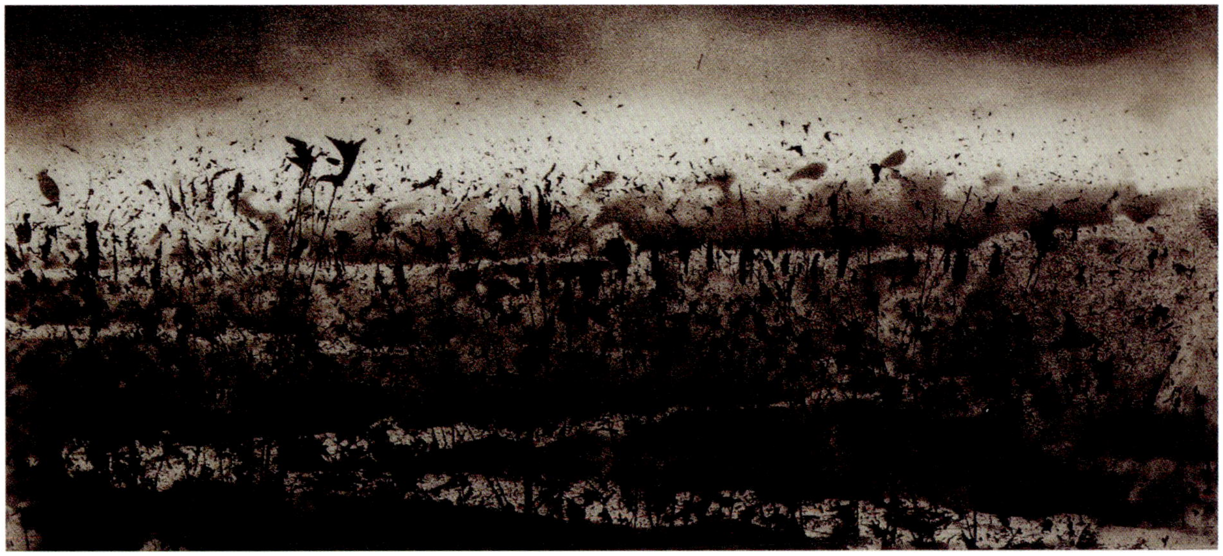

Over the Marsh, Burnham Overy Staithe, polymer on gesso board

Sitting down, and positioning the mirror to reflect his chosen scene in reverse (so that the printed image will be true), he loads a pen with sugar solution and then sweeps and glides over the surface of the copper.

Any ensuing mark that displeases him can be easily washed away. But the remainder of what is now a sugar-lift print will be taken back to his London studio – part of a former leather factory in Bermondsey which he (barely) converted into a warren-like workplace and home. There he sets to work swiftly, while the image and its special atmosphere are still fresh. Sometimes he will dash back to the scene with all the etcher's paraphernalia of acids and inks to complete the desired picture. By such means – plus added notes from watercolour sketches – he conveys the precision and the urgency of his vision. And, like all vehicles, the working process continues to be refined and perfected.

But the idea of working in East Anglia evolved in his mind only slowly. It finally crystallised with an invitation to visit the then president of the Royal Academy, Sir Philip Dowson, at his home near Beccles. Norman Ackroyd remembers: 'One morning I was looking at the most far-flung of the Blasket Isles off County Kerry and the most westerly piece of land in Europe. And the next day we were having lunch in Southwold. I'd crossed the British archipelago within 24 hours, and I found that really exhilarating. I also loved the fact that fringes – and not just Celtic fringes – link up. There is an energy in being on the edge.'

So he explored the coast northwards, revelling in a diversity of scenery that belied our region's reputation for flat uniformity.

Ultimately he hit North Norfolk and the subjects for a first series of 10 etchings: Brancaster Roads. For boxed sets of the prints he revived Christopher Saxton's 1579 map of the area revised by John Speed in 1610.

Brancaster Sunset, etching

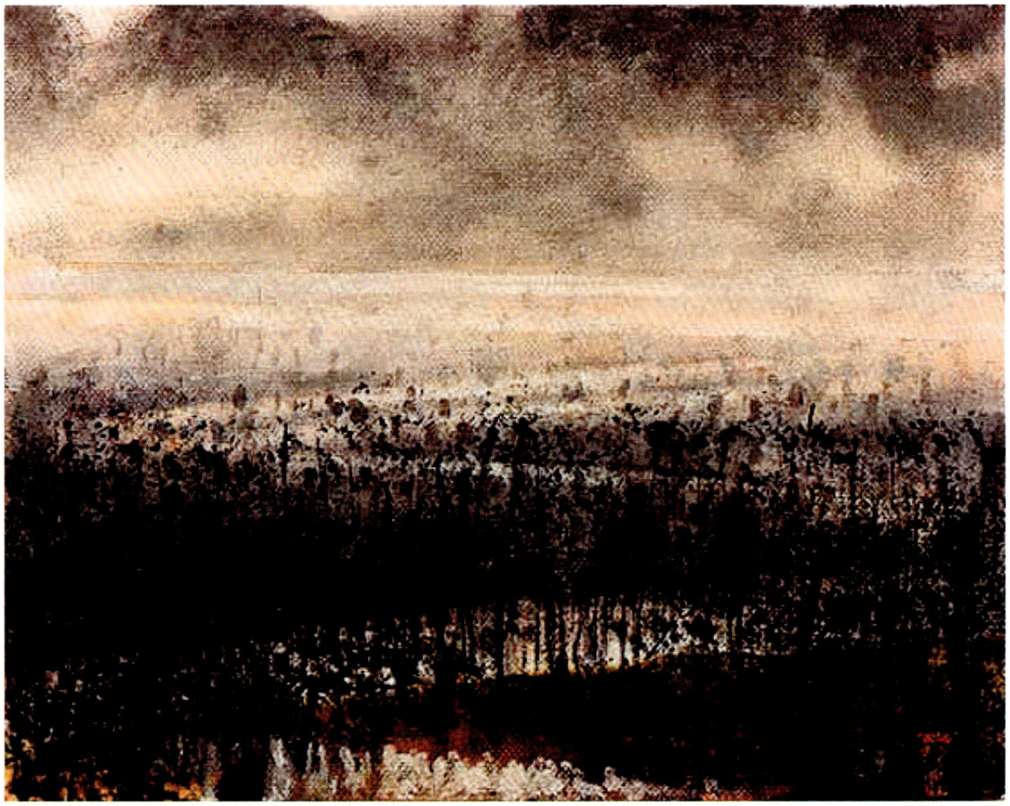

Extending from Snetsham to Cromere, it features hamlets such as Burnham Sutton and Berwick in the brakes which were subsequently swallowed up by history. Large chunks of coastline charted by Saxton were also to be amended and lost between the reigns of the two Elizabeths.

The artist says: 'The coastal sea roads of East Anglia, from King's Lynn to London, have been, for centuries, especially before the advent of road and rail, the fundamental routes for trade and communication. The North Sea relentlessly erodes the east-facing coast around the Yarmouth Roads and deposits its spoil on the North Norfolk coast in the form of enormous sand spits and an ever-changing and dangerous sea bed on the Brancaster Roads. The tides dominate the rhythms of life on this shore as they flood and drain the salt marshes, funnelling, often at deceptive speed, through the creeks leading to the chain of coastal settlements which, until recent times, boasted busy and bustling quays.'

This, then, is the elemental drama he relishes in his art – you just need to look a little longer and deeper to appreciate the broad picture. 'Over the last few years I have had much involvement with the immense and obvious power of the Atlantic on the hard rocks of the west coasts of Ireland and Scotland,' Ackroyd continues. 'The power of the North Sea is much less obvious but equally dangerous and influential on the softer, vulnerable geology of the Norfolk coast.

'These extensive salt marshes constitute one of the most important nature reserves in the British Isles. They still seem to belong more to the ocean than to the land. The wide expanses of dunes and marsh grasses, teeming with wildlife on a summer afternoon, contrast starkly with the threatening desolation conveyed at flood tide on a winter evening. So as well as all that beauty there is also something rather sinister. When that winter tide is gurgling through the reeds there is also the feeling that it can't be resisted.'

For this artist the essence of coastal North Norfolk lies in sparse detail – plants, posts, banks and dunes. Without the huge intrusion of peaks and troughs we can see more clearly. But in one print the outline of Brancaster church soars before us like some celestial cathedral. And mountain ranges do loom above Ackroyd's Norfolk – echoes of the Pennines and Cairngorms etched in cumulus clouds.

Sharpies Racing at Wells, Brian Lewis, 2001, oil on canvas

Surrey-raised **Brian Lewis** was lucky enough to attend one of only two secondary schools in the country to run an arts stream (another pupil was the future rock star Eric Clapton). He then served a long art-school apprenticeship which ended only with a chance discovery of the North Norfolk coast in 1980. The artist has been based there ever since, focusing fully on deceptively-innocent paintings which take a wry and sly view of humanity at play.

While Brian Lewis has long looked like a Norfolk painter – first selling his pictures in the street at Walsingham – his adopted patch is now starting to look like a Brian Lewis. As with Stanley Spencer's Cookham and L S Lowry's Salford, coastal outposts such as Cley, Blakeney and Wells-next-the-Sea can be seen in the sharp new light of idiosyncratic paint.

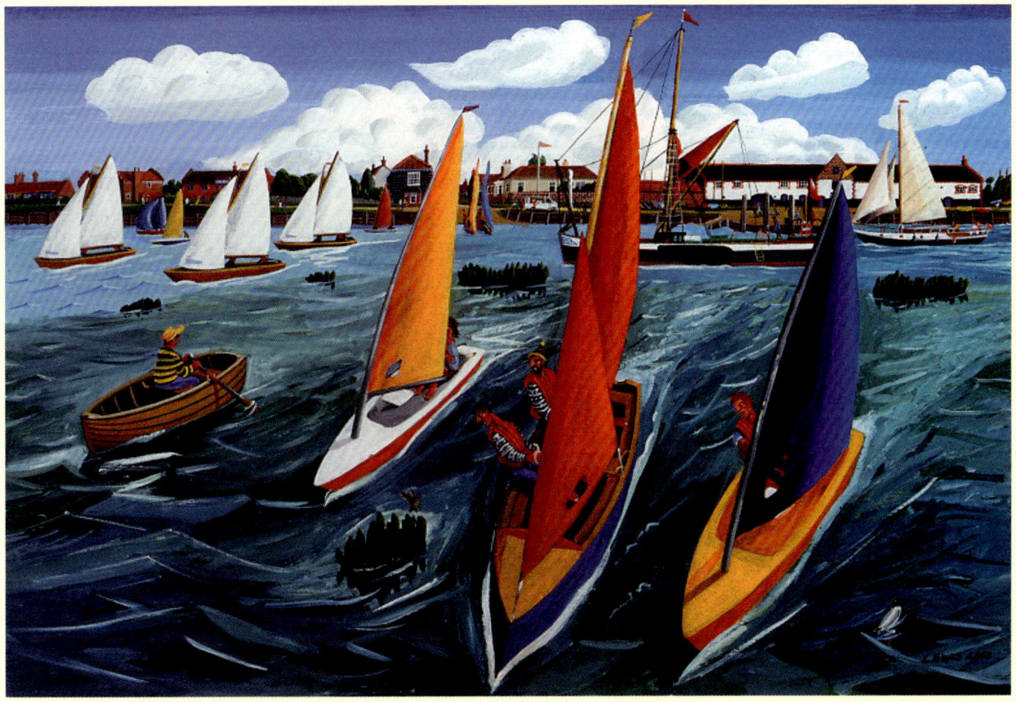

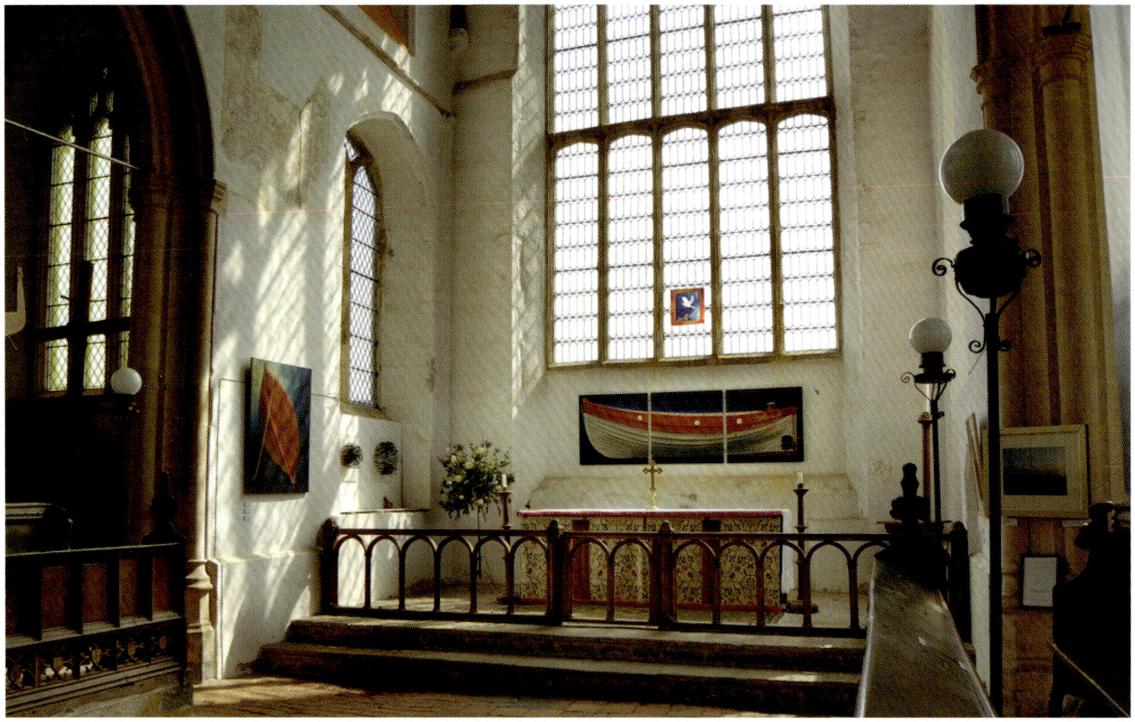

The chancel with James Dodds' *Salthouse Altarpiece* (see below), and *Out of the Marvellous*, both oil on linen

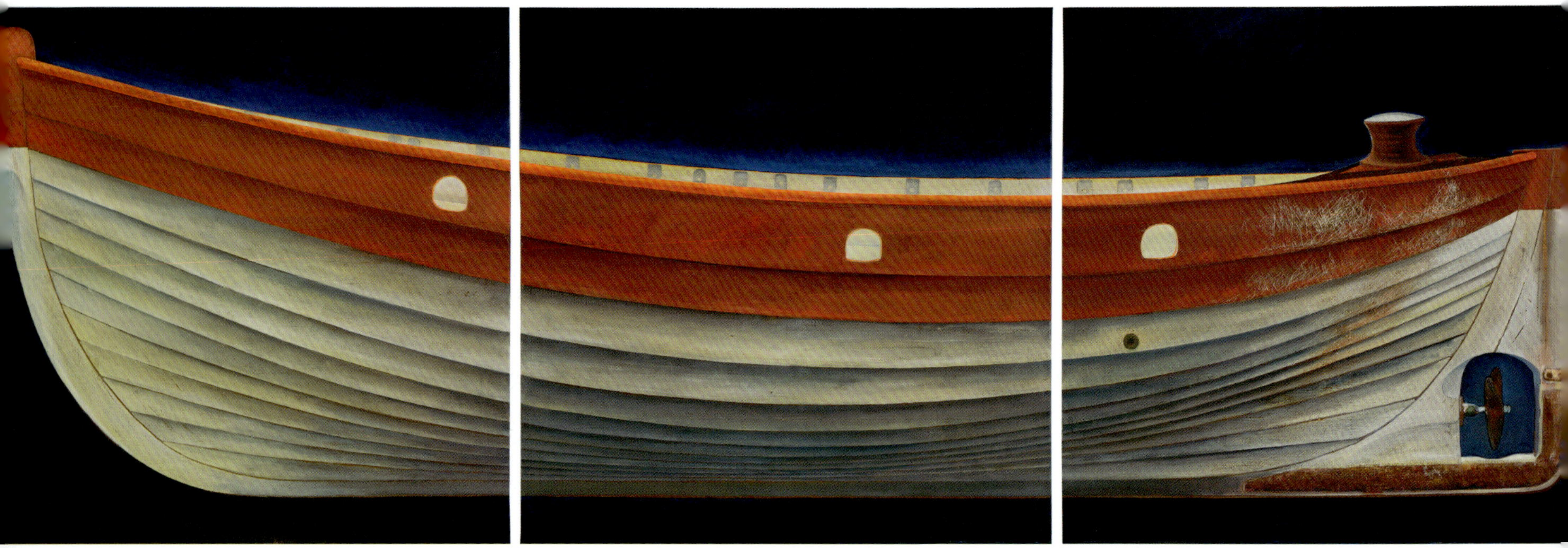

Out of the Marvellous

Salthouse 08

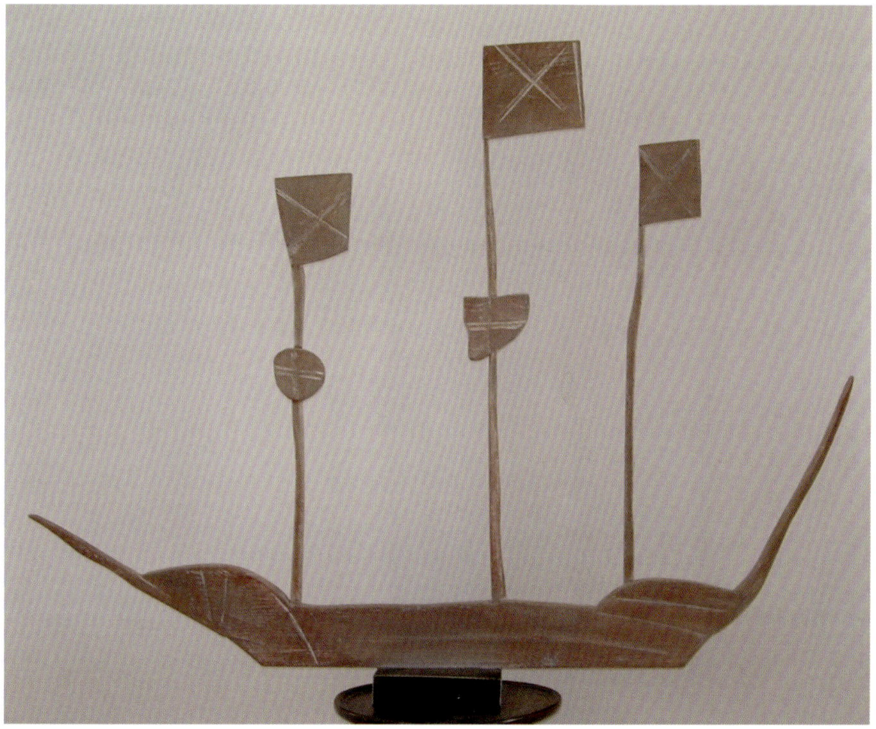

Salthouse Ship, Derek Nice, oak

Imagine a beacon church on the North Norfolk coast turned into a boat. I did. And, thanks to an invitation to curate Salthouse 08, that dream was realised in a ship-shape show.

Drawing thousands of visitors, annual Salthouse displays have been held every 21st-century July in the sublime medieval church near Cley. They are run by the North Norfolk Exhibition Project, whose stalwart organisers – mostly practising artists – pick a different curator each time. I was preceded by James Colman and succeeded by Pallant House curator Simon Martin.

Works by 70 artists addressed the title SEAhouse LIGHThouse SPIRIThouse. For my focus was the magical building, its history and setting above the coast and in that marvellous northern light. For good and ill, the sea has been central to the Salthouse story and to a building which for centuries was literally a lighthouse. I love the medieval view of a church as a ship carrying us safely through the storms of life to the shores of paradise. While more swimmer than sailor, I hail from a long line of Broadland boat builders and also wanted to pay tribute to the strong traditions of craftsmanship keeping Norfolk afloat down the ages.

I pictured a James Dodds Cromer crabber as a 21st-century version of a medieval altarpiece – like the great retable surviving at Thornham Magna, near Eye, but lost almost everywhere else in the smashing and sackings of the Reformation, which hit Salthouse most grievously. Here rood screen fragments resurrected as choir stall divides were to be

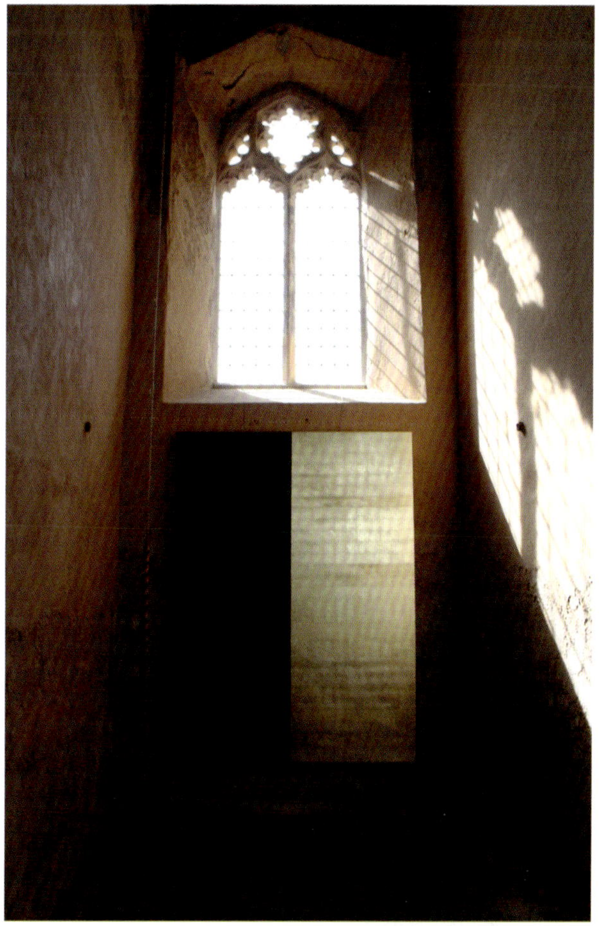

Sacro Terra, Susan Gunn, Salthouse 07, Gold leaf, gesso, pigment & wax on linen & board (right)

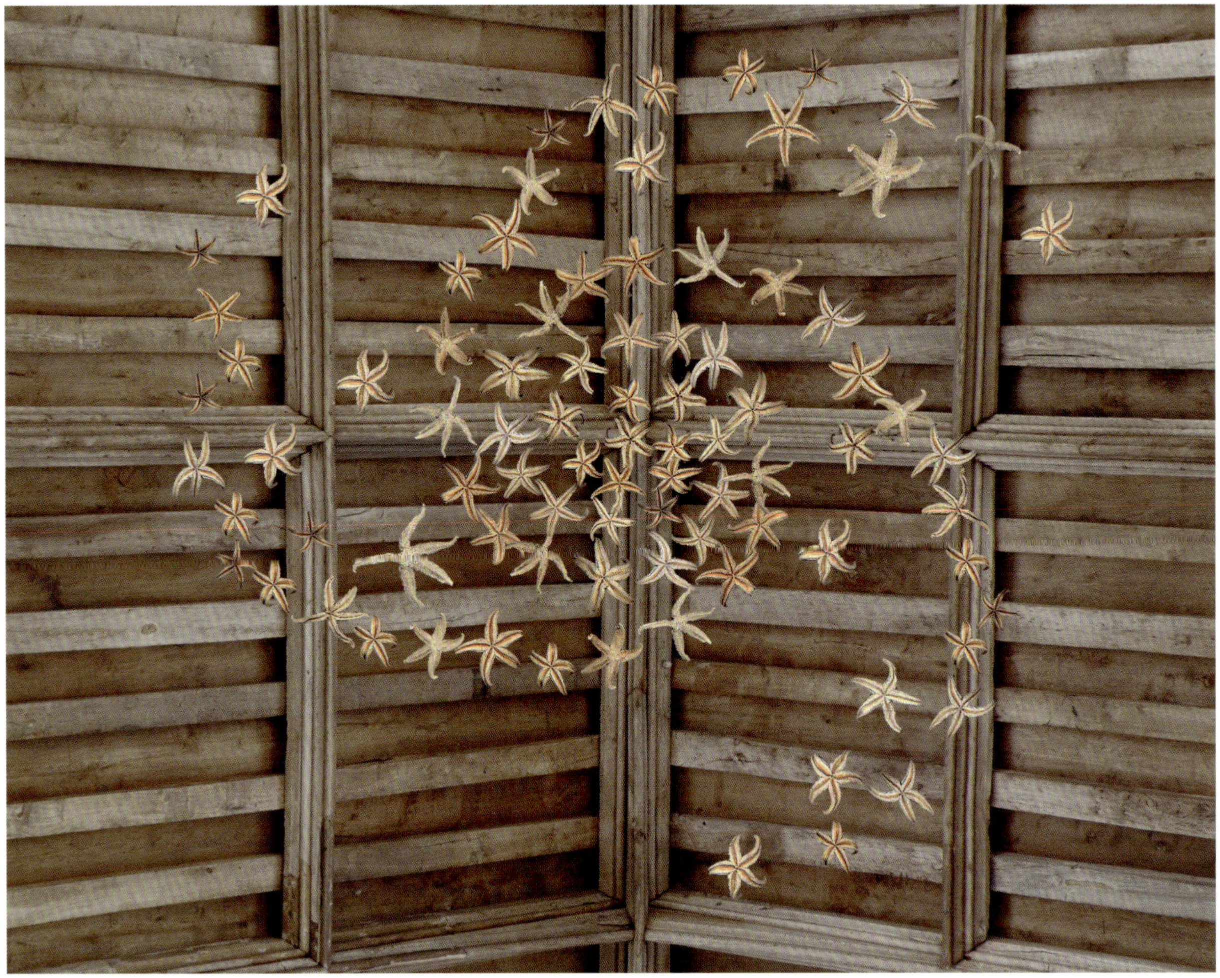

Azimuth – Navigation by the Stars,
Liz McGowan, Norfolk starfish (left)

Waiting for the Winch,
H J Jackson, linocut

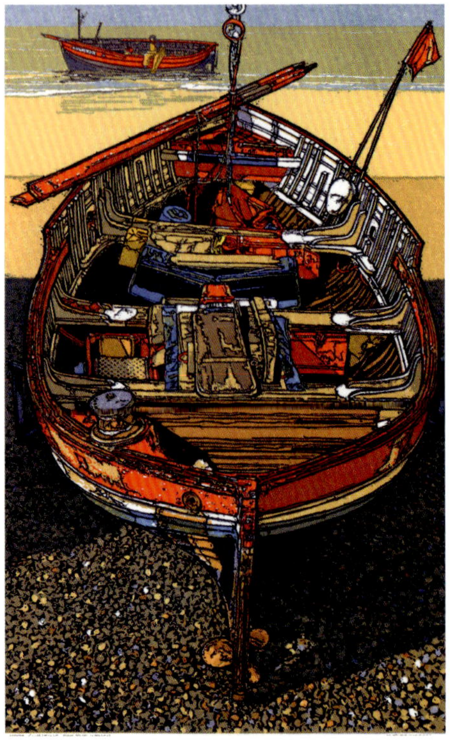

scratched with 18th-century graffiti ships – less vandalism by bored choirboys, perhaps, than pleas for safe passage by anxious crewmen.

James depicted the traditional north Norfolk inshore fishing vessel in the triptych form beloved of religious painters. And so, all at once, we saw a monumental boat split apart as if on the point of wreckage on this perilous coastline. Then a copper-leaf laminated mainsail by Alison Mitchell was tied to the outside of the tower, at a stroke turning the church itself into a glittering vessel.

In church and churchyard a site-specific display ranged across words, pictures, crafts, sculptures, music and light – taking in painting, print-making, drawing, collage, photography, textiles, stained glass, installations, mobiles, mirrors and models. The assembly moved from the avowedly abstract to the resolutely representational.

Jane Frost connected beach and churchyard shelters with lanterns strung across the marshes, while Viv Allen offered a camera obscura – a sort of igloo where shelterers watched sky and surrounding scenes along the lines of a popular Victorian seaside attraction.

With works by Norfolk sculptors Charlotte

The Beach, Salthouse,
Angie Lewin, linocut

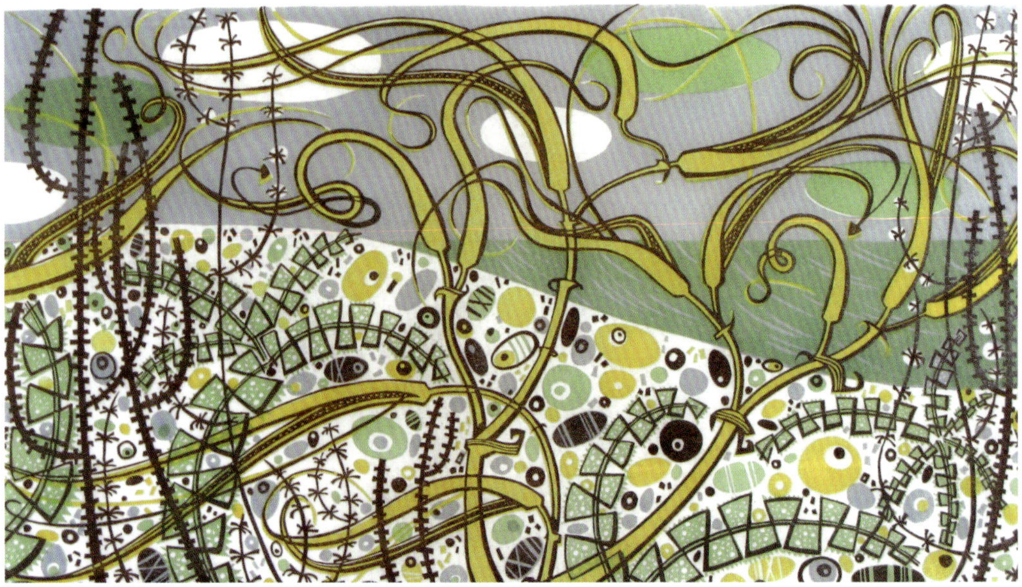

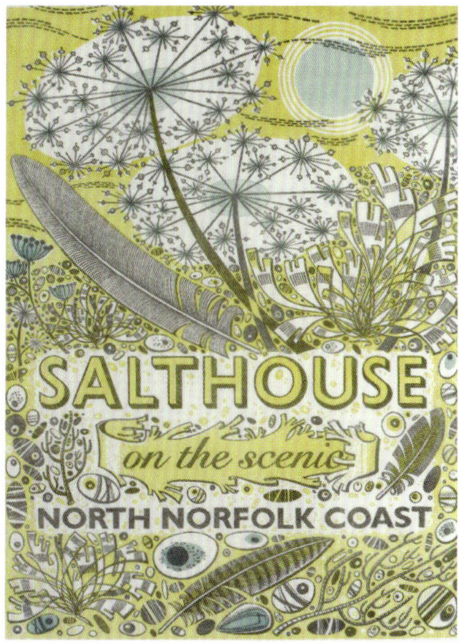

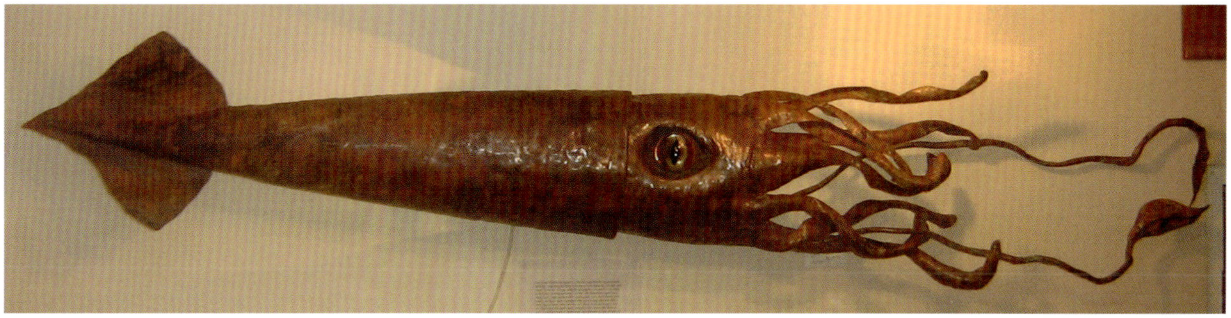

Salthouse poster, Angie Lewin, 2010

Squid, Geoffrey Image, copper and glass (above right)

Essex Mermaid, Guy Taplin, painted wood (right)

Miracle of the Holy House of Walsingham, Brian Whelan, acrylic & tin foil on canvas

Howarth, David Holgate and Teucer Wilson I also honoured Harriet Frazer's Snape-based Memorials by Artists, which a few decades ago began the beautification of English churchyards with a splendid tombstone at Salle, near Reepham.

Andrew Schumann constructed a tower of painted steel and glass and salt crystals, and Nick Ball a tower of light. In the hollow of the church tower Karen Whiterod created a LumenEssence mass of lit plastic mimicking a luminous kelp forest. In the porch an internally-lit copper squid by Blakeney-raised sculptor Geoffrey Image swam in the air as if in a submarine cavern.

Essex Mermaid – part mermaid, part barmaid and perfect ship's figurehead – by Guy Taplin was transformed into an icon by its setting in an aisle niche. The aisle was hung with banners by Harry Cory Wright in which his two immaculate photographs of Salthouse appeared to be

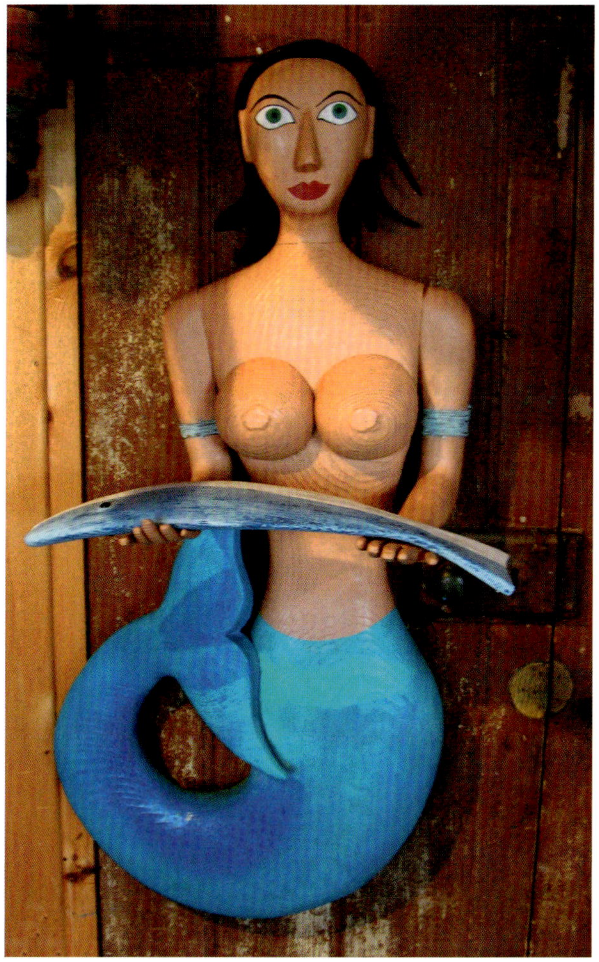

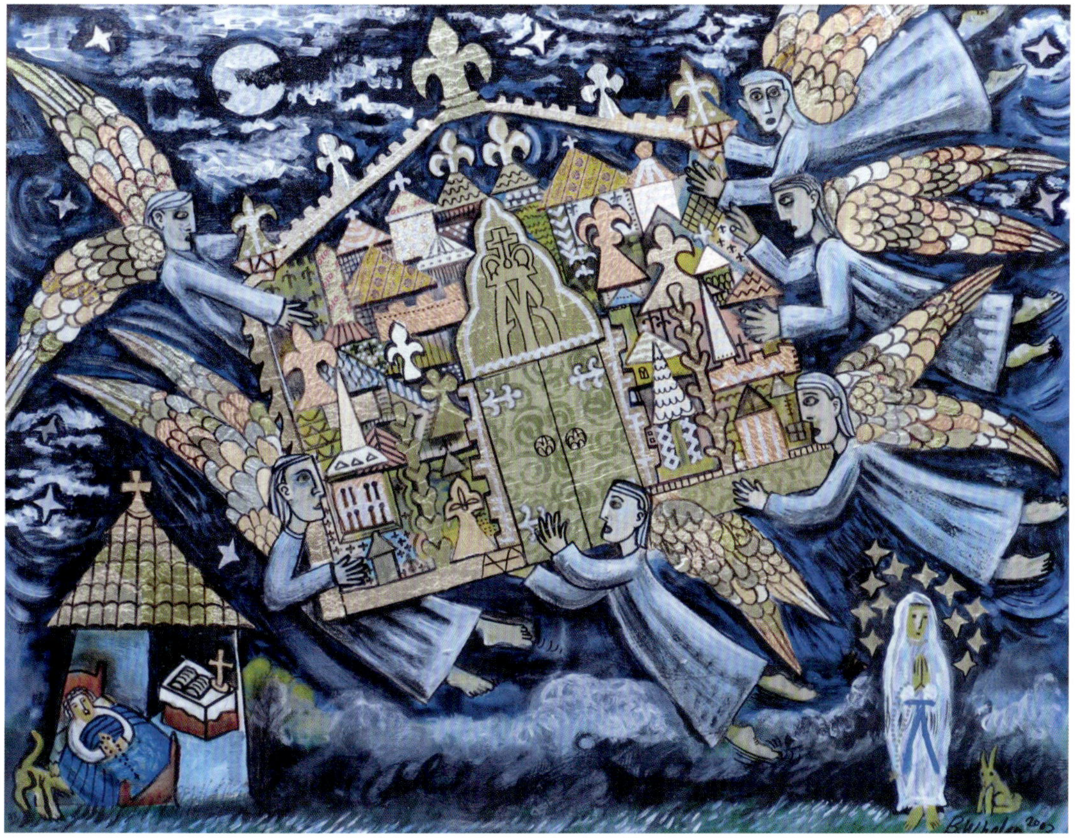

disintegrating. Elizabeth Peer's lit copper ship floated above the font, while her field of anchors grew in the churchyard.

Margie Britz used different coloured sand and clay from Hunstanton, Weybourne and Overstrand for a subtle installation in the clerestory window sills, while above spun a

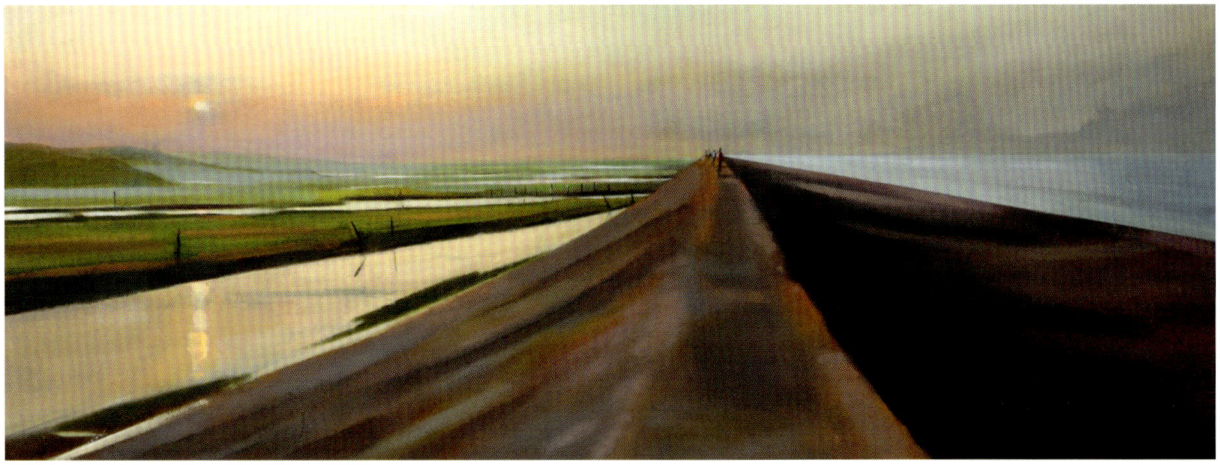

October Marsh, Salthouse,
Katherine Hamilton, oil on canvas

gigantic sail motif by Colin Miller and a constellation of starfish by Liz McGowan entitled *Azimuth – Navigation by the Stars*. Scottish abstract artist John McLean, later designing a sequence of stained glass windows for Norwich Cathedral, suspended a *Jacob's Ladder* series of paintings in the north aisle, where rivers of pigment ran like molten medieval glass.

Print-makers perfected the art of the linocut – from boats by Norfolk veteran H J Jackson to a pair of images based on wildflowers in Salthouse churchyard and on the shingle bank by Angie Lewin of the St Jude's Gallery at Itteringham, near Aylsham. A *Flood* collaboration between Bungay-based composer Roger Eno and abstract artist Dom Theobald saw a suite of pictures hanging in the south aisle and a soundtrack looped at intervals through the show. And, in a show-within-a-show, the meditative space of the Lady Chapel was underlined by Brian Whelan's paint-and-tin-foil depiction of the Walsingham legend, of angels moving the original shrine building to safer ground, and further reflections on the role and nature of lady chapels.

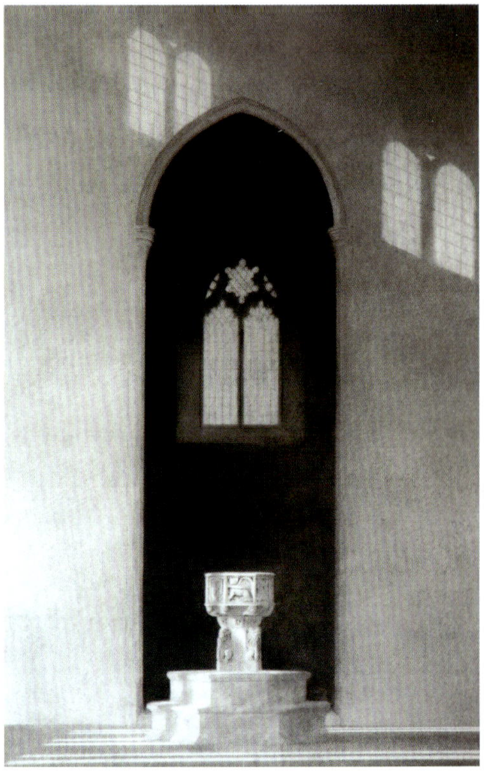

Salthouse Light 1,
Gerard Stamp, charcoal

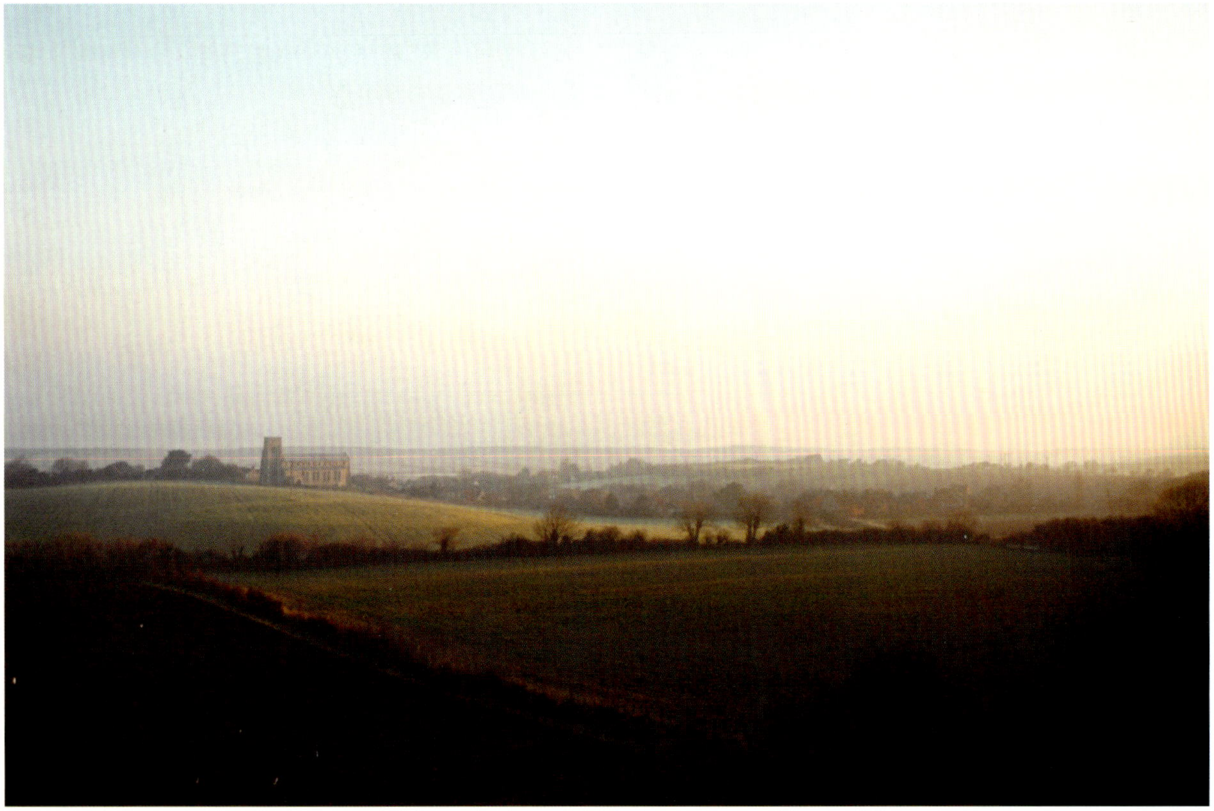

Salthouse Church from the South,
Harry Cory Wright, photograph

And James Dodds further confirmed a voyage into poetry by addressing one of the most beautiful and mystical poems by Nobel Laureate Seamus Heaney. *From Lightenings VIII* retells the saga of an Irish monastery whose altar-rail snagged the anchor of a flying ship. A sailor climbed down the rope to free the stricken vessel but struggled in vain. Seeing him flailing and drowning, the abbot told the monks to help him:

They did, the freed ship sailed, and the man climbed
Back
Out of the marvellous as he had known it.

Sister Wendy Beckett, who opened Salthouse 08 and marvelled at the altarpiece, says the poem 'reveals its fullness only right at the end, when we understand that the marvellous, out of which the man climbs, is this very ordinary world of ours. We live in the marvellous. We just don't see it.' But James Dodds sees it – and showed it in an *Out of the Marvellous* oil painting and a linocut entitled *The Monks of Clonmacnoise*. They hung on either side of the altar.

Having encouraged this project, Seamus Heaney was delighted with the outcome. On receiving a copy of the print, he wrote: 'Magnificent. A re-vision. The marvellous as he has shown it.'

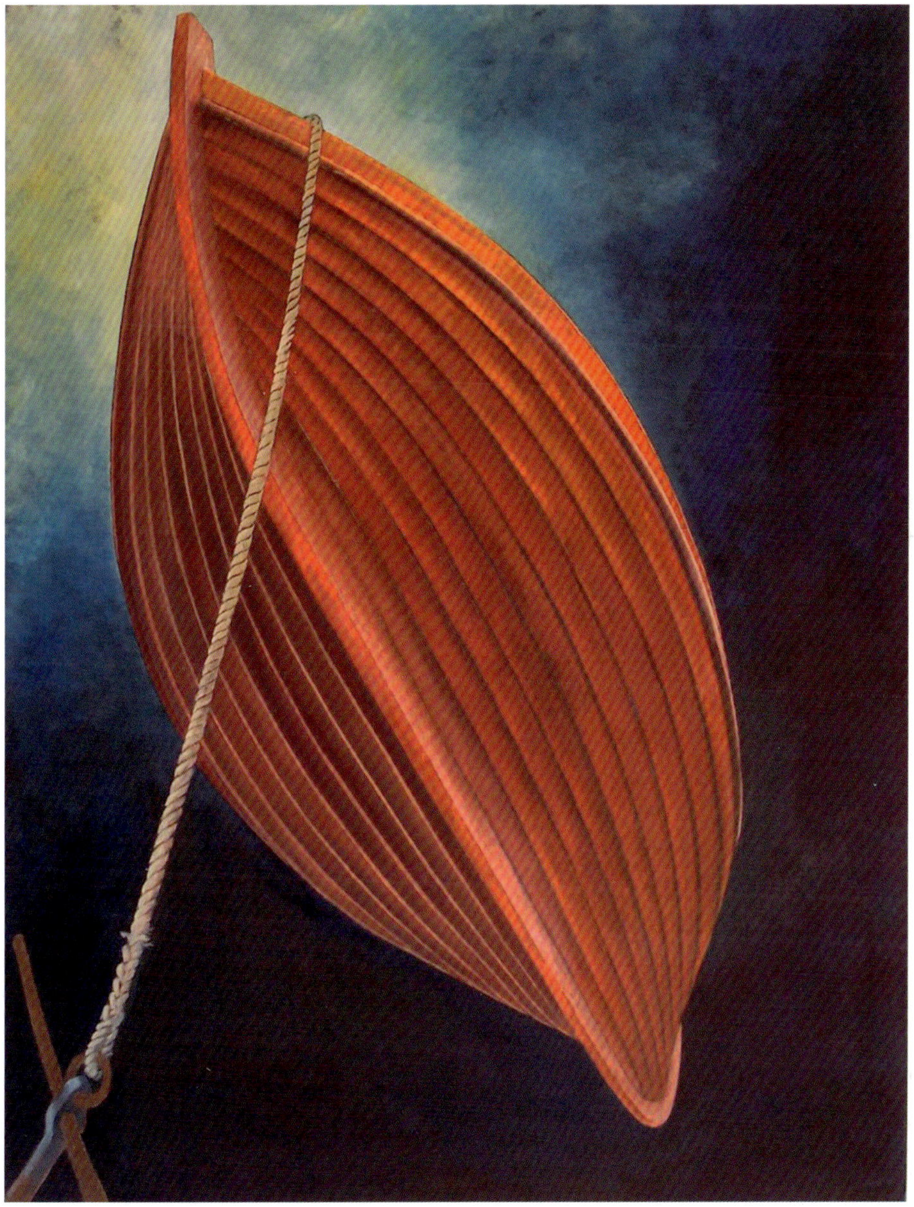

Out of the Marvellous,
James Dodds, oil on canvas

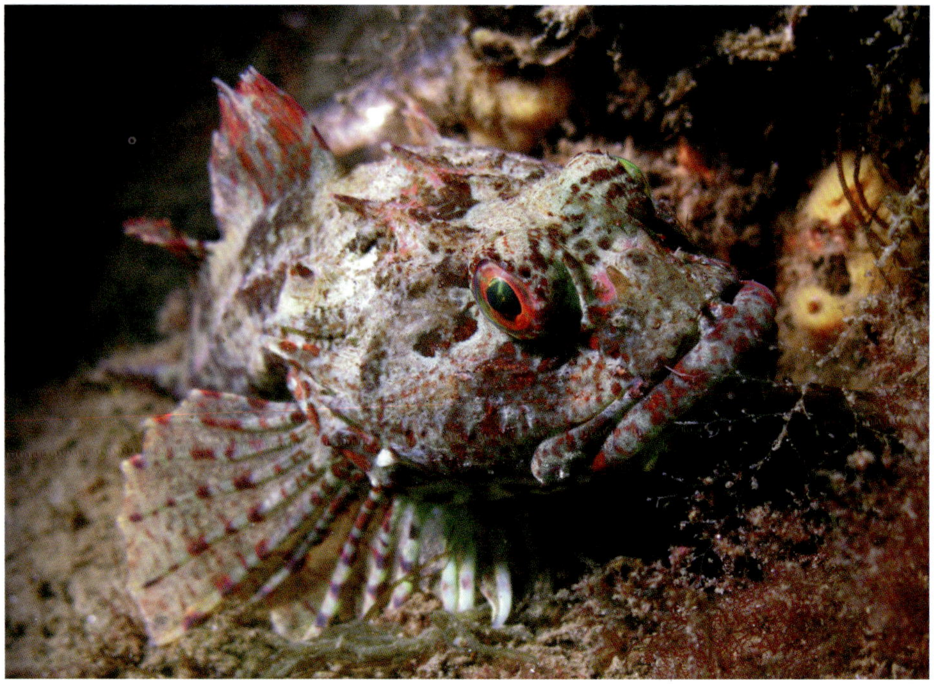

Long-spined sea scorpion

Lightbulb sea squirts

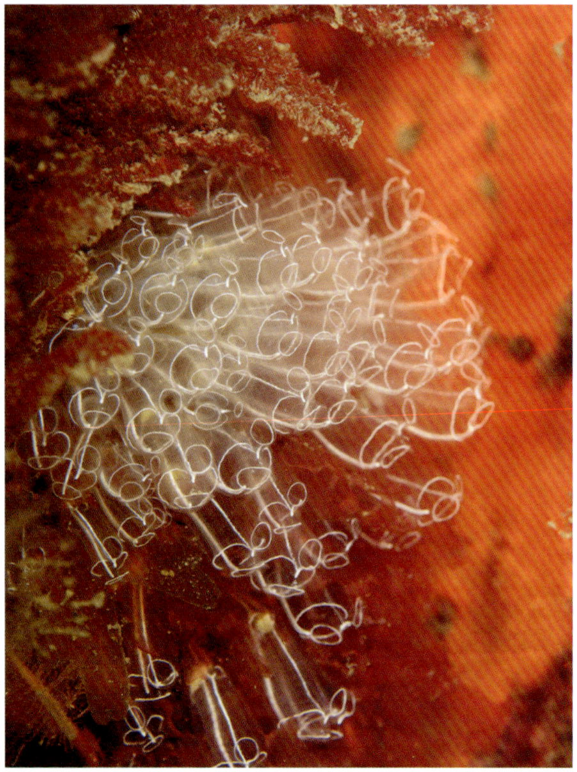

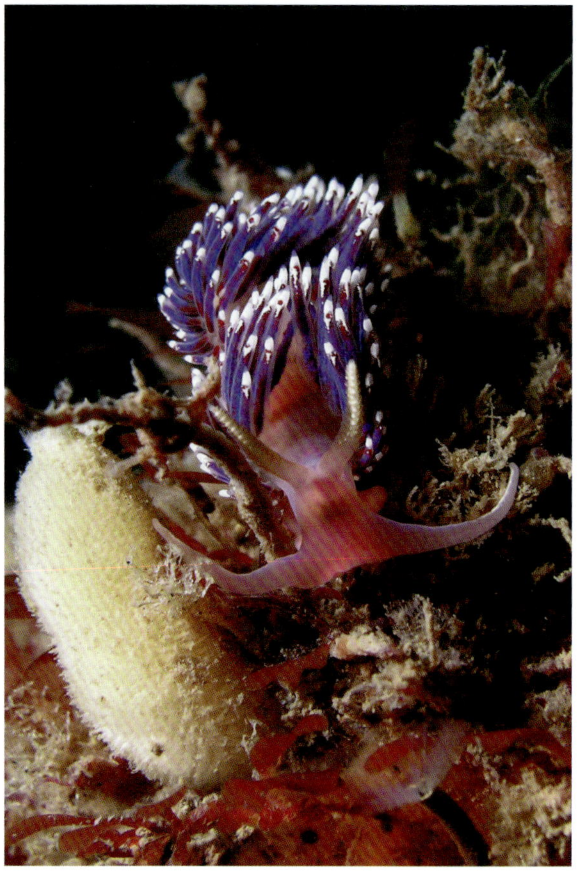

Facelina auriculata

Crystal sea slug

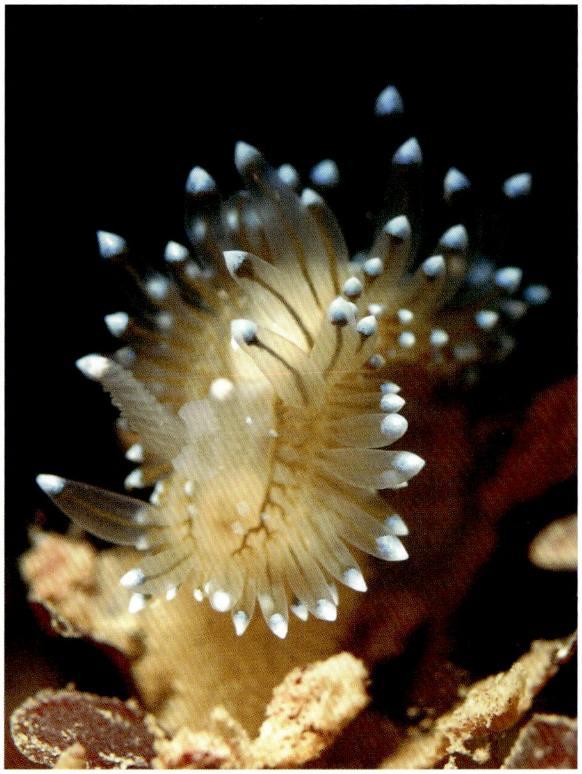

Sea Searching

Wrecks of *Vera* and *Rosalie*

Despite decades of disturbance by shipping, fishing, dredging and oil and gas extraction, the wildlife of the North Sea remains astonishingly diverse – with riches just off North Norfolk's shifting shoreline.

Here submarine prairies are broken by raised features such as chalk reefs – rising near Weybourne and running past Sheringham and Cromer to make landfall as rock pools at West Runton – but also shipwrecks, ruins of submerged buildings and even high-rise colonies of tube worms. All host colourful reef communities.

In the 1980s Suffolk's **Rob Spray** and **Dawn Watson** bought a fish tank for their first shared home, in Ipswich, which soon became a dozen. The engineer and microbiologist then joined a Martlesham diving club to watch non-pets in the wild. Now they dive for advanced ventures in digital photography all over the world up to 120 times a year.

Off Indonesia a sudden current dragged them down 23 metres when they were about to surface, disorientating them in a fog of bubbles until the force subsided just as suddenly. Off Norfolk's Sea Palling, when sealed in duvet-like dry suits, they mistimed the slack – the pause between tidal ebb and flow which is the divers' window – and hit a wall of water. They dropped into a cloud of sand, clinging to a wreck as starfish flew past until they were able to struggle to the surface.

Their favourite hunting grounds are the wrecks of two World War One cargo vessels – the *Vera* at Cley and the *Rosalie* at Weybourne – still visible at low tide having been beached to save their crews. Their resulting photo-chemical prints of our most dazzling Norfolk neighbours have a deceptive calm and a hard-won clarity. See shoaled or solitary fish (bib, horse mackerel, snake pipefish, scorpion fish), vivid sea slugs and sea anemones, luxuriant peacock fanworms, luminous creatures such as lightbulb sea squirts and sea gooseberries and Norfolk's famous edible crustaceans – most notably Cromer crabs the size of dinner plates which can crack bone with their claws but prefer to

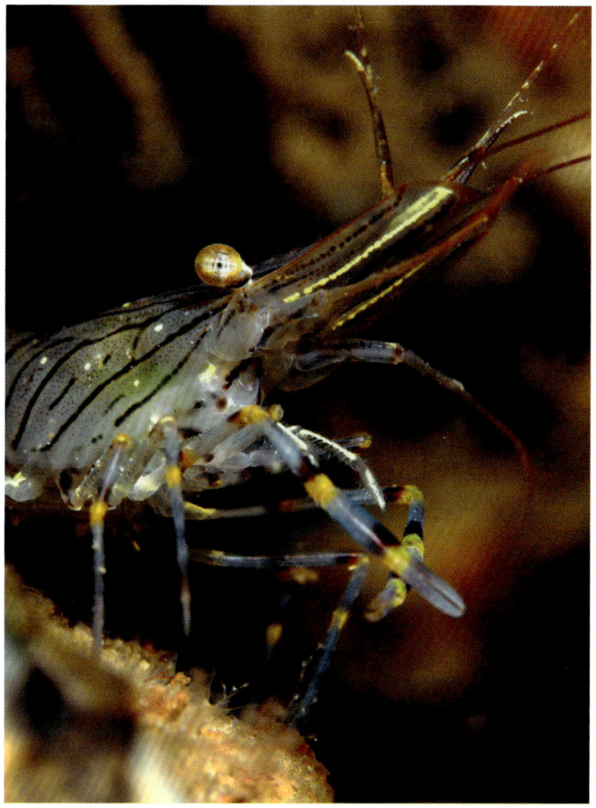

Common Prawn

lodge in lairs by their elbows, and lobsters which advance in curiosity rather than aggression and can live as long as we do.

Dawn and Robert help Seasearch to map the sea-bed around Britain and the wider campaign for marine reserves. They were delighted when the first tompot blenny, brightly smiling poster fish for this conservation project, was recently snapped at Weybourne.

Beach Scene (The Foreshore), 1931, needlework, Britten-Pears Foundation

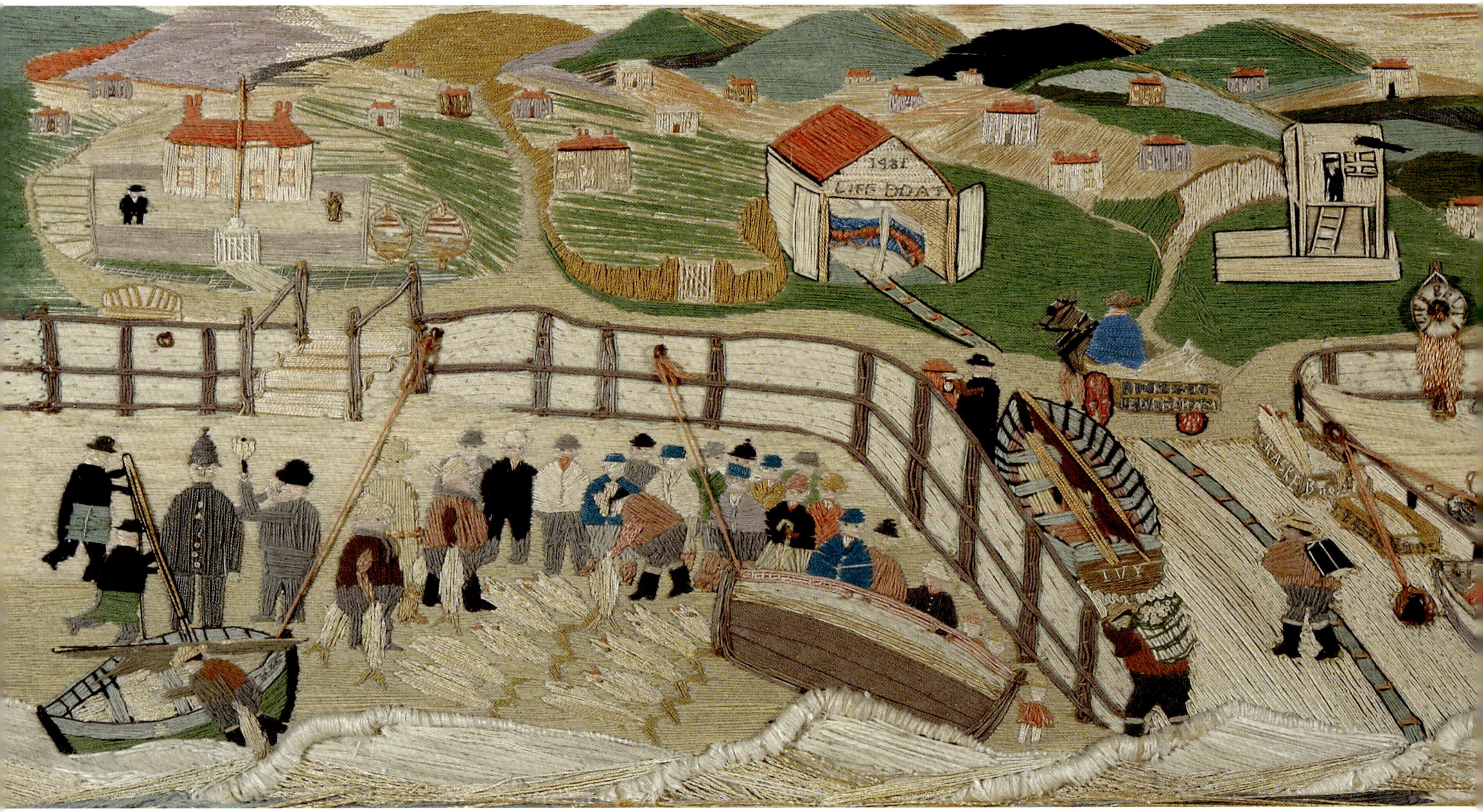

The Yarn Spinner

John Craske the Sheringham Wool Artist

In 1927 a poet called Valentine Ackland visited a fisherman's cottage in Hemsby on the Norfolk coast to buy a model boat and found paintings of ships sailing, waves surging and lighthouse signalling on every surface – doors, lids, trays, ornaments and pastry board. Valentine (well-named because she looked the spit of matinée idol Rudolph Valentino) had just discovered **John Craske**, one of Britain's greatest naïve artists.

Craske was frail but the visitor was amazed by the vitality of his work. She begged to buy a portrait of a ship called *The James Edward* for 30 shillings (£1.50). She noted later that it was 'the utmost money I dared spend'. Although the image was Mrs Craske's pride and joy, so vast a sum was gladly accepted in a stricken household often reduced to barter. Plus, it was the artist's very first sale.

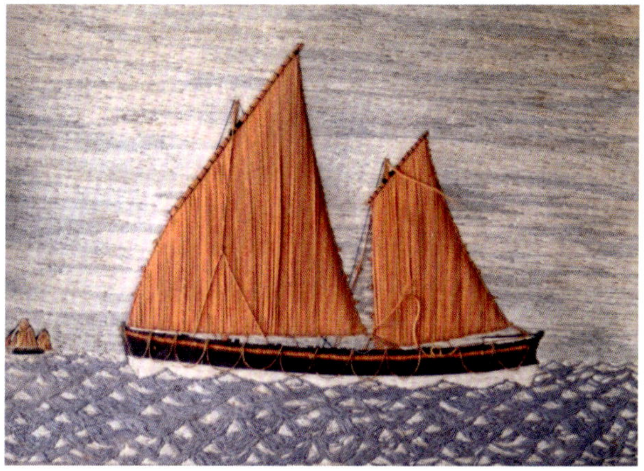

Fishing Smack, embroidery, Sheringham Museum (right)

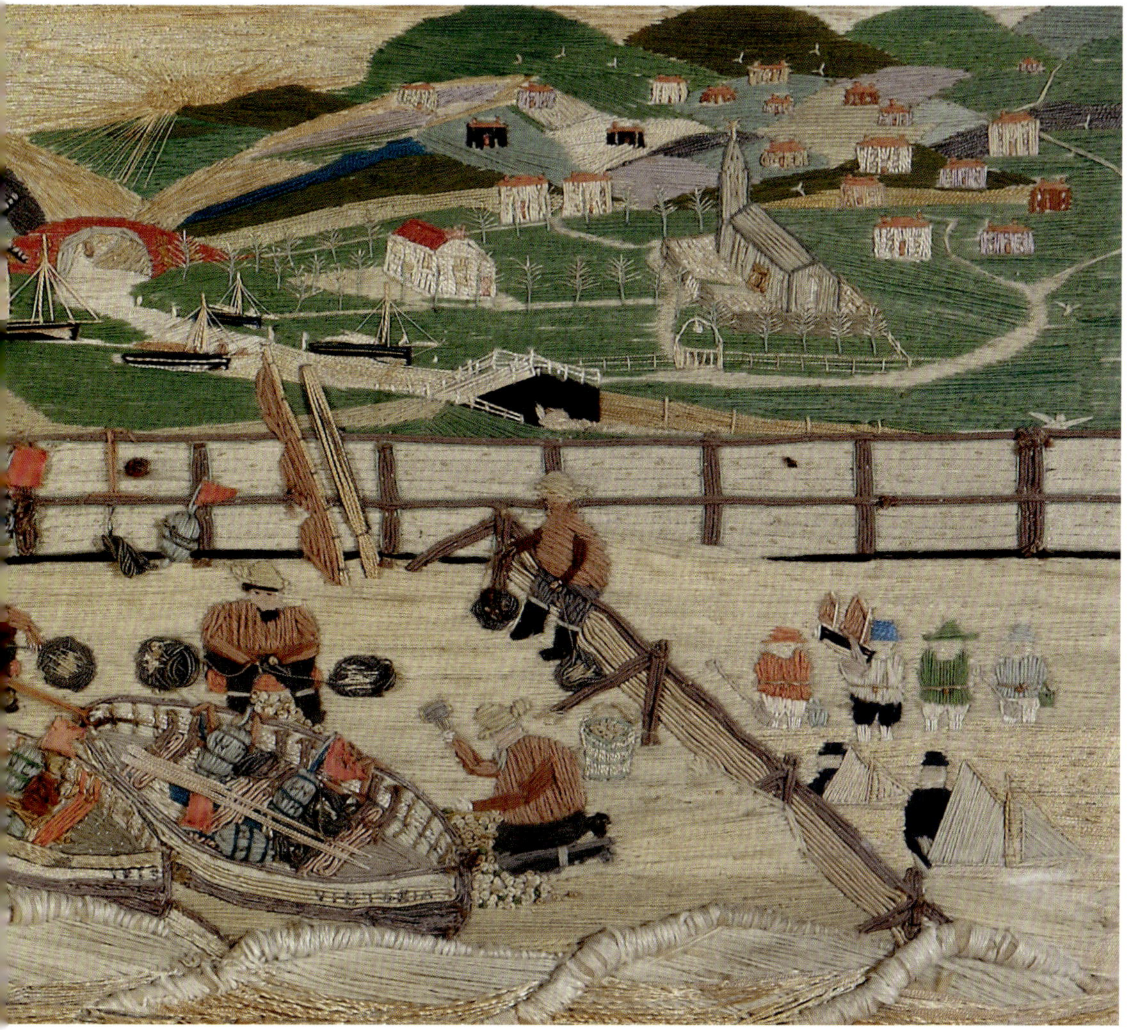

Two years later the work was spotted in Valentine's London flat by a West End art dealer and the poet was sent back to Hemsby to trawl for an exhibition. First fearing a demand for a refund, the painter's wife sorted the transfer of paintings and tapestries while her spouse was in one of many comas.

Successful shows followed in London and the United States, along with a commission for the Courtauld family yacht. But the disabled fisherman, who died in 1943, never himself saw his work exhibited. After Valentine's death, in 1969, the images she had collected formed an Aldeburgh Festival show arranged by her partner, the writer Sylvia Townsend Warner, who bequeathed them to Snape Maltings to celebrate her friendship with Peter Pears. By that point other Craske pictures had been given to the Red House home of Pears and Benjamin Britten.

Born in Sheringham in 1881, one of nine

children, Craske had followed generations of forebears to sea. He worked out of Grimsby for a time, before the family moved in 1905 to East Dereham, to open a fishmonger's shop. The staunch Salvation Army member married Laura Eke in 1908 – the bride recalling their first meeting in the town thus: 'There was a soap box in the centre of the ring upon which a tall young man in a fisherman's blue jersey stands, his black curly hair is ruffled by the breeze. He is nervous. But he starts to sing: Since Christ my soul from sin set free ...' For the next nine years they worked in happy hardship, smoking and curing fish which the tireless young man then hawked around mid-Norfolk from baskets on two ponies – toiling 17-hour days bar Sundays.

Saved from the trenches on health grounds, he appealed and was called up in May 1917. Within weeks he was felled by influenza and, after a 'brain abscess' left him prone to nervous collapse, moved to the mental wing of Norwich War Hospital. He then became one of those veterans for whom an internal war never ceased.

In October 1918 the invalid was discharged with 'harmless mental stupors' into the care of his stalwart wife. In fact, his nervous afflictions were compounded by undiagnosed diabetes. The couple opened a fish shop in Dereham but in 1920, on the death of his father, John Craske collapsed and was confined to a wheelchair.

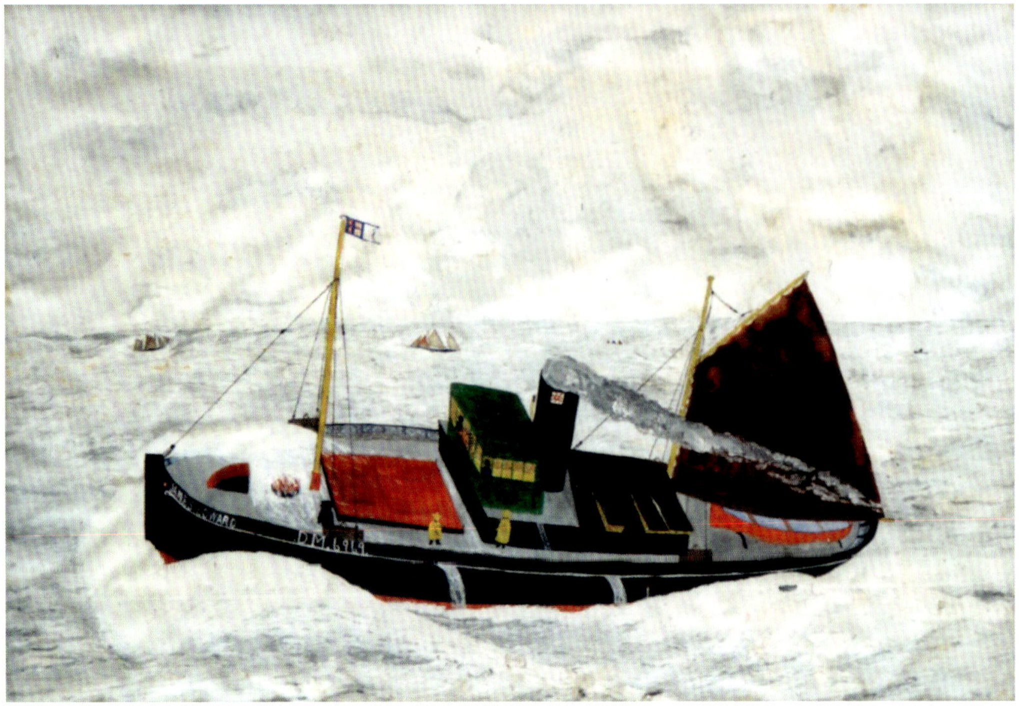

The James Edward, gouache, Aldeburgh Music

During a bid for recovery at Wiveton he carved, painted and sailed to Blakeney Point in a little boat. This period is recalled in an epic feat of needlework – a 4.5-metre map of the North Norfolk coast, now in Glandford Shell Museum, near Holt.

The materials of his art were found oddments

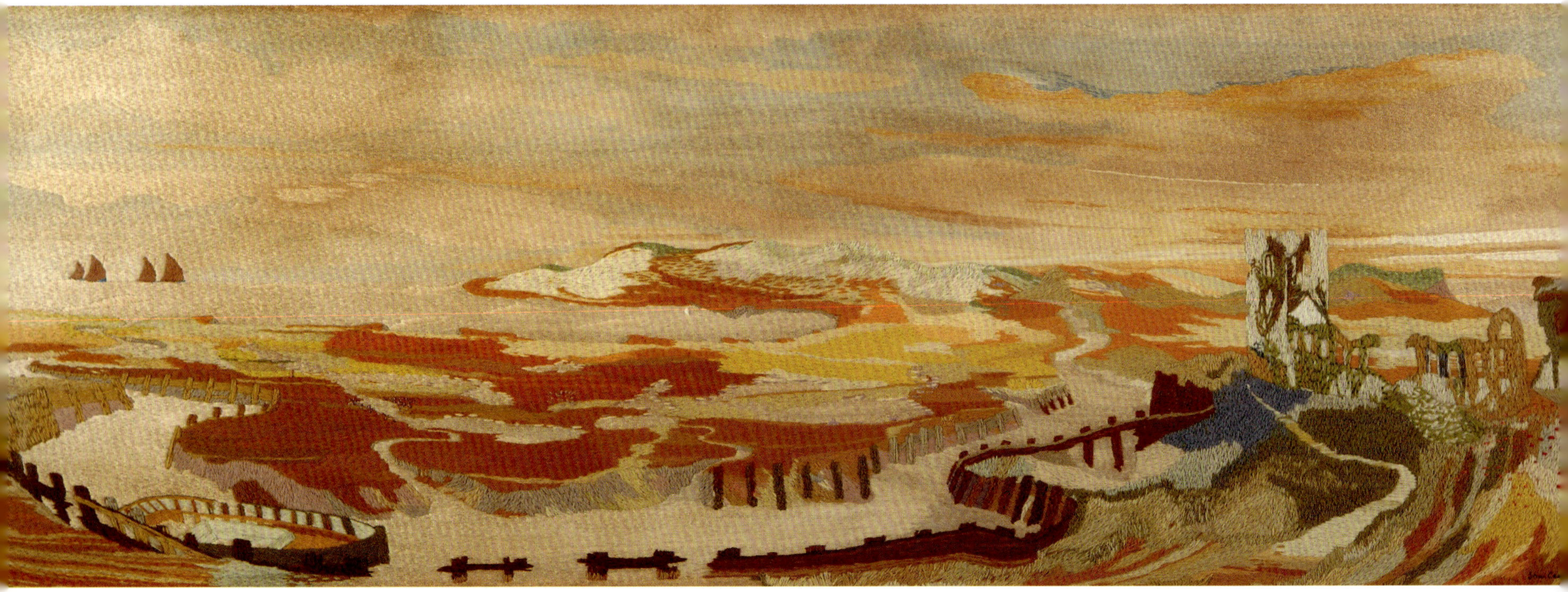

Saltings with Ruin, Norfolk Coast, the Foreshore, embroidery, silk on calico, Britten-Pears Foundation

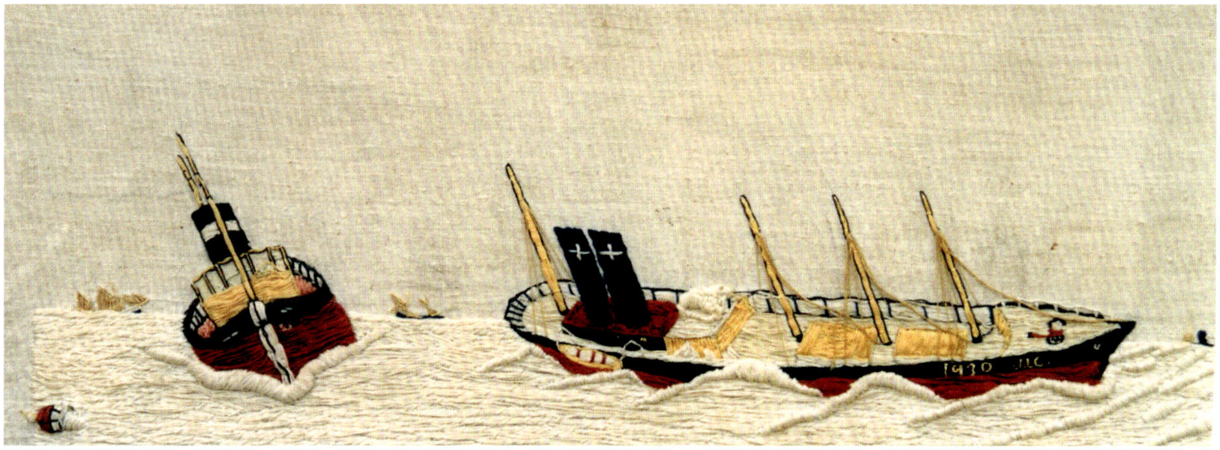

Ships in Heavy Seas, overmantle embroidery on calico with fringe, Aldeburgh Music

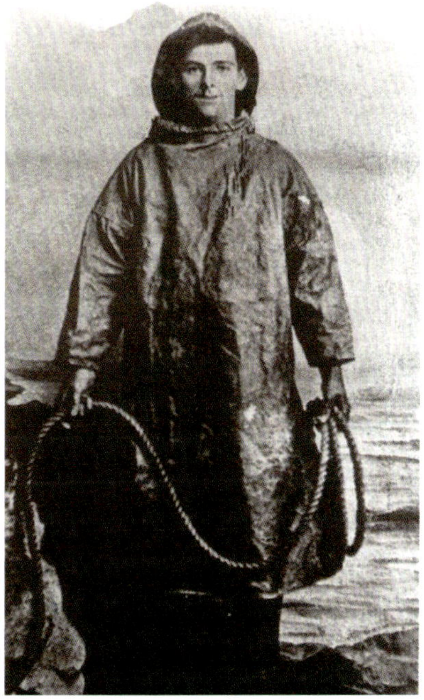

John Craske (1881-1943)

– old wood, lining paper, distemper, housepaint, whitewash, children's watercolours. Home-made frames were decorated with shells and pebbles. To save the price of nails, models were held together by old gramophone needles. However poor the media, the artist's imagination was rich. His talent was wholly free.

As Craske told his tale: 'I was ill in bed for three years, which I remember very little about, after which I just felt something that I cannot explain urging me on to make pictures of the sea and ships. Continually fresh ideas are flashing through my mind and when I hear the thrilling stories of sea rescues on the wireless, I make a note of them and hope some day to put them in pictures. I thank God for this gift as I realise it comes from Him!' Sylvia Townsend Warner wrote: 'He painted like a man giving witness under oath to a wild story… Most artists know the sea from its edge. Craske knew it from the middle, from experience of being a small upright movement in a vast swaying horizontality…'

When those coastal vigils failed to secure convalescence, John and Laura returned to Dereham. Here they were visited in 1931 by Valentine and Sylvia – the latter recording in her diary: 'He was lying in bed by the window, a crumpled-faced man with darting eyes, and large pale hands. Mrs C was short, upstanding, pale, sallow. Her knobbed hair and folded hands gave her the air of something by Craske – a model of a woman.' Guided by his wife, the bed-ridden artist now took to weaving nautical pictures from scraps of wool and cheap silk thread. The first was sewn on a piece of calico intended for a Christmas pudding, with a blue bag and distempered clouds completing the sky when the wools ran out.

There is a striking parallel with Alfred Wallis – the Cornish fisherman-turned-shopkeeper and abiding Salvationist whose naïve paintings, produced amid mounting infirmity, now fetch many thousands of pounds. Both men depicted a marine world of storms and shipwrecks, of boats afloat or berthed on slipways and of cottage terraces seemingly set to slide into the sea. Each scene may be read as a metaphor for rocky life encrusted with firm faith and wild

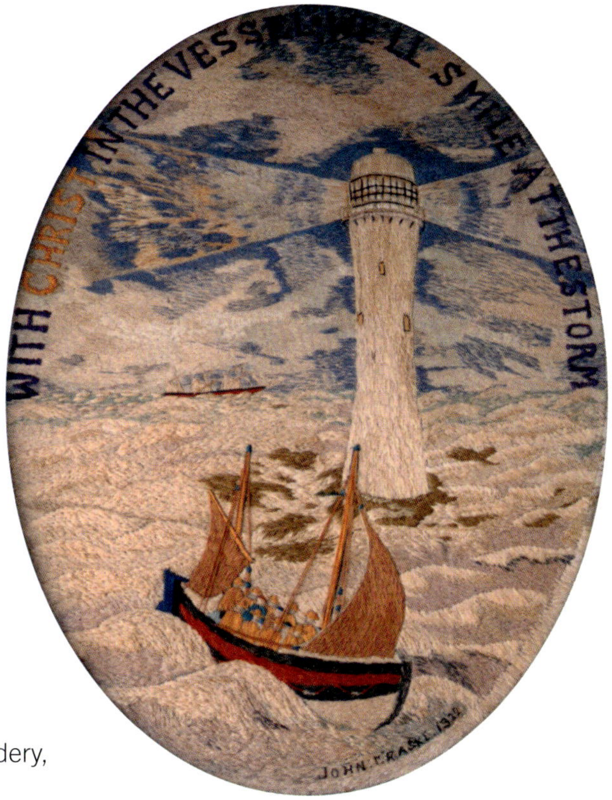

Lighthouse and Lifeboat with Religious Text, 1932, embroidery, Sheringham Museum

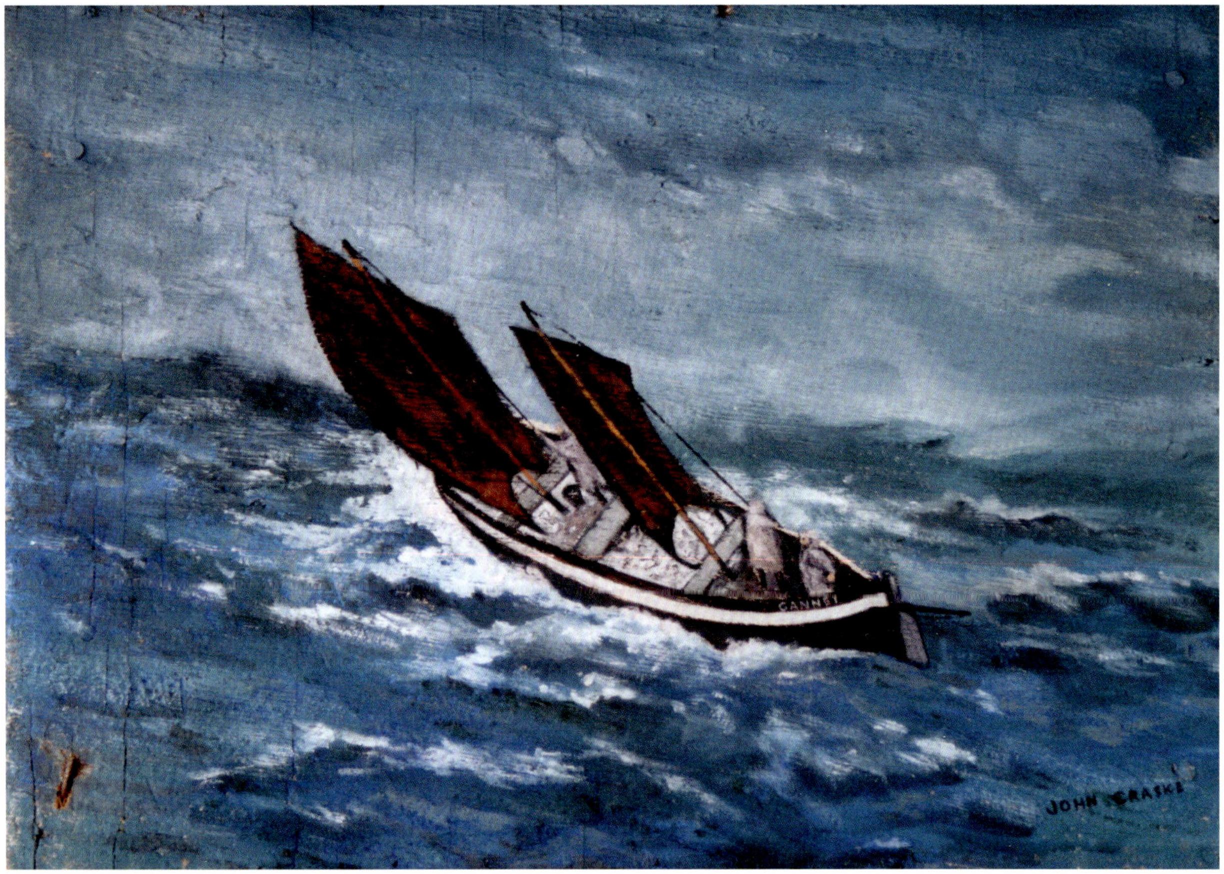

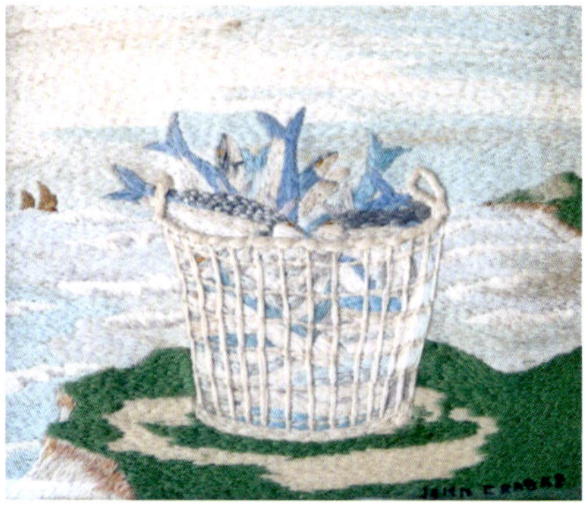

Basket of Fish on Cliff, embroidery, Sheringham Museum

The Fishing Smack Gannet, oil on bait board, Sheringham Museum

beauty. Craske often recalled prayer meetings on rolling ships as the moon's reflection on the sea was scanned for shoals of whiting.

And a final piece of needlework, held by Norfolk Museums and Archaeology Service, is a 3.5-metre Dunkirk panorama with soldiers wading towards waiting vessels beneath flaming, falling planes. Unfinished on the artist's death, the last campaign in a life of struggle contains a hole in the sky – where a doggedly devout artist was sure God would be.

And as for Valentine and Sylvia – well, the latter produced two fine historical novels set in Norfolk, *The Flint Anchor* and *The Corner That Held Them*. The two writers were sustained by Sylvia's earnings, chiefly from short stories published in the *New Yorker*. The couple often visited Valentine's family in Winterton and lived for a time at Sloley, near North Walsham.

They braved the winter of 1950 at Great Eye Folly – a gaunt turret on the exposed shore at Salthouse, built by Victorian speculative builder and womaniser Onesiphorous Randall and subsequently used as a coastguard station. Later they tried to buy this forbidding fortress, where Sylvia noted in her diary that 'The east wind sobs and whimpers like a Brontë in the kitchen', but wisely moved on, for the building was to vanish beneath the Great Flood of 1953.

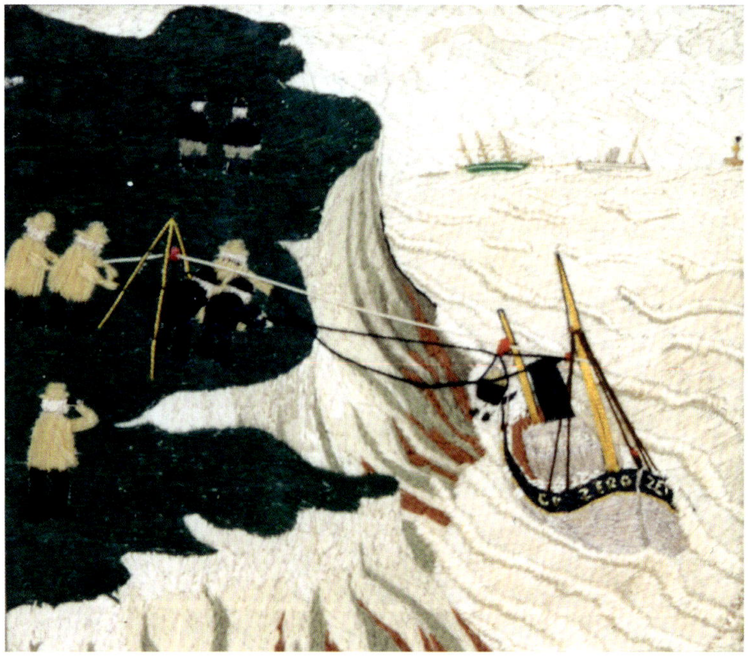

Rescue by Breeches Buoy from the Ship Zero, embroidery, Aldeburgh Music

Creativity is at the heart of meaningful human existence – and most especially to those on the edge. How fitting, then, that a world centre of 'outsider art' should be a barn at Walcott. Here, at the Barrington Farm Day Services Centre, tutors are merely assistants who give the artists the freedom to express all the dazzling ideas and images in their heads and at their finger-tips. Each striking and startling vision is unique to its owner.

With conditions such as epilepsy, autism, schizophrenia and Downs Syndrome, they haven't heard of Picasso, let alone of Jean Dubuffet – the great artist who coined the term Art Brut ('outsider art') in the 1950s for the work of the untrained and intuitive and often marginalised. They just get on with the job of being artists and making sense of this peculiar world.

In the 1970s the late Janith Bastow adopted an adult with learning problems and then gradually turned her farmhouse into a refuge. Back from art school, her son, Martin, started to turn a potato shed into a studio but found his vocation when Michael Smith, one of Janith's adoptees, borrowed some paint and sketched a brilliant cow on a cart.

The art barn gradually took shape, with kiln and textile room and print workshop added – for user artists came to range over every medium. Today, alongside a working farm, there's a creative hub for 50 residents and day visitors referred by Norfolk social services and others. All are here in farthest-flung do-different Norfolk because art has never ceased to be central to their lives.

Now presented by the RoaR Outsider Art Archive charity, the art of Barrington Farm has been shown throughout East Anglia, in London and New York and at the Prague Biennale. Stellar talents include Barbara Symmons, James Gladwell, Ian Partridge and the late Leofric Baron.

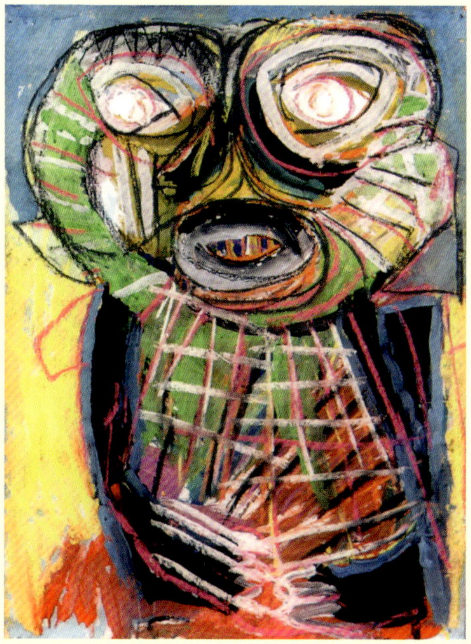

Owl, Leofric Baron, 2007, mixed media

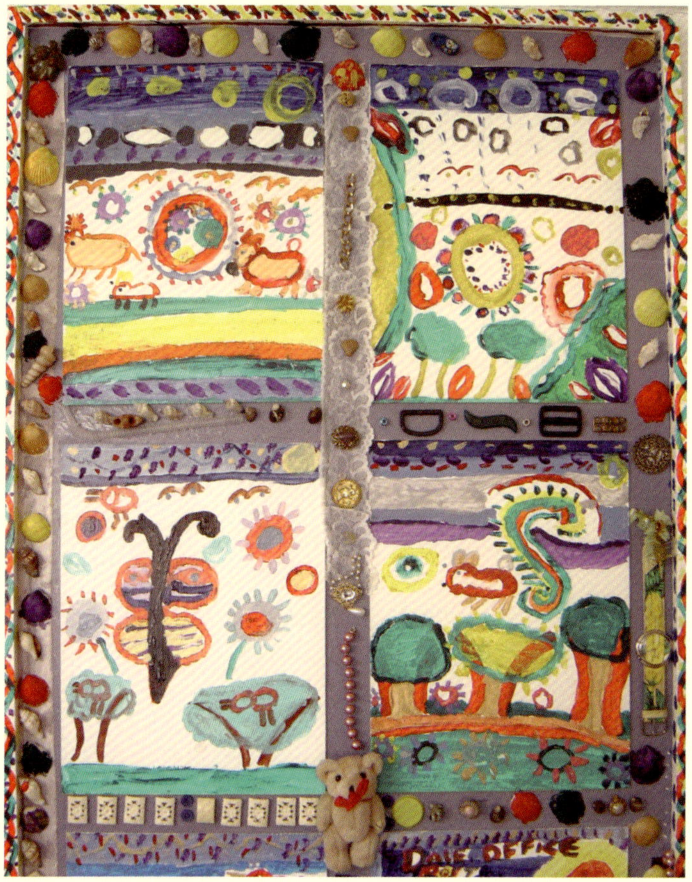

Panel with Shells, Barbara Symmons, 2001, acrylic on mdf

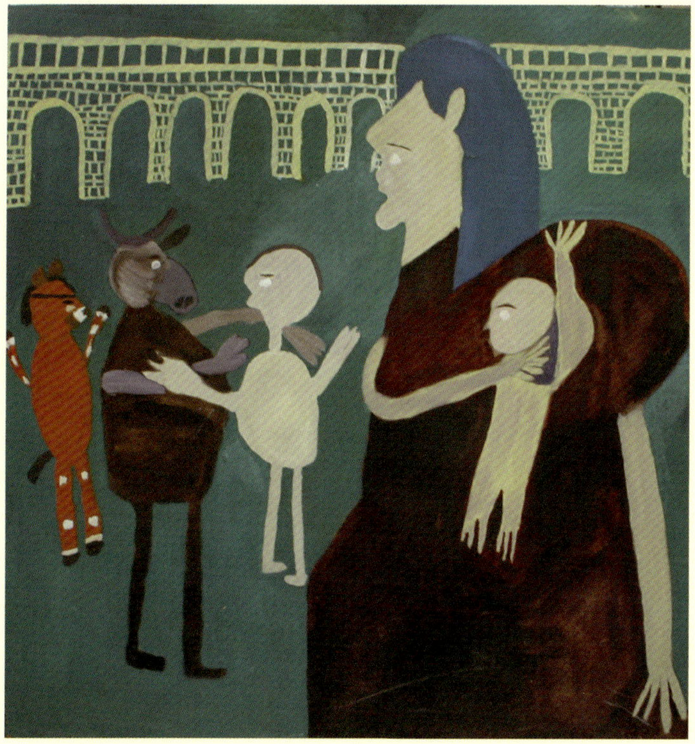

Cleopatra, James Gladwell, 2002, oil on board

Reclining Figure, Henry Moore, 1930, ironstone, Sainsbury Centre, Norwich

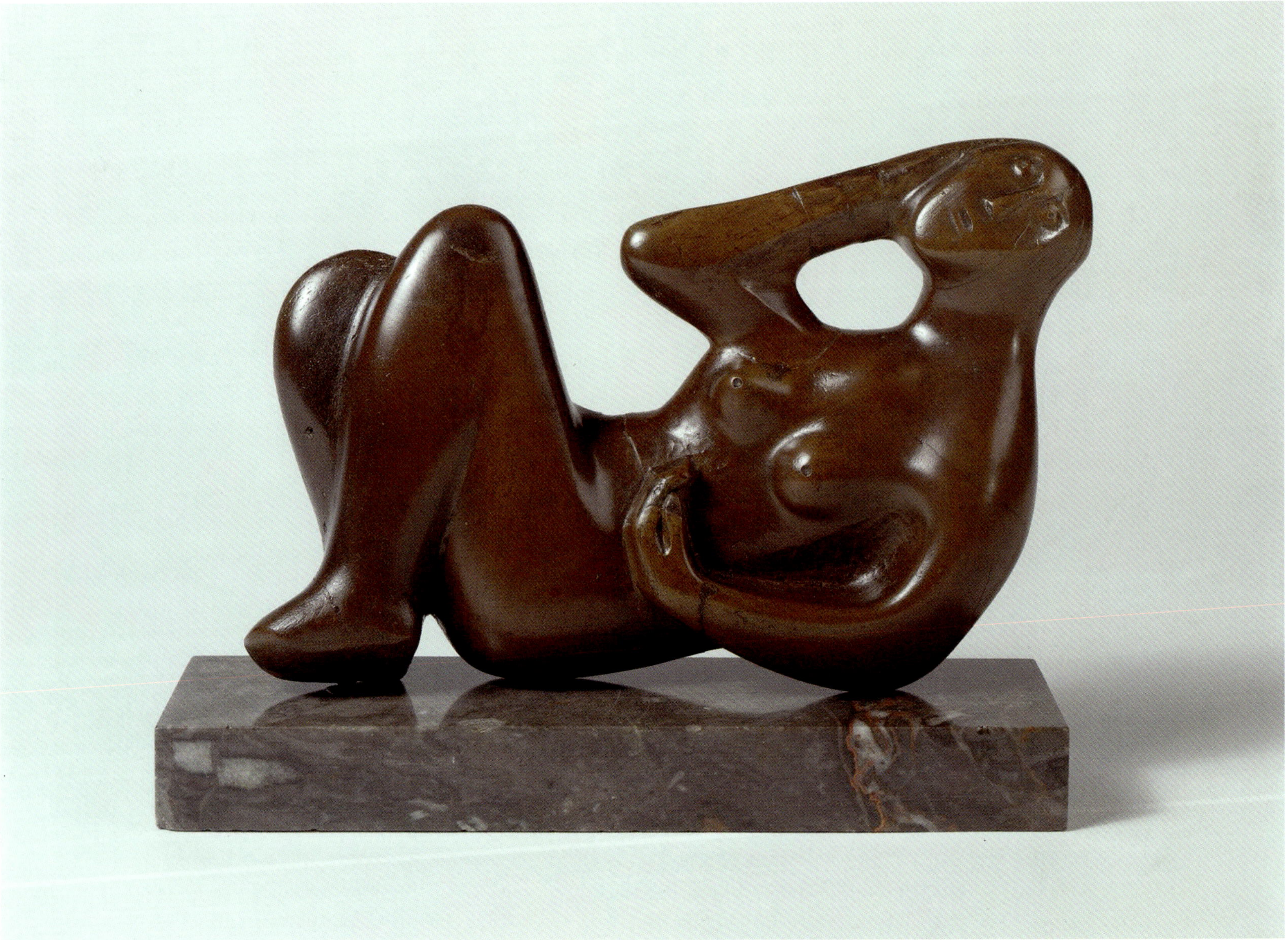

Happisburgh Holidays

Henry Moore and Barbara Hepworth

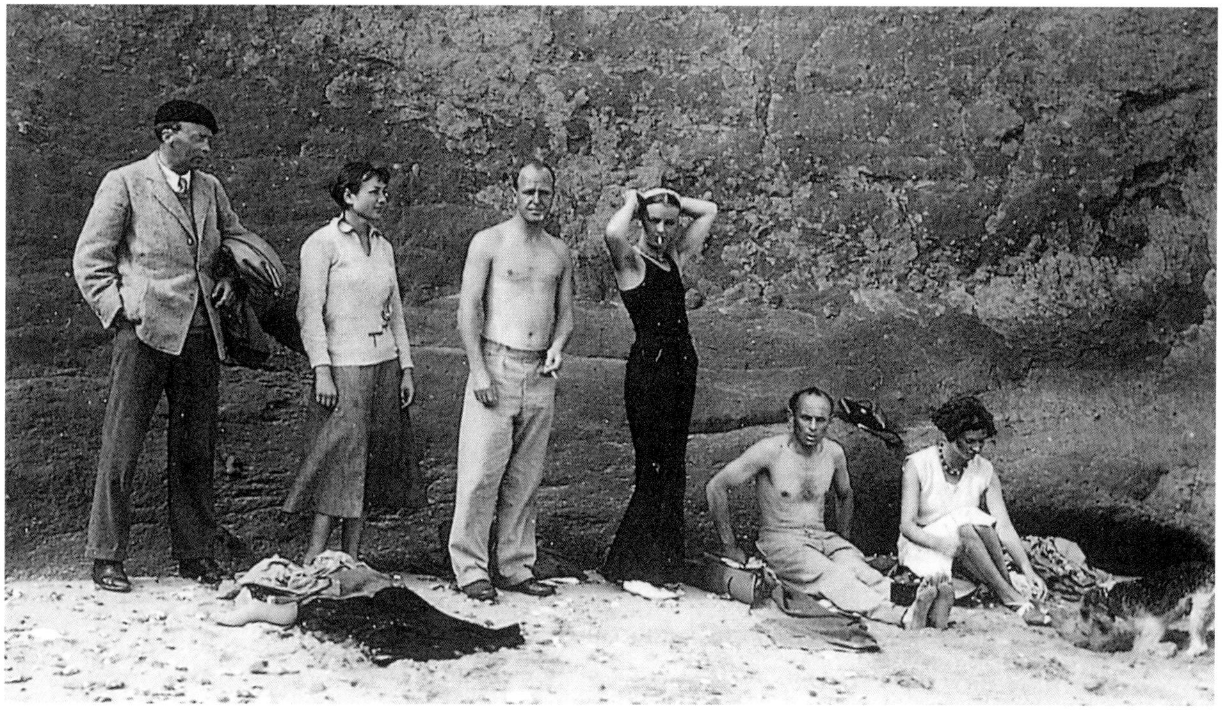

(left to right)
Ivon Hitchens, Irina Moore, Henry Moore, Barbara Hepworth, Ben Nicholson and Mary Jenkins, Happisburgh beach, 1931

A black-and-white snapshot exists of six artistic friends on the beach at Happisburgh in September 1931. Three look away from the camera and three stare rather startlingly out at us. The figures gazing straight ahead, and apparently into the future, are **Henry Moore, Barbara Hepworth** and Ben Nicholson – the latter seated but all set to spring. So much of the story of progressive 20th-century British art will rest on them.

Any sense of tension from this holiday snap is not entirely due to the fomenting of radical art on a working holiday, though Moore and Hepworth, modernist sculptors sharing Yorkshire roots (and a smoking habit), are even now rivals as well as allies.

No, the electricity is more personal. Barbara – serpentine as a Norfolk flint as she fixes her hair – has just fallen in love with Ben. Her sculptor husband John Skeaping will soon arrive from London in a last-ditch bid to save the marriage and find he is too late. Up in Cumberland with her children and paints, Winifred Nicholson is in for bad news.

But the group is here because of Henry Moore. In 1922, while at London's Royal College of Art, he heard that his coalminer father, Raymond, was dangerously ill and a decision was made to move the family from Castleford to the purer air of Norfolk.

Henry's elder sister, Mary, became headteacher of Wighton village school, near Wells-next-the-Sea. She and their parents moved into the adjoining schoolhouse, but Raymond's decline continued and, after a brief spell in a Walsingham nursing home, he died within a month of reaching Norfolk. He is buried in Wighton churchyard.

Born in 1849, Raymond Moore toiled as a crow-scarer on a Lincolnshire farm from the age of nine, penury and bondage then forcing his migration to the mines as a young man.

Marrying at 35, and fathering eight children, he urged his offspring to train as teachers. Several did. Henry taught in Castleford. Raymond became headmaster at Stoke Ferry near Downham Market while Rowland Howarth, husband of sister Betty, presided over Mulbarton school near Norwich.

Henry spent most of his art school holidays in Norfolk at Wighton and Mulbarton, where he developed his passion for carving outdoors, steadying stone blocks between his feet or lodging them in the ground. The reaction of local folk can only be imagined.

Writing from Mulbarton in the summer of 1925, he said: 'I'm thankful for these two spots in Norfolk where I can sit in the open air, crosslegged on patches of grass & chip stone – though I was nearly sent loopy this afternoon by the incessant lowing of a cow that the farmer next door is starving for killing.'

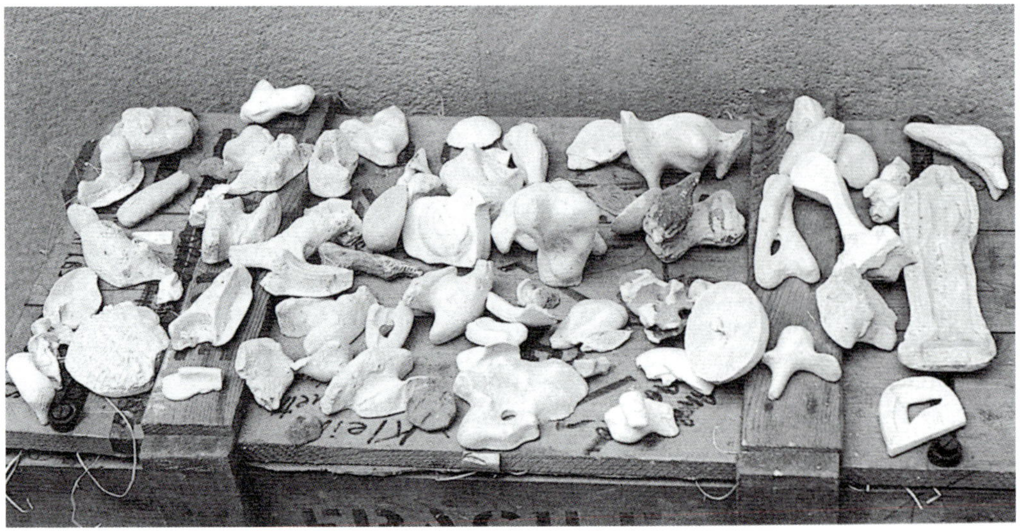

Part of Moore's flint collection begun with finds from Norfolk

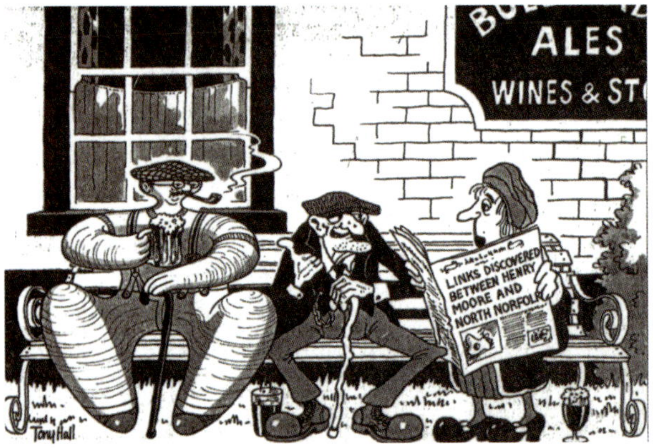

'Course oi remember him livin' in Wighton ... O' Cyril, hare, used to pose for him.

Eastern Daily Press cartoon, Tony Hall, 1980 (left)

A further letter from Mulbarton mentioned a half-figure carving of a woman reaching upwards. 'It's not coming on as well as I expected – but I may get something into it before it's finished,' he said. The work in progress turned into *Woman with Upraised Arms*, whose 'primitive' appearance confirms the artist's love of ancient and non-western sculpture and seems to owe nothing to the place where it was made.

And yet. In 1925 Mary Moore married bank manager George Garrould and moved to Wells (then to Colchester 18 months later). From their house that summer Moore wrote that, given enough money, he would make for 'somewhere like Wighton or Walsingham, and stay there until I'd found and wedded one of those richly formed, big-limbed, fresh faced, full blooded country wenches, built for breeding, honest, simple minded, practical, common sensed, healthily sexed lasses that I've seen about here'. Here were the inspirations for a harem of reclining figures.

A faded photo also survives from this period of the young sculptor carving a dog. His first *Mother and Child* can be seen in the background. The picture further includes a piece of white marble from which a head and shoulders are emerging. When the subsequent owners of Wighton Schoolhouse – painter Alfred Cohen and his wife Diana – were clearing the overgrown garden in the 1980s, they found the unfinished sculpture.

Henry Moore had a life-long interest in

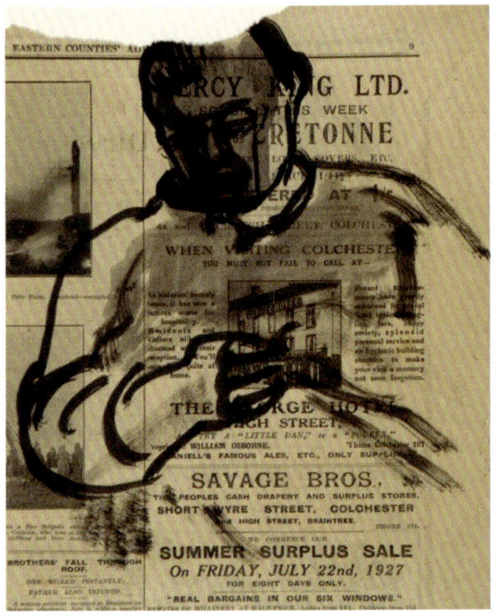

Henry Moore, 1927, pen, ink and wash on newspaper, Henry Moore Foundation

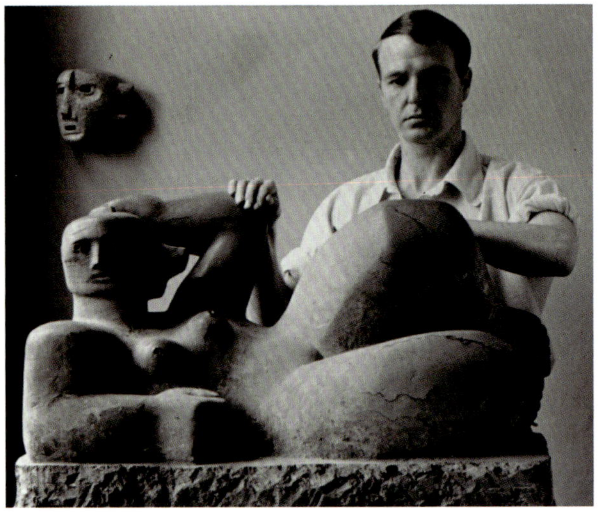

Henry Moore and *Reclining Figure,* 1929, brown Hornton stone

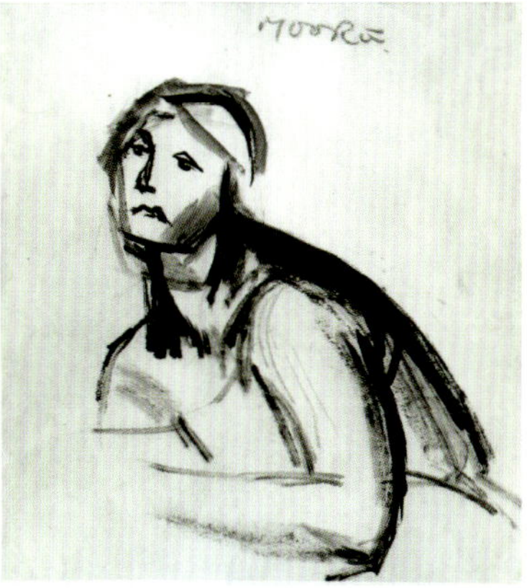

Head and Shoulders, Henry Moore, 1922, brush and ink, Henry Moore Foundation

natural forms and found objects and it was in Norfolk that he began to collect the flints abounding on beaches and in fields. As the natural stone building blocks of East Anglia, they had been set and knapped in walls, houses and a mass of medieval churches. The more twisted shapes, often suggesting female figures in repose, were prototypes for a sculptor's future works of art.

When, in 1930, Barbara Hepworth proposed a seaside holiday for their group of kindred spirits, including her friends Mary and Douglas Jenkins, and the painter Ivon Hitchens, Moore, who would be accompanied by his Russian-born wife Irina, recommended Church Farm, Happisburgh. As well as working amid stimulating company, Barbara wanted space and peace to rescue her marriage to John Skeaping. Her husband had taught her carving and both had found early success. But, despite the birth of a son, in 1929, the union was soon in trouble.

John Skeaping was to recall: 'Henry, Barbara and I used to pick up large iron-stone pebbles from the beach which were ideal for carving and polished up like bronze. I rode and fished on the Broads. Henry accompanied me on one of my fishing trips but he couldn't leave sculpture alone for long and took with him a piece of iron-stone and a rasp. Sitting at one end of the boat he filed away continuously, occasionally hauling in his line to see if he had got anything on the end.'

Back in London the Skeapings held a joint exhibition of 47 sculptures – John showing five ironstone carvings (ox, duck, stag, animal mask and torso) and Barbara two (a fish and a half-figure called *Carving*). Four more appeared in Henry's 1931 show (two heads, a mother and child and a reclining figure).

The disc-like Norfolk pebbles determined a flatness of carved forms – small wonder John and Barbara, working to the maxim of 'truth to material', released fish from these shallow pools of stone. Stylistic similarities led the Tate to buy the Skeaping *Fish* in the belief it was a Hepworth.

But the personal partnership still drifted and in spring 1931 John and Barbara met and befriended Ben and Winifred Nicholson – both painters in a faux-naïve style, though Ben had lately turned to Cubism on a path to

Alfred Cohen (1920-2001) was a Chicago-raised painter and print-maker who came to Europe after war-time service in the Pacific, ending in the old School House at Wighton near Wells-next-the-Sea from 1978 and perfecting what Anita Brookner had identified early on as 'an acute charm of colour'. His restless energy lit brilliantly expressive seascape, flower, exterior and interior studies such as this 1994 oil on board of *Cley Smokehouse* (below left) – from a series of real and imaginary North Norfolk shopfronts – and the 1997 screenprint showing *The Best Room,* where the Moore family had once gathered (below right).

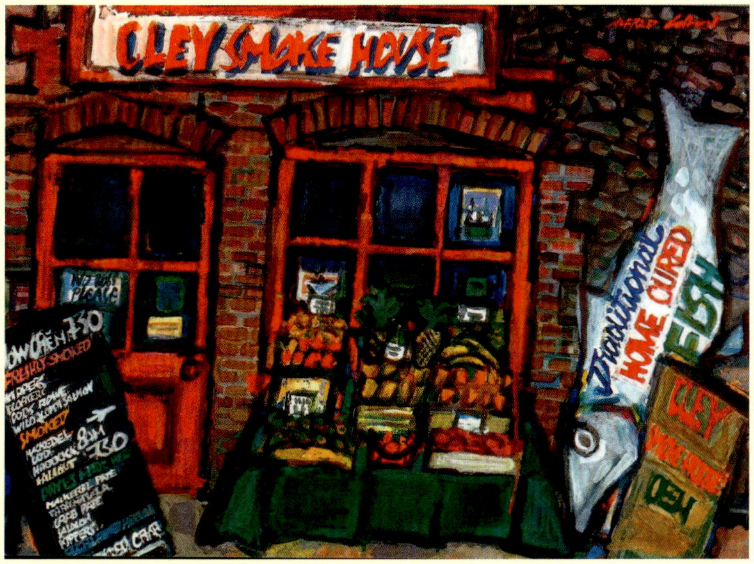

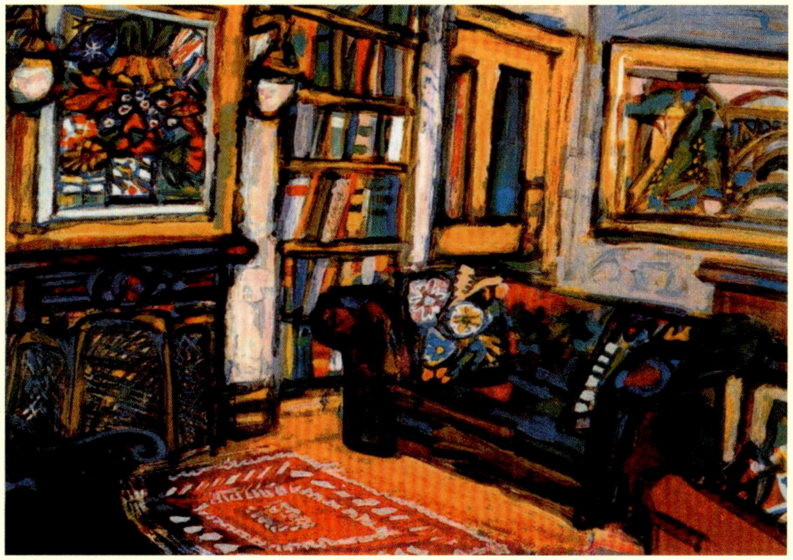

eventual abstraction.

When a second Norfolk holiday was mooted, Barbara wrote to the Nicholsons: 'Do come and stay with us at Happisburgh… I enclose a photo of the farm – the colour is lovely. The country is quite flat but for a little hill with a tall flint church and a lighthouse… The beach is a ribbon of pale sand as far as the eye can see. The Moores and ourselves should be so pleased if you came…'

But that summer John asked Barbara for a divorce and she left for Norfolk without him. Family duties kept Winifred at home, where she heard from her ecstatic husband: 'I do like these sort of free creative people they are alive and vital – you know like we thought of Derain & Picasso in Paris, with the same imagination and power and purpose.'

When John Skeaping had a change of heart and hastened to Happisburgh it was too late. His wife was lost forever. He returned to London and to the margins of British art.

Ben Nicholson left early also, his departure prompting a flow of love letters in which Barbara likened his head to 'the most lovely pebble ever seen' and related how she and Moore had carted four large crates of beach stones to Stalham for the London train.

In *The Listener*, in 1937, Henry Moore wrote: 'Although it is the human figure which interests me most deeply, I have always paid great attention to the natural, such as bones, shells and pebbles etc. For several years running I have been to the same part of the sea-shore – but each year a new shape of pebble has caught my eye, which the year before, although it was there in hundreds, I never saw… Pebbles show nature's way of working stone. Some of the pebbles I pick up have holes right through them.'

Those lucky stones, or witch stones, attracted Barbara and Henry on that 1931 holiday as a way of connecting both sides of a sculpture and making it more three-dimensional. Soon there was a small Hepworth pierced form in pink alabaster and soon after – or was it before? – a holed Moore. Whoever spotted it first, the motif discovered in Norfolk claimed a central

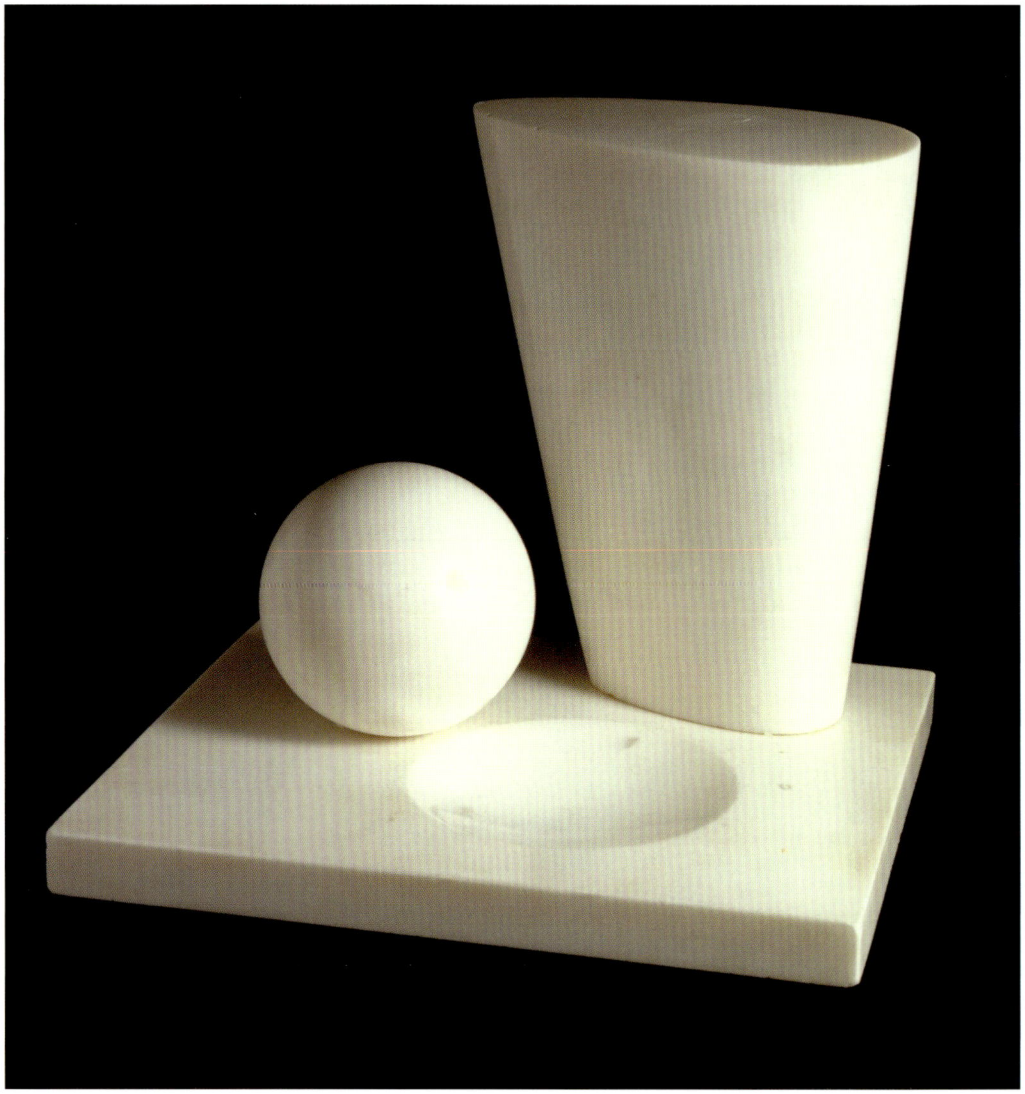

Conoid, Sphere & Hollow II, Barbara Hepworth, 1937, marble, Government Art Collection

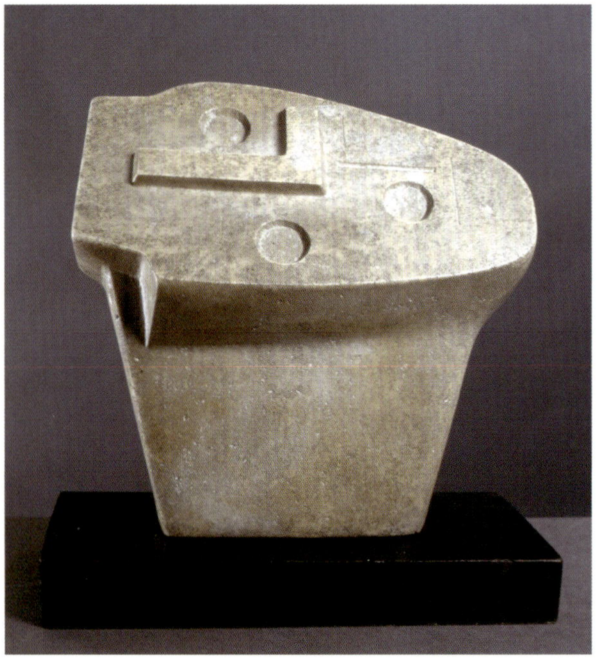

Carving, 1936, Henry Moore, Travertine marble (left), Henry Moore Foundation

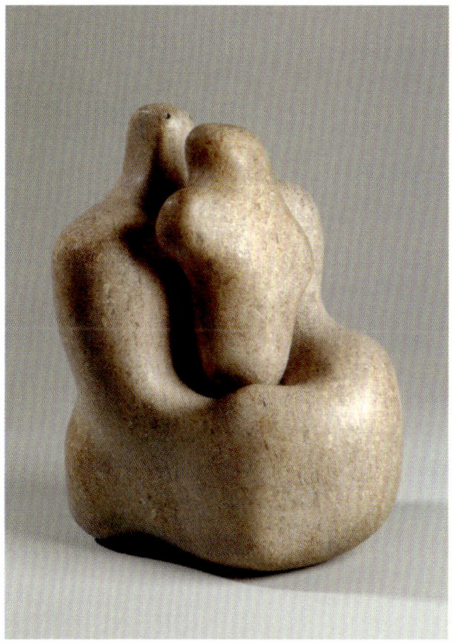

Mother and Child,
Barbara Hepworth, 1934,
pink Ancaster stone,
The Hepworth Wakefield

place in both careers. And for several years the two artists made sculptures drawing on natural, organic forms.

Ben Nicholson's paintings became increasingly sculptural, and from 1933 he made carved reliefs which also suggest the flatness of Norfolk ironstone pebbles.

In Hampstead the three pioneers were to be joined by art critic Adrian Stokes and his artist wife Margaret Mellis, and by leading international Constructivists Naum Gabo and Piet Mondrian, until all their creativity was threatened by looming war. Barbara suggested Happisburgh as a place of escape.

Adrian and Margaret were charged with finding a rural bolthole where Ben and Barbara would join them. They searched coastal Norfolk and Suffolk in vain – the Martello tower at Slaughden being rejected as dungeon-like and the track from Aldeburgh menaced by drifts of stones. In the end they found a haven outside St Ives, which Ben had visited with Christopher Wood in 1928. Ben and Barbara duly arrived and the focus of British modern art shifted from east to west.

Both the Stokes and Nicholson unions foundered – Barbara remaining in Cornwall, Adrian returning to London, Ben eventually settling in Switzerland and Margaret moving with second husband Francis Davison first to Syleham, near Harleston, and finally to Southwold.

With Margaret and a film crew in Cornwall in 1993, I took her to the Barbara Hepworth studio museum. 'That's my chair!' she cried at one point. 'Typical of Barbara to borrow something and then keep it as her own.' The same charge was widely made about art borrowings in what Herbert Read had rather inaptly called a 'nest of gentle artists'.

Some years later, in Southwold, Margaret and I watched a TV documentary in which it was claimed that Ben's move from Winifred to Barbara had mirrored his artistic impulse as it shifted from representation to abstraction. 'Absolute balls!' shouted Margaret at the screen. 'Ben left Winifred because she was so untidy!'

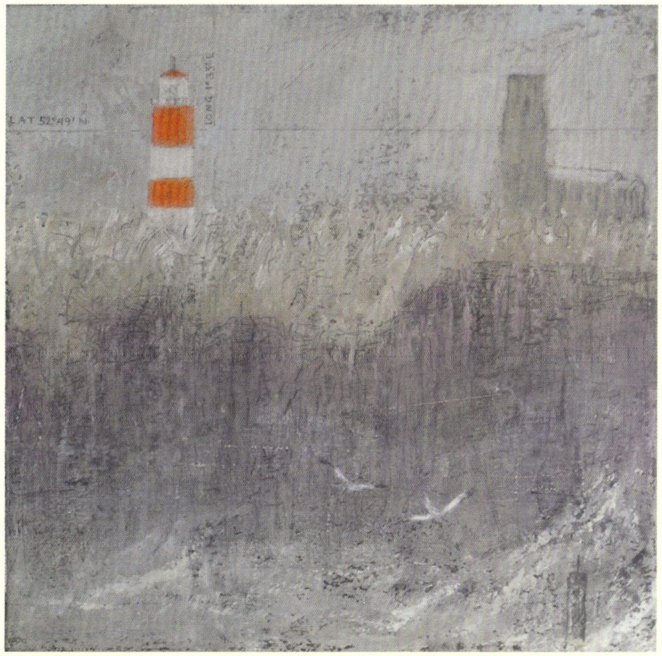

Caroline McAdam Clark's *Happisburgh*, 2005, oil and pencil on canvas (left), and Julian Perry's *Happisburgh*, 2010, oil on panel (below), draw back and zoom in on the same elemental drama.

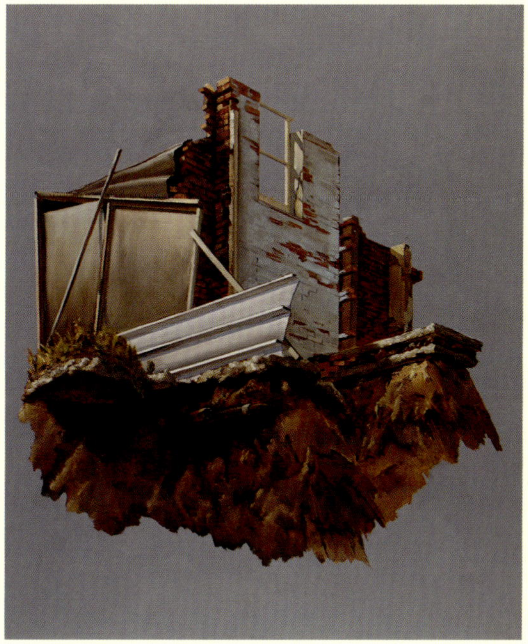

Erosion to East Anglia's coastline in recent decades has been most marked at Happisburgh – as more and more of the village, with towering church and lighthouse, topples over the cliff.

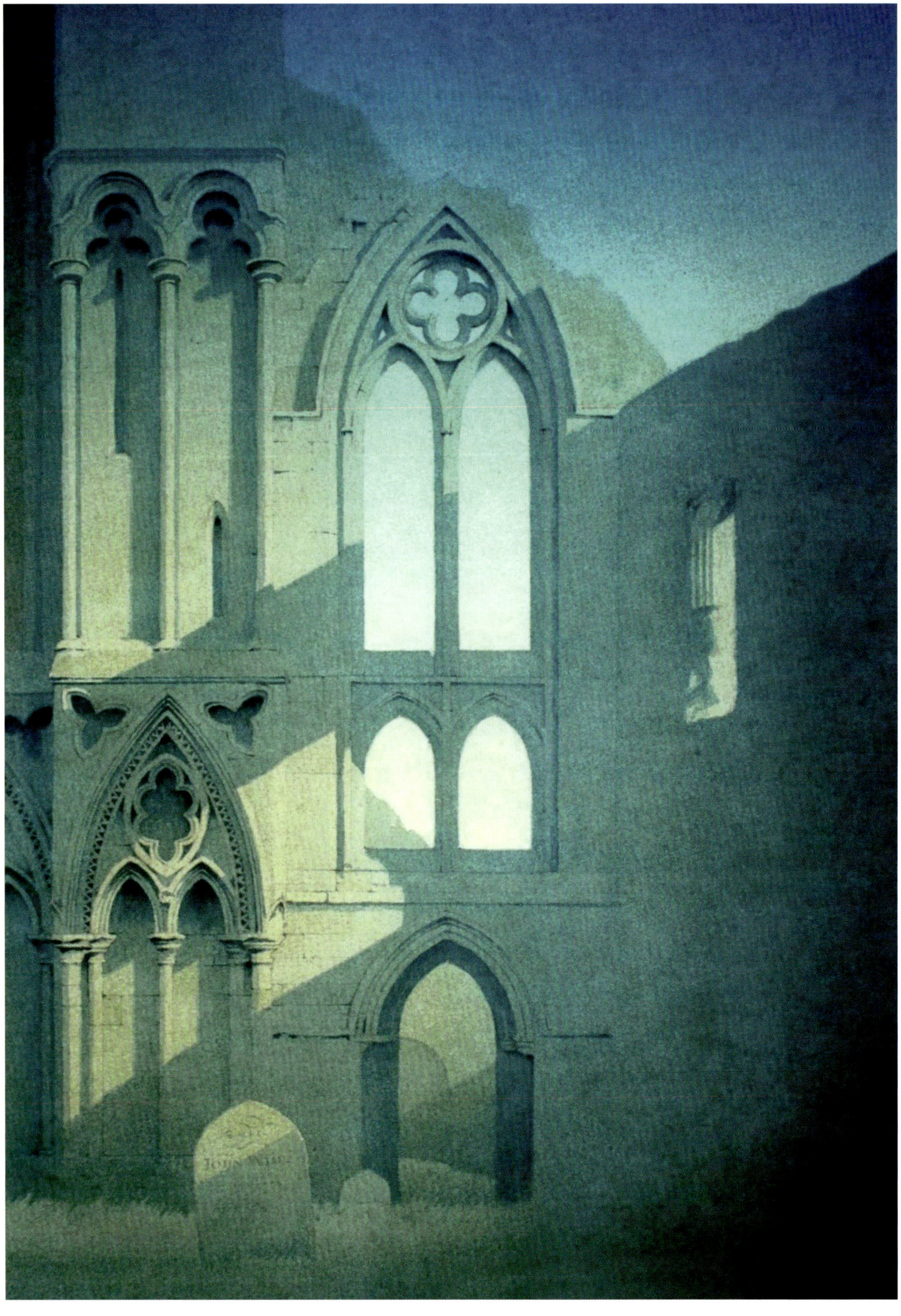

Binham Priory Shadows,
2005, watercolour

Water Coloured

Gerard Stamp's Churches

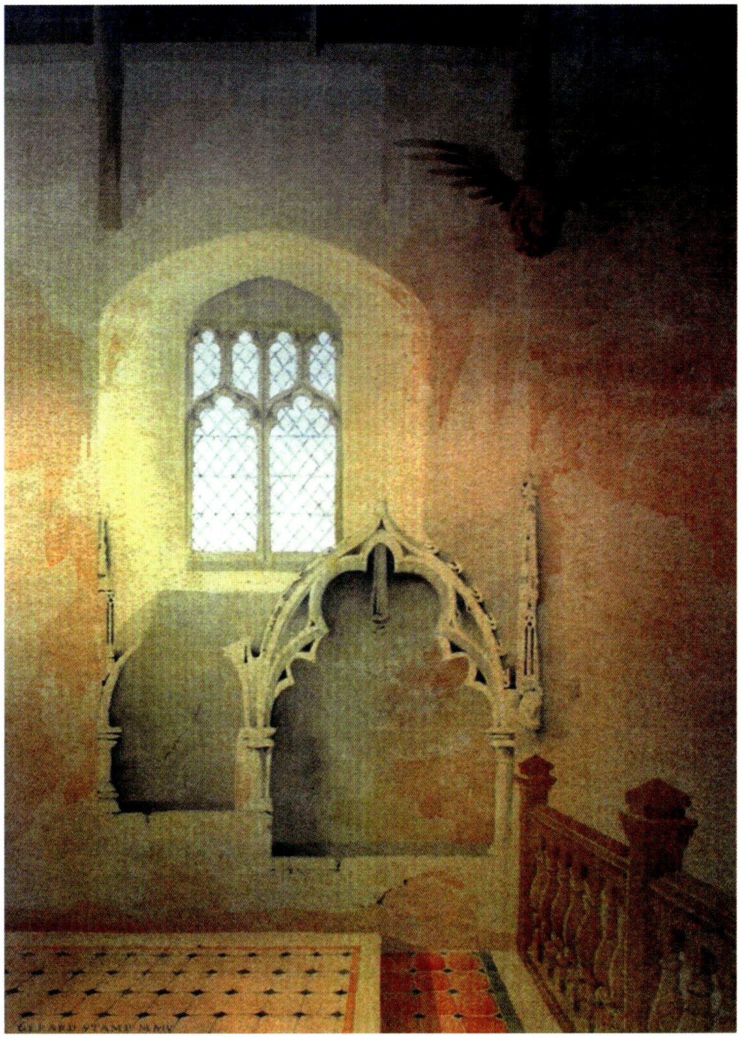

North Barningham Sedilia and Piscina, 2005, watercolour

In 2010, at the official exhibition to launch the Norwich Cathedral Hostry, watercolourist and draughtsman **Gerard Stamp** was surely forgiven his former trespasses.

He attended Norwich School from 1964 to 1972, with six years as a boarder. 'My first tearful night away from home was in a dormitory with a view of the cathedral framed by a Georgian sash window,' he remembers. 'It became a constant influence on my school life.'

The cathedral was substantially shrouded in scaffolding during the 1960s. A lot of structural work was being done to the spire, and the north side underwent an extensive programme of cleaning and repairs. Gerard says: 'Scaffolding to an adventurous schoolboy was too much of a temptation, and in those days it was easy to climb past the rudimentary obstacle designed to deter such activities.

'I went everywhere: round the tower and up the spire (I'm not ashamed to confess that my initials can be found on the inside wall by the top window), up and down all the Norman spiral stairs, on the roof under the flying buttresses, over the nave between the vaulting and the roof, round the triforium and the clerestory. All is now heavily padlocked but back then a friendly steward let me into the one door that opened up a world of medieval adventure.'

That door features in *Steps to the Triforium*, one of the immaculate images in the inaugural exhibition to celebrate the completion of the £10-million Hostry and its opening by the Queen. Designed by Snape-based architect Sir Michael Hopkins, and complementing his recent Refectory on the south side, the building incorporates a big and brilliant new gallery.

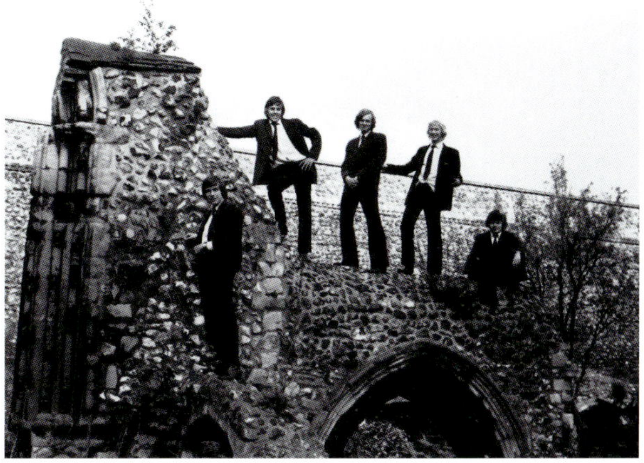

Gerard Stamp (far left) & Norwich School friends on the Hostry arch, 1972

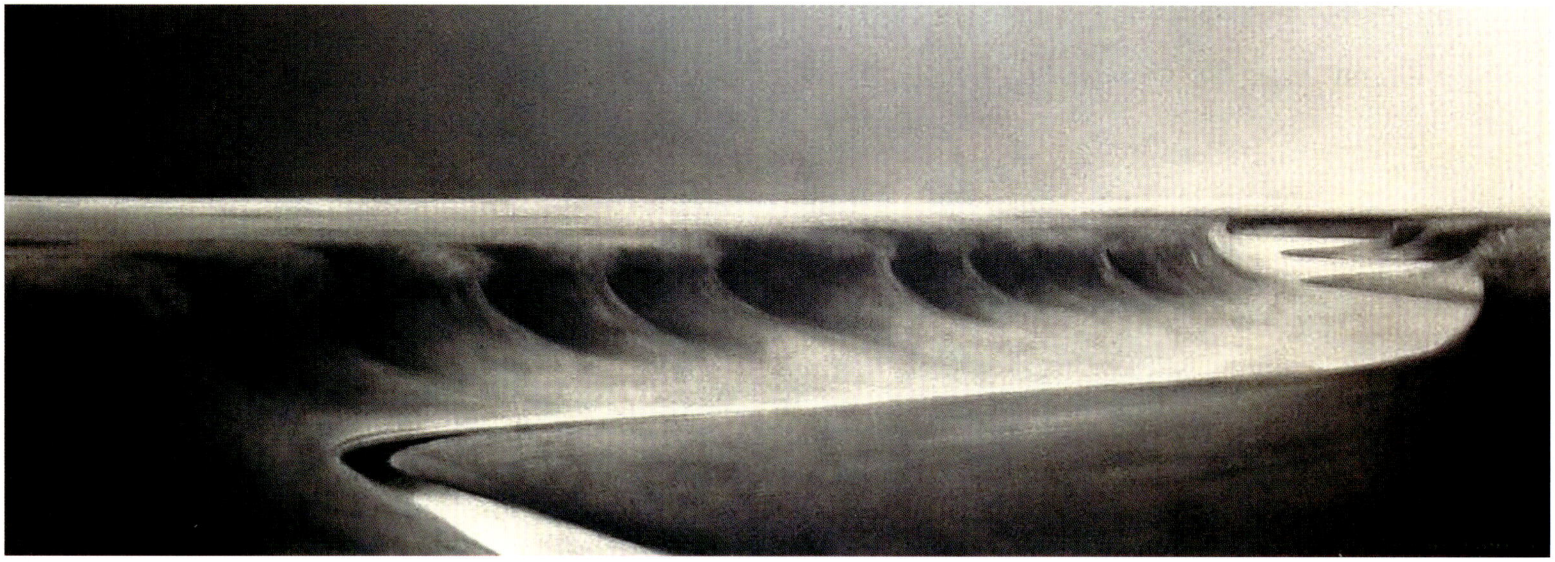

Morston Panorama, 2005, charcoal, Archant Art Collection

Gerard Stamp was taught art at Norwich School in the old chapel above Ethelbert Gate into the Close. Tutor A V Humphris imparted 'everything from the history of art and architecture, calligraphy, print-making, stage design, graphics, to composition, perspective, colour theory, and tonal values'. Hating team sports, Gerard was transferred to the school's History Society, for which he chose to record in words and drawings every Norwich church font. That led to a thesis on the then-forgotten Victorian architect Thomas Jeckyll, via cycle tours across Norfolk to study and sketch churches in particular.

And that led in turn to a love of ruins, a passion shared with his artistic heroes – especially the Norwich School's John Sell Cotman in the early 19th century and John Piper in the 20th century. 'This fascination with decay, romance, and echoes in the wind, are all tangled up with my love of Norfolk,' he says. 'There is a wonderful chapter in Lilias Rider Haggard's *Norfolk Notebook* in which, referring to the area around Binham but summing up the entire county for me, she writes: "The whole place is so heavy with history that in certain moods it gives you the feeling that you have but to put out a finger to touch the past".'

While really hankering to be an architect Gerard was steered towards studying illustration and design, and then he enjoyed a successful career in advertising. Now he longed

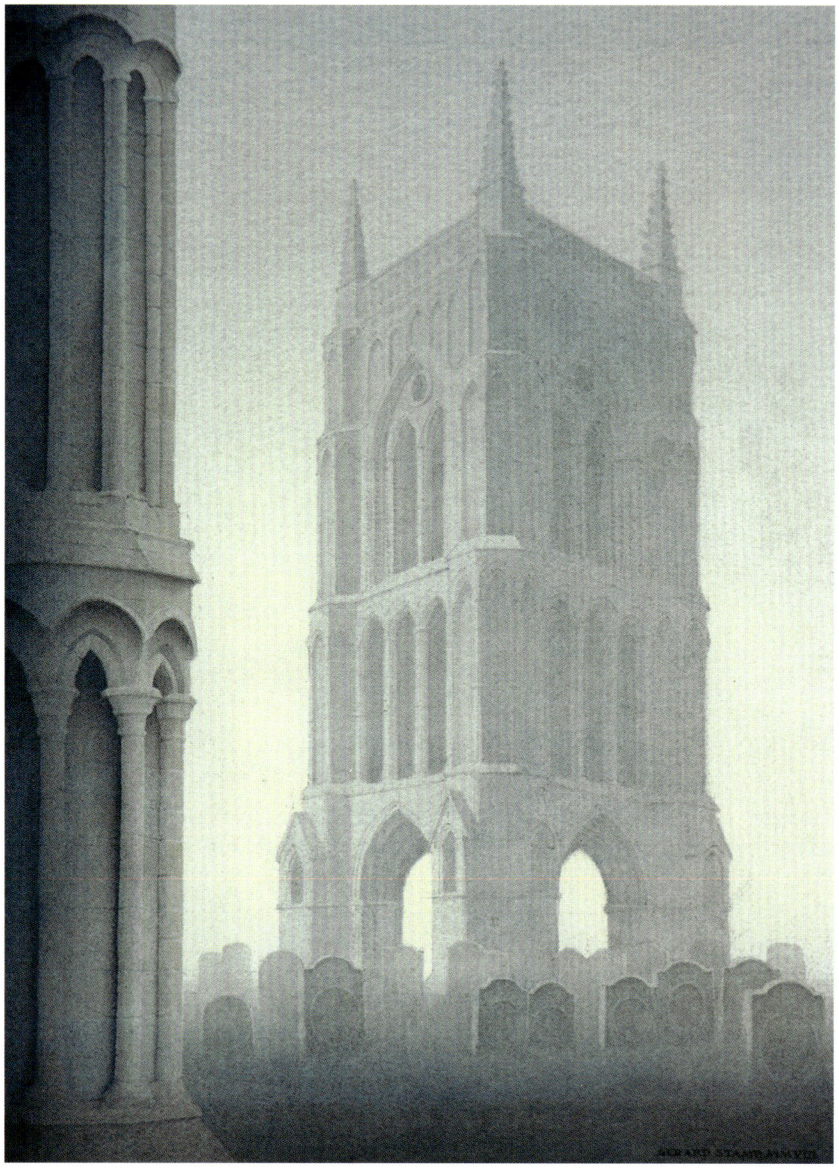

West Walton Tower, 2008, watercolour

for art and kept on vowing to become a full-time painter – the dream eventually clinched as late as 2001.

In London from the 1980s he studied the techniques of the great watercolourists, loving watercolour for its closeness to drawing and also to poetry. Loving Cotman most of all, for the 'melancholy and stillness' of his best pictures, he spent many hours in the Victoria & Albert Museum and British Museum, copying his images and then tracing his footsteps further afield.

When finally he returned to Norfolk to paint, he moved with his wife and family to the converted kitchens of Gunton Hall, near Cromer. So great was his devotion to Cotman that ensuing pictures verged on pastiches of the master – so dozens ended up burning in the kitchen fireplace.

Those purging flames heralded a new line in watercolour. An image – of a weathered building or monumental swathes of North Norfolk saltmarsh stretching like prairies split by muddy channels soaring like Grand Canyons – would be meticulously sketched out and painted on thick, rough Arches paper, plunged into a sink and sponged. The surviving painting, now minus most of the pencil marks and considerably softened, would then be dried and reworked – and maybe soaked, wiped and worked all over again.

What emerges is the thrill of the familiar rendered in a fresh light. It's that happy marriage of ancient and modern – perfect for a celebration of Norwich Cathedral. The

Steps to the Presbytery, Norwich Cathedral, 2009, watercolour (below)

Salle Choir Stalls, 2005, watercolour (below right)

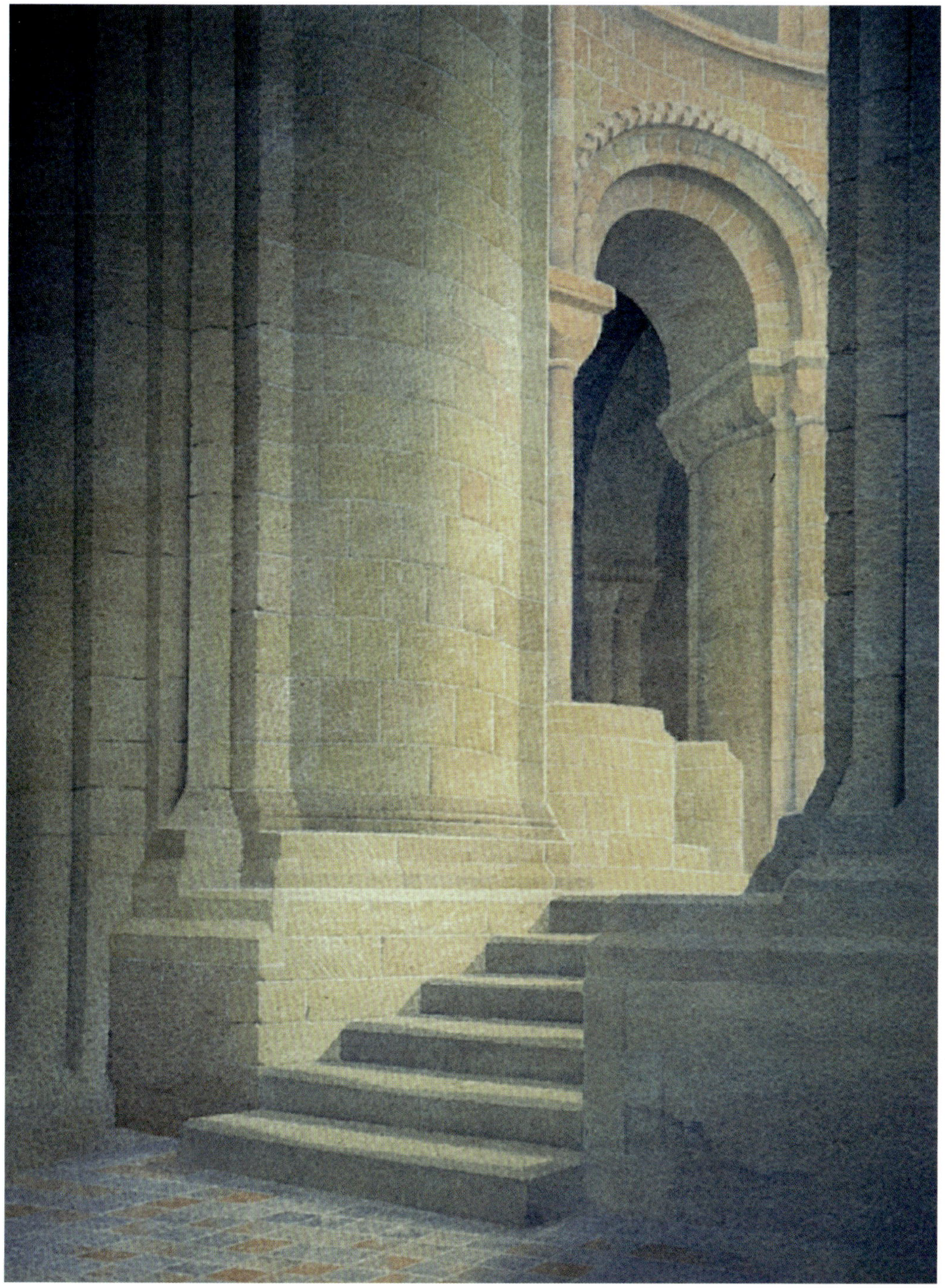

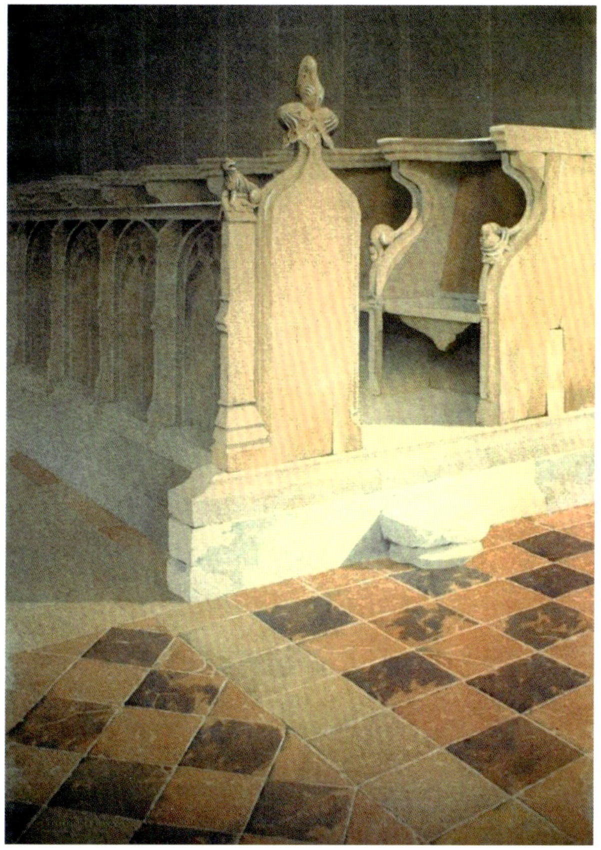

inspirational structure arose through ingenuity and industry and yet appears so natural – just like the paintings.

His focus on the cathedral comes amid an ongoing journey to chart the glory of medieval churches, most glorious of all in East Anglia – be they the grand Fen churches (West Walton, Wiggenhall St Margaret) beloved of Sir John Betjeman and the towering splendour of Salle and Cawston in mid Norfolk, or the overlooked riches of obscure parishes in his adopted North Norfolk most especially.

As Simon Jenkins has written: 'Gerard Stamp turns architecture into art. He converts stone and brick, light and shadow, the tilt of a roof and the line of a wall into a living, exhilarating picture. His eye for the power of style is unerring, whether the fluting on a pillar or the tracery in a window. He gives depth and character to the simplest buttress or the blandest patch of limestone. Above all, his pictures evoke the mystery of English churches.'

And, save for yellow hard hats, the workmen held forever in Gerard Stamp's painted grid of the Hostry building site are much like their medieval forebears who toiled to sculpt a hallowed space that the artist has adored from his schooldays. 'I just love the building,' he concludes. 'It has its own smell, its own warmth. There are many grander, more beautiful cathedrals, but none more welcoming, or more intimate. Norwich Cathedral is a close friend.'

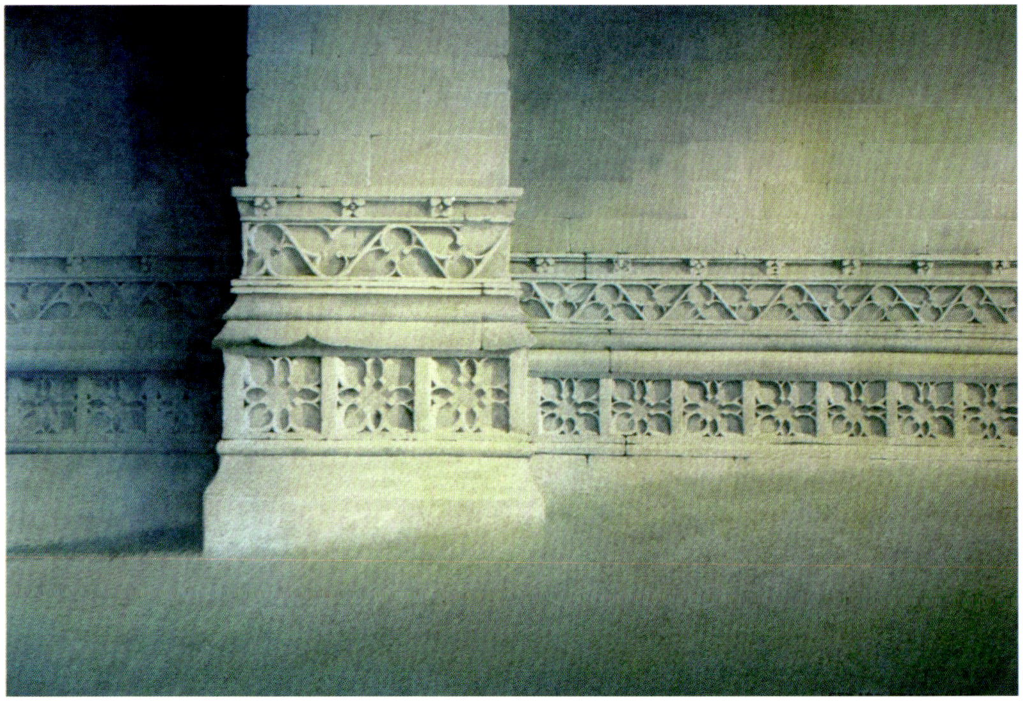

The Base of Cawston Tower,
2005, watercolour

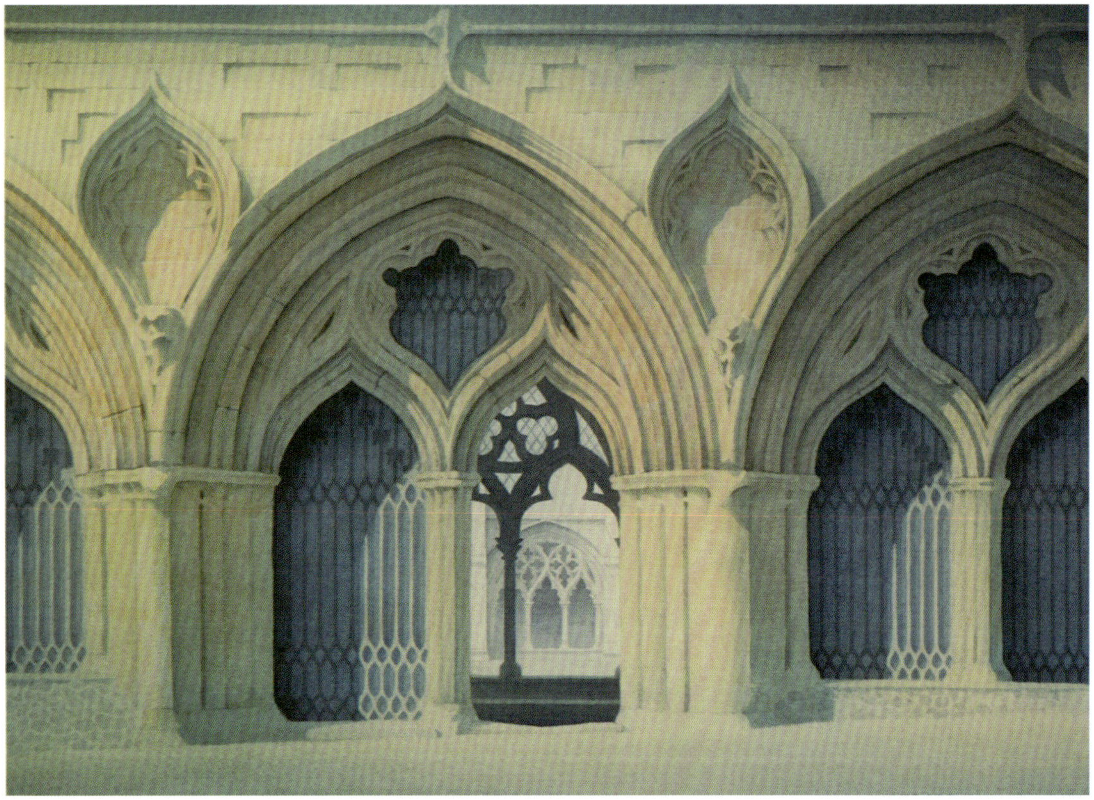

Chapter House Doors,
Norwich Cathedral,
2009, watercolour

YARMOUTH AND THE BROADS

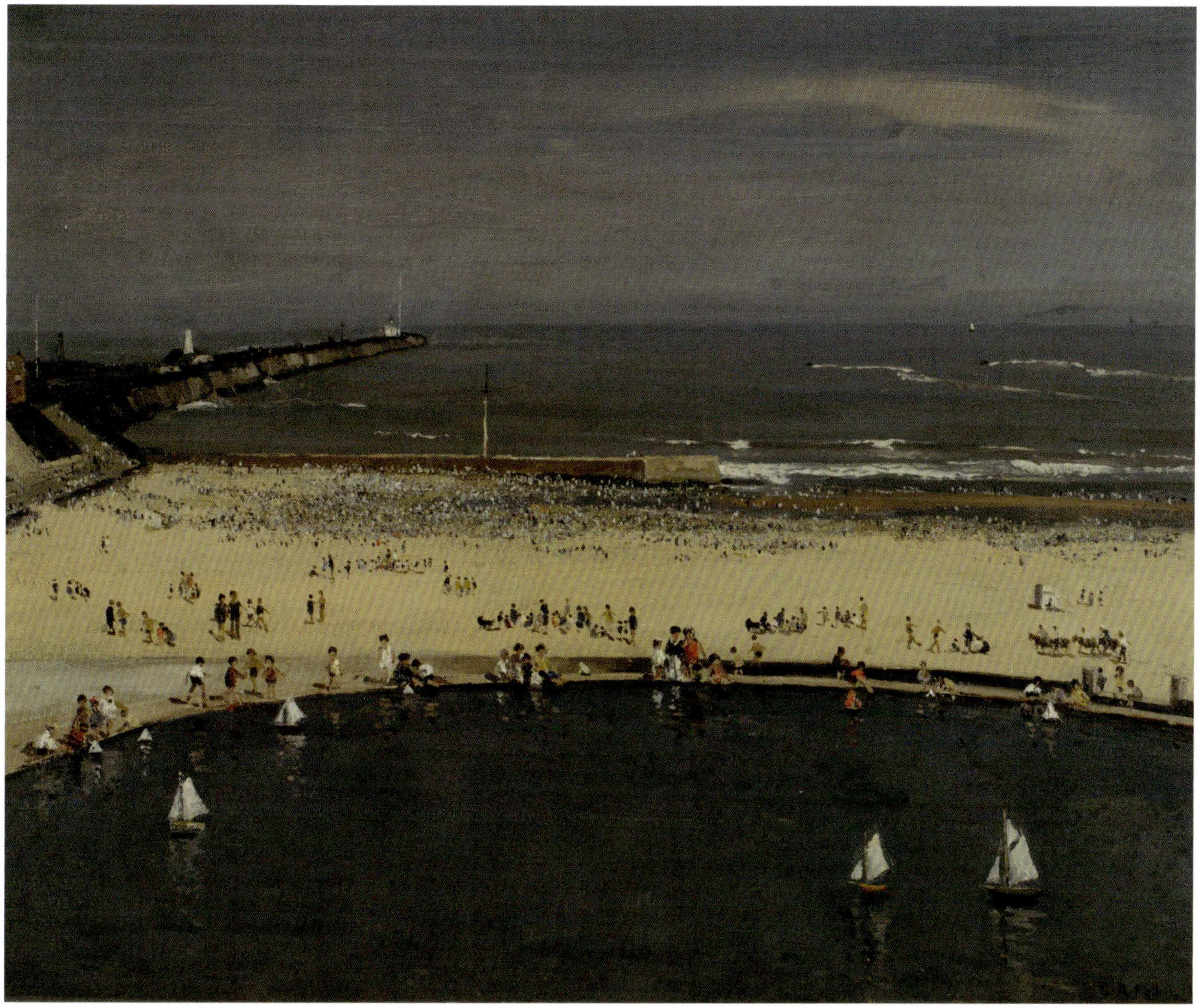

Gorleston Yacht Pond and Sands, Campbell Mellon (1876-1955), oil on canvas.

In the Barley Harvest, from *Pictures of East Anglian Life,* Plate VII, P H Emerson,

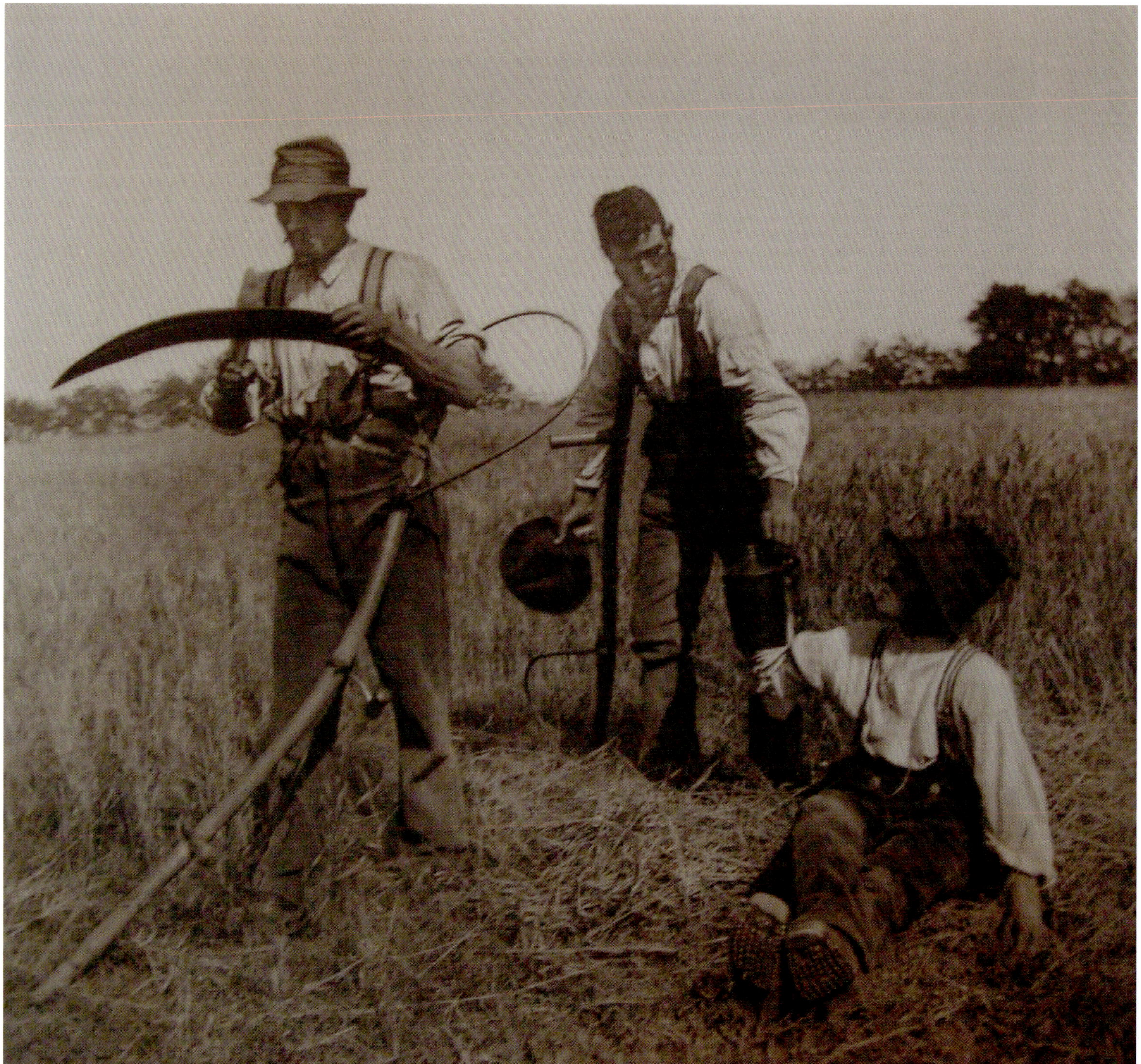

Gathering Water-Lilies

P H Emerson and T F Goodall

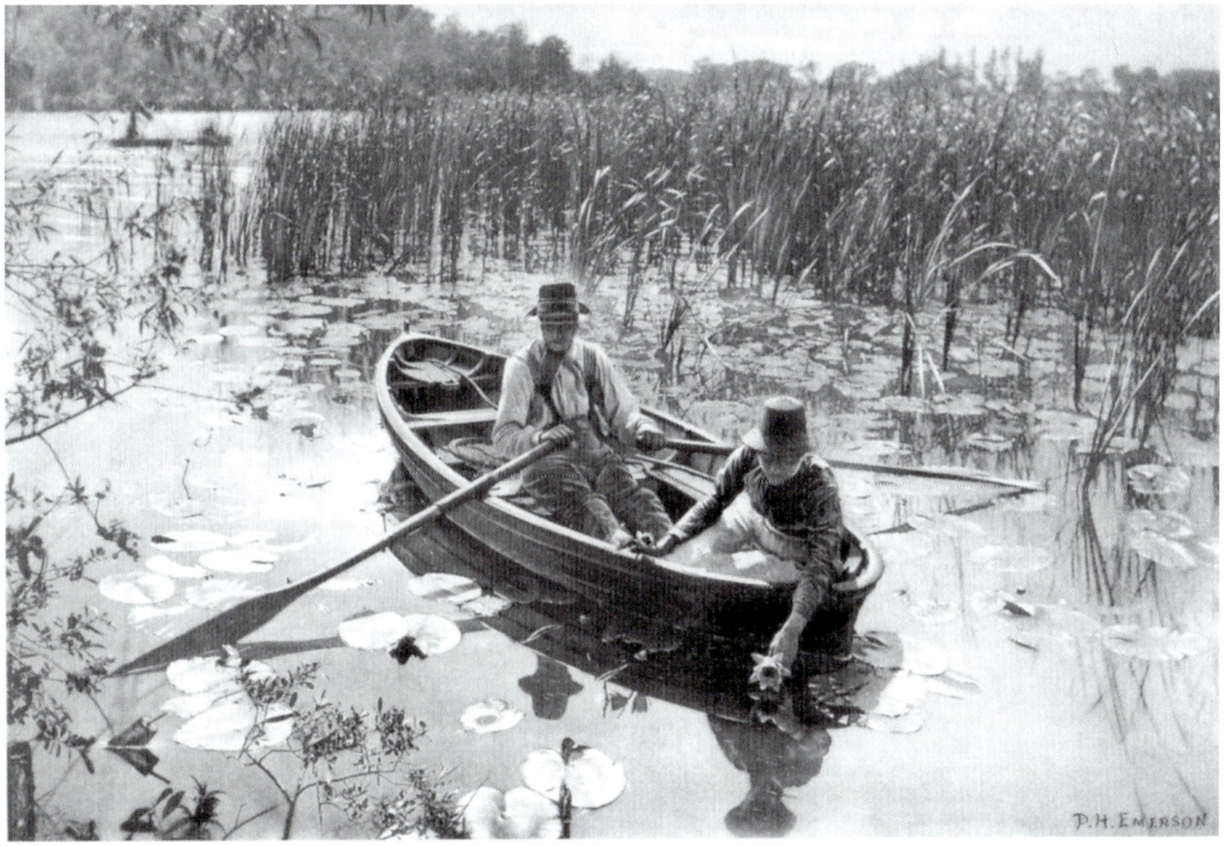

Gathering Water-Lilies, from *Life and Landscape on the Norfolk Broads,* Plate IX, 1887, P H Emerson

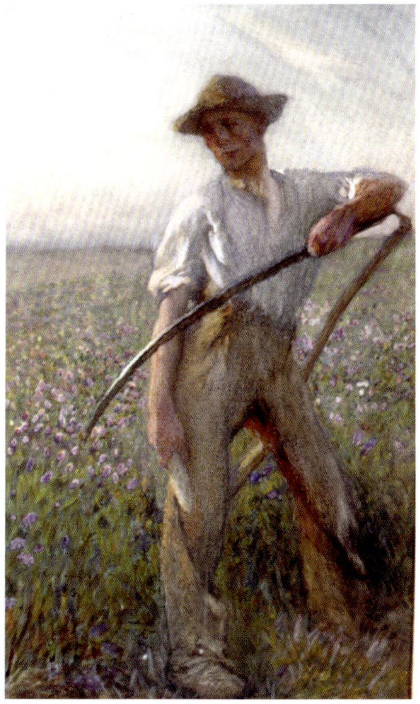

The Tired Mower, Sir George Clausen, 1896, watercolour

In May 1886 naturalist photographer **P H Emerson** published a study of Broadland bliss. The photogravure *Gathering Water-Lilies* – with an old man steadying a rowing boat so that a young woman can pick lilies from a liquid mirror – soon sold out in two limited editions.

An ideal poster for burgeoning holidays on the Norfolk and Suffolk Broads, the single and supposedly unstaged shot was really rather artful. But a focus on the foreground figures and a romantic blurring of the reedy backdrop mimicked, this former medic insisted, the action of the human eye.

The new gravure process saw an albumen print engraved by a skilled craftsman using printer's ink – though not skilled enough for an exacting master who railed against retouching of an original composition which actually survives in two forms. He himself edited nature more than he cared to admit.

And when, later in 1886, the peaceful study appeared in Emerson's first book – *Life and Landscape on the Norfolk Broads* – it seemed to stand out as the only unsore thumb in an album of hard labour: reed-cutting, hay-making, eel-fishing, wild-fowling. Until, peering into the immaculate platinum plate, we spy the collapsed bow net behind the boatman.

While Emerson's text waxes lyrical on the symbolism of water-lilies, elsewhere his overshadowed collaborator **Thomas Frederick Goodall** describes a girl braiding a bow net and her father making a cylindrical cage by stretching the mesh over hoops of split hazel separated and held taut by notched sticks. The structure surrounds a cone-shaped inner net to trap incoming prey.

Baited with white and yellow blooms, the weighted bow net will be sunk below the lily pads in tench swims. These olive-backed, golden-bellied edible fish thrive in brackish water with little oxygen where even carp struggle. With such tenacity, the invisible tench in *Gathering Water-Lilies* reflect the hardy Broadlanders just keeping their heads above water economically.

Peter Henry (né Pedro Enriques) Emerson had been born in 1856 on a slave-worked sugar plantation in Cuba, to an American father and English mother. Childhood dramas – the American Civil War, Cuba's revolt against Spanish rule, the deaths of his father from dysentery and his sister from typhoid – brought scope for added embroidery. Our young hero claimed, for instance, to have saved a ship from foundering in stormy seas amid sailors drunken, diseased or mutinous.

Confessing to a general genius in everything from meteorology to billiards, this human meteor quit medical studies for explorations with the aid of his new-discovery: a camera. Abandoning his wife and family in Southwold

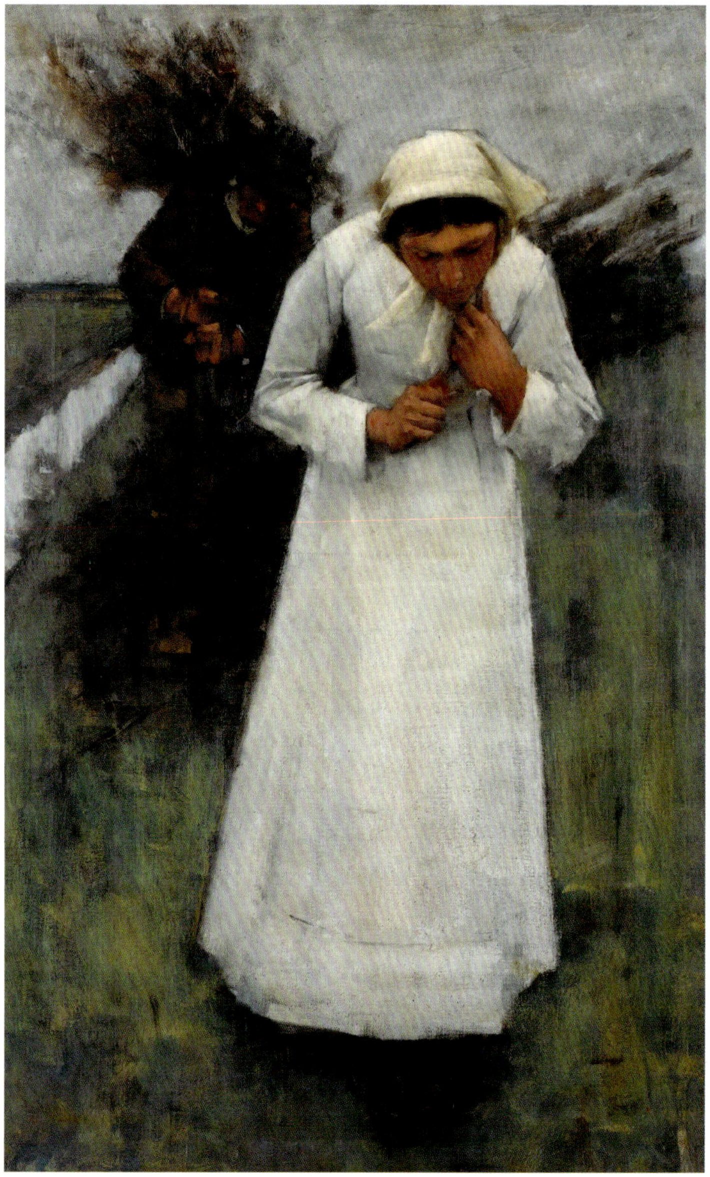

Gathering Faggots, Henry Herbert La Thangue, (1859-1929), oil on canvas

in 1884, he hired a yacht to tour the Broads with his brother – dropping him, too, on meeting painter T F Goodall and moving into his South Walsham Broad houseboat.

Amid the instant fame of 1886, and after snapping two sequel volumes *Idyls of the Norfolk Broads* and *Pictures from Life in Field and Fen*, the Emerson brood was hauled back to London, though the rover returned the following year to join Goodall in his new houseboat on Breydon Water to plot *Wild Life on a Tidal Water*.

Vowing to spend a year aboard a wherry he actually landed in Anglesey, revisiting Lowestoft in 1895 by way of Ramsgate and Broadstairs. The next year he was near the Goodall family in

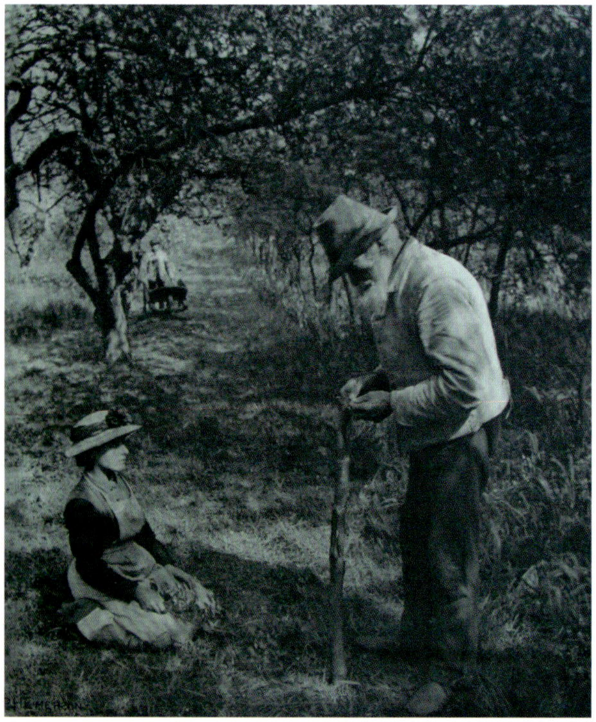

The Grafter, from *Pictures from Life in Field and Fen*, Plate VI, 1887, P H Emerson

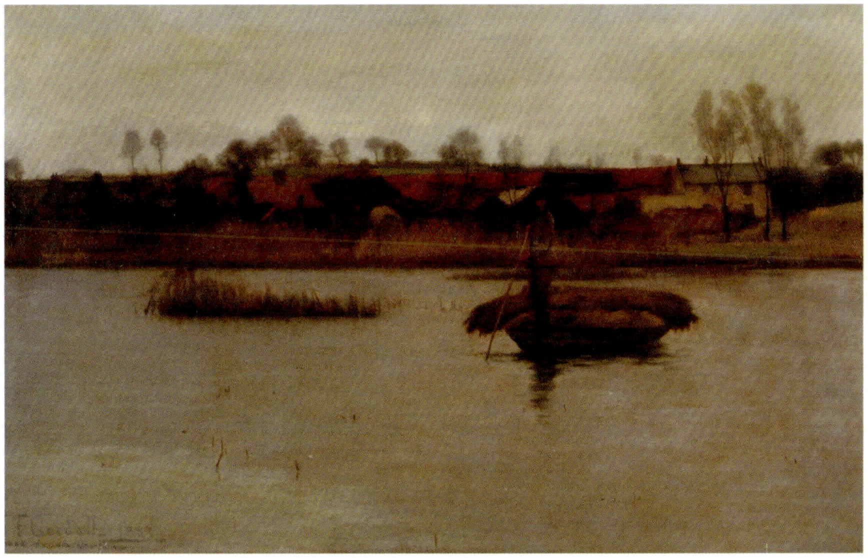

Rockland Broad, T F Goodall, 1883, oil on canvas, Norwich Castle Museum

Oulton Broad, before the friendship was abruptly and mysteriously broken. Maybe the mystery was that it had lasted so long.

At the end of the 1880s he had written a book on naturalistic photography – aiming to emulate with a camera the achievement on canvas by pioneer painters Henry Herbert La Thangue in North Walsham, Philip Wilson Steer and friends in Southwold and Walberswick and George Clausen, later on, in the Essex villages of Widdington and Duton Hill.

Likened by one writer to 'dropping a bomb at a tea-party' the explosive thesis was soon being described by Emerson himself as a 'tempest in a teapot'. For he had turned violently against his own vision – destroying every plate he could find in his angry conclusion that photography could never equal art.

Luckily those four East Anglian albums survive – together with a tantalising handful of Goodall paintings, notably *The Bow Net* of 1886, now in Liverpool's Walker Art Gallery. Credit for *Gathering Water-Lilies* should surely be shared.

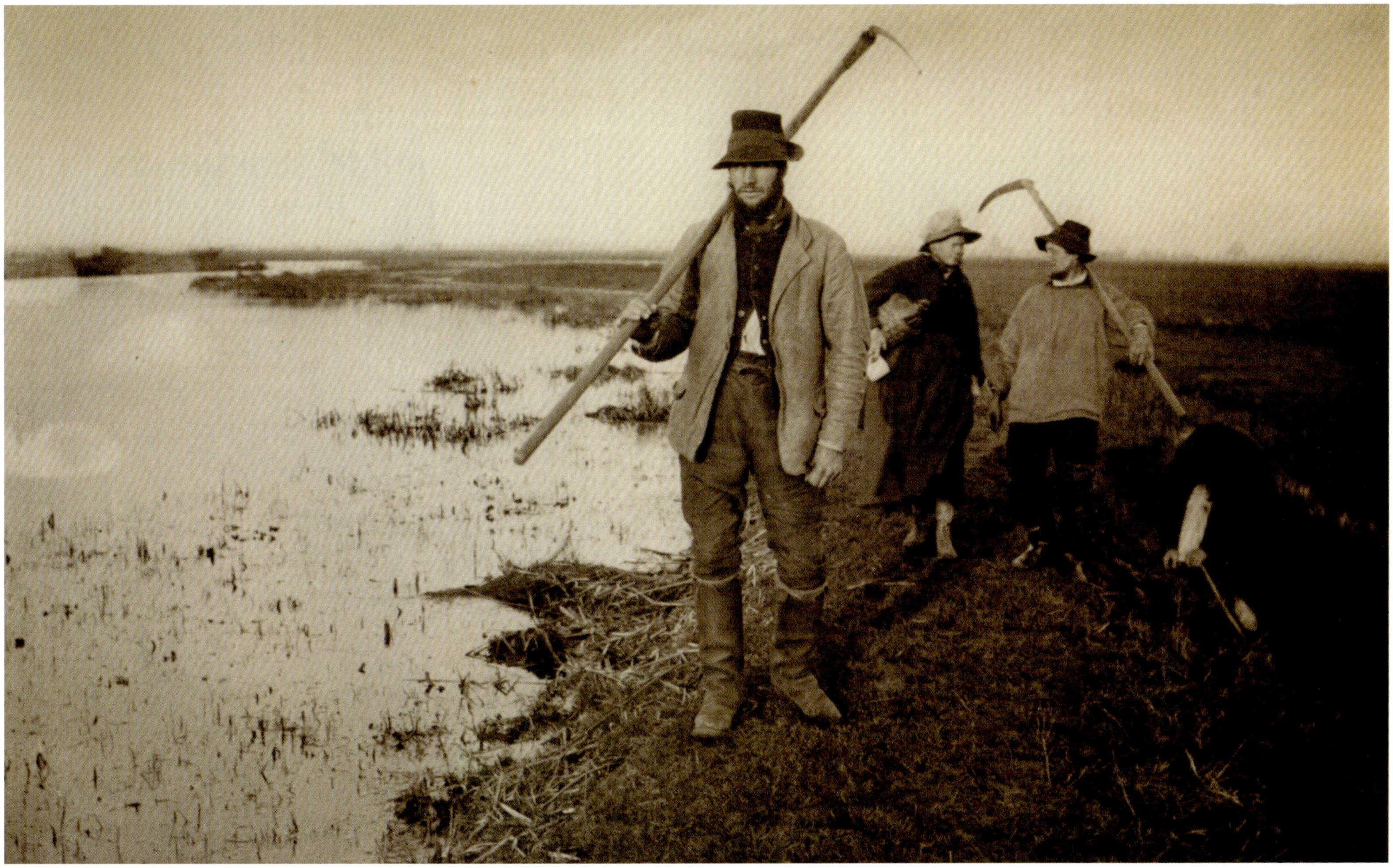

Coming Home from the Marshes, from *Life and Landscape on the Norfolk Broads,* Plate I, 1887, P H Emerson and T F Goodall

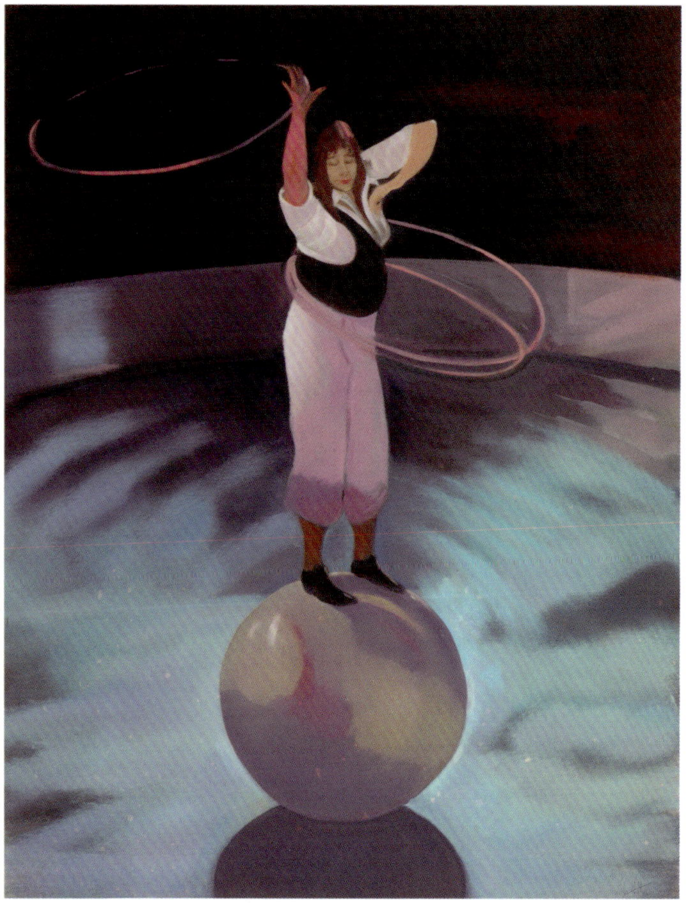

Girl on a Ball with Hoops,
Katherine Hamilton, 2008,
oil on canvas (left)

Fire Breather,
Katherine Hamilton, 2008,
oil on canvas (below left)

Roller Blades,
Katherine Hamilton, 2008,
oil on canvas (below)

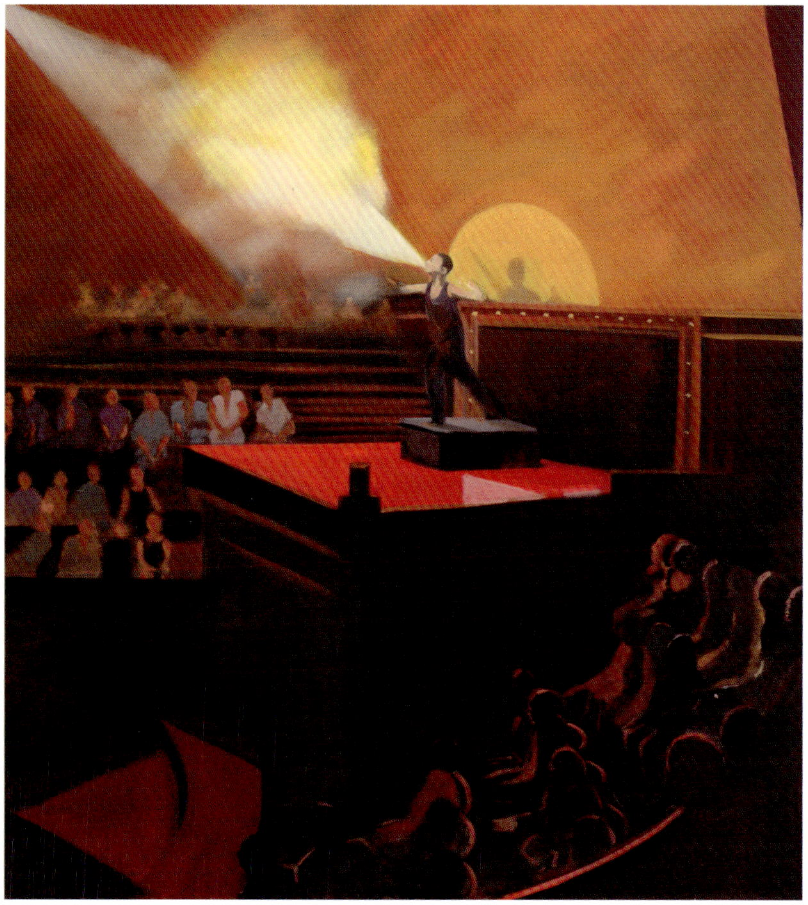

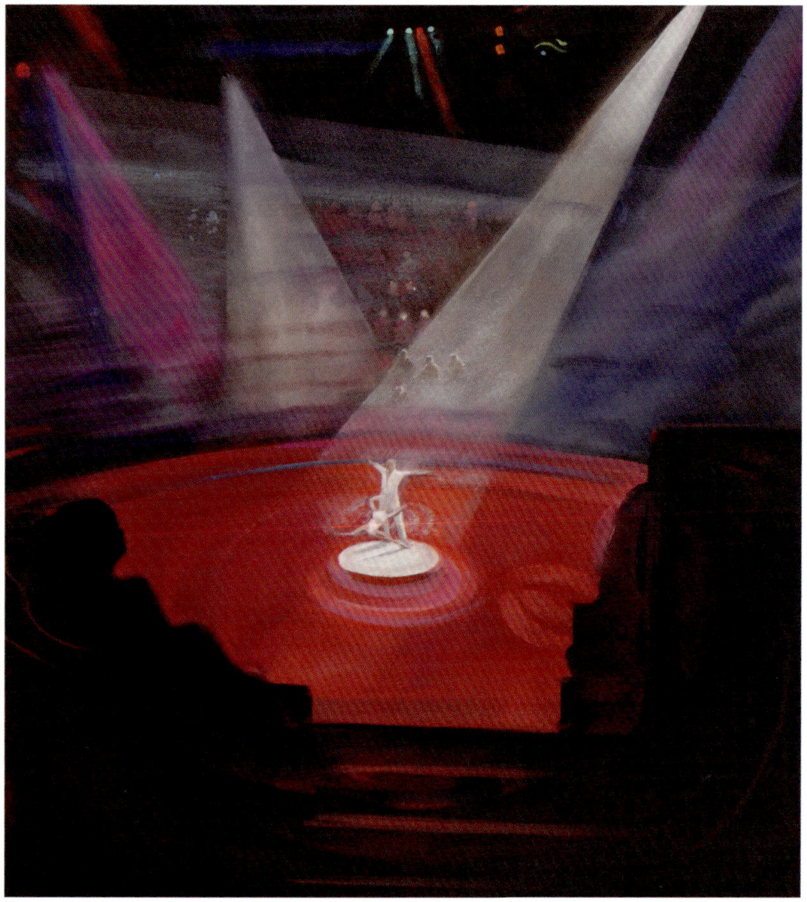

Show Time

Great Yarmouth Hippodrome

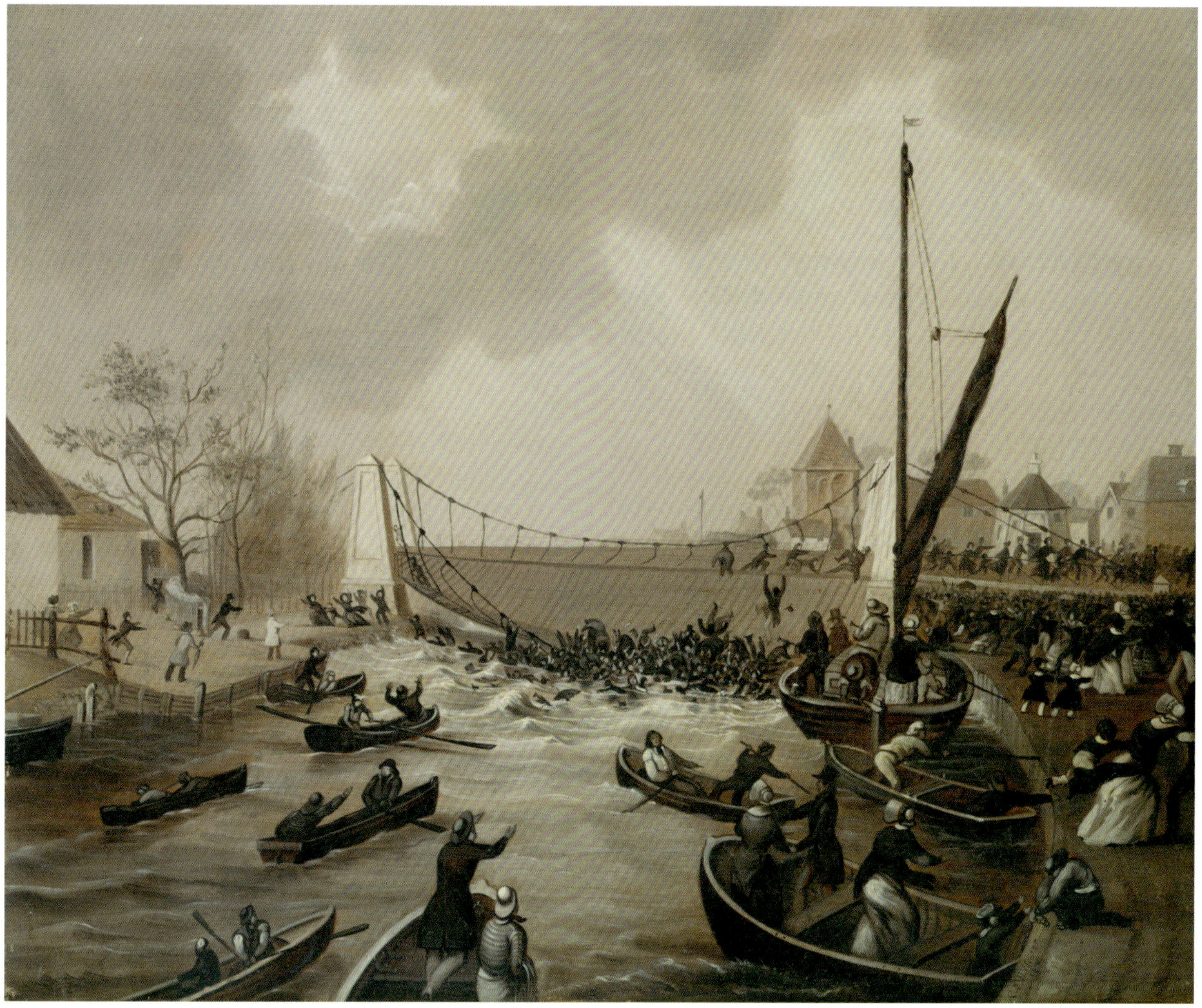

Falling of the Suspension Bridge Great Yarmouth, Cornelius Winter, 1845, oil on canvas, Archant Art Collection

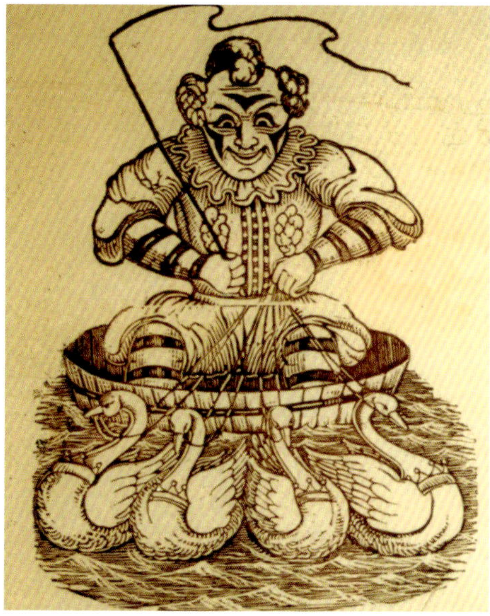

Nelson the Clown, 1845 handbill

In the spring of 1845 Cooke's Royal Circus posted handbills around Great Yarmouth advertising a bizarre benefit performance. Nelson the Clown was to be pulled in a wash tub by four geese from the Quay to the Suspension Bridge over the River Bure. The beneficiary of the ensuing whip-round would be himself.

Spectators came to line both banks, but the crowds massed thickest on the bridge, launched with a fanfare in 1829, for the best vantage point of all. When the tub reached Bessey's Wharf, 400 people rushed to the southern side of the elegant span, throwing all their weight on one badly welded chain. It snapped.

A few heard a warning creak and leapt ashore, but most were thrown into the river as the bridge collapsed – those plunging last crushing the ones below. A boy called Jay would recall that when he was under the water the people had seemed to be hugging each other.

A pandemonium of panic swept the separated families on either bank as all

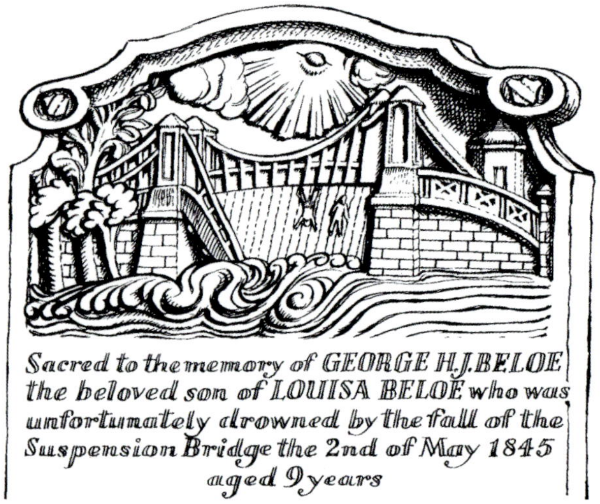

Noel Spencer, 1977, line drawing

available craft were commandeered for lifeboats and arms were outstretched and human chains formed to pull flailing kith and kin to safety. Mrs Gillings swam free with her baby's clothes clamped between her teeth. Lucky young Mr Simmonds was trapped on the wrecked bridge by his leg, which a rescuer broke with a crowbar. Mrs Livingstone, of King Street, clung to one child, but her six-year-old son Joseph and daughter Matilda, seven, were lost.

Corpses were laid out in the Norwich Arms, Admiral Collingwood and White Swan pubs, and many of the 79 coffins later assembled in St Nicholas's Church proved pathetically tiny. For 54 of the victims were aged 15 and under – one being nine-year-old George Beloe, whose tombstone in the churchyard displays a relief carving of the disaster (left).

Many of the victims came from Rows 1 to 99 – a network of hovels leading from the harbour and finally levelled after the last war. One is now splendidly recreated in the Time and Tide museum, where a monochrome oil painting of the collapsing bridge by eye-witness Cornelius Winter can also be seen.

Circus had evolved from trick horse riding performances in Georgian London, and then took in a cast of tumblers, jugglers, comedians and animal tamers for an art form spreading nationwide and world-wide. From 1845 six circus buildings were constructed in Yarmouth, the last and greatest being the Hippodrome.

A fantasy castle complete with Art Nouveau friezes of peacocks, owls, foliage and faces – and, once upon a time, stained glass windows depicting a chariot race – the Grade Two* listed

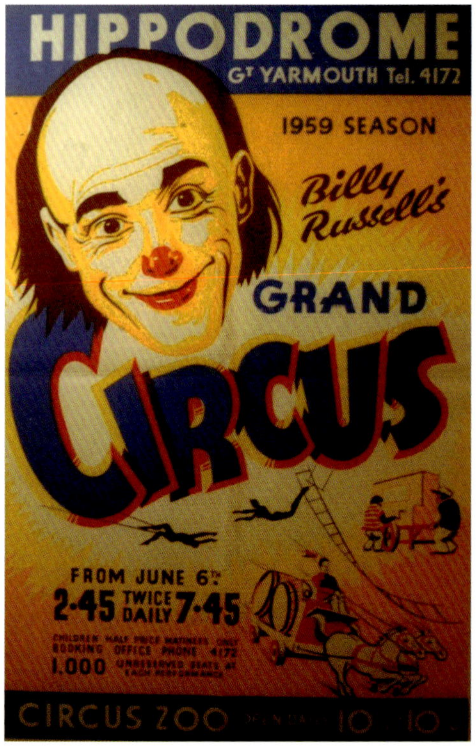

Bill poster, 1959

Beryl Cook (1926-2008) was a one-woman circus. The former showgirl and model lived in Southend and Leigh-on-Sea before serving as a Suffolk pub landlady – at Nayland's White Hart in the mid-1950s. After a decade in Africa she found fame in Plymouth as a self-taught painter of larger than life good time girls who might just be pensioners (and possibly with an East Coast ancestry). *Granny the Lion Tamer* was painted for Nanette Newman's book *My Granny Was A Frightful Bore (But She Isn't Anymore).*

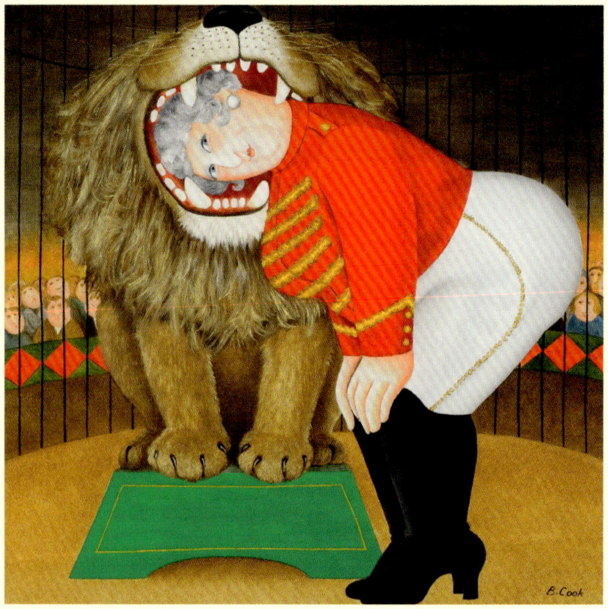

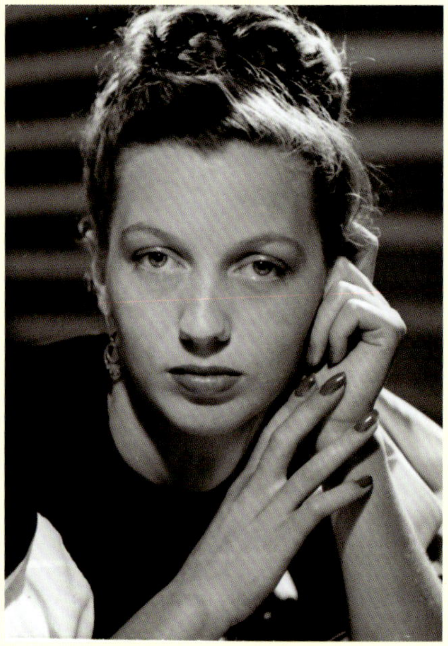

Granny the Lion Tamer,
Beryl Cook, 1983,
oil on canvas (far left)

Model Beryl (left)

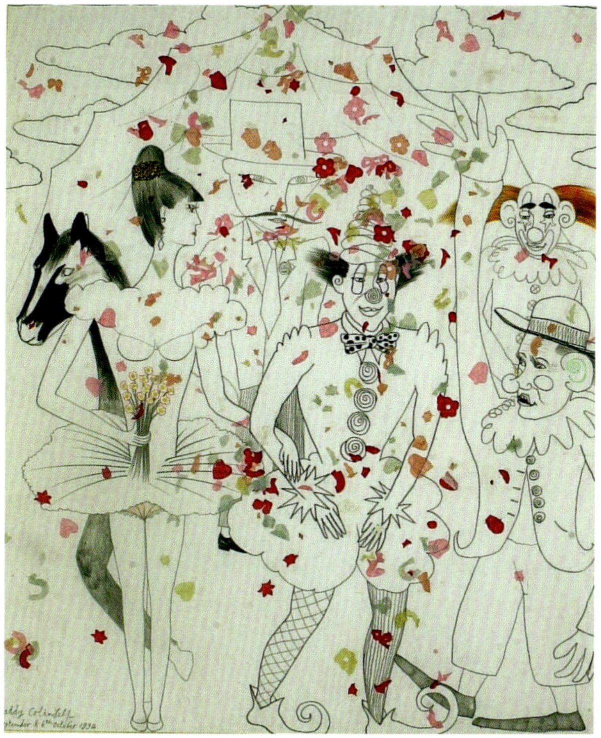

Clown's Wedding,
Colin Self, 1982, mixed media,
Archant Art Collection

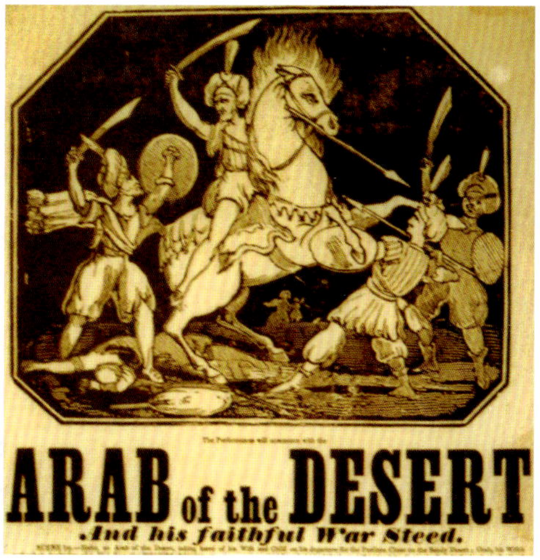

Hippodrome poster,
19th century

structure behind the Golden Mile was built in 1903 by legendary showman George Gilbert. That was the year when the cast iron and glass Winter Gardens were shipped by barge from Torquay to the present site beside Wellington Pier with not a pane broken in transit.

Lily Langtry sang here, Max Miller joked, Houdini escaped, and Lloyd George (political performer extraordinaire) addressed a rousing rally. Charlie Chaplin is said to have featured as a child actor before finding fame in America.

The Hippodrome is Britain's only surviving purpose-built circus building still true to its original purpose – and one of only four world-wide with a stage which sinks and floods into a pool for synchronised swimming. It is a beautiful shell since war-time service as a shooting range blitzed an interior of fabulous plaster carvings.

The Jay family has enjoyed a record spell running the Hippodrome. Jack and his former pop star son Peter bought the building in 1978 intending to turn it into a bowling alley. But soon they had fallen for the circus. Now Peter and wife Christine co-produce the twice-yearly seasons which also involve their three sons (Jack as ringmaster, Joe as lighting operator and Ben as general manager).

Painters have been drawn into the spectacle – most notably Yarmouth-based Bruer Tidman, artist in residence here from the 1980s, and Norfolk Pop Artist Colin Self. And a hugely popular 2010 exhibition of art and artefacts at Time and Tide – Show Time: Great Yarmouth's Circus Story – featured a parade of pictures by **Katherine Hamilton**.

This dancer turned painter searched the world for flowing colour and frozen movement – until finding her perfect subject in a magical arena just up the coast from her home near Southwold. She meant to visit the Hippodrome just the once, but kept returning. Through successive summer and Christmas seasons, this former performer was busy sketching. Between shows she produced panoramic oils in the peace and quiet of her garden studio. She says: 'There is a whole world in the circus – it is about a global family where all are accepted, and many are actually related, because

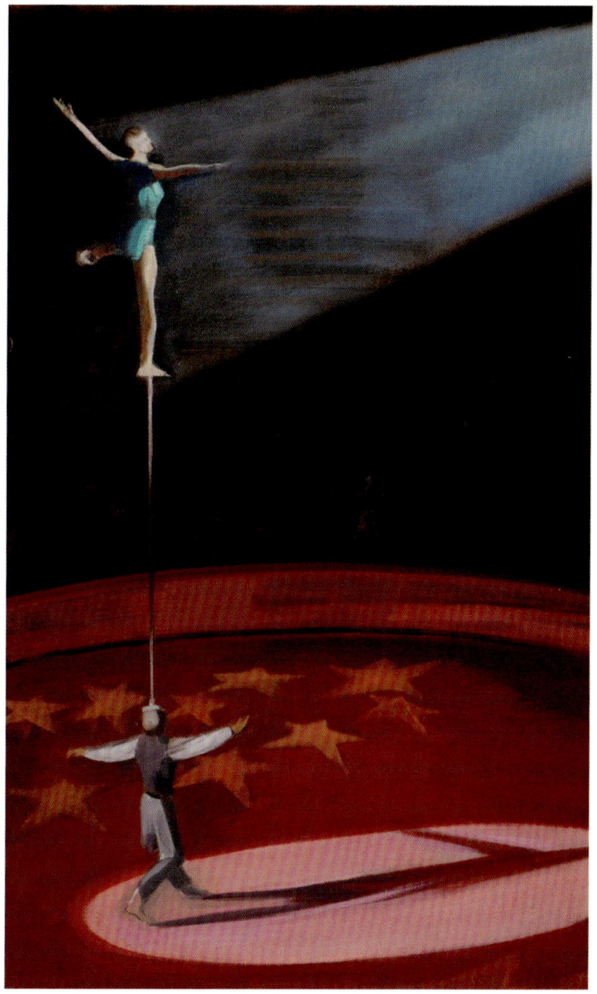

Balance,
Katherine Hamilton, 2008,
oil on canvas

everyone has a brilliant skill to bring to the spectacle. It's a portrait of shared dedication.

'The excitement of the acts – hailing from all over Europe, Africa, Asia and South America, as well as being home-grown in Yarmouth – is what I wanted to show in paint. It's about movement, colour and atmosphere. And it is also about the ghosts of all the aerial, acrobatic and comic artistes that have appeared at the Hippodrome over more than a century. There is something wonderfully eerie about the circus. The magic is still there when the building is empty.'

As a teenager Katherine Hamilton studied painting in Florence and then in London

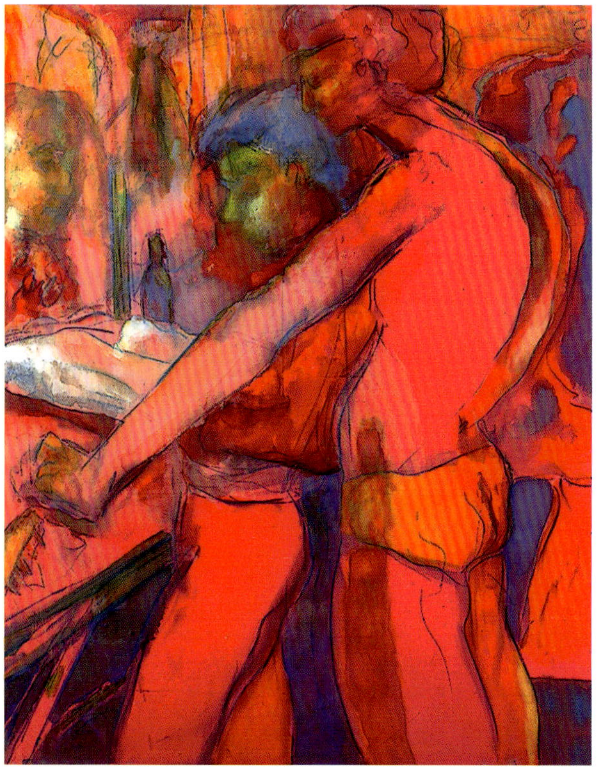

The Dressing Room, Bruer Tidman, 1987, acrylic on canvas (left) Norwich Castle Museum

where she switched to the London School of Contemporary Dance. She worked as a dancer and choreographer in New York and set up a dance school in Ethiopia.

After that it was back to painting – based in Italy, then France and Spain. She moved to East Anglia in 1992 and has worked here ever since, especially on panoramic seascapes, apart from frequent and far-flung travels from Guatemala to Kerala to paint everything from markets and harbours to beach football matches and bull fights.

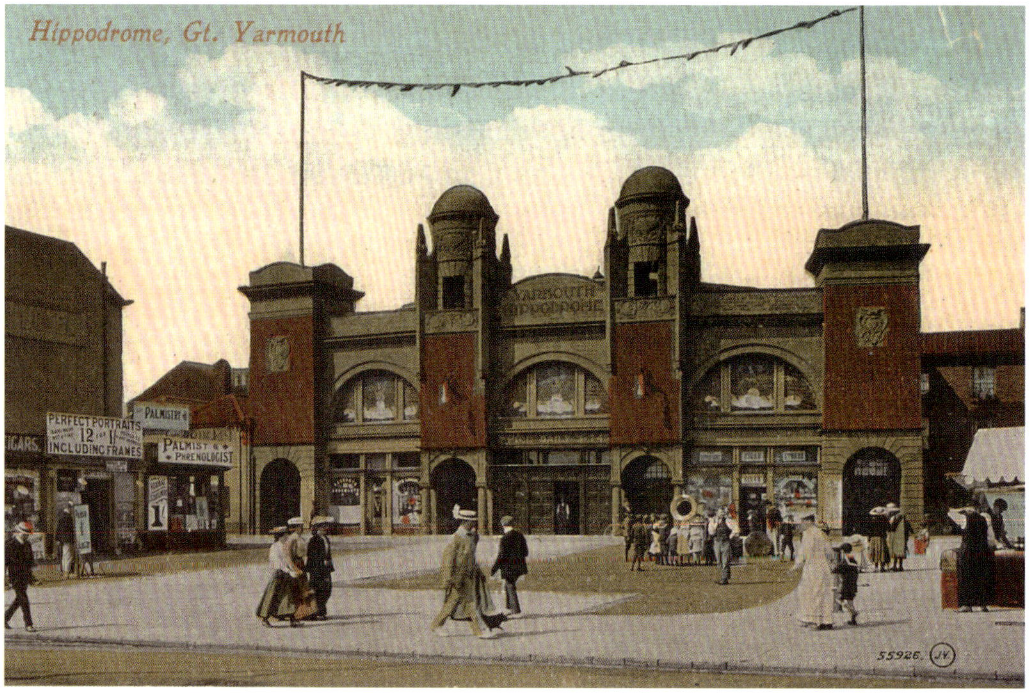

Yarmouth Hippodrome c.1900

Human relationships are paramount to her and yet she is also supremely committed to pursuing a singular path as an artist. The easy route is rejected. What appears to be a veering creative journey has been all the more impressive because Kate herself generally has no idea where it will lead.

She just throws herself into the process and seizes each new visual opportunity. Her two careers are ultimately united. What she's after is diverse vitality. 'Katherine Hamilton does what all true artists should,' says Southwold's

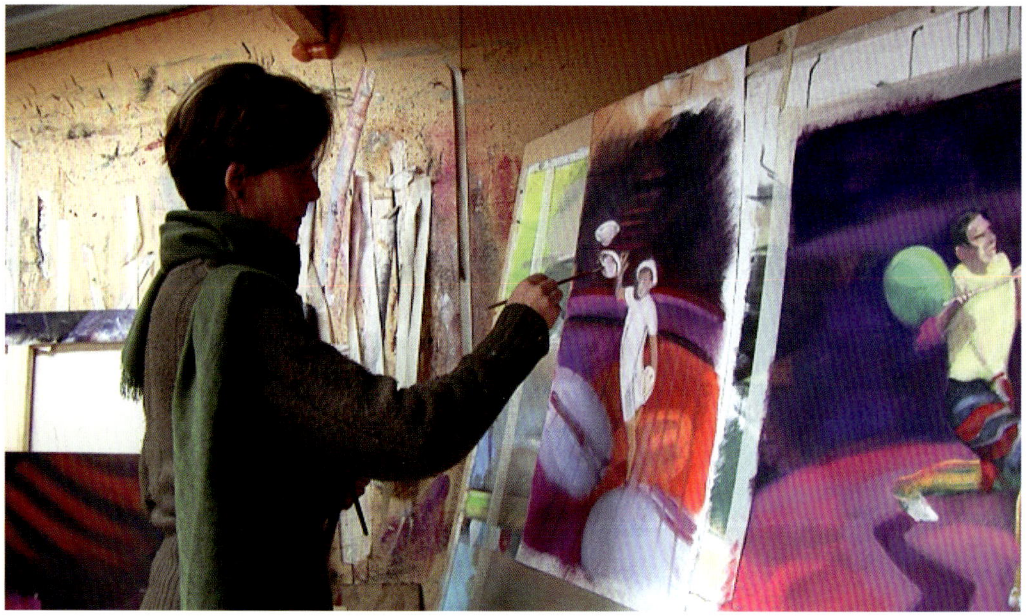

Katherine Hamilton in her studio

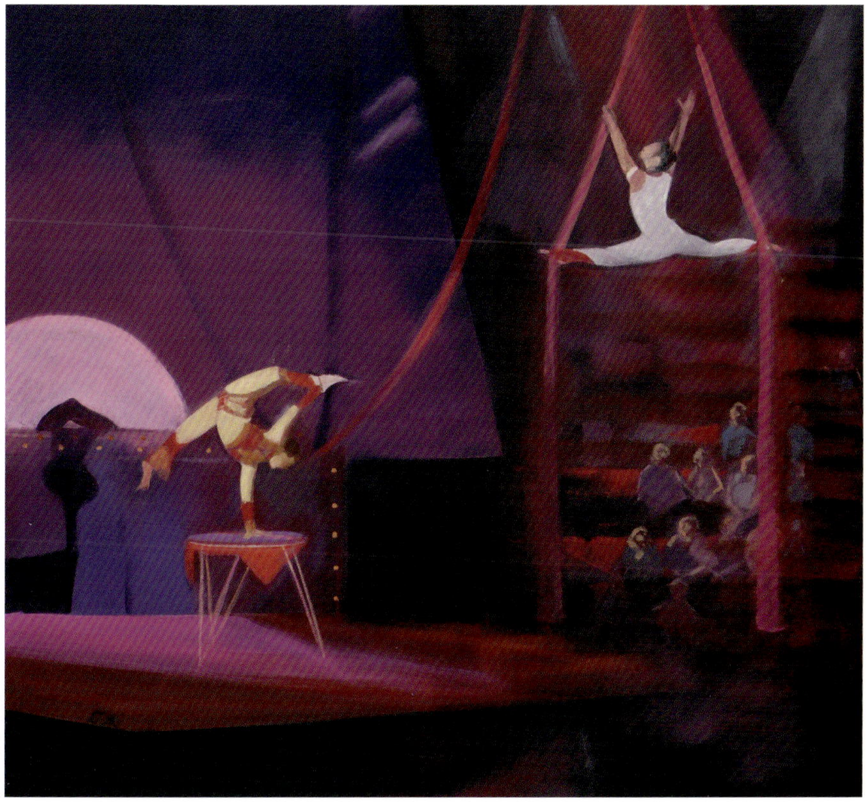

Double Acrobats, Katherine Hamilton, 2008, oil on canvas

P D James. 'She celebrates and interprets the beauty and variety of the world in which all of us have to live and it is this truth to what she sees that draws us powerfully to her art.'

She spares us the terrible journeys she undertakes with glee. When a plane to Mali was cancelled she waited a day to fly to neighbouring Senegal, then suffered a 12-hour taxi ride to reach a hotel where a column of ants flowed through the lobby bearing away creepy crawlies fallen from the walls and ceilings.

She leaves the comfort of any haven for the authentic experience which might land her in a mud hut with a hurricane looming and no rescue boat in sight. Her pictures can indeed reveal the calm before the storm – a deceptive ease summing up the circus, where delight is spiced with danger.

'The illusion of circus is like the illusion of making a painting,' she says. 'We don't want to see behind it or tear it apart by analysis. The aim is visual joy – and being transported by magic.'

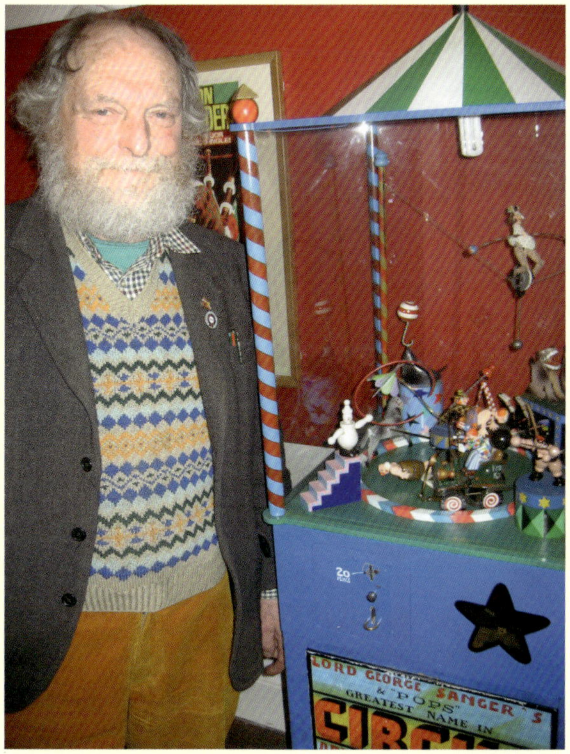

Artist-craftsman **Ron Fuller** (left) has been making automata at Laxfield near Halesworth since 1972. He has set 11 acts within one moving, musical Big Top (left), and produced stand-alone models such as *The Lion Tamer* (below) and *The World's Strongest Woman*. His watercolours of circus toys appeared in a 2002 set of postage stamps.

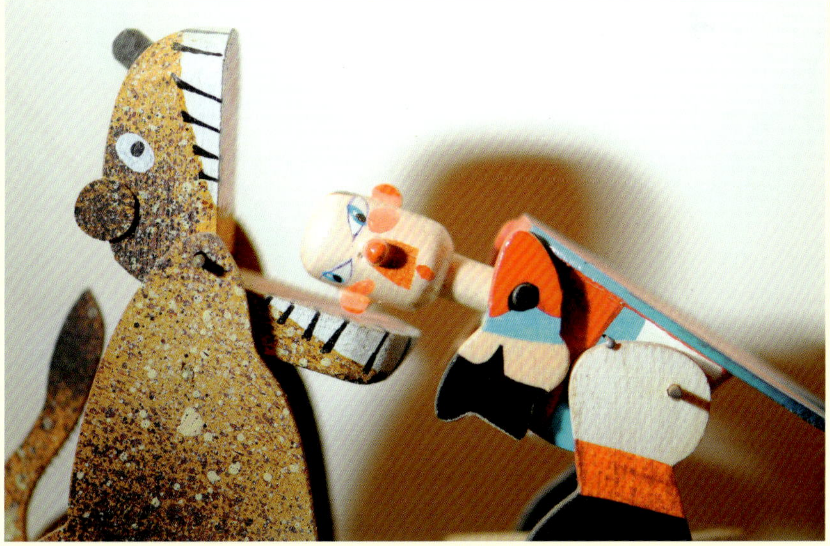

A Norfolk Village, Aldeby, oil on canvas, Norwich Castle Museum

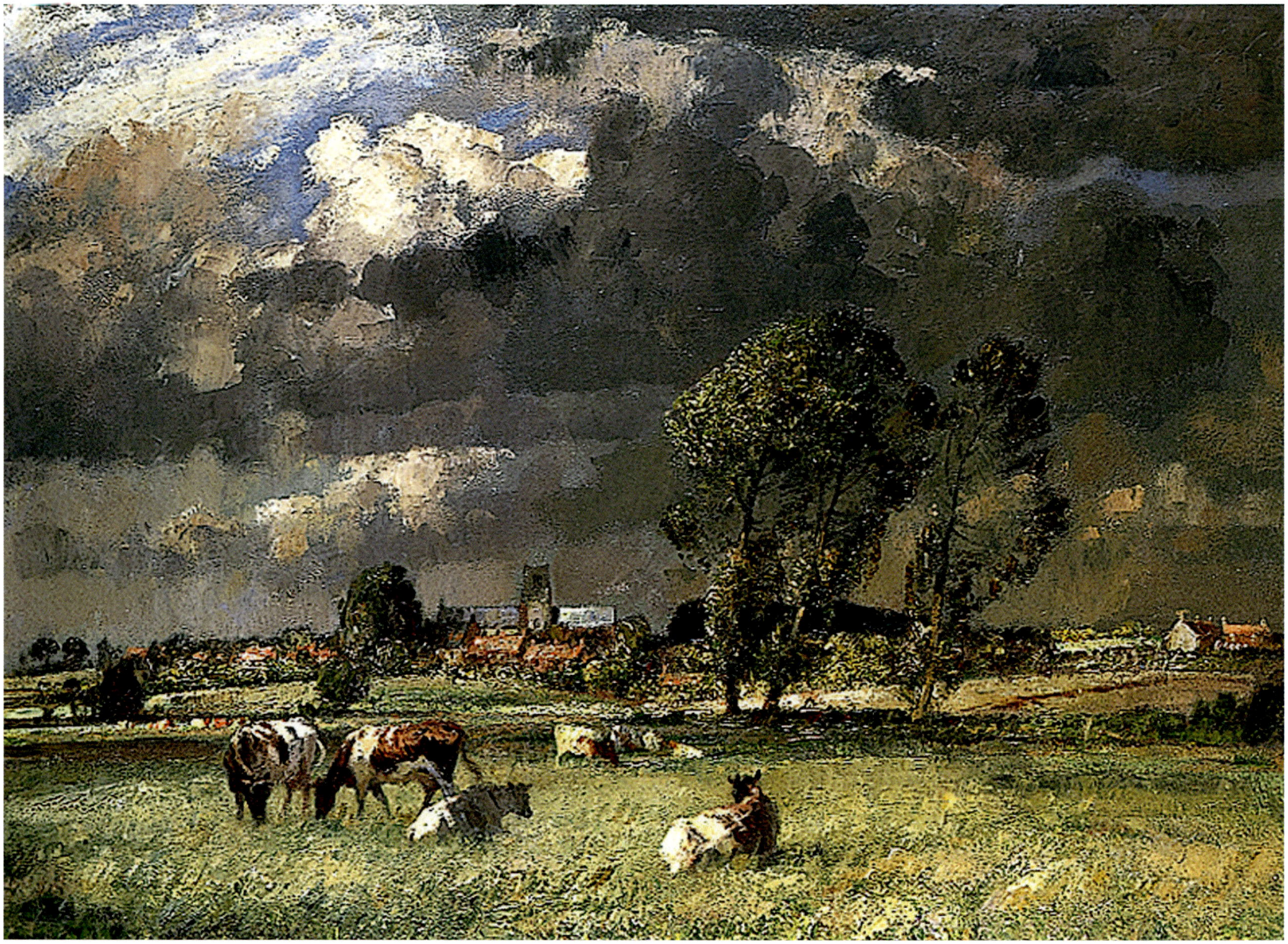

A Broads Canvas

Edward Seago

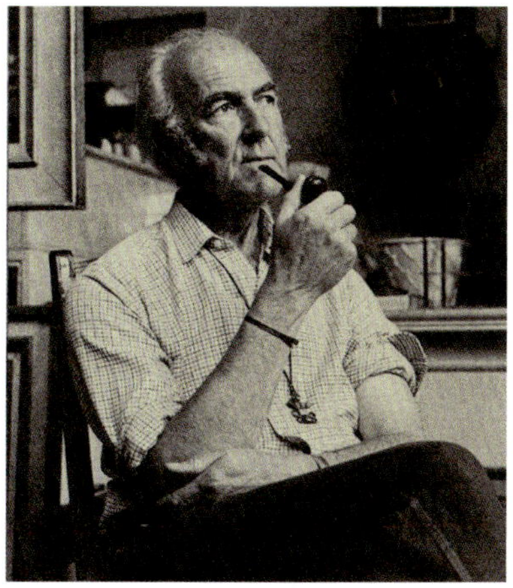

Edward Seago

Edward Seago sailed seas and oceans in search of scenic subjects to paint, but his fugitive heart was most firmly anchored in his native East Anglia.

Then again, here was a haven holding hope of further artistic adventure, for which he need only cast off from the edge of his Broadland garden. With a longing to escape key to his nature, he found himself most at home in what appeared a lost idyll and which he painted to the last.

Edward Brian Seago was born on 31 March 1910, at 13 Christchurch Road, Norwich, the younger son of a coal merchant. His mother, an amateur watercolourist and former governess to the Bacon family at Raveningham Hall, was the daughter of a Beccles boatbuilder.

From the age of eight Ted was often laid low by a mysterious – and probably psychosomatic – heart ailment, which left him debilitated and even delirious and for which baffled doctors could prescribe only prolonged rest cures.

Gypsy Encampment, oil on panel

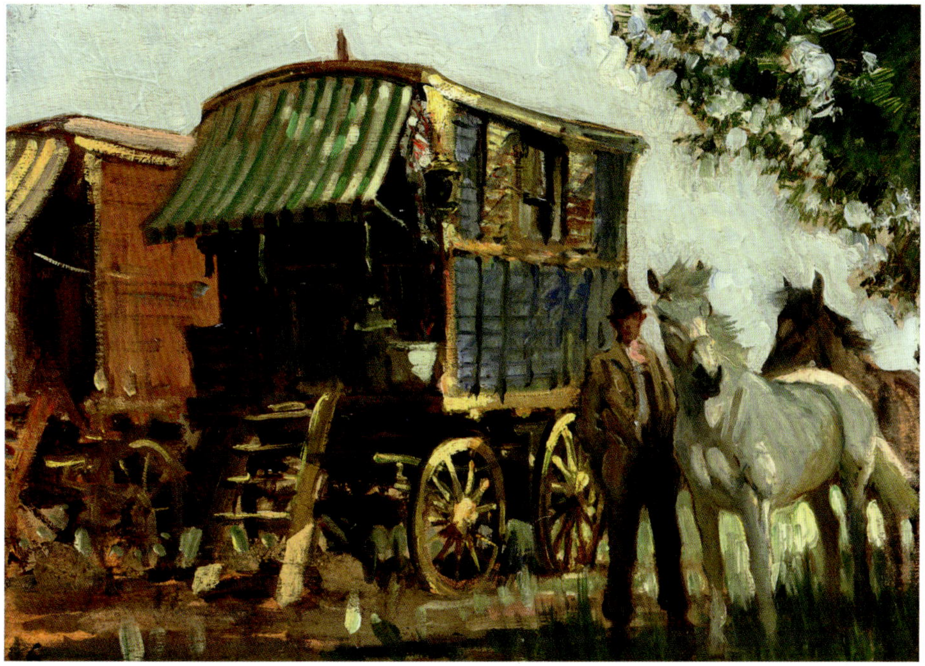

Like Benjamin Britten he attended South Lodge Preparatory School in Lowestoft – where sea spray came through windows open even in winter – but was withdrawn due to ill-health.

Further terms closer to home were terminated by recurring frailty, and when, in 1924, the Seagos moved to Brooke Lodge, six miles south of Norwich, it was chiefly to provide fresh air and quiet for an invalid son who wanted only to paint. Not that there was much peace in the household given parental tensions via a fearful and controlling mother and a father's resentment.

Ted spent long days lying in the garden looking at the sky and its constant movement – with clouds racing like yacht sails across a blue infinity and then piling up above a level landscape in vaporous mountain ranges of grey and black.

He charted the shifting aerial drama of light in sketches which became crucial notes for later East Anglian paintings where majestic skies would comprise more than two-thirds of most compositions. In 1947 he was to write: 'Light and atmosphere. To my mind there is more magic in those two words than in all the others of the English language. They embody form and colour, space and substance.'

Eager for mentors, the teenager sought out the much-travelled Royal Academician Bertram Priestman, lately settling in Walberswick, and also Nugent Monck, the actor, artist, writer and director of Norwich's Maddermarket Theatre, where the young Ted Seago would perform and paint scenery.

He also fell under the spell of Alfred Munnings, who had previously lived in nearby Swainsthorpe and had painted at Brooke Lodge. Resulting horse-rife pictures were soon selling to patrons in the country house set – who ensured the success of his first solo show in London at the age of 19 – but which rather too obviously mimicked the master.

There is even a photo in which the young pretender is painting horses while wearing an eye patch, in homage to the fact that Munnings had been blinded in one eye by a Norfolk thorn bush at 21. It was a pose and Seago was no poseur.

Whatever else his critics might attack him for in a career allegedly showing precious little development, his vision was absolutely sincere. He often quoted his hero John Constable's line that painting was another word for feeling – and his own feelings ran deep and true.

They also ran to thoughts of running away. He had yearned for a nomadic existence since creeping off to a gypsy encampment outside Brooke, there to sketch the horses, caravans and figures of freedom briefly settled to the tasks of making paper flowers and clothes pegs.

He loved travelling fairs but most of all he adored circuses. He had been taken to see Sanger's Circus in Norwich at six or seven, but was transported at 20 by a Bertram Mills show in the city – and particularly by the thrilling sight of three young men riding bareback and

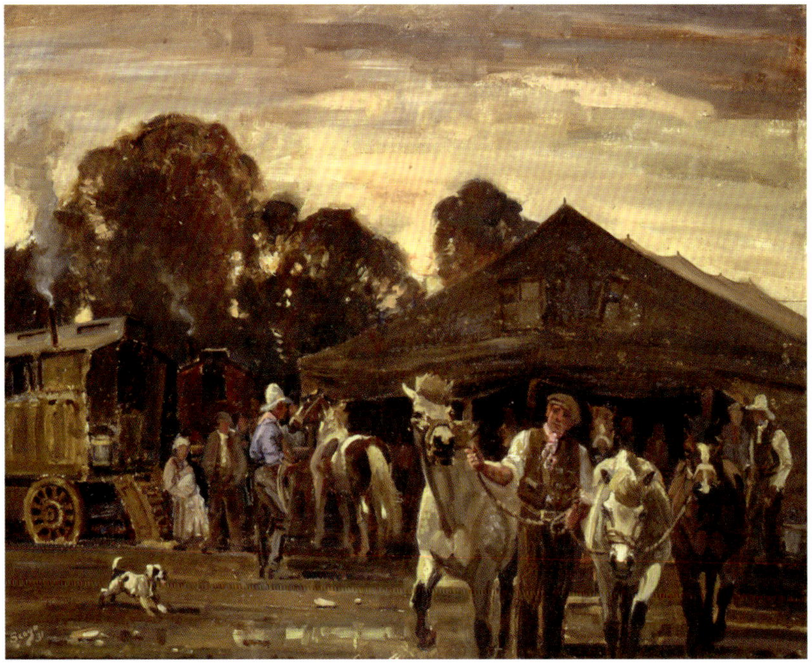

Circus Encampment, 1931, oil on panel

performing comic and daredevil feats on a galloping horse: The Baker Brothers. At the next port of call, Ipswich, he watched every performance for a week.

Like Munnings, Augustus John, Laura Knight and Lucy Kemp-Welch before him, he set out to follow the circus. But, with his family impressed by sales from that first London exhibition, he didn't exactly run away. He went with a parental allowance, and was driven to the Big Top, on its latest stop in Colchester, by his brother.

At first a distanced camp follower was widely ignored and consigned to dismal lodgings. But finally winning the trust of Tommy Baker, he was taken in by the all-male family and shared their cramped caravan. For Ted Seago it was the height of heaven.

In his 1933 memoir *Circus Company*, in which names were changed and the nature of his feelings often emerged only between the lines, he recorded that the first blissful months of touring ended after an animal trainer was mauled to death by a polar bear while having his portrait painted.

But he returned to the Bakers for a tour of Belgium, stints at Olympia and in Paris and then more roams through the regions, this time with a journey up the East Anglian coast – and an unexpected pause at Wells-next-the-Sea,

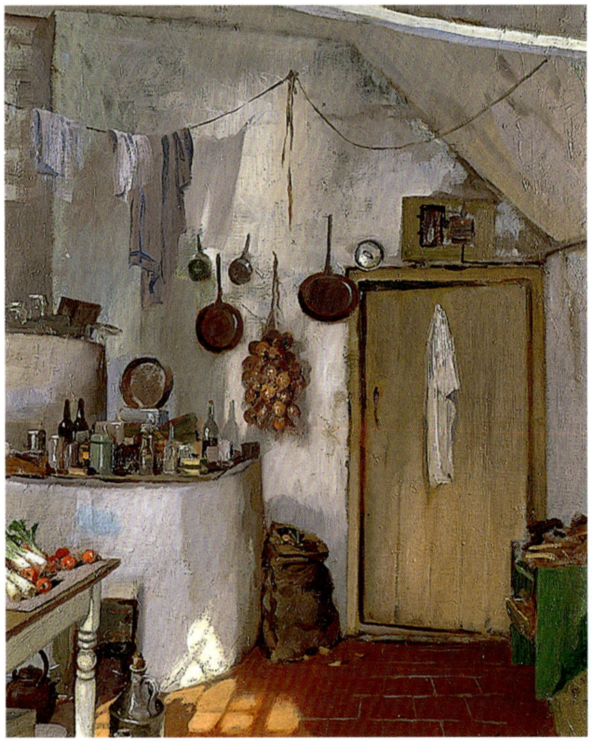

The White Kitchen, oil on canvas, Norwich Castle Museum (left)

where a broken-down lorry had to be pushed by a Burmese elephant.

Seago left the party when Tommy made plans to marry, but within months was summoned to his deathbed in Liverpool – appendicitis having turned to peritonitis – to share a sad vigil with the young man's pregnant wife. This was the first of three beloved male (and largely or wholly heterosexual) companions who would die before the age of 30.

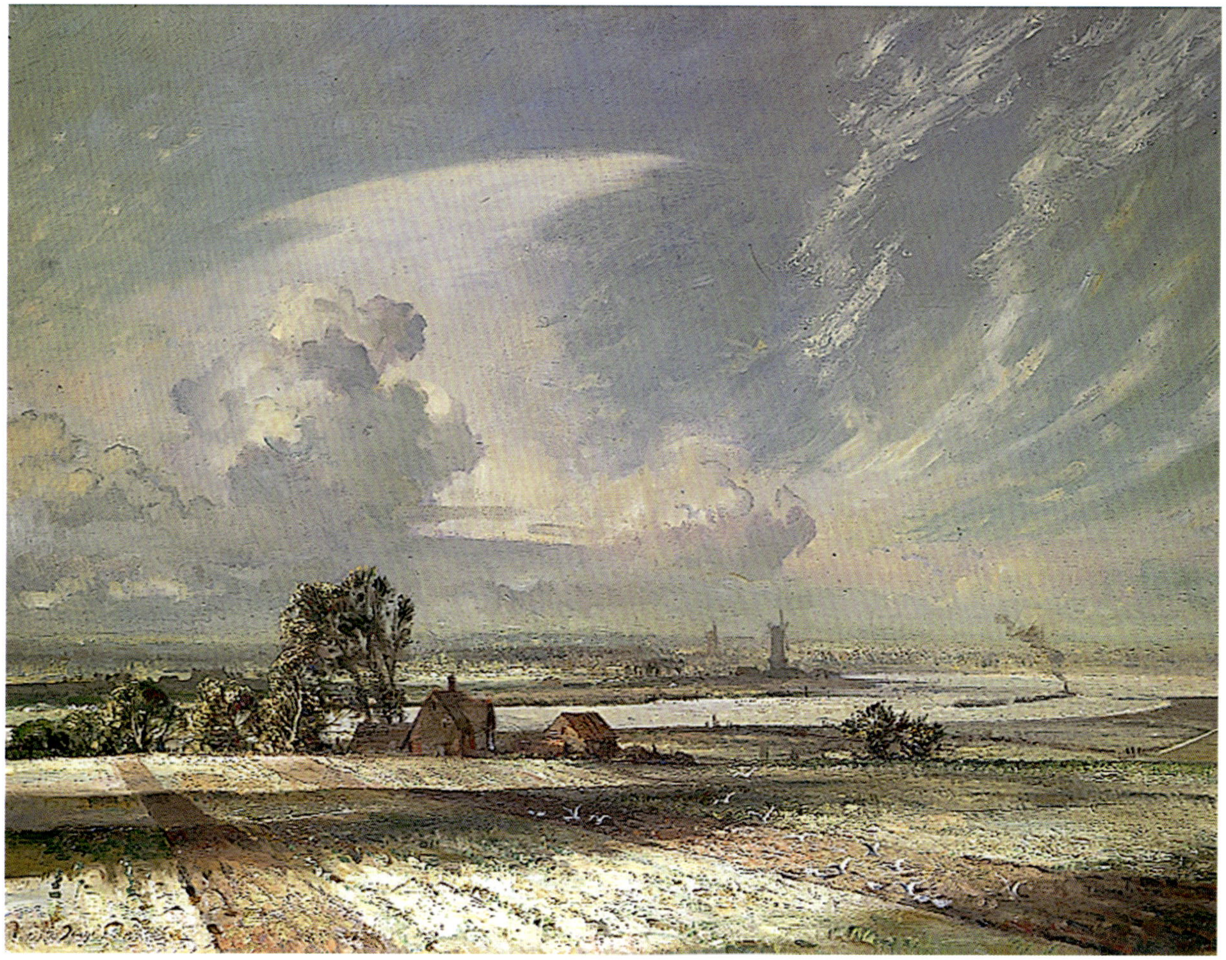

The Anvil Cloud, oil on canvas, Norwich Castle Museum

The circus travels had also brought a meeting with Poet Laureate John Masefield, a fellow rover and lover of boats, wind and saltwater, with whom he would collaborate on three popular books: *The Country Scene, Tribute to Ballet* and *A Generation Risen.*

The last and best of these, a 1942 salute to the young people of England busy battling barbarism, savours a shy but shining humanity. The most heroic portrait, entitled *A Reconnaissance Pilot*, is armed only with what looks like a sketchbook. This was Seago's beloved Bernard Clegg, who was to be killed in the war before the same fate befell the similarly adored Derek Mond.

With powerful patrons, Edward Seago travelled widely and seemed a picture of success. Serving as a camouflage officer he was befriended by generals Auchinleck and Alexander – the latter coming to the rescue when Seago failed a medical (grief having brought on the old heart problem), flying him out in his own plane to join the Italian campaign as his official artist.

Edward Seago returned to Norfolk at the end of the war in many ways a broken man, alone and pretty much unable to paint. What rescued him was a complete absorption in the scenes of his youth, and most especially by his finding the Dutch House on the edge of the Norfolk Broads at Ludham.

And when a young man called Peter

Seymour knocked on his door he had found the perfect soulmate for the rest of his life. They explored East Anglia's waterways, and they sailed across the channel, along the coast and then up the Seine to Paris, to moor near the Place de la Concorde. Or else they would tackle the Thames and tie up at the Chelsea embankment for a walk to another Seago exhibition selling out on its first day.

For two decades from 1947 annual shows at Colnaghi Galleries in Bond Street alternated oils and watercolours and drew long queues from which buyers were restricted to one picture apiece.

Every January and June for 21 years this well-connected artist visited Sandringham, and the Queen and Princess Margaret were at the Dutch House on the day George VI died. In 1956 he joined Prince Philip on a trip to Antarctica, New Zealand and West Africa, painting grand works now in the Royal Collection.

Other water-borne trips would take in the Mediterranean, Hong Kong, Burma and Thailand and in the end he bought a flat in Sardinia from where he was taken ill with the brain tumour which killed him, in hospital in London, in January 1974.

Edward Seago was shunned by art critics and the Royal Academy but his hundreds of oils and thousands of watercolours were and remain hugely popular. And, with a ruthless eye for quality some never suspected, he ordered that a third of his studio pictures should be destroyed after his death.

He always said he was very relaxed painting oils because he knew mistakes could be rectified. But with watercolours he was 'taut as a bowstring' – focusing his nervy energy to avoid a single slip that would ruin the picture.

And for all those travels, the liquid East Anglian pictures may move us most. As Munnings declared in his memoirs: 'Art is long – life is short.... So many things to see besides circuses. A river even!'

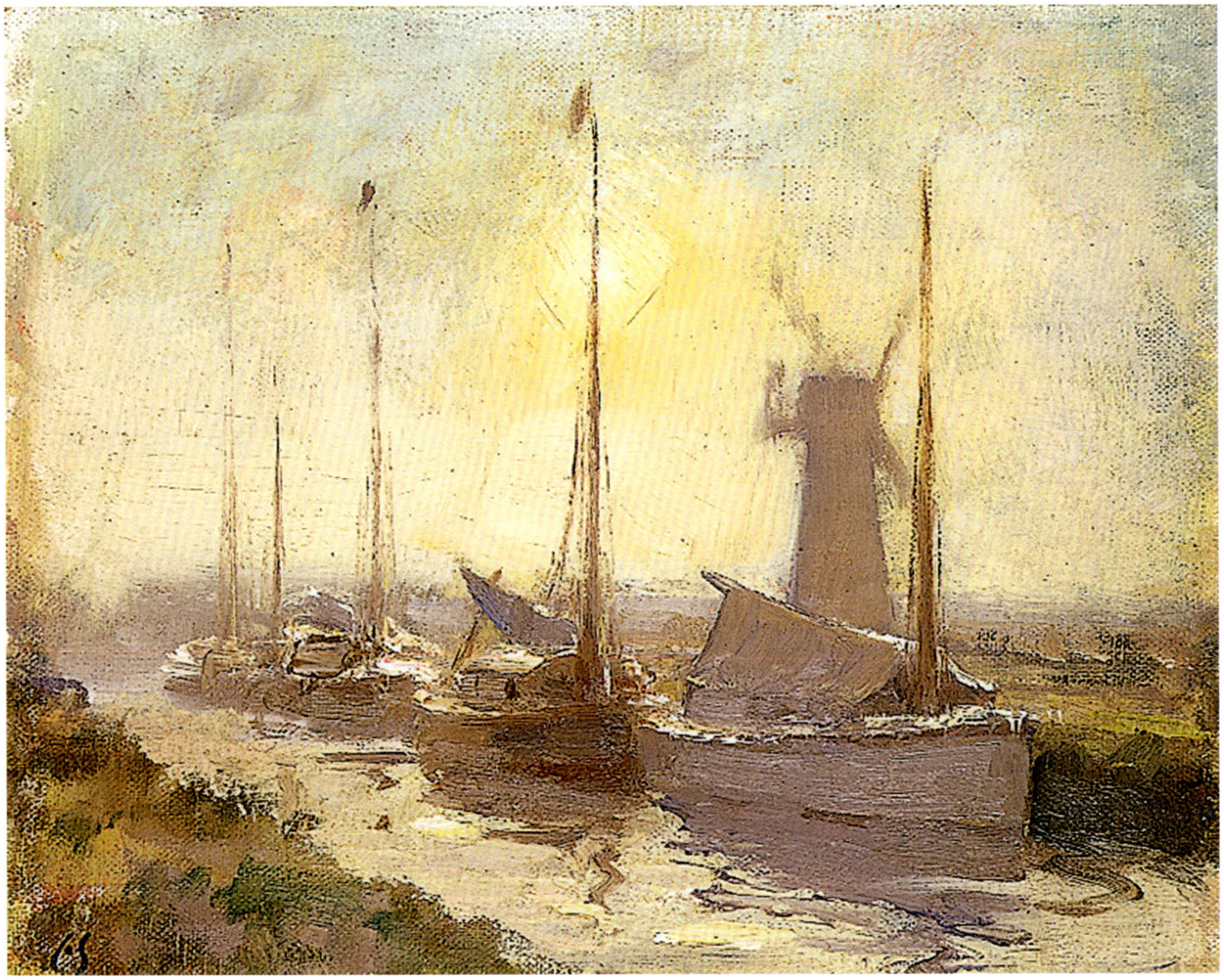

Evening Haze, Thurne Dyke, oil on canvas board, Norwich Castle Museum

Gilded Glory

Ninian Comper and Lound Church

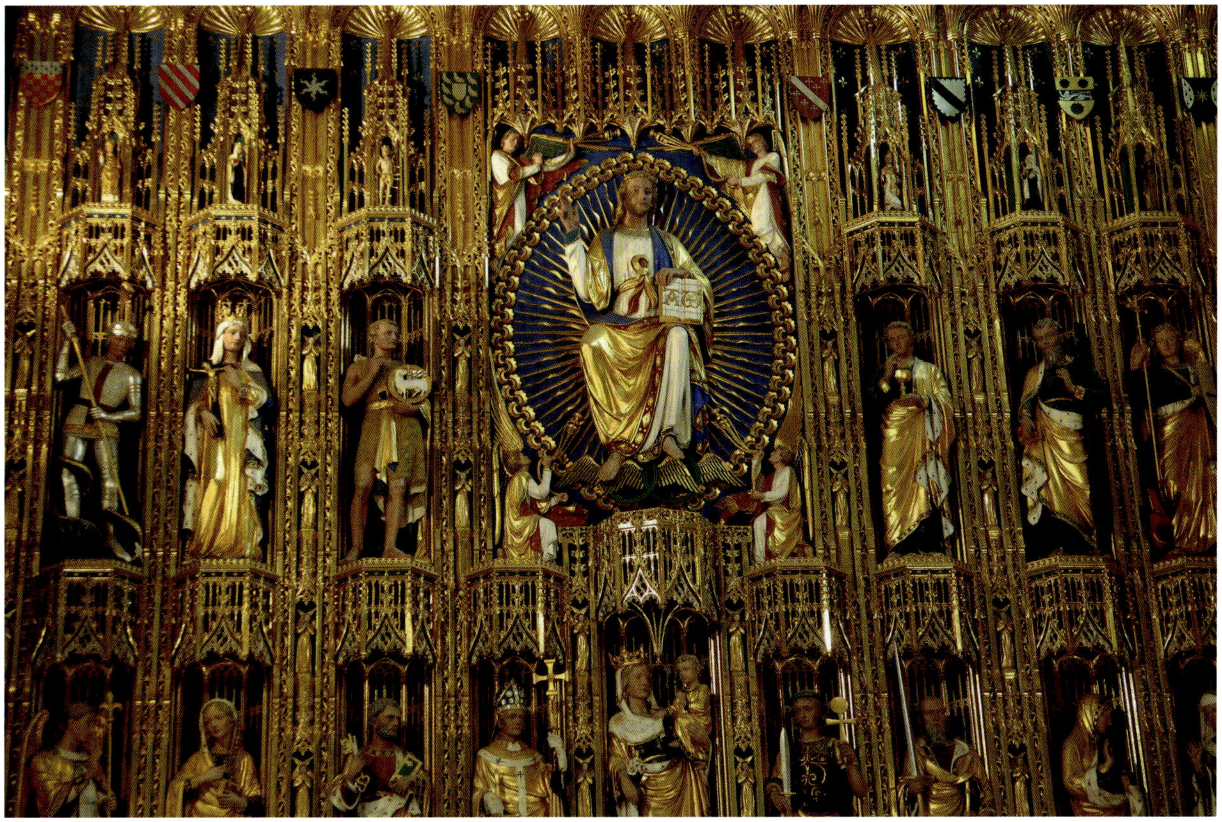

Reredos (detail), Wymondham Abbey, 1922

As battlefields go, the twin-towered parish church of Wymondham Abbey and monastic ruins beyond may be unsurpassed in beauty. Here medieval conflict had a decorous modern echo.

Lately celebrating the 900th anniversary of its founding, the building resembled a rural Norwich cathedral when, in 1209, rights disputed between monks and townsfolk brought a papally decreed division.

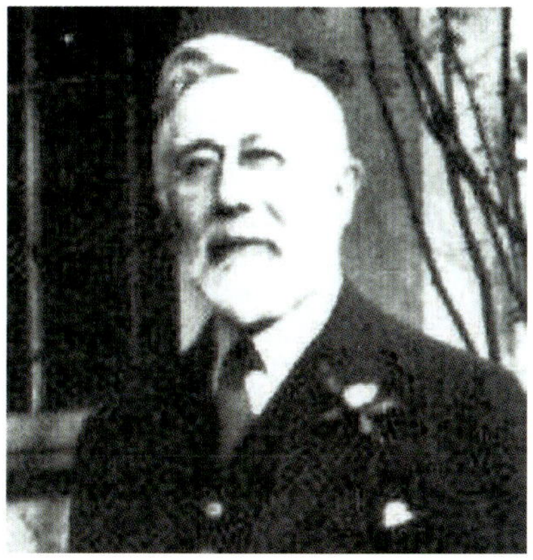

Sir Ninian Comper

But still the feud persisted – and exploded after 1409 when the monks' tower collapsed, and a replacement encroached upon the nave. A blocking wall was then breached by civic pickaxes, with bell warfare waged between the two sides until the town triumphed at the Reformation.

Diminished and denuded, the Protestant church was carved from the arcaded Norman nave until another conflict – World War One – prompted a new burst of golden decoration via a memorial altar screen. This vast but incomplete reredos, with three tiers of saints and a glorious Christ in Majesty, is the greatest work of **Sir Ninian Comper** (1864-1960).

Sir Ninian was the key 20th-century architect and artist of the Anglo-Catholic revival, merging Oxford Movement theology with Arts and Crafts aesthetics – enraging puritans with a love of spectacle and ritual from gilded screens to robed processions and from incantations to incense.

Architectural historian Nikolaus Pevsner thought him sentimental, and firm(ly-tongue-in-cheek) fan Sir John Betjeman mocked 'Sir Niminy Piminy' by hailing a camp sense of

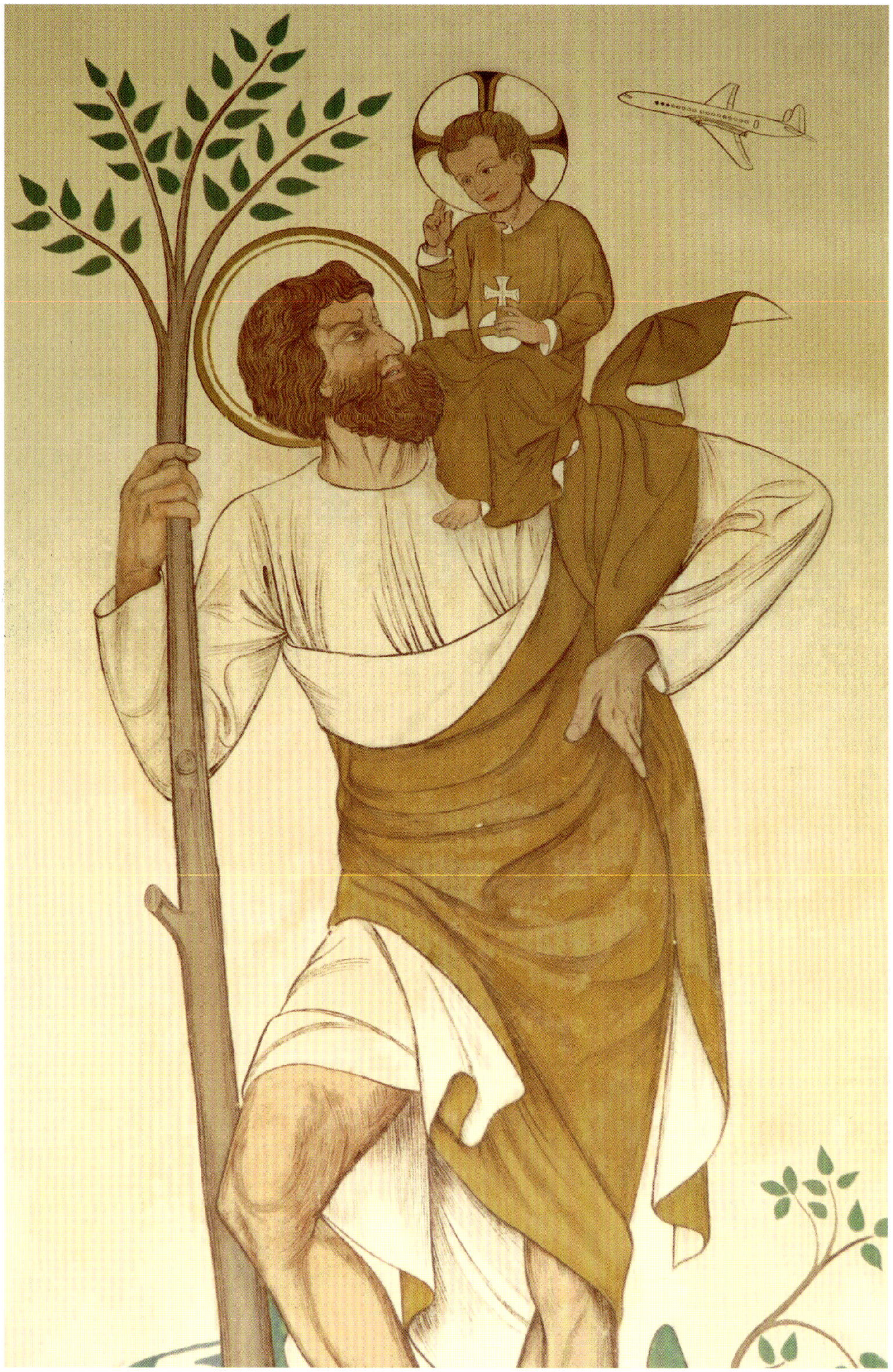

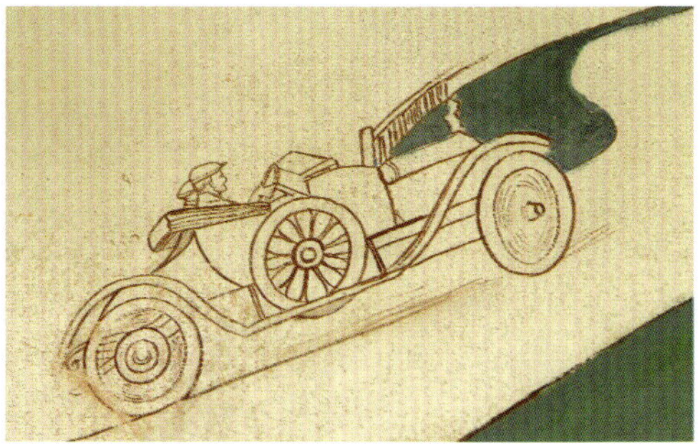

Inset detail (above), Comper's Rolls Royce, from the St Christopher

St Christopher, north wall, Lound church, Suffolk

theatre rather than a seriousness of awe-inspiring purpose.

Then again Sir Ninian's 'unity by inclusion' credo, blending any historic style that took his fancy, Baroque and High Gothic being favourites, was easy to knock as eclecticism at its most hectic. But for the undogmatic his designs are visually thrilling, especially when a tad mad.

The Scotsman's long career saw churches across East Anglia screened, stained, gilded and painted, and adorned with carvings and hangings. The illuminated roll-call ran from Bourn in Cambridgeshire to Bocking in Essex, and from Hunstanton, Great Ryburgh, Mundford and Norwich St Peter Mancroft in Norfolk, to Eye, Ufford, Kettlebaston, Ipswich St Mary Elms, Southwold and Lowestoft St Margaret's in Suffolk.

But the ravishing rescue of a humble, round-towered medieval shell at Lound, to the north of Lowestoft, is truly inComperable. Behold a marvellous shrine and a magpie's summer pudding.

Thanks to the passion and deep pockets of the local vicar, the beautification programme began in 1912 with a raised High Altar boasting opulent posts surmounted by gilded, torch-bearing bronze angels supporting silk curtains dyed to Comper's favourite shade of unblushing pink. Between Johns Baptist and Evangelist, Christ admires an ornate Sisters of Bethany-worked embroidery.

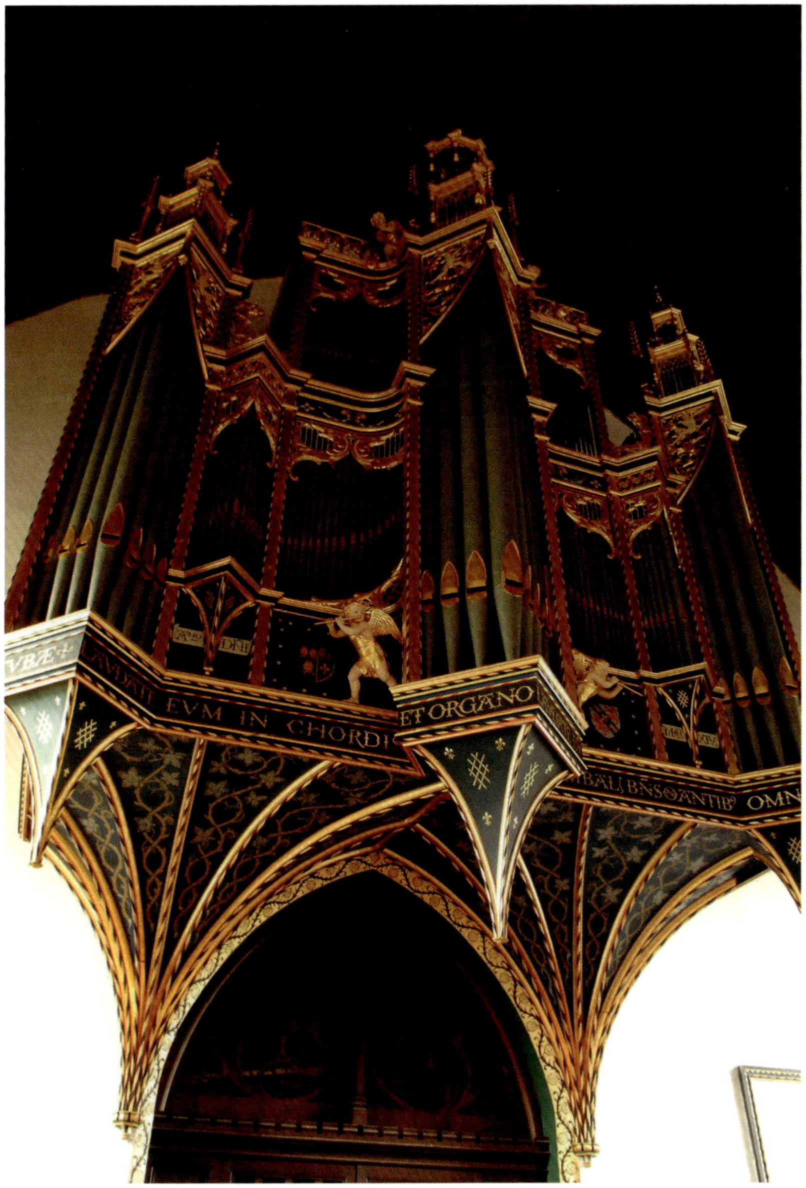

Organ case, Lound church, Suffolk

Next came a gilded, buttressed and giddily Gothic font cover ending in a crocketed steeple, and then a massive mural portrait of St Christopher cheered up the north wall as the traditional comfort to travellers. To modernise the message, Comper added himself and a friend jauntily departing in his open-topped Rolls Royce. Restoration in 1964, for the artist-architect's centenary, saw a Bristol Britannia plane added overhead.

On a roll after the Roller episode, Comper went wild in Lound with a rood screen depicting the cross as a dragon-crushing tree of glory and heraldry hailing favoured bishops as well as sundry royals from Edward III to George V and Queen Mary.

The donor vicar, Father Lynes, was in there too – with a further exhortation, at a side altar with portraits of the three Marys, to pray for his welfare (not his soul, since he wasn't yet dead).

What should have been the final flourish came, in 1913, with a Gothic-Baroque organ case in green and gold. But that was not the finish. Comper had barely motored away from Lound when the world was changed forever by war. He was back in 1920 to design a poignantly restrained crucifix for the exterior of the nave's south wall as the memorial to the village dead.

More slowly, the war killed everything he stood for. Comper's designs demanded large crowds but churches steadily emptied of choirs and congregations. Near the end of the 20th century, the ordination of women priests saw much of an Anglo-Catholic rump flouncing off to Rome with a last rustle of vestments and waft of incense.

All that remained was the gaudy glory of gilded ghosts.

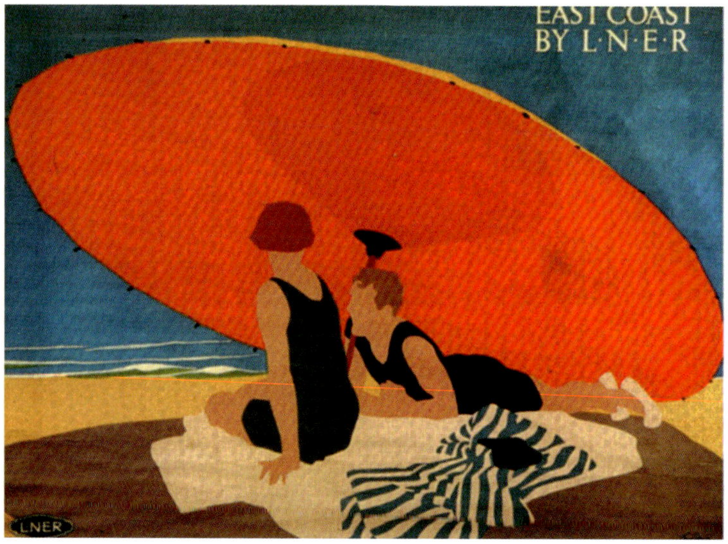

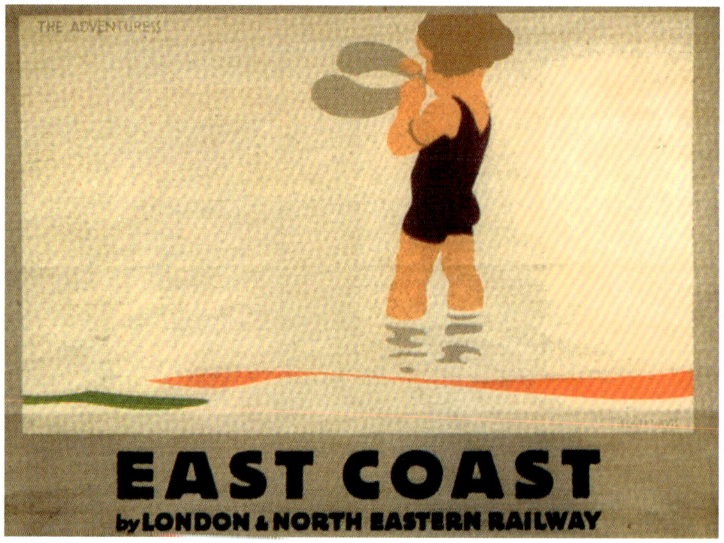

Six LNER posters, Tom Purvis, 1930s (top, sides and bottom of page)

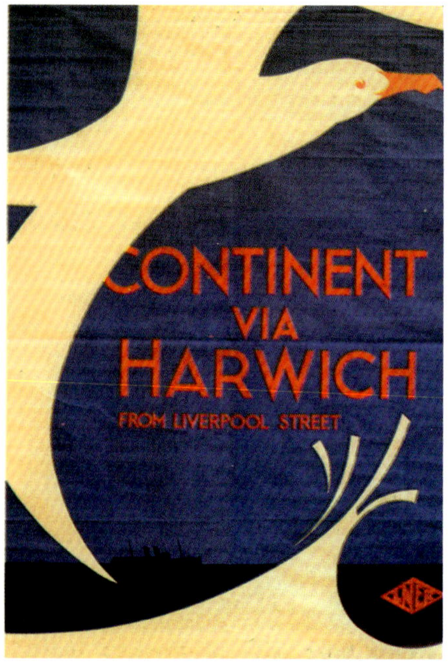

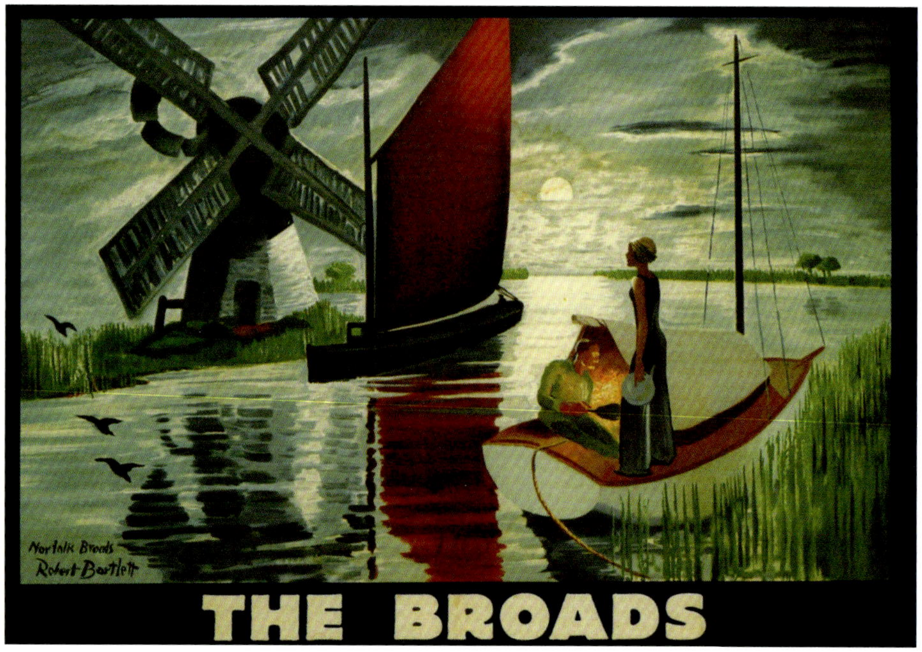

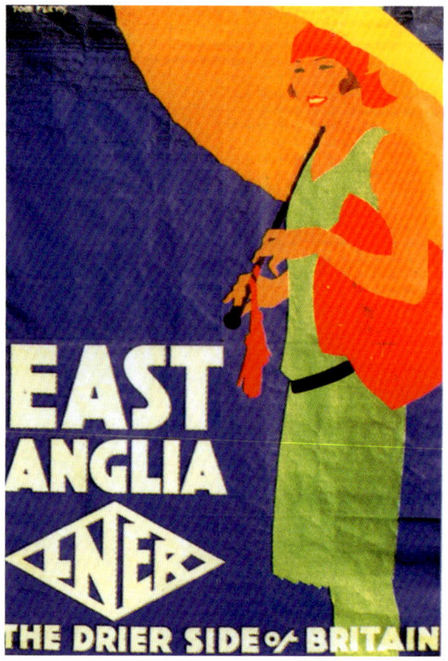

LNER poster, *The Broads*, Robert Bartlett, 1930s

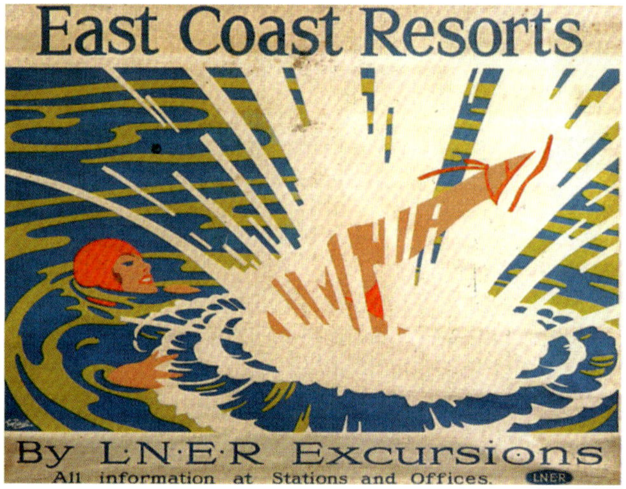

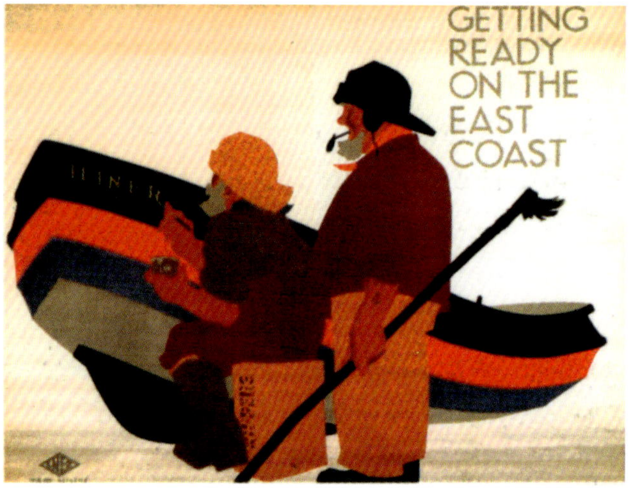

Wish You Were Here

Resort Posters and Reg Carter

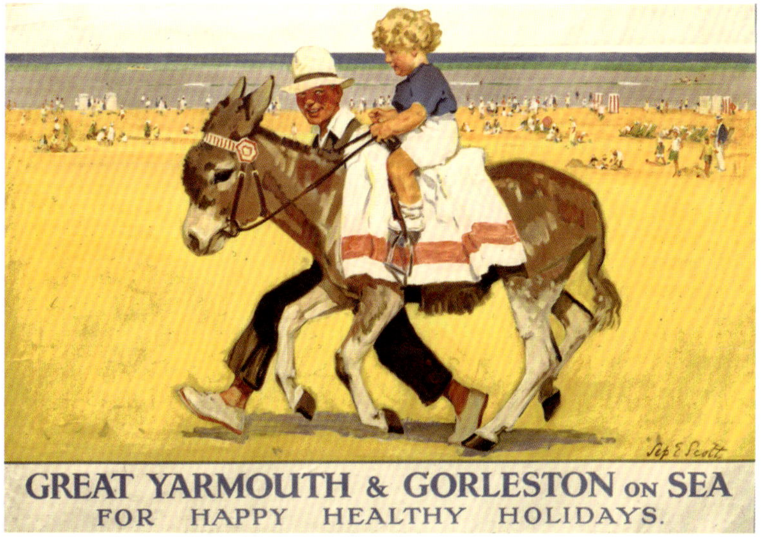

LNER poster,
Septimus Scott

Trips to the seaside began in the 18th century as an alternative to fashionable inland spas, with sea bathing seen as a healthy shock to the system. The popularity of coastal resorts grew in contrast to the grim conditions of Victorian towns and cities, and leapt with the spread of the railways. Consolidation of the rail network into four regional operators, in 1923, coincided with seaside holidays coming within reach of the industrial working classes. Competition between resorts was then promoted by the companies serving them, with the London & North Eastern Railway securing the most spectacular inter-war posters of all.

The LNER bagged the 'big five' designers of the day – Austin Cooper, Frank H Mason, Frank Newbould, Fred Taylor and **Tom Purvis** (1888-1959). Born in Bristol, the son of a master mariner turned marine artist, Purvis had studied under Degas and Sickert before training with an advertising agency and a lithographic press. He aspired to being a master craftsman rather than an artist as he developed his distinctive style of adjoining areas of flat, brilliant colours.

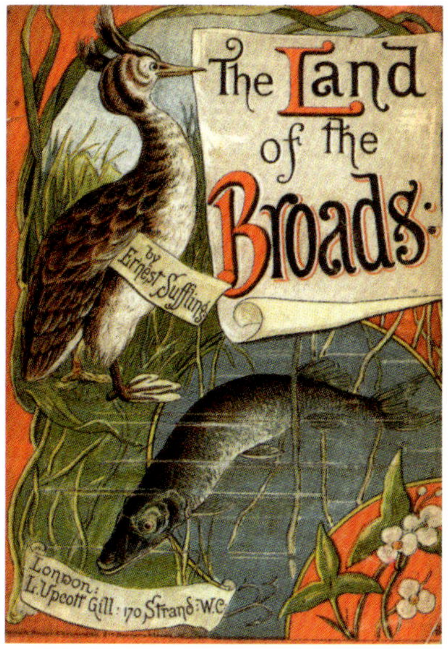

The Land of the Broads,
E R Suffling, 1885

Lowestoft Town Guide cover,
Philippa Miller, 1929 (right)

The standard size of railway posters measured 50 by 40 inches and demanded major feats in colour lithography. As recession deepened in the 1930s, the need for graphic simplification produced dramatic designs from Tom Purvis in particular. His pared-down images caught the new cult of sun-bathing so that Bracing East Anglia was also The Drier Side of Britain.

Other East Anglian poster artists included Septimus Scott, Robert Bartlett and Philippa Miller (1905-2006), daughter of an Oulton Broad boat designer, who glorified Lowestoft for the 1929 town guide. Sailing across her beloved Broadland until well into her nineties, she had two popular shows in Norwich Cathedral in her centenary year.

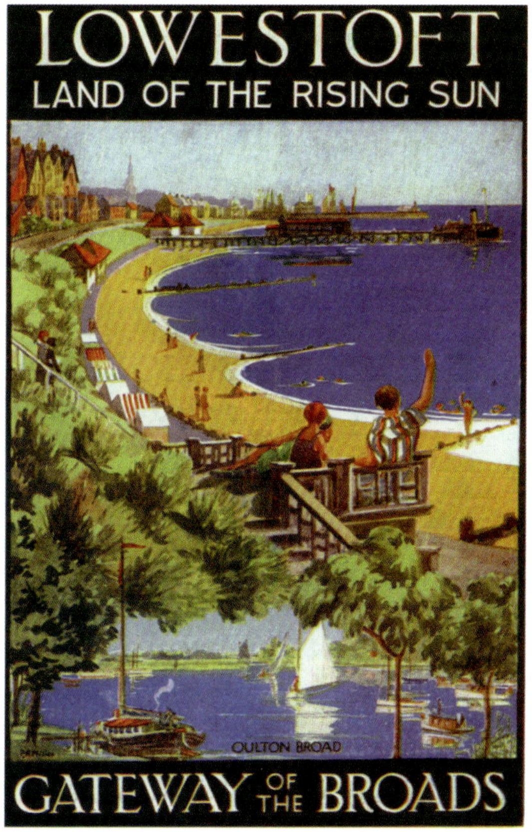

Southwold-raised **Reg Carter** (1886-1949) was a cartoonist best-known for penning the front-page of *The Beano* for its first decade from 1938. But he also plotted a lively line in saucy seaside postcards and caricatures of his long-suffering neighbours.

In 1902 Britain became the first country in the world to permit postcard senders to write on the same side as the address, and a year later a former Southwold solicitor's junior clerk launched himself as a commercial artist, with a garden studio at Granville House in the High Street. After that he never stopped working –

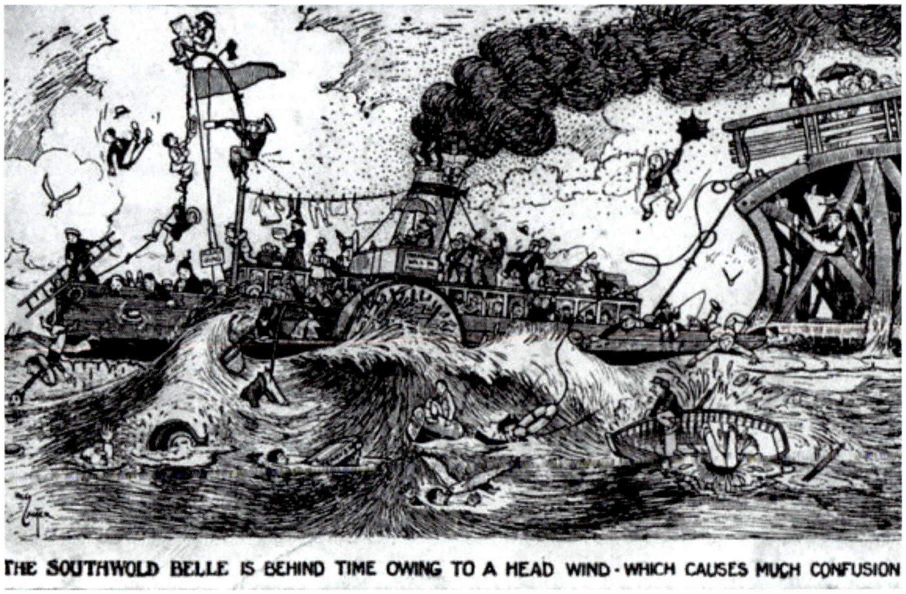

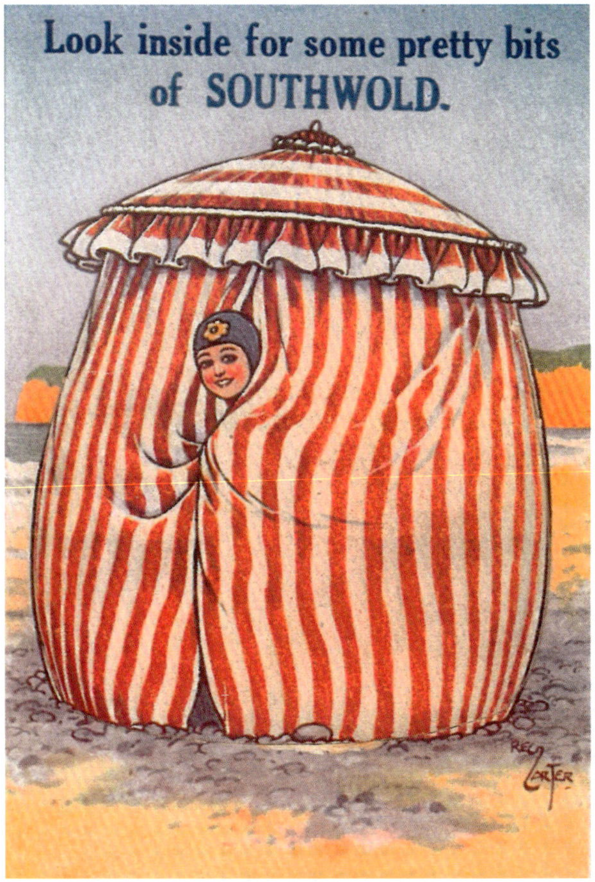

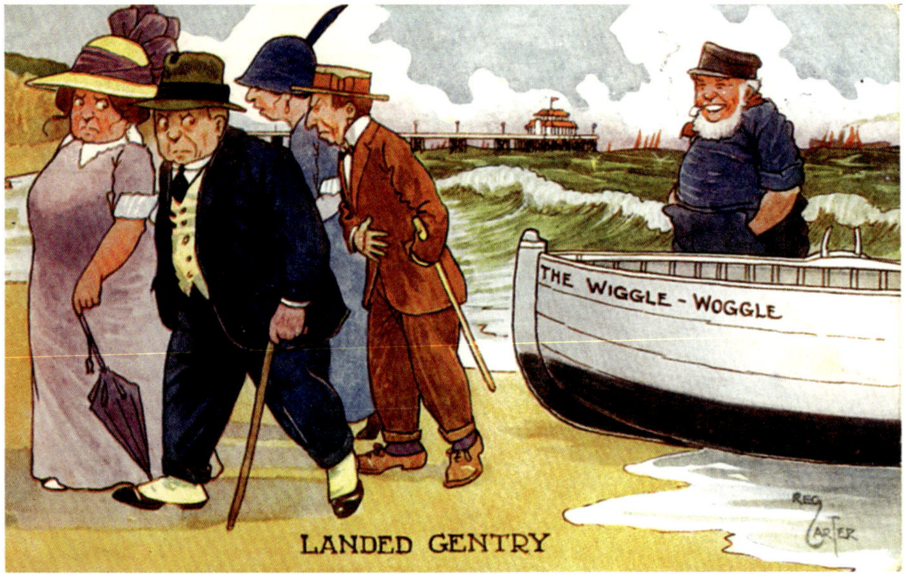

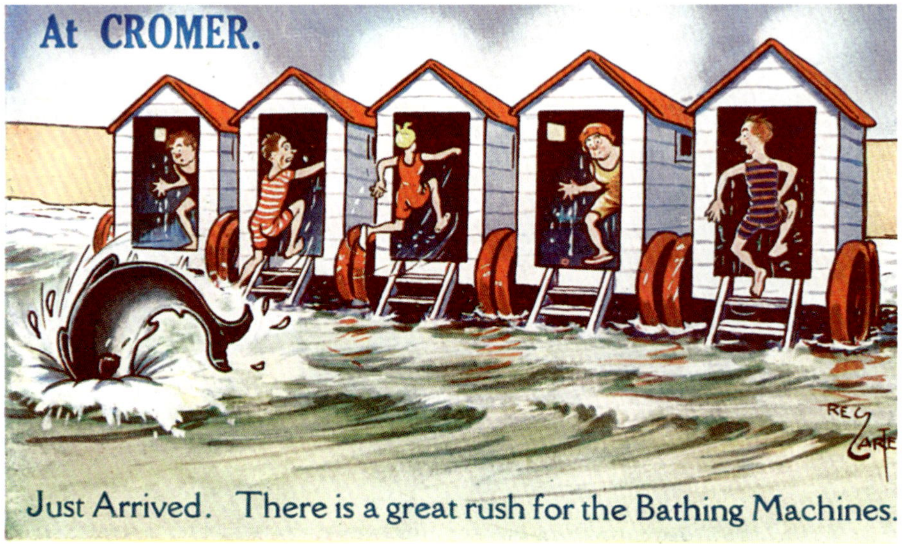

supplying 1,500 ink or watercolour images on a wide variety of topics to at least 32 postcard printers, and also illustrating sports books and children's annuals and compiling comic strips.

His most (in)famous black-and-white images comprised six *Sorrows of Southwold* cards lampooning Southwold's miniature branch railway from Halesworth, published 'with apologies to all' in what turned out to be the seriously unfunny year of 1914. A similarly

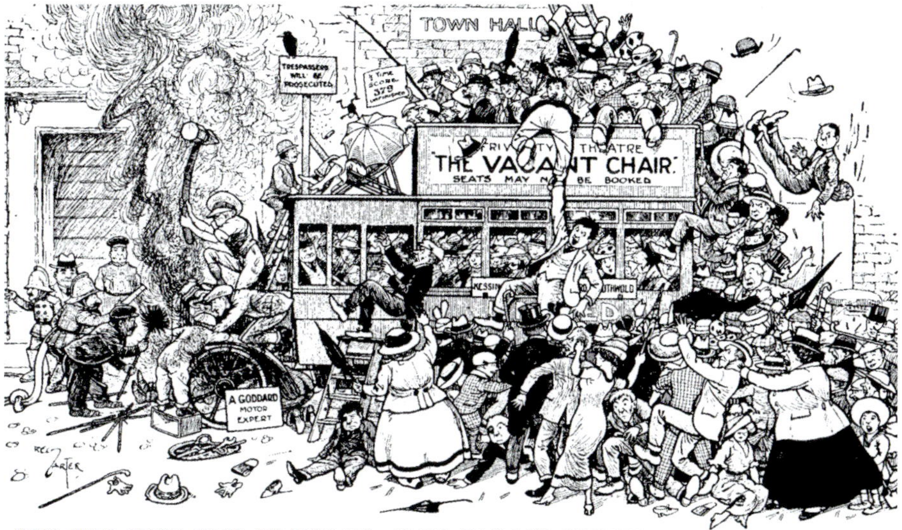

SLIGHT ENGINE TROUBLE DELAYS THE MOTOR BUS – TO THE JOY OF LATE PASSENGERS WHO WOULD OTHERWISE HAVE MISSED IT

hilarious sequel set followed seven years later. The twig line finally snapped in 1929 on nearing its 50th birthday.

The man whose incendiary imagination ran to showing Suffragettes blowing up Southwold Town Hall, the railway bridge over the Blyth collapsing under the weight of trippers and a Belle steamer crashing into the resort's pier, also pictured the stalled motor bus for Lowestoft engulfed in a riot of late arrivals.

Colourful and general seaside images were stamped with the names of resorts around East Anglia and indeed the entire country. But

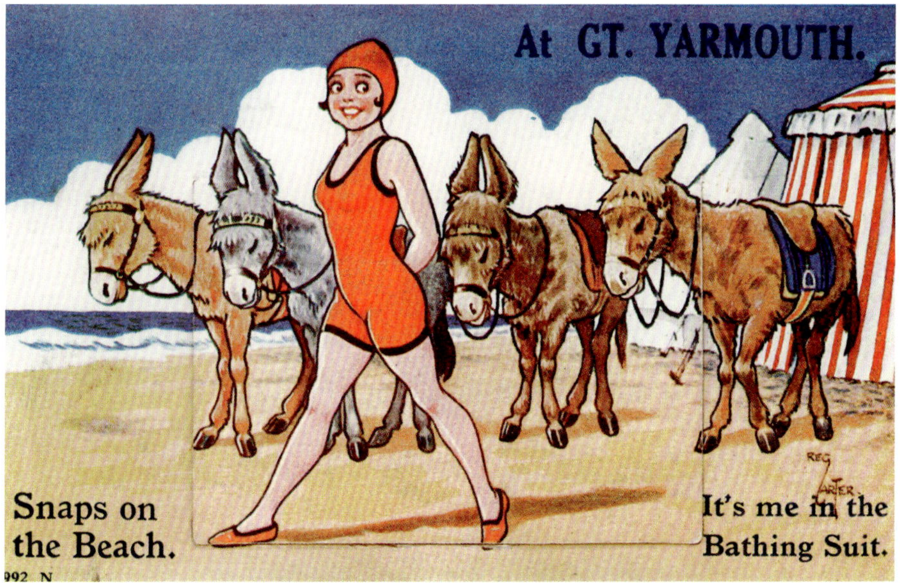

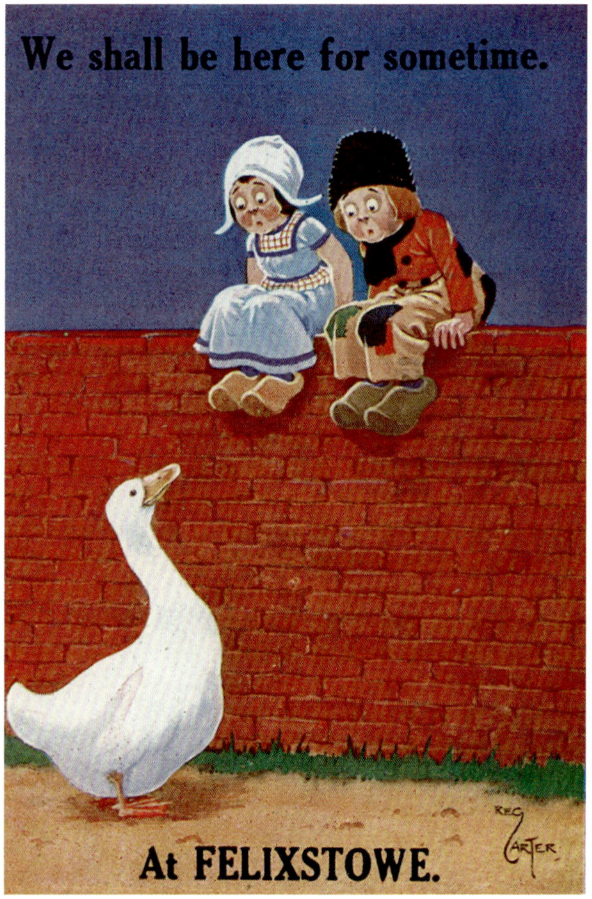

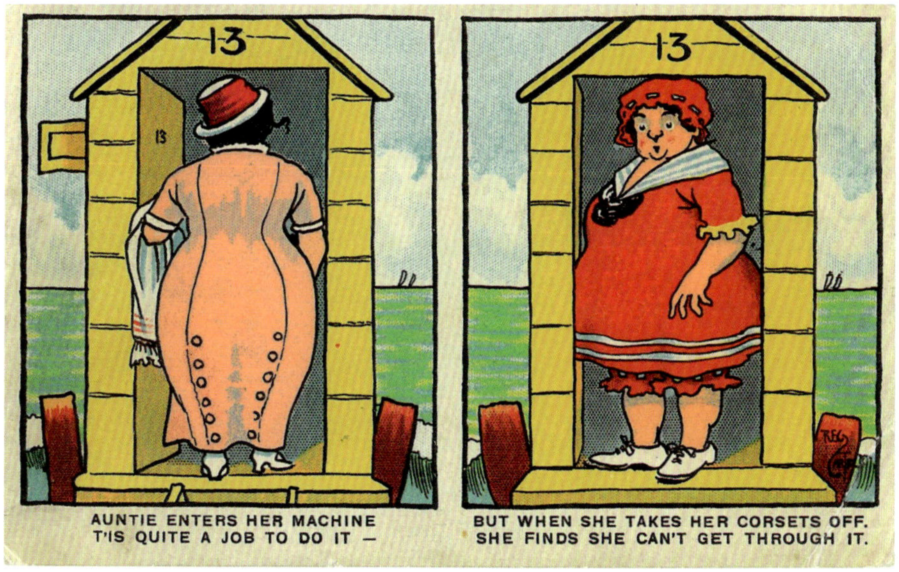

clearly Reg Carter's chief inspiration came from Southwold, where spouses and classes clashed on the beach and belles leapt from bathing machines while matrons freed from corsets risked imprisonment.

It's easy to imagine how the relentless joke wore rather thin in a small town – and to guess the key reason why this most subversive son of Southwold moved to Sussex on marrying in 1923.

LT 120, F Love, 1890, oil on strawboard

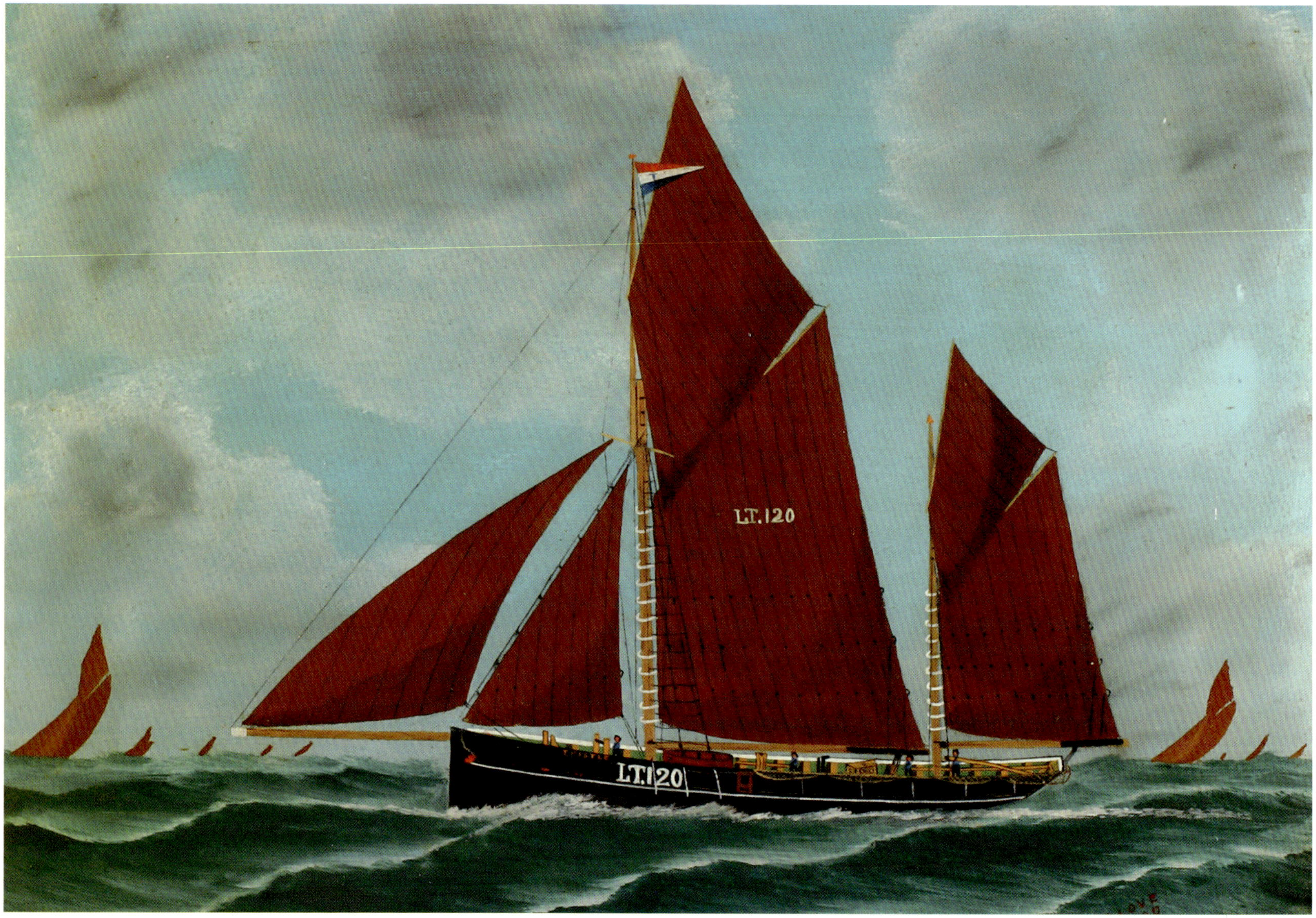

Pierhead Painters

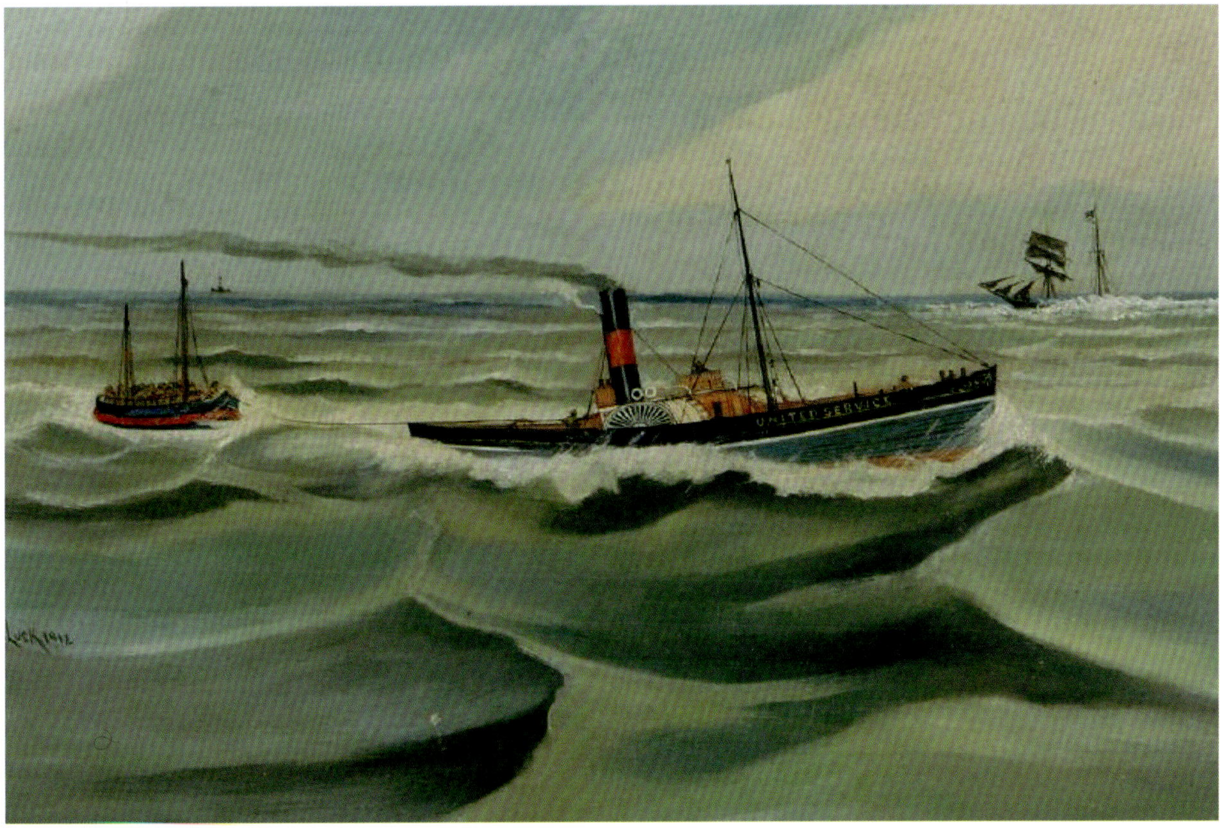

Steam Tug United Service Towing the Caister Lifeboat Covent Garden, Claude Mowle and Kenneth Luck, 1912, oil on board, Great Yarmouth Museums

England's rich tradition of marine painting was launched in the third quarter of the 17th century when Willem van de Velde and his namesake son switched sides as official war artists in recurring Anglo-Dutch naval conflicts. Commissioned to record the 1665 Battle of Lowestoft from a continental viewpoint – no painting emerging when victory went the wrong way – they designed tapestries for Hampton Court based on the 1672 Battle of Sole Bay, even though both sides were the losers.

This genre has sailed a wide ocean between fine and folk art, and in East Anglia it has been most marked in the latter with a host of 'pierhead painters' working in the ports of Great Yarmouth and Lowestoft in particular for a century from the coronation of Queen Victoria to the onset of World War Two.

Portraits of vessels, swiftly executed for owners and skippers, or else as souvenirs of daring rescues, were most in demand in decades on either side of 1900 when fishers and gutters followed teeming herring ('silver darlings') on annual migrations down the east coast, to end as far south as Southwold every September. At the peak of this killing spree, berthed boats formed a bobbing bridge between Yarmouth and Gorleston.

Little is known about most of these artisan artists – some remaining anonymous, others identified only by names or initials – but a handful of the most skilled and prolific recorders have secured a degree of posthumous fame. Lowestoft Maritime Museum has a haul of images by George Vemply Burwood (1845-1917), who lived on

Mariner's Score. Besides his trade as cooper (barrel-maker), this 'Marine Illuminator and Artist' made model boats bought by royalty and oils and watercolours for nautical visitors and neighbours. Lowestoft's George Race (1872-1957) painted likenesses at night which he would dry by the fire, set in lifebelt frames and then rush to the harbour for an agreed exchange for two and sixpence (12.5p) before the ship sailed in the morning.

Yarmouth's pierhead fleet was headed by **Claude Mowle** (1871-1950) and **Kenneth Luck** (1873-1935), working together in the early 20th century. Mowle had a photographer's studio in Gorleston where Luck taught woodwork at the East Anglian Blind and Deaf School. The lensman snapped fishing vessels, taking proofs to the boats to solicit orders and passing them to Luck as guides. Mowle also projected lantern slides on to board or canvas and marked in the outline of the vessels for his artist friend. The painter and framer signed the works with both names and split each £1 sale equally. As pierhead paintings were being scuttled on a rising tide of photography, here was a unique partnership which died with the painter.

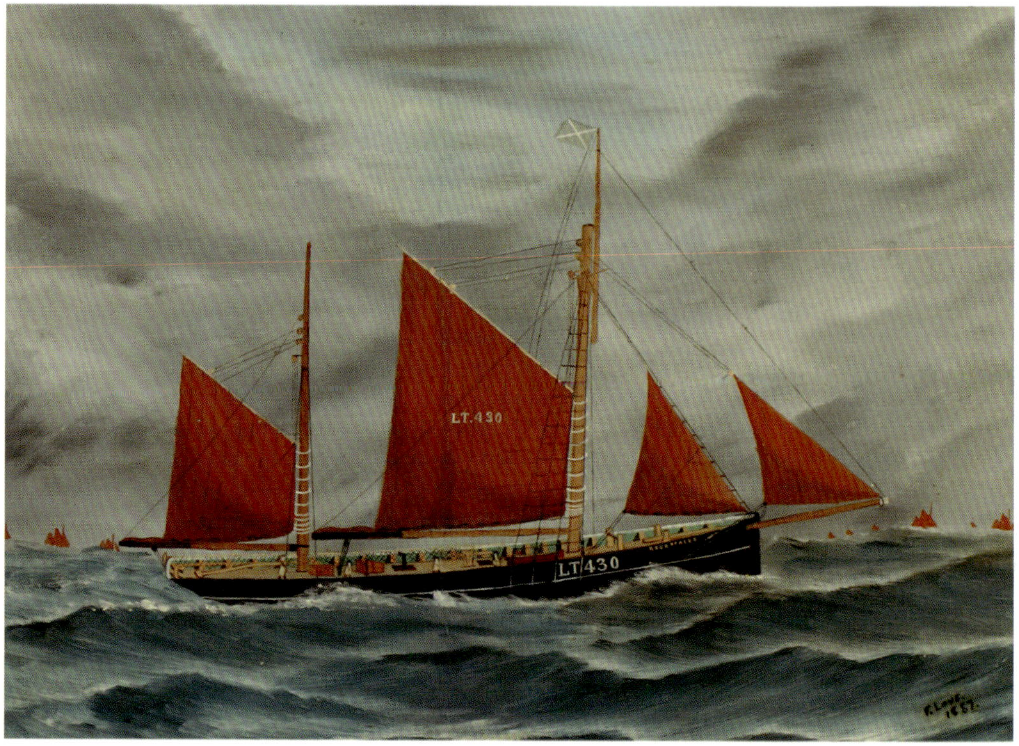

LT 430, F Love, 1887, oil on strawboard

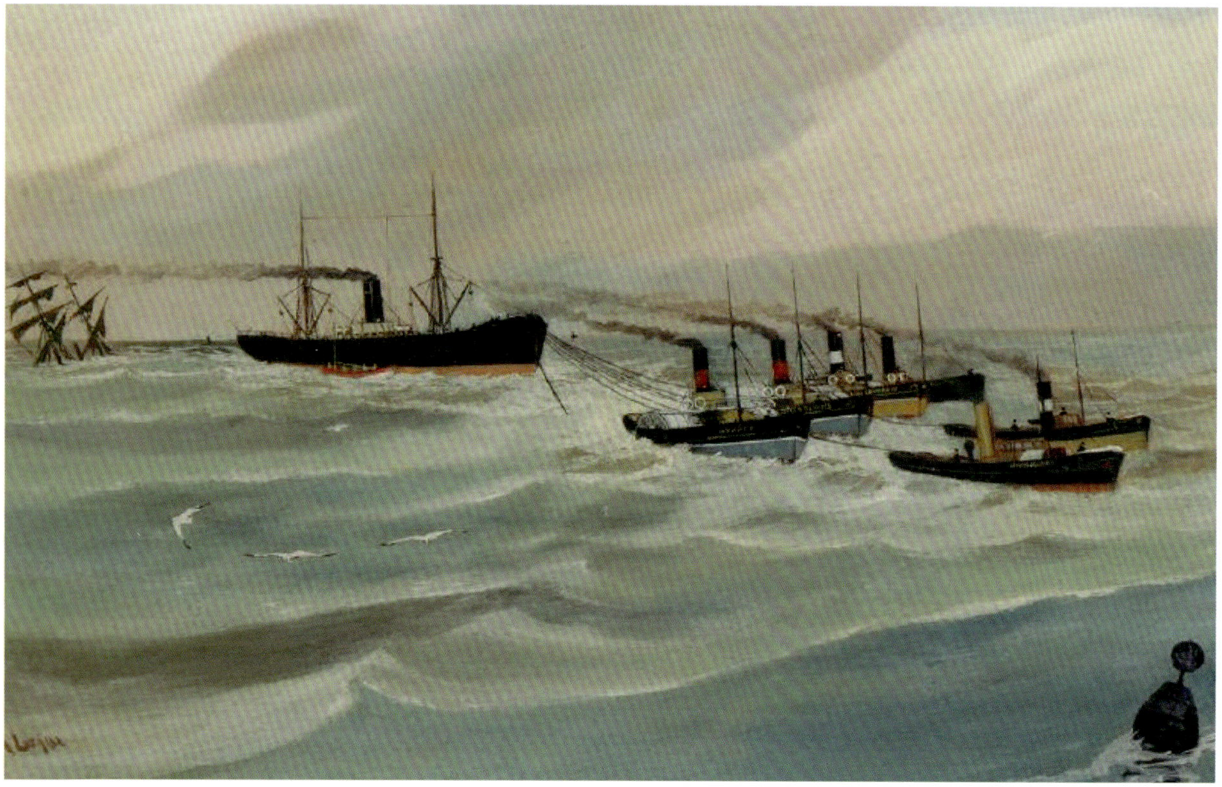

The Rescue of the S S Adriatico, Claude Mowle and Kenneth Luck, 1912, oil on board, Great Yarmouth Museums

The *Adriatico* went aground on Happisburgh Sands in February, 1912 and was dragged off by six tugs. This scene also shows the German sailing ship *Walkurie*, stranded two months earlier.

SUFFOLK COAST AND VALLEYS

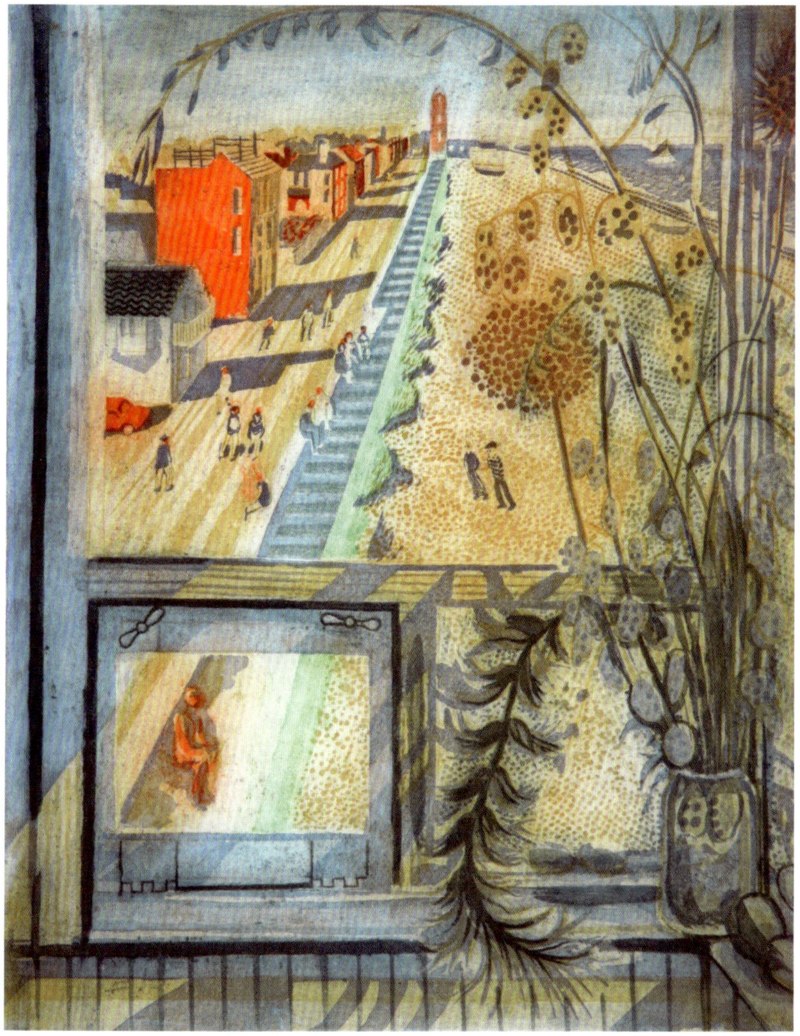

Aldeburgh from the Tower, Richard Bawden, 2008, etching

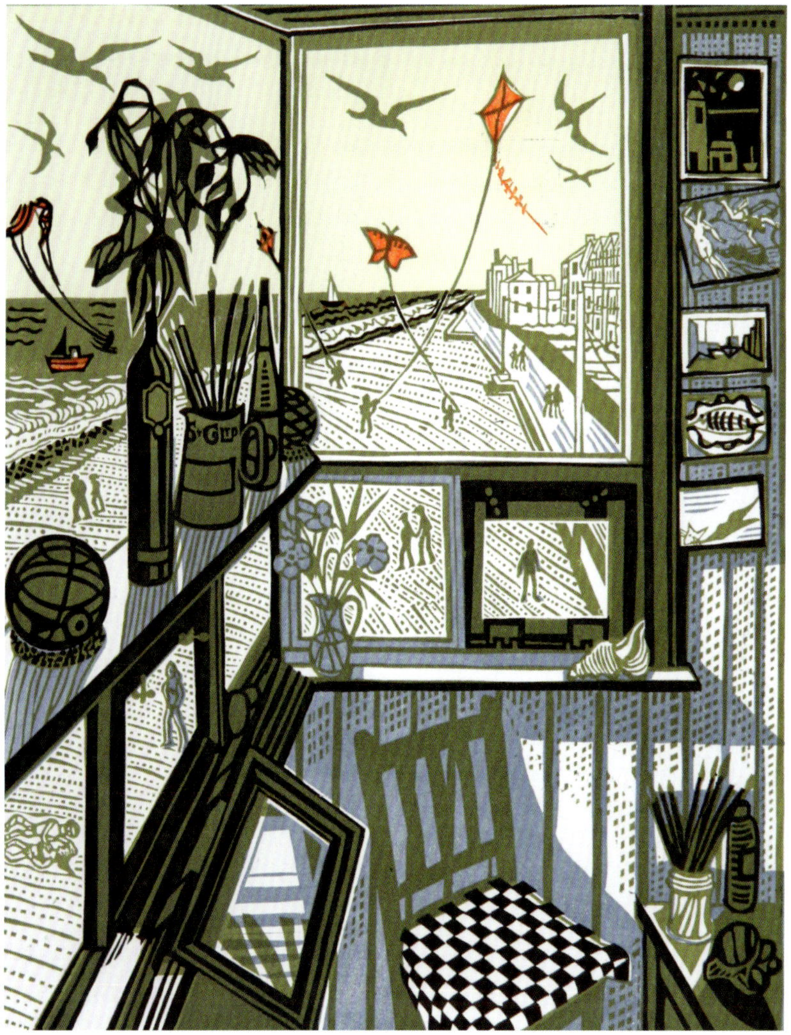

Kites at Aldeburgh, Richard Bawden, 2009, linocut

The Three Wherry Tour on the Waveney, 1995-6, oil on canvas

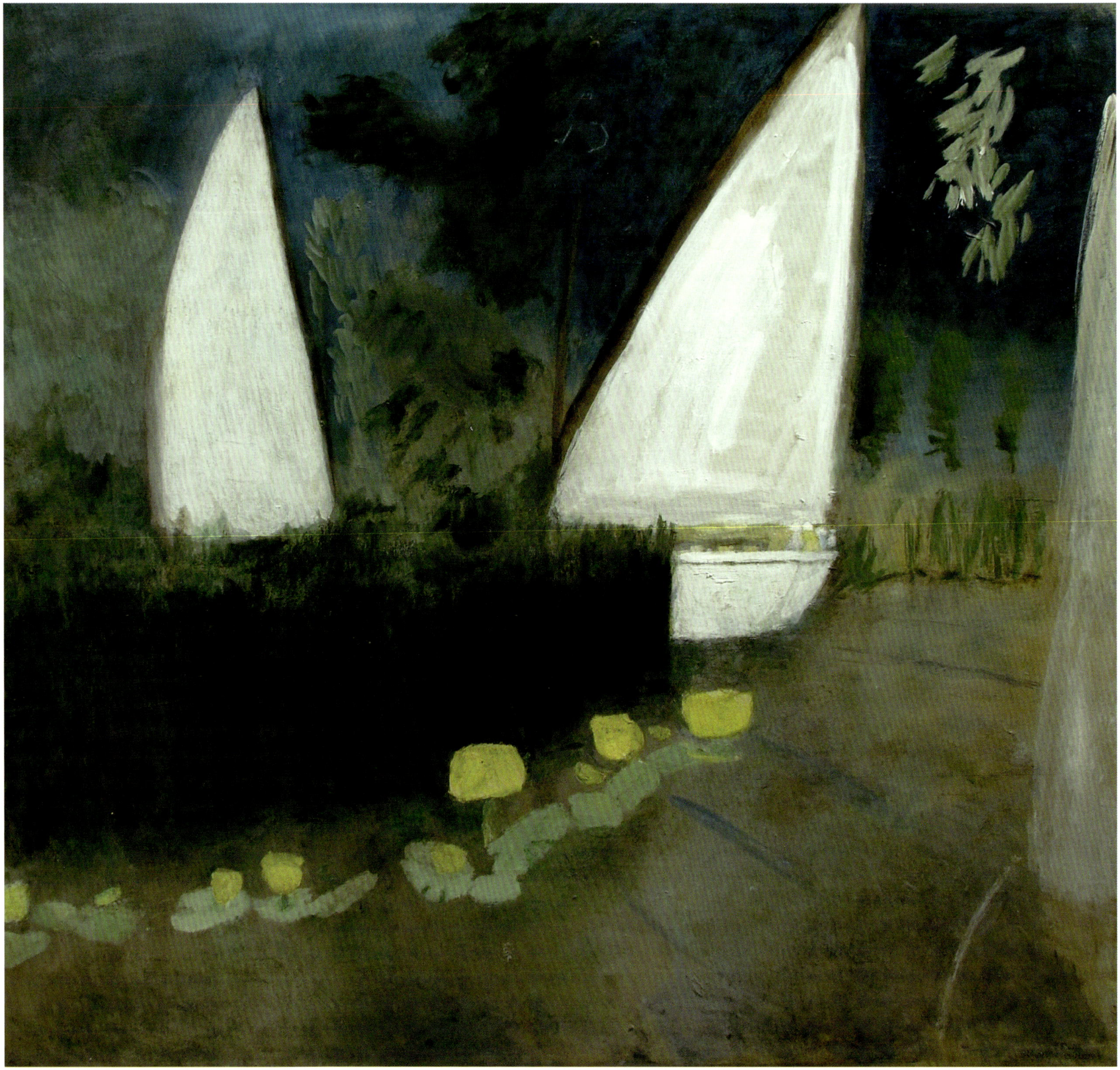

An Odd Universe

Mary Newcomb in the Waveney Valley

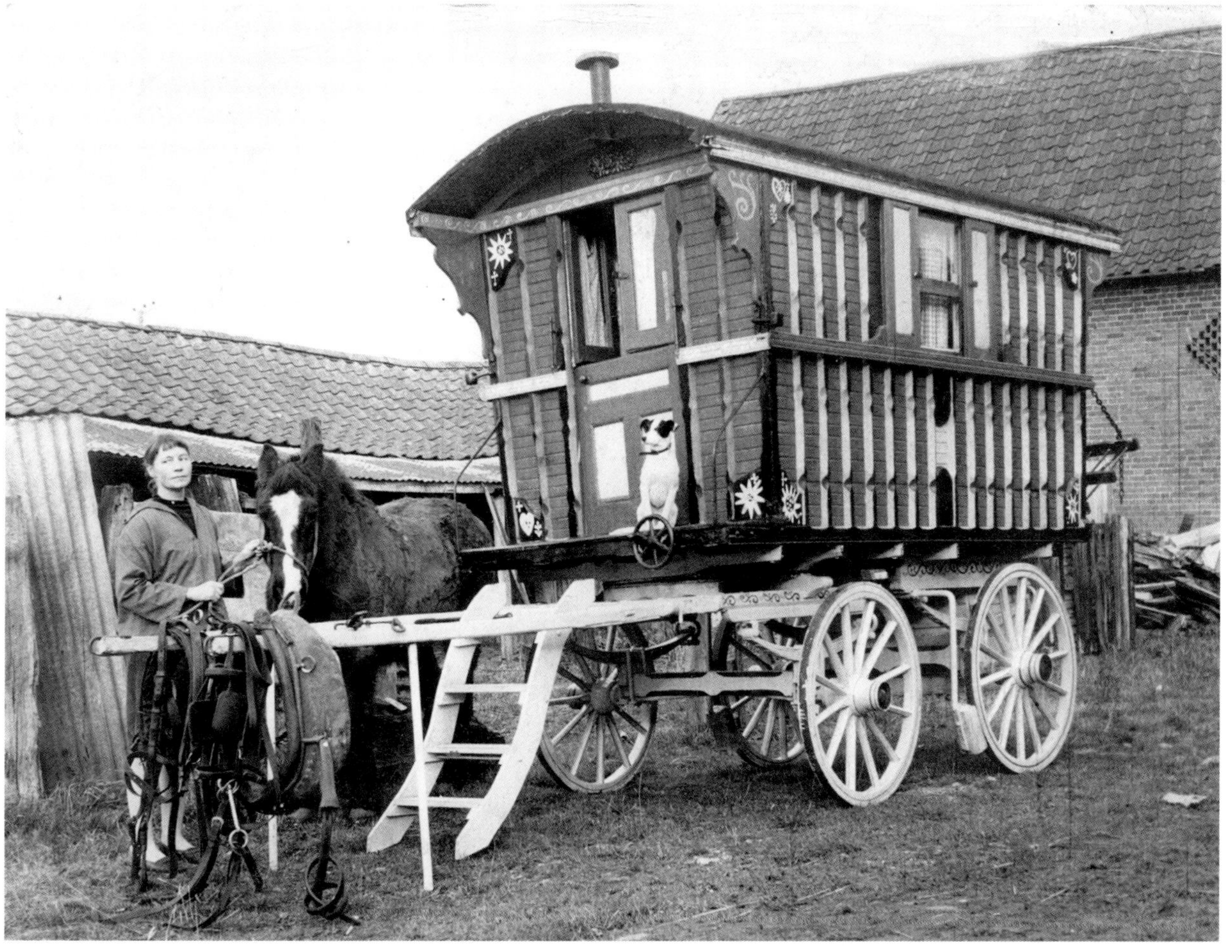

Mary Newcomb and the gypsy caravan at Mill Farm, Needham, early 1960s

Mary Newcomb's odd universe seems a place of unearthly enchantment – but she came from a long line of visionary East Anglian painters who show that paradise is on our doorstep and we have only to open our eyes to see it.

She once spent an afternoon watching two terns in Southwold harbour. One bird sat on a green post, above the grey tide, while the other hovered overhead, offering sand eels. Making notes and drawings on the spot, Mary translated what she took to be a courtship display into two paintings. They were later reproduced in a beautiful book complete with her caption commentary. Soon after publication she received a fan letter from Sir David Attenborough ending in a small point of correction. The learned naturalist informed the self-taught artist that what she had actually been watching at the mouth of the River Blyth was a parent bird feeding a fledgling. 'How would he know?' said Mary. 'He wasn't there.'

Although Mary Slatford had taken a science degree at Reading University, and then trained as a maths teacher, she had always insisted that seeing was believing. However much proportion and perspective might run amok, as she focused on the colourful incident within the wider scene exciting her interest, hers remained acutely observed pictures.

Born at Harrow-on-the-Hill in 1922, she grew up in rural Wiltshire. Her world fell into place weeks after the war while she was a helper at the Flatford Mill Field Studies Centre being set up by bird painter Eric Ennion on the Suffolk-Essex border. Her mentor had been a Fenland doctor before his art took flight. Lodging in Willy Lott's Cottage, overlooking a favourite scene of Constable, Mary learned the art of careful study – taking copious notes and sketches to keep an image fresh in the mind's eye.

With Peter Scott she went to assist the setting up of a new avocet-attracting nature reserve at Minsmere on a wild stretch of the Suffolk coast still barbed-wired and tank-trapped to prevent a monstrous migration by Hitler. And on an Ennion-led trip to boost reedbeds for bitterns at Walberswick she met trainee farmer Godfrey Newcomb. After their marriage they lived on Waveney Valley farms, where an outsider's outsider would find everything she needed for her emergent art.

Their first base, at Needham near Harleston, ran down to the Norfolk bank of the border river. Here hard graft in tough times was lightened by revelatory encounters with nature. In a letter to the writer and film-maker Roger Deakin, who lived on Mellis Common, near Eye, Mary described watching a fight between two dog otters beneath her window one night: 'They were on their back legs, teeth in each other's necks, and balanced by their tails. In the morning I saw their bloody trails in the dew on the marsh, going in different directions.'

In the early days the Newcombs restored

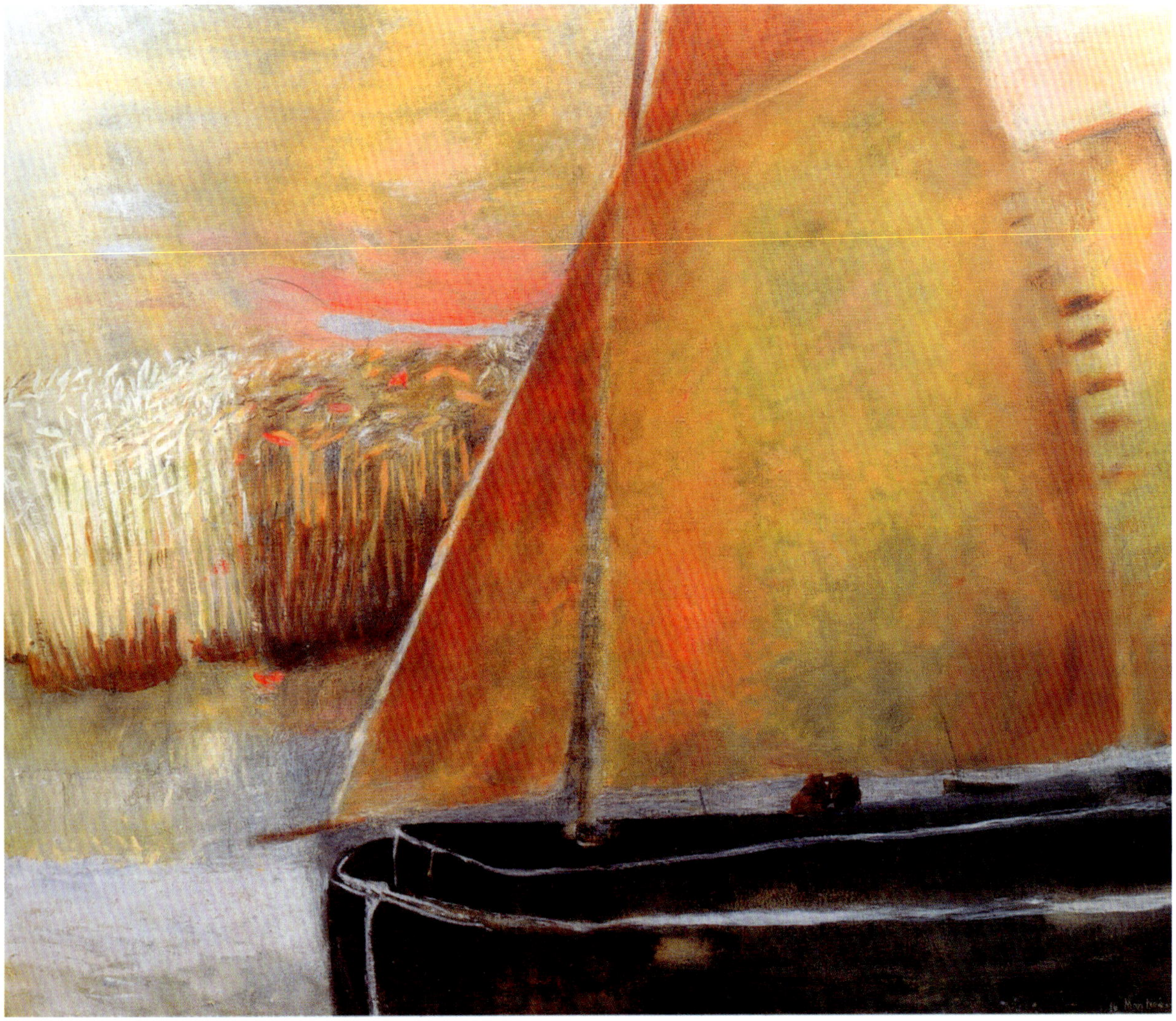

Boat in a low setting sun casting its shadow over the reeds as it passes, 1986, oil on canvas

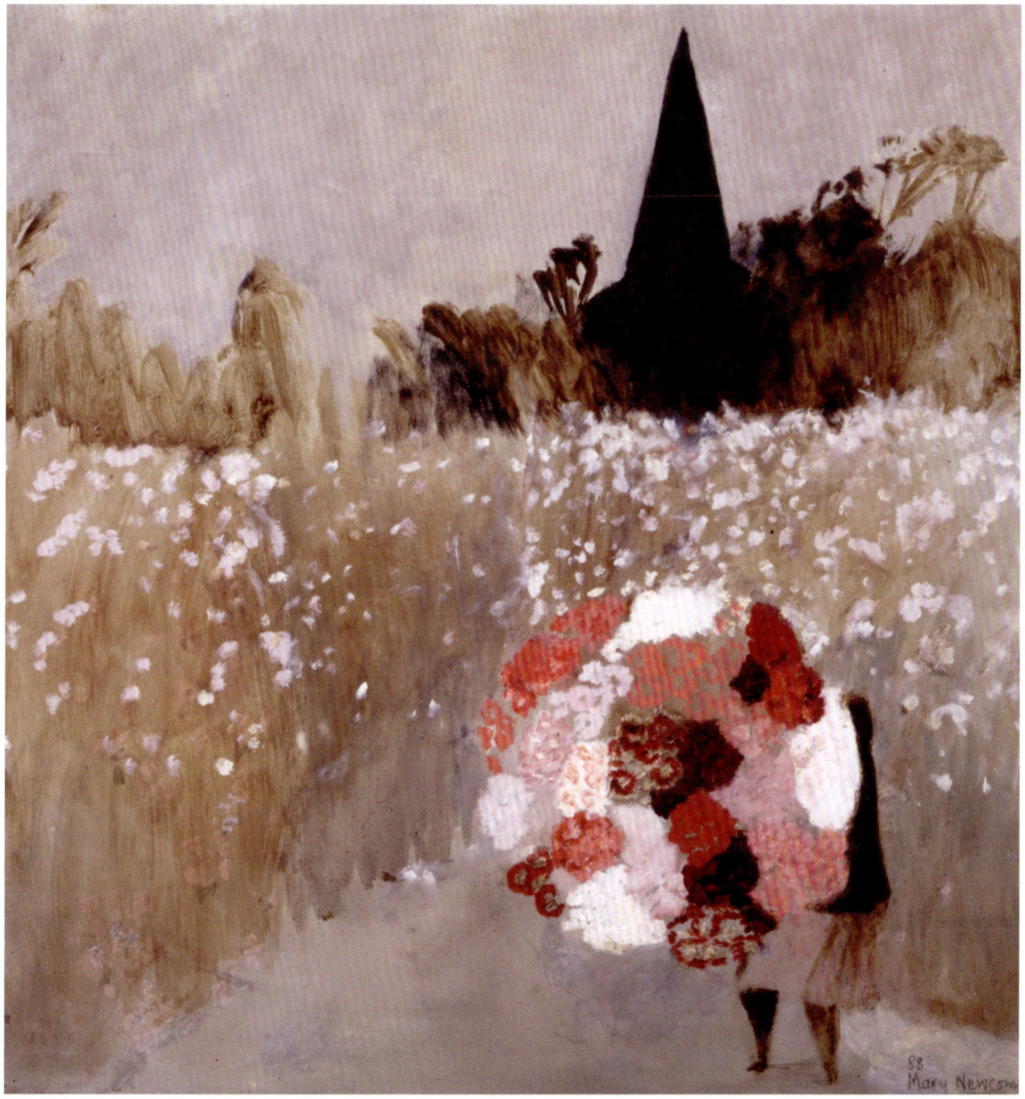

The lady with a bunch of sweet williams, 1988, oil on board

gypsy caravans and set up a pottery together – Mary having taken evening classes in ceramics at Corsham Court, the Wiltshire arts school and bucolic idyll run by Clifford and Rosemary Ellis. They turned out decorative slipware harking back to medieval pots and popular with a new wave of craft shops. These pieces still turn up at local car boot sales, where they are bought by the eagle-eyed for a song.

Within a few years Godfrey was running the farm and pottery – spinning the wool from a small flock of very mixed and often escaping sheep. For Mary was finding her vocation in painting while also raising daughters Hannah and Tessa. She became a stalwart of the Norwich Twenty Group – for years selling major pictures at £20 apiece – before daring to take a bag of work to London dealer Andras Kalman, the Hungarian refugee who had championed L S Lowry in his first gallery in Manchester. On that occasion the Knightsbridge premises were packed with people, so Mary fled home. But her second attempt marked the start of a model relationship between artist and dealer. With a dozen solo exhibitions at Crane Kalman Gallery from 1970, and further shows across Europe and in America, the Newcomb name was firmly on the map.

She came to be collected by magnates and media stars. There were purchases by public galleries including the Tate. But throughout Mary remained entirely unaffected, armed with a watchful eye, a rich interior vision and a quiet but resolute determination to paint exactly how and what she wished.

Her art lay in the rhythms of nature and the rituals of rural life – in her chickens, guinea fowl and, best of all, sheep, in village fetes and country shows, or in incidents glimpsed as she travelled on the bus or train, or walked or bicycled. Akin to visual poetry, her canvas ranged from the tiniest insects to the night sky and showed, however unwittingly, how everything links up within the harmony of the universe.

Lyrical titles could underline the poem of each picture. A view of an ancient farmhouse

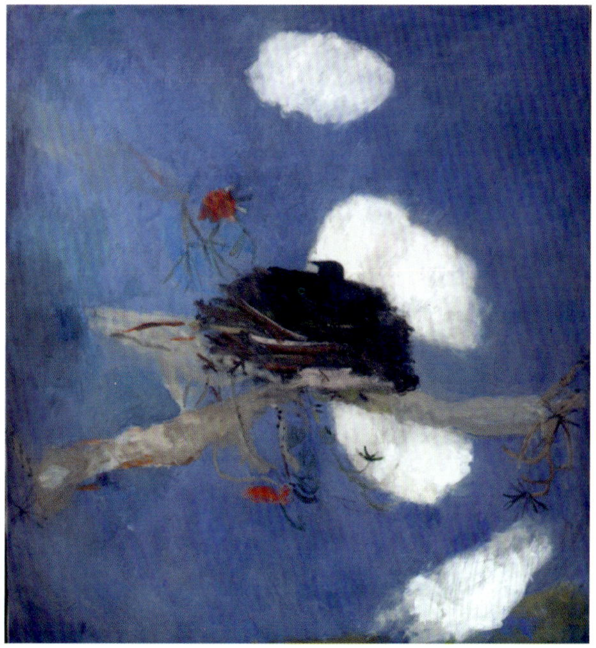

The brooding rook's heaven, 2001, oil on canvas (right)

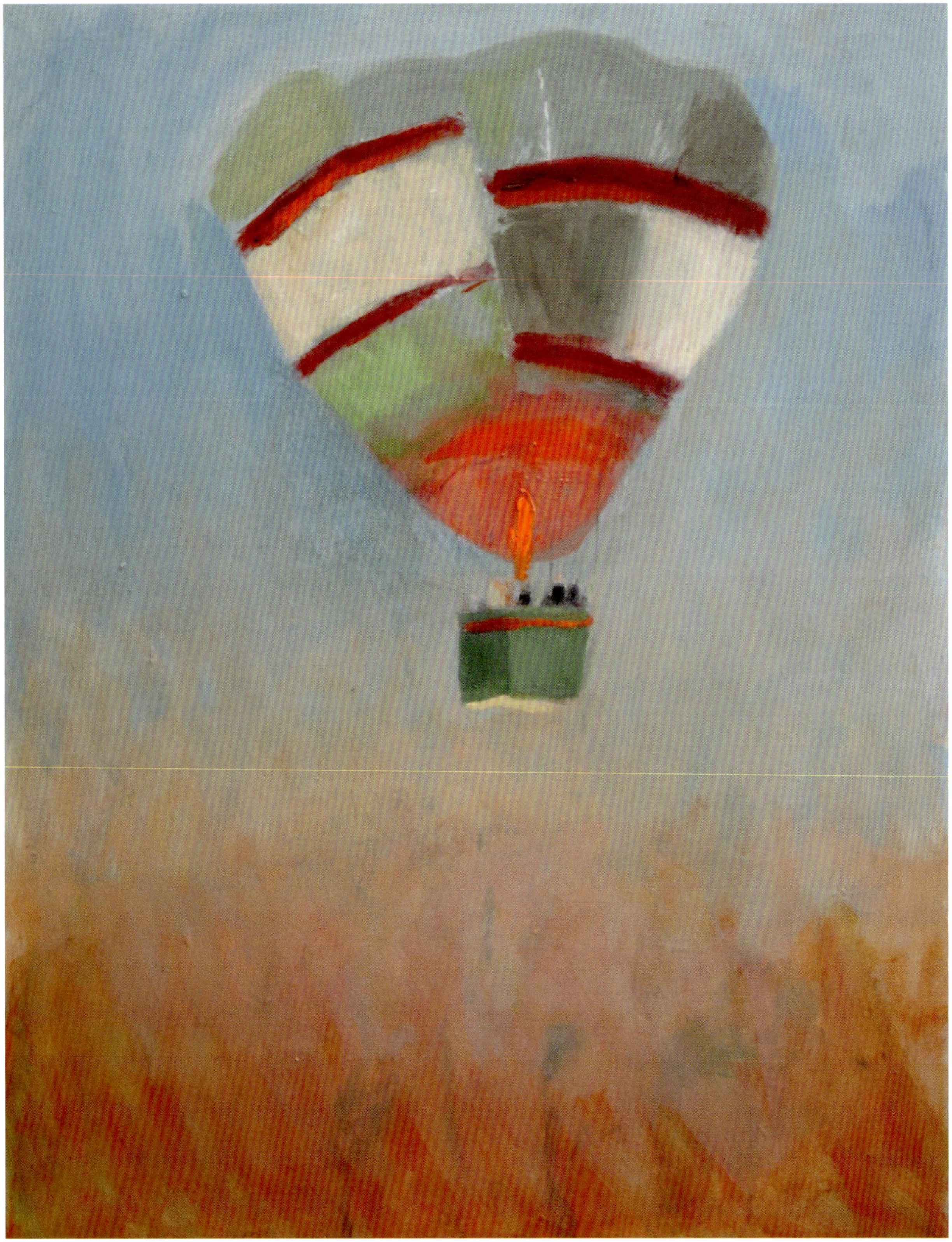

Drift me home at the end of the day, 2000, oil on board

lost in a field and closed-up save for a tiny attic pane was called *Mrs Meek ppens her window to the larks*. With pictures such as *Ewes watching shooting stars* and *Some bees do not die but remain on their backs confused* Mary shows an overwhelming sense of awe combined with a note of wry comedy about the strange nature of existence.

Her successive studios contained jumbled notes and drawings and souvenirs from rural

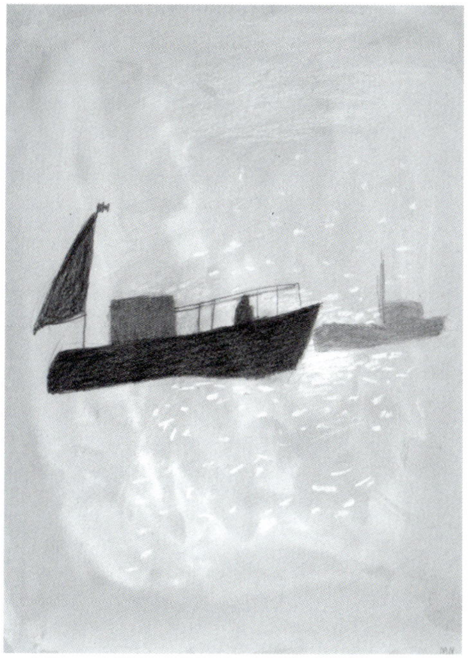

Boats, 1988, pencil and crayon

journeys as far afield as Ireland and Holland, Orkney and the South of France. Several pictures would be in progress at any one time – first streaked with vibrant combinations of abstract colour, then propped against the wall, and turned into new positions until they suggested a remembered scene. New images could be brushed on top of upside-down old ones. Towards the end her paintings became sparer, lighter, larger and increasingly abstract – works which hold their place on the walls of major museums.

Acclaimed by fellow artists from Ben Nicholson to Mary Fedden, she was also admired by numerous writers. J G Farrell ended his novel *The Singapore Grip* by detailing her paintings on the wall above him as he wrote. She found in East Anglian author Ronald Blythe an especially kindred spirit – his words and her pictures memorably combining in the *Borderland* book of essays. Soon afterwards, the cover painting, showing goldfinches whirring around a thistle like ponies on a carousel was destroyed in a fire in Andras Kalman's flat.

Down the decades the Newcombs moved to Linstead Magna near Halesworth, Newton Flotman near Norwich and Peasenhall near Saxmundham – each rambling old house much like the last. Godfrey died in April 2003 and Mary suffered a severe stroke in the October from which she was not expected to recover. But she had a tenacious hold on life even in extremis. Although severely paralysed, and unable to eat or speak, she continued to draw pictures in the air and her mind remained her own to the last bright morning four and a half years later.

The atmosphere in her Darsham nursing home recalled her successive houses – an old cat might be asleep on a bedside armchair, birds thronged window feeders and chickens pecked at a glass door. Mary, who had always existed primarily in a rich interior world, wasn't so much stoic as endlessly interested and very often amused. She was perfectly aware that she had painted some wonderful pictures.

One late, great work of a balloon above East Anglian fields was called *Drift me home at the end of the day*. It became the poster for her uplifting memorial exhibition Mary Newcomb's Odd Universe: Fire, Earth, Water, Air, seen by 21,500 visitors to Norwich Castle over 50 spring days in 2009.

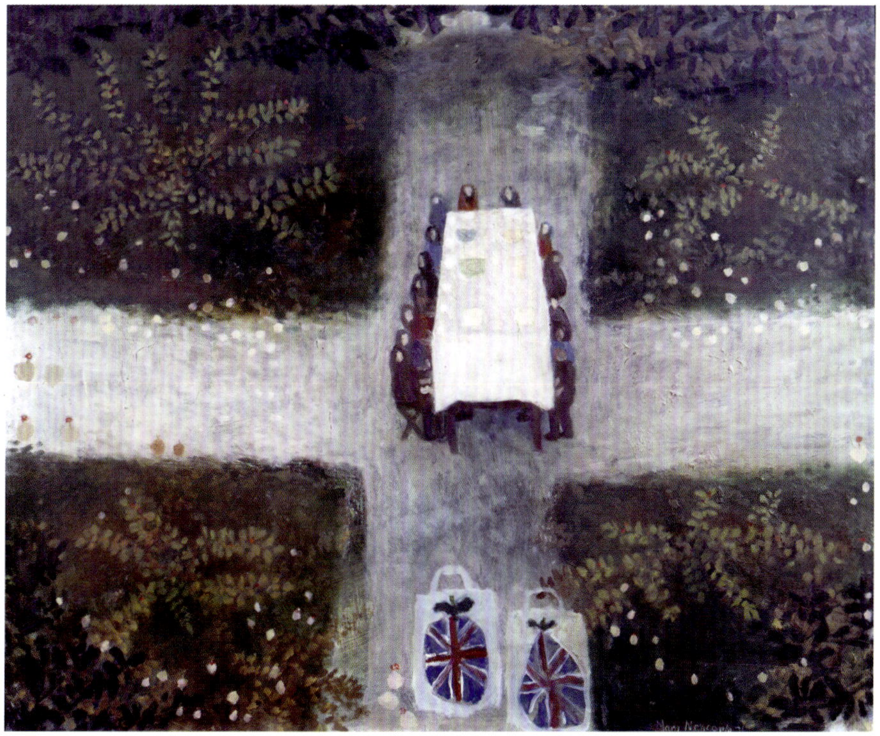

The apple pickers' feast, 1971, oil on board

Winter Floods, 2001, oil on board

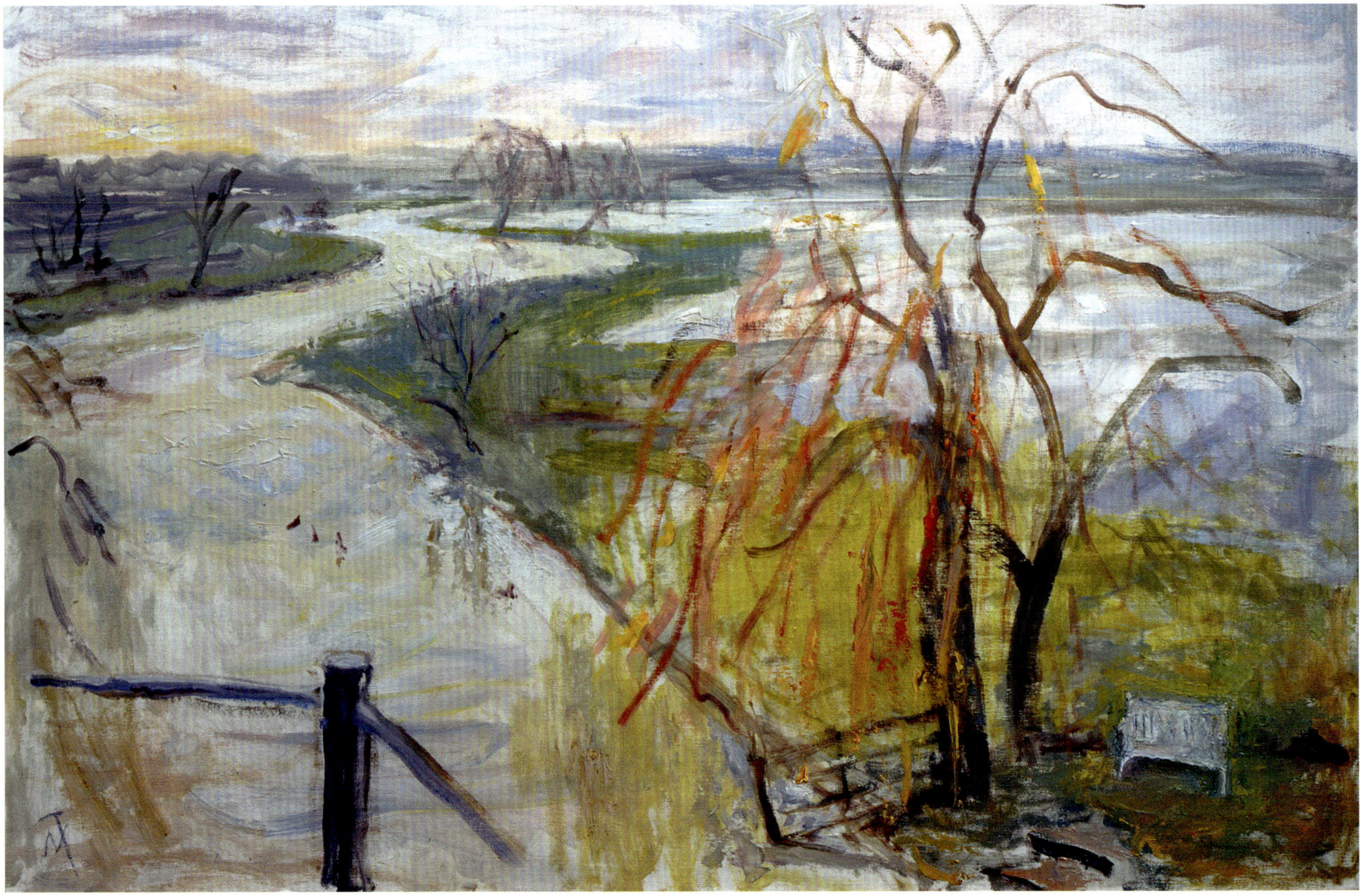

A Clear View

Margaret Thomas and the River Waveney

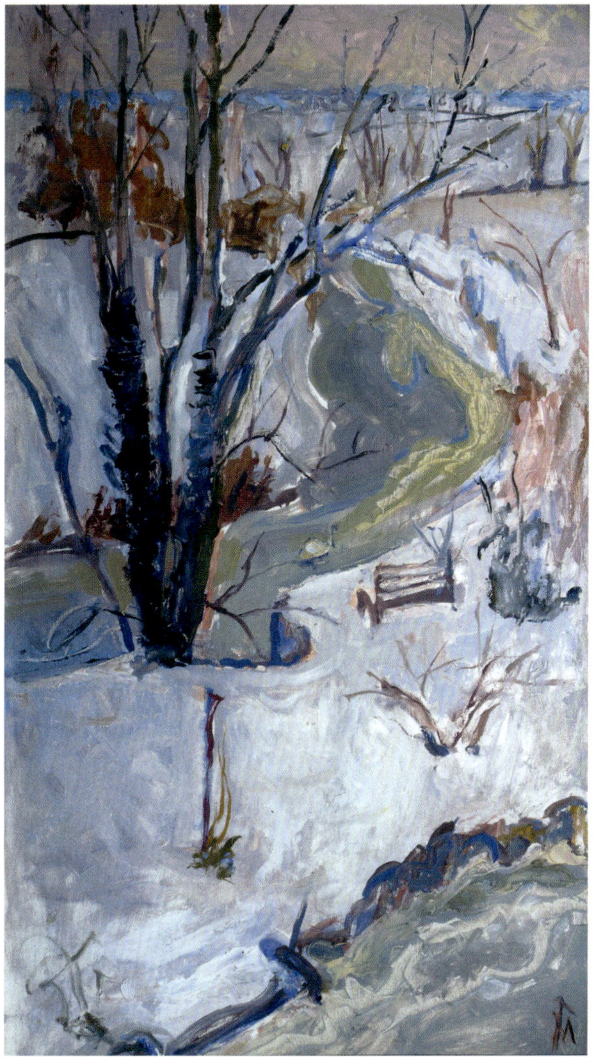

Snow Beck, 1991, oil on board

Margaret Thomas is a painter of clear views – revelling in a vantage point high above water and most especially from December to March. She says: 'As I see it, the visual world is magically transformed by winter – by wind and rain, frost and snow, mist and fog. Whereas in summer, with its cloudless blue skies and exhausting humidity, everything that really matters is obscured by glare or draped in wraps of unpaintable GREEN.'

Disregarding birthdays, with the belief that every day should be special, she was compelled to celebrate her 85th with a retrospective show at Messum's gallery which drew queues down London's Cork Street. Expressing firm opinions in a catalogue note, she led an 'I Love' list with 'A good view' and 'Looking down from a height'. Other favourites comprised twilight, peace and quiet, old roses, gardening, milking cows, swimming in the rain, people, dogs, bees, teddy bears, mime, auctions, kitchen antiques, good fruit cake, trams, driving, not travelling abroad and Indian art and ballet.

Then an 'I Dislike' tally began with 'Mountains' (they impede the view) and extended to hot sunshine, painting out of doors, linseed oil, snobbery, hair-dressing salons, make-up, expensive clothes, luxurious furnishings, television, supermarkets, raucous 'music', committees, coffee mornings, cream teas, peanuts, crisps, garlic, gravel, plastic flowers and orange plastic watering cans.

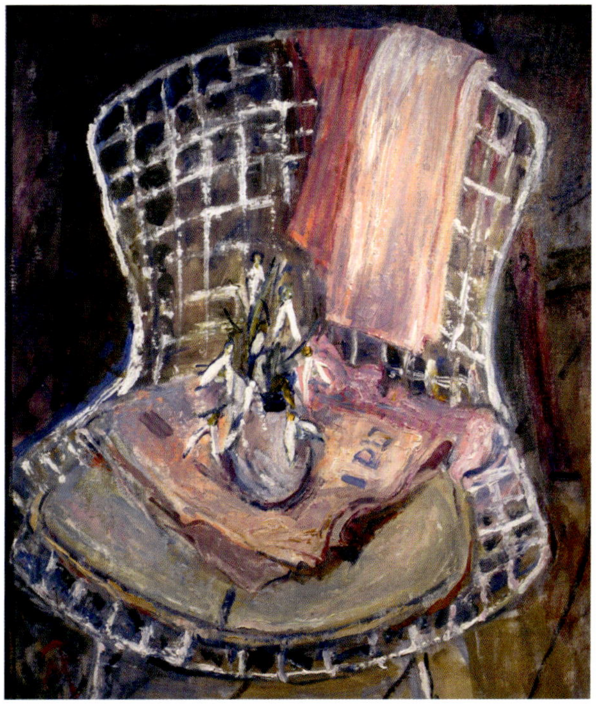

The Snowdrops are Posing Again, oil on board (right)

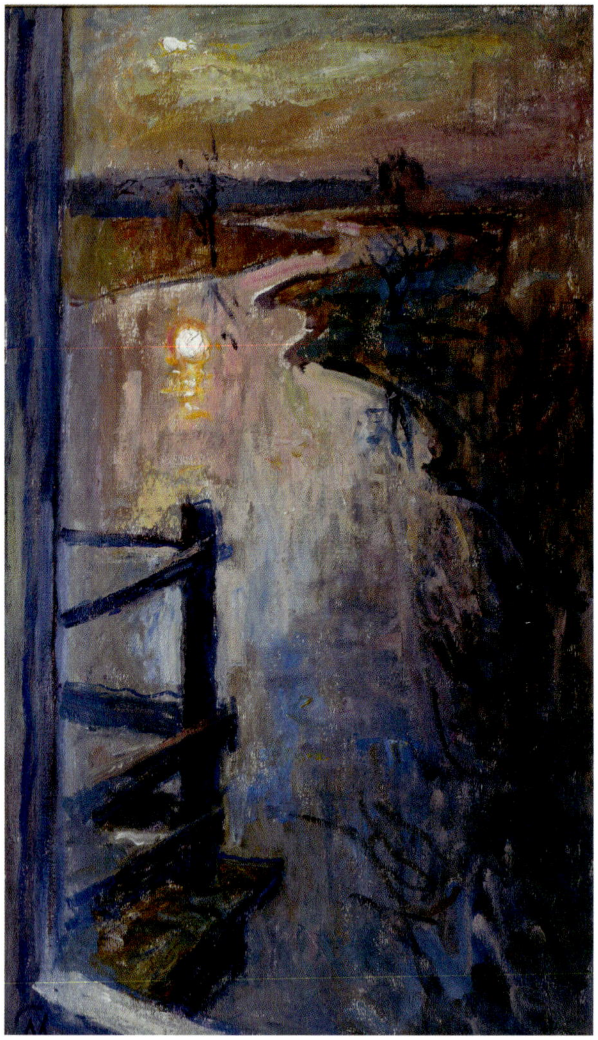

Sunset River, 1995, oil on board

Raised as a Londoner – in suitably elevated Highgate – Margaret Thomas always felt drawn to the Norfolk roots of her timber merchant father, first in childhood holidays afloat on the Broads, and latterly via a painterly migration up the East Anglian coast for a final landing on the Norfolk bank of the River Waveney with some of the finest views in the region.

As an only child taught at home, she longed for a school uniform but finally conformed to a paternal urging to be herself and not to copy others. From the age of 12 she was tutored by Dora Sulman, who had been at the Slade with Ethel Walker in the golden age before the Great War. ('We did Art & Literature & History, no Science as Sully said she had never understood it.')

A scholarship to the Slade proved a bitter disappointment, and Margaret transferred to the Royal Academy Schools where, in a markedly happy life, she was to be at her happiest. As an ardent pacifist, she worked on a dairy farm and also in an apiary in Wiltshire for much of the war. Returned to London in 1945, to her family's temporary home in a Highgate hall, Margaret found herself perfectly and harmlessly framed amid broken glass when a huge window was blown in by a Doodle Bug.

Building a career with portrait commissions, she had her first solo show at the Leicester Galleries in 1949. She became a stalwart member of the New English Art Club after her election in 1951, and showed in Royal Academy summer exhibitions for 46 consecutive years.

Always with a river running through her life, Margaret Thomas first painted along the Thames from Bankside to Gravesend, and – drawn to Scotland by Anne Redpath's suggestion that she should exhibit in Edinburgh – she had an eyrie on top of The Mound commanding a panoramic view over the city and the Firth of Forth to the Ochil Hills of Fife for 45 years from 1956.

Meanwhile, from 1972, she had established another outpost in a boathouse studio on the Suffolk coast – on the quay at Orford, where the Alde estuary runs from Snape Maltings. This soon became her main painting base, to be vacated, 12 years later, only when the major part of a converted watermill on the Waveney, became available – and she moved there fully on acquiring the rest of the historic property in 2001.

Naturally she immediately made a studio in the attic with the most magnificent of westward views over water, willow and meadow, the scene sometimes flooding so that she felt like Mrs Noah in her Ark. This scintillating vista has now been depicted in moonlight, sunlight, snow, rain, storm and mist – and especially in its myriad guises at sunset.

Margaret Thomas has robust ideas on the composition of a painting – latterly landscapes, still-life studies and her favourite motif of dead flowers – just as she does on the construction of a home and a life. A great loyalist and stylist, she loves 'intrepid old ladies' and friendships have remained her anchor.

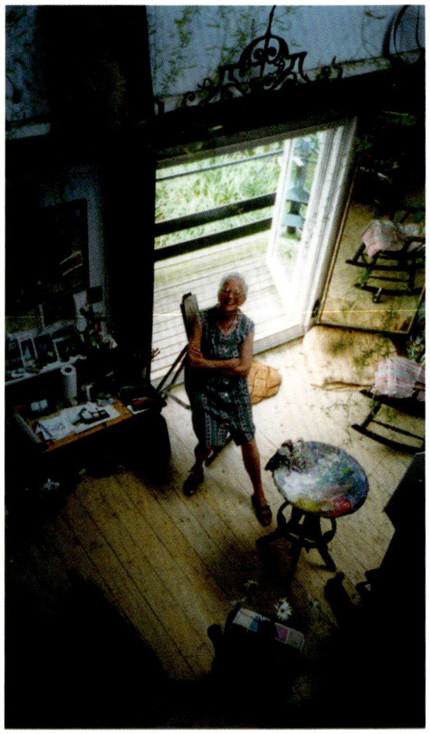

Margaret Thomas
in her mill studio

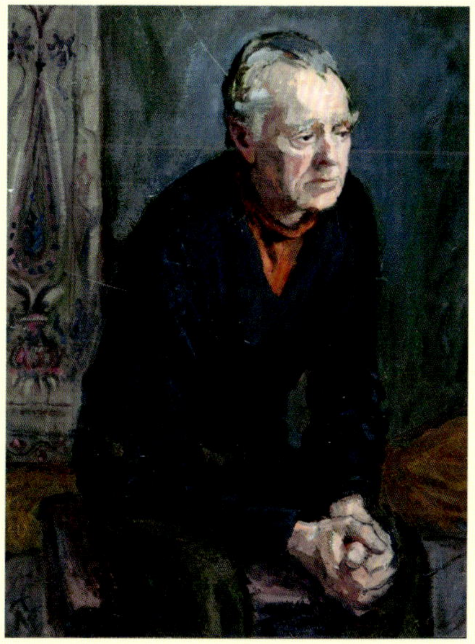

John Gay, oil on canvas

John Gay (1909-1999), born Hans Gohler, was a German Jewish refugee who recorded his love of England in more than 40,000 photos – of grand and humble architecture, the coast (see pages 86 & 104) and countryside, railway stations and his adopted home of Highgate – now with English Heritage. He and his wife Marie often visited their painter friend Margaret Thomas in East Anglia, first at Orford and then in the Waveney Valley.

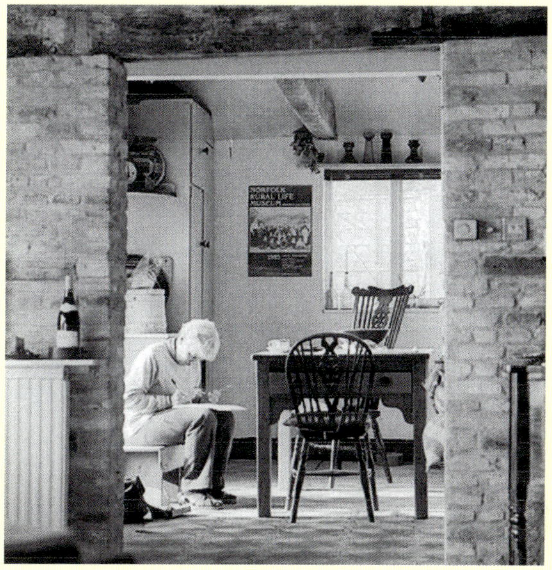

The Waveney Mill, John Gay, 1986

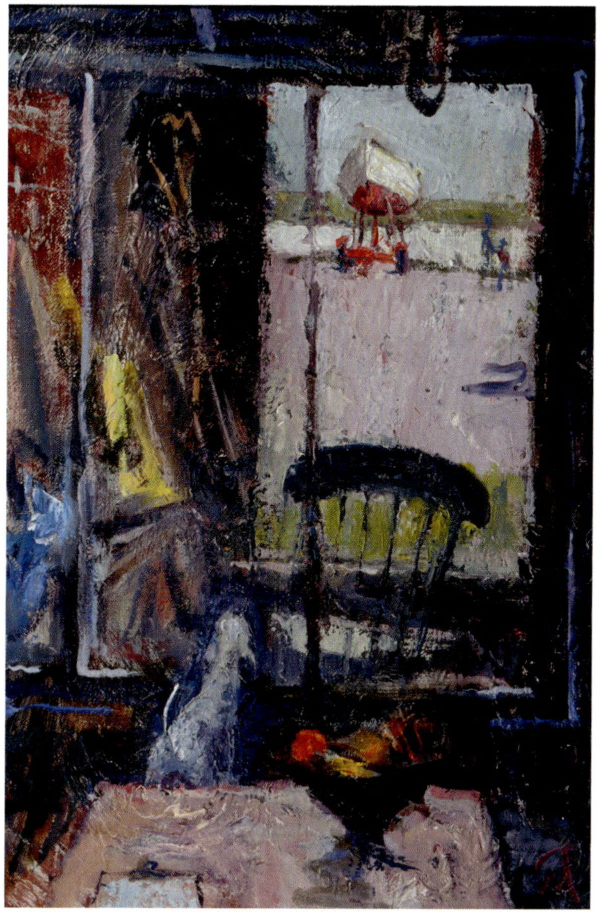

The Watch House Door, Orford, c. 1986, oil on board

Each of her houses and studios has been stamped with her superb decorative hallmark: doors and skirting boards in matt black, and walls either mushroom or white – all above bare wooden floors long before the fashion for stripped boards. Her favourite car, Miss (Zuleika) Dobson, is a 1925 Bullnose Morris. Her dog of choice is a Bedlington terrier, providing a succession of pets named Larry. Her childhood companion, Sir Edward Bear – ultimately raised to the bearage as Lord Bruin – continues, despite the onset of gout, to preside over Christmas Open House parties, for which Margaret bakes and sculpts a spectacular cake, and once personally thanked some rather startled firemen who had just doused down a chimney blaze.

But, however settled in the domestic scene with its widest horizons, to the end Margaret Thomas enjoys an alternative view. How she has loved, into her nineties, to pack her painting gear into Maria, her trusty Land Wagon, and drive to the coast. Best of all has been climbing to the top of a lookout tower on the beach at Aldeburgh and taking stock of another shifting and shimmering panorama.

Sea, 1991, found painted wood

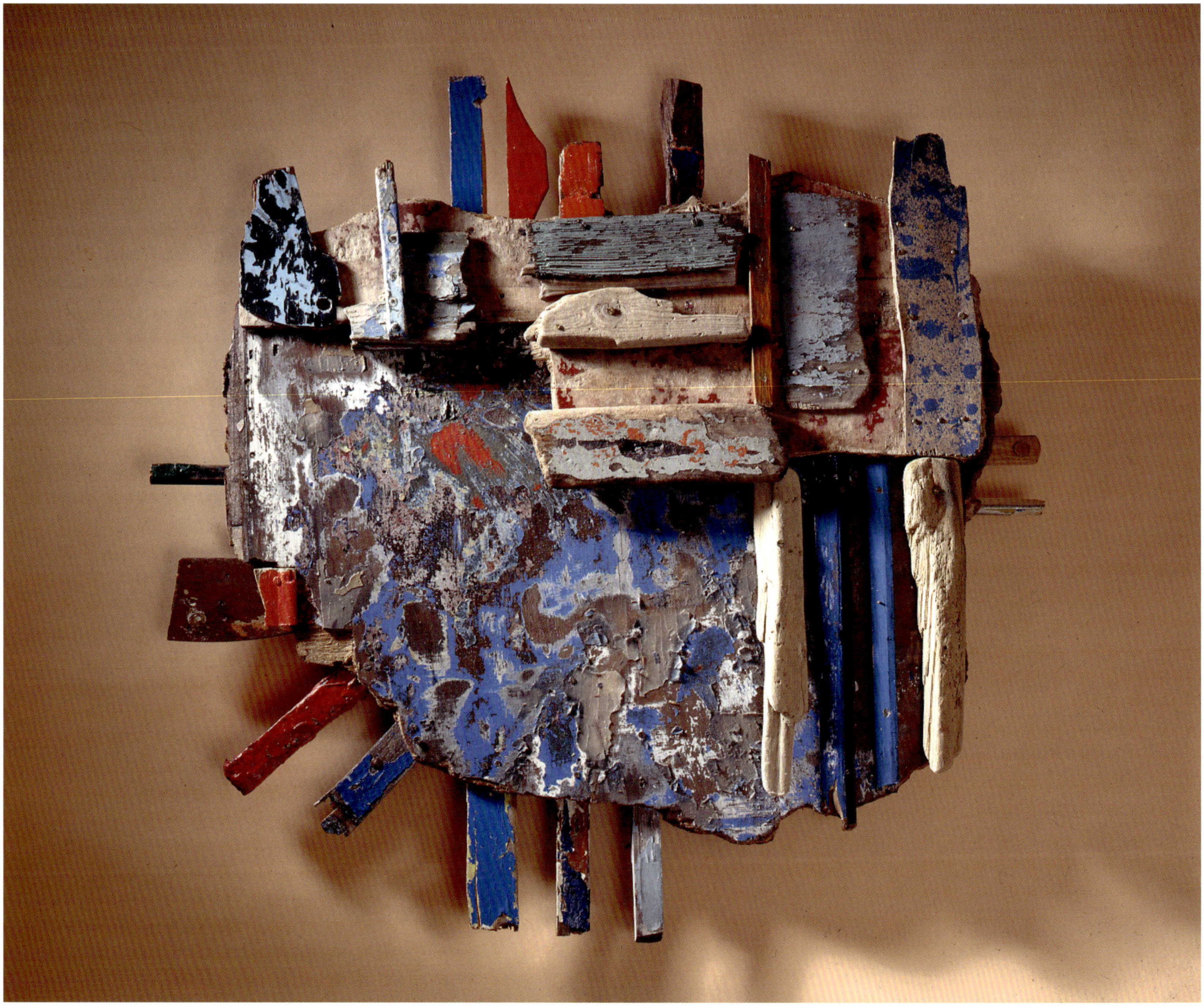

The Art of Salvage

Margaret Mellis, Frank Jennings and Walberswick

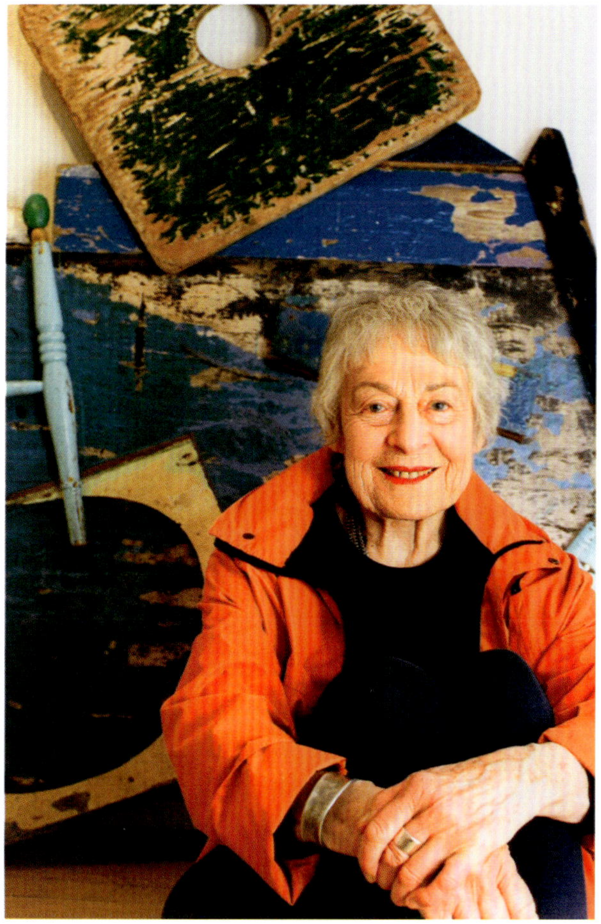

Margaret Mellis in her studio

Margaret Mellis (1914-2009) was a pivotal figure in modernist British art. Born in China to a missionary father, she spent her first birthday on the boat returning the family to their native Scotland at the start of World War One. Her earliest memory was of 'being bathed in a blue and white china basin with dragons on it and lying on an orange sofa'. Absorption in brilliant colour would be the key to her life.

Margaret entered Edinburgh's College of Art at 15, went to Paris on a scholarship to train with André Lhote and when returning for the Cézanne exhibition of 1936 met Adrian Stokes, an established art theorist and emergent painter with magnetic looks and charm. They married two years later, visiting Ezra Pound during their Italian honeymoon.

Amid the false hopes of Munich, Margaret and Adrian searched for a coastal refuge from the predicted London Blitz, first in East Anglia. The discovery of an ideal house near St Ives changed the course of British art. In August 1939 these escapees were joined by Ben Nicholson and Barbara Hepworth – bringing with them triplets, nursemaid and cook. The constructivist Naum Gabo and his wife Miriam followed shortly afterwards, as did Peter Lanyon. Nicholson went on to incorporate aspects of local landscapes into his abstracted paintings, to teach Lanyon and influence the next wave of artists drawn to the St Ives area – Roger Hilton, Patrick Heron, Terry Frost and Bryan Wynter. Hepworth remained in Cornwall for the rest of her life.

For mere shillings Mellis and Stokes – like Nicholson and other modernists – bought masterly primitive marine pictures on scrap paper and card by an old St Ives tar, and later rag and bone man, called Alfred Wallis. But when he died, at Madron workhouse hospital in 1942, they halted his pauper's send-off – funding the Salvationist funeral he would have wished and paying for a grave above Porthmeor Beach with a fine ceramic memorial by Bernard Leach adorned with motifs from Wallis' paintings.

Far from the social realism of London's Euston Road School towards which Stokes had unwisely steered her, Margaret was encouraged by Nicholson and Gabo to produce small abstract compositions in card and paper – springboards to all her daring works of the future. But conflict abounded. Someone said the St Ives artists 'fought like ferrets in a sack' and Adrian was the most jealous of all. Margaret was meant to be a submissive housekeeper, even before her husband's attentions shifted to her sister, Ann. In 1946 the marriage ended. Adrian left and Margaret would have killed herself, but for the need to care for their young son, Telfer.

Patrick and Delia Heron went to stay and invited a lately-divorced schoolfriend of Patrick's – Francis Davison. Similarly wounded, Margaret and Francis struck up an immediate rapport. They married in 1948 and were rarely parted thereafter. At first the couple, together with Telfer, camped in the spartan Davison chateau on the Cap d'Antibes. They returned to England in 1950, borrowing a fisherman's shack at Walberswick.

Here their lives of self-sufficiency and mutually-supportive creativity really started. Margaret explored still-life painting; Francis pared down his pictures into simple, flat forms, switching to collage from 1952. Both journeyed into abstraction along personal but parallel routes.

Soon a small legacy paid for a cottage and four-acre smallholding at Syleham, near Harleston. Here, for 25 years, they thrived in splendid isolation – selling eggs and chickens; growing barley and the herbs, fruit and vegetables of a French-style kitchen garden. Only a few painter friends were welcomed, among them Patrick Heron, Roger Hilton, Mary Potter and Mary Newcomb.

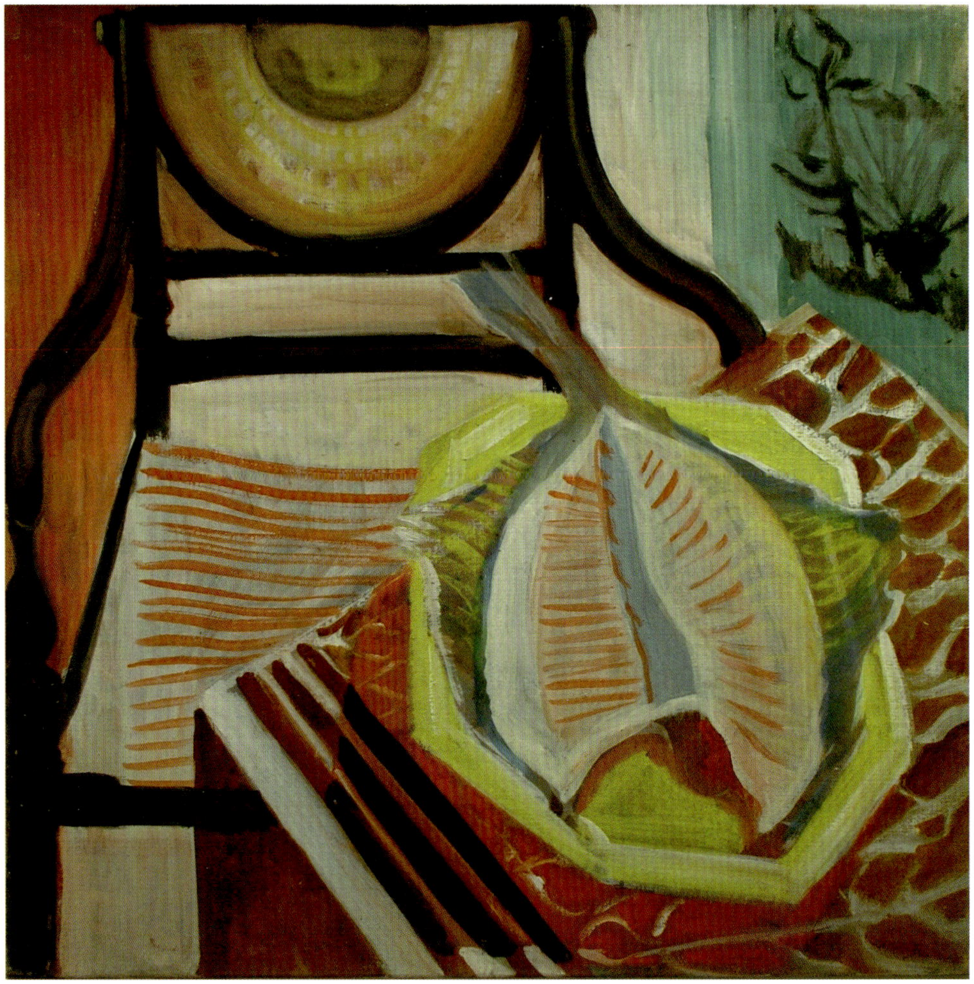

Fish on a Yellow Plate, c. 1951, oil on canvas

The artists had produced a mass of mostly-unseen work when fowlpest and Margaret's rheumatoid arthritis made life at Syleham untenable. With help from Ann – by now Adrian's widow – they moved to Southwold in 1976.

Margaret, with rigorous exercise and rigid diet, regained her lithe form and boundless energy. By 1978 she had turned from painting to driftwood constructions – combining beachcombed finds of vividly-coloured bits of boats and beach-huts, kippering boards and medieval timbers from Blythburgh church gouged by deathwatch beetles into honeycomb.

Working solely on colour, as affirmed and amended by form and structure, she produced relief sculptures with great wit and verve, in which semi-representational images unintended at the outset – soaring

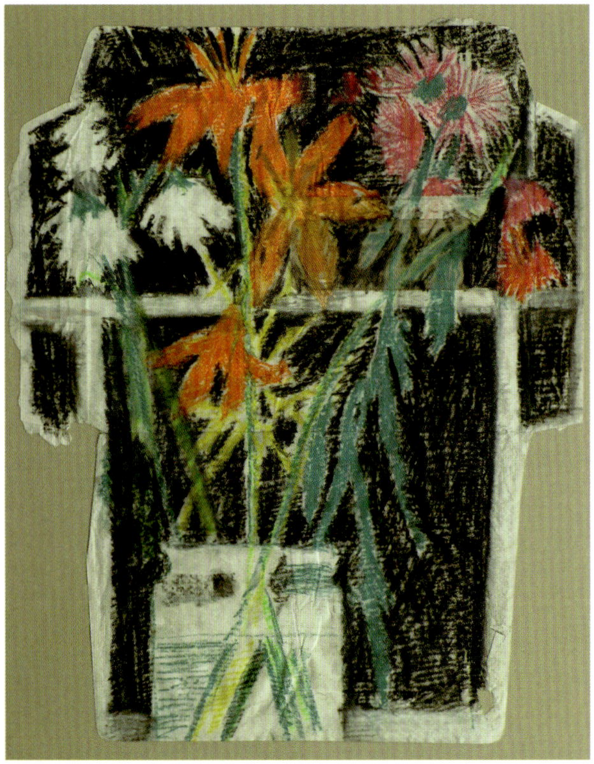

Red Lilies and Daisies, 1988, pastel on envelope (left)

angels, dipping boats, surging seas – appeared as if by magic. Francis, exhilarated by the coastal light and views, worked in a frenzy on ever-brighter and more complex collages. Then, just as Margaret recovered, he began to ail with the brain tumour that killed him in 1984.

Margaret worked on in Southwold, filling her attic studio and garden with mountains of driftwood. In 1986 she received a card from would-be art student Damien Hirst, who had 'been equally blown away' by her constructions and Francis's collages. He visited and they swam, walked and worked together.

In a foreword to Margaret's 2001 show in Newlyn and at Austin/Desmond Fine Art in London, Hirst recalled: 'We lost touch. I don't really know why. Maybe it was the age difference, maybe it was because I got into art school. I think it was also because I felt such an affinity with her.'

The 1995 Turner Prize winner concluded that Margaret had been neglected by critics and curators and deserved to be 'up there – large on the map with her contemporaries' and her work in 'the museums where it belongs'. Prophetic words for their work has now been hung side by side in Tate Britain.

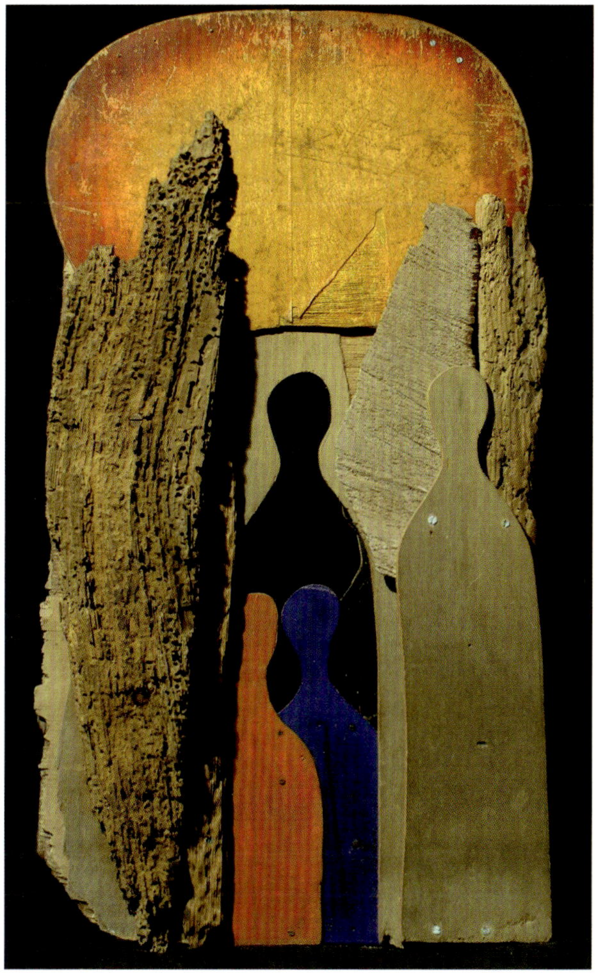

Garden of Eden, 1988, found painted wood

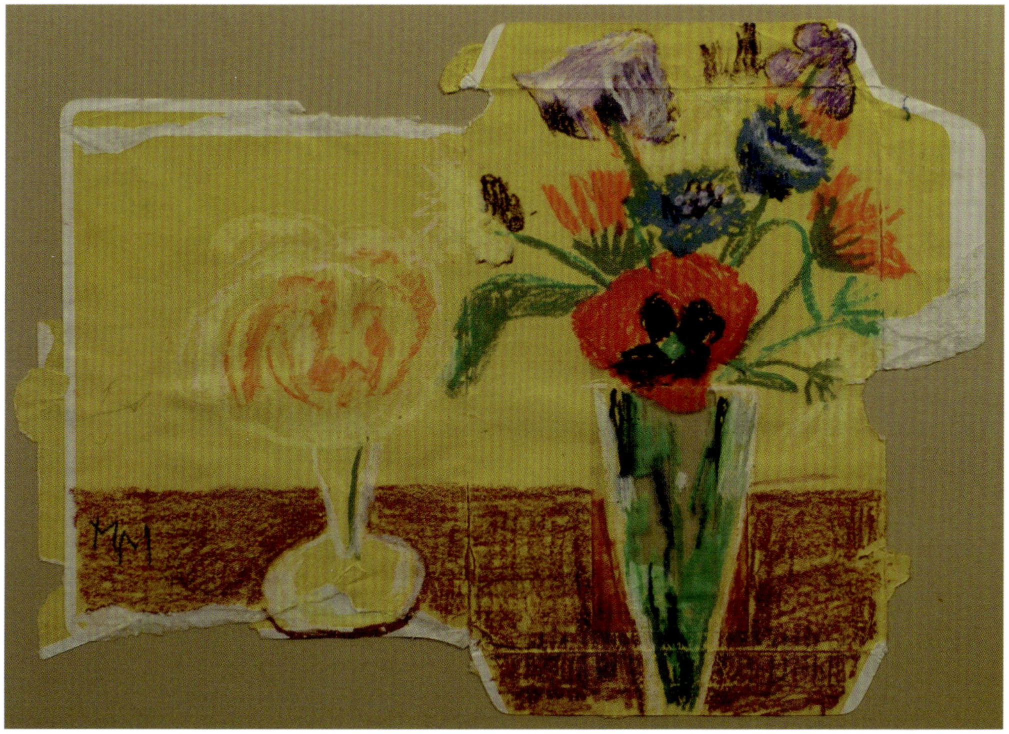

Yellow Envelope, 1998, pastel

Surrounded by friends after the death of the more reclusive Francis, she had seen fresh possibilities from the letters cascading from her mantelpiece – opening out the envelopes and producing pastel drawings of flowers on the coloured or patterned insides. Exploring these irregular shapes, she paid unconscious tribute to marine painter Alfred Wallis, whose house she had helped to clear in St Ives in 1942. She had left a heap of his oddly-shaped pictures of boats and lighthouses – later hailed as highlights of modern British art – for anyone who wanted them; but no one did.

Filmed in Suffolk and Cornwall in 1993, for a profile screened on Anglia TV, Margaret Mellis swam, danced, bicycled and created a construction on camera called Marsh Music. Her first and last loves came together towards the end. 'If I were on my death bed and I heard a good tune, I'd get up and dance,' she said. 'It would be a good way to go, actually.'

Margaret and Francis are buried in a corner of Walberswick churchyard – the village across the Blyth where architect **Frank Jennings** (1877-1961) built ten Arts and Crafts houses for himself, his family – including painter brother George – and friends in a decade from 1903.

A forebear was reputedly the richest commoner in England until dying intestate, prompting an 80-year battle in chancery and providing the model for Charles Dickens in *Bleak House*. Frank had little money but, imbued with the ideals of William Morris, a magpie collecting impulse and the nascent spirit of recycling, he incorporated salvaged artefacts into his architecture, as well as giving 200 pieces to the Victoria & Albert Museum.

So discarded medieval screens and stained glass fragments, Tudor beams and panels, an ornate Jacobean staircase from Stanton near Bury St Edmunds and 17th-century bolts and hinges found new life in singular Edwardian structures. Furious, in 1908, to find a 15th-century timber-framed dwelling about to be demolished in Lavenham, he bought the building for £80, then dismantled and reassembled it as Mercer's Hall in Walberswick.

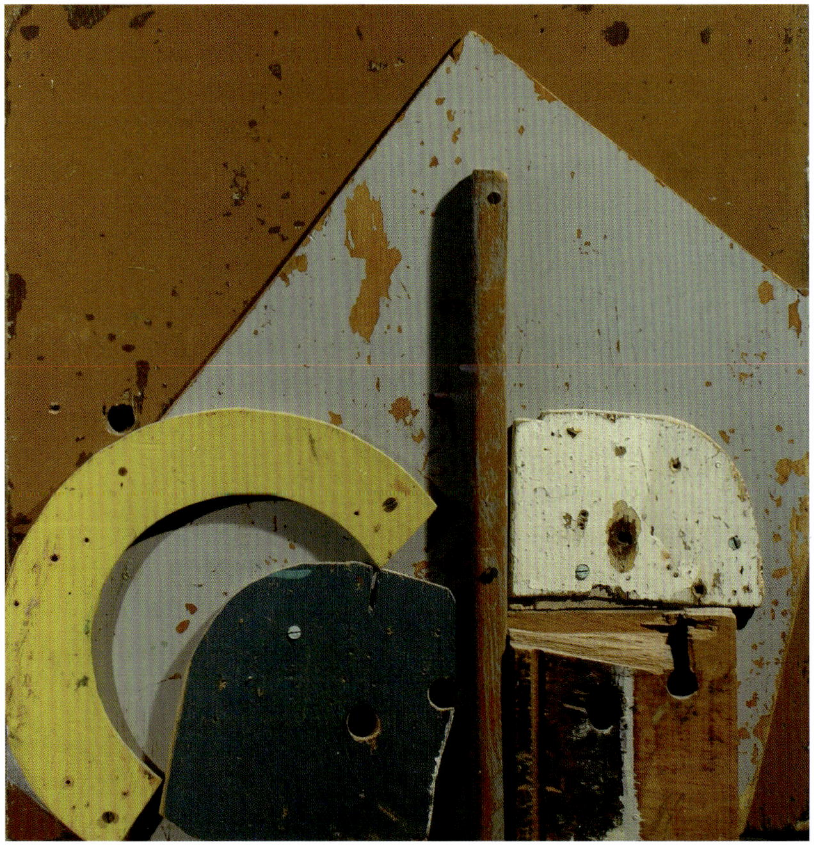

The Saint, the Clown and the Devil, 1990, found painted wood

Frank Jennings was in Walberswick in 1914 when artist and architect Charles Rennie Mackintosh and his wife Margaret fled rejection in Glasgow to take refuge with patron

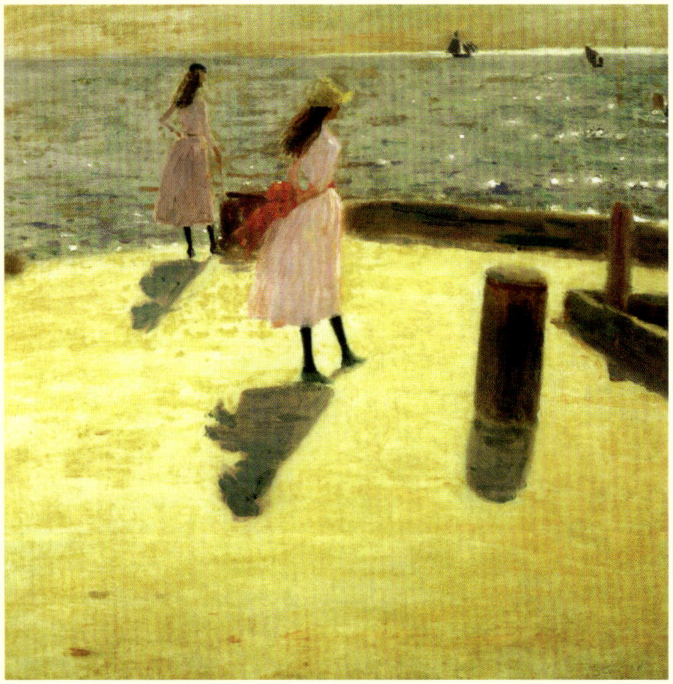

Paying lengthy and almost annual summer visits to Walberswick between 1884 and 1891, **Philip Wilson Steer** (1860-1942) created an English Impressionism on the Suffolk coast with dazzling images of sun-lit, dancer-like girls on and around the pier. Witness this lovely oil of 1887-8, *Two Girls on a Pierhead* (left).

Then the girls left, the painter's nerve failed and the old pier was ravaged and replaced. It was reduced to rotted, weeded posts when photographed (right) in 1969 by **John Gay** (1909-1999).

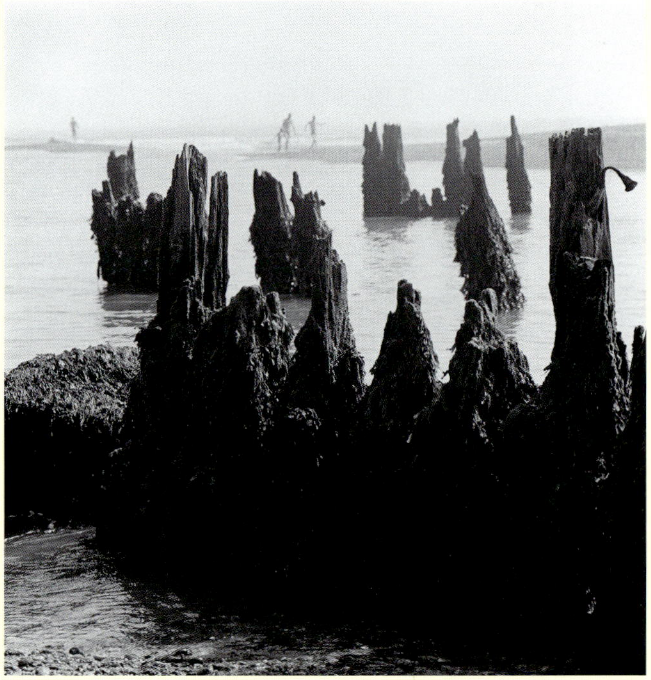

Francis Newbery and work on scores of ravishing floral watercolours for a book commission that never made it into print.

The two pioneers had persecution in common. Mackintosh was forced to leave Walberswick after nocturnal walks in the dunes

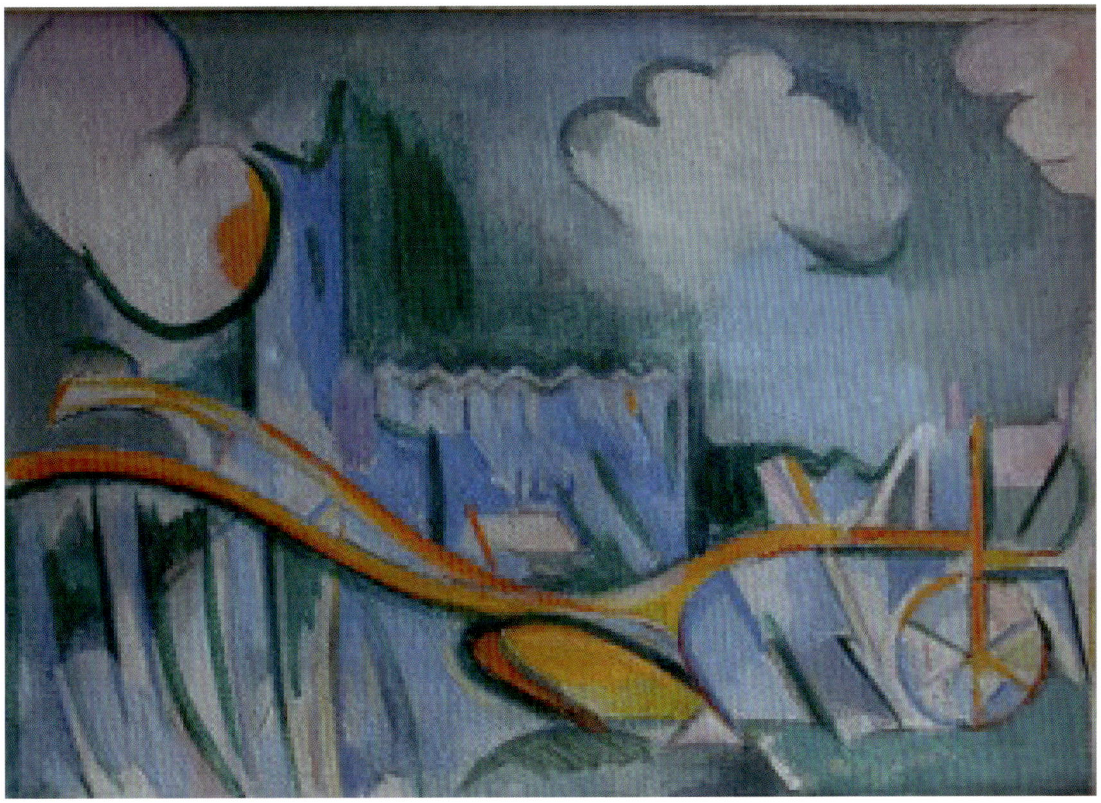

Blythburgh Church, Humphrey Jennings, c. 1946, oil on canvas

and disregard of blackout rules led to claims that he was signalling to the enemy – suspicions hardening when letters arrived from kindred Art Nouveau artists in the Vienna Secession. Jennings had similar trouble on a visit to London: smoking a cigarette on a balcony just before a Zeppelin hoved into view, he had to be rescued from an irate mob.

Later, the Jennings example of architectural salvage was echoed by Surrealist photographer Angus McBean (1904-1990) – who was to be jailed in World War Two for homosexuality – at Flemings Hall, Bedingfield near Eye.

Anyway, moving to London in 1919, and breaking ties with Walberswick from 1928, Frank Jennings had returned in the 1930s to revamp Valley Farm – where Philip Wilson Steer lodged 50 years earlier. In 1939 he had a 16th-century farmhouse moved from Brampton and re-erected near Saffron Walden, where he lived with friend and fellow Morris disciple Katherine Riley until his death.

Now he is best-known as the father of poet, painter, set designer and documentary film-maker **Humphrey Jennings** (1907-1950) who, in 1936, organised the Surrealist Exhibition in London with André Breton, Roland Penrose and Herbert Read, also displaying photos and paintings, and co-founded the Mass Observation project to record everyday life in Britain. A master of salvaged montage and collage, and of the surreal art of strange juxtaposition, he died in a fall in Greece when Margaret Mellis was moving from the South of France to Walberswick.

On their honeymoon in 1925 Stanley Spencer and Hilda Carline had searched the beach at Southwold for cornelians, which are far scarcer today, though not so rare as tiny nuggets of amber. But Margaret Mellis caught the last big wave of painted driftwood, before the marine harvest turned primarily to plastic, just as Frank Jennings had been in at the end of the mass destruction of our wooden heritage. Both breathed new life into an otherwise lost art.

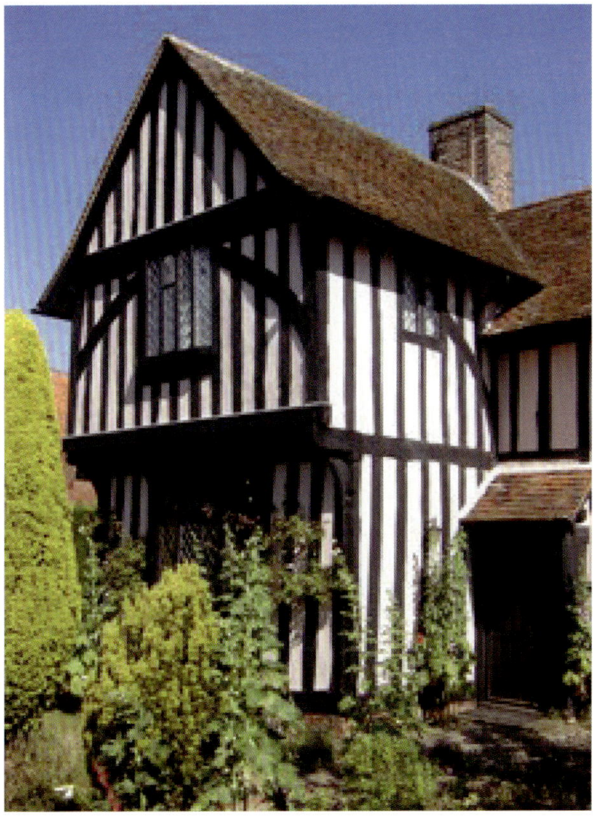

Mercer's Hall, Walberswick (right)

Walpole Church, 2005, oil on board

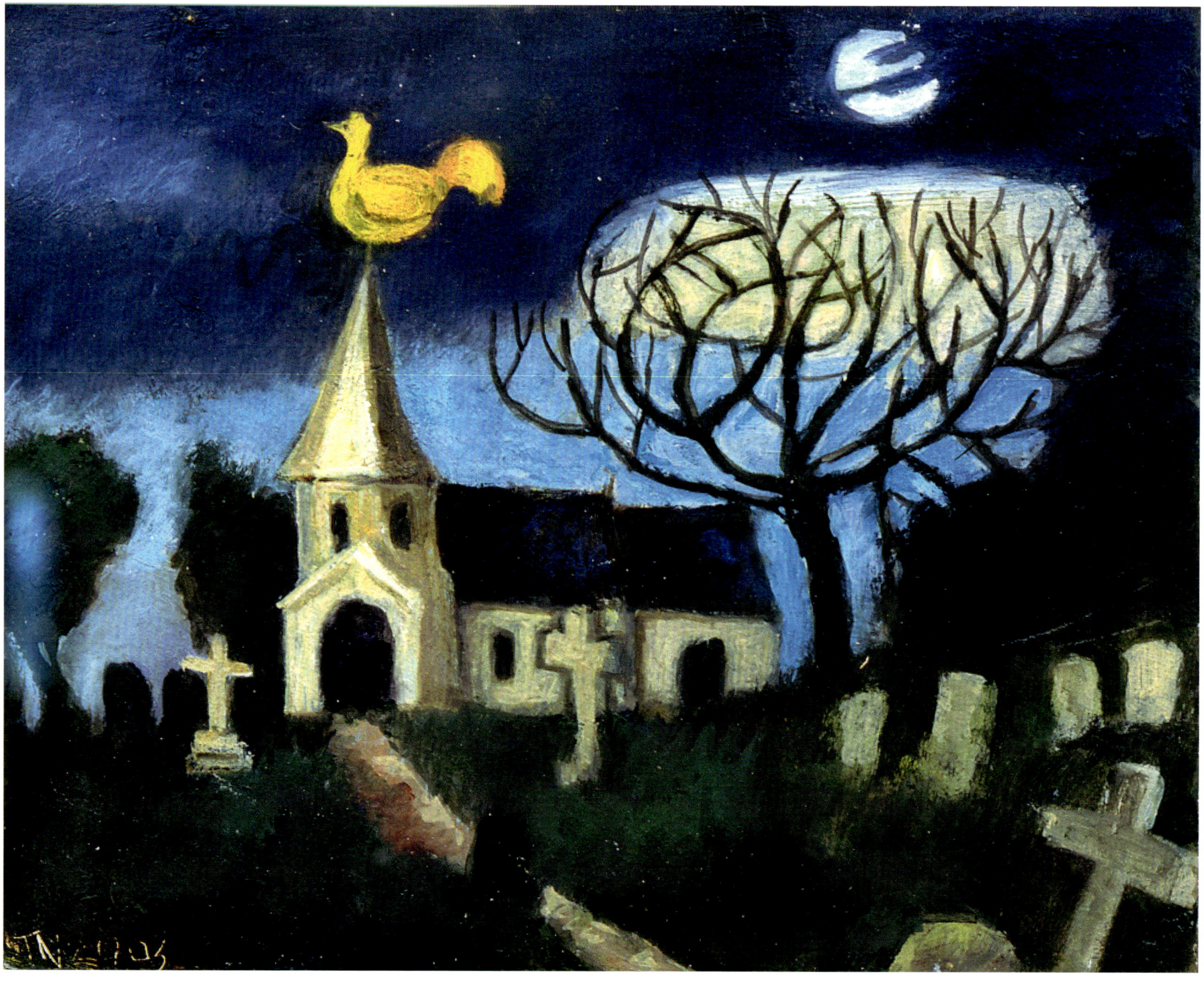

Eerie Encounters

Tessa Newcomb

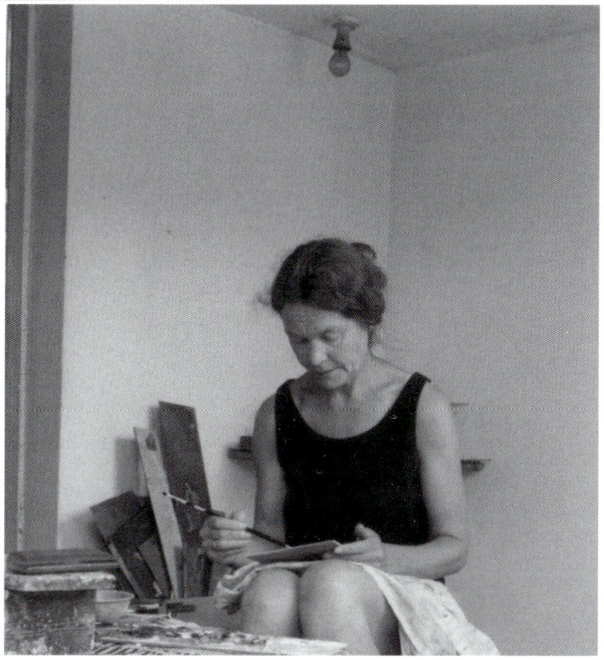

Tessa Newcomb in her studio

For Mary Newcomb's 2009 memorial show, at Norwich Castle, a talk was mooted on a topic of happy family outings and holidays as recalled in those pictures of rural bliss. That drew a wry laugh from her daughter **Tessa Newcomb**, a keen supporter of the exhibition but a stickler for the truth. 'There were some happy holidays with Mary – but mostly we were taken on research trips. We tagged along while she got notes and drawings for her paintings.'

Mary had started to paint around 1955 when Tessa, her younger daughter, was born, and she maintained that discipline and distance of dedication while her children were growing up and her husband, Godfrey, potted, pottered, farmed and played in jazz bands.

They lived in one of the wildest stretches of East Anglia, at Needham, near Harleston. Their farm was on the Norfolk bank of the Waveney – and the girls and their friends regularly swam in the river, crossing to Suffolk and back. But as a teenager, Tessa most liked to view the countryside from the back of a pony.

Nearby, at Syleham, she often visited another highly creative and largely self-sufficient household – that of Margaret Mellis and Francis Davison – and along with a love of a working landscape bordered by river and sea she acquired that sense of happiness-through-absorption which makes the lot of even the poorest artist priceless.

In what might seem to many the middle of nowhere she was thus close to two of the most remarkable women in the history of 20th-century British art. The link became closer still from 2003 when, with their own families all but grown, she and Margaret's artist son, Telfer Stokes, became partners.

Raised into the life of the artist before she had any clear idea of her own art, Tessa then

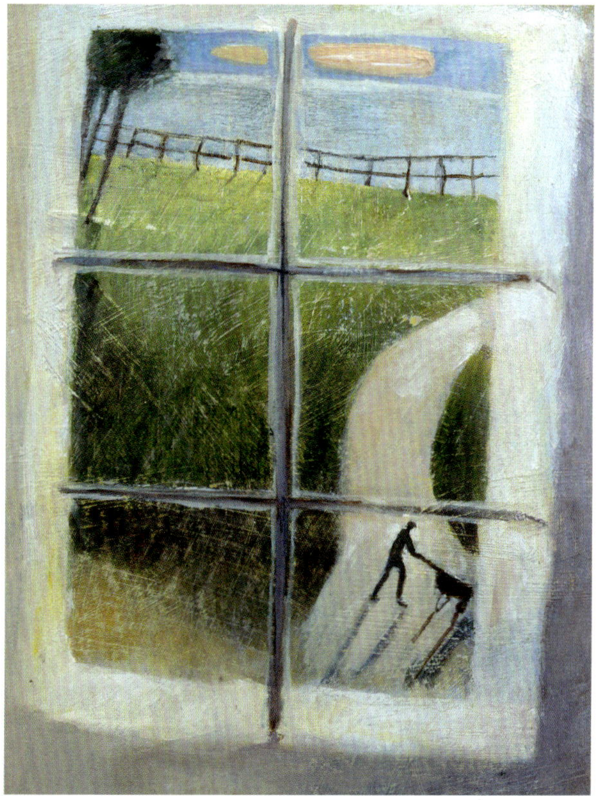

Wheeling Out of the Picture, 2005, oil on board (right)

studied painting and print-making in Norwich, Corsham and Wimbledon – with inspirational tutors such as Peter Kinley, Adrian Heath, Prunella Clough, Howard Hodgkin and William Scott. She also modelled for Euan Uglow and spent a bedazzled evening with Lucian Freud.

Since 1980 she has lived in the workaday village of Wenhaston near Halesworth and has toiled with a rare but inherited intensity on her painterly vision – an outlook which has grown ever more authentic after emerging from Mary's long shadow. Still, as she says: 'My paintings may look a bit like my mother's but then I do.' Now her work is so readily recognised, and so popular, that entire exhibitions can sell on opening days to other dealers.

Although Tessa's cottage is on the landward side of the A12 – and she takes working breaks from North Norfolk and London to France and Italy – she has really become the painter of the Suffolk Sandlings and especially of the least smart swathes of coastline (extending across harbours, boatyards and beaches, fields and gardens, pubs and cafés, churchyards, lanes and backstreets) between Kessingland and Bawdsey.

She is a painter of discomfort – quite literally so, since her 'studio' is a low, small, dark and cold backroom which seems all the starker and bleaker when she paints crouching through the night beneath a bare bulb. As a student in London she lived in an art dealer's garden shed and she has retained a warm regard for tarred huts collapsing on allotments or tilting in sand

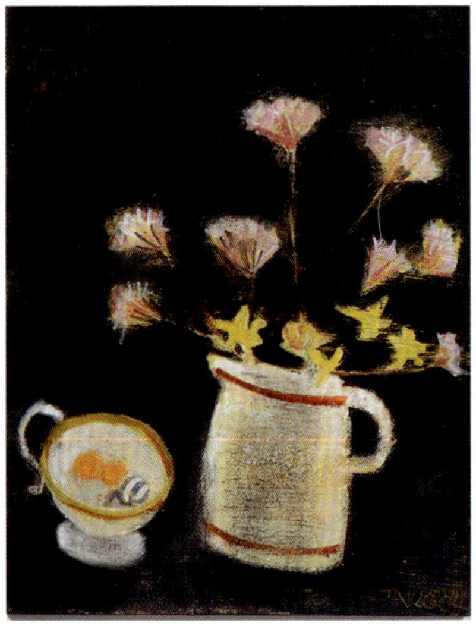

Spring Flowers Against Black, 2004, oil on board

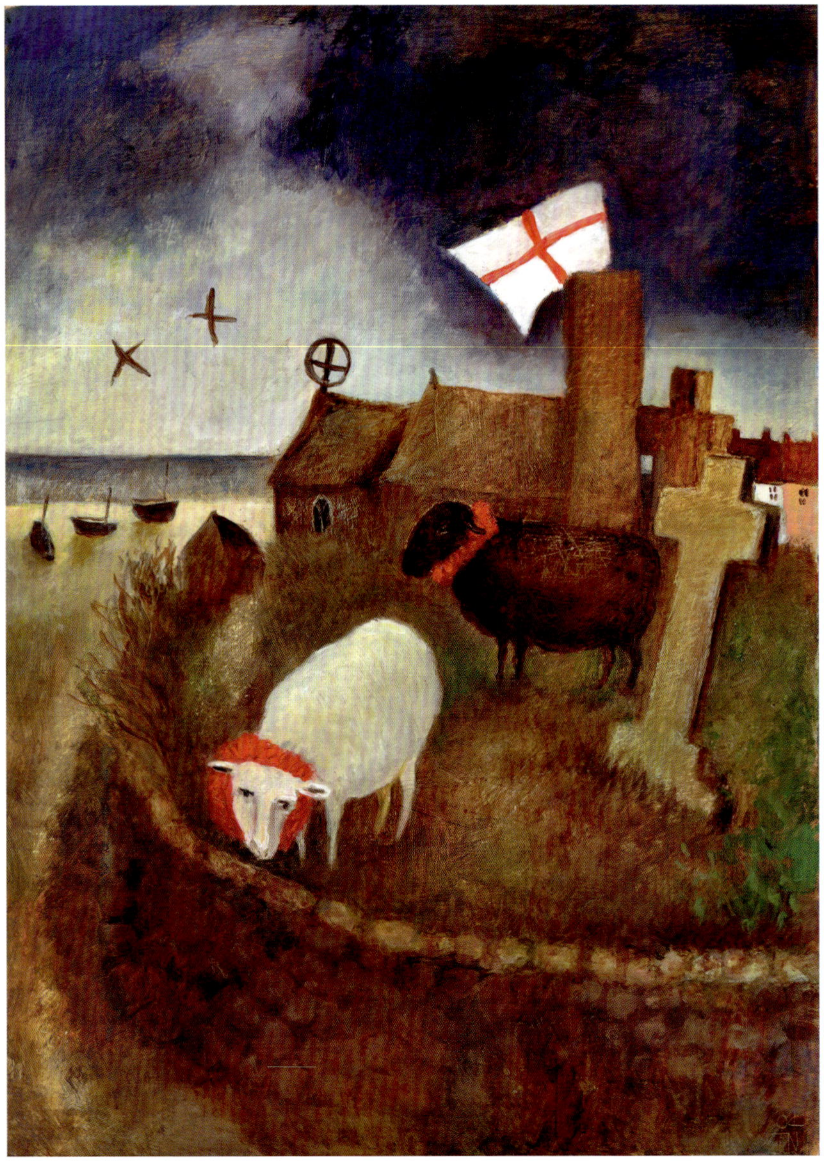

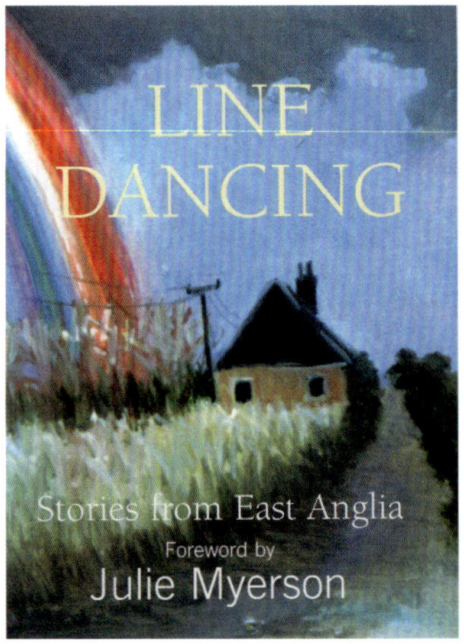

Never Ending Rainbow (detail), 2001, acrylic on board

Christmas Sheep, 2004, oil on board, cover for *Dead Men Talking* (2007)

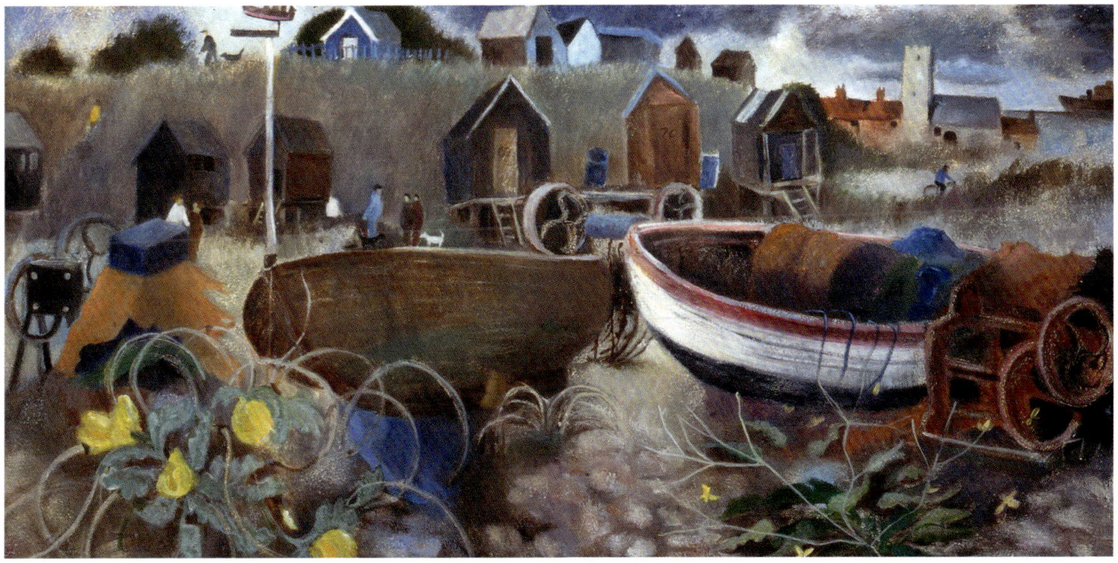

Foreshore with Fishing Vessels,
2001, acrylic on board

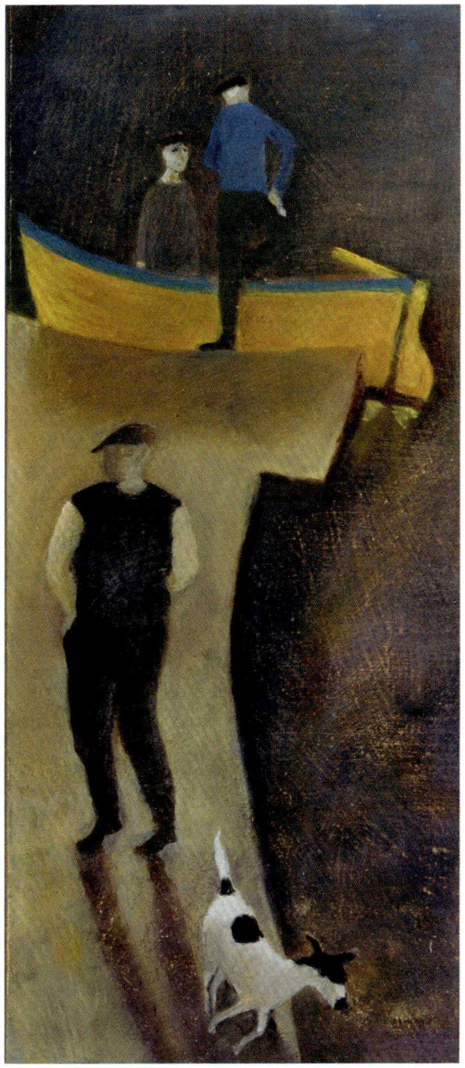

The Dog Got Off First,
2005, oil on board

dunes which seem a million miles from the prized and painted beaqch huts of Southwold (where she nevertheless often draws while Telfer works on his vegetable patch).

And work remains her mainspring. As she told biographer Philip Vann: 'My "boards" – sometimes they are paper or canvases – are pre-prepared with two coats of base colour then several washes of thin colour. These are allowed to dry. Then I go out to draw. Before I do I have an idea of what I'm going to do, and have a final look at the boards to see what colours will be in my mind.

'On returning I lay out drawings and boards, then paint very quickly, often several. Later when they are a bit dryer I have a second go at them which pulls them together.

'On less inspired days, I will use up paintings and frames, cut bits out of old paintings, paint bits out, bring bits up. Finish things.' If a picture comes back from a gallery unsold she is ready and very likely to paint over it. Would-be buyers had better be swift.

Whereas Mary worked with a slow, calm deliberation on a few pictures, Tessa works speedily on a lot – with a sense that she will explode if she doesn't. Her pictures spill beyond frames to cover mugs and jugs, tiles, trays, boxes, furniture and bits of driftwood. The atmosphere of spaces and silences she produces in her compositions derives from a maelstrom of compulsive creativity in cramped conditions.

If Mary Newcomb paintings are visual poems, those of Tessa Newcomb are more akin to short stories – with missing bits in the narrative providing the essential element of mystery which viewers are then invited to fill in via their own memories or imaginations.

The viewpoints of both Newcombs can be comic, but Tessa's work is by far the edgier, being the more sensuous and erotic and also the more sinister. In her hands a conversation takes on the image of a conspiracy; a man digging the garden seems to be burying a secret and a cyclist wheeling away from a harbour must surely have a saddlebag full of contraband. She is a brilliant portraitist of robbers' dogs.

For all that rather unkempt East Suffolk beauty she evokes so faithfully, here is a home-grown artist well aware that this is also the wild coastline of M R James and P D James. The ethereal merges into the eerie in a setting of marked separateness and strangeness dating back to ancient times. One Boxing Night, for instance, she painted the blacked-faced and ivy-wigged Molly Dancers at Middleton re-enacting the medieval hunting of a wren as the symbol of devilish darkness but stopping short of killing a tiny bird.

And she savours the surreal encounter. At Pakefield, one freezing mid-winter afternoon, she came upon a ram and ewe in the churchyard, still grazing but with their throats apparently cut. On closer inspection she found that the necks of the sheep had been hung with festive red wreaths – then she sped home to produce a haunting picture which in 2007 became the cover for *Dead Men Talking*, Volume III in the Black Dog Books trilogy of *Stories from East Anglia*.

Girl by the Sea, Margaret Green, c. 1958, oil on canvas

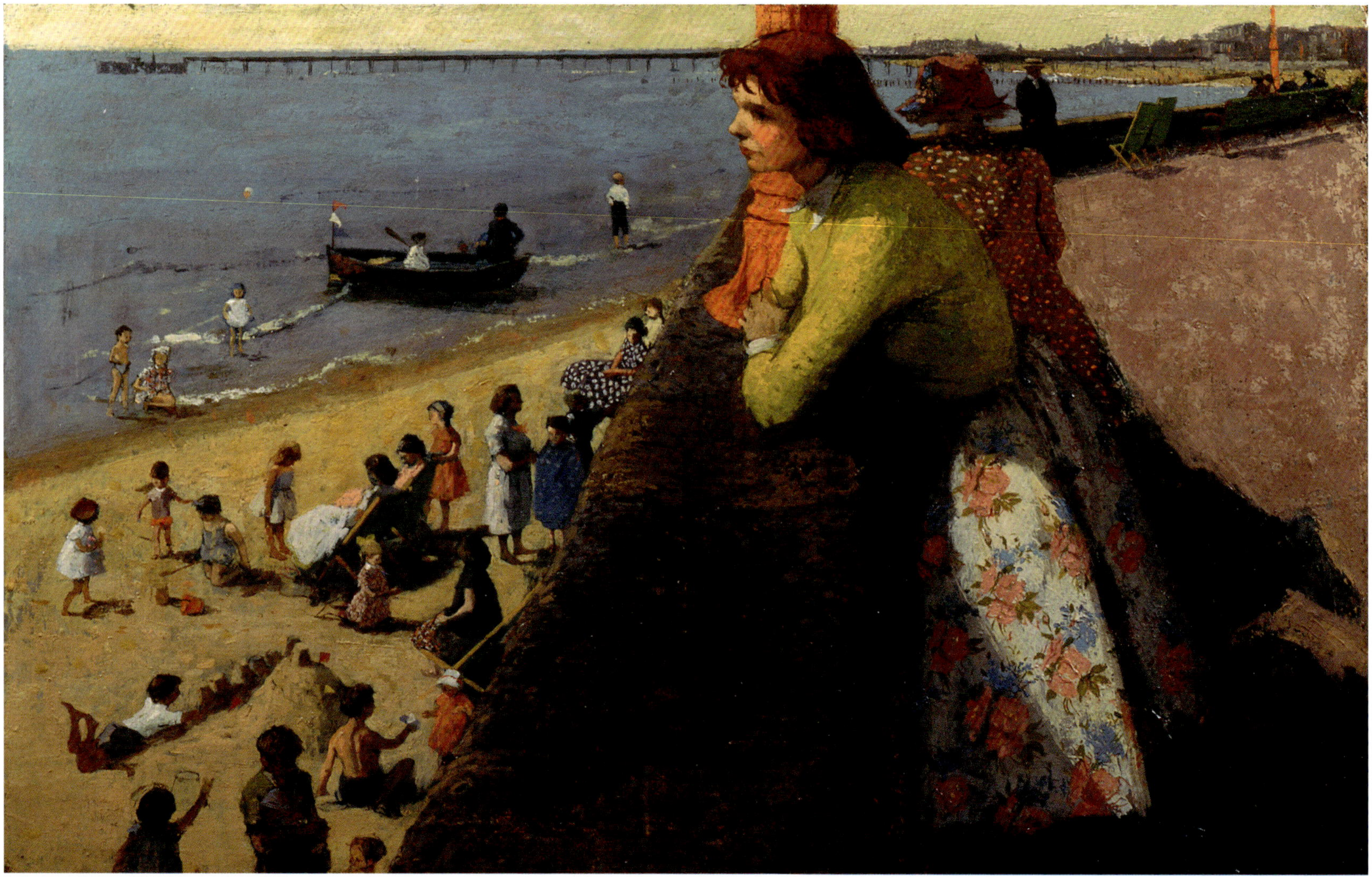

Partners in Paint

Margaret Green and Lionel Bulmer

Margaret Green and **Lionel Bulmer** were people and painters of singular convictions – but from their first meeting in 1944, until Lionel's last breath 48 years later, their lives simply merged. Friends called them MargaretandLionel. Theirs was one of the most remarkable partnerships in 20th-century British art.

With their diverse Northern and Southern backgrounds – Lionel, born 1919, the son of a London architect; Margaret, born 1925, the daughter of a West Hartlepool steel plant worker and art club secretary – they both had the luck and luxury of families in which creativity found free rein.

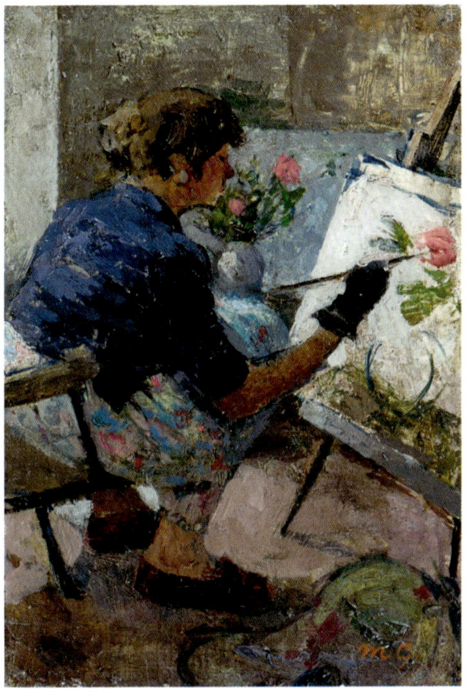

Self Portrait,
Margaret Green, oil on canvas

Carrying off hearts and prizes, the beautiful Margaret won a scholarship to the Royal Academy – then displaced by the Luftwaffe to the safety of the Lake District – where Lionel enrolled on being demobbed. By the time the RCA returned to South Kensington, they were joined at the hip. Their pattern of living simply but well, within a framework of mutual support and creative labour, was set when a £160 travelling scholarship allowed a year's tour of France and Ireland for two.

They shared Chelsea studios and taught at art schools in and around London, finding inspiration in streets, squares, parks and embankments, then returning to their private domain to work on their joint vision cheek by jowl.

Having already painted memorable images of blustery resorts on the County Durham coast, Margaret now led Lionel in a search for the sea. Weekend wanderings ended in the renting of a Spartan room above a Sussex boathouse – overlooking the Arun estuary at Littlehampton and inhabitable only in summer. So began the flow of sun-dazzled beach scenes by which these soul mates are best remembered.

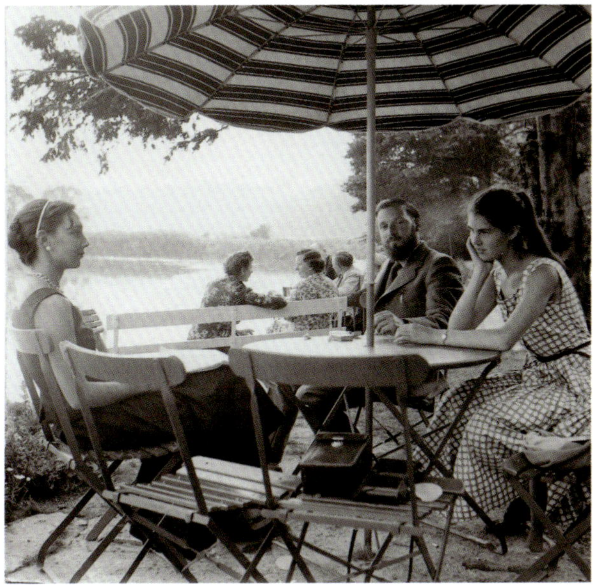

Margaret Green (left), Lionel Bulmer (centre), 1950s

Keeping a toe-hold in London, they then searched for a more permanent rural base. Consulting *Dalton's Weekly*, and fanning out in an arc from London, they motored in the old Bedford van serving as their mobile studio until finding something within their modest price range. Suffolk was suitably cheap in those days. In the late 1950s £850 bought a medieval hall house in an overgrown wilderness running down to the River Rat.

Rethatched, whitewashed and with a new light-filled studio, fruitful garden and junk-shop furniture, Lodge Cottage, in Buxhall Vale, near Stowmarket, became the ideal painters' retreat. Margaret painted corners of this domestic paradise – window sills, mantelpieces, table tops – in tiny panel pictures; Lionel produced larger studies setting the patterns of rugs or curtains against the prevailing white.

An impression of Margaret and Lionel uniting against a hostile world firmed in the fact that both held out resolutely for representational painting at a time of doctrinaire abstraction. The strength of Lionel's talent in particular lay in fine draughtsmanship which was increasingly dismissed in art schools and leading galleries. The couple were left increasingly reliant on regular acceptances at Royal Academy summer shows and, most of all, on New English Art Club exhibitions.

It was ironic that, having hit upon Suffolk almost by accident, they – along with their friends William Bowyer, Fred Dubery and Margaret Thomas – discovered the scenes inspiring the most ravishing and revolutionary French Impressionist-inspired paintings by NEAC pioneer Philip Wilson Steer. Soon their trusty van took them to Walberswick and Southwold, where over successive summers between 1960 and 1990 they were invariably installed beside the harbour or on the beach. Margaret chose a vantage point with her back to a breakwater or harbour wall, so that no onlooker could peer over her shoulder; Lionel built himself a barricade of windbreaks and deckchairs like a castle in the sand. Often, however, they were driven to brave public exposure by the desire to paint side by side as at home, hunching their shoulders and closing ranks against the world around them.

Always similar, Lionel and Margaret's pictures were becoming indistinguishable, even to themselves. They talked it over, deciding that one needed to change direction and that the one making the break should be Lionel. Transforming the way he constructed a picture, Lionel overhauled his use of colour by reworking the Pointillism of Seurat – possibly guided by Wilson Steer's *Knucklebones*, on view in Ipswich's Christchurch Mansion. Lionel's and Margaret's paintings had tended to place gem-like patches in muted and monochrome settings. Now the jewel effect was expanded to cover the entire picture surface. It was a brilliant technique for evoking kaleidoscopic revels (with striped canvas, bright towels, bathing costumes, parasols, kites) beside a sun-dazzled sea. It was also extremely brave.

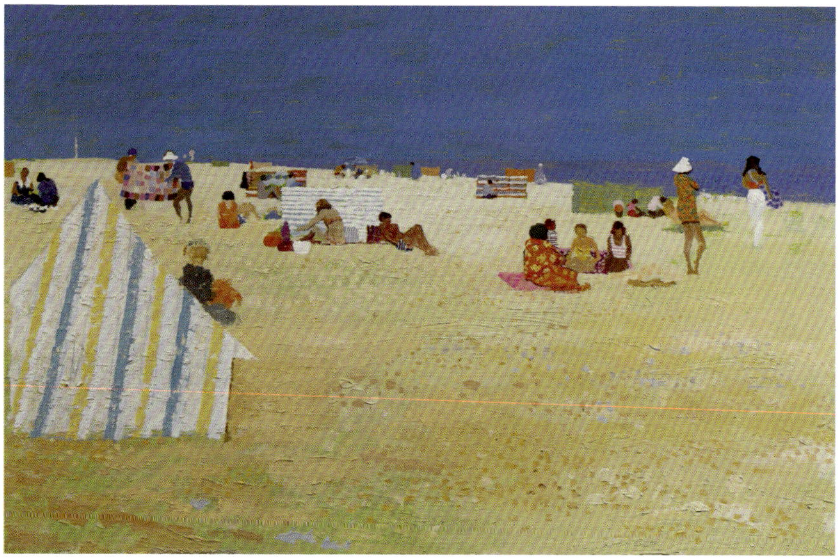

Summer Days on the Beach,
Lionel Bulmer, oil on canvas

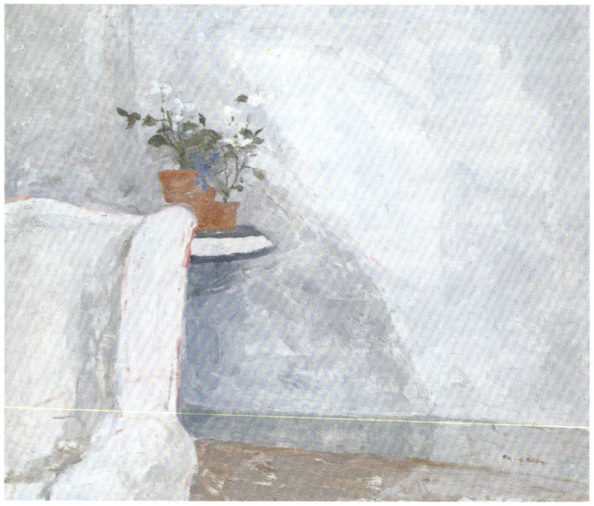

Light Interior,
Margaret Green,
oil on canvas (left)

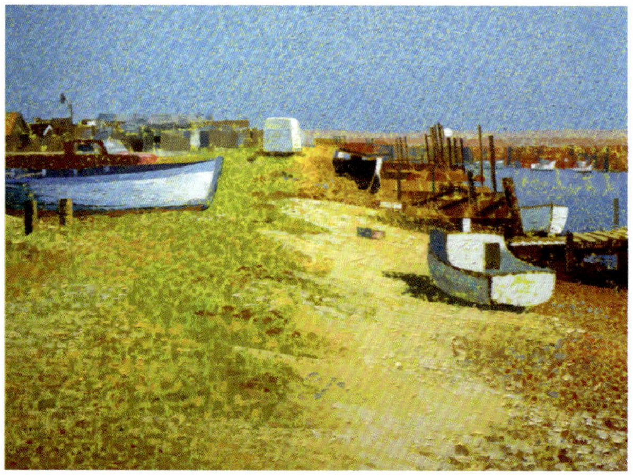

Fishing Boats on Southwold Quay,
Lionel Bulmer, oil on canvas

But then courage was a hallmark of this couple. Although she might appear to be made of glass, Margaret Green had a steel core tested to the hilt when she defeated cancer. Margaret and Lionel enjoyed an Indian summer before

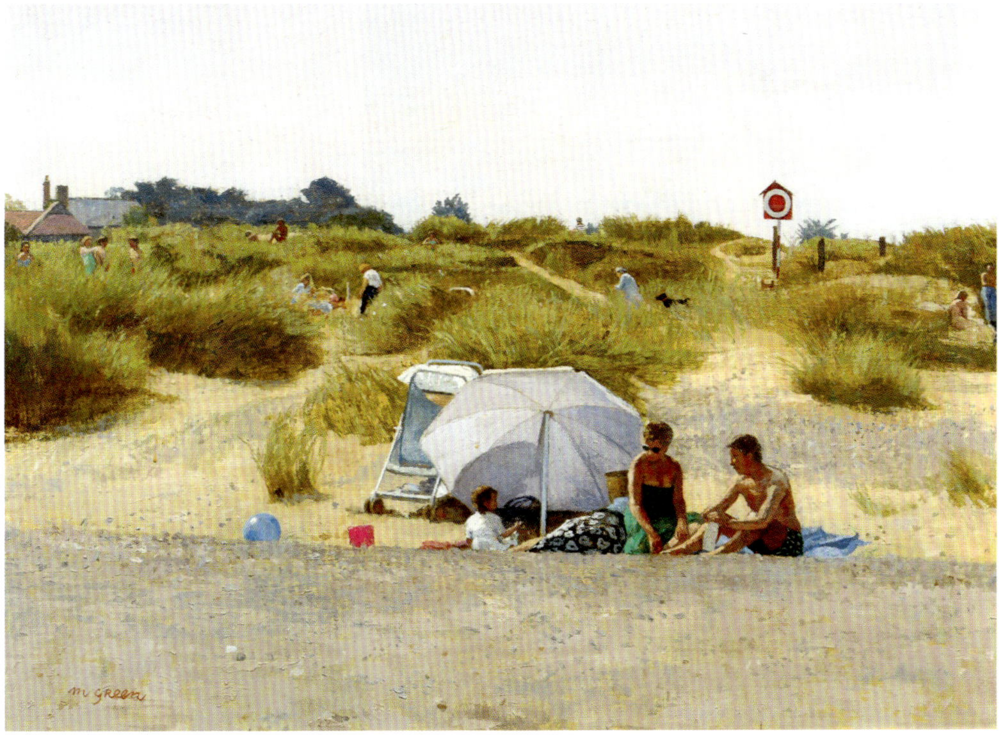

Summer, Walberswick Dunes,
Margaret Green, oil on canvas

the disease struck the second partner, this time advancing remorselessly. When Lionel could no longer paint he continued to draw, and when it became clear that his illness was terminal this most wedded of couples were married, on 2 October 1991, in the ancient house in Stowmarket where John Milton, poet of *Paradise Lost*, had stayed.

Lionel Bulmer died the following February. At the funeral Margaret was asked whether she would continue painting. 'Of course,' she replied. 'How else would I live?' But although she lived for another 11 years she never completed another picture. Artist Diana Armfield said: 'Margaret refused all consolation. I used to see her at the Royal Academy or at New English Art Club exhibitions, in which she would show old pictures. She was like a ghost wafting through the rooms. When I asked how she was coping, she answered, "I'm not coping at all." There could be no compromise, you see. Love was an absolute and so was its loss.'

In an address written for Margaret Green's funeral, in November 2003, her friend Ann Baer – whose husband, Bernhard, founded the Ganymed Press – looked back from the sad ending to a triumphant partnership: 'In their talk I have heard more "we" and less "I" than in any other couple I have known.' The same sentiment in a letter to Margaret a decade earlier had drawn the reply: 'I am not at all offended that you used to regard Lionel and I as one person. We did ourselves. On occasions in talking to friends and recounting something said or done, I frequently couldn't remember whether I said/did it or he.'

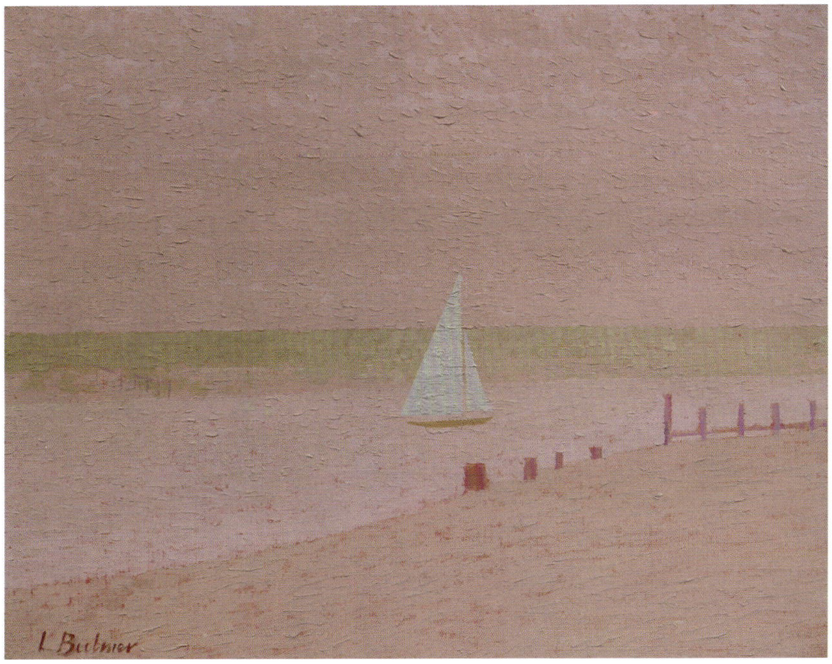

Heading Home, Summer Evening,
Lionel Bulmer, oil on canvas

Coney Barrow – Sizewell, 1935, oil on canvas

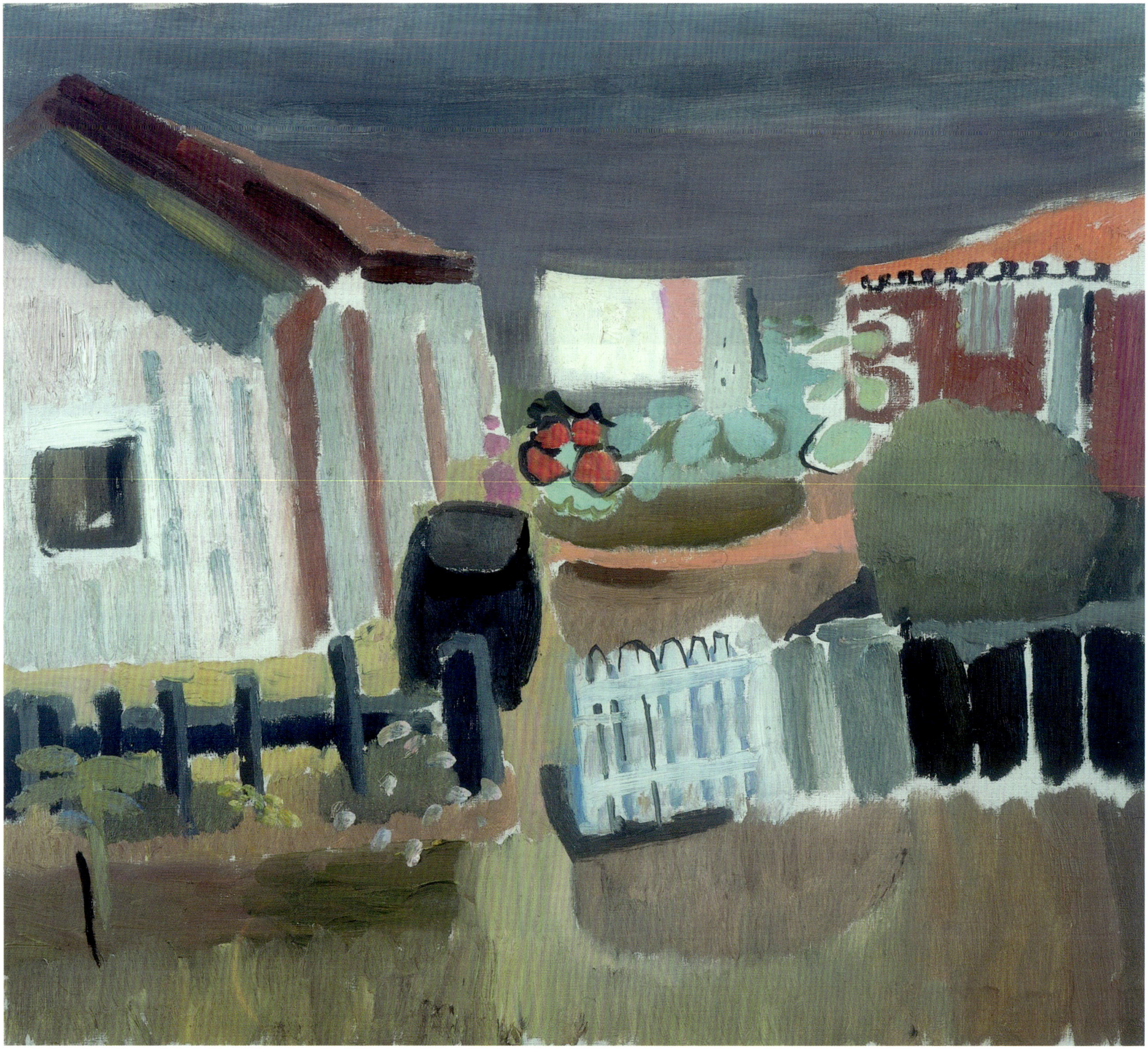

Wenhaston Doom

Stanley Spencer and the *Resurrection*

How fortunate that, in the driest part of the country, it rained heavily one night in 1892 – just after a late Victorian clear-out in Wenhaston church near Halesworth, and just before a churchyard bonfire.

Renovation of the sort William Morris hated – and which he opposed, largely successfully, in nearby Blythburgh in one of his last campaigns – had included a new chancel arch. Old whitened wooden panels were stripped out and thrown on the pending pyre.

Then came the overnight deluge and next morning, through rivulets of dissolving whitewash, a visitation of the Virgin Mary was noted. Other painted figures – heavenly, satanic and human – were emerging through the murk. It was indeed a miracle that, though mutilated and then obscured for centuries, the Wenhaston Doom's late 15th-century idea of Judgement Day (Doomsday) had survived.

Art historians were summoned, and the relic from a humble church – where antiquarian David Elisha Davy found 'Nil memorabile' in 1808 – was taken to London's Burlington House for a Society of Antiquaries display generating 'much excitement'.

The restored treasure still excites visitors in its church setting today – though not, alas, in the now-narrowed original overhead position where it and its ilk cowed medieval congregations into lowly submission in hope of heavenly elevation and fear of falling. The message and workmanship may be crude but as a picture of past faith the Doom is hugely illuminating.

An immense cross-shaped central shadow punctured with nail holes is flanked by blank columns where a carved rood and figures of the Virgin and John the Evangelist were torn out and destroyed during 1540s Protestant iconoclasm under Edward VI. The boards and whitewash then covering the painted scene, and an added biblical text similar to that still visible on the whitened rood screen at Norfolk's Binham Priory, proved a protector when Puritan vandals called a century later.

Red-robed Christ, the Divine Judge, sits top-left on a rainbow throne, with the Virgin and John the Baptist kneeling top-right. Below, a richly-attired St Peter holds the key to a castellated heavenly city – a papal tiara exuding maximum glory for a church dedicated in his honour.

The souls being judged are naked to show human equality in the eyes of God, but it just so happens that the four naturists poised for salvation wear the headgear of king, queen, bishop and cardinal.

Wenhaston began collecting for a supporting rood beam in the 1480s, with the resulting

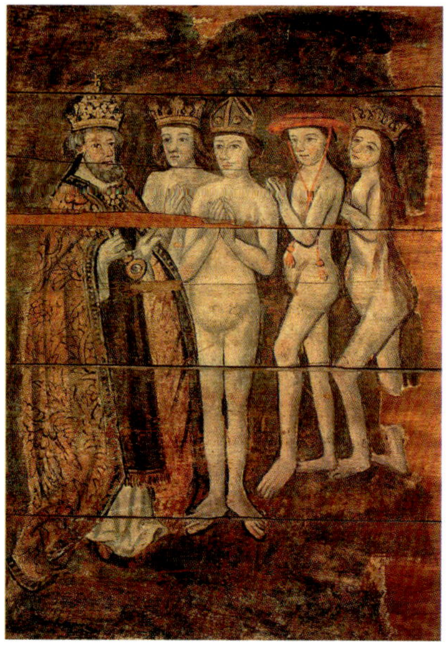

St Peter on Judgement Day receiving souls into heaven (detail)

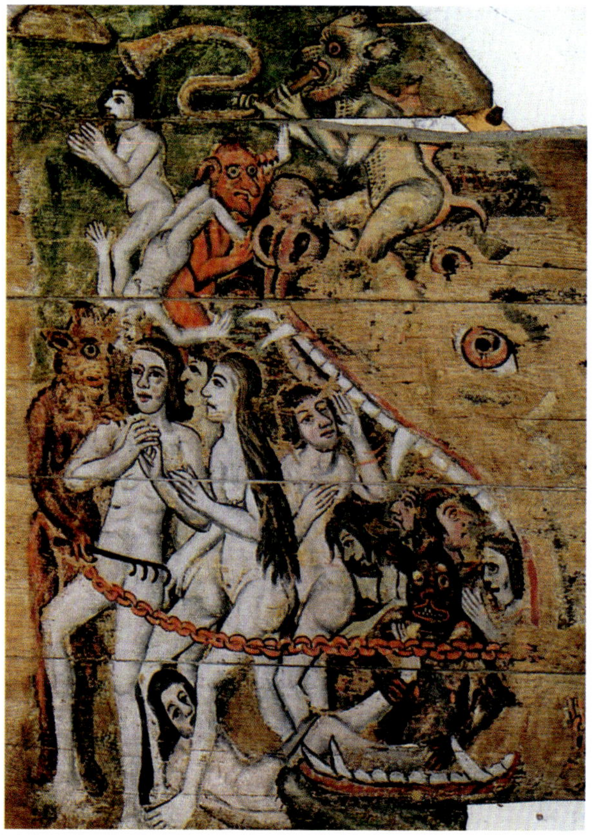

The damned descend into the jaws of hell (detail)

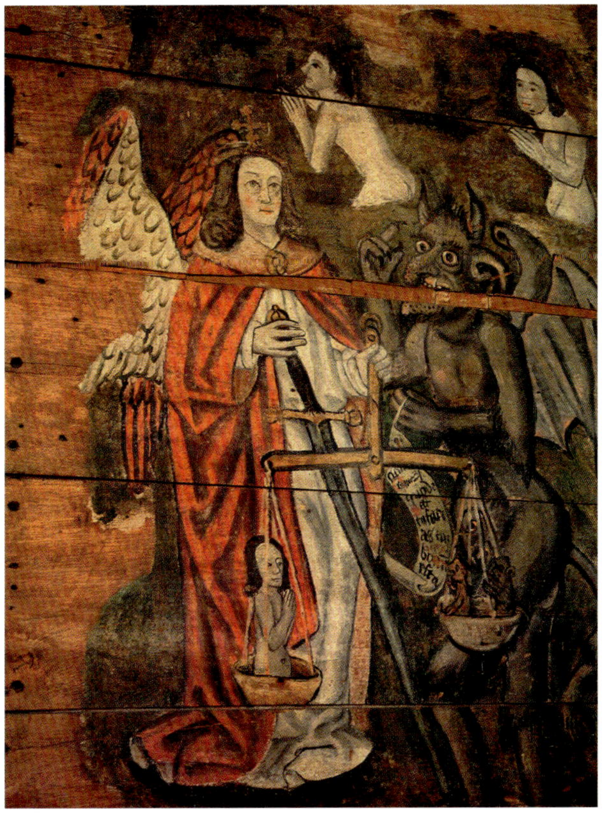

St Michael weighing souls (detail)

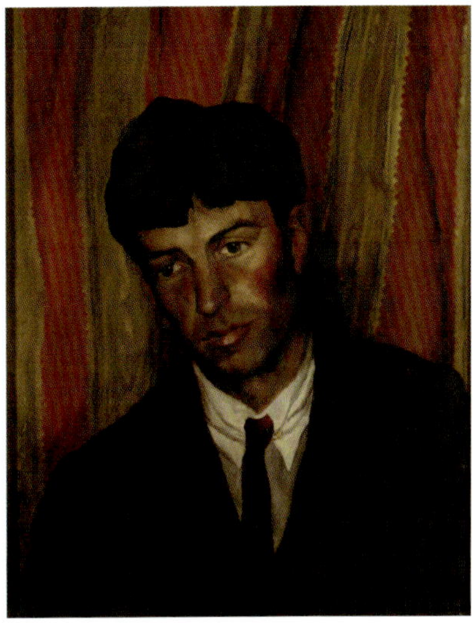

Stanley Spencer, Hilda Carline, 1923, oil on canvas

scene likely to have been painted either by a journeyman artist or a monk at Blythburgh Priory soon afterwards. The message of faith in the status quo was very timely given the new Tudor era – and the fact that the 1486 marriage of Elizabeth of York to Lancastrian Henry VII, five months after the Battle of Bosworth, had just confirmed the end of the Wars of the Roses.

To the right St Michael hovers on angel wings while wielding the sword and scales of justice. In the non-balancing dishes, one good soul outweighs two bad imps. The saint is too busy to notice a goading Satan – a bat-winged beast with a second face in his stomach to denote base appetite.

Above, five risen corpses – four naked and one shrouded after a recent funeral, and all around 33 (the age of Christ at his crucifixion) – are making their penitent way towards judgement.

But the main drama of the piece is in the left-most section, where poor souls are being pulled and prodded towards the sharp-toothed jaws of a hellish fish as a ghoul sounds a trumpet. For light relief, one doomed wretch thumbs his nose at his fate.

The Doom transcends the centuries. In the 1920s it was surely spied by painter **Stanley Spencer** (1891-1959), wooing and then marrying Hilda Carline in nearby Wangford, where she had worked as a land girl during World War One. For Stan, separated from Hilda by his infidelity and her mental collapse, incarceration and early death, this corner of coastal Suffolk would remain a lost heaven.

For all the beloved Thames Valley topography of his native Cookham, so often the backdrop for his scenes of paradise, he wrote that the figures in his great *Resurrection* painting now in the Tate echoed his memories of his and Hilda's feelings as they left the 1925 Wangford ('everywhere was this new place of our love').

Such a hopeful picture or rebirth has more than a faint hint of Wenhaston. Sadly, all the trauma that followed is in there also.

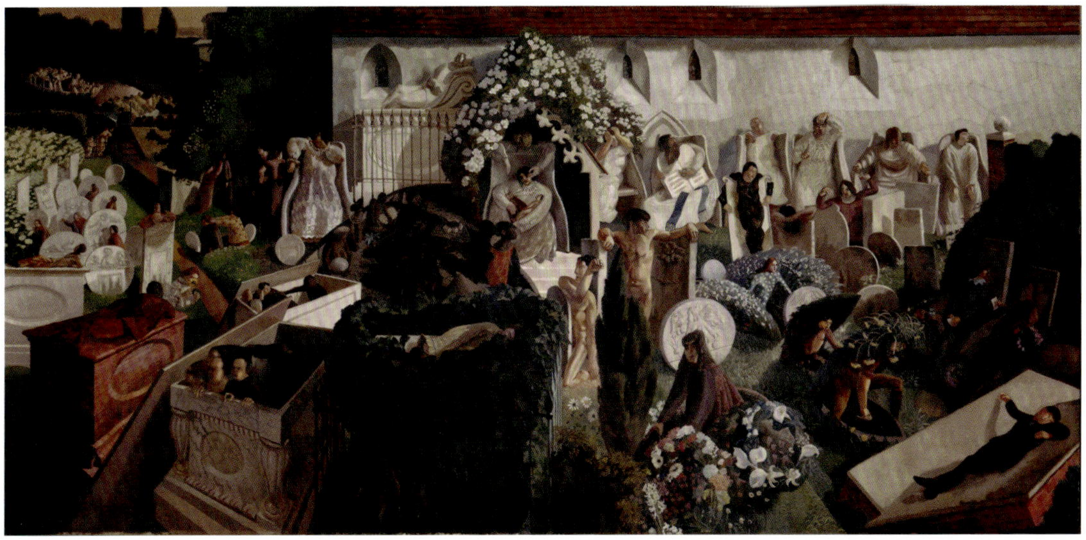

The Resurrection: Cookham
Stanley Spencer, 1923-6, oil on canvas, Tate Britain

Coney Barrow – Sizewell, 1935, oil on canvas

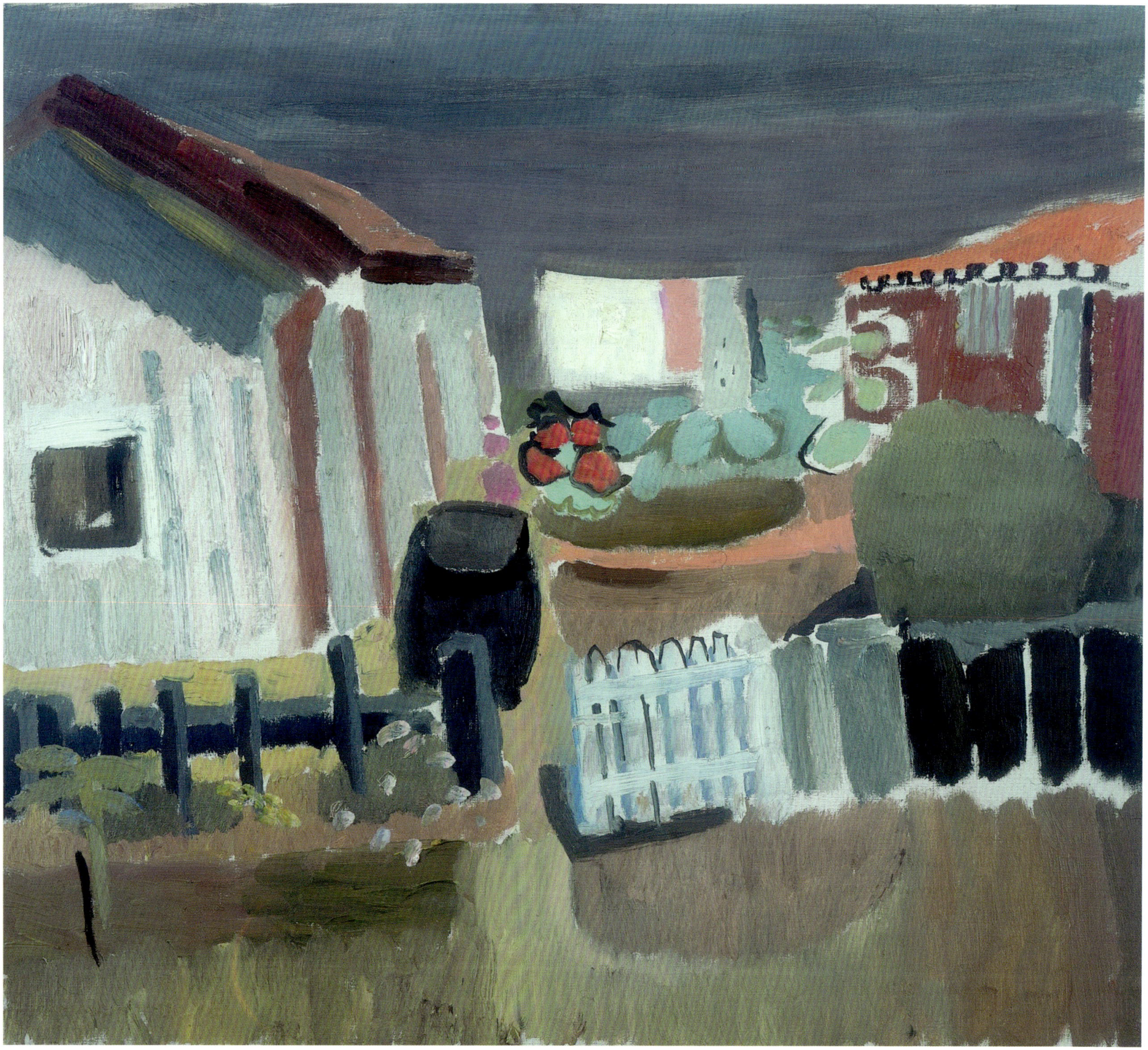

Sizewell Summers

Ivon Hitchens and the Pipers

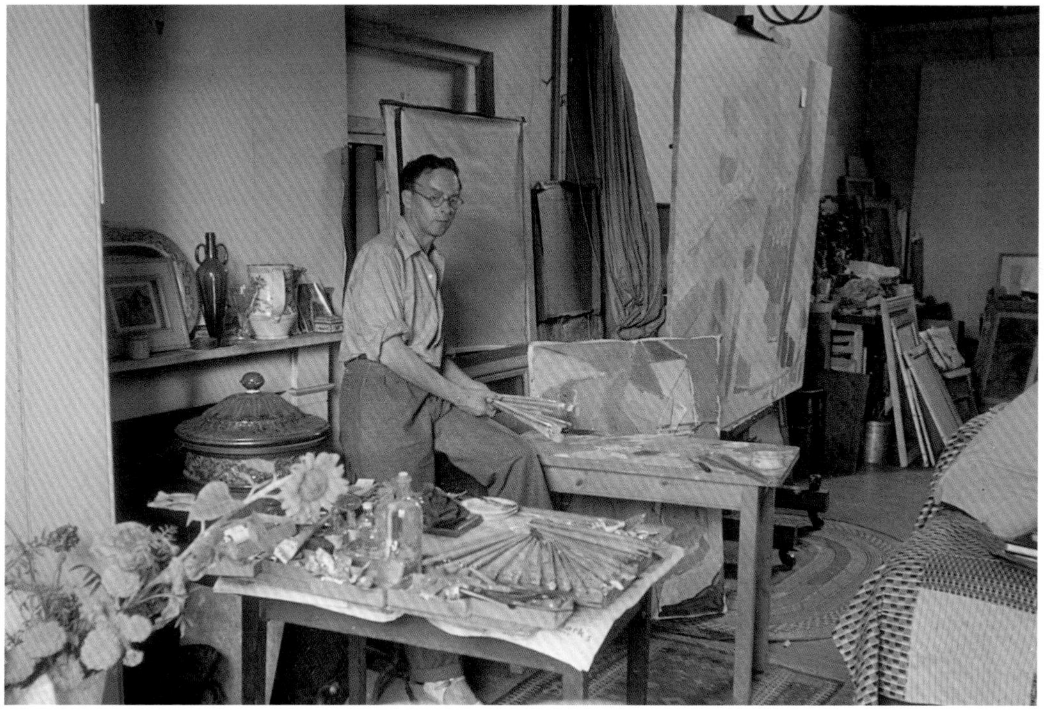

Ivon Hitchens in his studio, 1933

Today paired pylons, marching like giant metallic skeletons across the countryside, announce the presence of an alien intruder at the heart of the Suffolk Heritage Coast. Since 1966, an eroding shore just below the drowned medieval city of Dunwich has held an evolving nuclear power station – Sizewell A-C.

This modern energy producer so dominates the place that it is hard to conceive of a pre-war time when an outpost of the Ogilvie estate (stretching through Thorpeness to Aldeburgh) held only sheds, cottages and fishing boats drawn up on the shingle.

Imagine a tin-roofed shack called Coney Barrow, with a sand garden around which a wooden palisade proves no defence against an army of dune-occupying rabbits. This is a haven for Richard Perry Bedford, Keeper of Sculpture at the Victoria & Albert Museum (who will ultimately retire to West Mersea) and for his artist friends. And since the owner is for a time a sculptor-member of the pioneering Seven and Five society, those (mostly) friendly lodgers will include some of the leading avant-garde talents of the 1930s – and especially painter Ivon Hitchens, who alone will stay with the fractious and shifting Seven and Five from first show to finish.

London-born **Ivon Hitchens** (1893-1979) will be based in the capital until his Hampstead studio is bombed in 1940. By the time of his Sizewell visits, over four successive summers from 1933, this professional artist's son is in the thick of modernist circles but somehow set apart, anxious to develop his very personal response to Cézanne, Braque and Matisse in a restless, roving quest to celebrate the quiet green English scene.

In that famous photo of the pioneering artists' Happisburgh holiday of 1931 (see page

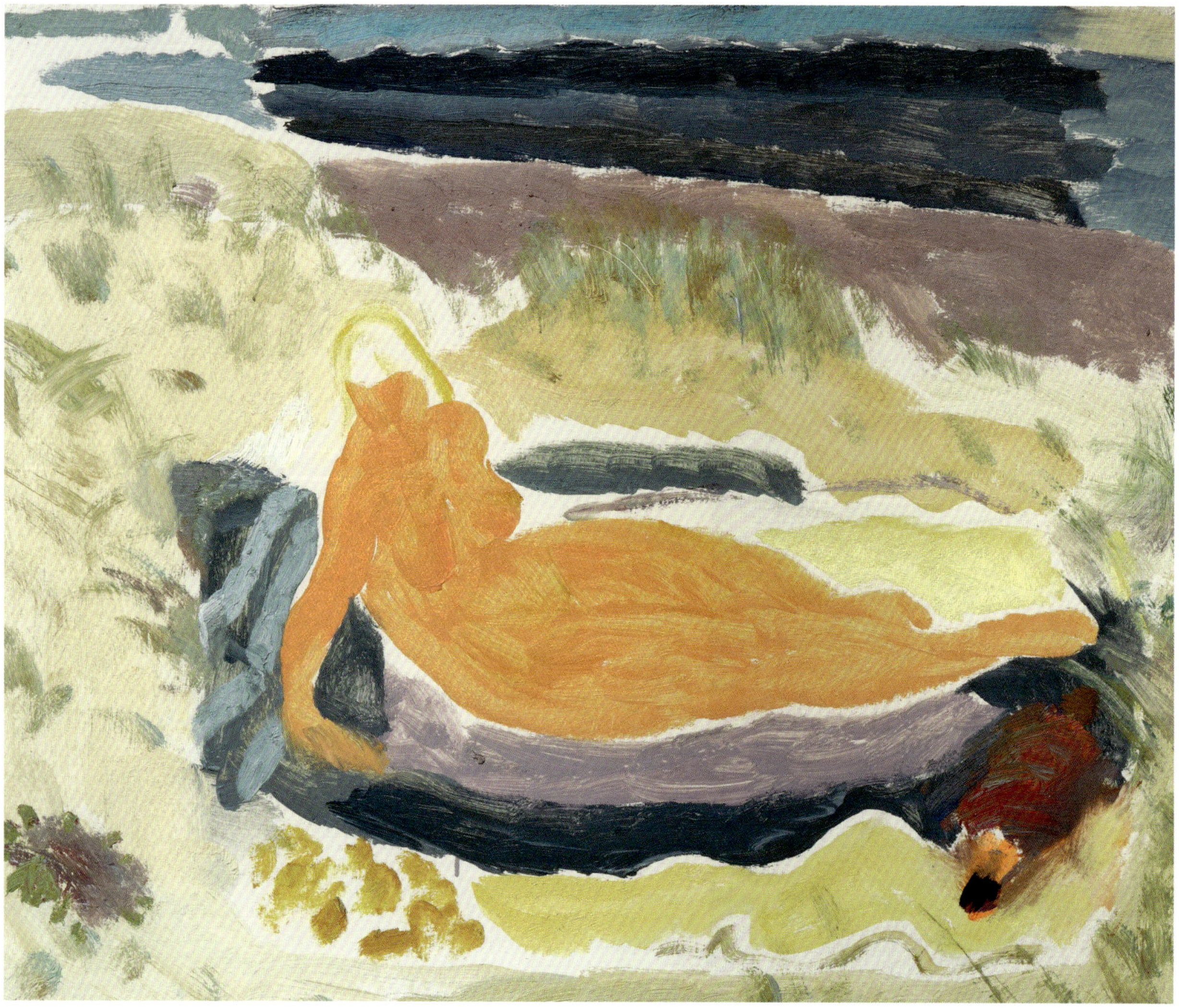

Sunbathing in the Dunes,
c. 1934, oil on canvas

35) he looks edged-out, buttoned-up and apparently askance at Ben Nicholson, Barbara Hepworth and Henry Moore. When the party partly reassembles, at Sizewell in 1934, he is glimpsed as being similarly at odds with his less inhibited allies, who readily discard conventions – clothes included – for a game of seaside cricket.

As Peter Khoroche, the Suffolk-based Hitchens biographer, has recorded: 'Henry Moore would spend each day drawing incessantly – stones, pebbles, rocks, bones, driftwood – and managed to get through reams of paper, tossing each sheet aside as he finished one drawing and began on another. The other members of the party would scrunch these up into balls and then bat them out to sea, whereupon Hitchens would, half-seriously, reprove them, prophesying that one day those sketches would be of great value. Nevertheless there were enough sketches to make quite a solid bat as well as innumerable balls; the game went on, and Ivon was told not to be such a fusspot.'

But the recent discovery of a trove of Hitchens' Suffolk oils, rolled up in a chest and stored away for almost 70 years, gives us a very different picture. It shows the artist, while also looking back to the landscape (garden, harvested field, wood, riverside willow), revelling in sea, sand, sun and back-to-nature nudity – as he strips each painting to elemental essences and his own emergent style.

Two of these brazen images date from around 1934, when Hitchens also stayed with the artists Ida and Blair Hughes-Stanton in their Stour Valley cottage at Higham. The extrovert Ida had posed for one study beside the River Brett, reclining on elbows and stomach in a red swimsuit. Peter Khoroche reports: 'Time passed. Tree shadows lengthened across the

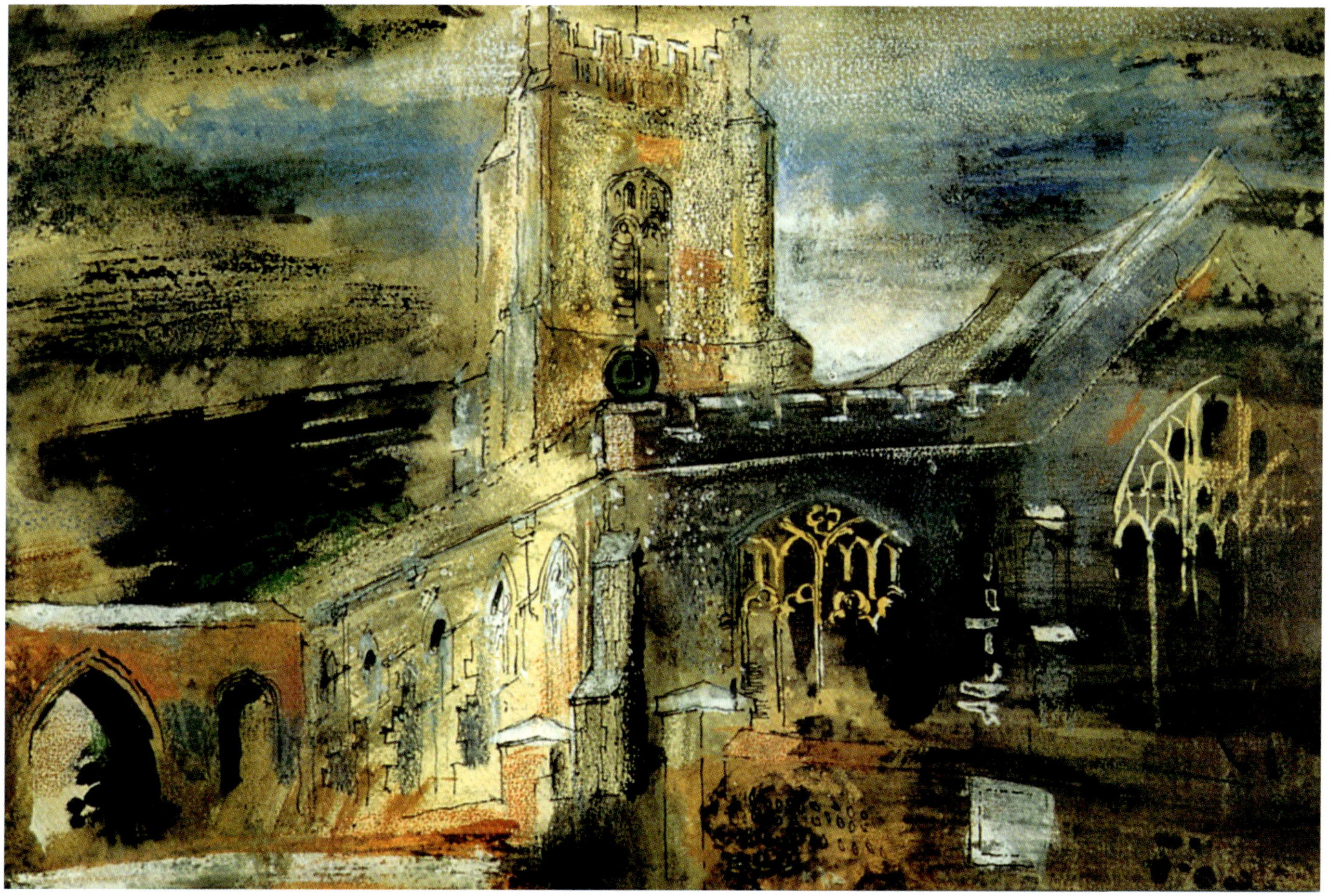

Aldeburgh Church, John Piper, watercolour

Punting, Suffolk, Ivon Hitchens, 1938, oil on canvas

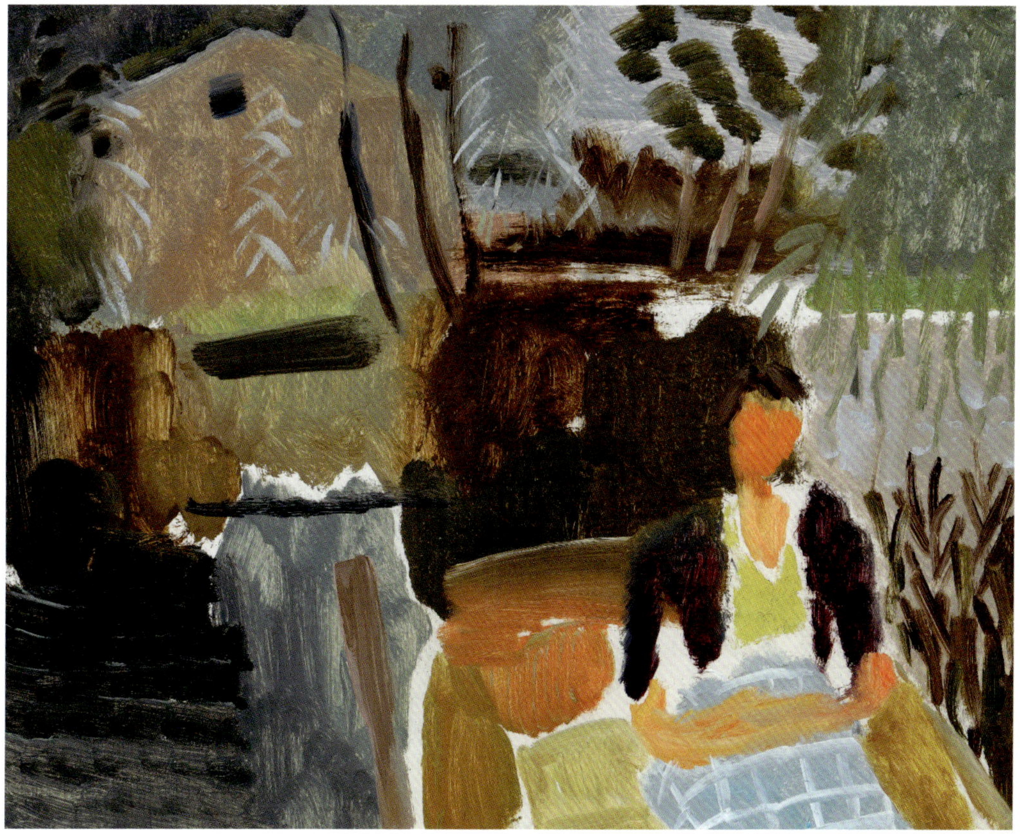

field. At last it was finished. With sore elbows and aching back the model eagerly asked to see the result. It was a large painting of trees with three small blobs of paint beneath them – two brown and one red. When she remonstrated gently, "Really, Ivon!", he replied: "Oh, but without you there could have been no picture".'

But the Sizewell pictures are more explicit and intimate and completely celebratory. They also accord with the first meeting of a key creative partnership, thanks to Hitchens, that June. He invited for the weekend a sympathetic *New Statesman* art critic, who had failed in the family law firm just as his marriage was now foundering. This was **John Piper** (1903-1992), really an aspiring painter.

Also on the guest list was Myfanwy Evans, acutely intelligent daughter of a London chemist. A Hitchens model in the capital and an avid *New Statesman* reader, she had just thrown in a job with the Times Book Club. When she caught the train to Saxmundham as directed, and then changed to the branch line for Leiston, she was amazed to be met by an admired critic – and at once the future lit up.

As Myfanwy recalled: 'The summer night was warm and the sea phosphorescent. We bathed before going to the cottage and dried ourselves by running along the strip of sand between the shingle and the shining water.'

They provoked umbrage by arriving late and then being absorbed in each other's company – John saying later that they 'spoilt the weekend and came home early'. Frances Spalding, their biographer, adds: 'But in years to come two local residents, Benjamin Britten and Peter Pears, would celebrate the meeting of John and Myfanwy by metaphorically raising their hats every time they drove over Sizewell level crossing.'

Their fertile, feisty and even fiery union lasted until John's death, after many whirlwind decades of creative work, in 1992. (For a special birthday tribute, Myfanwy wrote: 'I have lived with John for well over half his 80 years and I have enjoyed every other minute of it.')

A few years after Sizewell John Piper abandoned abstraction to record countless architectural treasures aglitter in light and landscape and at risk from bombers or bulldozers. He paid tribute to scores of East Anglian churches, stately homes and Norwich marketplace – also designing a marvellous 1979 stained-glass memorial window in Aldeburgh church for Benjamin Britten, having provided sets for six of his operas and both sets and costumes for two more. For three of those operas – *Owen Wingrave, Death in Venice* and, best of all, *The Turn of the Screw*, based on the

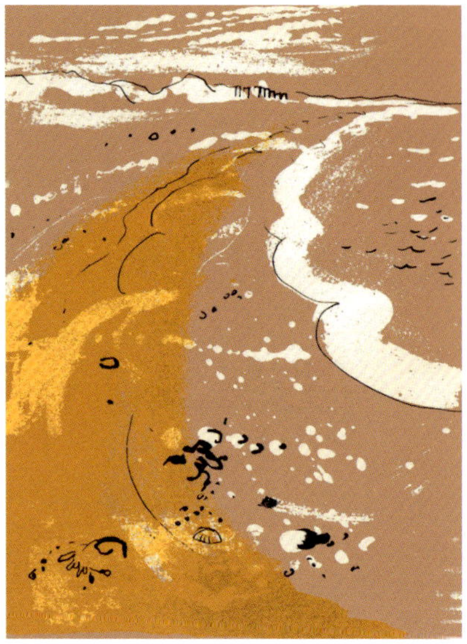

1954 Aldeburgh Festival Calendar, *July*, John Piper

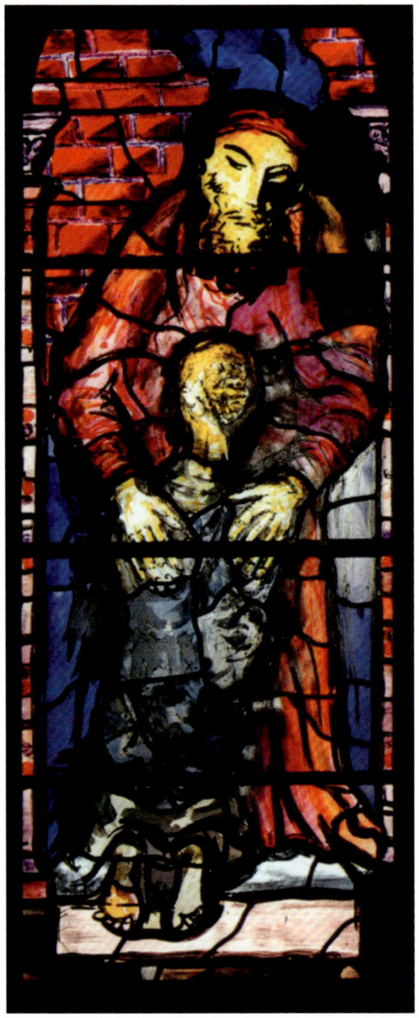

The Prodigal Son

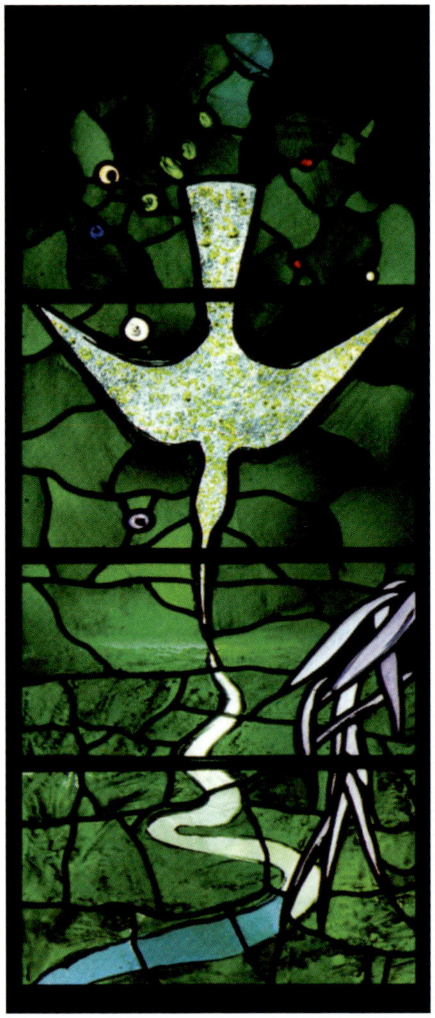

Curlew River

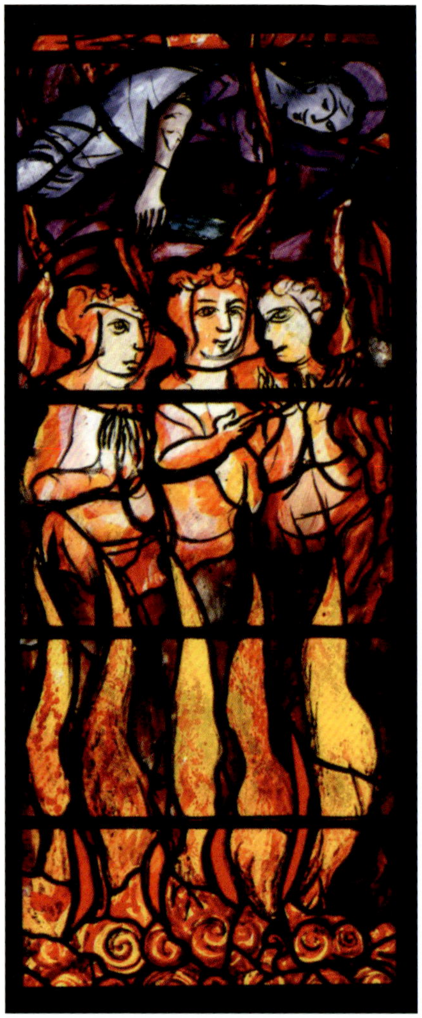

The Burning Fiery Furnace

Benjamin Britten memorial window designed by John Piper, glass by Patrick Reyntiens

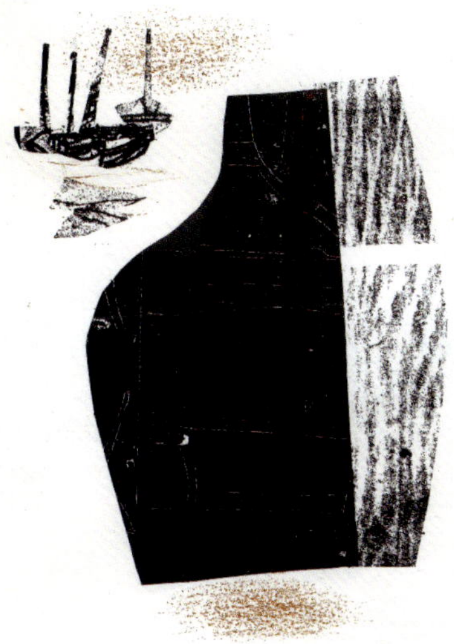

1954 Aldeburgh Festival Calendar, *February*, Prunella Clough

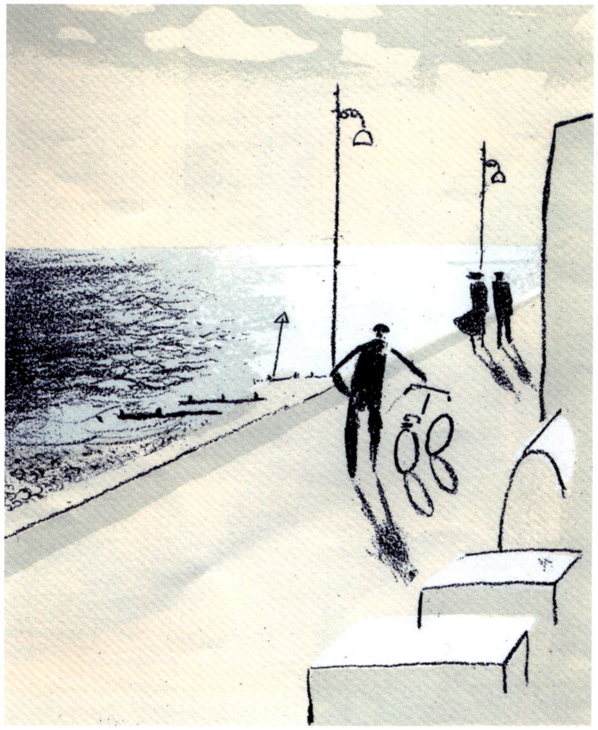

1954 Aldeburgh Festival Calendar, *March*, Mary Potter (right)

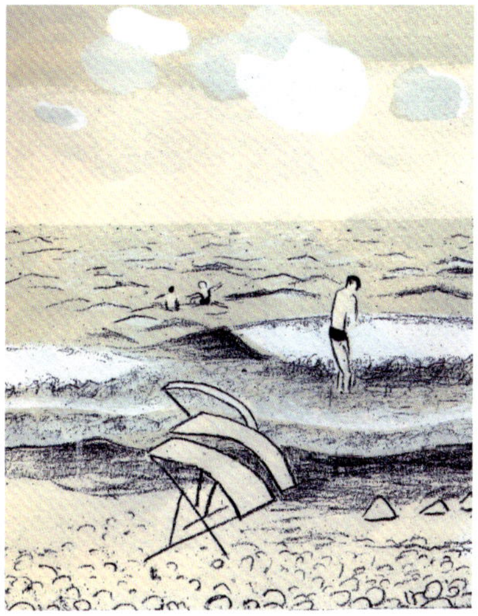

1954 Aldeburgh Festival Calendar, *June*, Mary Potter

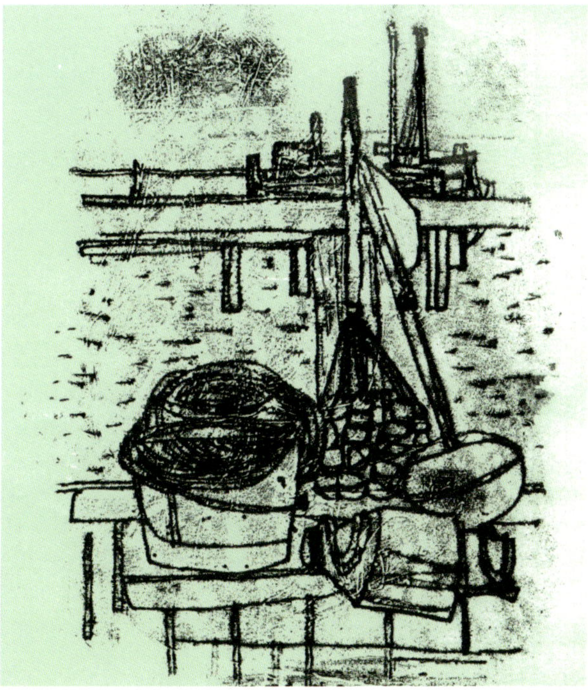

1954 Aldeburgh Festival Calendar, *November*, Prunella Clough

chilling Henry James story from the Essex coast – Myfanwy wrote the libretti.

The 'golden Myfanwy' of John Betjeman verses also championed Aldeburgh artist Mary Potter, having chosen the *Sea Poems* volume for the landmark 1944-46 *New Excursions in English Poetry* series which saluted local poet George Crabbe just as Britten was producing his Crabbe-inspired *Peter Grimes* with its ravishing Sea Interludes (an opera premiered in London in 1945, but not staged at the Aldeburgh Festival until 2000).

The Pipers paid frequent and fruitful visits to the Suffolk coast all their lives. But for Ivon Hitchens the intense attachment broke even before the Blitz. He honeymooned in Sizewell in 1935, after marriage to Mary ('Mollie') Cranford Coates. They both drew and Mollie modelled while Ivon painted. But after one last visit to the tin-roofed refuge, they spent two summer holidays – in 1938 and 1939 – in the 17th-century mill house at Holbrook, on the Shotley Peninsula.

Here, with a wide view of pools and tree-fringed river, he extended the elongated and exhilarated art for which he would later be known, albeit when living – first in a gypsy caravan – in a Sussex wood. Although the painter John Craxton claimed that those panoramic canvases were slyly designed to sit over mantelpieces, they certainly fit with that ecstatic child's sensation of spinning round in a landscape – bringing an all-around view of a small, beloved patch of rural England.

Meanwhile, **Prunella Clough** (1919-1999), who had spent childhood holidays in Southwold and owned a house there from 1945 until 1966, scoured the coast from Lowestoft to Aldeburgh for powerful, semi-Cubist 1940s images of bleached bird skeletons and tree roots, tank-trapped beaches, tarred sheds, fishermen, fish, nets, baskets, boats, floats and breakwaters.

After the Great Flood of 1953, having contributed four prints to an Aldeburgh Festival calendar along with John Piper and **Mary Potter** (1900-1981), she wrote to the Norfolk painter David Carr: 'Do you know that lovely beach at Sizewell has been smothered in shingle? – Not only that but the most appalling monsters have appeared. One is better than any Lynn Chadwick. It has its base in concrete with a long curving body, sickle jaws and hideous eye…(Spread of machine consciousness – of a kind…).'

The merest hint of the monstrous machine consciousness to come.

Seagulls, Aldeburgh Beach, John Gay, 1964, photograph

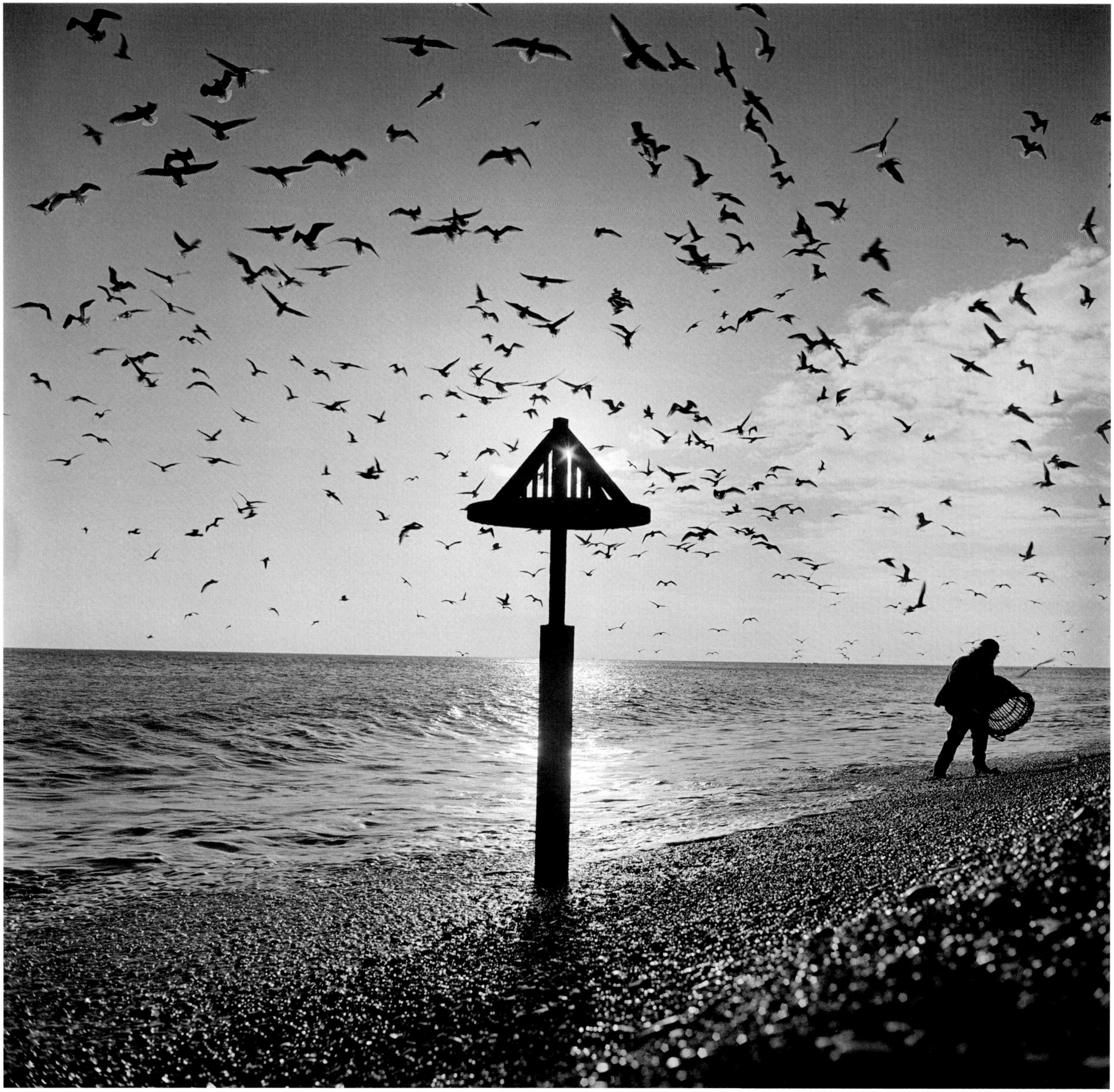

Maggi and Moggie

Maggi Hambling, Kathleen Hale and Aldeburgh

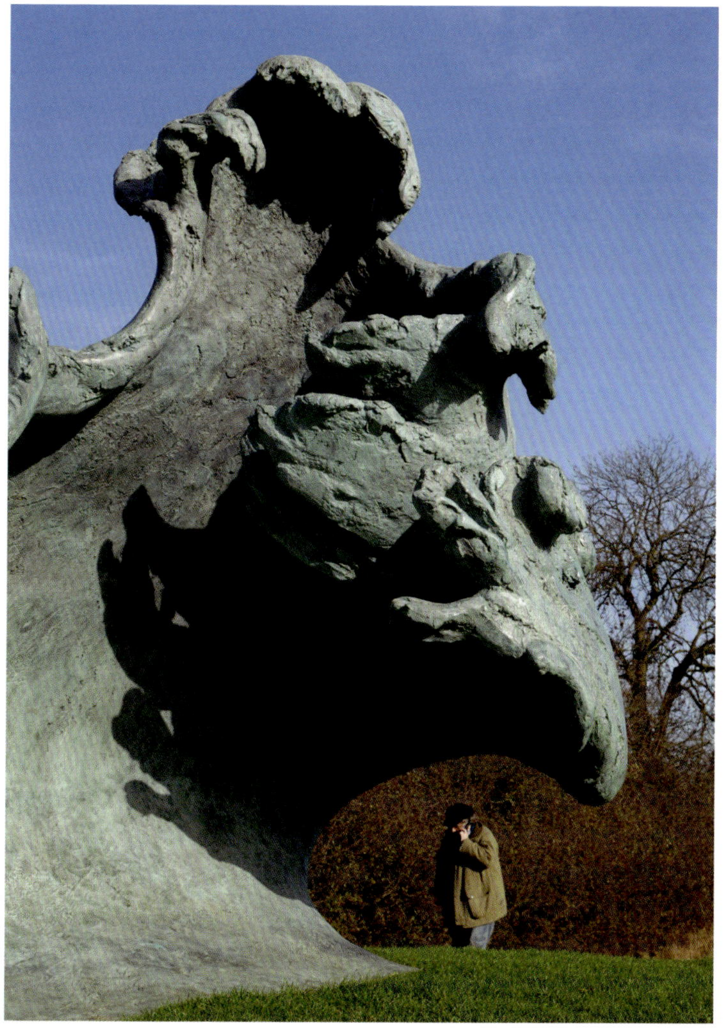

Maggi Hambling engulfed in *Rising Wave*, 2009, bronze. Rejected for Saffron Walden churchyard, now in a Suffolk private collection

Maggi Hambling surveys a landscape of bucolic bliss – an artist in a world steeped in myth and history. Here magic happens.

From studio windows she watches white geese wander from her garden to the watermeadows beyond, and then down to the River Alde where, in 1907, a schoolboy fished out a Roman head. Arthur Godbold happily swapped the bronze relic for five shillings, and still had no regrets when, six decades later, the British Museum bought it at auction for £15,500.

The treasure was a prized trophy – hacked from an equestrian statue in Colchester's temple to the deified Emperor Claudius, when Boudica and her Iceni army sacked the town in AD61. It was apparently tossed into the river on a rebel soldier's return journey to Norfolk.

Magic (or fate, or fortune) also brought Maggi to this village of traditional flint church and colour-washed houses in the fields behind Snape. That's where legions of her farming ancestors rest in the churchyard and also where her paintings of the nearby North Sea had a first sell-out exhibition.

After an Anglia Television profile, the artist received a fan letter from an elderly widow, who in 1994 left her favourite artist her Alde Valley cottage and a slice of the surrounding scenery. 'She thought Suffolk land should go back to Suffolk people,' says the Sudbury-born, Hadleigh-raised Maggi. 'I really feel I've come home.'

Margaret Hambling was laden with gifts from the outset. She drew so much that her inspirational tutor, Yvonne Drewry, suspected colour blindness until the demonstration of a vivid painting. At 14 she spent most of an art exam trying to attract the attention of the invigilating biology teacher on whom she had a crush. Then, with ten minutes to go, she dashed off a painting and finished top of the class.

But her biggest stroke of luck, and act of daring, came when, aged 15, she took her first two Suffolk landscape oils to what was known among suspicious Hadleigh folk as 'the artists' house'. This was Benton End – an excellent and eccentric art school presided over by Sir Cedric Morris and Arthur Lett-Haines, who had met on Armistice Night in 1918 and who remained together, despite an often icy chasm between their characters, until the latter's death 60 years later.

Margaret was shown into a kitchen where Lett was serving Cedric dish after astonishing dish. With the two tutors offering encouraging but wholly conflicting criticism, it was finally agreed that she should paint with them during holidays and help in the kitchen in lieu of fees.

'On the first day of the next school holiday I went along but was too shy to approach the house, so I just sat at the end of the drive painting a ditch. Then Lucy Harwood came out, ringing a cow bell and calling my name. So I went in and my life was transformed.'

At the East Anglian School of Painting and Drawing she was renamed Maggi – just as Kathleen Hale became Moggie and colonel's daughter Joan Warburton became Maudie.

Helping Lett Haines with his stupendous meals – generally served to a silent Cedric while the cook himself dined on gin and French plus a cigar – she fell under his spell. 'As I cut up the vegetables he told me I must make my work my best friend, so I could go to it no matter how good or bad I was feeling, to have a conversation. He also said an artist had to have imagination and everything must be an experiment. Whereas Cedric people tended to paint like Cedric, followers of Lett found themselves.'

Maggi and her fellow students – who had included Lucian Freud, Welsh-born Glyn Morgan and Constructivist David Carr – also learned that the artist's lot was one of insecurity and discomfort. It was about advancing by taking risks. She was to bask in the art of performance – in portraits of friends Max Wall, George Melly and Stephen Fry.

Quoting W H Auden about the artist's role being to break bread with the dead, she has been a stalwart recorder of the ageing process and death bed scenes – first of Cedric Morris, in a poignant pencil study now in the British Museum, then of her bank-manager-turned-painter father Harry and of Soho hell-raiser Henrietta Moraes.

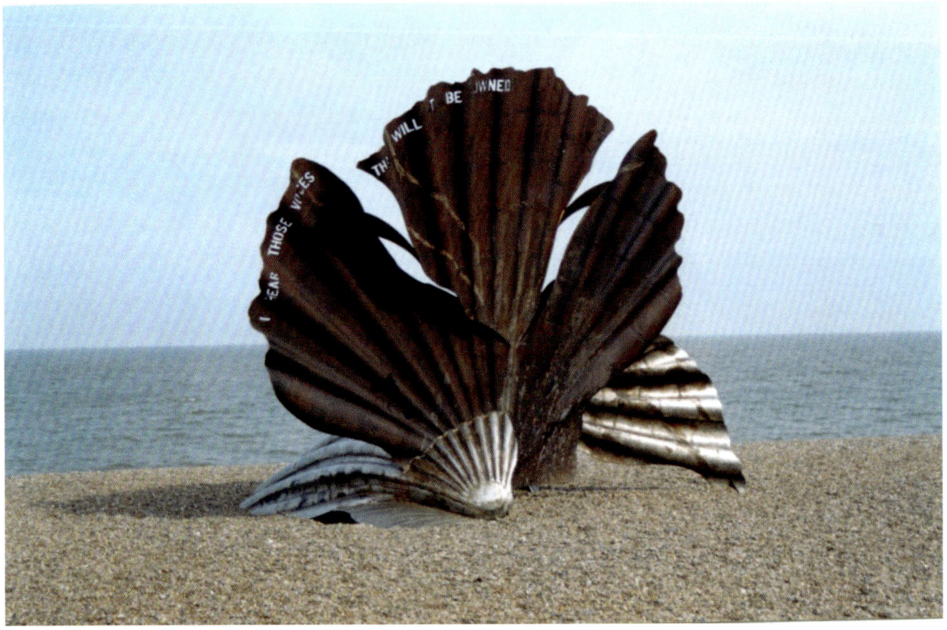

Scallop, Aldeburgh, 2003, stainless steel

One of the best Hambling images, now in the National Portrait Gallery, shows Beccles-raised Dorothy Hodgkin. The dynamic brain of a Nobel Prize-winning scientist, who cracked the structural codes of penicillin, vitamin B12 and insulin, is expressed in a flurry of agitated hands which also show the frailty of an old woman.

Loving the 'rawness' of East Suffolk, she relishes nature at its most elemental. In 1978 she produced black studies of sea and sky at Southwold and Corton – on the last morning witnessing, for the first time, the magic of the

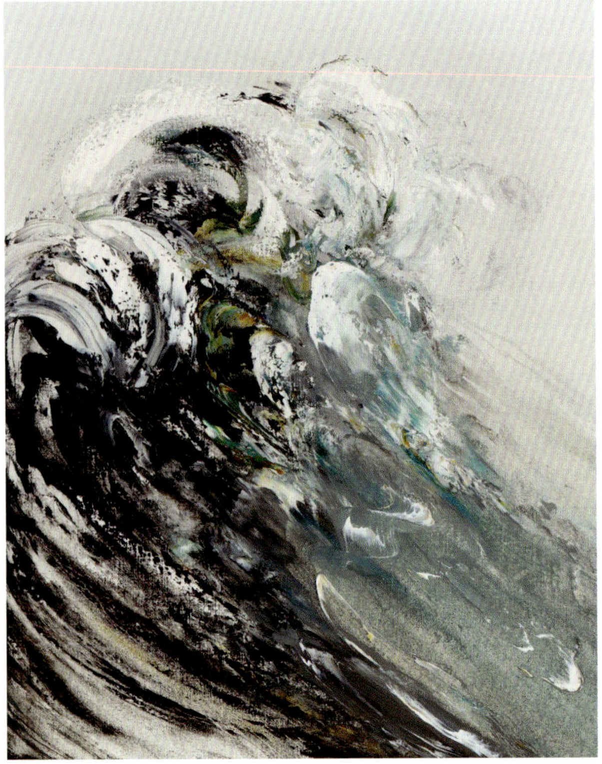

Rising Wave, 2009, oil on canvas

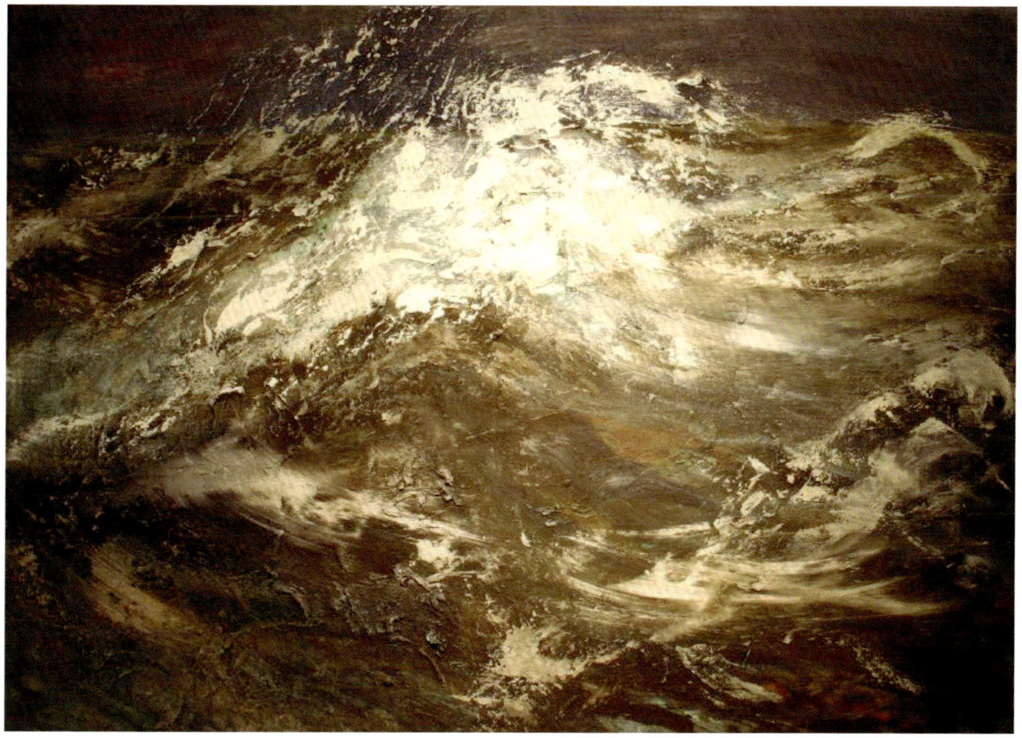

Big Sea, May 2005, oil on canvas, Great Yarmouth Museums

sun rising from the sea. That led to Orwell Estuary sunrises in oil and watercolour.

And now she has been working for years on maelstrom-like wave paintings. 'They began on a stormy day in November,' she says. 'Rather than talking to the sea, as I did during childhood, or making studies in situ, I remain silent, observe and absorb, then return to the studio and employ my visual memory.

'The sea bird paintings began after finding a dead oil-soaked gannet on Thorpeness beach on Boxing Day morning. I try to trap the particular moment of light, the seconds of a bird diving, the instant of a wave breaking. Colours of the sea are elusive, its rhythms mysterious, its space infinite.

'James Joyce likened the sea to a "sweet grey mother". It is a symbol of life itself: change is constant – calm, storm, crashing, lapping, raging, sucking, mist, tide, wind, moon, sunset, sunrise. Time is suspended in the birth, climax and death of a single wave.'

Sales from the initial Snape exhibition helped to fund a huge Hambling sculpture in celebration of Benjamin Britten, which rose from the shingle beach between Aldeburgh and Thorpeness in 2003 and above all protest ('It doesn't look at all like Benjamin Britten'; 'Ben hated seafood!'). Composed of two fractured and interlocking shells, and made by Aldeburgh iron founders Sam and Dennis Pegg, *Scallop* is pierced with words from the *Peter Grimes* opera – 'I hear those voices that will not be drowned' – to reveal the sky. A steely monument, by turns rusted and silvered, hints at fins and wings.

The artist adds: 'The rising striations of a scallop shell resemble the rays of the sun, its curved edge echoes Constable's "dome of the sky" and its corrugations suggest the waves of the sea. The scallop shell is the ancient symbol of pilgrimage, the sea and the cradle of Venus. I have destroyed and recreated its form in an attempt to reflect the original and explosive power of Britten's music.'

The composer's quicksilver genius is recalled as if in a gigantic ear by which we listen to nature and music. Every child knows that by holding up a shell we can hear the sea and the artist wanted her 'conversation with the sea' to provide a resting place for walkers, a climbing frame for children (the Pied Piper of Hambling) and a cover for lovers. As it does.

Orwell Estuary Sunrise I, II, III, July 1991, watercolour, Archant Art Collection

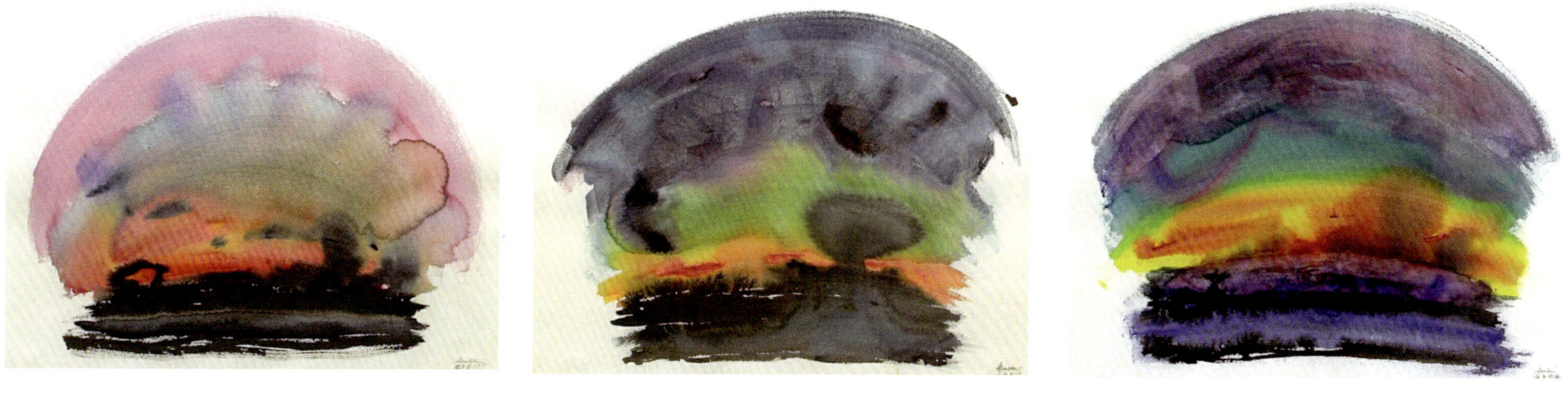

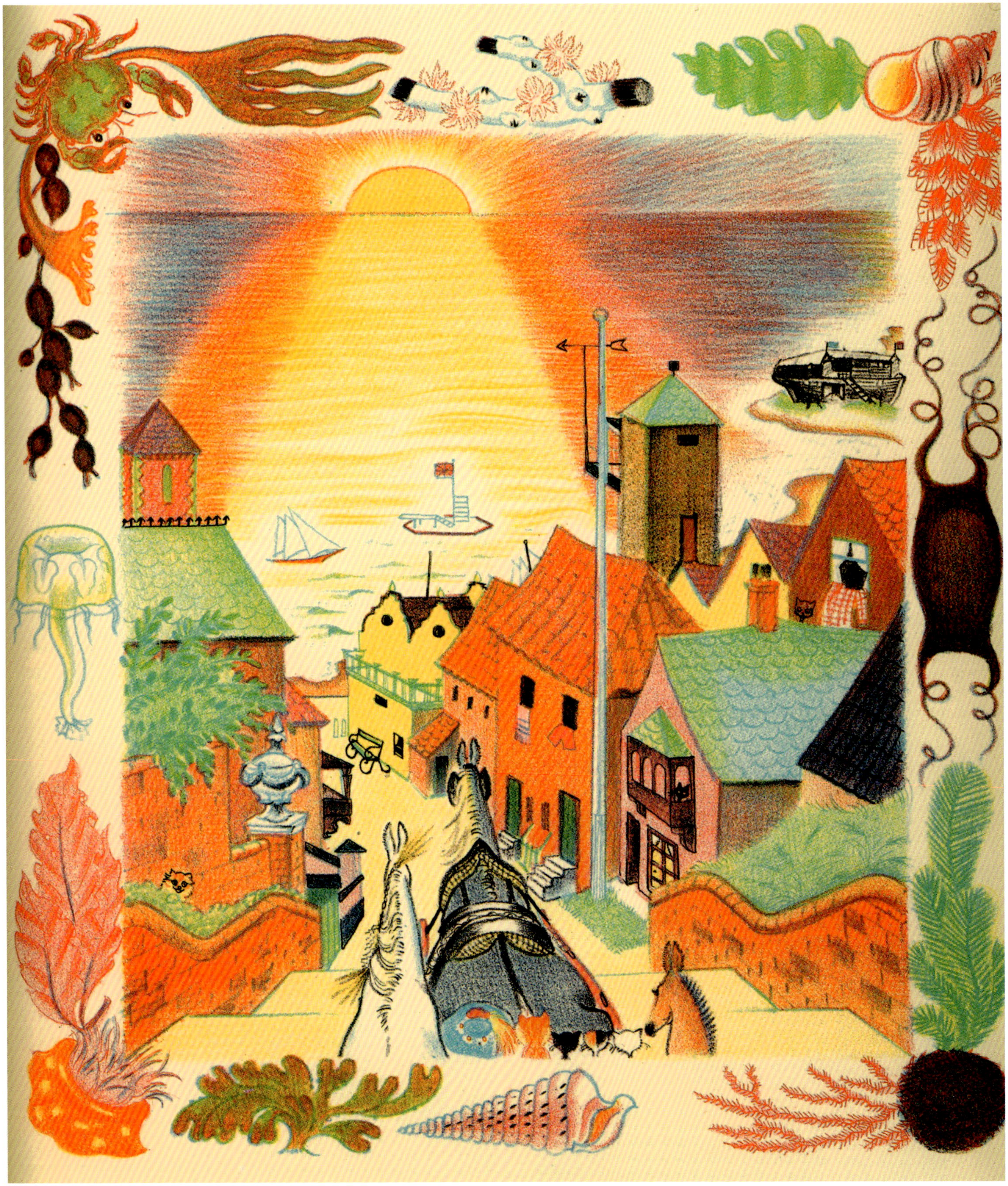

Orlando and family, drawn by Vulcan, arrive at Owlbarrow-on-sea; from *Orlando – A Sea-side Holiday*, 1952

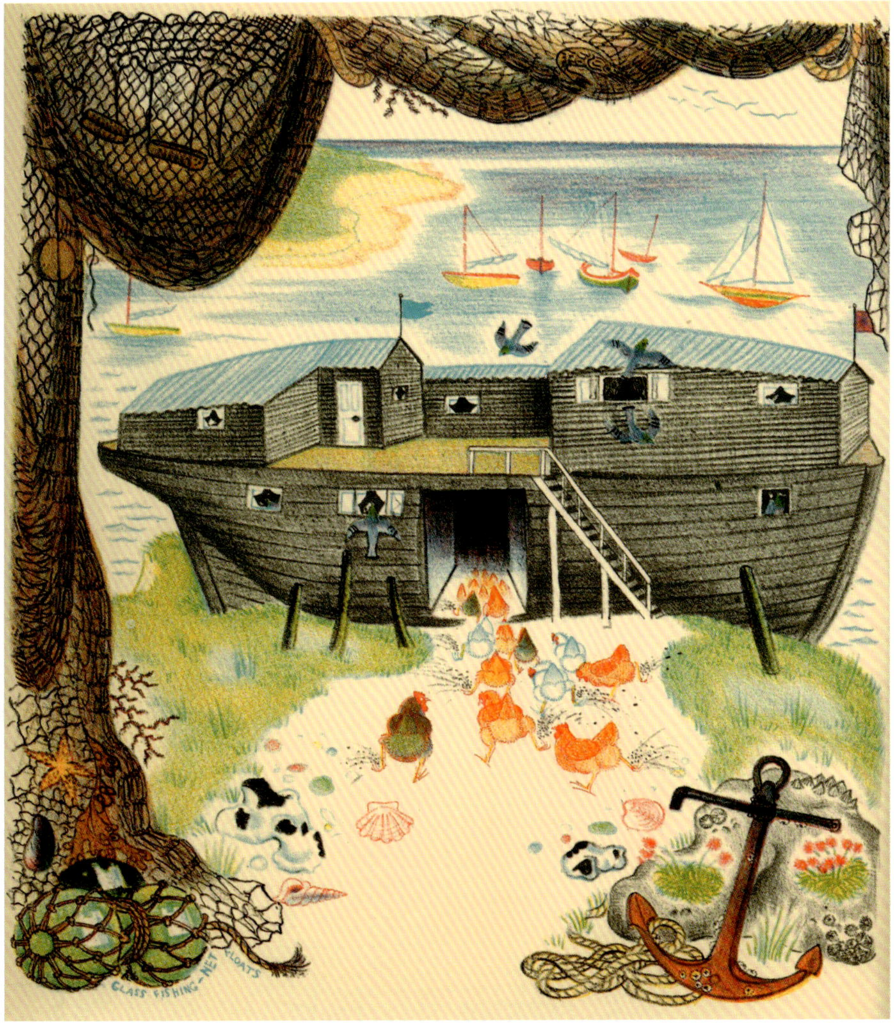

Orlando's holiday home

Dust jacket draft, 1952

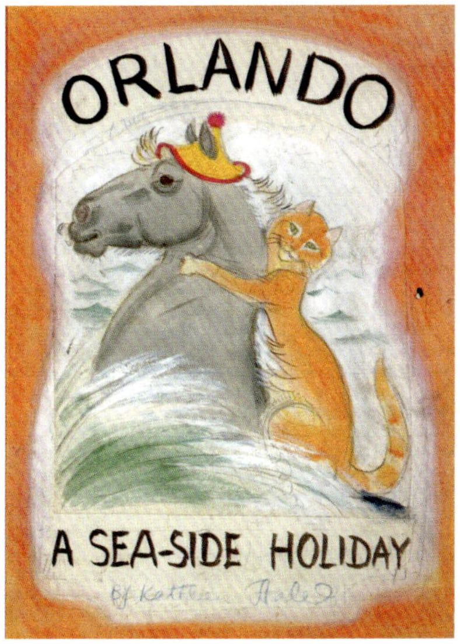

Kathleen Hale (1898-2000) wrote and illustrated 18 Orlando books for children, drawing mockery from her friend Cedric Morris that such a gifted artist had hung her slender reputation on the broad shoulders of a eunuch cat.

In the 1920s she had worked as Augustus John's secretary and met Morris and Lett Haines in Paris. For a time they were neighbours in London, and when the partner painters moved to the Essex-Suffolk border to open their art school, she often visited – adapting their initial home, at The Pound, in Higham, into a feline-shaped dwelling in *Orlando's Silver Wedding*, with a black marble torso by John Skeaping in the garden replaced by a stone cat madonna and kittens. Lett appeared as the Katnapper (darning a hole in his check tweed jacket with white wool and then painting on the pattern in watercolour just as he had done in real life). Cedric was to be the dancing master in *Orlando's Home Life*. No wonder they called her Moggie.

Her first book, *Orlando's Camping Holiday*, appeared in 1938 – printed by Cowells of Ipswich whose director, Geoffrey Smith, secured publication via *Country Life* and its editor, Noel Carrington. He in turn ensured that *Orlando's Evening Out* was the first Puffin Picture Book. The artist-author also produced the lithographic plates from her drawings – 128 for each book. She slogged for that slender reputation.

She wanted her books to portray the secure and happy home life she herself had not known in childhood – and which was a challenge in adulthood. As approved by her two sons, they were full of jokes and puzzles. In 1952 a family break to Aldeburgh produced the classic *Orlando – A Sea-side Holiday*.

Here Orlando, his wife Grace and their three kittens (the most wayward, Tinkle, a self-portrait of the artist when young) are taken by Vulcan, an old circus horse, plus spouse and foal, to the Suffolk town renamed Owlbarrow-on-Sea. They all stay in the *Iona*, a beached and blackened hulk which was a striking feature above the tide-line towards Slaughden in the decades around World War Two. It was depicted by artists including a visiting L S Lowry.

As Moggie recalled in her memoir: 'When

Rotting Boathouse, Slaughden, John Gay, 1973, photograph (right)

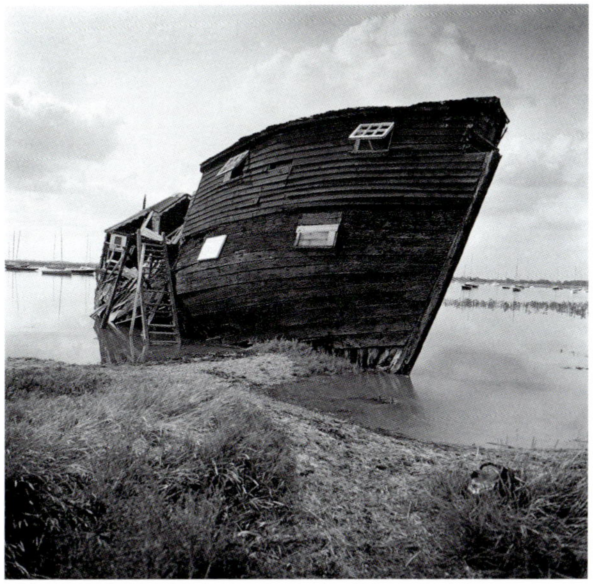

we arrived just as the sun was setting, we were entranced by the steep descent before us leading down to the tiled roofs of the lovely old town, with the unlimited expanse of the sea at our feet…I loved the "fantaisie" villas on the seafront, and found these bizarre constructions of red brick, white stone, turrets and battlements, which looked as though they were built of nursery bricks, much more amusing to draw than the elegant Georgian houses.'

She added that she had been compelled to alter the fantastical architecture of a villa meticulously recreated as the home of the bad-tempered Mr Curmudgeon, when warned of the case for libel if association with such a gloomy character deterred a potential house-buyer.

But she could never resist reproducing reality in her stories. A shiny black sofa with brown feet in the Owlbarrow ship-hostel turns out to be a dachshund modelled on the pet belonging to Cedric Morris's sister Nancy. The face of Mr Curmudgeon – whose misery derives from his dire cooking and domestic disarray and who eventually cheers up in the company of a ship-wrecked African queen – is also strangely familiar.

At a low point in her marriage, Moggie Hale had engineered an affair with the bisexual Lett Haines which had ended well before the 1952 book. It seems that she couldn't resist a dig at a former lover, and ongoing friend, in a dark portrait possibly removed from the realms of libel since the subject was a famously brilliant cook.

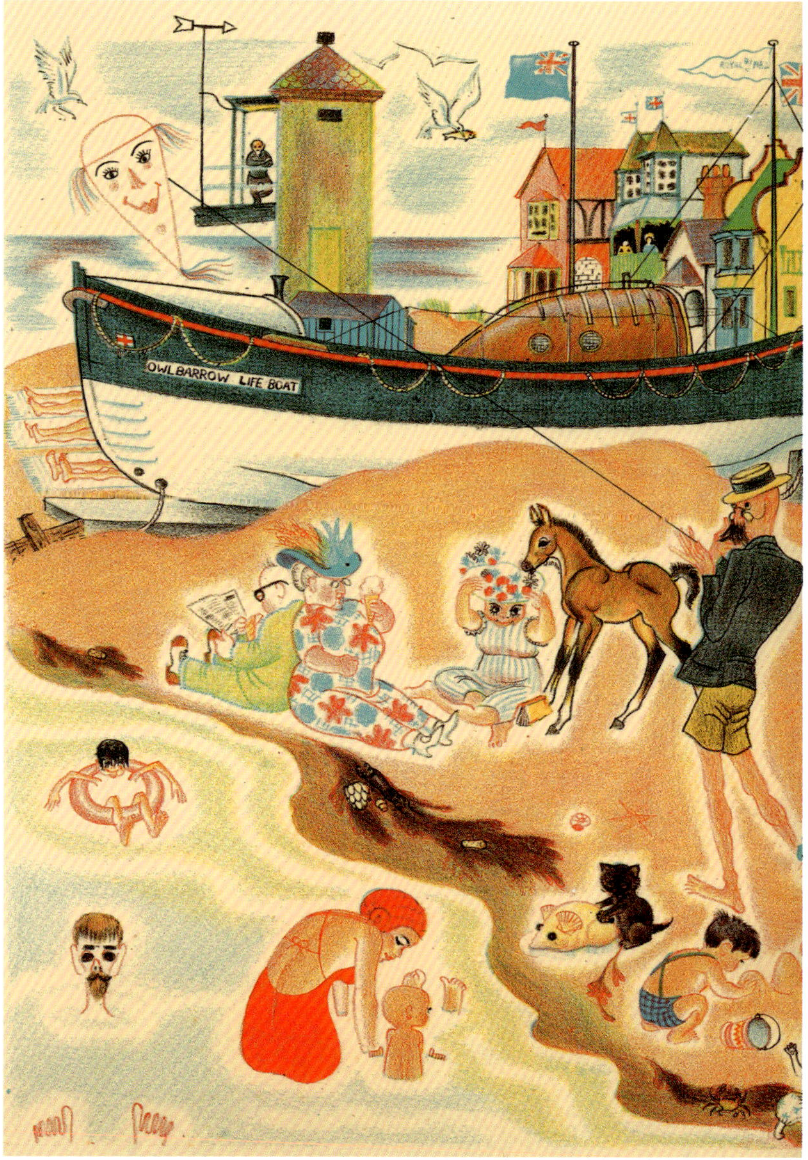

Owlbarrow Lifeboat

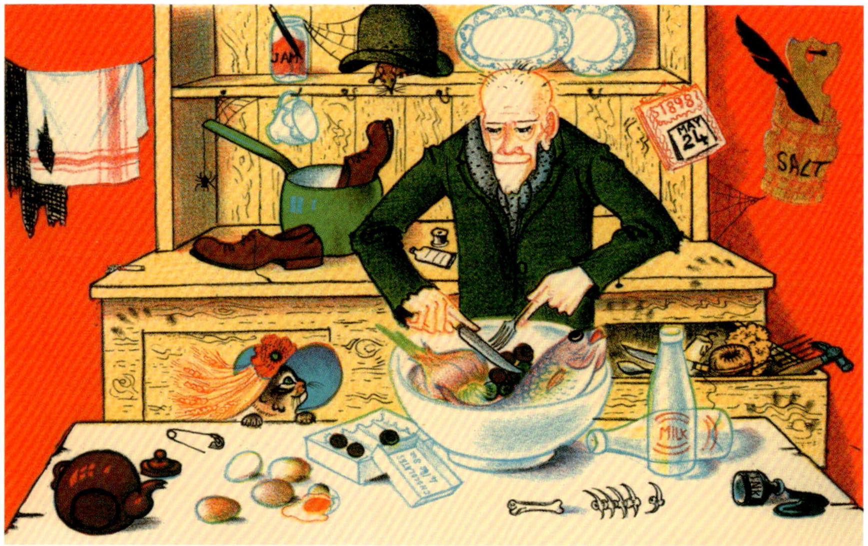

Mr Curmudgeon in his kitchen

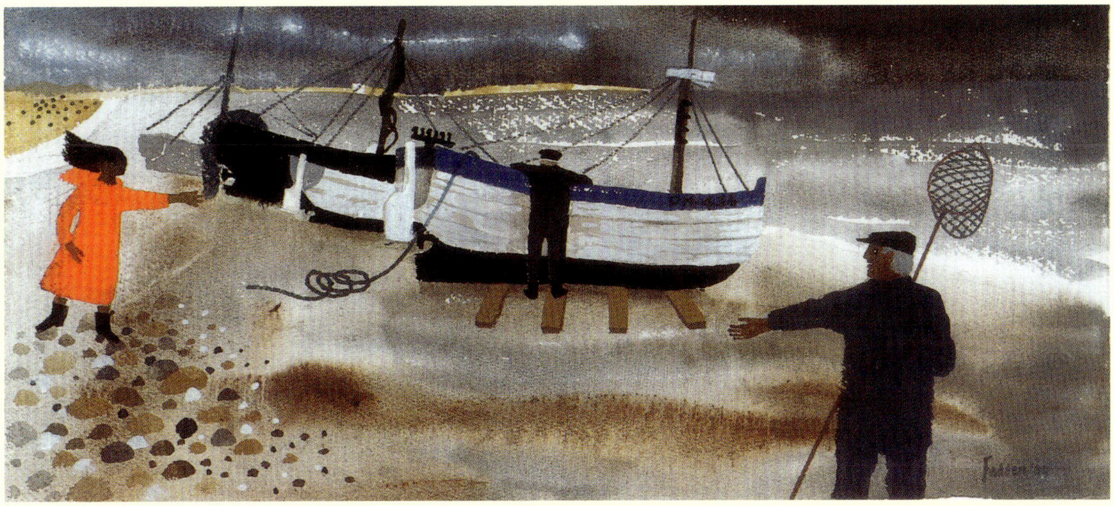

Dunwich, 2000, gouache

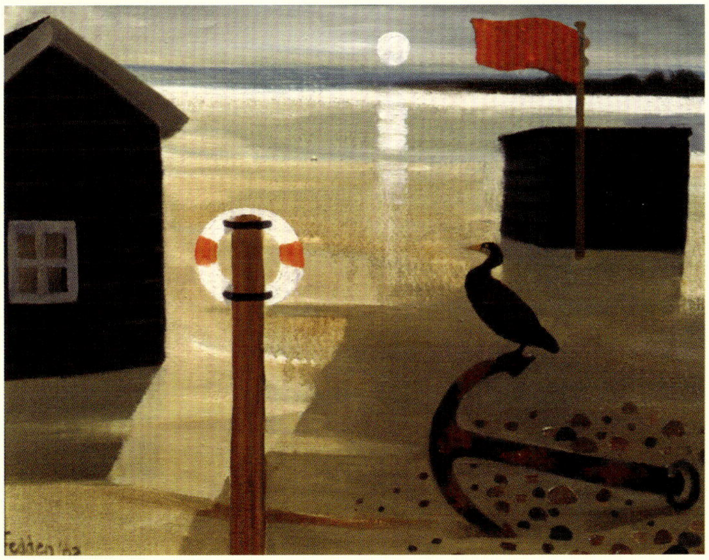

Born in Bristol in 1915, and long residing in London, **Mary Fedden** has produced some of the liveliest and best-loved still-lifes, seascapes and domestic interiors in post-war British art. They are the records of supreme happiness, pouring from her studio like postcards from an endless holiday.

Her love of the world and of other people has been fixed most firmly on her husband, the painter and print-maker Julian Trevelyan, with whom she lived, worked and travelled from 1949 until his death in 1988. Her recollected pictures cover numerous visits to friends in coastal East Anglia from Blakeney to Snape.

Cormorant, 2002, oil on canvas

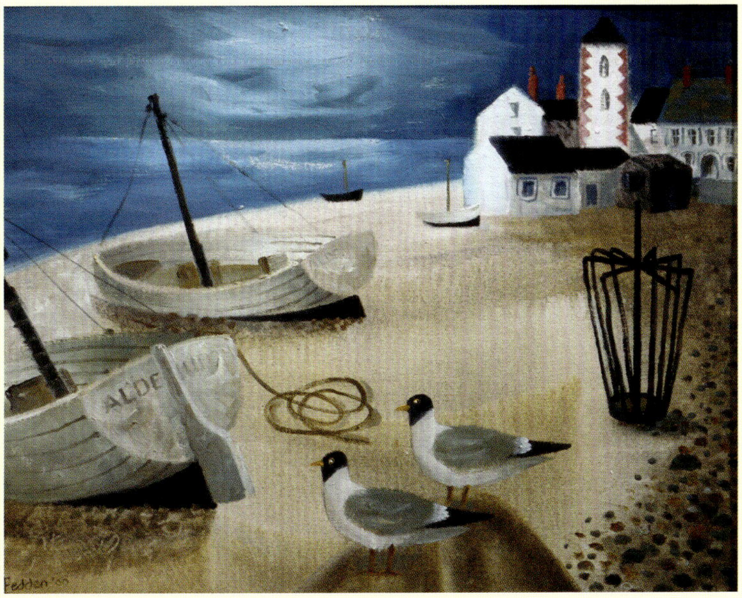

The artist's widowhood has brought more trips to Aldeburgh and Dunwich, with abstracted elements from real-life scenes – boats, birds, flowers, lookout towers – taking shape back in her old boatshed studio beside the Thames.

Distance and distillation lend the late Fedden art of East Anglia a rather ghostly air, and no wonder since glimpsed men – Dunwich boatmen, walkers on Aldeburgh beach in twilight – appear to be turning into Julian. And in one poignant image of 2000 a familiar figure with a shrimp net reaches across the shingle to his red-robed bride.

Aldeburgh, 2000, oil on canvas

Aldeburgh Beach, 1939, oil on canvas

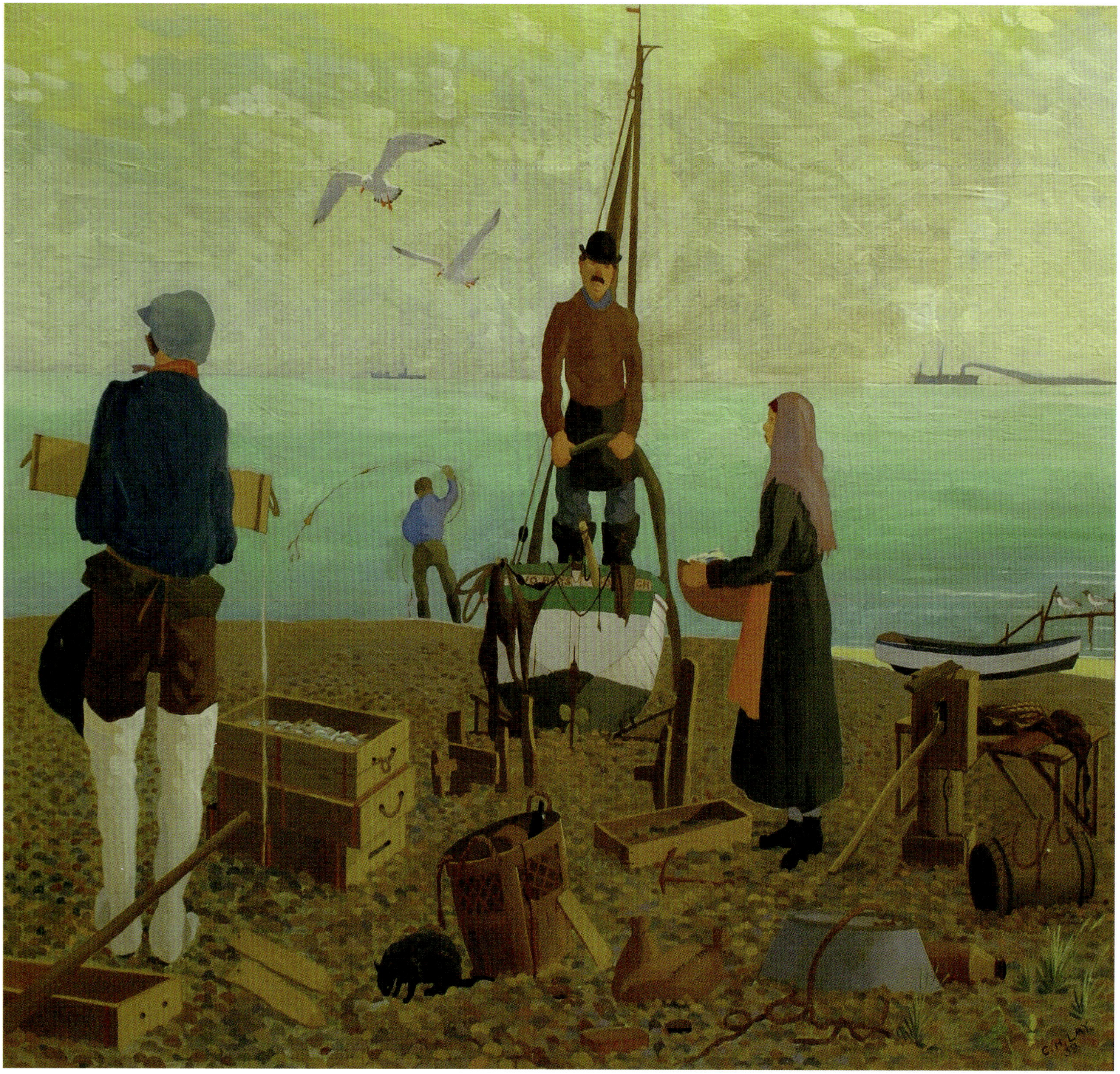

Seaside Surrealism

Cecil Lay and Peter Baldwin

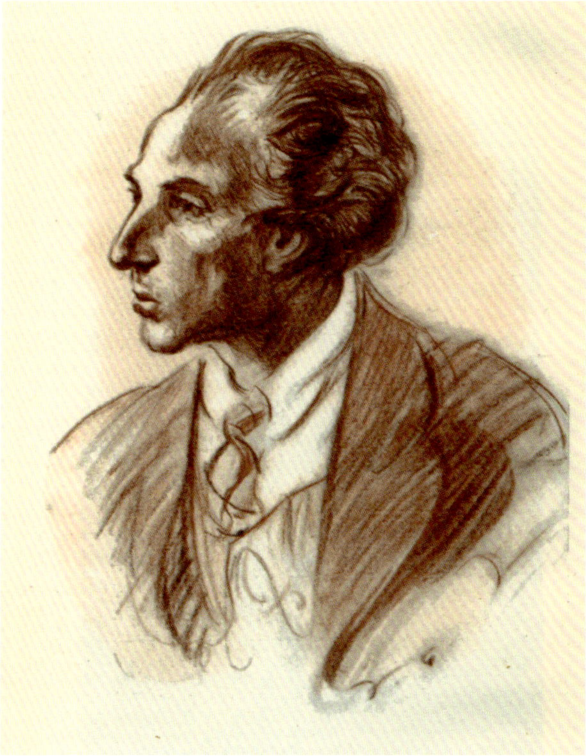

Cecil Lay, self-portrait, pencil

While clustered Thorpeness proclaims an Edwardian eccentricity, scattered around Aldeburgh and Aldringham are the hidden remains of the quirky Arts and Crafts genius of **Cecil Lay.** This near-forgotten local architect was no less remarkable as a poet and painter.

Cecil Howard Lay (1885-1956) was born in Aldringham, the son of the village schoolmaster who hailed from an Essex seafaring family, and a mother who came from Suffolk farming stock.

Hugely ambitious for the boy they seem virtually to have weaned on strong tea (and whose constitution they ultimately ruined), the cultured but snobbish parents hired a home tutor and discouraged the company of local lads.

Soon young Cecil was ripe for rebellion. As a student in Ipswich he haunted the music-hall theatre and boasted of having Marie Lloyd – bawdy legend and role model for Mae West – perched on his knee in the bar after the show.

Sitting in a box, he was even employed to respond to the star's invitation 'Wouldn't you like to spoon with me?' by jumping up and shouting out: 'Yes, why, rather!'

But one evening he leaned out too far and the balustrade gave way so that he and a group of relief plaster cherubs ended in a heap on the stage.

As a teenager he also went on dawn shoots at Thorpeness with a local farmer's son after which they would repair to Aldringham's Parrot and Punchbowl pub for a 'hunter's breakfast' washed down with a brew called Purl – a concoction of gin, beer, wormwood (a bitter herb) and sugar heated in a conical container among the coals.

After training with Suffolk architects, he left for London in 1907 to attend the Architectural Association Schools and soon joined progressive artists and musicians meeting at The Bombshell in Leicester Square. For a time he was a friend of the sculptor Jacob Epstein, who gave him a special stone which he afterwards kept in his pocket, and he remained close to painter Frank Brangwyn.

Cecil Lay cheered Roger Fry's championship of the Post-Impressionists. He penned a warm appreciation of Van Gogh in the *Journal of the Architectural Association* in 1910, but at the end of that year failed to persuade an uncle to buy one of Vincent's works from Fry's first Post-Impressionist Exhibition for £30.

He excelled in watercolours and drawing – the media on paper of the trainee architect – which he exhibited at the London Salon and the Albert Hall in 1913. The following year he fulfilled his mother's wish to have the grandest house in Aldringham, before a war began which changed his world forever.

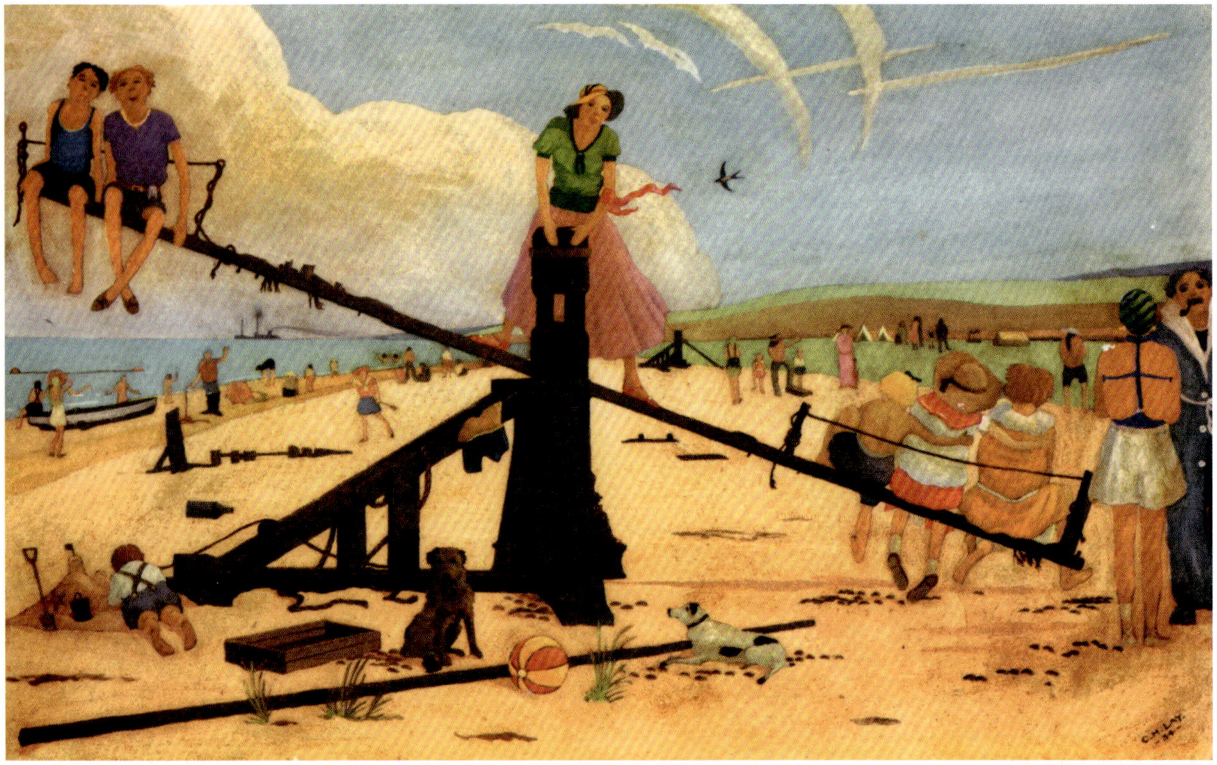

Sizewell, 1933, oil on canvas

Spared active service, he suffered trauma as the carnage mounted and torment afterwards, culminating, in 1921, in a nervous breakdown. Even after his recovery he rarely left Aldringham except to walk and work as an artist and architect in the neighbouring countryside.

Poetry inspired by rural Suffolk began to pour out of him, with nine volumes published between 1927 and 1934. His verses were admired by leading critics such as Middleton Murray and Desmond MacCarthy and writers A E Coppard and W H Davies – the last wishing he had written this prize-winning poem, *To a Bird*, himself:

When that mighty hand whose art
Flung the Earth and Sea apart,
Raised the mountain, rolled the plain,
Carved the tree and set the grain,
Drew upon the growing plan
Half the lineaments of man,
Then the God said, 'There must be
Song to set his spirit free,
Colour to inspire his heart,
Symmetry to nurse his art.'
Spoke the great Divinity,
'Three in one combined shall be.'
And the mighty hand that stirred
Trembling made a little bird.

There was also more than a touch of the music-hall ditty in witty rhymes inspired by nature. As in: 'The zebra's like a peppermint/ Not only by the even print/ That lies upon his shining hide,/ But also by his fire inside.'

In 1923, while overseeing alterations to a house in Middleton belonging to the artist Haworth Chadburn, Cecil Lay met the owner's daughter, Joan, and they married in 1932. He converted two cottages into a marital home lined with bookcases and suffused with the dim light of a woodland dell.

Then, for 13 years from 1927, he produced an amazing outpouring of oils in an architect's studio in the woods behind his home where no one – not even his wife – ever saw him painting.

Like a Suffolk L S Lowry, this solitary figure teemed his canvases with people – crowds spilling over parks and greens, flocking to fairs and from churches and attending sports fixtures from cricket matches to Benacre races. Best of all were the trippers relishing resorts from Lowestoft to Felixstowe, suggesting closest kinship with Gorleston

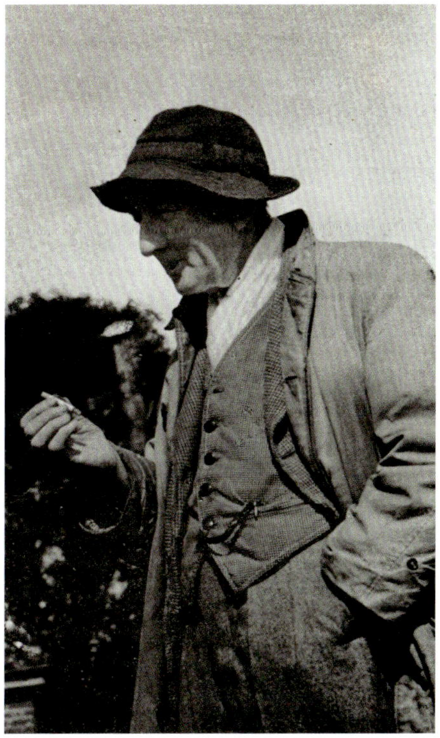

Cecil Lay

painter Campbell Mellon.

Seaside Seesaw shows a surreal scene of an old piece of timber and a capstan converted into a playground attraction on the beach at Sizewell in the summer of 1934.

Cecil Lay also painted figure-rife images of farming and fishing celebrating the harvests of fields and sea, but what was possibly his final image, *Spratters*, shows an eerie composition in which outsized mourners on Aldeburgh beach seem to be bidding such peaceful scenes farewell in a strange ceremony of parting.

This former wildfowler had grown to worship the birds which flew through his poetry but soon airbases were all around him and heaths and shores were practice battlegrounds. Minsmere, where the Dieppe landing was rehearsed, would be shot by Suffolk film-maker Humphrey Jennings in 1948 with commentary about 'the beaches mined and the trees blasted by shell-fire'.

With all these horrors pending, Cecil Lay put his oil paints away.

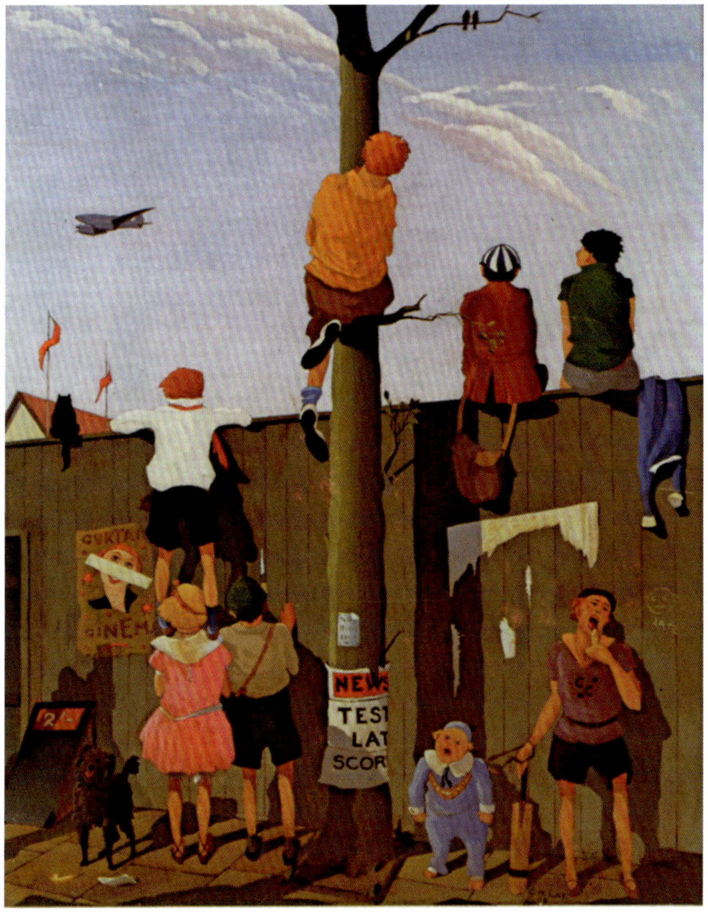

The Cricket Match,
oil on canvas

In 1955 the broadcaster Lance Sieveking, driving from Aldringham to Aldeburgh, noticed a pair of enormously tall, brick gateposts and a tattered For Sale sign.

At the end of an overgrown drive he found a Dutch-roofed house reminding him of William Morris or Edwin Lutyens and with an ornamental inscription above a window dated 1914.

Outside a cottage in the garden he found an old man talking to a white goose. The visitor recalled: 'He was dressed in very pale, faded Edwardian tweeds, and a white silk scarf; and on his head one of those round tweed hats that river fishermen wear. His eyes were clear dark grey.

'He answered my enquiry in a voice that belonged to a past far more remote than that of the Romans and Saxons: I mean that dim and almost incredible period, which, nevertheless, did have an actual existence once: the second decade of the 20th century.'

Gaining the key to the big house he found it filled with old clothes and sundry household items bursting from cases, chests and boxes, and large paintings stacked with their faces to the wall.

Asked who was the architect and the artist the old keyholder owned up – explaining that the building he had made for his mother had been untouched since a house auction after her death.

Lance Sieveking ensured that Lay's *Collected Poems* were published as a posthumous tribute in 1962, and two years later Anglia TV screened a profile documentary. Then, in 1978, Joan Lay offered 88 paintings, watercolours and drawings by her late husband for sale through the London gallery of Norfolk's Michael Parkin.

High time for another rediscovery.

A model of creativity, Cecil Lay was an extraordinarily talented recorder of everyday East Anglian miracles. As he wrote:

My eyes are filled with wonder
At any little bird:
On every tree and bush I see
A wing to give an ecstasy.
A goldfinch sitting on a thorn
Can make of me a man re-born,
But sparrows in the mud suffice
To carry me to Paradise.

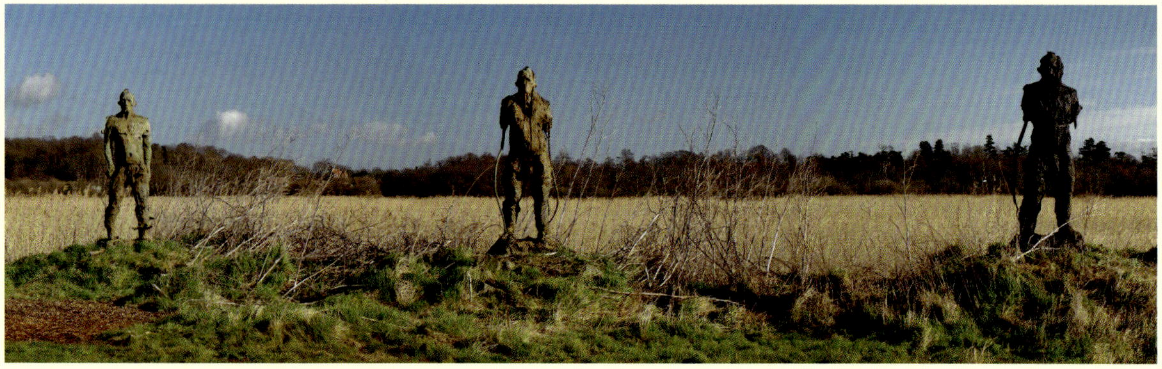

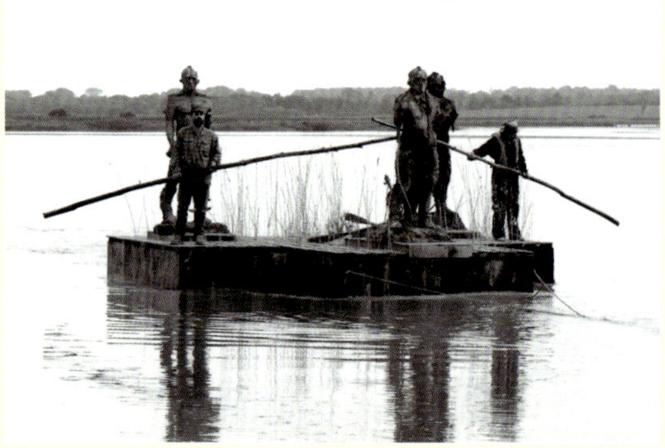

Suffolk sculptor, caster and draughtsman **Laurence Edwards** has produced a long line of monumental male figures in his foundry – first at Laxfield and now at Butley Mills, in a creative journey poised between modernism and antiquity. In 2009 he made the *Creek Men* pictured here, chronicling their transition from clay to bronze, and their transportation by reed-bedecked raft to Snape, in an Aldeburgh Festival exhibition and subsequent book. They are now at Heveningham Hall.

The first near-eight-foot bronze giant sprouts the 'Leather Strop' fungus found in birch trees close to his studio. There is a hint here of the Green Man, but a stronger tribute to the Saxon warrior-king at the centre of the Sutton Hoo ship burial, whose sceptre was a whetstone and whose followers are found in sand burials with their remains fused to buckles and sheaths. He is the heroic survivor.

The second figure, standing stoic and steadfast, has the hue of the East Suffolk landscape and the deer, hare, bittern and curlew found there. 'His face and body are gashed like a scarred oak,' Laurence Edwards says. 'The slits in the face imitate the strange scent glands found in the heads of deer. The figure's arms are cast from fronds of poisonous hemlock.'

And the third giant stands battered and burned, but still erect. The smoky colour references the ancient practice of pollarding oak for charcoal. The body has been wounded by dowel spears which also hold it together.

In 1956, the year of Cecil Lay's death, a 15-year-old Aldeburgh lad decided to become an artist. But **Peter Baldwin**, newly-enrolled at Lowestoft art school and revelling in Suffolk seascapes, was then uprooted to the Canadian prairies.

His idyllic infancy – with one kind grandfather Aldeburgh's coastguard and another licensee of the Mill Inn – had clouded when his father came back from the war to bring conflict to the family home. Tension grew. A teenager's free Saturday mornings messing about on boats at Slaughden was sabotaged with work as a butcher's boy. And when Peter took to following Benjamin Britten on afternoon walks, opening his sketchbook when the composer paused on the river wall to savour the clear view to Orford Ness and across the hulk of the *Iona* a little further up the Alde, dad was horrified. He led a swift migration to Alberta, destroying all his son's pictures and finding him work as a labourer in what seemed to be a Siberian landscape. Eighteen months later the exile had saved enough for a return passage, joining his maternal grandparents, who had retired to Sheringham.

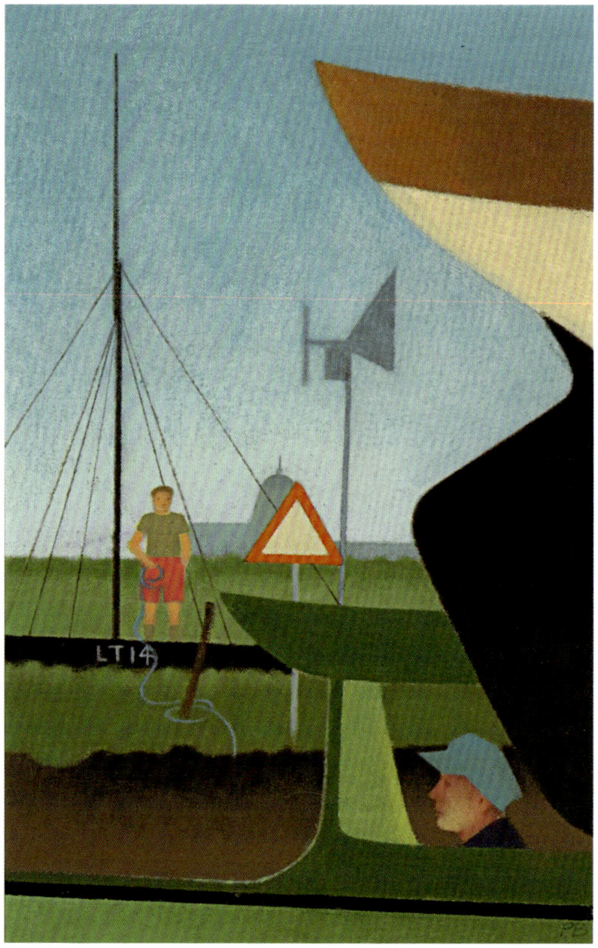

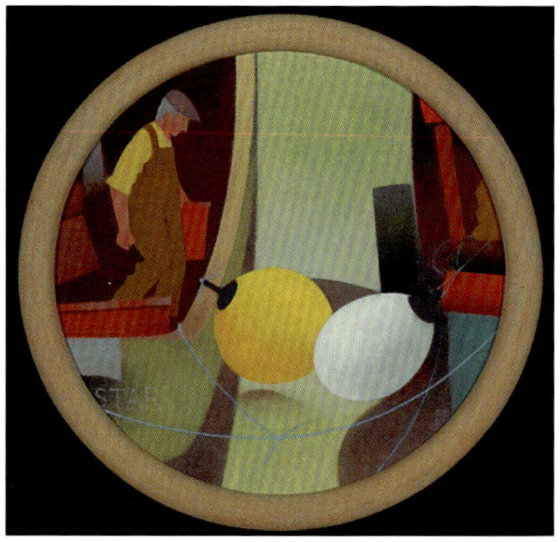

Porthole with Figure, 2008, oil on canvas

Alan in his Boat, Slaughden, 2009, oil on canvas

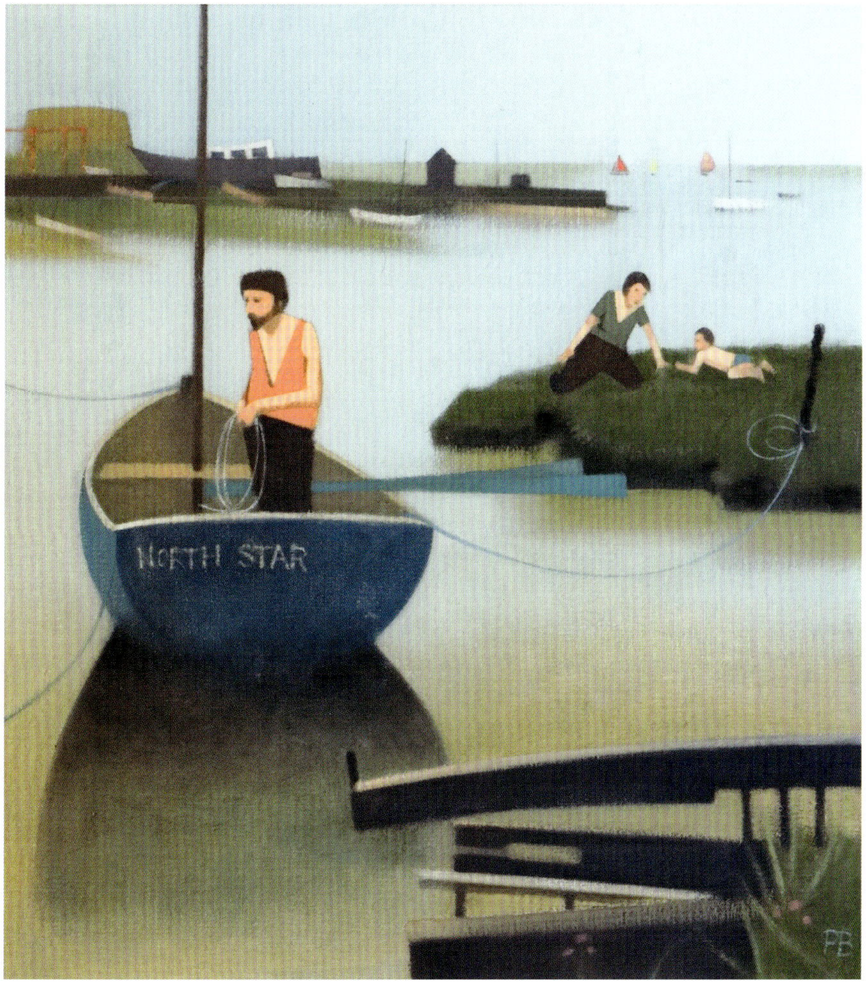

Slaughden – A Homage to Puvis de Chavannes, 2008, oil on canvas

Baldwin sees himself as a painter 'working within a modernist approach by means of implied narrative and cryptic symbol'. But his images of heightened reality owe much to harrowing memory. The figure in the boat in the Slaughden picture reproduced here is a self-portrait, recollected anguish undermining an air of deceptive calm.

In fact, Peter Baldwin was to chart his artistic craft as he wished. At Norwich art school he gained hugely from teachers Jeffery Camp and Michael Andrews, and mentor Leslie Davenport got him to show with the Norwich Twenty Group in its pioneering heyday. He then taught but mostly painted. Although living for much of his life on the North Norfolk coast – with a stint as county council chairman during a decade in local government – he remains haunted by childhood images and a stretch of coastline between Aldeburgh and Orford bounded by the citadels of a Napoleon Martello tower and a former nuclear testing ground.

Encouraged by Michael Andrews to develop ambiguous narratives touching on personal experience, he says now: 'I had noticed that when Michael was painting with us in the

Slaughden sent medieval sons to fish for cod off Iceland. By 1899 **R André** painted its last Three Mariners – an ancient pub in a final row of buildings unclaimed by the sea. By then the front and back doors were being left open so the tide could wash through. In 1908 the last landlady tended the injured when Slaughden Oil Works blew up, but waves soon erased everything save for the mightiest and most northerly of Martello towers.

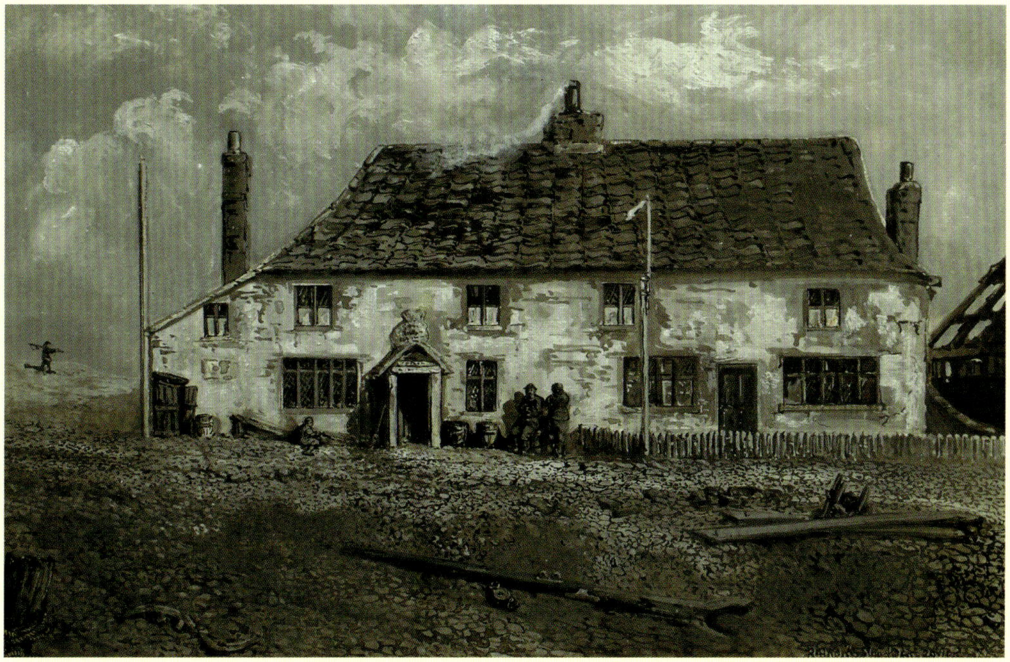

studio, he would sit still for long periods. The look was focused and intense with interior activity. The result was always that the ordinary was given magic and mystery. I had seen the same intense stare years before in the face of Benjamin Britten, the commonplace experience given transformative context.'

Art is about transformation and so is the sea, and few stretches of coastline have been transformed as much as this one. The *Iona* – where Kathleen Hale pictured a holidaying marmalade cat and which L S Lowry drew – was burned in 1974 when a rats' hostel was deemed unsafe for humans. Its blackened base can still be seen at low-tide.

And Orford Ness, that 16. kilometre shingle spit massing to strand Henry II's mighty tower and form a buffer zone from Slaughden to Shingle Street, was a top-secret military site from 1913 and is now a National Trust reserve (next to the RSPB haven of Havergate Island). A surreal assembly of buildings ranges from a red and white lighthouse of 1792 to two concrete pagodas – relics of the Cold War and the Atomic Weapons Research Establishment and currently home to a colony of mutant yellow-legged gulls.

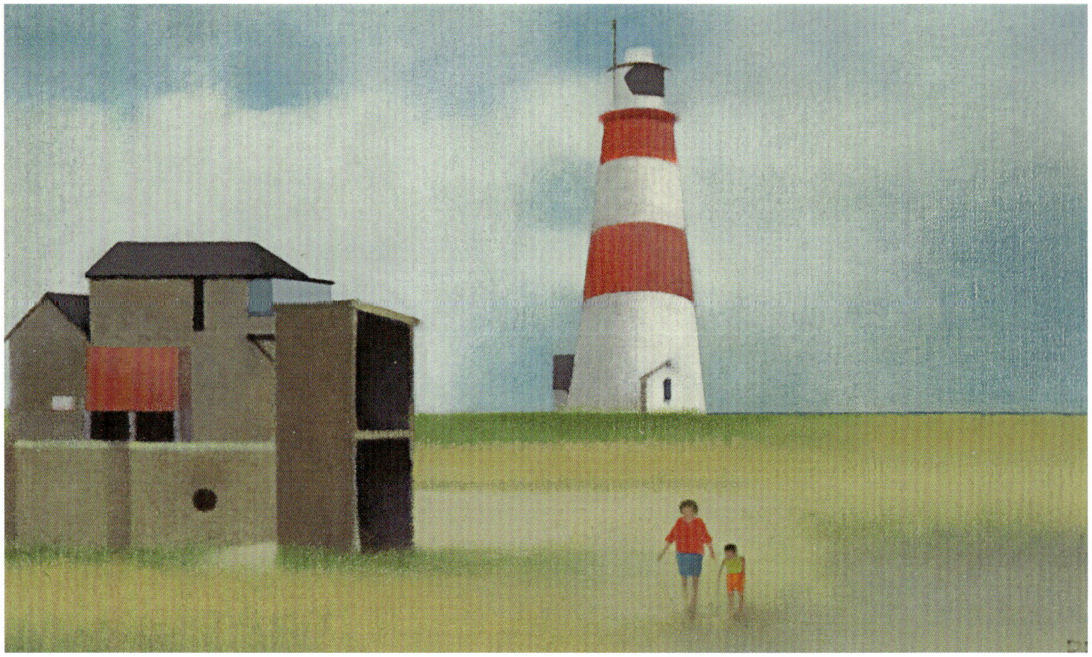

Lookout and Lighthouse – Orford Ness, 2009, oil on canvas

Orford Ness Warrior, 2009, oil on canvas

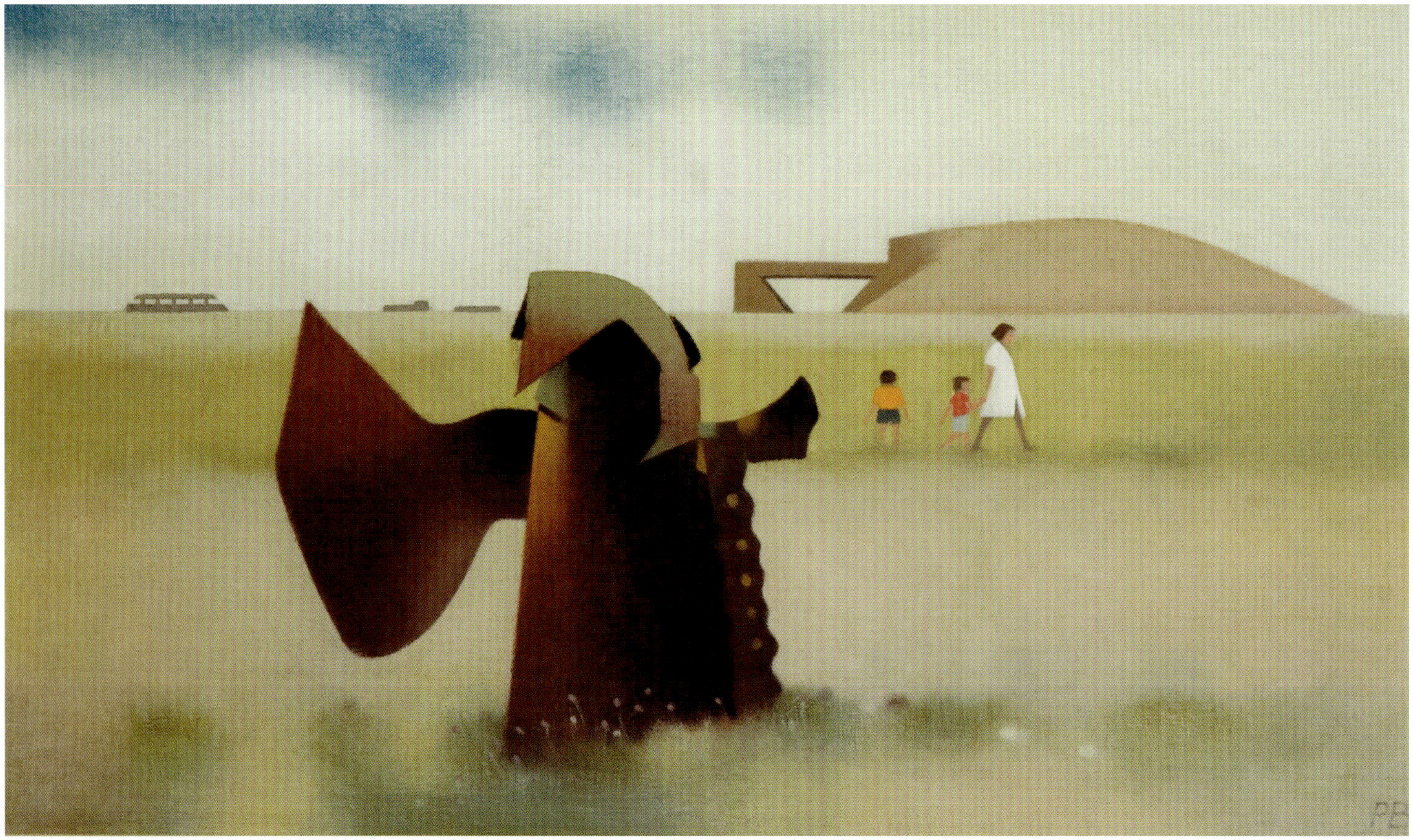

ESSEX FRINGES

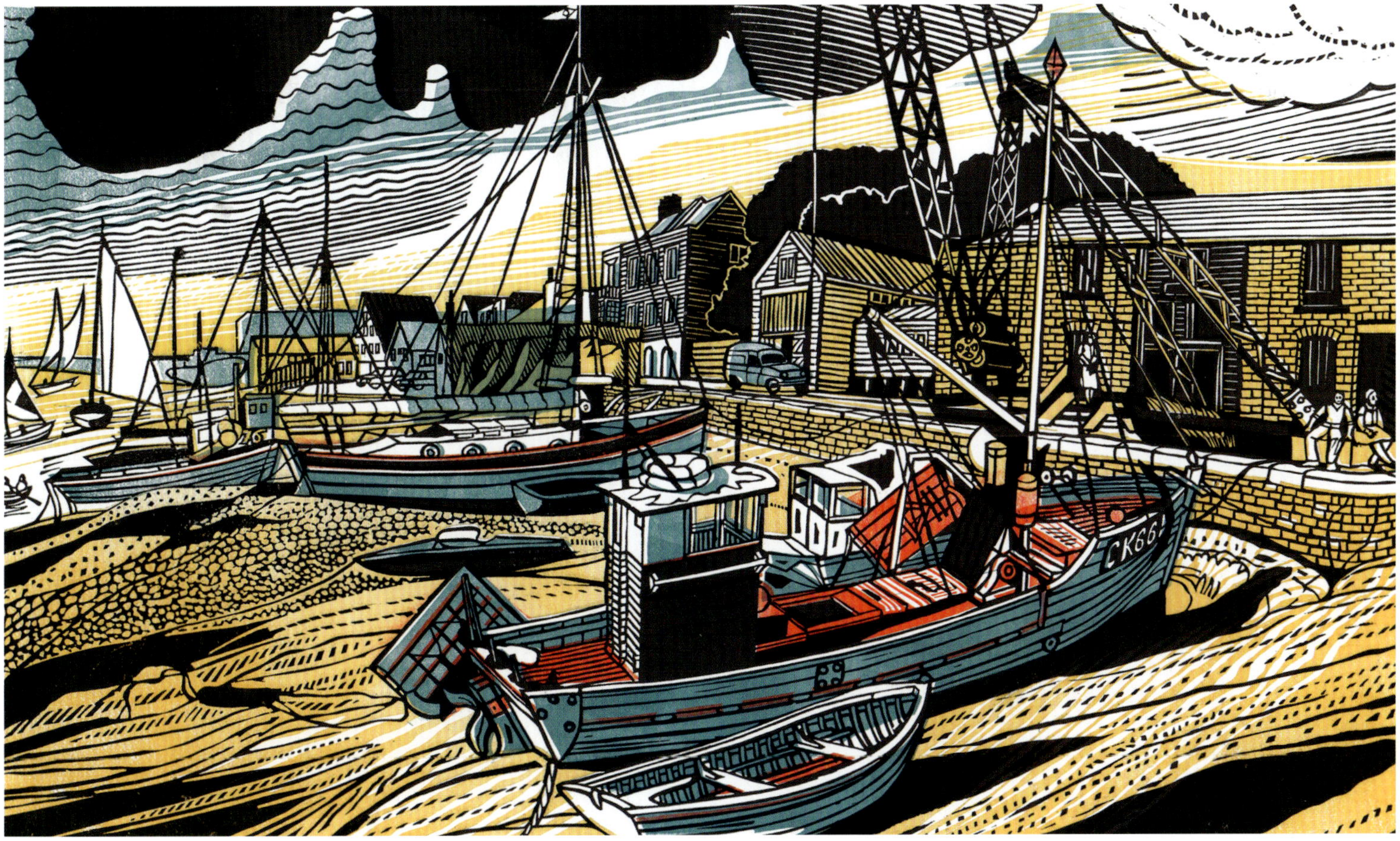

Wivenhoe Waterfront, Richard Bawden, 1985, linocut

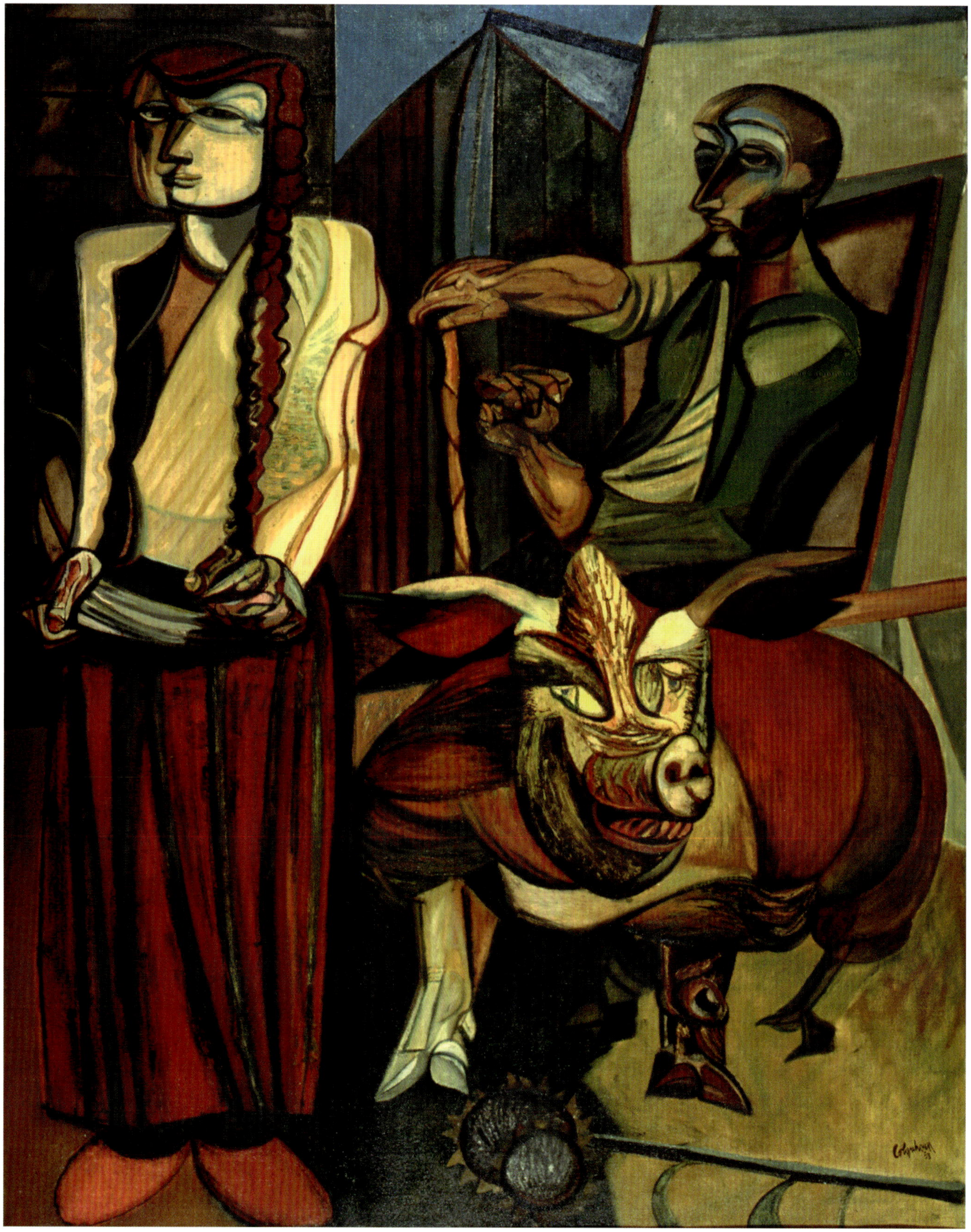

Figures in a Farmyard, Robert Colquhoun, 1953, oil on canvas, Scottish National Gallery of Modern Art

The Last Bohemia

The Two Roberts

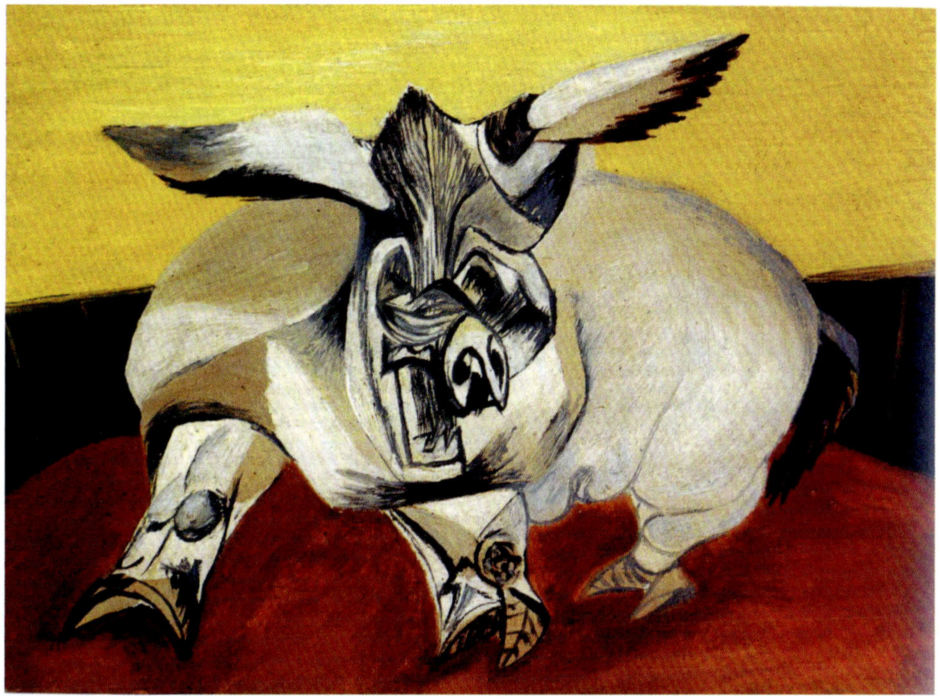

Pig, Robert Colquhoun, c. 1952, oil on canvas

A short Ken Russell film from 1959 opens with a dramatic, sky-dominated South Suffolk scene. Across the crushed terrain, a farmhand is riding a horse and pulling a cartload of canvases. As the wagon passes, we see the painters – **Roberts Colquhoun** and **MacBryde** – sitting on the tailboard. They look as blasted as the landscape.

Having started as an assistant in London's Lefèvre Gallery, and turning to photography and amateur film-making, Russell was making his professional directorial debut with the BBC's Monitor arts programme. Decades later he would tell his biographer: 'I was able to make a film of those two distant, dark heroes of my early gallery days, MacBryde and Colquhoun. It lasts ten minutes and is the most enjoyable film I've ever made. They were great guys, the last of the real Bohemian painters.'

He showed Bohemia moving into the picture-postcard village of Kersey, and an idyllic medieval weaver's cottage behind a garden of roses. Here MacBryde was seen depicting a random still-life on a table. Then footage of a shawl-covered woman walking on a bleak shoreline gave way to Colquhoun at work on one of the highly-charged female figures forming a long funeral procession

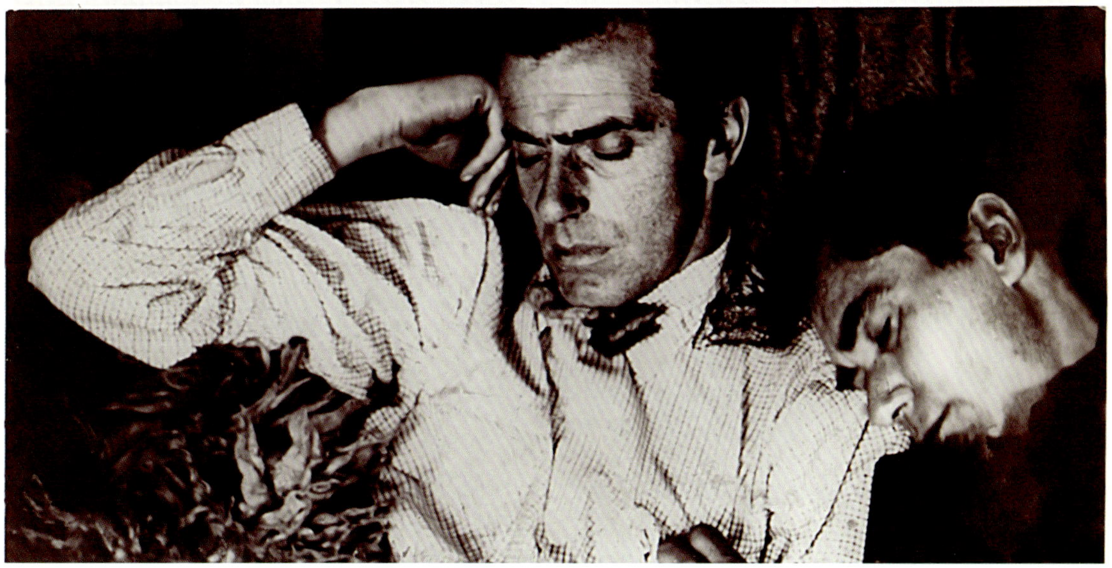

The Two Roberts, Colquhoun (left) and MacBryde (right) at Tilty Mill, John Deakin, photograph

through his briefly brilliant career.

A narrator said the artists were heading for their new home in East Anglia, far enough from London to live cheaply, but near enough to sell their pictures. In truth the Two Roberts, the former Golden Boys of 1940s Bond Street, also needed proximity to a capital supply of pubs, and rounds of Soho in particular.

Not that the relief of alcoholic oblivion was lacking close to hand. In his memoir Ken Russell recalled the mighty task of tracking the Roberts down for his artful documentary. Finally finding MacBryde in their rural retreat, he was then led over a field of stubble to a pub yard from which the collapsed Colquhoun was lifted, carried home and put to bed. That start of the film was very near their end.

But a decade earlier, the two working-class Scotsmen, who had met at Glasgow Art School and then stuck together for good or ill, had been among the great hopes of British modern art. It all went awry well before their energetic and elegantly coloured line in semi-Cubist figurative art, that owed so much to Picasso and also depended on each other, was all but eclipsed by abstraction.

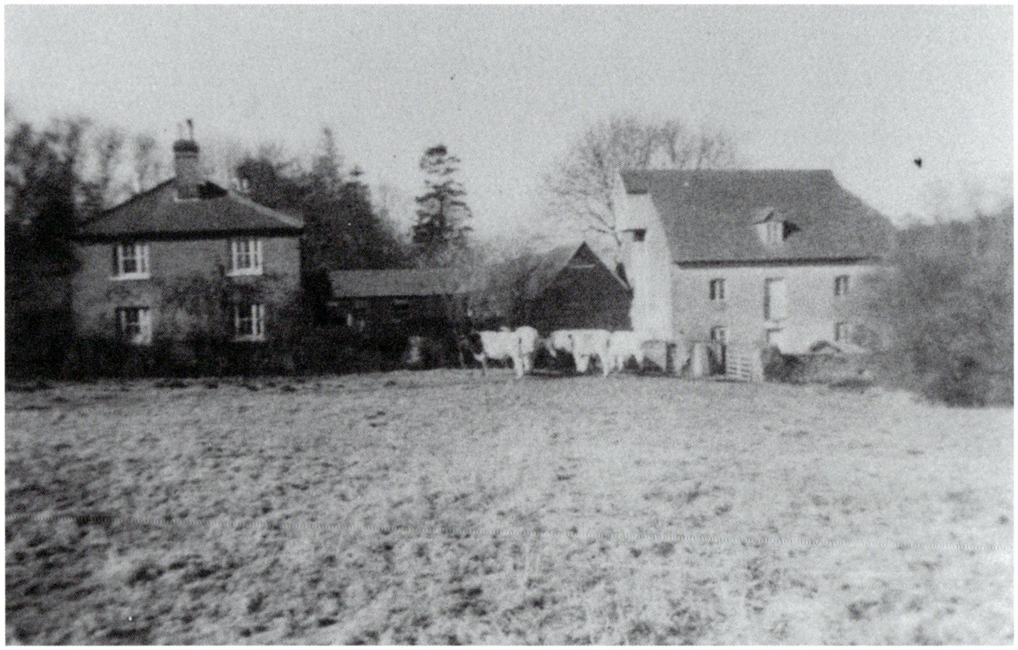

Tilty Mill, Essex, 1950s

Soon after moving to London during the war, MacBryde was confined to bed with what he called 'pernicious partyitis' and while they drank for pleasure among the early patrons and purchases, the Roberts drank for escape when troubles grew. In the end they just drank – Colquhoun dying of an alcohol-induced heart attack, aged 47, in 1962; MacBryde being killed by a car on leaving a Dublin bar four years later.

That short-lived Kersey episode, ending in an almost literally flaming row, was the last in a rural round of false respites set up by kindly and foolhardy friends. Late in 1957, Bobby and Sally Hunt had invited the Roberts to share the Old Forge at Groton near Sudbury – finally enforcing an eviction order when the latest of many nocturnal battles between the warring partners left an oil lamp thrown, smashed and burning.

In 1947 the writer Elizabeth Smart, whose affair with poet George Barker produced four children and the prose poem *By Grand Central Station I Sat Down And Wept*, had begun renting Tilty Mill in the North Essex wilds between Great Easton and Dunmow. She sub-let from Surrealist poet Ruthven Todd, who left behind his precious books and pictures. Now a single mother and magazine journalist, she

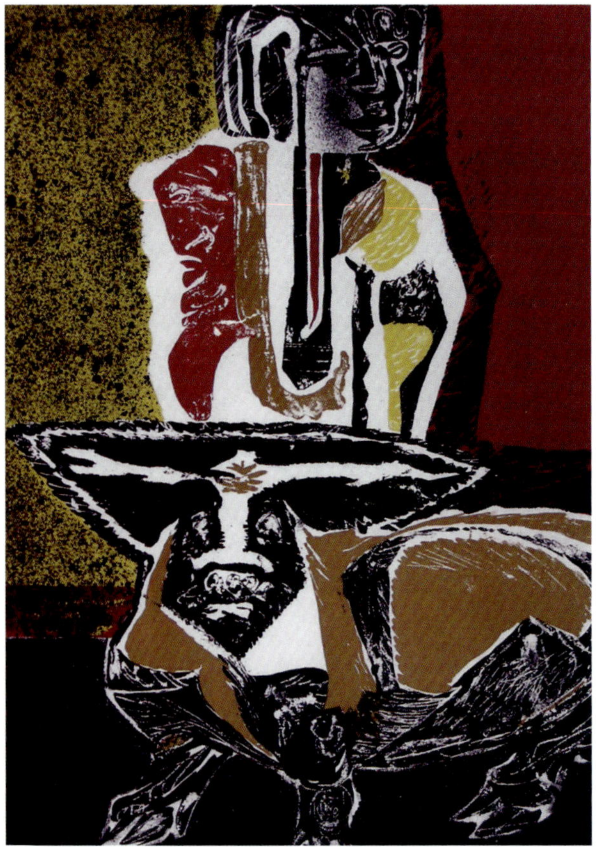

Man with Pig,
Robert Colquhoun, 1951,
lithograph (left)

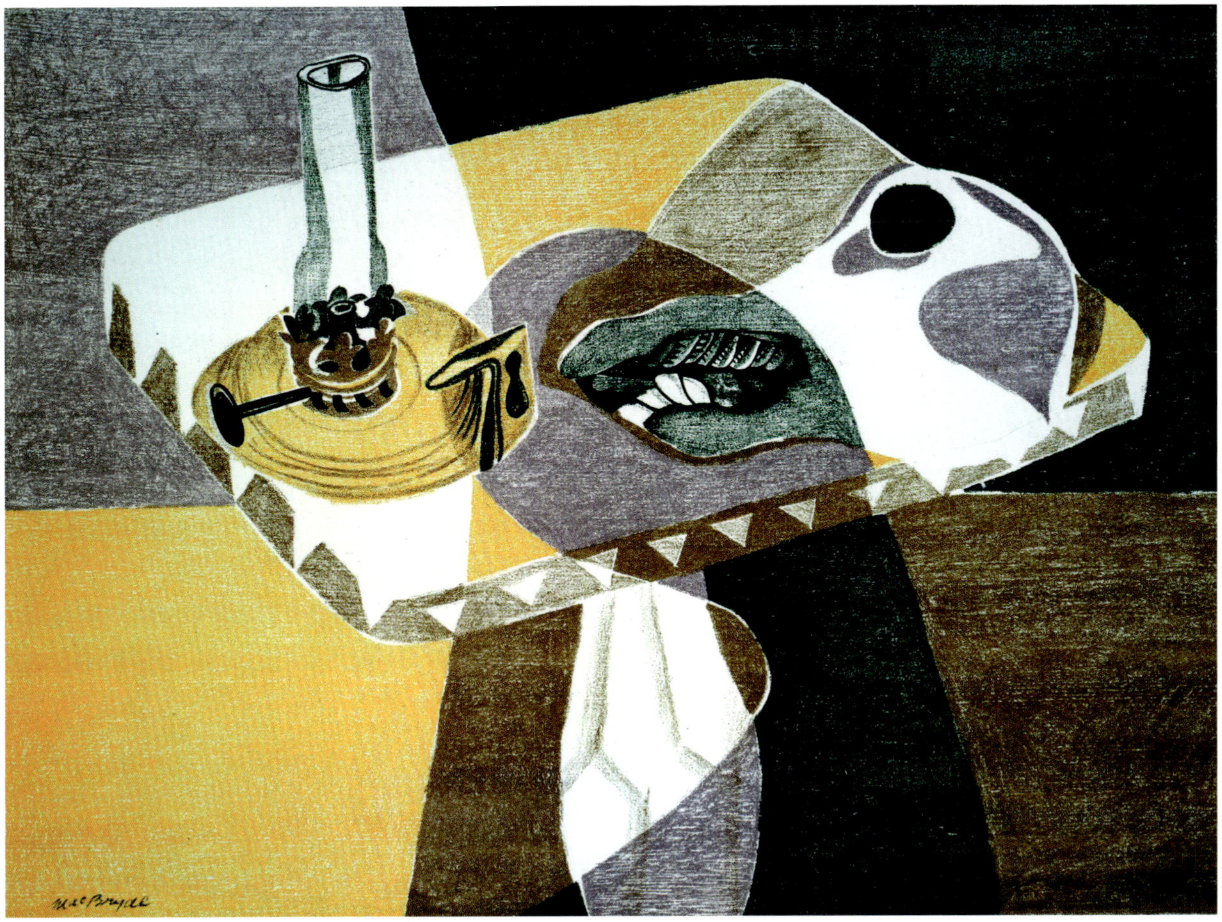

Still Life with Lamp,
Robert MacBryde,
c. 1953, lithograph

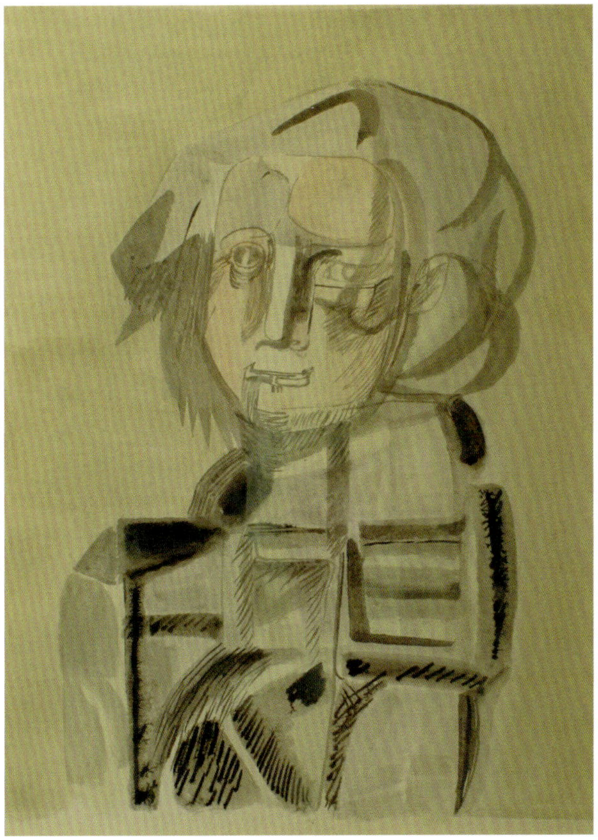

Georgina Barker,
Robert Colquhoun,
c. 1952, watercolour

needed help with childcare while working during the week in London. When a succession of housekeepers failed, she turned, as if asking for trouble, to her Soho chums Colquhoun and MacBryde.

But Georgina, Christopher, Sebastian and Rosie adored minders soon regarded as surrogate parents. Affectionate, amusing and intensely inventive, they showed that life was a great adventure. Even after late-night smashing sessions they took care to clear up the debris in the morning. Ruthven Todd's later complaint that the pair had wrecked and plundered the place – recalling an impression of a house 'gone blind' due to broken windows – was disputed by loyal witnesses.

In three years at Tilty Colquhoun worked on drawings and monotypes inspired by his surroundings – farm animals, gypsies and their dogs. He also produced the major and highly unusual 1953 painting *Figures in a Farmyard* (long unsold but now in the Scottish National Gallery of Modern Art) and several preceding

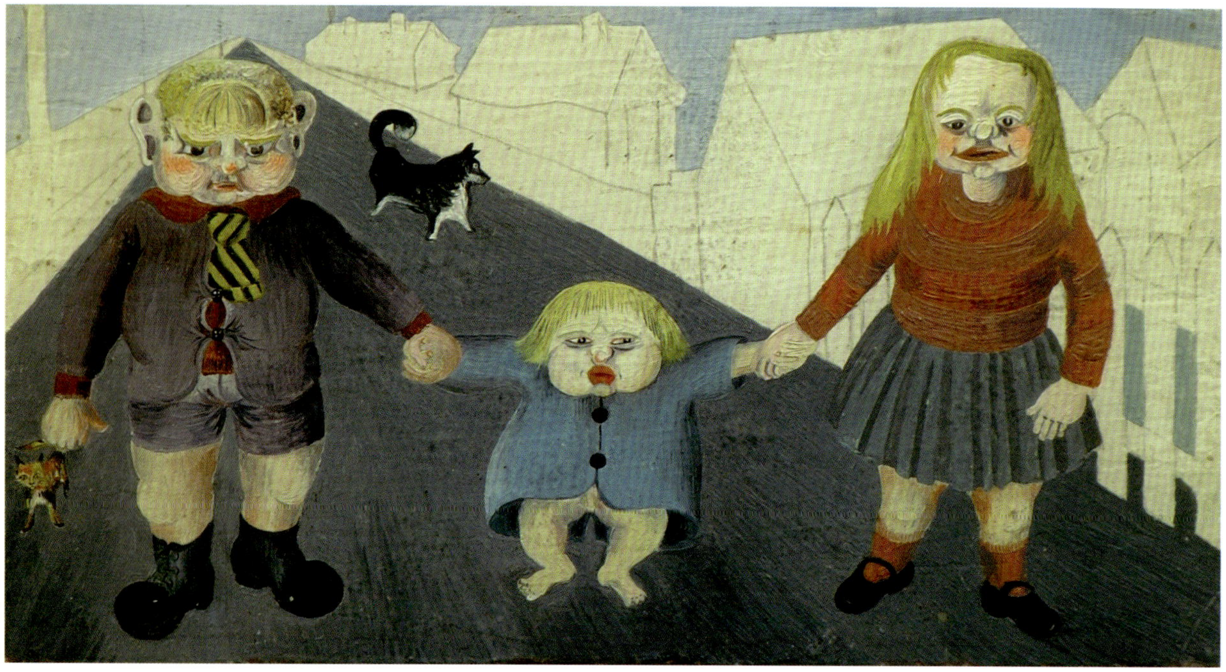

The Hearn Children,
Richard Chopping, c. 1940,
oil on board

studies. The conventional portrait of a family group is here subverted into an old man, a young girl and a leering pig trampling a sunflower. Bohemian Essex could be dark indeed.

But all had seemed so bright when, early in May 1945, close to the peak of their powers and the height of their fame, the Roberts had visited **Richard Chopping** and **Denis Wirth-Miller** in Wivenhoe. Here they drew River Colne scenery between frequent pauses for refreshment and one big party on Victory in Europe Day. Attending a fireworks display in Wivenhoe Park – painted by Constable and later the site of the University of Essex – the four artists had nabbed a dingy and rowed into the middle of the lake for a better view. Leaping up to raise a toast, the kilted MacBryde then toppled overboard and his companions feared an imminent drowning. But as Wirth-Miller told the Roberts' biographer, Roger Bristow, 'he soon bobbed up, encircled and supported by the kilt floating on the water's surface'.

Wivenhoe, the old port of Colchester turned university village, can lay claim to being East Anglia's truest Bohemia – boasting a creative community which had Wirth-Miller and Chopping, 'Denis and Dickey', at its fractious heart until the latter's death, three days after his 91st birthday, in 2008. Richard Wasey Chopping was born into a Colchester milling family, his love of art nurtured at Gresham's School, in Holt, where he was a contemporary of Benjamin Britten and the spy Donald Maclean. After studying at Cedric Morris's East Anglian School of Painting and Drawing, he produced the book *Butterflies in Britain* (1943) and worked for seven years with writer Frances Partridge on what was to have been a 22-volume encyclopaedia of British wildflowers before the publisher uprooted the project on cost grounds when the collaborators were still dug in on the letter C.

Meeting in 1937, Chopping and Wirth-Miller had lived for a time at Daffodil Cottage in Wormingford – where the former's dim view of three young neighbours (shown here) belied his later success as an author and illustrator of children's books. But he was to be best-known for his trompe l'oeil watercolour images of beauty and death on the dust jackets of nine of Ian Fleming's James Bond novels, starting with *From Russia, With Love* in 1957. Not that he cared for the stories, once he got round to reading them. He concluded: 'I don't mind a bit of sex, but there is enough violence in the world without needing to make it more glamorous.' That must have caused much mirth in Wivenhoe where the two Bohemians – the first couple to register a civil partnership in Colchester in December 2005 – staged

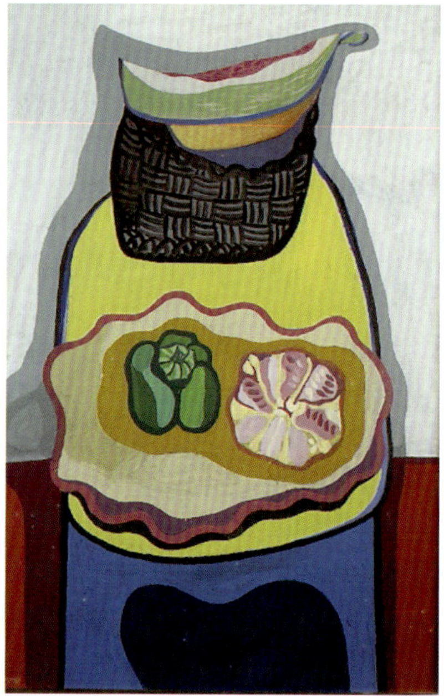

Still Life with Basket,
Robert MacBryde, 1953,
oil on canvas

legendary rows which Margaret Drabble likened to 'the kitchen scene, with dough and utensils flying, in pantomime'.

They had bought their quayside house in 1944, but war-time restrictions meant that they moved in the following year. Here Wirth-Miller worked on peaceful marshscape panoramas which featured in an Aldeburgh Festival exhibition and, reputedly, in the 1950s, collaborated with visitor Francis Bacon on several pictures. Lodging in a pub or with his friends, Bacon prompted further merry mayhem. In the early 1970s he acquired his own working base in Queens Road – the street name amused him – and there were riotous visits to Long Melford where the brother of his Cockney lover and eventual heir, John Edwards, had made Georgian Westgate House another Bohemian outpost.

Wirth-Miller once took Bacon to see Guy Taplin, but they never actually met. Taplin was detaining two Jehovah's Witnesses in lengthy debate at his front door, when the painter friends, having entered by the back door and waited in the kitchen for as long as their patience could bear, emerged from the side alley before vanishing down the street. Pointing at Bacon's departing head, Taplin told his evangelical canvassers: 'There goes the Jesus Christ of art.'

Portrayed by Epstein, Derain, Giacometti, Picasso and Bacon, **Isabel Rawsthorne** (1912-1992) was one of the great muses of modern times. She was also a notable painter and stage designer and an unsurpassed Bohemian.

The cat-like beauty born Isabel Nicholas was raised in London and Liverpool, her mariner father importing exotic animals which were housed in the family home before being sold to zoos. She came to love wildlife and wild life equally.

After the death of second husband Constant Lambert, she married Alan Rawsthorne – their close friend and another composer – in 1954. They moved to Sudbury Cottage, Thaxted, though Isabel still stalked Soho, being photographed by John Deakin for images passed to **Francis Bacon** for a sequence of sublime (distorted but instantly recognisable) portraits in the 1960s. As Isabel said: 'If you look at the details, they are fabulously accurate.' *Three Studies for a Portrait of Isabel Rawsthorne,* from 1965 (see below) is now at the Sainsbury Centre for Visual Arts. The Norwich treasure house also holds a bust of Isabel by Giacometti, with a second example in Cambridge's Fitzwilliam Museum.

After Rawsthorne's death in 1971, his unmerry widow shared an increasingly isolated rural life with cats and geese. Having depicted dancers, she wanted to portray the animals inhabiting her studio (weasels, swallows, owls), then turned to the airy filigree of bird skeletons and to campaigns to conserve the Essex countryside.

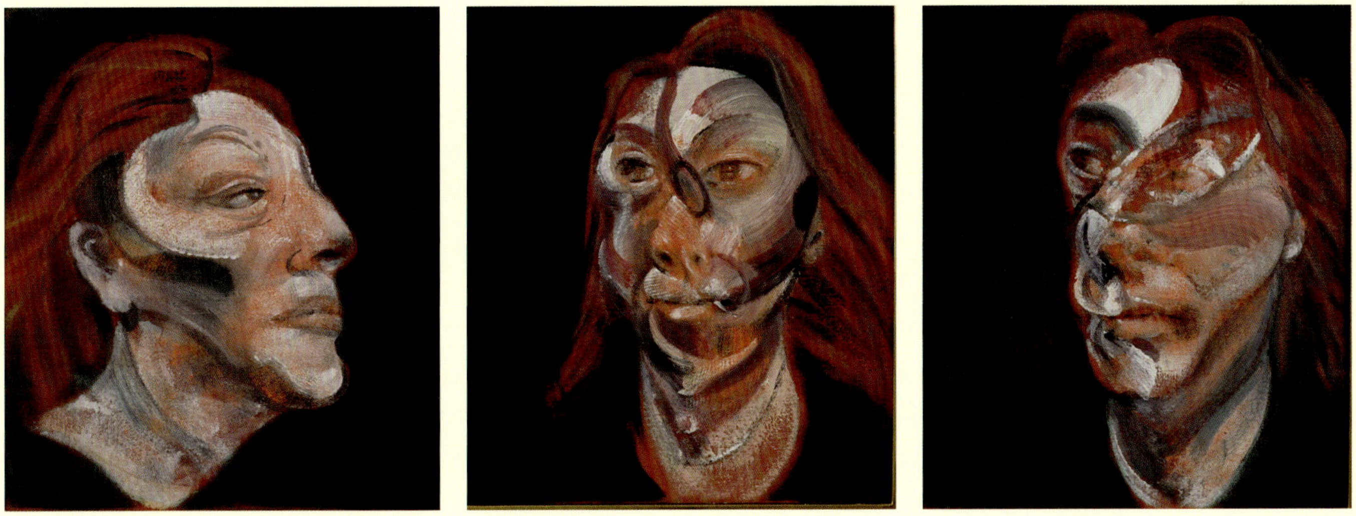

Cormorants, painted wood

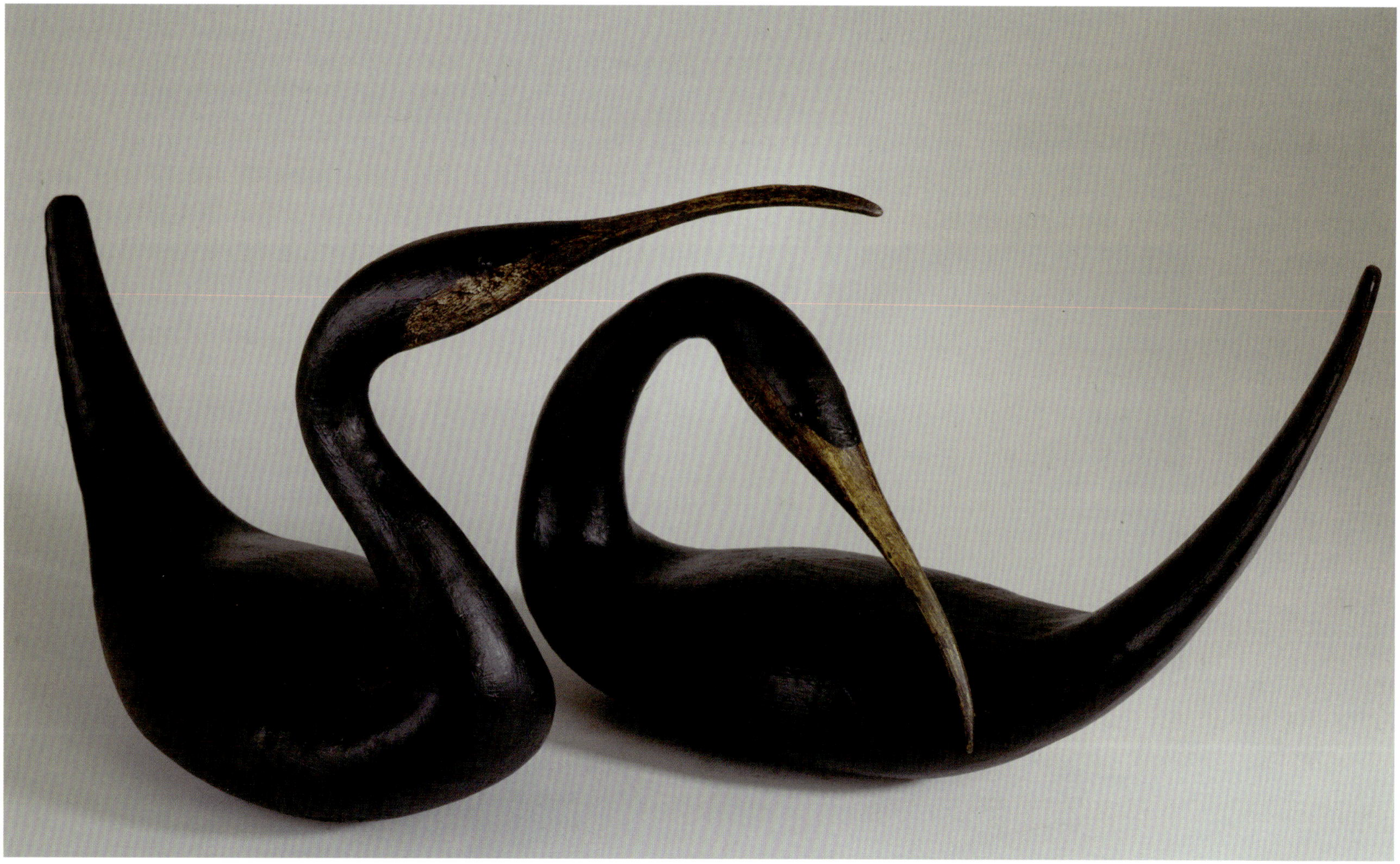

Wild Men of Wivenhoe

Guy Taplin and Ernie Turner

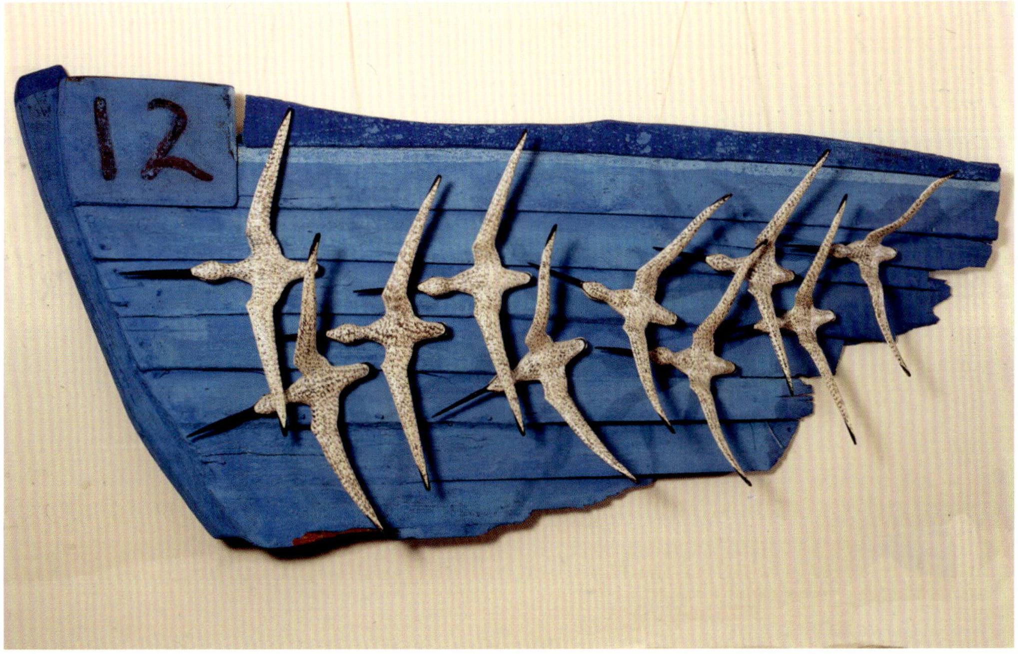

Ten Sanderlings, painted wood

Down the eastern edge of England winter migration brings huge flocks of waders and waterfowl from Scandinavia and the Arctic Circle and swans from Iceland and Siberia. Out on the Essex marshes these avian visitors are carved in stupendous flights and stands by Britain's premier bird sculptor, **Guy Taplin**.

Deeper yet, images of elemental creatures, breathing new life into salvaged wood with an eerie earlier existence, suggest the wildness we all yearn for via the wilderness embraced from the 1970s by a Cockney jack-of-all-trades turned Bird Man of Regent's Park. He narrowly avoided a calling as a Buddhist monk before fledging as a sculptor.

The keeper of the royal parks' foremost ornamental waterfowl collection first whittled on a whim a crude decoy-like model of one of his charges out of a piece of driftwood rescued from Thames mud. Obsession – and the transformation of forests of discarded timber, from chopped-up telegraph poles to chucked-out theatre seats and sculling boats – made perfect as an untrained craftsman evolved into an unmatched artist.

At times there appears precious little method in the Taplin creative madness. Asked for guidance on how to make a duck he has replied: 'You get a piece of wood and you chop off everything that don't look like a duck.' Nervy souls have quaked to see the sculptor approaching his most fragile masterpieces with a mallet, having somehow conjured them up with electric bandsaw, blowtorch, rasps and sanders, paintbrushes and scrubbing brushes, dabs of pigment and much rough handling.

Some of his best creations seem to have been liberated from sunken ships or caves or burial chambers, and then arrested on the brink of erosion and extinction. He says: 'Through sheer force of repetition your eye develops and

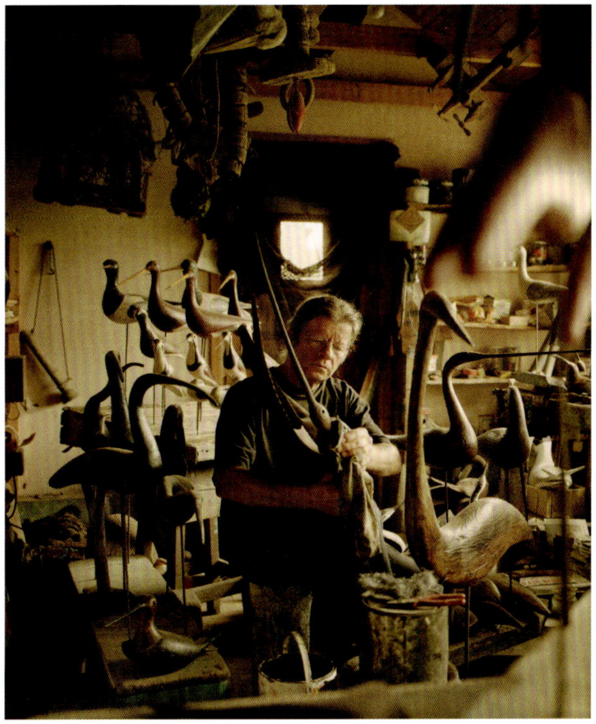

Guy Taplin in his studio

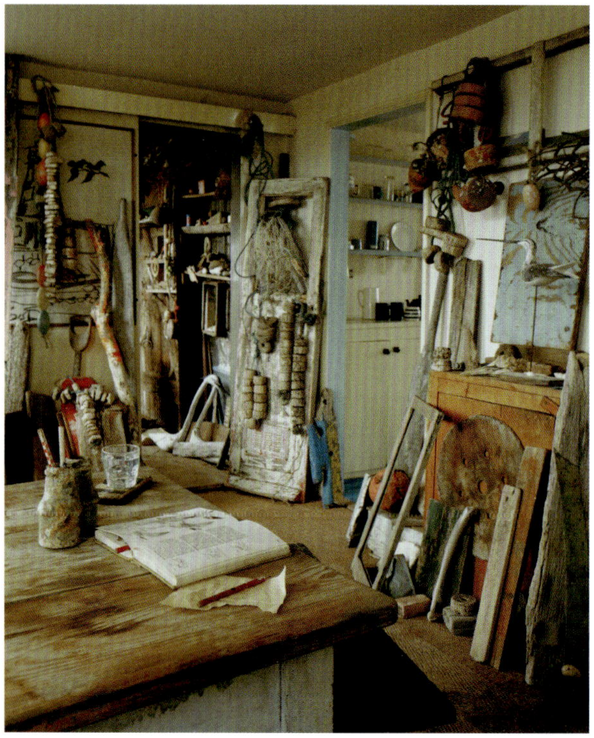

formed from salvaged russet hatch covers and the yellow-painted front of a beach-combed mahogany chest of drawers.

Other stands display the bleached blue of boat fragments which are the artist's favourite souvenirs from frequent visits to a bird reserve in the Algarve, where Atlantic storms and currents have created a haven for smashed and splintered vessels – debris awaiting rebirth. In fact, sharp as a heron, Guy Taplin has stalked ocean edges and estuaries from Africa to America, fishing for the raw materials of his art and then lugging home bright cargoes like a giant magpie.

But his greatest hunting ground remains coastal Essex: on the sandbanks and the mudflats where at night, from the sail-loft workshop beside his Wivenhoe sea captain's cottage, he can hear the curlews calling; or else on the shore barely below his studio in a pre-

Artist's studio (left)

you are able to get the length, width and depth of the bird correct very quickly. And then you find you've added the feeling of movement and the spirit as well.'

His flock of fans include Michael Palin, who owns typical Taplinesque birds and a singular *Guy Taplin*. That's the name writ large on a jaunty model fishing vessel on whose deck stand two figures in a pose the former Monty Python star associates with 'old British underwear catalogues, pipes clamped reassuringly in jaws as if they were modelling a new range of ocean-going vests and long johns'.

He adds: 'Guy has told me of his admiration for Alfred Wallis, another self-taught artist who drew inspiration from the sea. Wallis is generally classed as a primitive. I don't know if Guy is in the slightest bit interested in art labels. All I'd say is that if an artist can with so little fuss and such great assurance transport me and my home into the sky or onto the sea I wouldn't call him a primitive; I'd call him a magician.'

And so a six-foot panel of an old east coast tender might be transformed into a flank of white whale over which tiny sanderling flit and skim, while further groups of waders are

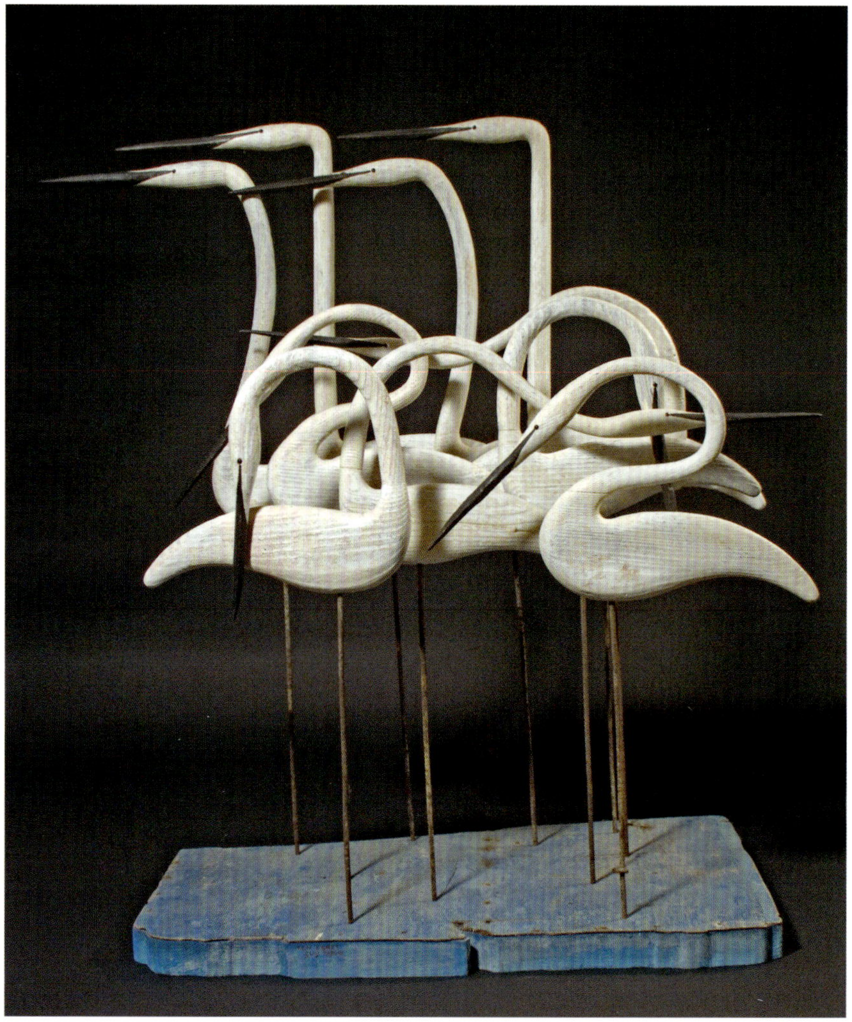

Egrets,
painted wood

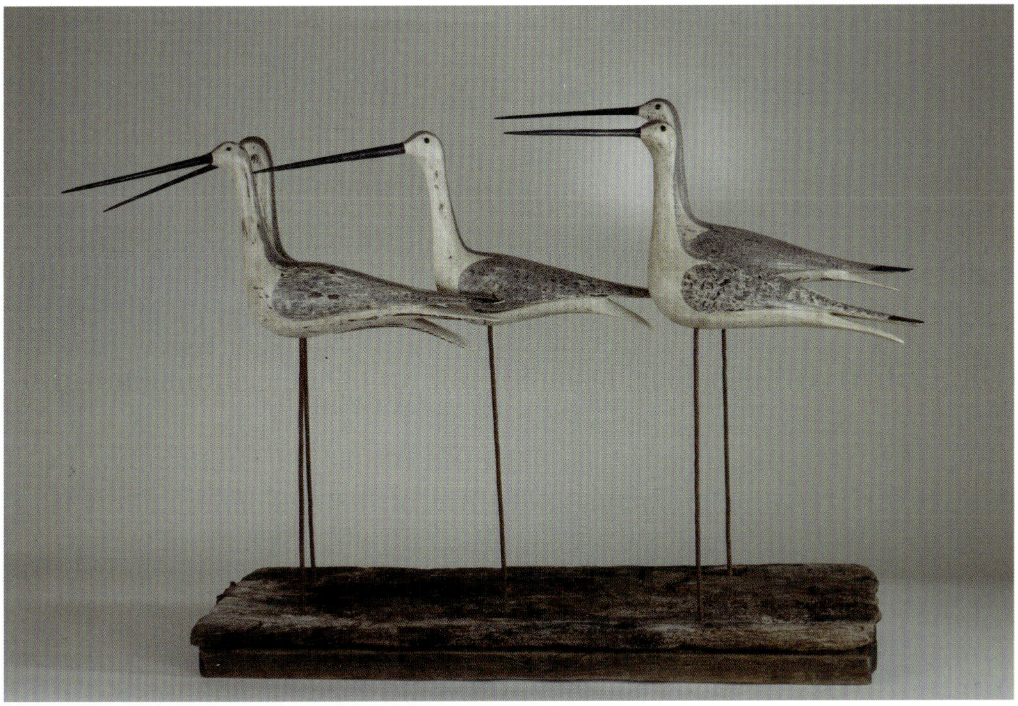

Godwits, painted wood

war holiday chalet which the tide sometimes maroons in a saline lake stretching as far as the eye can see.

Most especially in winter, birds are his friends and neighbours. Here, perfectly at home on the edge of everything, are certainly to be found the oystercatcher, the turnstone and the Taplin. And then… those strange cries, flutterings and shadows on a darkening afternoon just might be the ghost of a great auk or an albatross.

Nature writer Richard Mabey says: 'Being a bit of a beachcomber myself, I often expect to come across a fully-fledged Guy Taplin caught in the flotsam, tangled in the fish-egg-cases and old feathers, hatched and shiny. His pieces always have that sense of being wave-shaped and wind-honed themselves.

'I feel he is plugging into something ongoing, as well as adding his own grace notes. Putting it another way, if evolution had a strong sense of humour (it has) and was obliged to express the idea of birdishness in wood, these are the forms that might result.'

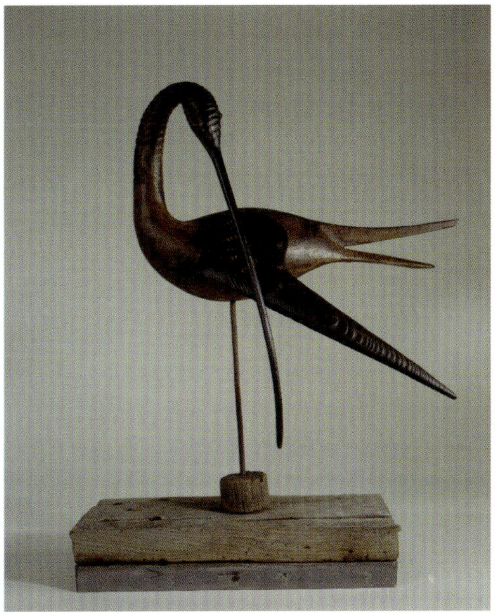

Preening Curlew, painted wood

And Ronald Blythe adds: 'What an enviable man he is. It must be wonderful to be in that shed at Point Clear with the sea offering up its materials and the gulls shouting, "make me!" "make me!"'

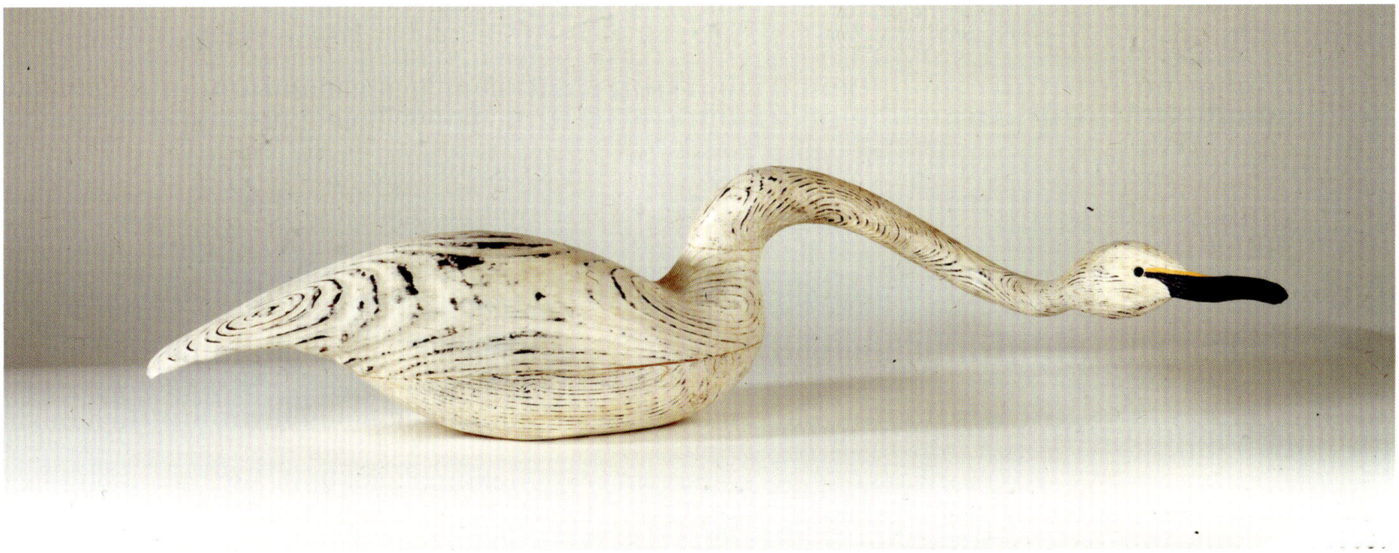

Reaching Swan, painted wood

Ernie Turner (1899-1977) was born into a large Wivenhoe family, his father being a shipwright and his seafarer clan crewing every variety of vessel from smacks to the royal yacht *Britannia* scuttled off the Isle of Wight after George V's death in 1936.

Details of his early voyages remain a mystery but when he married, in Southampton in 1920, his older bride hailed from the Channel Islands and they lived on Jersey until the pending Nazi invasion sent them fleeing to his childhood home. He then worked in the town as a shipwright – at Admiralty, Wivenhoe and Cook's shipyards – until retirement in 1964.

With an ailing second wife to care for, and in need of extra cash, he responded to an incoming tide of artists and academics by concluding that he could join or sell to them. This not-so-naïve folk artist was also well aware of Alfred Wallis – with whom he shared Salvationist as well as nautical interests. 'If those Cornish buggers can do it, so can I,' he was heard to comment from the 'Old Boys' bench on Wivenhoe Quay.

As Wallis had been championed by Christopher Wood and Ben Nicholson, so Ernie Turner was encouraged by Denis Wirth-Miller, who gave advice on painting and brought buyers from both sides of the Atlantic. The Essex Wallis duly obliged with hallmark pictures of the Wivenhoe waterfront – often painted to order and at prices to fit the pocket of the purchaser.

Although preferring hardboard, he worked on and with any materials to hand – scraps of old housepaint, combining with oil, ink and watercolour on paper, cardboard, formica or even canvas placed horizontally to stop the

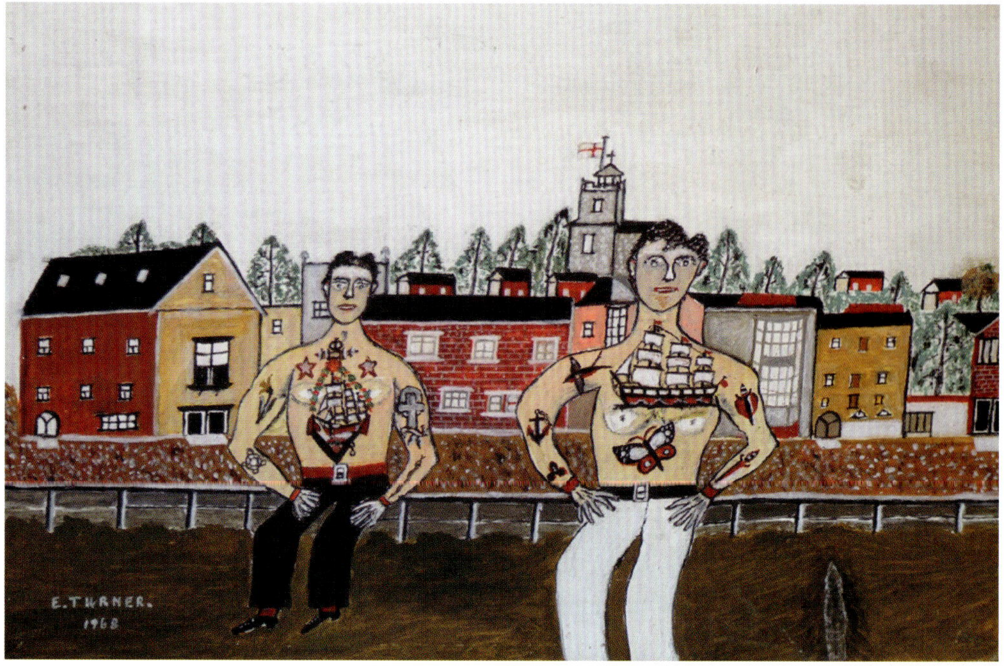

Tattooed Men,
1968, oil on hardboard

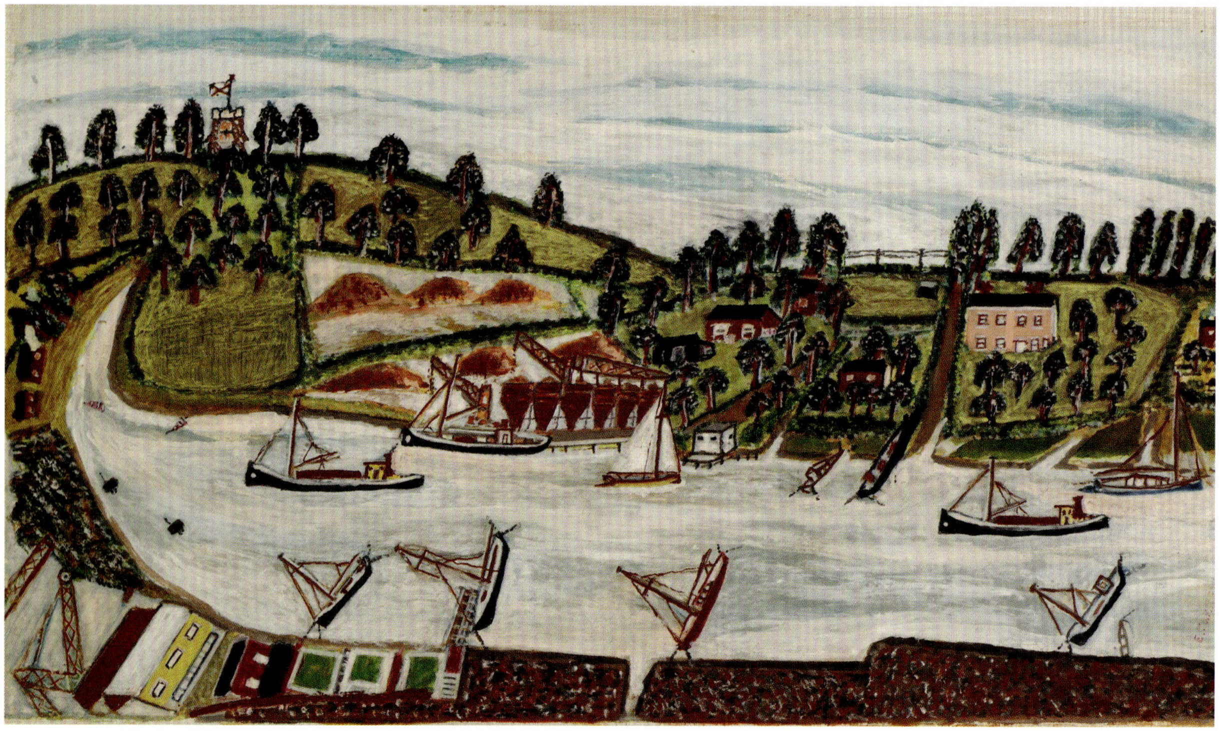

River Scene,
mixed paints on formica

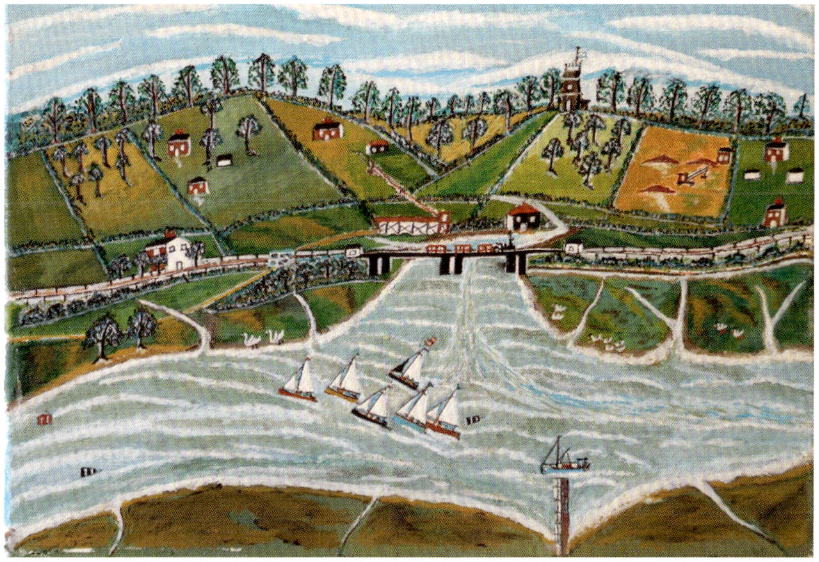

View of Alresford Creek, oil on canvas

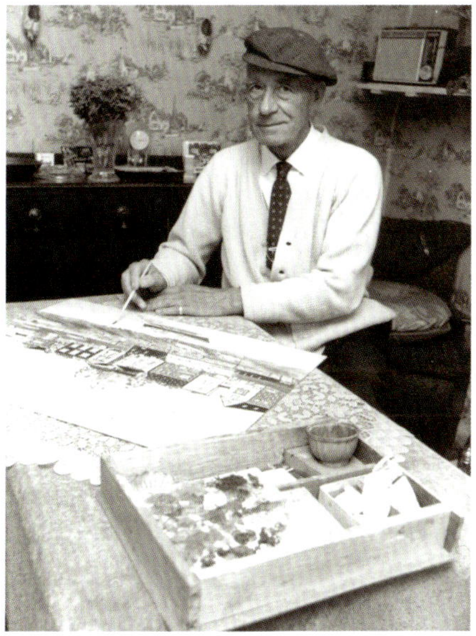

Ernie Turner at home

paint 'running away'. He also made model boats and performed the marine craftsman's trick of sailing miniature vessels in bottles.

For all the hints of hack work, his was a truly authentic localist vision – whether imagining Wirth-Miller and Richard Chopping as tattooed matelots on the quayside (see p.130) or recreating surrounding River Colne scenes. His view of Alresford Creek has the 'Crab and Winkle' steam train crossing the Iron Bridge while white-sailed yachts flock like geese between swans and shelduck.

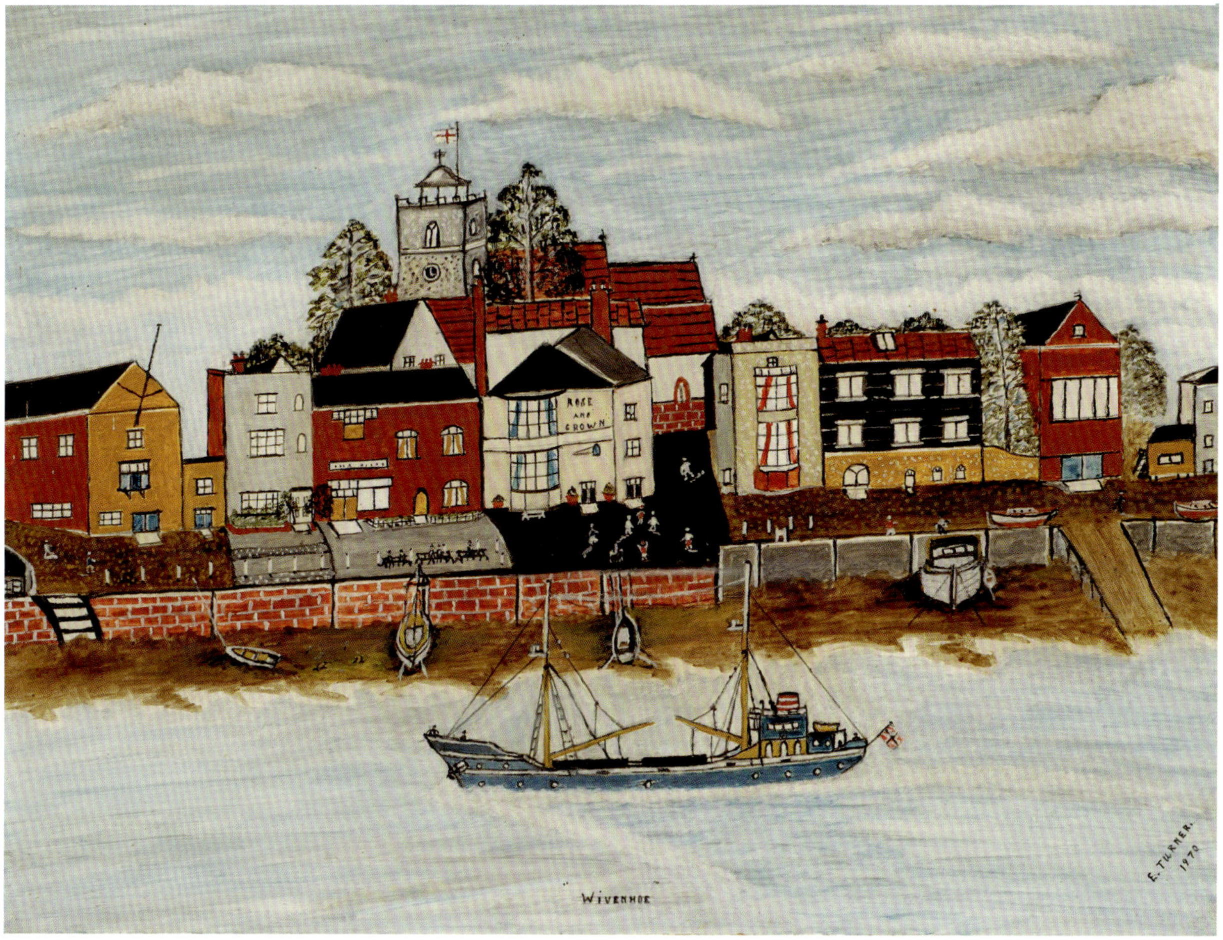

Wivenhoe, 1970, oil on board

Wivenhoe Past and Present, James Dodds, 1996, linocut

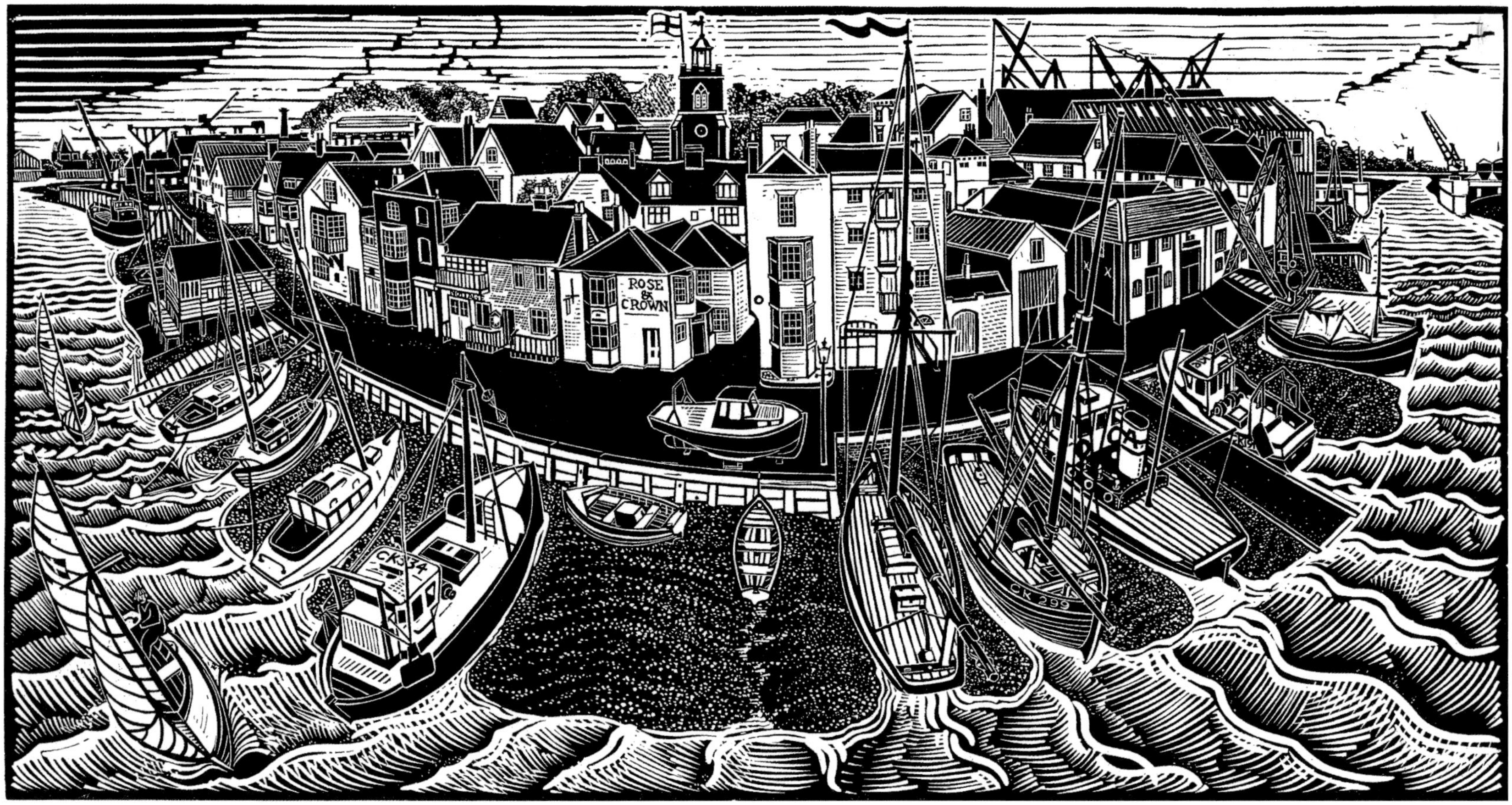

Ports and Boats

James Dodds and Derek Nice

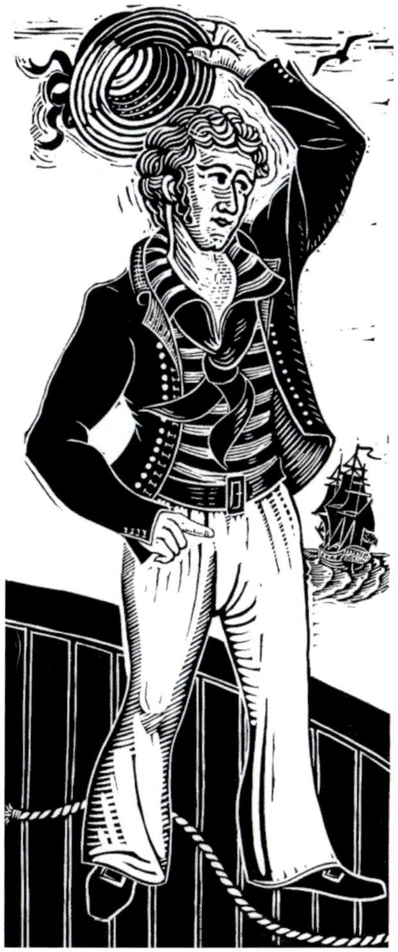

Billy Budd, 1993, linocut

A fleet of painted, gouged, sculpted and fine-press printed boats has floated from the water-side studio of shipwright turned maritime recorder **James Dodds**, whose current berth at Wivenhoe is a short sail down the River Colne from his birthplace at Brightlingsea.

He has portrayed – and fought to preserve – vernacular vessels from the Scillies to Orkney, but charted most lovingly the distinctive river and coastal craft of East Anglia, whose ports and boatyards he has also celebrated in gulls'-eye-view linocuts.

Having struggled in formal education due to undiagnosed dyslexia, James Dodds swapped school at 15 for a shipwright's apprenticeship at Walter Cook and Sons in Maldon. By that point he had already learned to sail in a smack and a winkle brig, and spent working weekends on a Baltic Trader, exploring East Coast estuaries and crossing the North Sea to France and Holland.

He learned by watching Alf Last, builder and restorer of smacks and Thames barges over seven decades – grasping the value of maths through the process of 'lofting', making moulds from full-scale drawings and then calculating the required amount of timber for the emerging boat. A gift for draughtsmanship was further honed in evening art classes and then in impromptu sketching sessions as a boatyard's self-appointed 'artist in residence'.

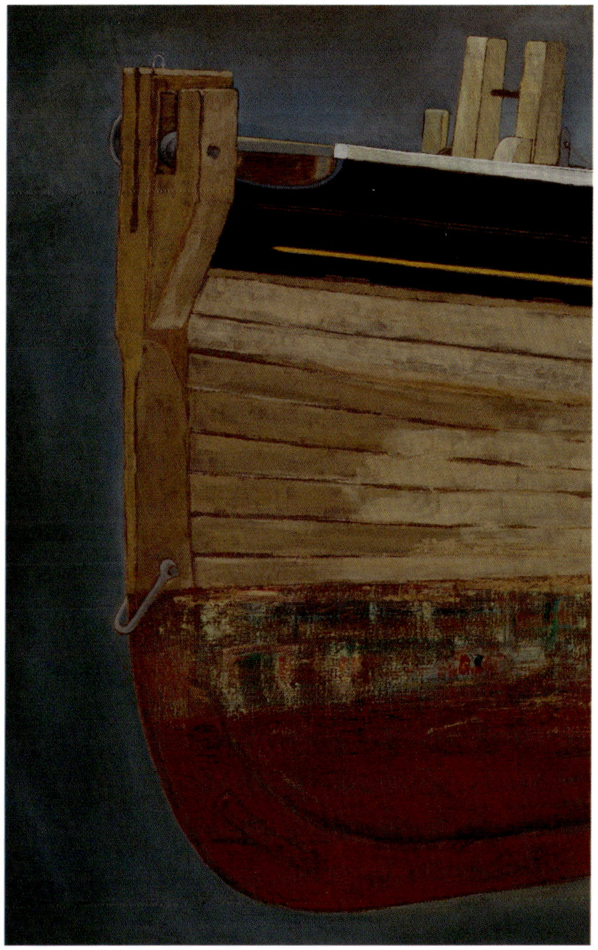

Bow of a Small Smack, 2007, native mud, pigment and oil on linen

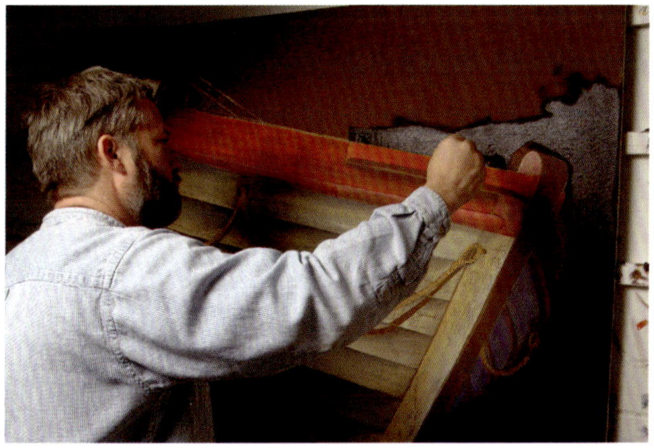

James Dodds at work

His was to be a long apprenticeship for training in Maldon gave way to art studies – with a foundation year in Colchester then a further six in London, at Chelsea and the Royal College. To an extent he was following his father, Andrew Dodds, who had left the family farm at Weeley to train as an artist and enjoy a prolific career as a watercolourist and illustrator (early on using his family as models for The Archers in sketches for the *Radio Times*).

As he told Paul Thompson in the book *Sea-*

change: *Wivenhoe Remembered*: 'It was only really in the final years at college, that I realised that the background I'd got was very rich. And from that point onwards, I've been making pictures about the boatyards, and the construction of boats, and the subtlety of the shapes of boats, the regional variations, and how boat shapes have evolved to suit the kind of fishing and the kind of harbours and sea conditions in the region.'

He had wrestled with strongly symbolic and allegoric imagery until, with a big show looming at The Minories in Colchester, he suddenly covered a long-unresolved picture with a long, blue boat. Now, decades into a master mariner's voyage, he says: 'The boat has become a metaphor for my identity, combining my boat-building and artistic selves. But the boat also has a broader analogy with that of a community within a defined space, whose differing and yet complementary characters can feel secure however uncertain the surrounding seas may appear.'

James's favourite vantage point – with the vessel up on the stocks and the sheer line at eye-level – gives the viewer the same perspective as the builder. But, like a nautical anatomist, he also picks apart the structure of a vessel and shows us the intricacy of internal congregations of linked timbers akin to medieval church roofs (the words 'nave' and 'navy' sharing the same root).

The first blue boat – monumental as a blue whale suspended in an indigo infinity – led a portrait fleet of local and regional vessels from a launch in Colchester to a four-year Shipshape voyage around the country, ranging from Thurso to Falmouth and with a final call at the National Maritime Museum in Greenwich. That epic journey then gave way to a sellout debut at Messum's in London's Cork Street.

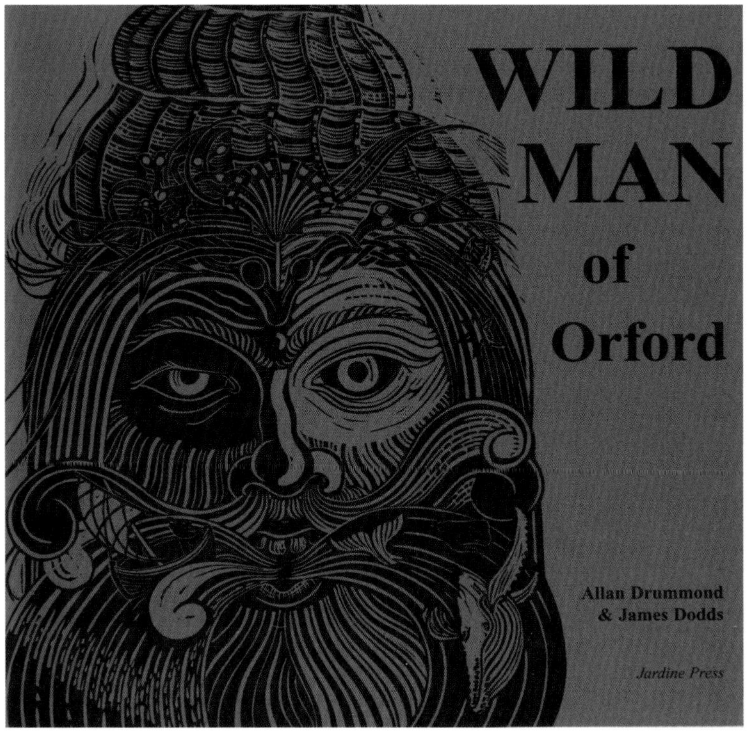

Cover illustration, 1997, linocut

Meanwhile the ancient boatyards on the River Colne were fast foundering. Over ensuing decades of dereliction James Dodds fought hard for the ghost sites to be reclaimed by the local community, but all were eventually sold for development. The last, Cook's Yard in Wivenhoe, brought the tide of housing almost to his studio door. The artist's first venture into carving was inspired by a discarded shard of pavement from the construction site. It now bears the image of a boat like a tombstone. A similar memorial shape was claimed for the monumental *River Colne Shipbuilders: A Portrait of Shipbuilding 1786-1988*, which

East Coast Boats, 2004, linocut

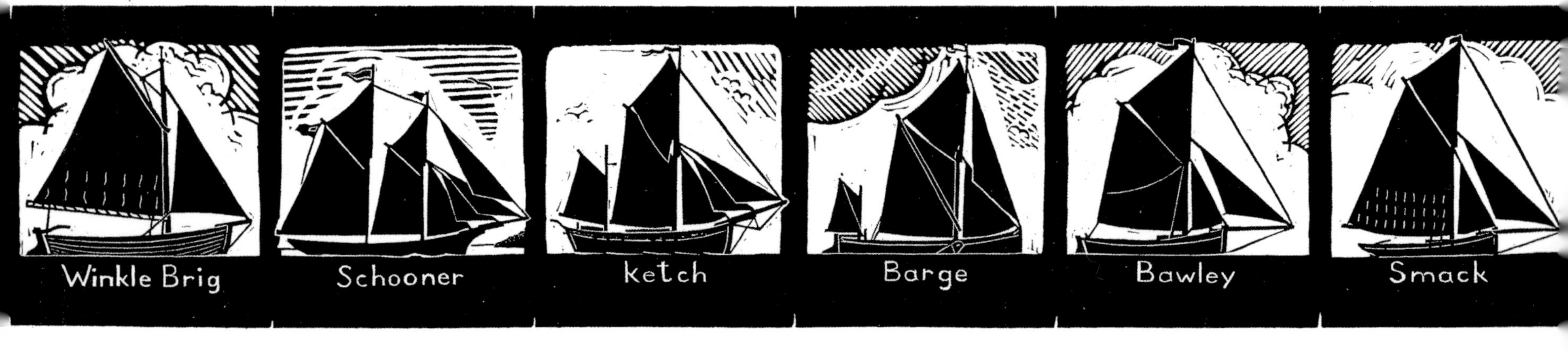

James's Jardine Press produced with historian John Collins in 2009.

But two strengthening communities, in both of which James now finds a place, keep the spirit of creativity alive. One is an artistic assembly – including poet Martin Newell, collaborator on Jardine Press titles including *The Wild Man of Wivenhoe*, an ironic take on the trials and ultimate triumph of an Essex student (and a neat echo of *The Wild Man of Orford* volume recounting the medieval saga of the merman caught off the Suffolk coast). The second is a university fraternity whose students and tutors now hail from all over the world. James, awarded an honorary degree for services to the community as an artist and campaigner, has paid tribute to this creative growth in his linocut *University Tree*: a grand old over-arching oak, already imposing when Constable painted his image of Wivenhoe Park in 1816, and shown by Dodds sheltering a young sapling planted after the 1987 hurricane.

In the multi-media art of James Dodds the connecting thread is not a straight line but an arc – an impulse both to move forward and return to the home port. A curving motif may also be discerned within each picture: the bow of a boat, the curl of a wave, the reaching and bending of figures engrossed in creative labour. The sea, which smoothes and rounds everything, albeit with great trauma and drama, is the artist's constant inspiration.

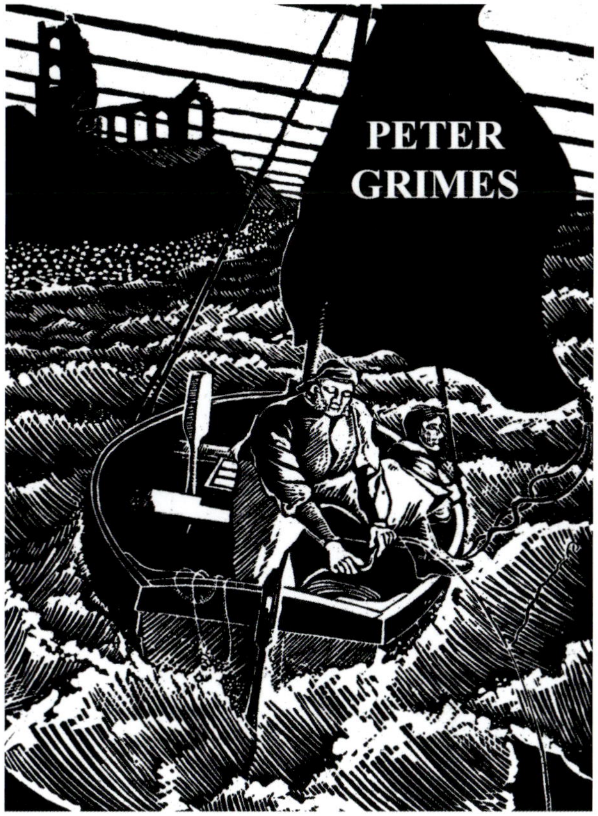

Cover illustration, James Dodds, 1984, linocut

Moving between Malta and a land-locked swathe of the Mendip Hills in Somerset, marine artist **Derek Nice** seems at first glance an unlikely East Anglian. But our sea-lapped region fairly claims him.

A born Londoner displaced early on to Essex, he has deeper East Anglian fishing and farming roots. Two great uncles ran a fishing boat out of West Mersea, while another tended a market garden on Colchester's North Hill. He himself has lived, worked and roamed here. But the French-originating name Nice – pronounced 'niece' – also reveals a wanderer's genes.

Having been a promising junior art student, Derek gained a National Service posting to RAF Waterbeach in Cambridgeshire, whose commander was in urgent need of a creative talent. He was duly despatched in a Tiger Moth with a former Battle of Britain Spitfire pilot to check out officers' mess decoration across the region. Securing the required intelligence, he then turned a humdrum hut into a French Impressionist fantasy and a sergeants' mess into a Wild West saloon.

So bizarre a mission proved a flying start for

White Beach,
Derek Nice, oil on canvas

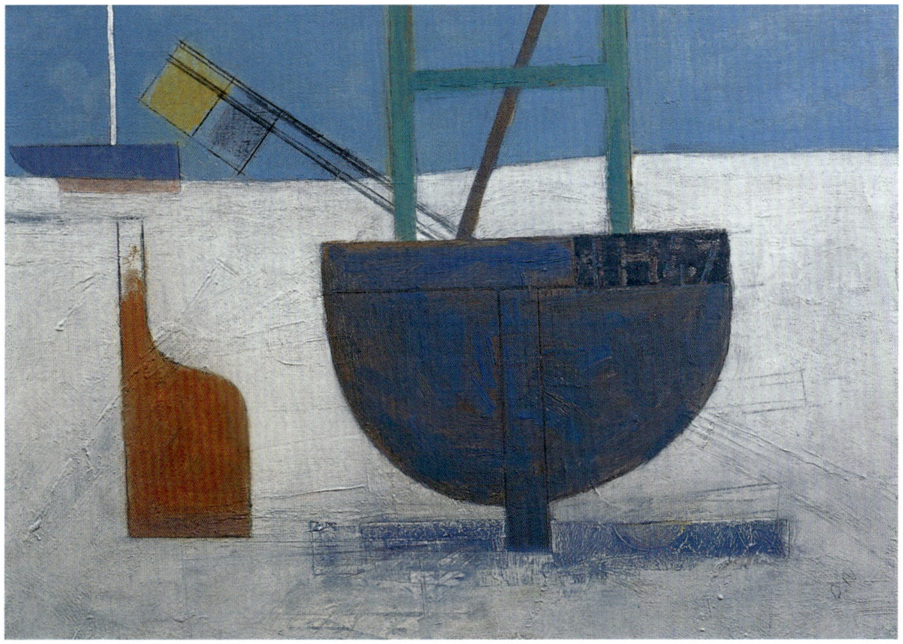

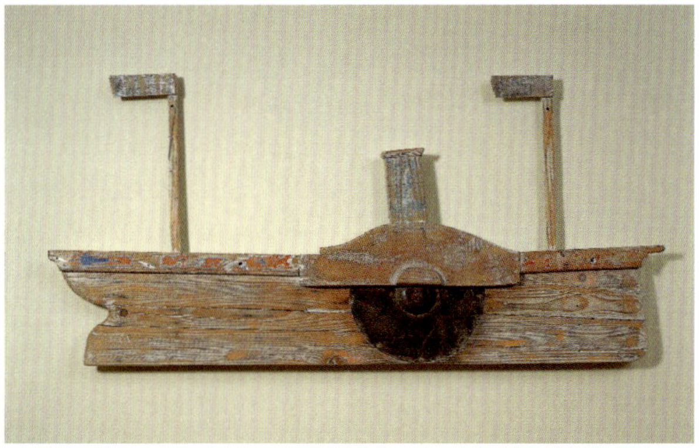

Paddleboat, mixed media

a man who, after spells of teaching and then a post-graduate design degree from London's Central School of Art, became an art director and designer for stage and screen. He worked on Ken Loach's first film, and with Ken Russell and John McGrath. He was the set decorator for Simon Gray's movie adaptation of the J L Carr novel *A Month in the Country* (with early roles for Kenneth Branagh and Colin Firth).

Then he extended his skills into museums – designing, for instance, the Trafalgar Story at Portsmouth, a replica Viking longship in Oslo and the Gozo Heritage Museum. A huge wooden ark carved as a visitor centre for Colchester Zoo was conceived and built with Essex farmer David Eagle.

In the 1970s he spent several months at Pin Mill on the River Orwell helping to restore a spritsail barge, and also crewed on another – *Millie* – on trips to Maldon. When, in the mid-1980s, there was a broad switch to boat-centred sculpture and painting, the first models were based on Belle steamers once ferrying passengers between Tower Bridge and Yarmouth and most piers in between. Then vernacular fishing craft gave way to images drawn from vessels painted on pyramid interiors or scratched on rocks in the Nubian desert.

Derek Nice has made much from driftwood found along our coastline, and also painted fishermen's haunts from Blakeney to Felixstowe Ferry, via Southwold, Sizewell and Aldeburgh. Pakefield's workaday beach offers an added air of mystery. He says: 'Everything has been wrapped up, so you're not sure whether the parcel contains a boat or a winch. And the wrapping is anything to hand – tarpaulin, striped awning, plastic sheets.'

Here is an ideal spur for images grounded in representation but floating towards abstraction, with hidden depths of meaning in blocks that may or may not be boats.

Visiting Greece as a student, Derek Nice fell for the history and colours and atmosphere of the Eastern Mediterranean. When wedded to the textile artist Mary Pasmore – daughter of artists Victor and Wendy – he also married into an obsession for Malta, and for the raw splendour of a rocky outcrop weathering waves of invasion, soaking up passing cultures and yet remaining resolutely itself. The island has also proved a rich hunting ground for a resourceful beach-comber.

Salvaged life in a found object, from a broken-up boat or an old oak floorboard, adds to those desired depths of meaning. Just as iron and copper nails pulled from the planking of lost clinker-built boats are resurrected as Lowry-like mariners in a model fleet.

Carving and constructing and painting and drawing concurrently – whether in East Anglia, Somerset or Malta – Derek Nice revels in the working process but contends that the message in the art is essentially the same. 'It's not the medium but the arrangement that matters,' he says.

Still, there is a love of materials. He savours the 'viscous, flexible performance of oil paint –

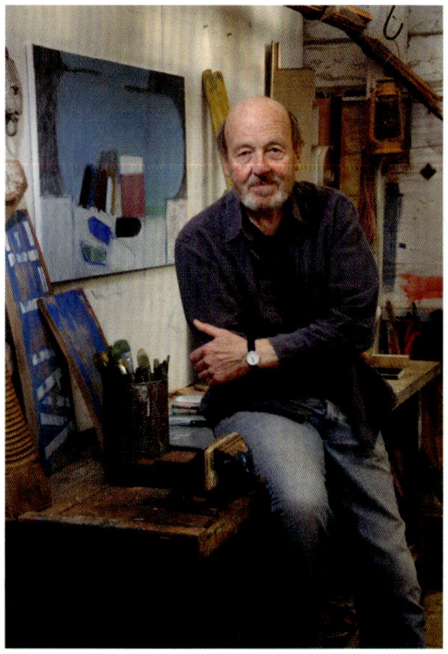

Derek Nice in his studio

Pakefield Beach III, oil on canvas

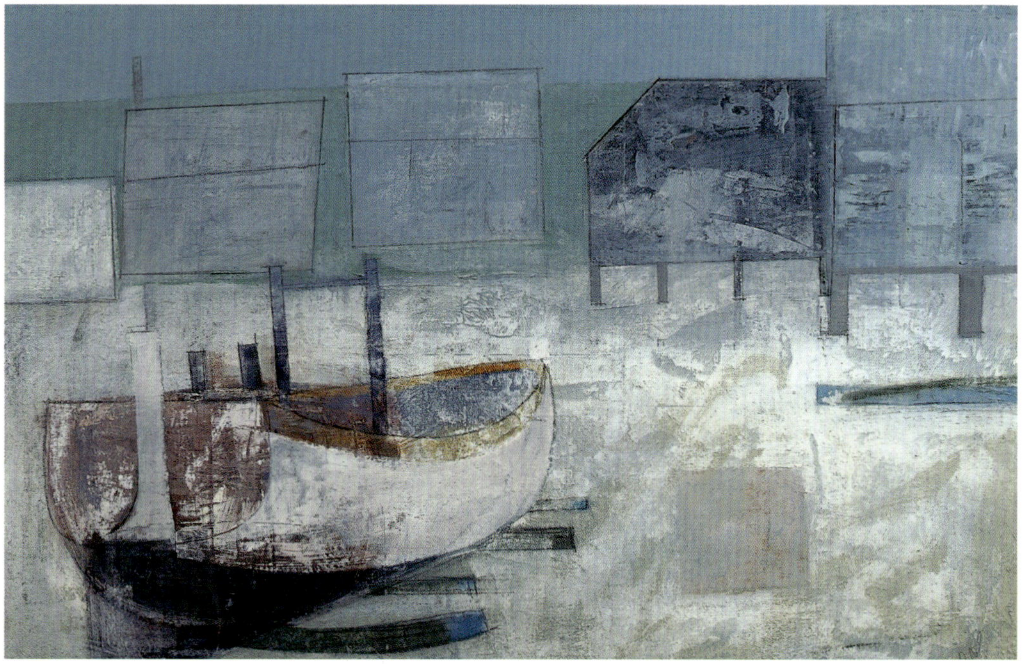

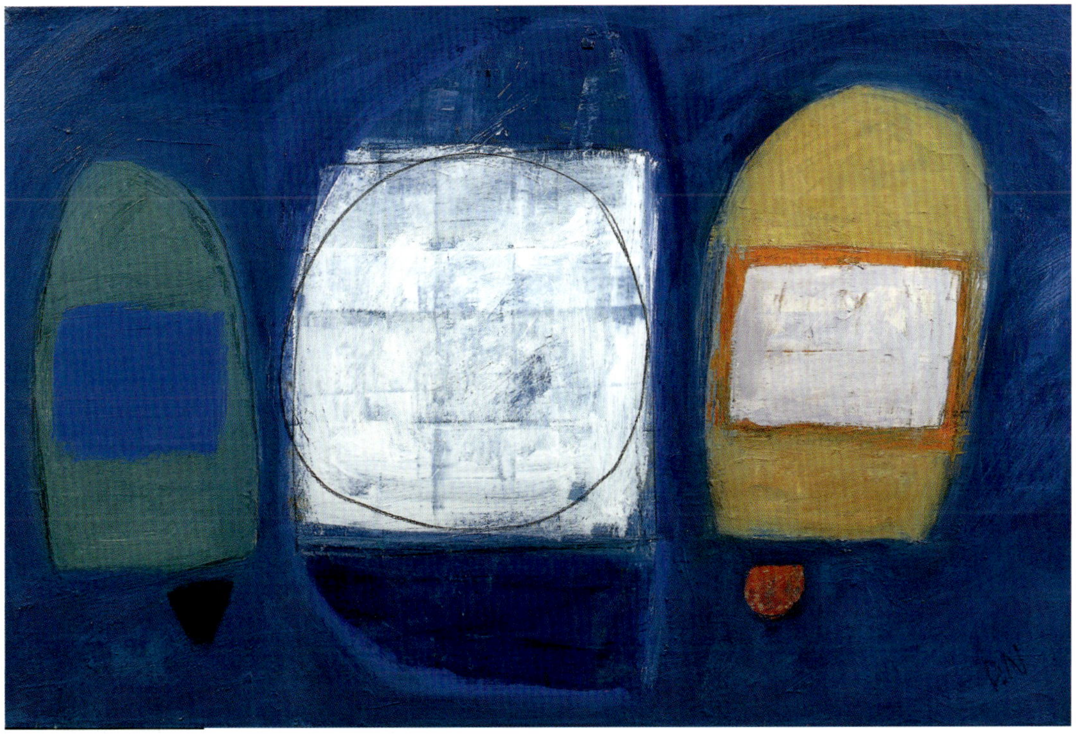

Three Spinnakers I, oil on canvas

and the way it dances and shimmers'. In deep pools of pigment he may press newspaper and then stamp the impression elsewhere on the composition in a ghostly echo.

'The whole idea is to stop the painting being over-calculated and slick,' he says. 'If willing to take risks and experiment you may fall on your face or you just could be uplifted by something unimagined at the start.'

As well as a serious purpose, there is also a playful wit here – a welcome hint of the seaside entertainer.

While his paternal grandfather gravitated from Colchester to end as chief steward in Piccadilly's Naval and Military Club, before a final working stint running the Fortnum & Mason wine cellar, his dad enjoyed a late career in and around Leigh-on-Sea, playing the washboard.

This is the art of enjoyment – to be toasted afresh amid the faint strains of an old sea shanty.

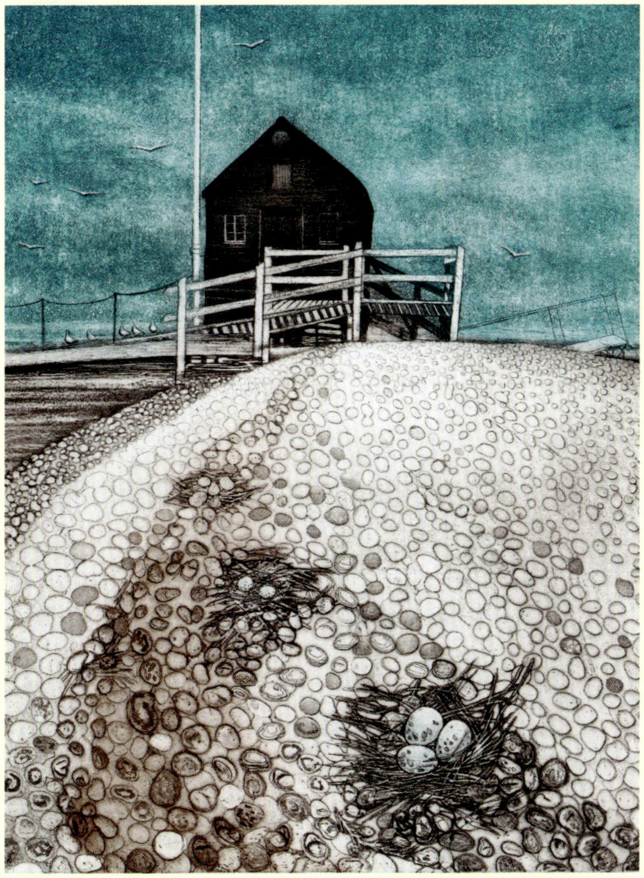

Gulls' Nests on Packing Marsh Island, 2003, etching

Elizabeth Morris trained as a painter in Bournemouth and then in London where, much later, she discovered etching at Morley College. Since a move to Mersea Island, in 1988, her lyrical prints have combined like movements in music – now forming a rhapsody in blue to the environment in which she walks, sails and dreams. 'Sea and sand patterns, shapes of stones, textures, imprints in mud and tracks, birds, fish and – most recently – sea myths and biblical stories with sea references, are all used as starting points for my prints,' she says.

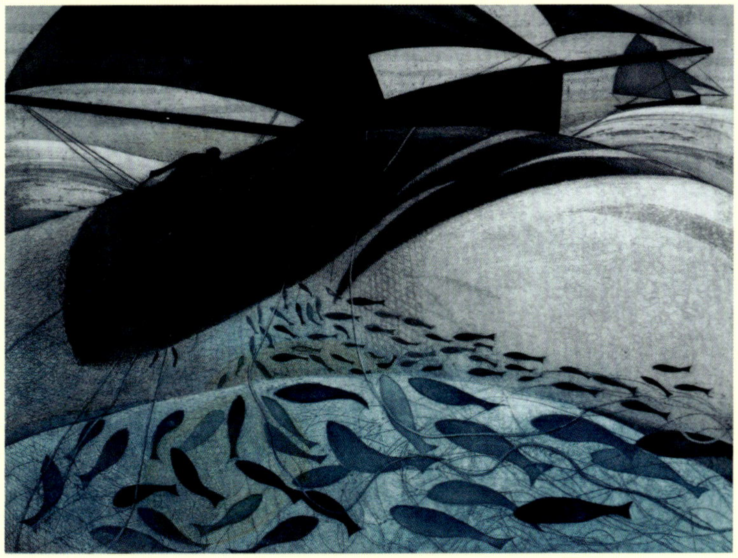

The Multitude of Fishes, 1997, etching

Garfish and Fry, Stephen Henderson, 2009, painted wood

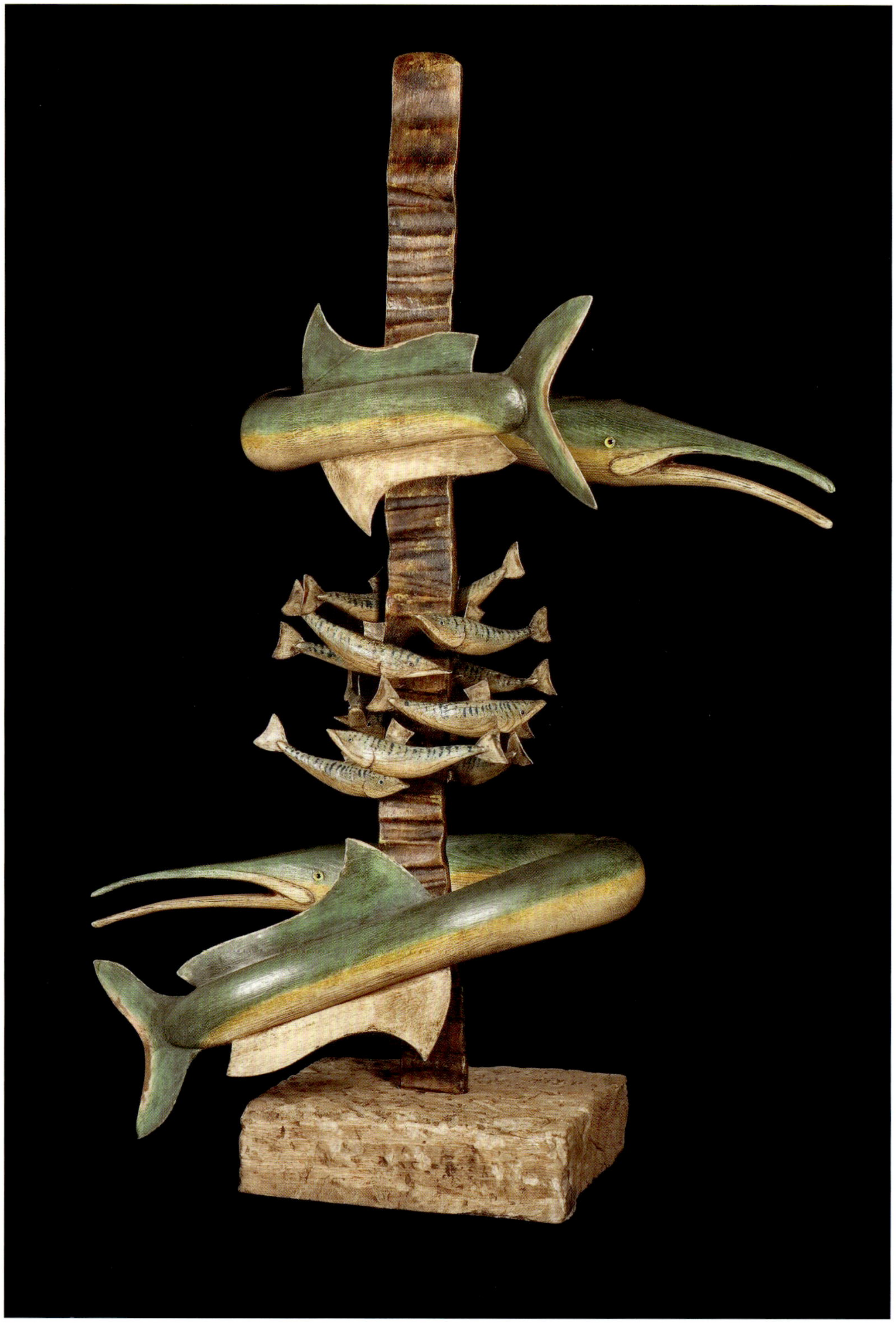

Secret Water

Simon Carter and Stephen Henderson

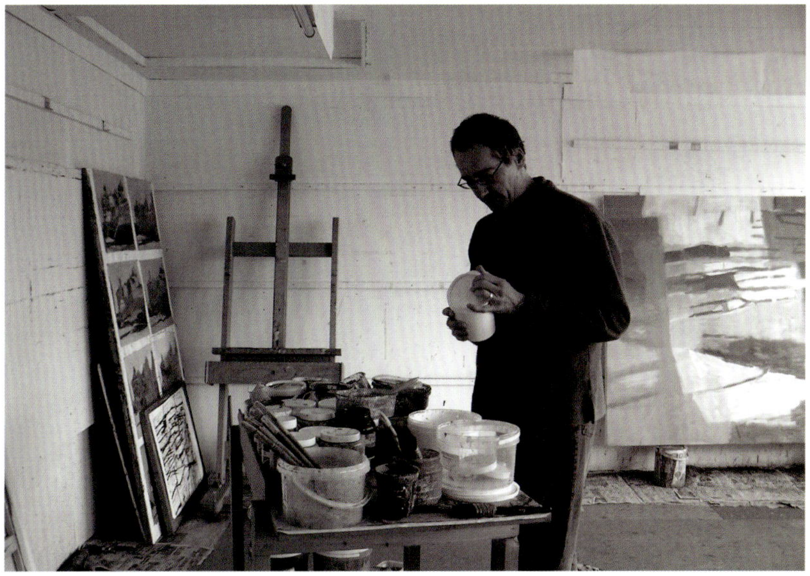

Simon Carter in his studio

The Pier and Beach,
2008, acrylic on canvas

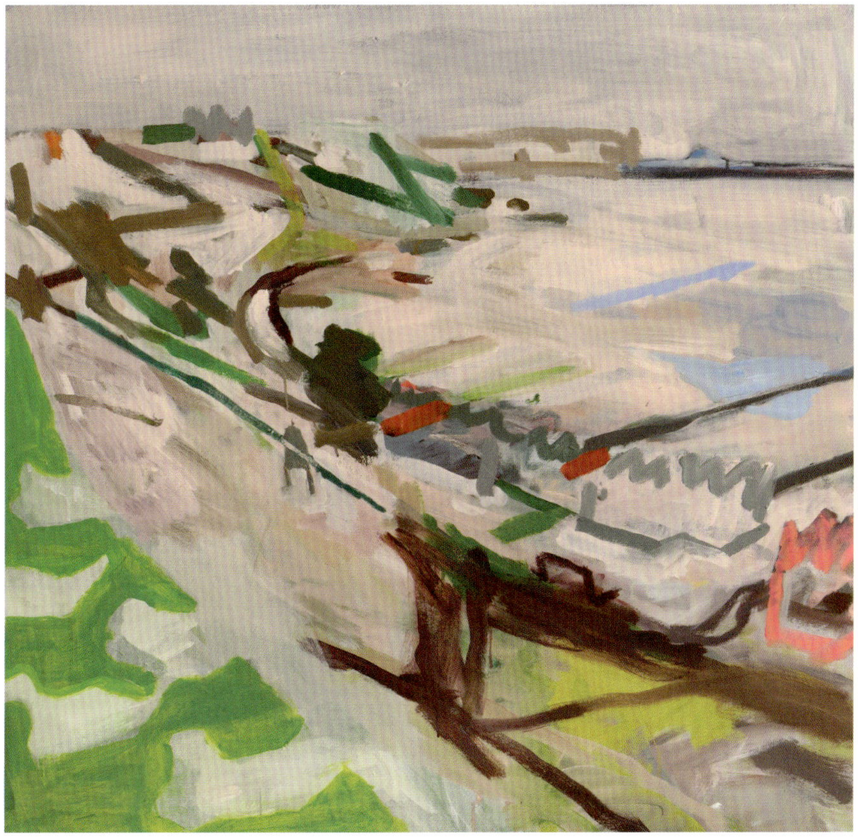

On his bike early each morning, as befits a former postman, painter **Simon Carter** explores the unsung treasures of the Tendring peninsula – where northernmost Essex meets the North Sea. Tellingly, the district council took its name from a small village so as not to favour or offend three neighbouring but poles-apart resorts: Walton, Frinton and Clacton. That solution also overcame the problem of Harwich, a wildly romantic port apparently positioned at the end of the world.

Here, beyond suburbia, there lies a horizon and a hinterland of hidden splendour – Dutch-style scenery around the aptly-named Great Holland, the glittering archipelago of the Walton Backwaters which was the *Secret Water* of novelist Arthur Ransome, wilderness next to industrial decay, beauty beside blight, the gem beside the gaudy. But always, sensed, glimpsed or sweeping, there's the sea, the sea. All this a local lad has made his own by drawing on it for first impressions in a highly expressionist and semi-abstracted vision.

In lightning sketches he sets down patterns

of marsh colliding with seawall, waves crashing on to beach and sun on to water, sand and mud, a lone house or a zig-zag of huts clinging to the edge of everything.

Here and there people (walkers, waders, swimmers) appear as anchors amid the airy elements. Or else there are vessels (canoe, yacht, ferry, freighter). Or birds which may be gulls or monstrous stork-like cranes unloading ships, akin to floating cities across the merging rivers Stour and Orwell at Felixstowe, now the largest container port in the land.

Before each journey of discovery he will doubtless have consulted his key text book – tables relaying the radically differing possibilities of scenes revealed at high and low tides.

Returning to his studio he trawls through his drawings for the element of surprise ('moments of revelation opening up new ways of seeing something noted hundreds of times before'). These he extends into watercolours, often lain and overlain on a light box to find the path to a new creative domain. 'Subjects are only starting points,' says Simon Carter. 'The further I get from that point of departure the more I can see the painting.'

Here, then, is an artist who has come a great distance by remaining essentially at home. Although a seemingly isolated figure he has been championed by Maggi Hambling,

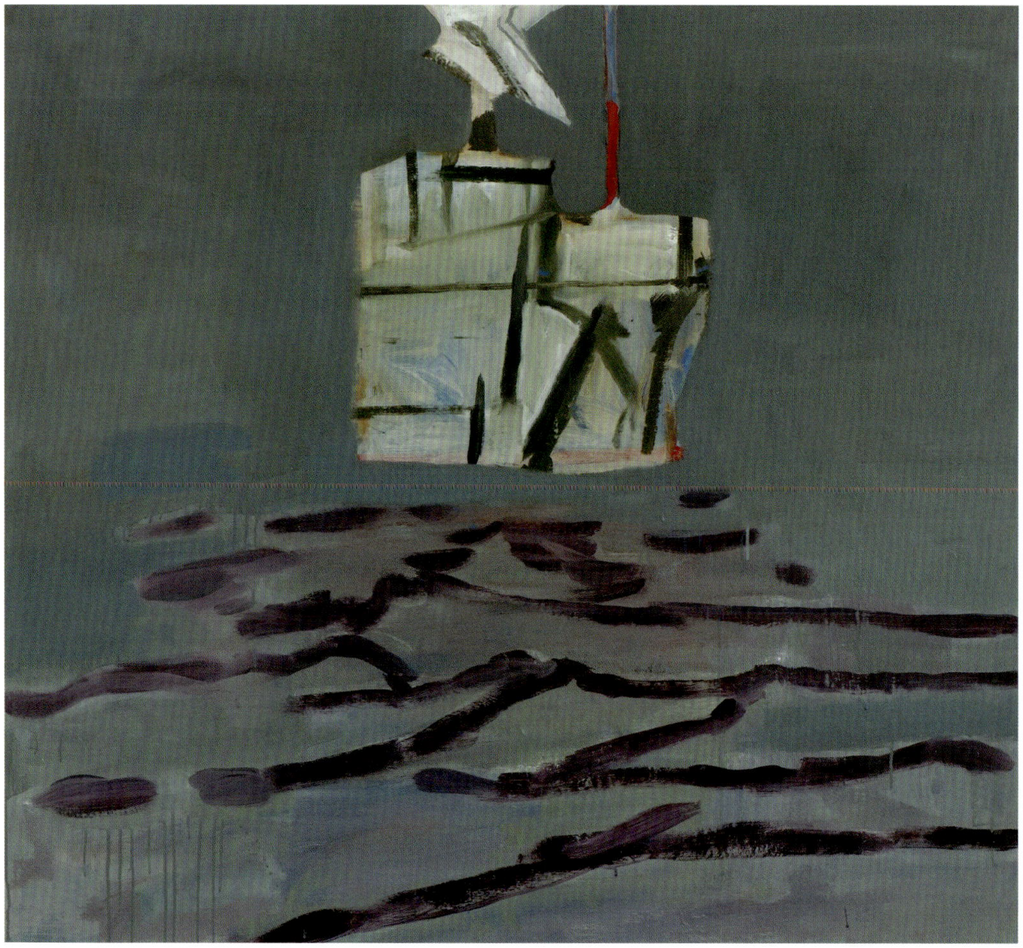

Freighter, 2005, acrylic on canvas

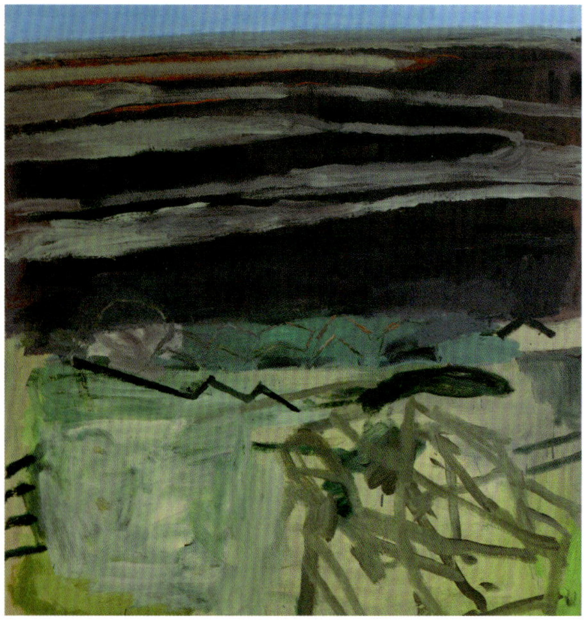

Shadows on the Sea, 2008-9, acrylic on canvas

George Melly and Gary Hume while stalking old giants who raised local documentary scenes to the level of high art. Take J M W Turner, who claimed to have had himself lashed to the mast to observe the wild scene inspiring his 1842 masterpiece *Snow Storm – Steamboat off a Harbour's Mouth making Signals in Shallow Water and going by the Lead. The Author was in this Storm on the Night the Ariel left Harwich.*

More crucial still is John Constable, whose family controlled trade on the River Stour – Tendring's northern border – between Sudbury and Mistley and who determined to record the beloved scenes of his childhood before he even picked up a brush. Carter's Get Constable homage exhibition, in Ipswich in 2007, reworked Flatford scenes known from both the paintings and from swan-feeding visits of childhood.

In a catalogue note he wrote of seeing Constable's sketch for *The Leaping Horse* where 'everything was visible on the surface; a

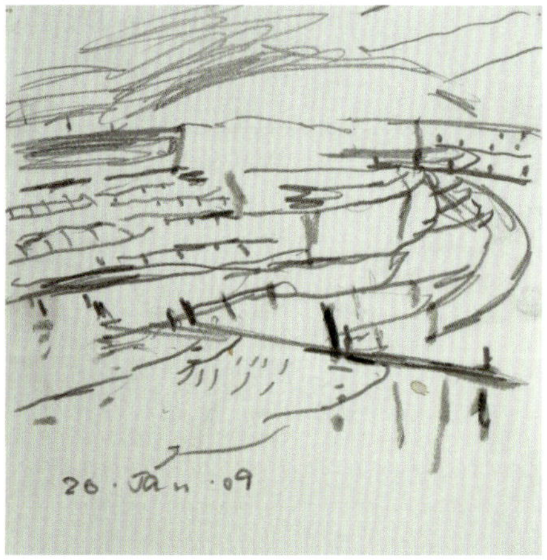

Drawing I for
North Sea, Winter Afternoon,
2009, graphite and oil pastel

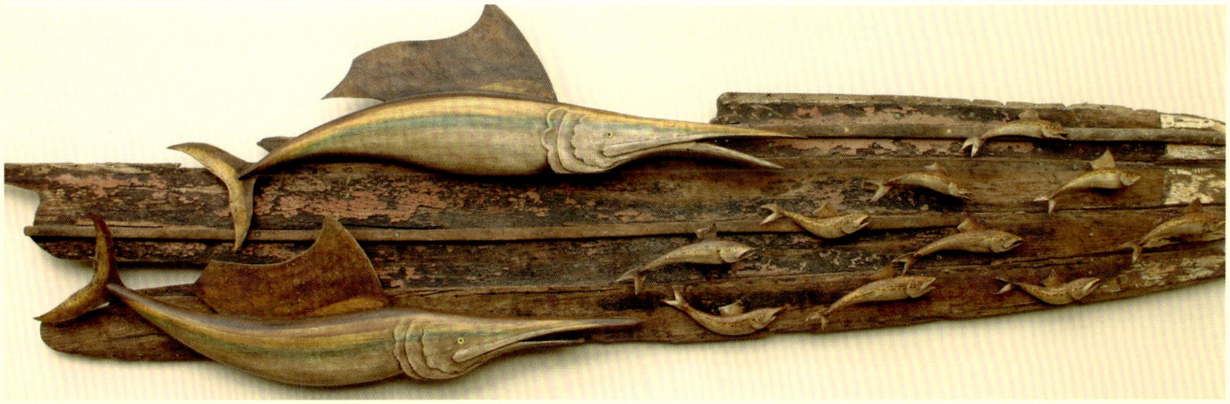

Sailfish Chasing Bait, Stephen Henderson, painted wood

Hamford Water and the Walton Backwaters are Essex at its most exotic – a changing scene of tidal creeks, mudflats, islands and saltmarshes, with small quays even built with stones from old London Bridge and once much-visited by Thames barges. Now the wild domain – celebrated in Arthur Ransome's *Secret Water* – is a nature reserve and a place of legend and ongoing creativity.

Landermere Quay was home to Sir William Gull, Queen Victoria's doctor and Jack the Ripper suspect, as well as Frederick the Great – an eight-foot-plus giant trapped as a freak show exhibit in Germany in 1914, who came back from internment to die in Schooner Villa (roofed with an upturned boat) aged 29.

Adrian Stephen and his wife Karin, pioneering Freudian psychoanalysts, moved to Landermere's former pub as World War One pacifists. They worked on a dairy farm and then stayed on, often visited by Bloomsbury Group kin and kindred spirits. The haven house passed in the 1950s to their daughter and her husband Nigel Henderson (1917-85), the Surrealist painter, collagist, photographer and veteran Norwich School of Art and Design tutor. They in turn brought in their friend Eduardo Paolozzi (1924-2005), sculptor, draughtsman, print-maker and mosaicist of London's Tottenham Court Road tube station, who for a time devised his influential designs on the edge of everything in remotest Essex.

Now the creative line is continued by **Stephen Henderson**, former boat-builder and producer of bespoke furniture, who was inspired by friend and neighbour Guy Taplin to carve out his own response to local wildlife in driftwood. His fluent images of fish and birds entwine with tradition and setting.

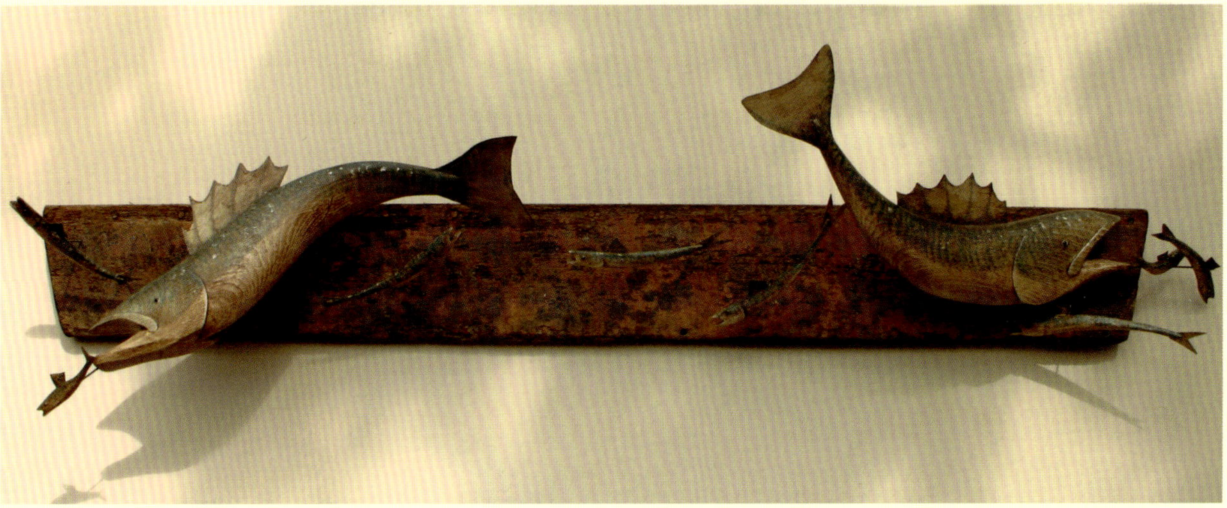

Bass and Fry, Stephen Henderson, painted wood

mad, flapping, exultant wreck of a surface; moving, demented and energised.' That exultation is exactly what he's after.

In great splashy acrylics he now paddles into pictures prompted by the watery domain of north-east Essex but even more by the potency of pigment. He says: 'I love seeing what paint can do – the way it slides around, the way one colour picks up or blots out another. I want the dynamism of the process to stay in the surface of the paint.'

Working on several images at once, he draws roughly and paints lengthily in colour. He tries to find the hue which will hold a picture together. He adds levels and layers, scratches and scrubs out – sometimes abandoning a canvas for weeks or months before retrieving it for a final brilliant flourish or a complete revision. 'The painting resolves itself through desperation rather than planned design,' he says. 'You just hang in there. At a point beyond desperation something magical can occur.'

Intense observation has shown him, for instance, how the acid light of winter sends colours off key – yellow goes into sharper citrus, blue into turquoise. And so icy Essex prompts a Mediterranean palette, via vibrant orange and acid green.

Many of his paintings flow from looking into bright light towards the sea in early morning, with the horizontals of sand bars and ripples and waves broken by the verticals of yachts and swimmers. These markers dissolve into light – being slashed and smashed as they move in and out of vision amid all the myriad ways in which sun plays on water.

And for years he has been haunted by a certain house on the Walton Backwaters. A typical tarred, weatherboarded and pantiled exercise in Essex vernacular architecture is now recast as a heap of deep and bright colours (yellow, scarlet, pink, purple) perched on a green plinth and teetering on the brink of a duck-egg-blue infinity of sea and sky.

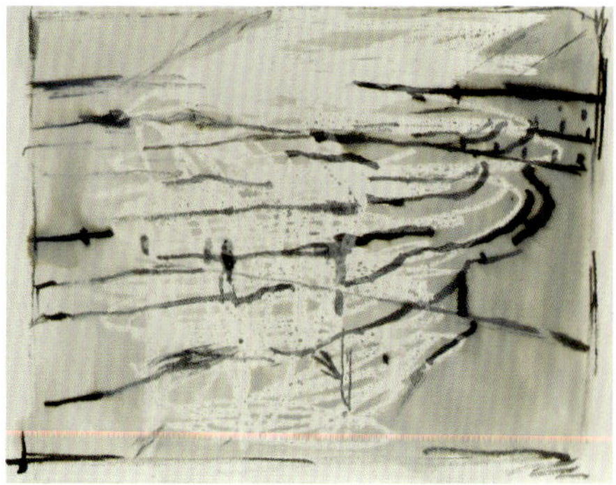

Drawing II for *North Sea, Winter Afternoon*, 2009, ink & wax crayon

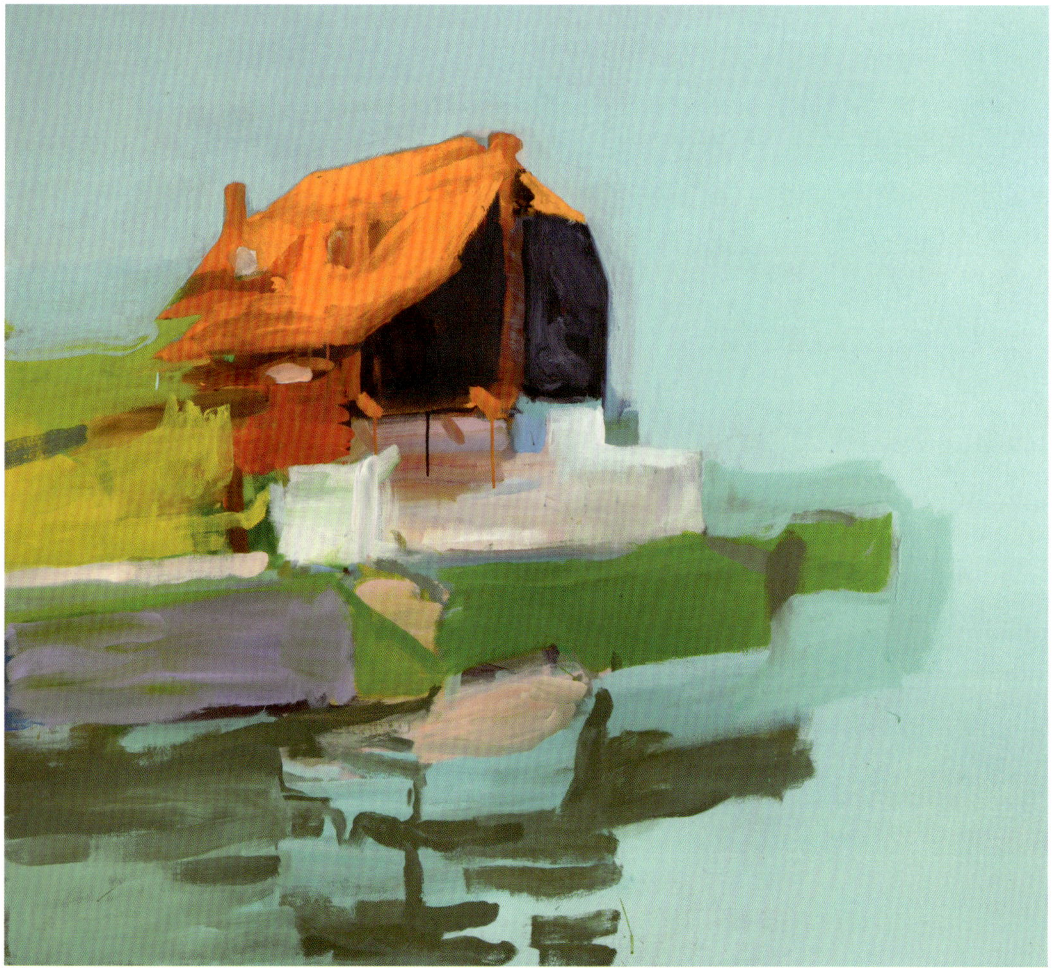

Quay House, 2008, acrylic on canvas

THE FENS

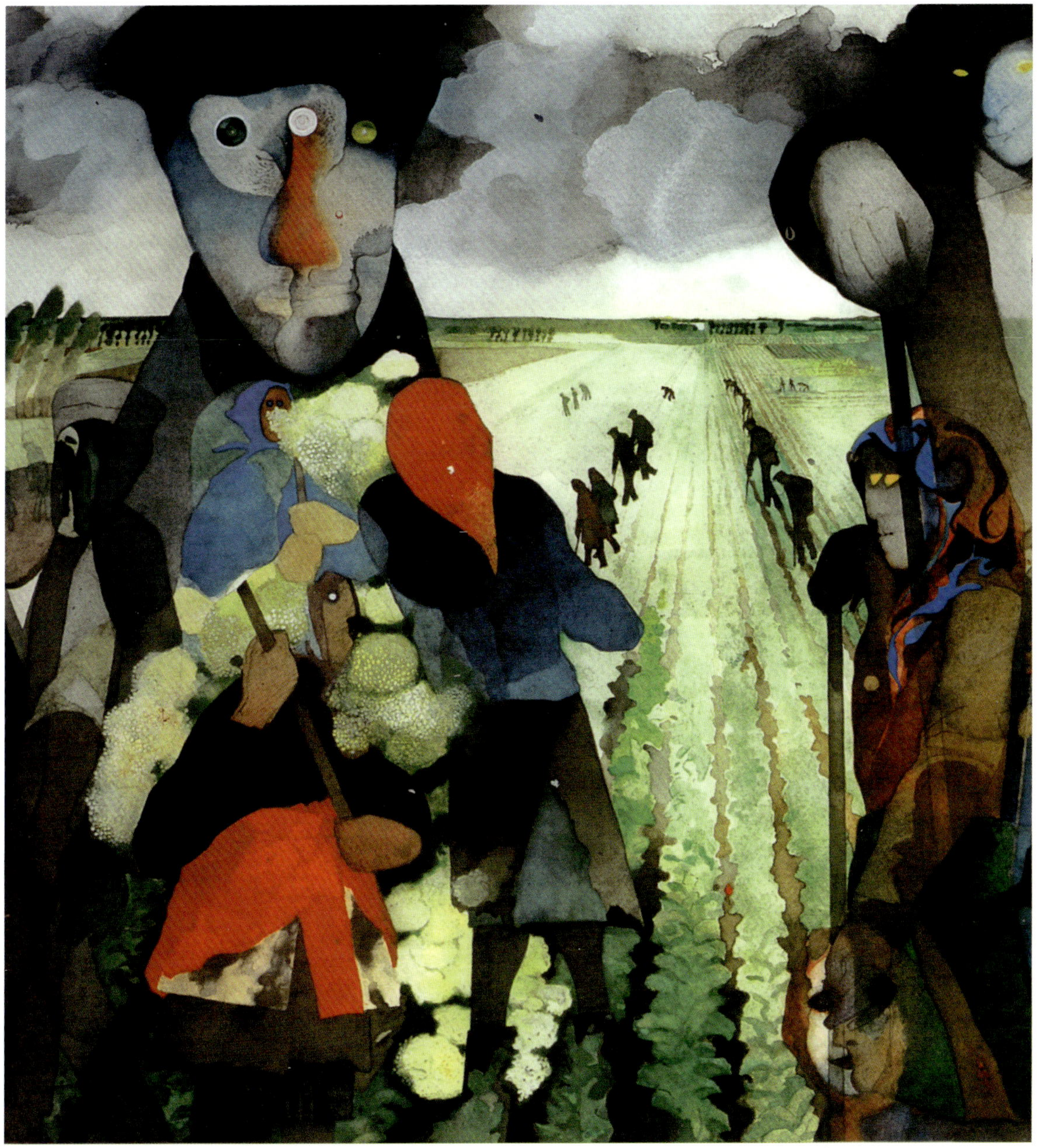

Sugar Beet, Edward Burra, 1972, watercolour (detail)

Brandon Camp, Vanessa Bell, 1913, oil on canvas

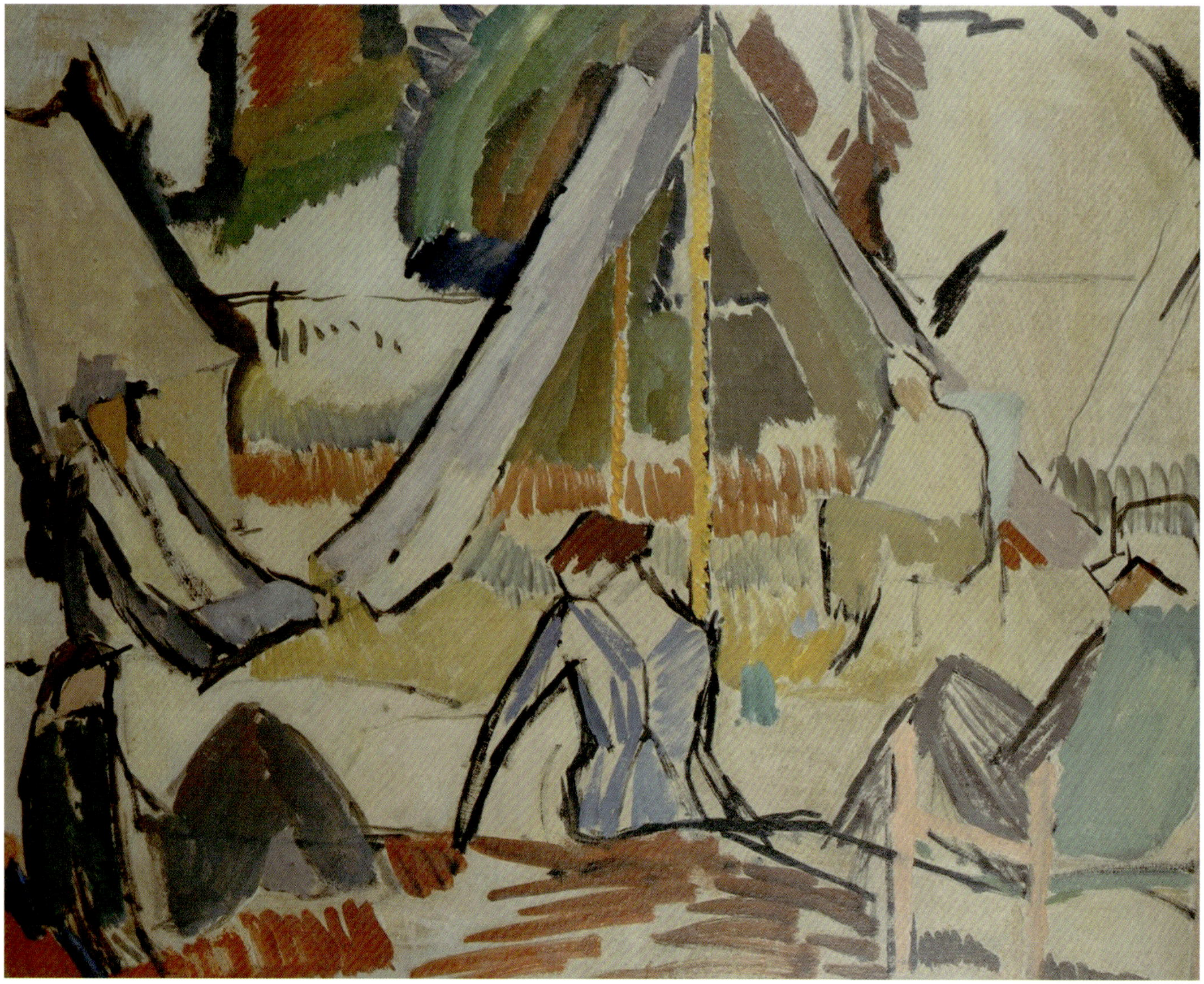

The Brandon Group

Bloomsbury in the Country

Shocking the conventions of Edwardian England, the Bloomsbury Group of painters, writers and intellectuals took its name from the London district where members chiefly gathered. But they all longed for the countryside and escaped for key periods to East Anglia.

The upper-class and inter-related group revolved around the two Stephen sisters, Vanessa and Virginia – the first a painter and the second a writer. Both became famous under their married names. Vanessa married art critic Clive Bell, and Virginia the Labour activist and author Leonard Woolf, but marriage was one of the conventions the group sought to shake.

The Bloomsberries were led by critic and painter Roger Fry who, in 1910, curated in London a Manet and the Post-Impressionists exhibition whose dazzling hues and dramatic distortions caused furore among the press and public and gave the group its modernist flag. More notoriety for Bloomsbury came via writer Lytton Strachey, whose *Eminent Victorians* best-seller poked fun at old icons.

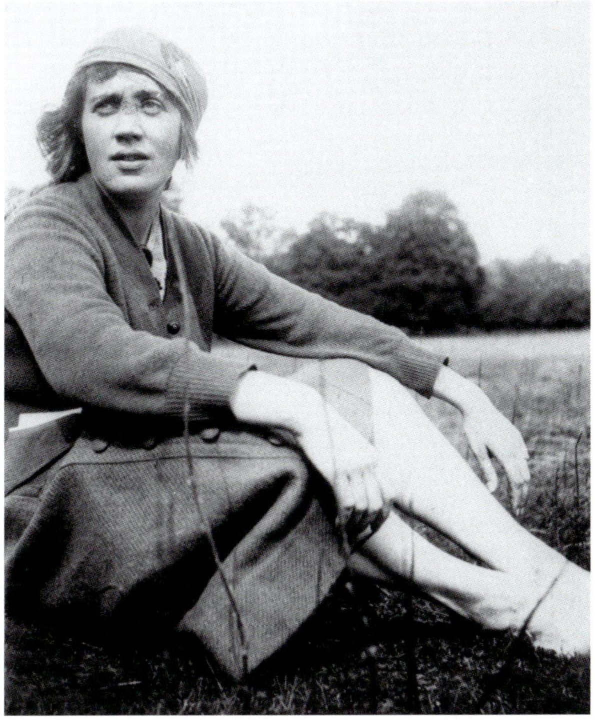

Vanessa Bell at Brandon camp, 1913

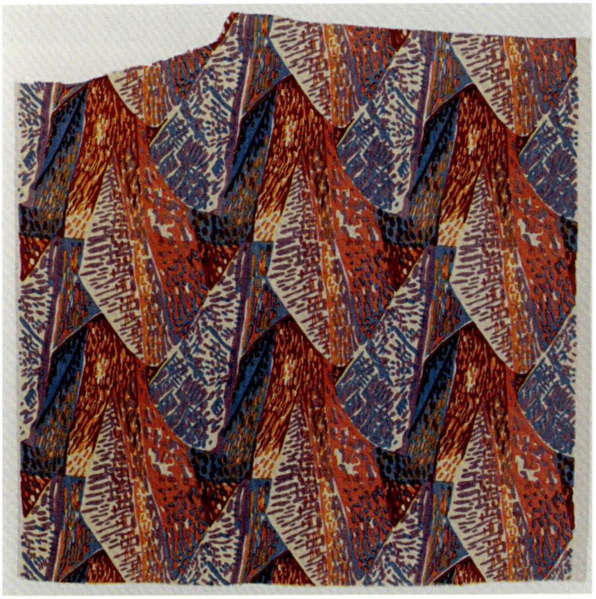

Omega fabric, *Margery*, 1913, printed linen, V and A Museum

Then came handsome, charming and quicksilver artist **Duncan Grant** and economist John Maynard Keynes. They were briefly lovers before Keynes married Russian ballet dancer Lydia Lopokova and set about rescuing the world from recession and despotism with the economic blueprint first for America's 1930s New Deal and then for post-war reconstruction.

The summer of 1913 proved a turning point for this band of brothers and sisters (many of whom were in fact cousins). It began in July with the launch of Roger Fry's Omega Workshops as a 'laboratory' for radical design ideas created by artists and used to produce rugs, upholstery, ceramics, furniture and clothing – all brightly coloured and emblazoned with dynamic abstract patterns.

Fired by the success of the opening fanfare for the enterprise in Bloomsbury's Fitzroy Square, and initial orders from artists and aristocrats, in August the leading members left for a camping holiday on the Norfolk-Suffolk border.

The Brandon camp was organised by the four daughters of Fabian socialist and colonial administrator Sir Sydney Olivier, all fans of the outdoor life and the poetry of their friend Rupert Brooke. Vanessa dubbed Margery, Daphne, Bryn and Noel the 'neo-Pagans' – and her brother Adrian trailed up to Norfolk in an unrequited swoon over the lovely Noel.

Frances Spalding, biographer of **Vanessa Bell**, writes: 'Vanessa, Clive… Maynard and Roger agreed to take part and at the last moment before they set out, Duncan also arrived at Gordon Square, wearing paint-stained clothes and a spotless white hat, clutching various packages, a collapsing easel and stool, and a bottle of champagne. For some the conditions of the camp were scarcely bearable; Clive never forgot the discomfort he endured…Vanessa, on the other hand, though she slept in a nearby farmhouse and not in a tent, found the simple life very much to her liking and sat guard over Roger's excellent chicken stew flavoured with apple and mint like a rustic peasant, full of ancient earthy wisdom.'

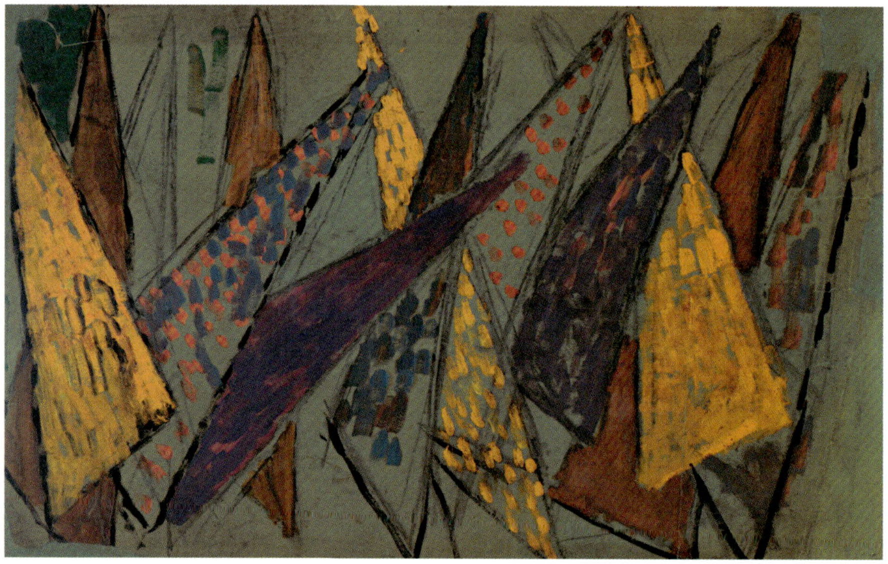

Design attributed to Duncan Grant, 1913-15, gouache on paper, Courtauld Gallery

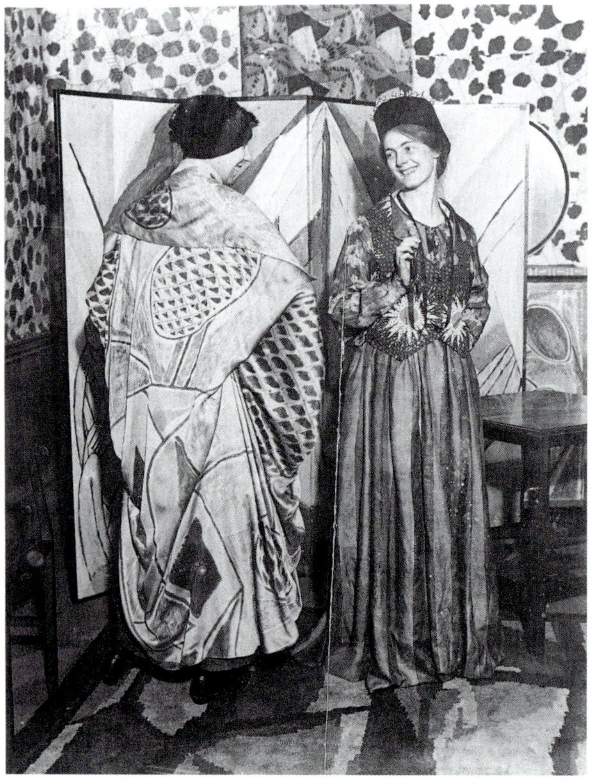

Nina Hamnett and Winifred Gill modelling Omega dresses, 1915 (left)

The Norfolk holiday also confirmed a shift in personal allegiances, Vanessa having ended an affair with Roger for life-long devotion to Duncan (who, initially in love with her brother, gave her a daughter, Angelica, in 1918, and much heartache thereafter). The 34-year-old Vanessa wrote to the absent and ailing Virginia about her 'grandmotherly' lectures to the young Brandon campers – adding: 'It will take years before they really reach our point of mature wisdom… .' Beyond her wise novels Virginia Woolf could be stupefied by depression. An attack building in that summer of 1913 broke, on the night of 9 September, with an overdose of sleeping pills and a timely discovery – one of several near-escapes before she drowned herself, in Sussex, in 1941.

Both Vanessa and Duncan painted Brandon camping scenes on the spot, which later set their imaginations alight. An ensuing Bell screen, *Tents and Figures*, shows naked and green modernist models arrayed in the foreground and across the folding panels amid arcs and broken triangles of brown, ochre, grey and green. In the centre two vertical tent poles rise beside an arching tree trunk. Three tents and four sisters in a wooded setting prompted the boldest work Vanessa Bell ever produced – giving her the greatest claim to being a significant contributor to modernism. Poised between easel painting and Omega design, and between representation and abstraction, this large-scale work of even larger ambition was bought by Roger Fry.

The screen motifs were also extended into a wealth of textile designs – with names like Maud, Margery and Pamela after kindred spirits of Bloomsbury – to suggest an abstracted rural idyll linked to the earlier Arts and Crafts ideals of William Morris.

A year later the world was broken by war; Omega fractured but struggled on. A feature in the *Illustrated Sunday Herald* of 24 October 1915 was rather ironically titled Women Who Do The Most Original War Work of All, given the pacifism of the ongoing company. Workshop manager Winifred Gill appeared as a model alongside artist-designer Nina Hamnett – the latter in a costume bearing motifs borne from that Brandon holiday.

As conscription threatened, Duncan's aunt, Florence Ewebank, died and so vacated Wissett Grange – a half-timbered farmhouse in six shabby acres near Halesworth. Duncan and David Garnett, his then lover, sped to Suffolk to escape the war as tenant farmers, putting visitors into harness since plough horses had been shipped off to France and further shocking the locals by painting tails of white leghorn chickens blue to deter thieves.

Vanessa, arriving with two sons and two servants, was instantly at home. On 27 April 1916 she wrote to Lytton Strachey: 'Today it's hot, and I'm so lazy, that I'm sitting out in the sun… If only there weren't a war and tribunals in the background it would be perfect. But perhaps one would then begin to think about fleas or money or something else… Anyhow, it seems the only thing to enjoy the present, and the only way of cheating one's fate.'

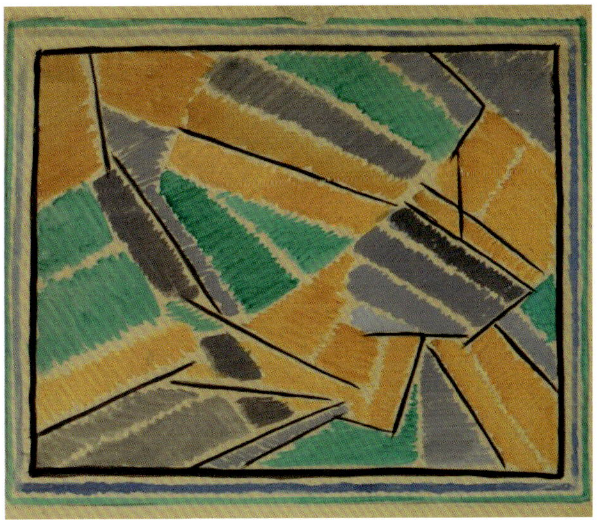

Rug design attributed to Vanessa Bell, 1913-14, gouache and pencil on paper, Courtauld Gallery (right)

Husband Clive, 'blinded to all else by the fleas and the cold', soon left with elegant mistress Mary Hutchinson. Maynard, Lytton and bohemian society hostess Lady Ottoline Morrell came and went. While Duncan and David toiled feebly in the fields and orchards, Vanessa painted walls and furniture in vivid hues and vibrant pictures, first in a barn and then in a bedroom studio.

Their peace was broken by the refusal of the Blything Tribunal to allow the two men conditional exemption from military service, despite the arguments of Maynard and Philip Morrell – Ottoline's husband and a Liberal MP close to PM Asquith. Vanessa railed against a panel of 'perfectly bovine country bumpkins, whose skulls couldn't be penetrated at all'.

But on 19 May an Ipswich appeal tribunal set in train a process which would save them from the army or jail. Later that summer Vanessa found Charleston, the Sussex farmhouse where she and Duncan would be based for the rest of their lives, and which is now a museum in their memory.

The Omega Workshops barely survived the war – being wound up in 1919 and so ending the dreams of the Brandon Group.

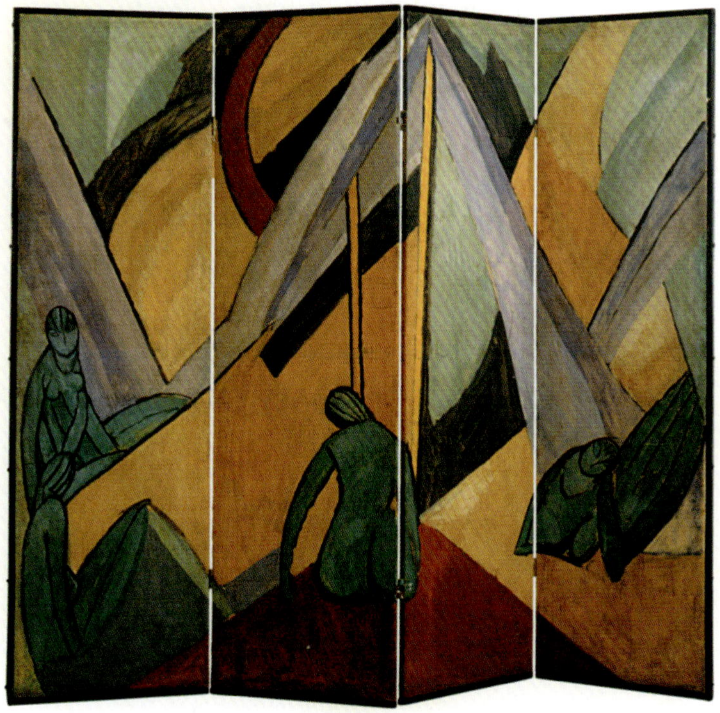

Painted screen, *Tents and Figures*, Vanessa Bell, 1913, gouache and pencil on paper, on canvas, V and A Museum

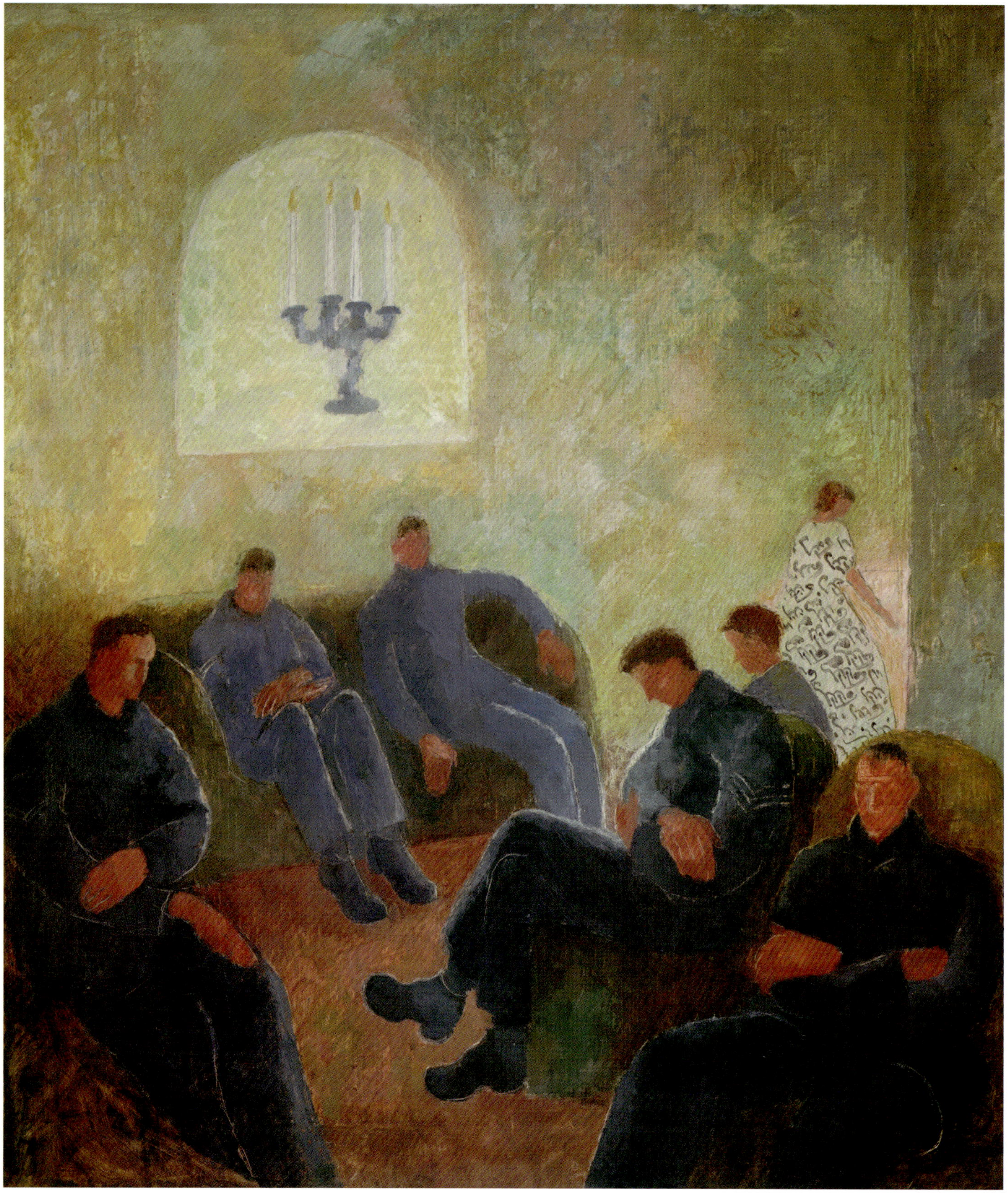

Airmen Seated, Elisabeth Vellacott, 1942-5, oil on canvas

Fenland Dreamers

John Craxton, the Bostons and Elisabeth Vellacott

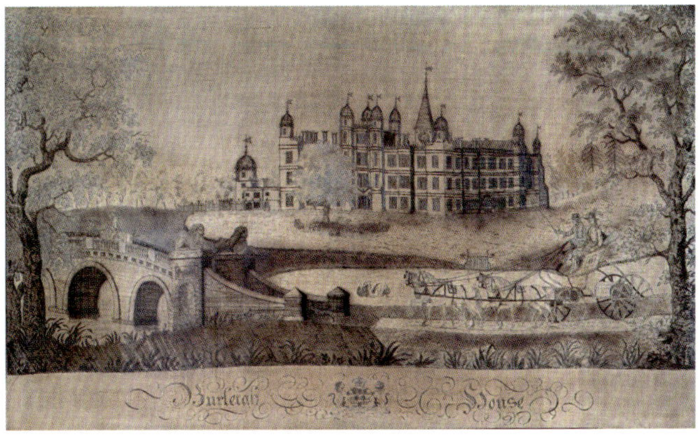

Burghley House, Napoleonic prisoner-of-war work, silk and human hair embroidery on linen

In the high summer of 1899 the Stephen siblings – future painter Vanessa Bell and future writer Virginia Woolf, and brothers Julian and Adrian – left London reluctantly for a family gathering deep in the Fen country. For six weeks they stayed near their cousin, Dorothea Stephen, in the old rectory at Warboys.

Virginia wrote in her diary of a melancholy place, beset by ghosts and graves and an elemental oppression. In sweltering heat she drifted in a punt on the moat, imagining a sensational drowning to break the stillness which perfectly prefigured her eventual suicide. 'Such melting gray of sky, land & water is the very spirit of monotony,' she noted. But, far into the visit, a transformation had occurred. Virginia wrote, enraptured: 'You don't see the sky until you live here. Wc have ceased to be dwellers on the earth. We are really made of clouds. We are mystical and dreamy… I shall think it a test of friends for the future whether they can appreciate the Fen country.'

A black-soiled landscape so drained, so level and so apparently laid-bare had revealed itself only slowly. Here were earthiness, over-arching grandeur and ancient secrets such as those Ralph Vaughan Williams found soon afterwards when collecting sea shanties and folk songs of age-old hardship and horror from King's Lynn and Fenland pubs to scatter across his orchestral tone poem *In the Fen Country*.

At the hamlet of Norman Cross beside the A1 a stone eagle swoops over a memorial raised in 1914 to 1,700 fatalities among 7,000 inmates of the world's first purpose-built prisoner of war camp. From 1797 it held Napoleonic captives marched overland from Lynn or landed at nearby Yaxley on Whittlesey Mere. To ward off boredom and hunger, detainees bartered food with woven pictures made from thread, hair or paper, and marquetry caskets and needle cases of plaited straw. But carving bone recycled from prison tables, worked with a knife, a little dye and glue from boiled fish bones, was the premier art of Norman Cross.

Sailors naturally favoured model vessels,

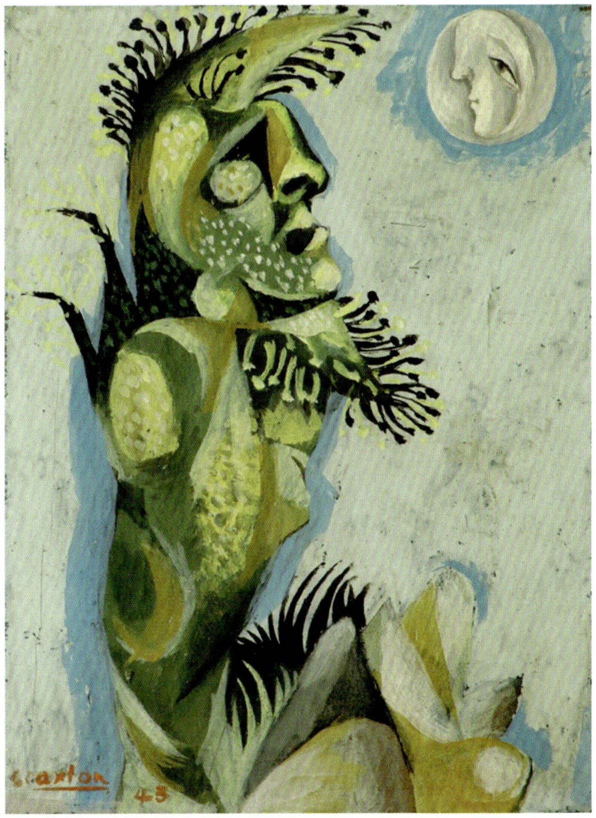

Metamorphic Willow and Moon, John Craxton, 1943, oil on canvas (right)

some producing amazing replicas of ships of the Napoleonic line. Others, witnesses to the Terror raging between the fall of the Bourbons and the rise of Bonaparte, turned out miniature guillotines with severed heads dropping into buckets at the twist of a handle. Many makers were marooned when the camp closed in 1814. Some stayed on, marrying into fen families and passing their skills into generational waves of East Anglian craftsmanship. The best assembly of prisoner-of-war work – art mirroring that of scrimshaw carvers confined in whaling ships – is in Peterborough Museum.

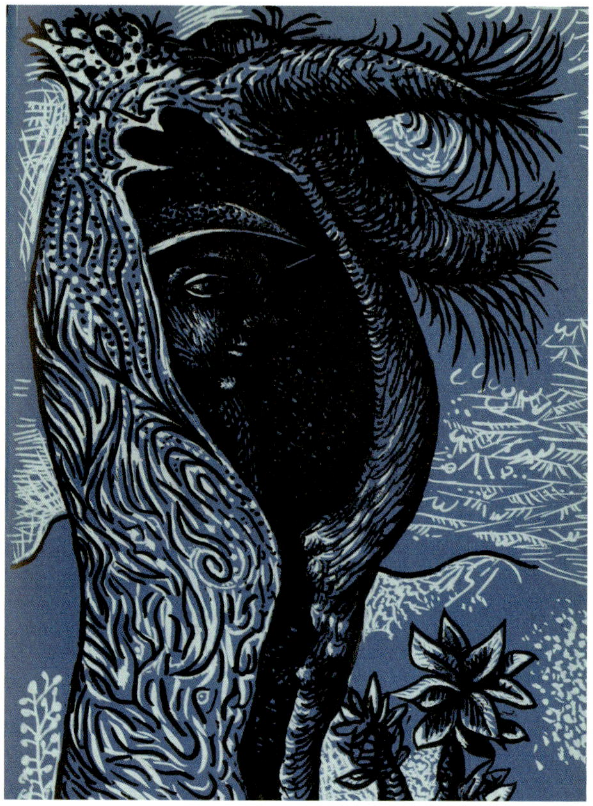

Lithograph from *The Poet's Eye,* John Craxton, 1944

Fenland is an exposed seabed, from which most of the water is long since expelled, but as late as 1972 **Edward Burra** (1905-1976), the painter of sinister satire, paused while driving through East Anglia to capture an ongoing drama. In a typically terrific and terrifying watercolour he depicted sugar-beet workers seemingly drowning in air, watched by grinning garden gnomes (see detail p143).

The old ocean is now confined to dykes and rivers and during World War Two the young painter **John Craxton** (1922-2009), romantic and at that time Surrealist, saw the moon glinting through Fenland willows and imagined the trees sheltering poets or shepherds or metamorphosing into monsters. Visiting Little Shelford, to stay with the family of pathologist H P Bayon, he and his friend Lucian Freud depicted animals sent to their host for autopsy, an exercise firing a longer Freudian interest in taxidermy. But Craxton returned to the hidden figures and anthropomorphic life force of pollarded willows in several of the lithographs he made in 1944 for Geoffrey Grigson's *The Poet's Eye* anthology, part of the New Excursions into English Poetry series printed by W S Cowell of Ipswich.

Cambridge drew another mythologist in **Cecil Collins** (1908-1989) who, with his equally visionary wife, Elisabeth, had a base in the town from 1944 to 1977, where they helped to found the Cambridge Society of Painters and Sculptors in 1955. He imagined an enchanted landscape of angels and fools all around him. Looking through his window, he perceived a Garden of Eden with vaguely Fenland trees but very far-flung mountains.

Lucy Boston (1892-1990) studied art in Vienna on the break-up of her marriage, before moving in 1937 to Cambridge, where her son Peter was training to be an architect. There she

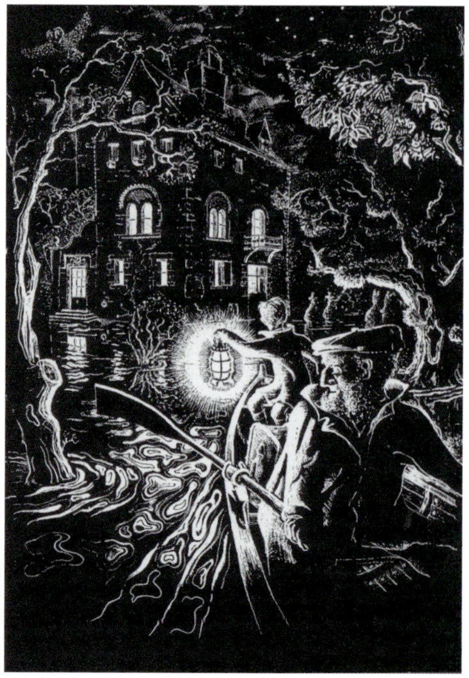

Illustration by Peter Boston from *The Children of Green Knowe,* 1975, by Lucy Boston

Landscape: Autumn, Cecil Collins, 1958, oil on canvas

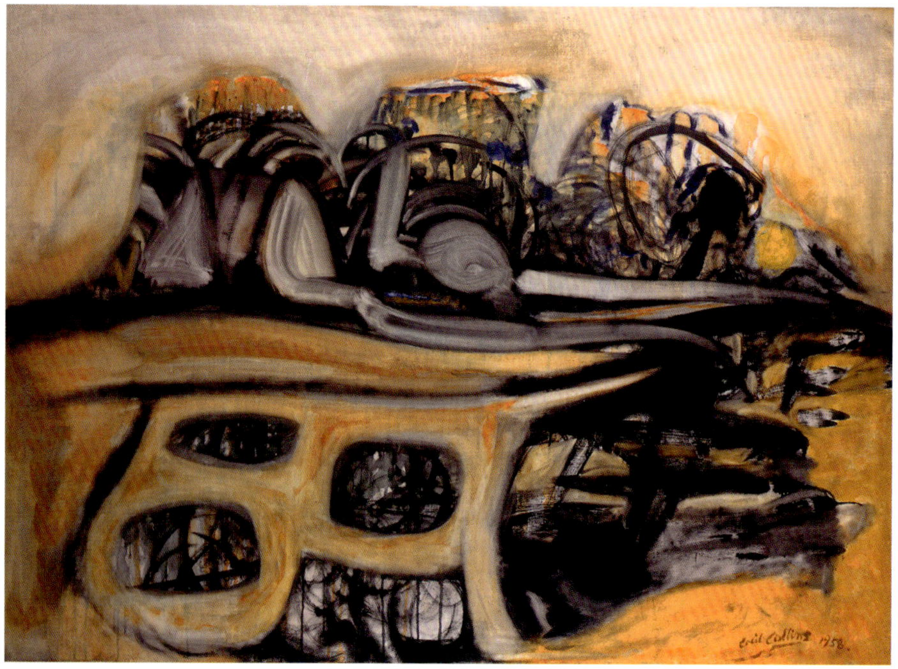

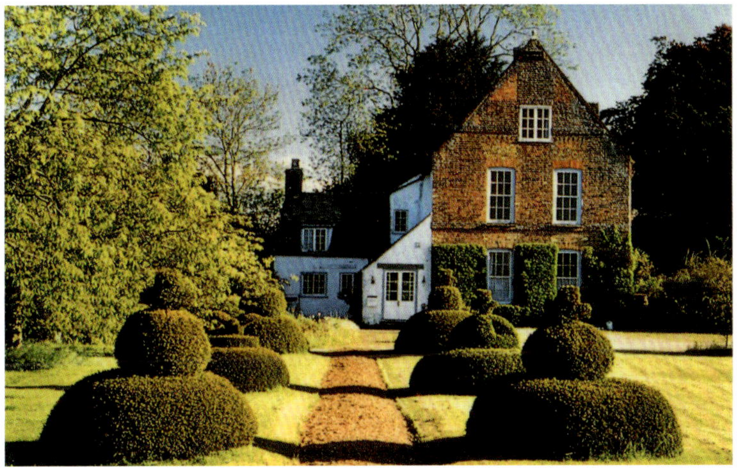

The Manor, Hemingford Grey

intended to settle down to paint still lifes and endless views of King's College Chapel. But soon she had bought the moated old manor at Hemingford Grey, having first seen its Georgian façade rising beside the River Ouse while punting in 1915. She and Peter then set about digging out a remarkable Norman interior – for this was once the private chamber of a 12th-century lord of the manor, whose hall would have stood nearby. Her memoir, entitled *Memory in a House*, charted what became a life-long obsession.

Lucy made patchwork quilts, gardened, fed birds on her dining table and deer at her door and, at 60, began to write about her manor – publishing six best-selling *Greene Knowe* stories, illustrated by Peter, between 1954 and 1976. Separated from his parents by war, young Tolly goes to stay with his grandmother in an old, isolated and often islanded Fenland house where his loneliness is eased as children step out of paintings or topiary animals spring to life. 'I like this house, it is like living in a book that keeps coming true,' he says.

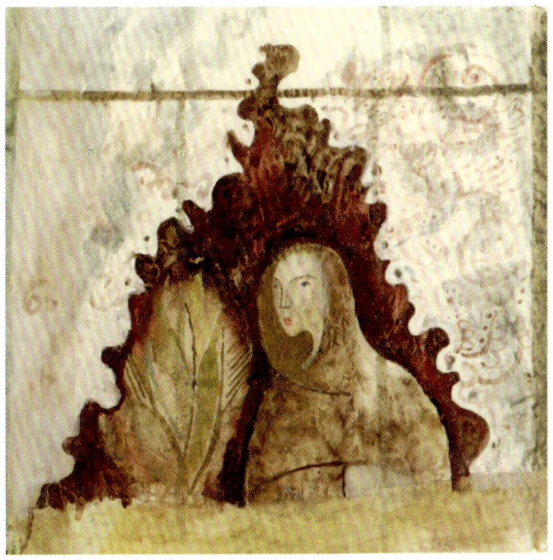

Woman at Window,
Elisabeth Vellacott,
1942-5, gouache

War brought artist **Elisabeth Vellacott** (1905-2002) to the setting for Green Knowe when a bomb fell on her Cambridge studio. Fragments of her abstracted and sequinned block-printed fabrics survive from linens, curtains and chair covers and her murals, like early Italian paintings, still adorn the manor walls. Locals took the two women for witches, and then for spies. In a double-height music room they donned evening dress to host gramophone concerts for airmen stationed nearby, Elisabeth portraying in attitudes of rapt attention listeners who might soon be killed in action. Refugees and prisoners of war were also welcomed.

When her next Cambridge house was demolished for a multi-storey carpark, Elisabeth bought a corner of a Hemingford Grey orchard where, in 1959, Peter Boston designed an A-framed house. Being all wood and glass and shingle tiles, save for an internal chimneystack ('a tree-trunk on which the whole house hangs', the owner said), it spared the unaffordable expense of walls. Even when the rest of the orchard was developed, Elisabeth remained in a perfect artist's studio amid a wilderness of

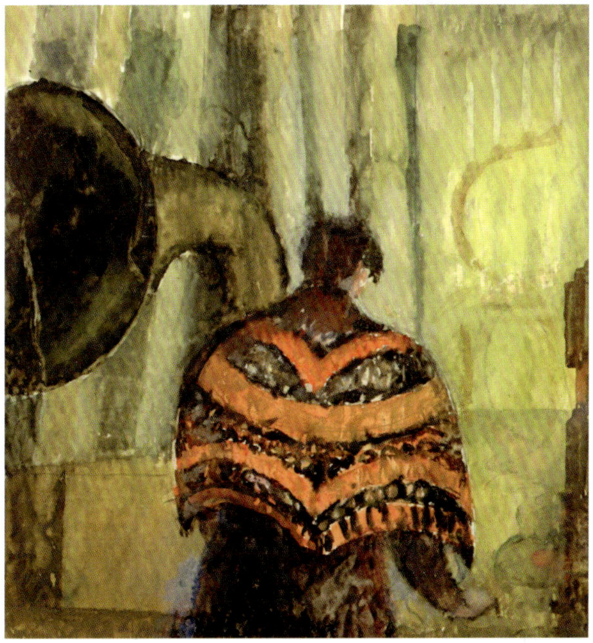

Lucy at the Gramophone,
Elisabeth Vellacott, 1942-5, gouache

apples, pears, roses and cats. Here she drew filigree trees in chalk and charcoal and painted, thinly and slowly on white-grounded panels, images of transfigured humanity – recreating the luminosity of frescoes for her own lyrical designs.

Although there were inspirational travels to Wales and Italy, the Scillies and Scotland, Vellacott art essentially portrays a mythical and magical Fenland. Dreamers and sleepwalkers appear at peace in a place where anything might happen and where a singular artist found her voice at 60 and painted her last magnificent picture at the age of 92.

Meadowsweet in the fen at dusk, 2007, acrylic on board

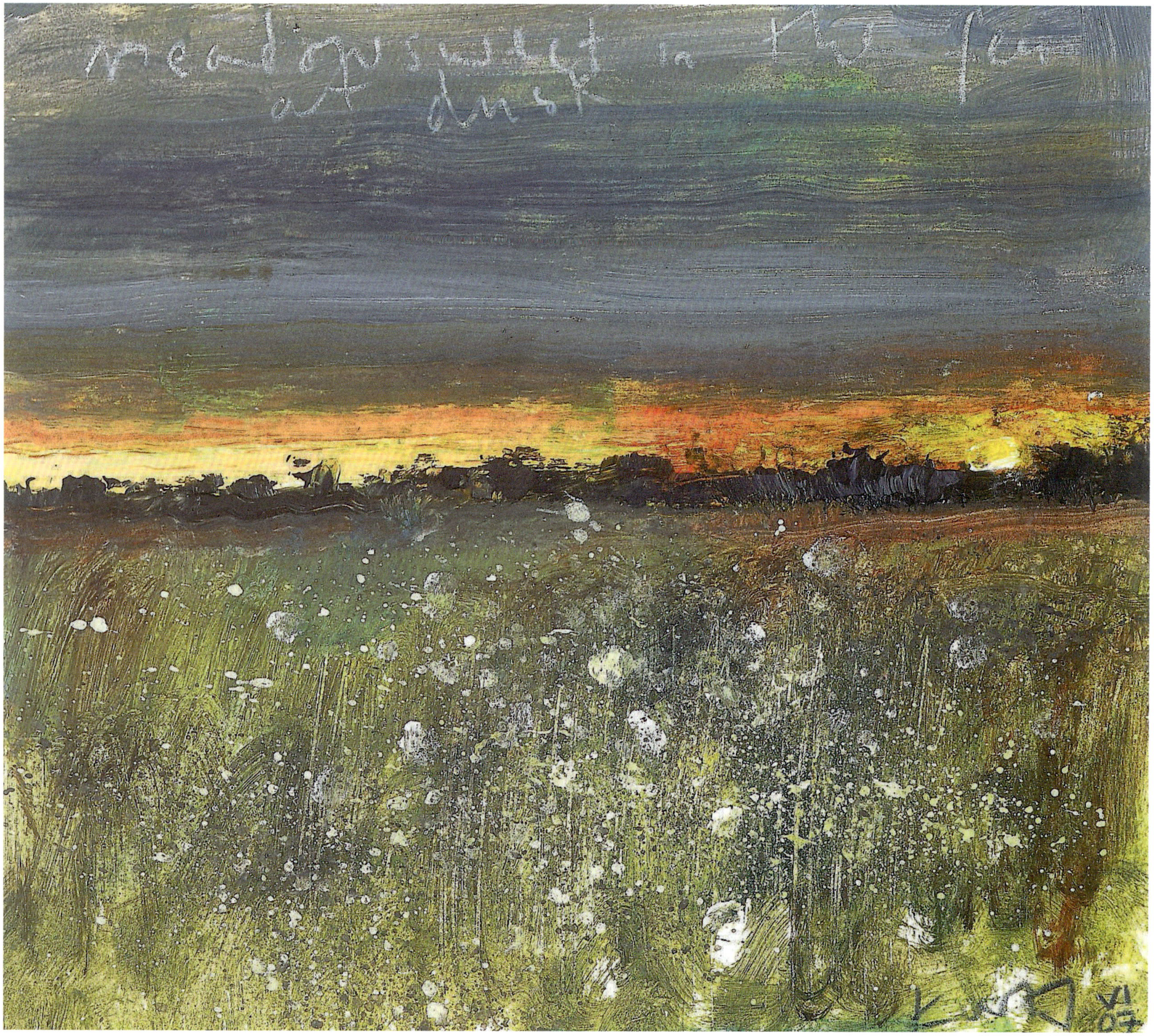

Waterland

Kurt Jackson at Wicken Fen

Kurt Jackson is an artist who seeks out wild places to celebrate, and then to save, through sequences of scintillating pictures which read like poetic documentaries. So it was only a matter of time before he came to Wicken Fen, one of the final fragments of the watery wilderness once forming East Anglia. And time is of the essence here.

Looking like a rock star – as befits a veteran Glastonbury Festival artist in residence – and armed with the off-beat expertise founded in scientific studies at Oxford and followed by many years of intense observation, he may be the very model of a 21st-century green campaigner.

And although firmly anchored with his family close to Land's End in Cornwall, he is also a natural nomad. Every year he travels to threatened spaces across edgy and elemental Britain, and into remote parts of France and Spain. 'I am an environmentalist,' he says. 'It's the springboard for everything else in my life. I want people to see the wonder and complexity of nature through my art, to appreciate the beauty.

'Beauty is not a sexy word in contemporary art, but beauty can open people's eyes and make them more likely to do something to protect the planet.'

He has had scores of best-selling and awareness-raising exhibitions in London and elsewhere, including King's Lynn Arts Centre, and has been an active supporter of conservation causes since a teenager. In 2007, he asked Friends of the Earth to recommend a site imperilled by climate change, his biggest concern of all, so that he might focus on the very local to help the battle against global warming, and was directed to Wicken Fen.

The site near Soham is the only nature reserve to be run by the National Trust, and it has been protected and painstakingly managed since 1899. Now it's recognised as one of the most important wetland sites in Europe.

This 1,500-acre peaty speck within the Cambridgeshire prairies is a tiny fragment of the marshy expanses once covering all of East Anglia and almost vanishing with the massive onset of drainage from the 17th century.

It is a paradox that somewhere so wild has to be so carefully nurtured, and even then its brilliance has been diminished as an island in a black sea of some of the most fertile (and fertilised) farmland in England.

Split by the man-made watercourse of Wicken Lode, and with the sails of its own windmill pointing higher than clumped and scattered trees, the reserve comprises two distinct sections. In addition, mere, dykes, ditches and the ponds of abandoned and

Kurt Jackson in the field

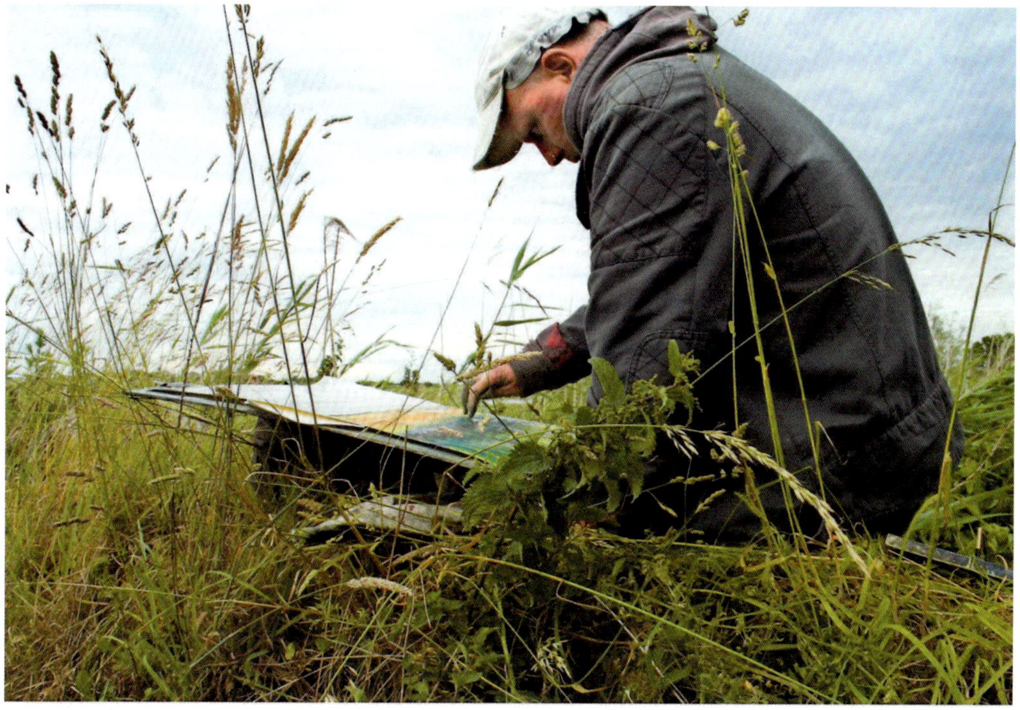

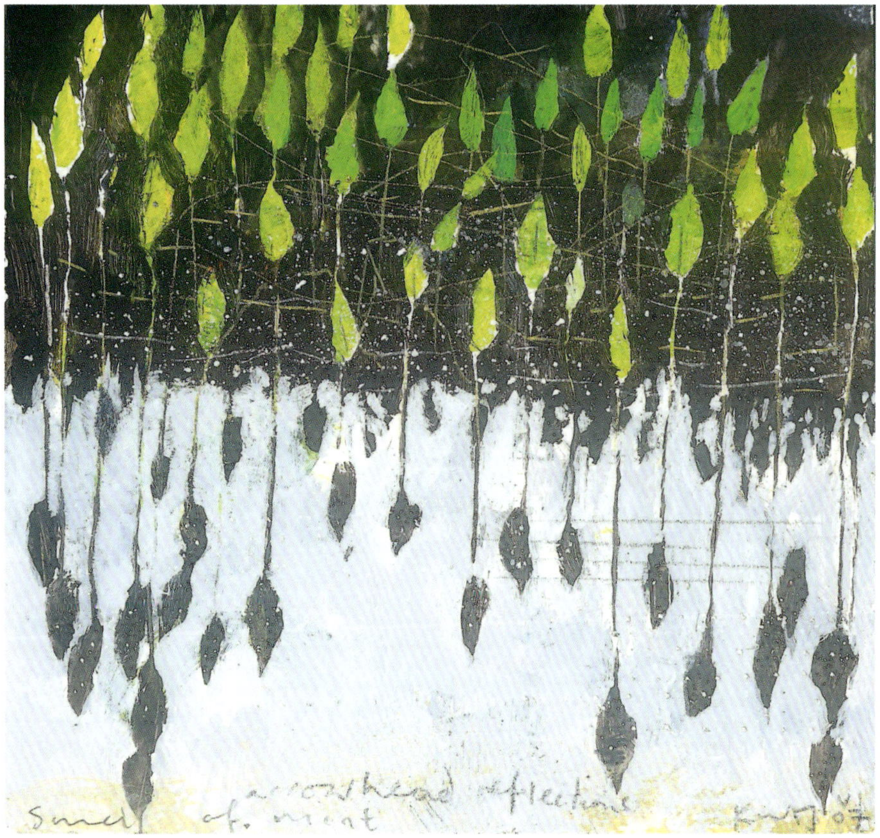

Arrowhead reflections, smell of mint, 2007, acrylic

drowned claypits provide further variety to this soggy, boggy miniature mosaic.

To the south, Adventurer's Fen has been drained in the past, and is now two metres lower than the Sedge Fen fragment to the north. This area is grazed – by cattle, sheep and Konik ponies, close relative of the primal ponies that once roamed Europe – or left for hay.

But the cutting of vegetation on the never-drained Wicken Sedge Fen continues all year, the exact pattern depending on the specific plants and locations.

Cycles range from annual to seven-year rotations. Sedge, harvested in summer, is still used for thatching – but these days only along the ridge rather than over the whole roof. The pitched sides are now composed of common reed which, since 1960, has also been harvested at Wicken Fen.

Rough hay made of a wide variety of grasses or herbs can no longer be used as fodder for most modern cattle, so it is left in rotting heaps which themselves form valuable natural habitats or else is distributed in bales as a seed source. There's a world of wonder to watch from hides, paths and boardwalks. Altogether, more than 7,800 species of plants, fungi and animals are recorded here. Kurt says: 'This freshwater fenland is a haven for a number of seriously endangered species, but it is an endangered ecosystem. Crucially the nature reserve also sits in an area that is under threat from sea-level rise as a result of climate change.'

So in June he set forth, and set to work – making himself, and then us, a part of the landscape via a full sensory immersion in 27 pictures.

Kurt is noted for working in all weathers, and for what his wife Caroline calls 'extreme painting'. He uses the elements and immediate materials in his resulting images – flotsam and jetsam from the sea may be set into his sun-seared and rain-, hail- and sleet-smeared canvases along with sand, mud and grass.

He doesn't just draw in paint – he literally draws the landscape into his painting and then throws his own spirit into the maelstrom mixture too. At the end of the vital and visceral process of producing a mixed-media image, a portrait of the artist himself might reveal an exhausted figure covered in pigment.

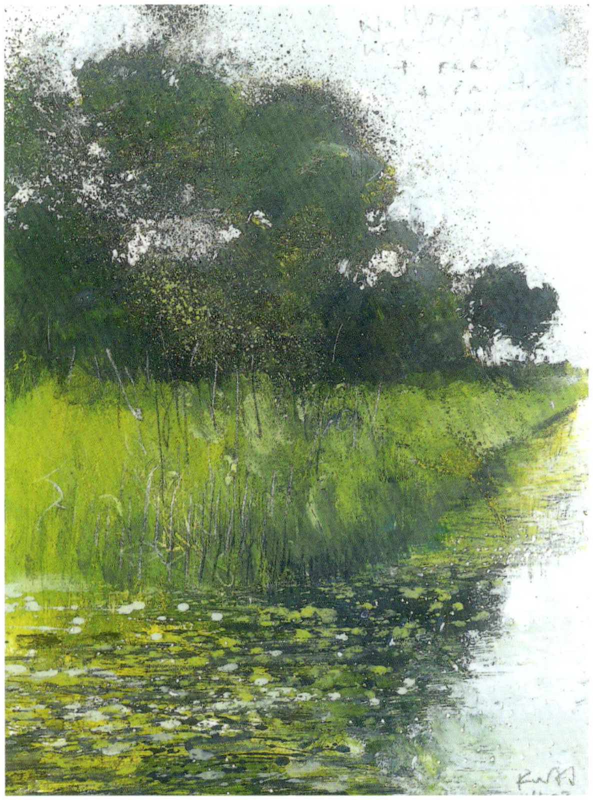

Willow and waterlilies, reeds and raindrops. Moorhens screech, 2007, acrylic (left)

His titles are like quickfire nature notes (*Squeaky reed warblers, distant cuckoo call, curlew choir; Lapwings are such sexy birds, reed beds full of bird twitter; The wind blows across the fen, the warblers sing, the clouds move, the reeds sway, the sedge dances*).

And then in pencil or chalk he may write these notes into the paint as titles or narratives – captions capturing precise moments. His pictures of the low-lying fen scale heights of beauty, but what unsettles the viewer is not only a close encounter with a typically fleeting English summer's day. It is that wider illusion of timelessness.

Kurt says: 'I wanted to celebrate the flora and fauna of Wicken Fen under those huge East Anglian skies. Saturated with colour and light I painted these mixed media works in the open air. For me they resonate with the scents and sounds of this fragile landscape.'

Backing for the Jackson venture has also come from the National Trust, which has its own grand plans for the long-term preservation of Wicken Fen. The aim is to create a new 22-square-mile (56-square-kilometre) reserve stretching from Wicken to a point beyond its Anglesey Abbey estate near Cambridge in order to increase a wild treasure and reduce the present danger of wipeout.

Welcome to the art of rescue.

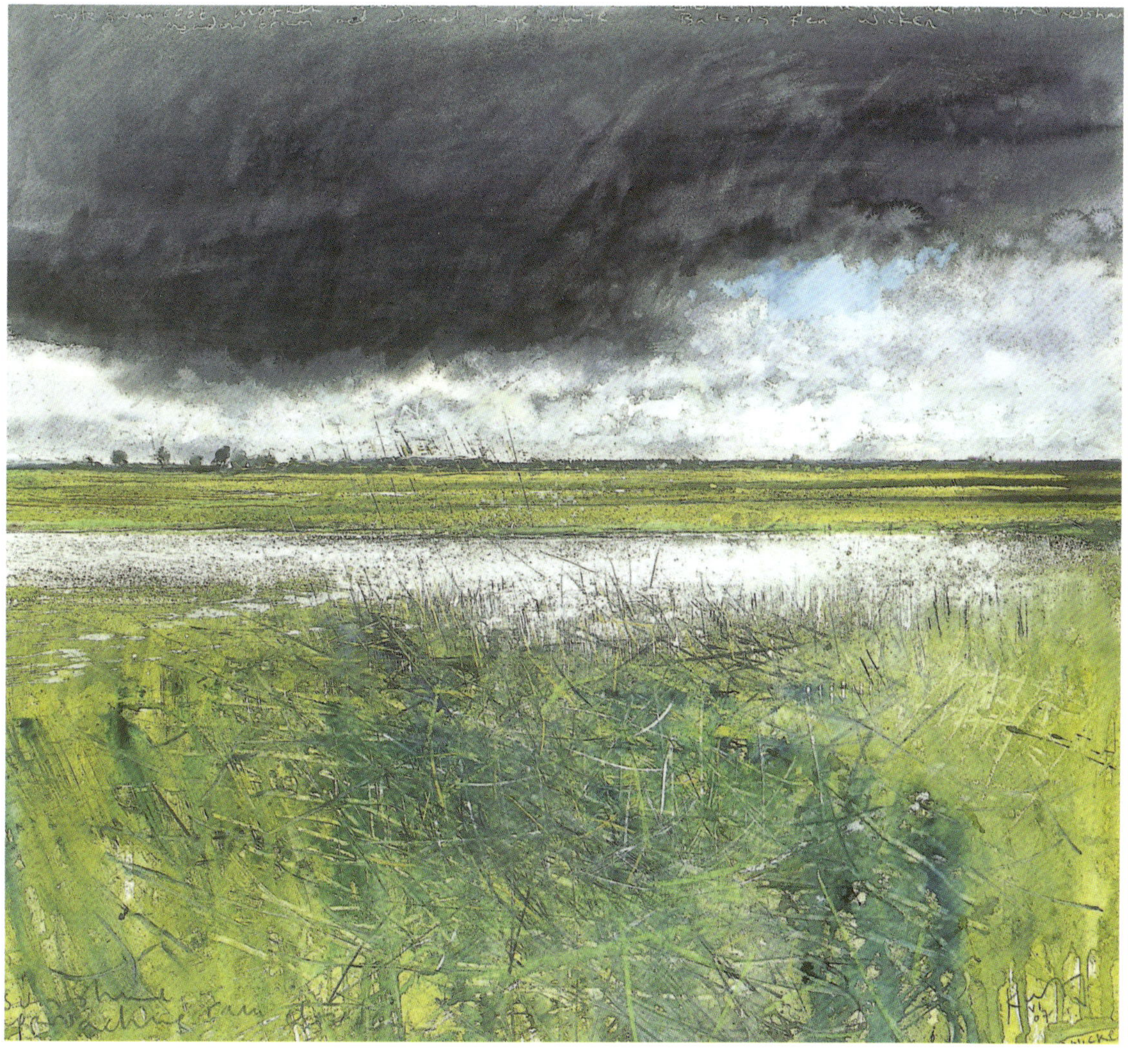

Sunshine with approaching rain clouds, Baker's fen, 2007, mixed media

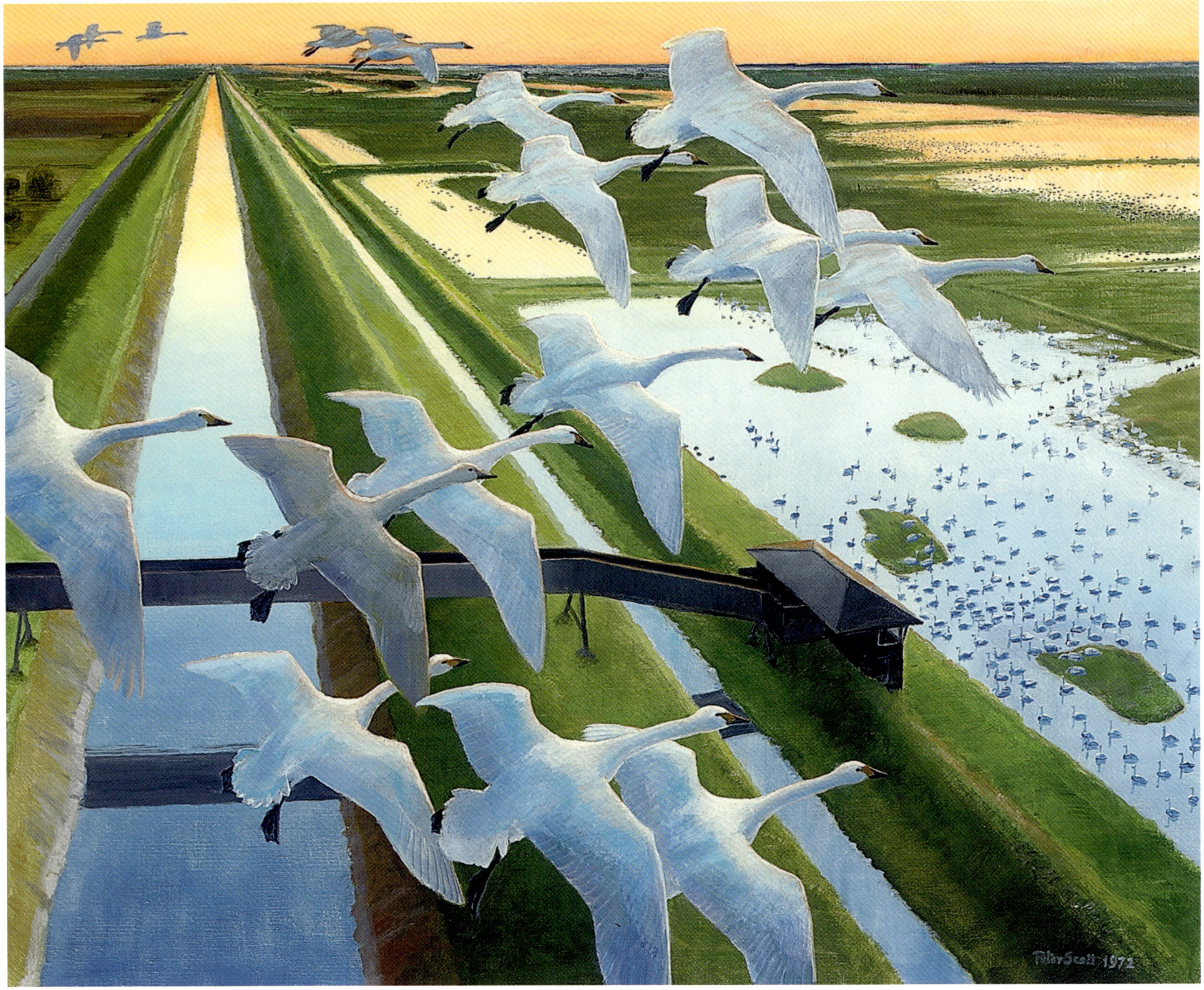

Swan Fall at Welney, 1972, oil on canvas

East Light

Peter Scott at Sutton Bridge

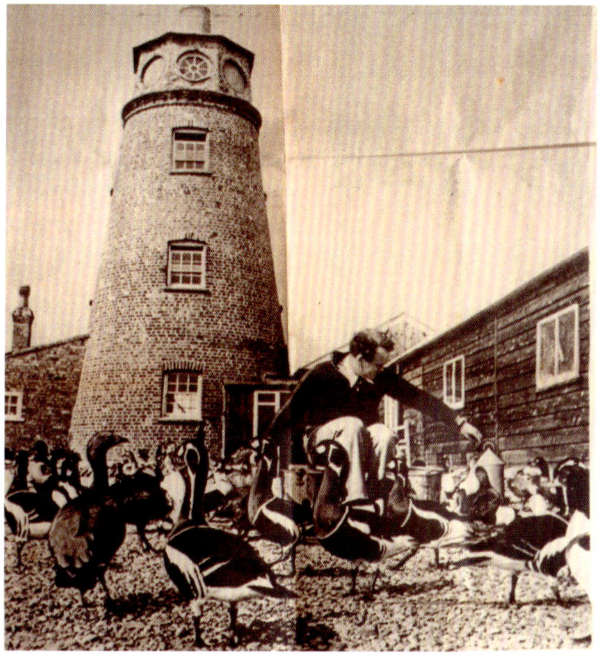

Peter Scott, feeding red-breasted geese, East Lighthouse, 1939

When explorer Robert Falcon Scott died in the Antarctic in 1912, he left a letter for his no-less-redoubtable sculptor wife, Kathleen, concerning the care of their two-year-old son. 'Make the boy interested in natural history if you can,' he wrote. 'It is better than games.' She could and did. The boy became, in Sir David Attenborough's words, the 'patron saint' of conservation. He was to be a painter with a mission.

Sir Peter Scott (1909-1989) also excelled at sport – at ice skating and sailing (landing a bronze medal at the 1936 Berlin Olympics and later seeing heroic war service in the Royal Navy, though Britain's future Open Gliding Champion was a loss to the RAF). Most of all he loved shooting. As a Cambridge student of 18, he downed a snipe on the Ouse Washes at Welney and then became a wildfowler to the last. He was fascinated by Northborough's Borough Fen Duck Decoy, near Peterborough, a rare survival where he made his first film. He also saw the light in the Fens, turning from bird shooter to saviour after seeing the suffering of a goose he had maimed and could not despatch.

From the summer of 1933 Peter Scott leased the East Lighthouse at Sutton Bridge from the Nene Catchment Board for £5 a year. The pair of beacons flanking the river where it enters the Wash had never been lit. Dating from 1829, and designed by Waterloo Bridge architect John Pennie, these twin towers were a monument to the draining of the Great Fens. A century later a customs officer still arrived for two hour-long stints each day to hail arriving or departing vessels via a megaphone.

Otherwise the East Light was surrounded by the noise of nature, being all but engulfed at

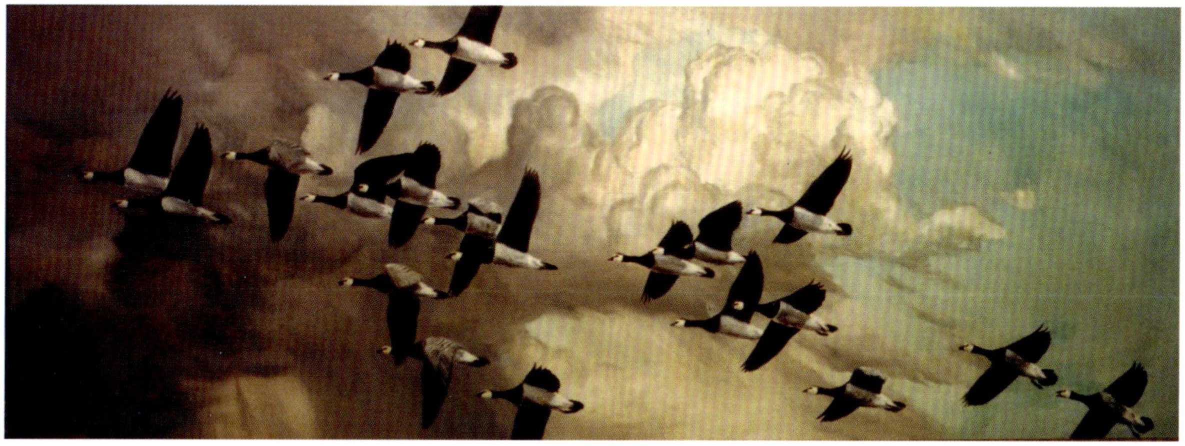

Barnacle Geese, oil on canvas

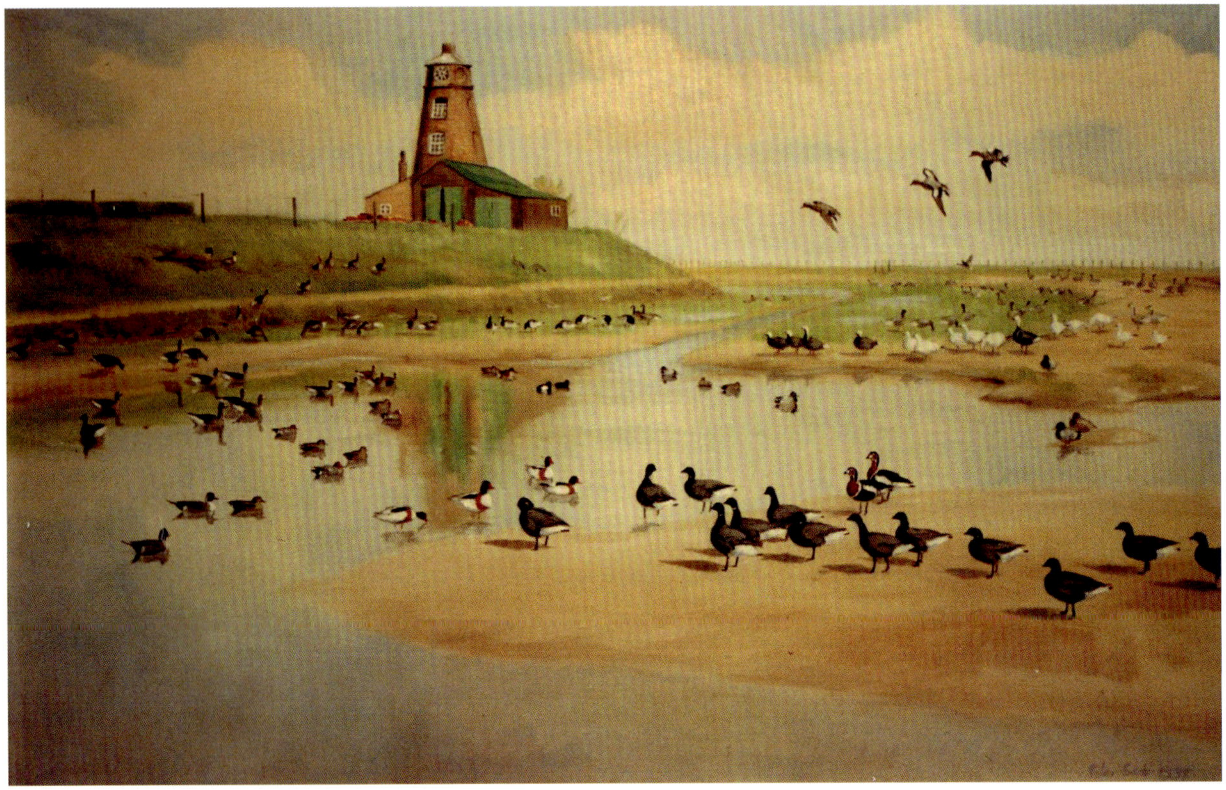

East Lighthouse,
1934, oil on canvas

high tide save for a thin land link – the grass-topped embankment along which the tenant navigated his battered, open-topped Morris. Winds and spray lashed the lonely building. And then the sea receded to reveal a haven of saltings and wildfowl and waders in their thousands.

As a highly successful portrait sculptor and society figure, Kathleen Scott (née Bruce) made sure Peter was feted also. She orchestrated his annual shows at Ackermann's Galleries in London between 1933 and 1940, each opened by a famous friend and selling out at ever-rising prices. She pressed her talented but easily diverted son to the business of painting (48 works for the 1936 exhibition finally emerging in under six weeks) or writing on his avian passion. Early profits funded a lighthouse extension, with bedroom and bathroom skylights for viewing flights of birds and a boathouse where a punt-gunner could store the transport to their destruction.

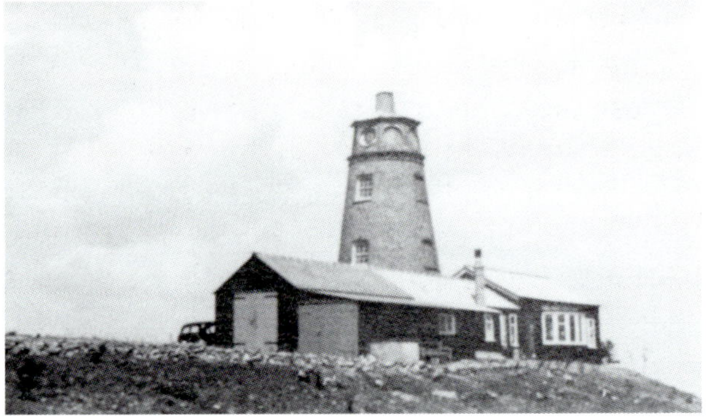

East Lighthouse, 1930s

Peter Scott's ornithologically accurate and scenically dramatic pictures had immense appeal. One 1930s oil entitled *Norfolk Spring – Shovellers and a Pair of Garganey* was renamed *Taking to Wing* for a mass version selling 350,000 copies in prints, cards and tablemats by 1959. His pictures adorned Wedgwood plates and 25 watercolours made in the East Light became Player's cigarette cards. His first illustrated book, *Morning Flight*, a hymn to the Wash and Fens, appeared in a signed and limited edition in 1935 – a ninth ordinary edition being part of a literary flock 12 years later.

Geese incised by Scott in the concrete pond at East Lighthouse, 1935 (left)

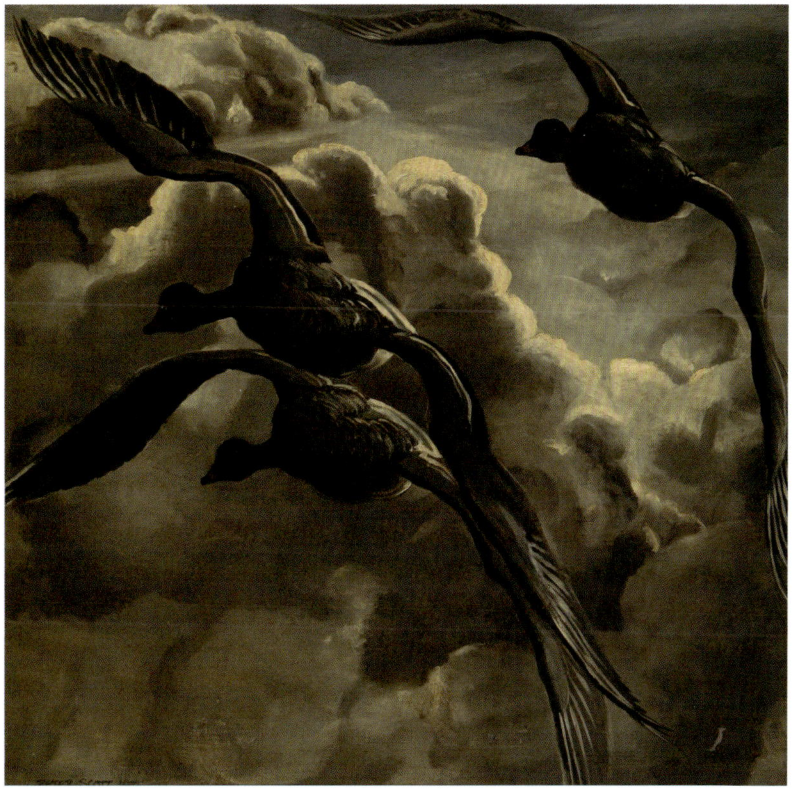

Pinkfeet Migrate High, 1935, oil on canvas

Through war and urbanisation, Peter Scott's pictures sent a comforting call of the wild across the continents long before he helped to found the World Wildlife Fund (doodling what became its panda logo during early meetings). As he concluded *Morning Flight*: 'And I hear the geese calling – a music of indescribable beauty and wildness, and fitness for the flat marsh which is their home. The moon has just risen, very large and orange over the sea, and the tide is high, half covering the salting, and filling the creeks right up to the sea wall... Suddenly there is a little burst of calling – the first ones are up – they are coming.'

In a single December night in 1932 he and a friend had shot 80 pink-footed geese, a troubling memory for the man writing *Morning Flight*. By then he had fenced in a small pond beside the lighthouse for a dozen pinioned pinkfoots bought from netters at nearby Terrington marsh. Soon the party was taken by the tide, but eight returned to found the world's best wildfowl collection.

In Peter Scott's absence the menagerie was cared for – in a high-risk appointment – by poacher and boxer **Mackenzie Thorpe** (1908-

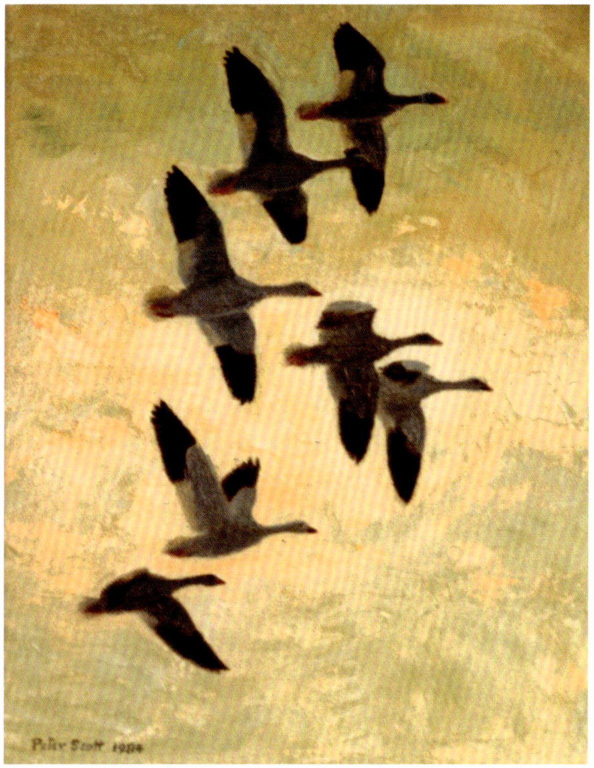

Snow Geese, 1984, oil on board

1976), who had a gypsy grandmother named Leviathon, an uncle called Emperor and was himself king of the saltmarshes. When Kenzie came on the scene, in 1936, the collection comprised 32 ducks (pintail, wigeon, mallard, shelduck) and 20 geese – pinkfoots, brent, greylag and a solitary bean goose he had himself caught and sold for £1. Regretting he hadn't asked a higher price, he helped himself to his

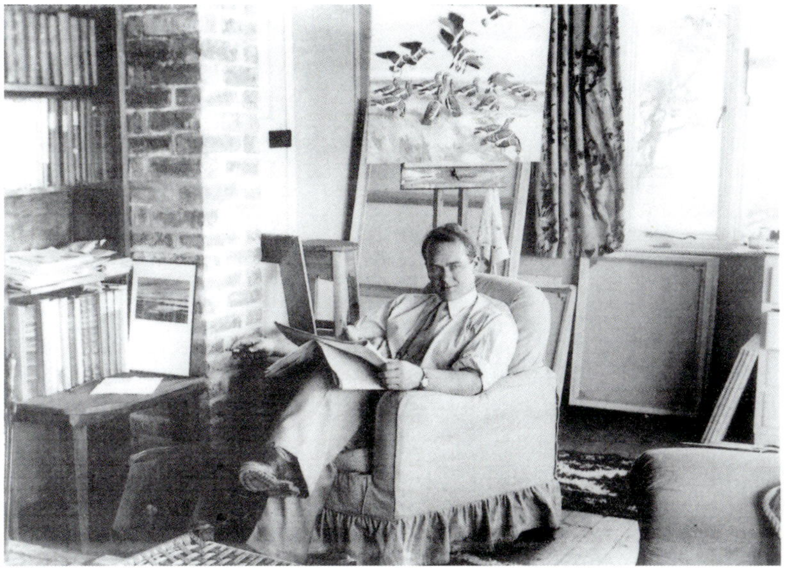

Peter Scott at East Lighthouse

boss's brushes, paints and canvas and sold skilful paintings to visitors as 'genuine Peter Scotts'. Later he fathered a large family and lived on a houseboat which, with all his possessions, was burned in Romany style after his death.

In 1922 Kathleen had married Edward Hilton Young – the future Lord Kennet, who was then an MP for Norwich. They had a son Wayland (father of sculptor Emily Young). In February 1936 they acquired a rural retreat at Fritton Hithe near Great Yarmouth, with a garden running to a lake where they and an endless stream of visitors could fish, swim and sail.

But war ended this east coast idyll. The wildfowl collection was dispersed among friends – some to Horsey Island in the Walton Backwaters of Essex – and Peter put to sea. In June 1940, just before the Battle of Britain, Kathleen wrote in her diary: 'The worst of things has happened. They are going to put guns in Pete's lighthouse, they are going to blow the top off and put on a concrete roof. I cried for the first time since the war.' She got the planned explosion halted, but billeted troops blitzed the interior. Worst of all, a new drainage scheme to boost food production left the lighthouse stranded in arable fields. The Scott dream of a wildfowl research station flew elsewhere – with a site located in 1945 on the Severn Estuary at Slimbridge becoming a first reserve for the future Wildfowl and Wetlands Trust. Sir Peter then oversaw the trust's purchase of a site at Peakirk, to help fund the nearby Borough Fen Decoy, but it was sold after his death. More happily, in 1970 he began the progressive rescue of the Ouse Washes, where he had shot that first snipe.

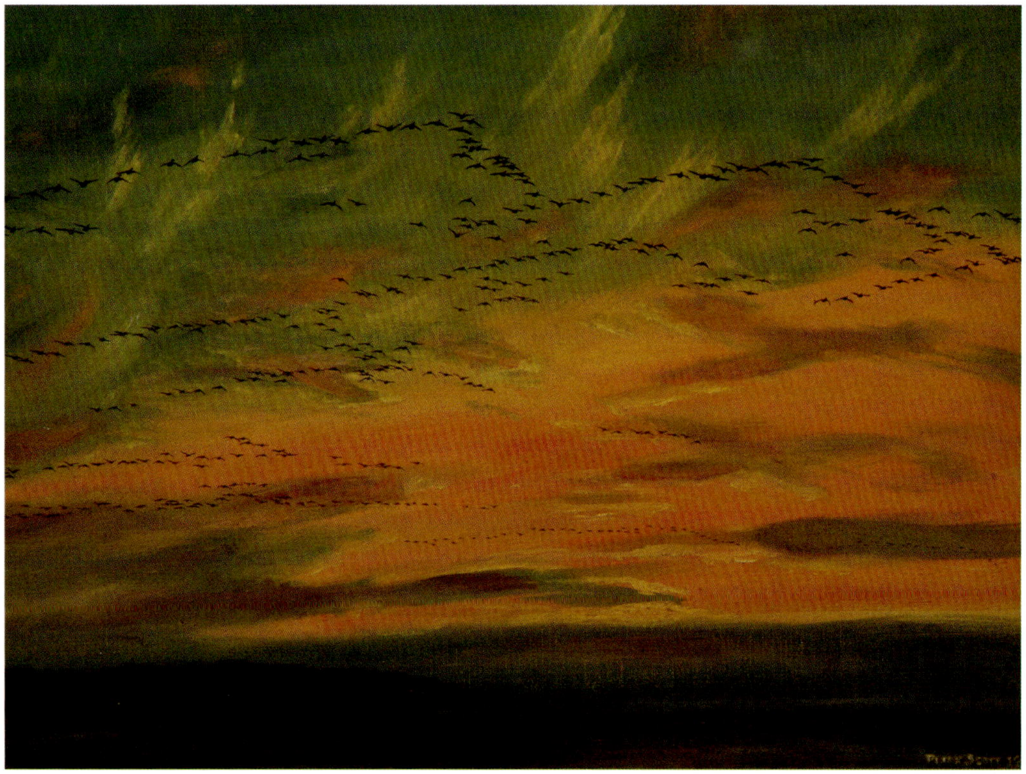

Pinkfeet in huge skeins fly from Holkham Fresh Marshes at dusk, 1933, oil on canvas board

The WWT now manages nearly 1,000 Welney acres. With further tracts rescued by the RSPB and county wildlife trusts, more than two-thirds of the Ouse Washes are protected. Here we see how the Fens looked 400 years ago, when among Europe's largest wetlands: shallow lakes, broad rivers, reed beds and pastures submerged in winter. The 17th century brought large-scale drainage, with a flagship Hundred Foot Washes scheme launched by Dutch engineer Sir Cornelius Vermuyden for the Earl of Bedford. Parallel Old Bedford and New Bedford rivers separated a strip of flood meadow half a mile wide and 22 miles long. When the River Ouse risks overflowing, an Earith sluice opens to discharge water into the River Delph which in turn rises and floods. This surge then runs into the New Bedford at the Welmore sluice further downstream.

So the Ouse Washes could still host the traditional Fen way of life – cattle-grazing in summer and wildfowling in winter, eel-trapping under bankside willows and skating on frozen meres. But now the man-made environment works for nature. Spring and autumn bring migrant mayhem, summer key nesting populations of godwit, avocet, redshank and

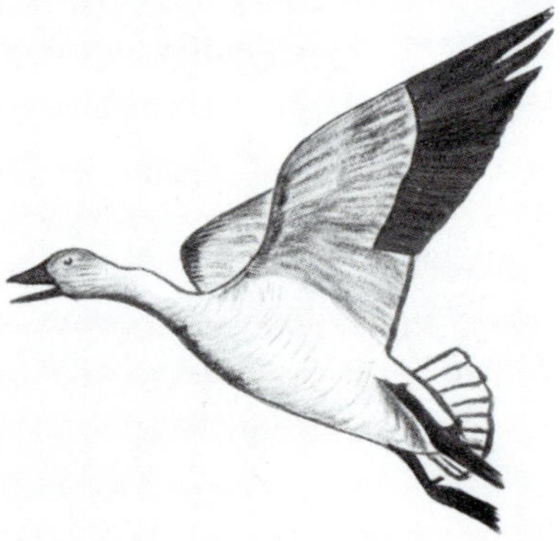

Snow Goose, Mackenzie Thorpe

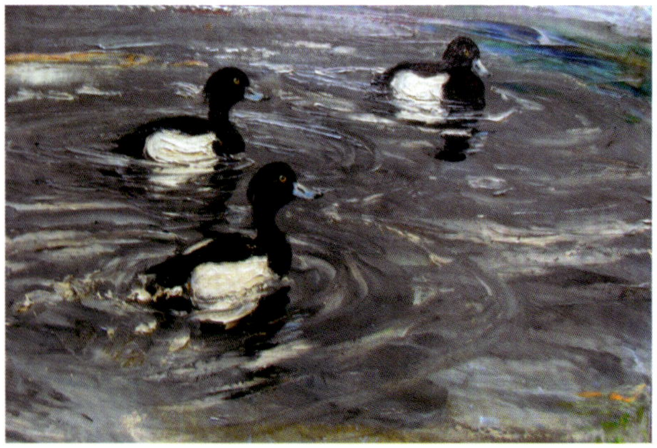

Tufted Ducks Diving, 1935, oil on canvas

snipe. Winter hosts swan lake, as thousands of whoopers and Bewicks wing in from Iceland and Siberia. At Welney in 1964 Peter Scott noticed the latter swan's unique bill patterning. Many were later named and monitored thanks largely to his younger daughter Dafila (the Latin name for pintail), herself now a Cambridgeshire-based wildfowl artist.

Today most of the old Fens form a flat geometric grid plotted on an epic scale. Long straight lines of roads and dykes cutting through enormous fields look from an aerial view like a vast Mondrian painting. Windmills have given way to windfarms, but between Ely and Peterborough cathedrals and abbey ruins at Croyland a score of church towers on medieval isles seems to be stretching out – growing taller and taller as if through an elemental tug of war. In paint and print John Piper hailed the churches at West Walton, Walsoken, Walpole St Peter (deemed by collaborator Sir John Betjeman the finest in England), the Tilneys, Terringtons and Wiggenhalls. He wrote that all were built by masons 'using majestically the Fens as a plinth – the best plinth for sculptural architecture in the whole country'.

On its plinth next to the Nene, no longer lapped by the North Sea, the East Lighthouse was rescued from dereliction in 1984 by the Happisburgh-raised bird artist and retired naval commander David Joel. He rescued a concrete fireplace fresco of 12 mallard scratched with a nail, and found another of flying ducks edging a pond (p.158). He restocked the wildfowl pen, rearing geese to

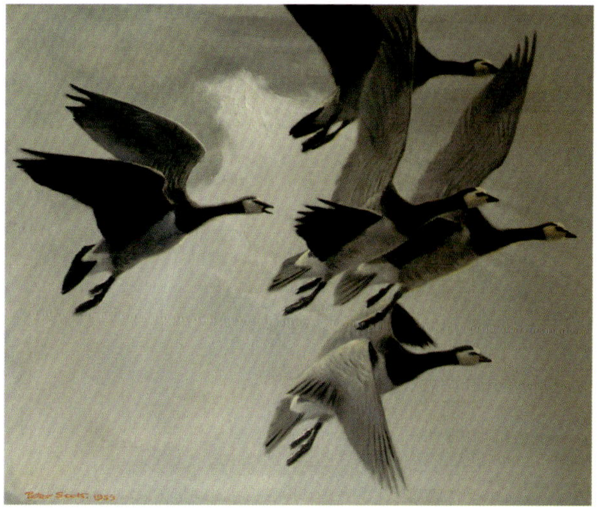

Barnacles in Flight,
1939, oil on canvas (right)

fly free. Twitchers have been aghast to find snow geese among the introduced species feeding in nearby fields.

For several 1930s winters a wild pink-footed goose dubbed Anabel had joined the pinioned party. The story inspired Paul Gallico to write *The Snow Goose*, a war-time saga set on the Essex coast and later filmed on Horsey Island. Peter Scott illustrated one best-selling edition, with a cover portrait of novelist Elizabeth Jane Howard, his first wife who later lived in Bungay. He also raised the snow geese stars of the TV film.

But art really is next to awesome nature. From the East Light – where a 10-mile Sir Peter Scott Walk now runs along the sea wall between the Nene and the Ouse ferry at West Lynn – David Joel has often looked up to see incoming flights of swans spotting a familiar marker and turning for the descent to Welney.

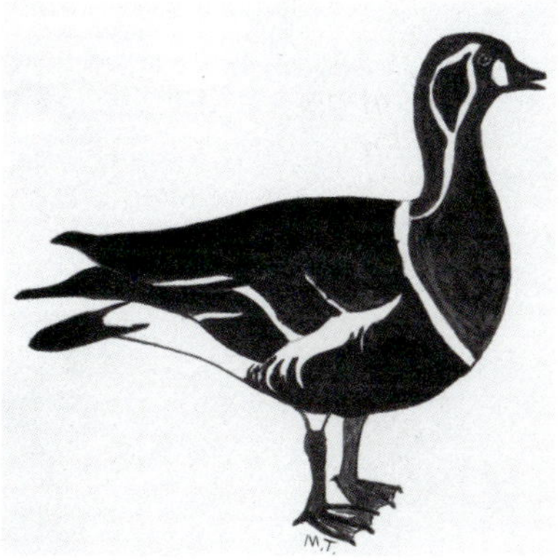

Red-Breasted Goose,
Mackenzie Thorpe

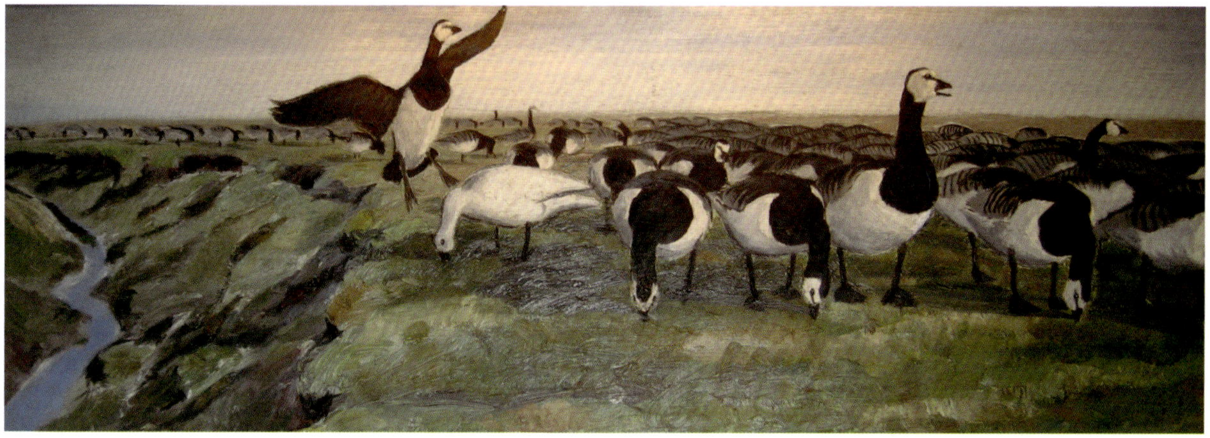

Barnacles Feeding on the Marsh,
1933, oil on canvas

Index of Artists

Numbers in bold indicate illustrations

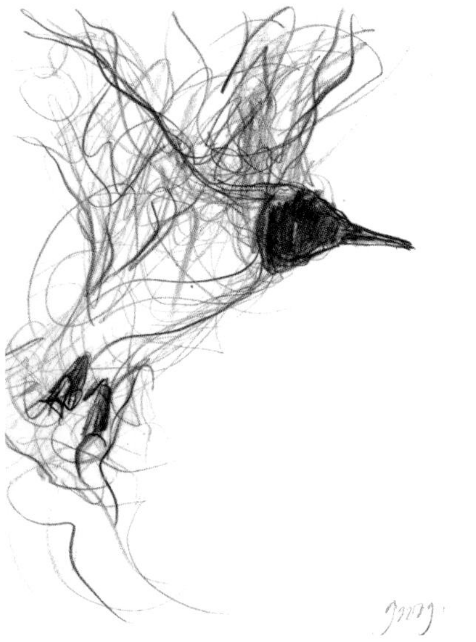

Black Headed Gulls, Slaughden, Jason Gathorne-Hardy, graphite, 2009

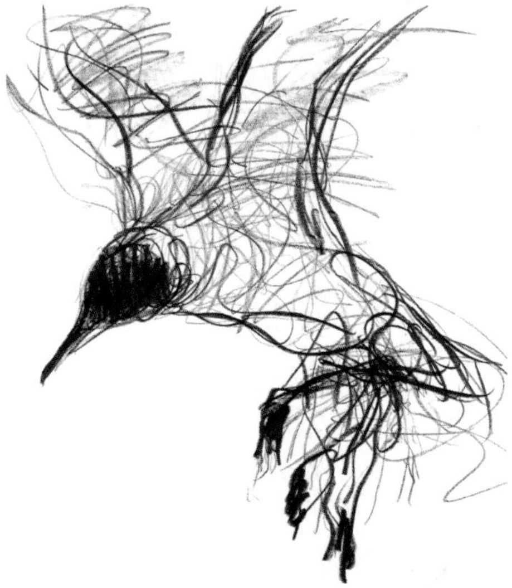

Boat and Hut, Southwold Blackshore, Jason Bowyer, 2009, oil on canvas

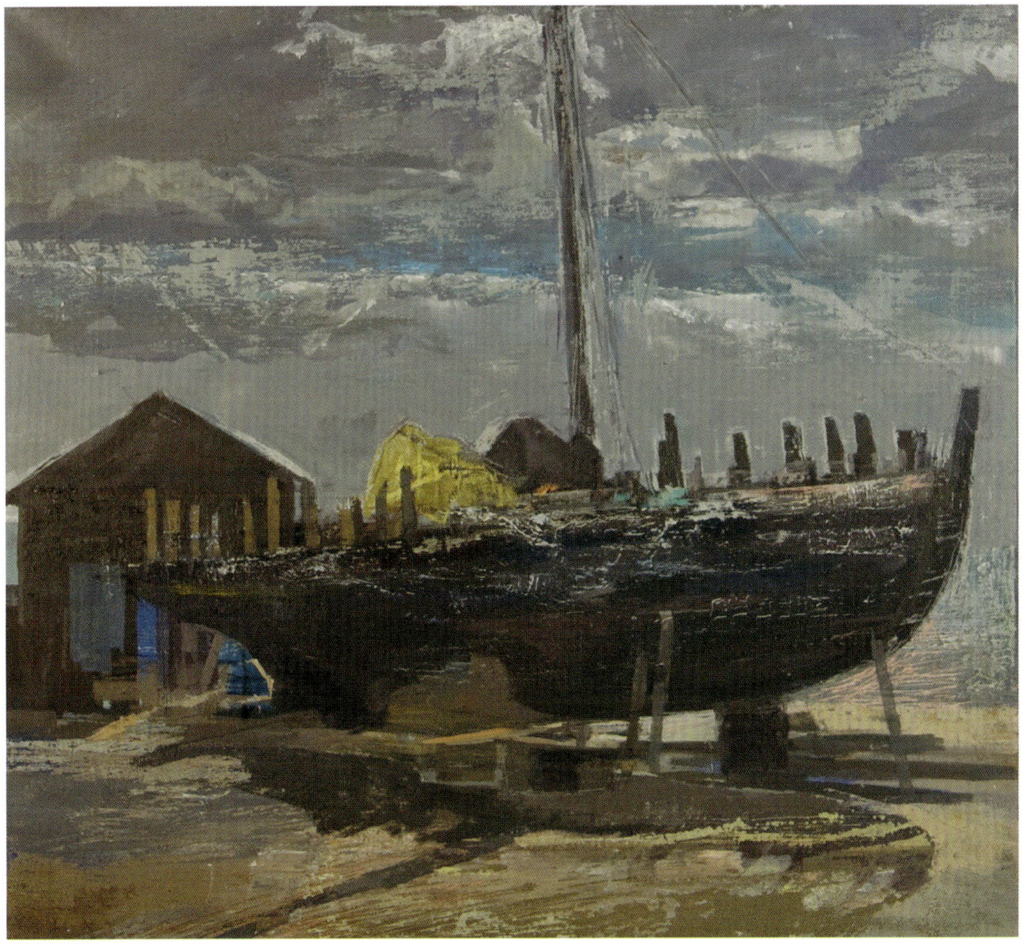

Acknowledgements

Reproduced works are in private collections unless otherwise stated. The help of all owners is much appreciated.

Warmest thanks to all the artists in this book, living and dead, who have inspired me through their work and, in many cases, their friendship. All errors remain my own. Thanks also to quoted writers, film-makers Clive Dunn (Margaret Mellis), Siri-Susanna Taylor (Katherine Hamilton) and Bill Ungless (Frank and Humphrey Jennings), photographers Doug Atfield, Robert Cotton, Andrew Montgomery, Susan Sunter and Simon Trapnell – and Helen Douglas for my jacket photo with Margaret Mellis.

I am deeply indebted to publisher Peter Tolhurst, editor Ann Kay, computer wizard and Reg Carter expert Hilary Huckstep, Eastern Daily Press, East Anglian Daily Times, Norfolk Museums and Archaeology Service, Britten-Pears Foundation, Aldeburgh Music, Sheringham Museum, Sainsbury Centre for Visual Arts, East Anglia Art Fund, Friends of the Earth, Henry Moore Foundation, North Norfolk Exhibition Project, Dean and Chapter of Norwich Cathedral, Wildfowl and Wetlands Trust, Bircham Gallery, Christie's, HarperCollins, Offer Waterman Fine Art, Pinkfoot Gallery, Sarah Ballard and the RoaR Archive (for Barrington Farm), Sister Wendy Beckett, Father Phil Blamire, Ronald Blythe, Diana Boston, Diana Cohen, James Colman, John Cook, Chris Cordingly, Charlotte Crawley, Rosie Glasgow, James Glennie, Jane Hamilton, Simon Hucker, Mrs Lawrence Hughes, Joachim Jacobs, Christine and Peter Jay, Marie Loise Jennings, Commander David Joel, Sally and David Kibble, Simon Martin, David Messum, Johnathan Messum, John and Yvonne Millwood, Judy Novak, Fiona Oates, Julian Potter, Camilla Purdon, Max Saunders, Peyton Skipwith, Judy Spindler, Quentin Stevenson, Telfer Stokes and Carol Tee.

I most gratefully acknowledge the help of galleries and artist estates as follows: Edward Bawden – The Fine Art Society; Vanessa Bell – Henrietta Garnett; Lionel Bulmer, Margaret Green and Peggy Somerville – Messum's (also supplying photos of works by Simon Carter, James Dodds, Mary Fedden, Derek Nice, Guy Taplin and Henry Herbert La Thangue); Edward Burra – Lefevre Gallery; Alfred Cohen – Wighton School House Gallery; Beryl Cook – Portal Gallery; John Craxton – Richard Riley; John Gay – English Heritage; Barbara Hepworth – Sir Alan Bowness; Ivon Hitchens – Jonathan Clark Fine Art; Margaret Mellis – Austin/Desmond Fine Art; Mary Newcomb – Crane Kalman Gallery; John Piper – Clarissa Lewis; Mary Potter – Julian Potter; Eric Ravilious – Anne Ullman; Peter Scott – Dafila Scott; Edward Seago – Portland Gallery; Elisabeth Vellacott – Redfern Gallery.

Every effort has been made to trace copyright holders of pictures illustrated. The publisher will be pleased to hear from any omitted party for redress and amendment to any future edition.

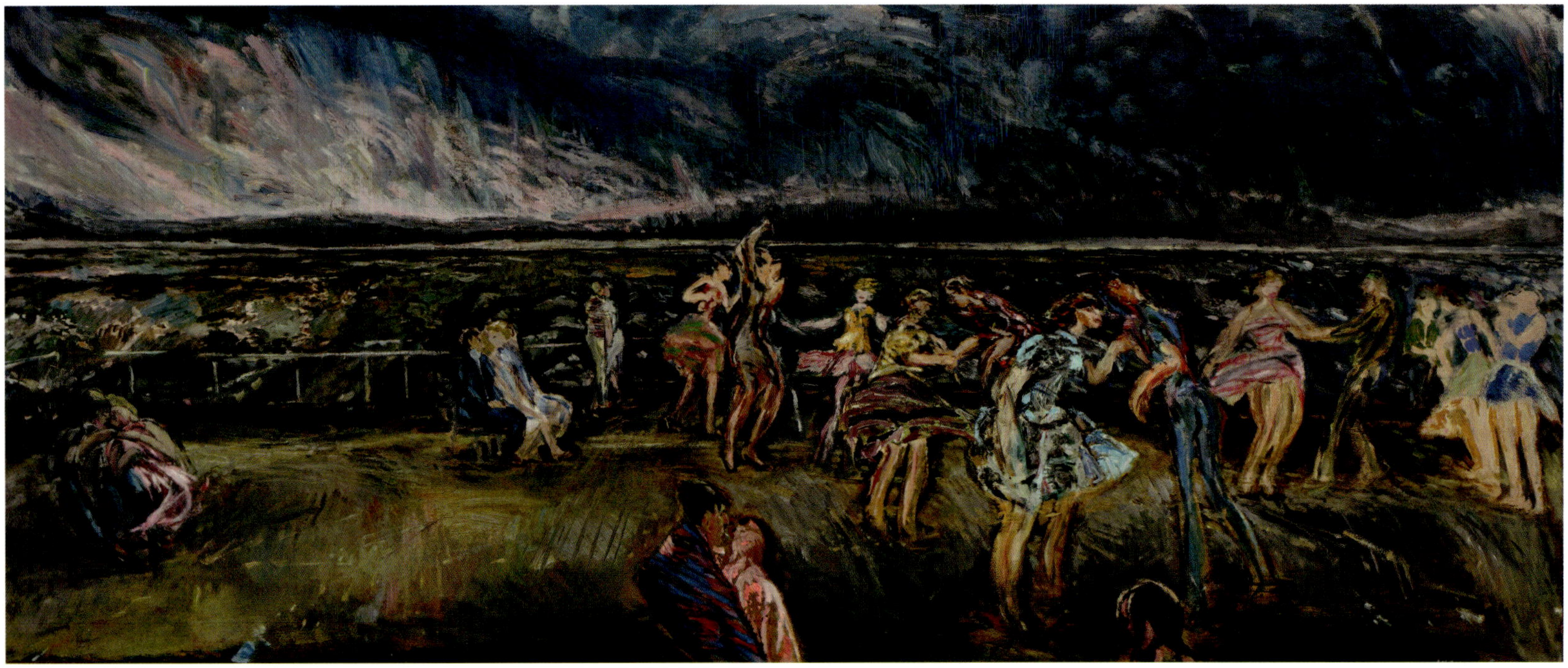

Jiving to the Rolling Stones, Lowestoft South Pier, January 23 1964, Jeffery Camp, oil on canvas